Penguin Education

Penguin Modern Economics
General Editor: B. J. McCormick

Introducing Economics

B. J. McCormick
P. D. Kitchin, G. P. Marshall,
A. A. Sampson, R. Sedgwick

Introducing Economics

B. J. McCormick

P. D. Kitchin, G. P. Marshall,
A. A. Sampson, R. Sedgwick

Second Edition

Penguin Books

Penguin Books Ltd,
Harmondsworth, Middlesex, England
Penguin Books, 625 Madison Avenue,
New York, New York 10022, U.S.A.
Penguin Books Australia Ltd,
Ringwood, Victoria, Australia
Penguin Books Canada Ltd,
2801 John Street, Markham,
Ontario. Canada L3R 1B4
Penguin Books (N.Z.) Ltd,
182–190 Wairau Road,
Auckland 10, New Zealand

First published 1974
Second edition 1977
Reprinted 1978

Made and printed in Great Britain by
Hazell Watson & Viney Ltd, Aylesbury, Bucks
Set in Monotype Times

Contents

Acknowledgements 8
Preface 9

Part One
A Panorama of Problems 17
1 The Wealth and Welfare of Nations 19
2 Wants and Goods 36
3 Production 46
4 Exchange and Trade 65
5 Money and Trade 74
6 Production and Trading over Time 79

Part Two
Markets, Demand and Supply 95
7 Demand 99
8 Supply 121
9 The Market 125
10 The Market Continued 144

Part Three
Utility and Cost 175
11 Consumer Behaviour 179
Appendix: Other Approaches 192
12 Costs and Supply: Economic Costs 201

Part Four
A Mathematical Interlude 219
13 The Calculus 229

Part Five
The Social Institutions of Production 261
14 The Social Institutions of Production 263
15 The Corporation 274
Appendix: Accounting for Information and Control 284

Part Six
Market Structures 303
16 Organizational Behaviour 305
17 Perfect Competition 319
18 Monopoly 337
19 Accounting for Ignorance 354
20 The Regulation of Monopoly 364
21 Public Ownership 384

Part Seven
**The Theory of Distribution:
A Preliminary Survey** 395
22 The Global Problem of Distribution 397
23 The Demand for Productive Resources 403
24 The Demand and Supply of Factors of Production 416
25 Interest 421
26 Profit 424
27 Labour 436

Part Eight
Money, Output and Growth 453
28 The Demand for Money 463
29 The Supply of Money 478
30 The Income–Expenditure Approach 508
31 Income Determination: Aggregate Demand and Supply 518
32 The Multiplier 535
33 Households: Their Contribution to Aggregate Demand 545
34 Aggregate Demand: Investment by Firms 566
35 Aggregate Demand: Exports and Imports 592
36 The Foreign Exchange Market and the Balance of Payments 604
37 Aggregate Supply and Inflation 634
38 Government Expenditure and Control of Aggregate Demand 660
39 Development and Growth 678
40 Fitting the Pieces Together 691

Part Nine
The State 729
41 The Role of the State 731
42 Financing the State 756
43 Poverty and Inequality 780

44 Political Processes 794
   References 803
   Further Reading 806
   Index 809

Acknowledgements

In the conduct of the seminars and the writing of this book we have had a great deal of help from our students, who patiently corrected our mistakes and tried to understand what we were getting at. In addition our colleagues at Sheffield and members of the Penguin Modern Economics Advisory Board gave us unstinting help. For all the assistance we are grateful, though for any blunders still embalmed we are eternally responsible.

Western Bank, Sheffield
January 1974

Preface

This book is an attempt to design an introductory course which reflects the changes in subject matter and techniques of analysis of modern economics. The contents of the book were tested with university students, some Open University students, extramural classes and sixth formers over a three-year period.

At the outset we were faced with the problem of how to approach economics. Three approaches suggested themselves – historical; market analysis; and non-market analysis.

Historical

An historical approach could start with the relationship between men and natural resources, drawing upon the experiences of Robinson Crusoe to demonstrate the problems encountered at the beginning of civilization. But it would be more appropriate to indicate how the socio-economic problems of production, distribution and accumulation were resolved within the institutional framework known as *feudalism*. The tenant would hire land from the landlord or he would be employed directly as a wage-labourer. Irrespective of the contract in force he would receive a certain income and the remainder would go to the landlord for his consumption and for communal defence and accumulation. Because this agrarian system was dependent upon a power source – solar energy – which was uncontrollable by Man's actions, labour was often idle between spells of sowing and reaping, with the consequence that the system of feudalism had to cope with the problems of unemployment as well as the pressures of over-population spasmodically relieved by epidemics and drought. Yet the principle problem was that of the distribution of output between landlord and tenant.

Feudalism can then be depicted as giving way to industrialization as a result of the exploitation of fossil fuels and new technologies. By its release from dependence upon solar energy, innovations made in agriculture and the reduction of population pressure the industrial economy could become a fully developed *market economy* in which all resources are relatively scarce, and in which surpluses could be invested in all kinds of activities as a result of market mobility. In such an economy the distribution of output would somehow be determined by the market. In an industrial market economy the distribution of output is not between landlord and tenant but between capitalist and wage-earner. Should accumulation of capital over time increase the total amount of goods available, the conflict implicit in determining distribution might be reduced, but alternatively it would be heightened if capitalists attempted to increase their share. The conflict could widen and deepen into a triangular struggle between rentiers (those who financed economic activity), capitalists (those who directed economic activity) and wage-earners (those who endured economic activity) as specialization created a difference between owners (financiers) and controllers (directors). And, finally, the conflict could be shown to be world-wide as industrial economies destroyed agrarian economies in their pursuit of raw materials, new markets and new centres of production.

Market analysis

Historical analysis has many virtues: it emphasizes the economic activity and stresses the uniqueness of different periods of time in terms of institutions and problems. But because it is a dialectical method it is apt to blur the differences; it does not allow the cutting edge of analysis to provide those deep insights which are so necessary to an understanding of how a particular economy works, or how an efficient economic system might be developed to deal with a particular problem. The dialectic is a barrier to measurement, since in emphasizing the qualitative it ignores the fact that many phenomena are capable of measurement. We murder to dissect but even post-mortem can advance understanding.

So an alternative line of advance would be to pick out the obvious in modern society – the market – and to analyse the way in which markets work, and from such an approach it would be possible to explain why markets sometimes break down.

Non-market analysis

Much human activity is undertaken outside the market situation. We are born and live in families, go to youth clubs and attend churches, and receive innumerable benefits from a Welfare State. Moreover, some economies and about nine-tenths of the human drama has been enacted in non-market economies. It would therefore be interesting to begin with the assumption that the state makes all the decisions and takes responsibility for the organization of all economic activities, in order to see why markets might sometimes be useful.

A compromise

Each approach has its merits. The historical approach brings out the importance of class and class conflict but tends to neglect the large element of co-operation in society. The market approach is class-less and ignores the importance of the state. A non-market approach would fail to emphasize the important rise in the use of the market over the last two hundred years. A compromise was necessary. We have dealt at greater length than most writers with the state, with non-market economies and the way in which theory has emerged out of historical problems. And to a basic approach we have fused the necessary mathematics because we believe that further advances in economics can be greatly assisted by the use of mathematics. Furthermore, we have introduced statistical testing as a necessary antidote to armchair theorizing and to indicate the scope and limitations of measurement. Finally, since economics is a moral science, we have not hesitated to introduce value judgements.

In Part One (*A Panorama of Problems*) the task of the economist is defined as being the analysis of the causes of the possibilities of civilization, the economist's role being that of aiding Man in his attempts to control his environment, and attain some satisfaction of his basic wants, so as to make possible the development of a culture. The indicators of material well-being and possibilities of civilization in the UK (national income) are measured over two centuries and explanations looked for to explain the variations in these indicators.

The nature of wants and the concept of a hierarchy of wants are discussed in connection with the indicators of society's ability to produce its material needs. From this the obvious step is made to study goods and their relationships with wants. Goods are classified as to whether or not property rights can be allocated to them, and it becomes apparent that although some goods can be privately produced, others require some form of collective action.

Following on from the initial discussion of the meaning of scarcity and the relationships between wants and the goods which satisfy them, a study is made of the processes and institutions used and devised by man to overcome the scarcity problem. Included in the illustration of the production problem is a discussion of over-population and pollution.

Production is not the only means of increasing a community's well-being: another is exchange and trade. The initial discussion concerns the world of barter exchange – the next stage is concerned with the institution of money as a means of further improving the material well-being of the trading partners.

'What is the function of money?' is a question answered primarily in terms of its use as a unit of account and medium of exchange. Finally the time dimension is introduced, and the concepts already developed used to show how the use of resources can be spread over time so that beneficial trade-offs can be affected between present and further consumption.

Part Two (*Markets, Demand and Supply*) turns the discussion from universal economic problems to something more specific – how resources are allocated – and to the different methods man has adopted to do this. The market is viewed as a mechanism for allocation, treated as an information system and compared with a system of central planning. Analysis of the demand side of the market is carried out by reviewing the concept of a function and the relationships between individual and market demand curves; discussing the different treatments of private and collective goods; and exploring the important concept of elasticity. The supply side is treated in a similar way, illustrating volume and rate effects. Demand and supply are brought together to show price determination. The concept of equilibrium is discussed and ideas of consumer and producer surplus explained. Some potential consequences of state interference with market processes are considered with particular reference to housing and the labour market. The concept of a 'charity market' is considered, and the idea of expressing market relationships as a set of simultaneous equations is explained.

Relative price and output effects are considered in discussing the implications of shifts in market demand and supply curves. The impact of taxes and subsidies is illuminated by such current problems as stabilizing farmers' incomes via UK or EEC methods; manpower planning, etc. We complete our analysis of the market with some simple tests of the theory including a look at the identification problem.

Part Three (*Utility and Cost*) turns to the subjective base of economics to look behind demand and supply curves in order to explain the underlying behaviour of economic agents. The logic of choice will be developed in a way which indicates how economists create a theory and how they develop and generalize it. Utility or benefit is a recurrent theme and costs are presented as the loss of benefits from rejected choices – a sharp distinction is drawn between the economist's subjective theory of costs and the accountant's objective approach. The law of diminishing returns is strongly revived for the whole section.

Part Four (*A Mathematical Interlude*) is concerned with the mathematical tools used earlier in the book, but only implicitly. There are two reasons for doing this. The first is that having covered quite considerable ground in this study of economics, some revision should prove beneficial for the student. Secondly, the theory of the firm often involves simple mechanical relationships best expressed mathematically – and this is the next topic to be analysed.

The concept of a function is revised in this section, and total and marginal values reconsidered in the context of some simple differential calculus. The examples used draw heavily on the sections on production; demand and supply; utility and cost theory.

Part Five (*The Social Institutions of Production*) deals with the theory of the firm – really a continuation of the exploration of market behaviour. The firm is introduced as an alternative mechanism for monitoring the work of factors of production, particularly labour. Various firms – households, corporations and the State – are considered.

Part Six (*Market Structures*) begins with some general principles of organizational behaviour irrespective of market structure. All organizations need rules by which to attain their objectives and the rule stressed here is that, at the margin, expected benefits must equal expected costs.

Both models used to show firms' reaction to their environment – perfect competition and monopoly – are presented as politico-economic systems to emphasize our interest in both the positive predictions from thse models and their normative implications. The analysis proceeds by finding the equilibrium position for the firm and comparing long- and short-run situations, and the relationship between the firm and the industry is studied with special reference to the nature of the supply curve in each case. Particular attention is paid to the mechanics of price discrimination and to the comparison of perfect competition and monopoly as means of maximizing community well-being. This discussion includes an appraisal of the methods by which the state can control the monopoly problem – destruction, regulation, or public ownership. Optimizing behaviour requires the use of a rule, but in a world of ignorance and uncertainty the rules are apt to be rules of thumb. We examine the implications of certain accounting conventions.

Part Seven (*The Theory of Distribution*) views the topic in the light of the social contract and the historical interpretations of Marx and Keynes. An examination is made of factor pricing according to the marginal rules, and the reward to a factor is classified into opportunity earning plus surplus at a point in time and over time. There then follows a discussion of the meanings and origins of profit and the surplus. The marginal-productivity doctrine is subjected to severe criticism and its limitations exposed. Finally, there is a discussion of the labour market.

Part Eight (*Money, Output and Growth*) deals with the overall behaviour of an economy – the subject matter of macroeconomics. We begin with a discussion of the part played by money in economic activity. Money is demanded as a medium of exchange and a store of value. The second function leads to a link between money and the rate of interest. Testing the nature of the link depends upon defining carefully what is actually used as money. This has changed over time and there have been variations in the importance of private and public sources of money and difficulties in exercising public control over the money supply.

A version of the Keynesian model of income determination is given, based on the circular flow of income. The withdrawals from and injections into the flow of income are considered under saving, imports, taxes and investment, exports, government expenditure. The conditions for the equilibrium level of income are then analysed by means of an aggregate demand and supply apparatus.

The use of money makes it meaningful to speak of a general level of prices and of the aggregate demand for, and aggregate supply of, goods whose equality yields a general price level and the levels of income and output. Two aggregate demand and supply models are developed: in one prices are constant and changes in demand give rise to changes in output and incomes, whilst the other model allows for price variations. The multiplier is defined and analysed. The next step is to examine the components of demand – consumer spending, investment spending, exports and government spending. Theories are developed and tested with UK data. Finally the problems of inflation and growth are analysed.

Part Nine (*The State*) deals again with the market system which is seen to give rise to the under-consumption of some goods and the over-consumption of others. The intervention of the state and the alternatives of taxation, printing money and borrowing are analysed. The problems of poverty and inequality in a community are analysed. Finally we look at the problems of decision making in the state.

We are indebted to Miss Julia Linton and Miss Sue Wardle who struggled to produce a coherent typescript from our chaotic handwriting. Good secretaries are scarcer than economists.

Part One
A Panorama of Problems

Chapter 1
The Wealth and Welfare of Nations

Economics and economists

Inflation and unemployment, poverty and monopoly are examples of the types of problem which economists consider. But if there has to be a generalization of what economists study, a capsule definition, then it is that they study how men and women obtain their livelihoods. What constitutes a livelihood varies, of course, from country to country and from generation to generation, and economists try to provide some explanation of these differences. Furthermore, economists must also consider in a particular context, the subtle relationship between livelihood, or 'life-style', and civilization – the life-style of some civilizations revolves around a bowl of rice, for others it centres on surfing. Economists do not pretend to study how a civilization is created, but they do believe themselves to be, in the words of Lord Keynes, 'the trustees of the *possibility* of civilization' (Harrod, 1951).

What does it mean to be the trustees of the *possibility* of civilization? First, it conveys the belief that only if men and women possess some control over their environment and have attained some satisfaction of their basic wants can they be said to enjoy the possibilities of a cultured life. Secondly, it indicates that it is the economists' task to seek out those methods of control over the environment which are most conducive to the development of the nobler arts of life. In a world of scarcity satisfaction of wants can be achieved through theft, rape and war as well as production and trade. But the former methods lead to fear, suspicion and the degradation of the human spirit. It is, of course, the moral philosopher, the poet and the artist who create a civilization, but their work is made easier by the economist. So the economist sees himself as protecting and conserving the good qualities and he hopes that through his recommendations he can ultimately increase the virtues and eliminate the vices.

How do economists explore, create and sustain the possibilities of civilization? Some, the great economists, are possessed of powerful visions of the workings of society and they embody these visions in systems of thought which transcend their times. Late in the eighteenth century Scottish economist and philosopher, Adam Smith, delved into the causes of the wealth of nations. He was followed by a stockbroker and MP, David Ricardo, who enquired into the distribution of the rewards from economic activity, and the Reverend T. R. Malthus who warned of the dangers of overpopulation. In the middle of the nineteenth century came Marx with his penetrating analysis of the evolution of capitalist society. Towards the end of the century Alfred Marshall took the ideas of Smith, Ricardo and Malthus, infused them with additional insights and used sharper tools of analysis to produce a synthesis. At the same time Leon Walras captured the essence and interrelations of production, exchange and distribution in a few mathematical equations. In the twentieth century J. M. Keynes prescribed for slumps and A. C. Pigou for the problems of the affluent society.

But these are the great names. What of the ordinary, work-a-day economists, what do they do? Some work in government departments advising on such issues as unemployment, inflation, poverty and monopoly, the location of industry, and exports and imports. Others work in private firms on the problems of pricing products, appraising investment opportunities, forecasting sales and manpower planning. In international agencies economists can be found to be preoccupied with the diffusion of new technologies to developing countries, the flow of foreign aid, the stabilization of prices and incomes for producers of primary products such as cocoa and tin. In all these spheres, in all these enquiries into the ways by which men and women seek to obtain a livelihood, economists apply and create methods for the efficient use of resources.

In this chapter an examination is made of how the possibilities of civilization in the United Kingdom have altered over time. This enables us to isolate the causes of change in material living standards and thus to present a preliminary enquiry into the territory that forms the bulk of this book. The information obtained about the United Kingdom will then be used to throw light on the possibilities of civilization in other countries, a subject investigated by Adam Smith in 1776 and which served as the starting point of modern economics.

The behaviour of the United Kingdom national output

One of the simplest methods of examining the foundations of civilization is to trace the behaviour of the national output, or national income as it is more usually termed. The national income measures the vast outpouring of goods and services that a country's citizens produce and *sell* during a given period, usually a year. The term 'sell' is important because sales records are the simplest means of checking that economic activity has been undertaken during a given time period; unpaid services, such as those performed by a housewife for the rest of her family, go unrecorded by the national income statisticians.

Statistics of the United Kingdom national income have been compiled for as far back as the middle of the nineteenth century. For earlier periods information is only available for Great Britain. In the nineteenth century the behaviour of the economies of Britain and Ireland diverged sharply: Britain underwent industrialization whereas Ireland was little affected by the Industrial Revolution; Ireland had a calamitous fall both in population (through deaths and migration) and in living standards as a result of the Famine whereas Britain did not. Of course, we must not expect that the recording of transactions in the nineteenth century was as rigorous and as accurate as nowadays and we do find great variations in both the quantity and the quality of information gathered over a century. These difficulties are compounded by the fact that there have been changes in the types of goods produced and consumed over the past one hundred and fifty years – motor cars and aeroplanes did not exist in 1800 and charcoal and candles have long since ceased to be significant items of consumption, save for those who enjoy barbecues and intimate dinners. But, despite the drawbacks, year to year changes can be compared and thereby, with some heroic assumptions, longer term comparisons can be made. Figure 1 shows the behaviour of the United Kingdom national income statistics since 1855. National income is measured in money terms because money is a convenient common denominator: only by using monetary values is it possible to add the (annual) physical output of ice cream to the physical output of motor cars.

In looking at the movement of national income figures over time we need to know how much income each person receives. We know what was available during the time period in question but we also

I.E. – 2

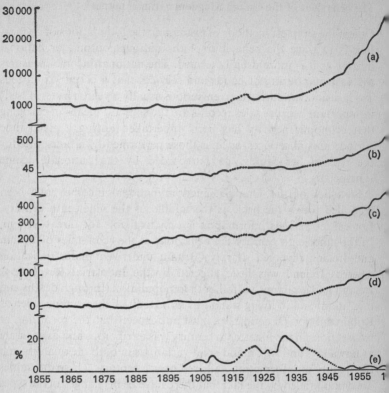

Figure 1 The material basis of civilization, UK 1855–1970.
(a) National income at current prices.
(b) National income per head at current prices.
(c) National income per head in real terms.
(d) Retail prices (1963 = 100). (e) Unemployment

know that the total population was changing. We must therefore divide the total income figures by the total population at various dates in order to get some idea of what the average standard of living was. This procedure is the best that can be done. We know that some people seem to get more of the available goods than do others but we have no reliable estimates of the disparities until recent decades. Dividing what is available by the number of potential recipients gives a measure of the standard of living that would have resulted if everyone had got equal absolute amounts of the community's goods and services. In this manner we obtain the national income per head at current prices (Figure 1a) and we see that this tends to follow the same path as the national income total (Figure 1b). (*Care should be observed in looking at these two time series since they are based on different scales.*)

The difficulty when using the money prices of goods and services, however, is that money prices can change from time to time without there being any change in the volume of physical output. Last year a particular make of car may have cost £1000 and this year it may cost £1500. Some of the difference might reflect quality differences but a more likely explanation might be changes in the value of money. Ideally what we need to do is to have constant prices for all goods and services so that we can look at output in physical terms. We need to take the prices of goods in one period and assume that these prices obtain in all periods, only then can we get a measure of national income per head *in real terms*, that is, at constant prices, and this is the time series in Figure 1c.

We have now obtained what we set out to obtain – changes in the physical output of goods and services over time, and in doing so have uncovered three important questions. First, there is the general question of why has real income per head increased over time? Secondly, there is the question of the part played by the population in determining income per head. People work but they also eat and there is often a delicate balance between the two which is considered in Chapter 3. Finally, there is the influence of changes in prices. In Figure 1 we notice that the elimination of price changes reveals divergences between calculations in current prices and calculations in the prices of a given date. Figure 1d illustrates the behaviour of prices and this reveals considerable fluctuations. What we need to know is what caused these fluctuations? This is the subject of Part Six.

The shift in the composition of output

How was the increase in the total output of the United Kingdom brought about? First, there was the emergence of a surplus in agricultural production (a product of good harvests and new methods of production) which released labour for other activities. Secondly, there were the great inventions which enabled more and more goods and

Table 1 The composition of the British national product, 1801–1955 (percentages of the total national income)

	Agriculture, forestry, fishing	Manufactures, mining, building	Trade, transport, income from abroad	Government, domestic, other services	Housing
1801	32·5	23·4	17·4	21·3	5·3
1851	20·3	34·3	20·7	18·4	8·1
1901	6·1	40·2	29·8	15·5	6·2
1955	4·7	48·1	24·9	19·2	3·2

Source: Deane and Cole (1960), table 1

services to be produced with the same inputs of resources. Thirdly, there was the development of new lines of economic activity.

Let us not proceed further with the process of sub-dividing the total output into finer and finer classifications of industries. Instead, let us see what we can glean from the broad groups. The striking feature to note is the relative unimportance of agriculture, forestry and fishing, and government (see Table 1). By the end of the period the contribution of agriculture is minute. The period under observation is one where economic activity is dominated by industry and trade, and mainly industry. What we see in Table 1 is the continuation of a process which began some time in the second half of the eighteenth century and which has been dubbed the Industrial Revolution.

Economic historians have long debated the significance and causes of the Industrial Revolution. Was it a Revolution, meaning thereby a sharp break with the past? Was it unique? Was it merely a revolution in industry and, if so, was it confined to particular industries? Some economic historians have pointed to a Neolithic Revolution which occurred around 4000 BC and brought about a shift from hunting and food-gathering to farming. Others have detected an industrial revolution in the thirteenth-century clothing industry and a later one in the sixteenth century connected with brass and glass. Thus, if there was a revolution in the eighteenth century then perhaps it was not historically unique.

The debate on the Industrial Revolution has also considered the question of whether the revolution was concentrated on cotton, coal or iron. Recent research has tended to reduce the importance of cotton and to emphasize the simultaneous revolutions in agriculture, industry, transport and communications. And even though it is conceded that there was some perceptible quickening in economic activity in the eighteenth century it is now considered to be the cumulation of many small changes that occurred from the seventeenth century onwards.

No doubt the debate concerning the Industrial Revolution will continue. If we wanted to single out any important feature it would be the factory system, and if we are to single out one important feature of the last fifty years then it must be the reassertion of government relative to private enterprise. Before the Industrial Revolution the systems known as feudalism and mercantilism had stressed the importance of collective regulation of economic activity. This declined in the nineteenth century but collective regulation has now reappeared in a different form and is concerned with different issues.

The increases in output and the shifts in the composition of output were accompanied by changes in the size, composition and distribution of the labour force. The first marked change was the movement of labour from the land into urban factories. Attendant upon that shift were changes in methods of work and in attitudes towards work. The factory system introduced greater regularity into the working lives of its operatives. Seasonal influences, bouts of enforced idleness, began to disappear. There was also a great increase in the participation of women and children in the labour market.

Latterly, the shift towards a service economy is making itself felt in the decline in the relative importance of manual workers in manufacturing. Indeed by the year 2000 if present trends continue the manual worker will have become relatively unimportant as compared to the white-collar worker.

Foreign trade

The task of feeding an increasing population has been partly met by increasing the output of domestic agriculture, but more so by exchanging our manufactures for the agricultural products of other countries. What we observe is a *substitution* of foreign produced foodstuffs for domestically produced foodstuffs. Presumably this must have represented a gain or it would never have been undertaken.

Table 2 Changing pattern of British exports, 1830–1950
(percentages of total exports)

	1830	1850	1870	1910	1930	1950
cotton yarn and cloth	50·8	39·6	35·8	24·4	15·3	7·3
wool yarn and cloth	12·7	14·1	13·4	8·7	6·5	6·5
iron and steel	10·2	12·3	14·2	11·4	10·3	9·5
machinery	0·5	0·8	1·5	6·8	8·2	14·3
coal	0·5	1·8	2·8	8·7	8·6	5·3
vehicles	—	—	1·1	3·8	9·0	18·6
chemicals	—	0·5	0·6	4·3	3·8	5·0
electrical goods	—	—	—	—	2·1	3·9

Source: Deane and Cole (1960), table 2

Table 3 Changing pattern of British imports, 1840–1950
(percentages of total imports)

	1840	1880	1910	1950
food, drink and tobacco	39·7	44·1	38·0	39·5
raw materials and semi-manufactures	56·6	38·6	38·5	38·2
manufactures and miscellaneous	3·7	17·3	23·5	22·3

Source: Deane and Cole (1960), table 3

The exploration of the gains from trade is the task of Chapter 4. What needs to be noted at this stage, however, is that if there were gains from trade, then their persistence has been due to a continual change in the kinds of goods that we exported, the kinds of goods that we imported and the countries from whom we imported. The process of substitution is continually occurring, as is well brought out in Tables 2 and 3. In the nineteenth century exports were dominated by textiles, coal, iron and steel, whereas the twentieth century reveals a shift towards machinery and vehicles. Likewise imports show a concentration on foodstuffs and raw materials though manufactured goods have become important in the last fifty years.

Inputs

The material basis of civilization has been created by man working and wrestling with Nature and in the process creating and using what have been termed capital goods – machines, buildings, etc. Casual

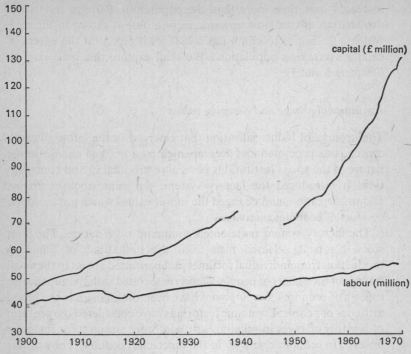

Figure 2 UK 1900–1970.
Source: Times Newspapers (1971)

observation suggests that how much a man produces may depend upon whether he uses a spade or merely his hands. More generally we can say that what man produces is crucially dependent upon the amount of capital goods available. In Figure 2 we show the behaviour of population and the capital stock since 1900. Since capital is heterogeneous – machines, buildings, etc. – it is measured in money terms because, as we have seen, money is a common denominator. However, because prices change, we have assumed that the prices occurring in 1963 ruled throughout the period. It is the same measurement problem that we encountered with the national income. Although people do differ we follow the statisticians and Robert Burns and say: 'A man's a man for a' that'. There are assumed to be no measurement problems with people.

What comes out from Figure 2 is that the stock of capital has increased over time more than the population. Perhaps this is the explanation of that slow upward creep in output shown in Figure 1 which later begins to climb rapidly. Does it represent the effects of capital overtaking population? We shall explore this issue later in Chapters 3 and 39.

Institutional change and changing values

The upsurge of industrialization that emerged in the late eighteenth century was promoted and accompanied by a marked change in the nature of the social institutions governing production and consumption. It introduced the factory system, the joint stock company, and urbanization, and changed the moral values which governed the conduct of economic activity.

The factory system represented command over nature. The joint stock company released men from the limitations of financing production from individual fortunes and permitted access to the small savings of thousands of people. Closely associated with the measurable aspects of economic development have been the changes in the moral attitudes of people. Economic historians have considered the problem of whether changes in religious attitudes were essential for the great upsurge in economic activity in the nineteenth century. The answers have been inconclusive. But there were some definite changes in attitudes, despite the fact that the new views on work, income and the accumulation of wealth were not the products of a smooth and gradual process. Men did not accept readily the doctrine of *laissez-faire*, a doctrine which may be defined as a belief that few restrictions should be placed on men's pursuit of wealth. Yet by the end of the nineteenth century there could be discerned a change in outlook. James Watt and his steam engine and Charles Darwin and the Beagle had done their work. The theory of evolution suggested that behind Nature lay not God but random forces, and the steam engine was one means of controlling those forces.

Other aspects of well-being

So far we have examined the changes in the output of goods and services and used those changes as an indicator of economic well-being and as a provider of a basis for a civilized life. We can, however, find

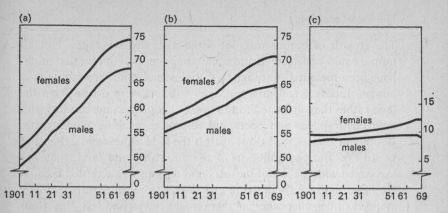

Figure 3 Expectation of life in Great Britain.
(a) At birth. (b) Five years old. (c) Seventy years old.
Source: *Social Trends,* no. 3, 1972, HMSO

alternative measures of well-being and an important one is the
expectation of life. As Figure 3 shows, expectation of life has increased
for all age-groups. Surely to generations succumbing to increasing
scepticism about a life hereafter this must be counted as a blessing?

Two further aspects of well-being need to be noted. The first is that
hours of work have declined over the period under observation.
From fifty-four hours a week in the late nineteenth century they fell
to around forty-six hours in the sixties. These changes have seen the
elimination of Saturday and Sunday from the normal work-week.
Leisure has in fact been an important indicator of the growth in
well-being and since 1900 people have consumed more of both
leisure and material goods. The second aspect has been the raising of
the age at which young persons commence their working lives; they
now enjoy longer periods in full-time education.

When obtaining our estimates of real national income per head we
took into account changes in the size of the population. These changes
in population have been considerable. Some economic historians have
seen the problem of the eighteenth century as the task of feeding an
increasing population and the Industrial Revolution as a solution to
this problem. Others have questioned whether population change is
a cause or consequence of economic prosperity.

The growth of output was not without its disadvantages. Not all output could be measured and some components of output that might have been measured were ignored. Industrialization brought with it human upheaval and misery. Many workers were driven from the land rather than attracted to the towns. People became careless with their environment and poets and reformers, such as Wordsworth, Booth and Engels, spoke out against the hideousness and ugliness of urban life. But the pollution of the air, rivers and land, that was associated with the rise of industry and output, was accepted because the basic wants of food, drink and shelter were being satisfied. Few stopped to consider whether there might be devised less obnoxious methods of production and it has been left to the materially affluent middle class of the twentieth century to be concerned with mass aesthetics.

The Industrial Revolution also brought with it marked fluctuations in economic activity. In agrarian societies such fluctuations were due to Nature and men attempted to insulate themselves from its effects by the social institution known as feudalism which permitted everyone a claim on what output was available. In industrial market economies, known sometimes as capitalist or *laissez-faire*, the fluctuations seemed to be due to forces within the system rather than to the forces without. Moreover, there seemed to be no methods of offsetting unemployment. Figure 1 shows some marked fluctuations in economic activity. In the nineteenth century 8 per cent of the labour force could be reckoned to be permanently trying to find jobs, in the period 1919–39 it rose as high as 20 per cent (in 1931) and thereafter the percentage never rose above 3 per cent. What caused these variations is the subject of Part Eight. It is worth noting, however, that if we compare real income per head in the slump years of the twenties and thirties with that of the boom years of the nineteenth century, then the *employed* people were in some sense better off in the twentieth-century depressions. Why this should be so is a question of the causes of growth and progress, the subject of Chapter 39. It is also interesting to note that in the nineteenth century prices tended to be stable when unemployment was about 8 per cent; fell in the inter-war years when unemployment was around 12 per cent, and have risen with unemployment below 3 per cent in the post-war period. This suggests a theory relating the behaviour of prices to the level of unemployment which is explored in Chapter 37.

Recapitulation

We started from a belief that changes in material well-being were conducive to the attainment of the good life and sought to measure such changes and isolate possible causes. We discovered that:

1 Changes in total output were accompanied by changes in the composition of output.

2 Some part of material well-being was created through foreign trade.

3 Change seemed to be accompanied by changes in mental and social attitudes.

4 Change seemed to have certain side effects – unemployment, pollution, etc. – whose significance has increased over time.

From a brief examination of the United Kingdom experience we now turn to ask the same questions of the rest of the world.

Other countries

The trend of economic activity and of economic well-being in the United Kingdom poses the question: do other countries exhibit similar characteristics? This question is really three questions:

1 Do the poor countries of the world share the characteristics possessed by the United Kingdom of one or even two hundred years ago?

2 Do the rich countries have much in common with the United Kingdom?

3 Must the poor countries follow the same paths trodden by the rich countries?

Lack of statistics

The most notable feature of the poorer countries of the world is the lack of statistics. Some measures of national income are available but such figures tend to refer only to the sector of the economy where goods are bought and sold for money, to what is sometimes referred to as the market sector. But a great deal of trade takes place in markets where there is little or no use of money so the volume of trade is not recorded. And an enormous amount of production and exchange takes place within the family, which in the poorer countries is frequently an extended family of considerable size. What economists sometimes do is to use information from the market sector to make guesses about the subsistence sector. We need therefore to treat the national income data for these countries with caution.

Agriculture

One of the simplest methods of determining the well-being of a country is to look at the proportion of its labour force employed in agriculture. The vagaries of the weather make agricultural output uncertain and threaten livelihoods, so that agricultural communities tend to be poor communities – though there are the exceptions such as Denmark, New Zealand and Australia.

Life expectancy

Agricultural economies seem to have low incomes per head and the people have a short expectation of life. Lack of nourishment means that illnesses and diseases often become fatal. Undernourishment can also lead to lack of mental development and general debility and so prevent attempts to work better and harder to increase output.

Literacy

A further indicator of poverty is the low level of literacy in the developing countries. Literacy makes possible efficient communication between peoples and thereby leads to an increase in the output of goods and services.

Combining fragments

Although we have tended to caution in using the national income figures of poorer countries, they have some usefulness. In so far as they refer to the market sector they refer to that sector of the economy

Table 4 Percentage of the labour force *not* in agriculture, by selected areas at various dates

	England and Wales	USA	Germany	Russia	Japan	India
1700–75	55–60					
1801	65	28				
1870–80	85	50	58		17	
about 1900	91	63	65	25	30	28
about 1950–60	95	91	77	60	67	27

Table 5 Crude death rates per thousand of total population, by selected areas at various dates

	England and Wales	USA	Germany	Russia	Japan	India
about 1700	32					
about 1800	25	25				
about 1850	23	23	27	40		
1900–9	15	16	19	30	21	43
1955–59	12	9	11	8	8	20

Table 6 Illiteracy (percentage of population) in the major world regions, 1930 and 1950, and in developed and developing countries, 1950

	All countries		Developed 1950	Developing 1950
	1930	1950		
World	59	47	6	71
North America	4	2	2	
Europe	15	8	4	23
Oceania	14	11	1	88
USSR	40	11	11	
South America	54	42	17	51
Middle America	59	48	22	53
Asia	81	70	2	75
Africa	88	88	56	91

which statesmen are interested in developing. If we then relate the national income data to other pieces of evidence we find:

1 Countries with low incomes per head tend to have a large proportion of their labour force in agriculture;

2 Countries with low incomes per head tend to have low literacy rates, low life-expectancy rates and high infant-mortality rates.

Alternative routes to affluence

An examination of the characteristics and problems of other countries serves to remind us how unique the UK growth in prosperity has been. It was:

1 The first major industrial revolution.

2 It was accompanied by the removal of restrictions on trade.

3 It was achieved with little or no foreign aid or investment, though some have seen in slavery and piracy the foundations of UK glory.

4 It produced social and political changes without the extreme violence that occurred in some other countries.

The contrast is marked even with those countries which began to industrialize in the second half of the nineteenth century. America and Germany imposed tariffs because they felt that their infant manufacturing industries would not be able to withstand the severe competition from the British economy. The British pattern of development was one which seemed to be associated with private enterprise and free trade. Today that association does not seem obvious to the underdeveloped countries. Some are inclined to follow the Russian example of centralized control of development with public ownership of the means of production, but even when the Russian pattern is rejected there is no acceptance of the UK example. There is, in fact, a tendency to imitate by example, if not intent, the French and German methods of state encouragement of industry as practised in the nineteenth century. But perhaps all countries, including the UK, have to follow a policy of state control in the preparatory and take-off stages and then allow a relaxation of controls at a later stage.

The problems of the poorer countries are of course tremendously difficult. Contact with the developed countries has created an immediate demand for Western standards of health, education and industrial relations. But these standards have been a relatively recent development in the West and their attempted introduction into the poorer countries may bring social tension and conflict and may inhibit social development. Moreover, the past experiences of colonialism have created a distrust of foreign investment and foreign aid.

Questions

1 'The gross national product does not allow for the health of our youth, the quality of their education or the joy of their play. It does not include the beauty of our poetry or the strength of our marriage, the intelligence of our public debate or the integrity of our public officials. It measures neither our wit nor our courage, neither our wisdom nor our learning, neither our compassion nor our devotion to country. It measures everything, in short, except that which makes life worthwhile . . .' Robert Kennedy, *The Times*, 10 February 1968. Comment.

2 How should we measure the difference in the national income of Denmark and Eire created by the ability to buy pornographic literature in Denmark?

3 What conclusions would you draw from the following (hypothetical) observations:

(a) In 1970 the outputs of steel in China and the UK were each valued at 1 million US dollars.

(b) The cost of water supply in Kuwait was 20 US dollars per gallon as compared with 0·25 dollars per gallon in the UK.

4 Is the national income per head lower in Morocco than in Ireland because the former enjoys a warm climate?

Chapter 2
Wants and Goods

The characteristics of the UK national income over time have been those of changing size and composition. Why has this been so? It has occurred because what has been produced has been in response to the wants of the community and, through foreign trade, the wants of other communities. Economists, we said in the previous chapter, study how men and women obtain their livelihood. What we concentrated on in that chapter was the size and composition of the things that constitute that livelihood. But we said nothing about the *wants* that dictated the types of goods and services bought, nor did we say anything about *production* which is the process by which things, undesirable in themselves, are transformed into things which are desirable. Production is the mechanism by which resources are transformed into goods which satisfy wants. Evidently we cannot produce everything immediately, for that would imply that Neolithic Man should have had a motor car and an aeroplane. In fact production is dogged by scarcity of knowledge, of time, and of materials, and because of the scarcity there must be choice. Economics, we have said, is the study of how men and women obtain a livelihood but at a more philosophical level economics is the study of choice, of what methods are used to obtain what kind of livelihood.

The economic problem

As the study of choice, economics ranges over all kinds of decisions: to take a particular job, get married, go to a film, buy a house. Its techniques are general, though sometimes confined to business and the market place. But it is a mistake to think of economics as a subject with a specific area of enquiry: its usefulness lies in the possession of a method for obtaining solutions to problems of choice. Choice arises because innumerable wants are constrained by limited resources.

Without scarcity there would be no need for decisions, no choice and life could be meaningless.[1]

Natural resources are essential to existence and comprise the potentialities of Nature. Such resources are limited because the earth is not boundless. But being limited is not synonymous with scarcity. Worn tyres are not scarce because they are *not wanted*. Water in the Indian Ocean is limited but it is not scarce. Only if everyone demanded a million gallons of water per day from the Indian Ocean might scarcity exist. Nor is scarcity a property only of physical things – time is a scarce resource and life is not eternal; time must be allowed for eating, sleeping, work and leisure and so a choice must be made as to how to allocate time.

Goods are the link between wants and resources. Goods are derived from resources and are necessary to satisfy wants. Goods need not be physical things and often economists use the more abstract term, 'services'. A symphony is a good even though it cannot be measured or weighed. Bread is a good, a motor car is a good and so are the words of the orator. Scarce resources are used to produce goods but which goods and hence which resources are used will depend upon choice, for people will attempt to obtain those goods which yield the greatest satisfaction from given resources. Alternatives are ranked according to their capacity to fulfil the objective of the individual, firm or country. Objectives can refer to 'satisfaction', 'well-being', 'utility', 'profit', 'national prestige' or 'duty'. In exercising choice an individual (or firm or country) will try to be consistent. If a man prefers a house to a car and a car to an aeroplane he will be inconsistent if he prefers an aeroplane to a house.

Sometimes contradictions or inconsistencies do occur or appear to occur. In complex situations fraught with uncertainty, apparently inconsistent choices are sometimes made. There is lack of complete information and what appears to be contradictory behaviour may often be experimentation, an attempt to obtain more information.

Choice links wants to resources through the selection of goods. Out of the myriad of wants some are given priority and given the limitations of time and other resources some goods are chosen to satisfy those wants. How is the choice made? According to the economist it is made through the principle of choosing the cheapest good to satisfy

1. This raises the thorny problem of whether there is such a thing as free will.

a given set of wants. If two cars will equally satisfy the want to travel then the cheaper is bought.

Wants

Because wants are so important and occupy a key position in economics it is useful to explore their nature and see what problems they present for economists.

Some wants are obvious – the need for food and drink stems from biological requirements. Others appear to be culturally determined – eating in cafes, watching football matches, going to pop festivals. And sometimes curiosity is the source of wants. Undoubtedly, the exploration of the deeper recesses of human behaviour is the task of the psychologist, but the economist has an interest in some of the more obvious aspects of wants. Two things attract his attention. First, there are the *cultural determinants of wants*. Secondly, there is the apparent existence of a *hierarchy of wants*.

Although economists cannot say why Britons like cricket and Americans like baseball, the notion that within communities there are certain needs, concerning which there is such universal agreement that they must be satisfied, is of use to the economist interested in making policy recommendations. If there is a general belief that no one should live in poverty then an economist may confidently propose various policies which redistribute income from the rich to the poor. If no such consensus exists then an economist can only record the existence of poverty and hope to play an educative role. The existence of a consensus can enable an economist to bridge the gap between *positive economics*, concerned with 'what is', and *normative economics*, concerned with 'what ought to be'.

The second aspect of wants that interests the economist is the commonplace observation that wants can be ordered, that there is a hierarchy of wants. Some wants, such as the need for food and drink, must be satisfied before others can be considered. This means that there is an irreducibility of wants in the sense that we must first satisfy some wants before attempting to satisfy others. This notion helps to explain why Americans can contemplate space flights whilst Asians must be preoccupied with food production. In exercising choice an individual, firm or country attempts to satisfy the greatest number of wants starting with the most important and going down the hierarchy.

For simplicity we can number a person's wants, $W_1, \ldots, W_n$. Let us assume that his first requirement is drink and can be satisfied by water G_1. If we join W_1 and G_1 then we can say that there is a one-to-one correspondence between W_1 and G_1 as in Figure 4. This need not always be so. Consider his second need, food. It can be satisfied by meat, G_2 and potatoes, G_3. Hence we can join W_2 to G_2 and G_3. Meat and potatoes may be thought of as a composite good created out of two other goods. In a similar manner, a blue car, G_4, can satisfy his need for transport, W_3, and colour, W_4. Here we can notice that the primary want is travel and so a blue house would be unacceptable whereas a red car or green car would satisfy the more pressing need.

Why should we emphasize a trivial point concerning a blue car? The answer is that when people are asked why they made a particular purchase they often give what is an apparently trivial reason – ' because it is blue'. Such a reply seems to indicate a lack of seriousness, yet to draw such a conclusion would be misleading for what the answer implies is that a *blue* car satisfies the lesser want.

The existence of a hierarchy of wants provides us with some reasons why a consensus might not exist. If individuals are seeking to satisfy different wants then, given the existence of limited resources to satisfy those wants, there will be a conflict of interest which may be difficult to resolve. If one group of stockbroker citizens want fast urban motorways in order to get to and from the office then they may require a motorway to be built close to the houses of those who wish to live in the towns. General agreement can usually be reached on basic needs – food and shelter – but conflict arises over the satisfaction of low-order wants. Should land be used for roads, or pony-trekking, or bird-sanctuaries?

We can go a little further in our exploration of wants by observing that the satisfaction of wants usually involves human services as well as inanimate objects. Suppose a man wants to live in a well-educated society. This want, W_5, can be achieved by combining schools, G_6, with other people $H_1, \ldots, H_n$. Again we suppose that he likes congenial company, W_6, which can be satisfied by H_2, a one-to-one relationship which takes economics into the realms of love and marriage, and contrasts monogamy with polygamy, the aloof with the gregarious.

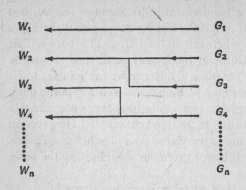

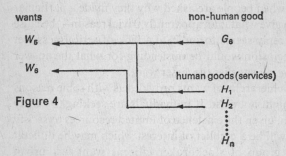

Figure 4

The classification of goods

1 Private goods
2 Collective goods
   (a) Privately produced
   (b) Produced by the State
   (c) Free goods

Private goods

The analysis of wants leads naturally on to the investigation of the sources of want satisfaction: that is, to the nature of goods. We begin with private goods. These are privately owned and privately consumed. They are the goods that we normally think of when people exchange goods for goods, or goods for money. Such goods are, however, probably rare, for most goods give rise to spillover effects (sometimes called *externalities*).

Collective goods

But many goods do not fit into the private category. Many goods, even when privately owned, are collectively consumed. For example, the bee-keeper owns his bees but his neighbour's gardens benefit from the bees' activities; a privately owned cigarette smoked in a crowded bus creates unpleasant effects for all the other passengers (such effects are often referred to as *spillovers* or *externalities*). This characteristic of collectiveness may appear on a grand scale as in the case of many goods produced by the State – moon trips and national defence confer benefits (or disbenefits) upon a host of consumers. Although this category of goods can be refined in detail our present aim is to convey the point that 'collectiveness' is independent of the actual number of consumers – the good may be consumed simultaneously by two consumers or by two hundred.

Free goods

A special class of collective goods are the so-called free goods. They cost nothing to produce and represent the free gifts of nature. But because they are free they are often squandered. Rubbish is dumped in rivers causing pollution and a scarcity of clean, pure water. Wild birds are slaughtered and wild flowers are picked indiscriminately. Into this category we also place the stately homes, English literature and other works of art, for they form, as much as the countryside, part of the cultural heritage which is shared by all. It is, in fact, interesting to observe the long line of distinguished economists who have sought to sustain the Arts largely through pressing for state financing and protection.

Reality and the politics of economists

Where does reality lie? Does it lie in assuming that the world is dominated by private goods which are privately owned and privately consumed and traded through markets? Pick up almost any economics

I.E. – 3

textbook and the impression given is of a world of private goods. This emphasis may be due to the fact that economics, as a distinct discipline, emerged at a time when the market was beginning to seem more important in everyday life. Moreover, it was also the period when individualism became the byword so that market economics tended to colour people's political and social thinking. Economists may be conservatives, but, if they are, then that arises not from their consciousness of the difficulties of making social changes, but from a presumption that reality is a world of private goods subject to some peripheral interference by the state.

Yet it is possible to see reality as a world of collective goods, of spillovers of goods and bads. A world in which people collectively seek to prevent standards of health, education and nutrition falling below certain social minima. A world in which many goods – neighbourliness, wonderful scenery – are not provided by markets, and where markets are continually crumbling under the forces prompting monopoly. Economic history suggests that the market economy is but two hundred years old in the thousands of mankind's existence, and from such a vantage point an economist might become a socialist or a communist.

The fascination of economics lies in its unravelling of the ways in which people cope with the problems of spillovers. For two similar goods may be classified differently according to their immediate environments. Thus, the words on this page are private goods in so far as the owner of this book has established a unique property right. But if these same words were to be read aloud to an audience then, in that context, they would constitute a collective good (or bad depending upon the tastes of the audience). Furthermore, the right to read this book may be disputed by some if it is felt to be seditious, pornographic and 'contrary to faith and morals'. Decisions concerning private and collective goods strike therefore at social behaviour and, in particular, at that faith known as liberalism which believes that each should be allowed to do that which enriches his own personality, but then discovers that this might mean subjugating the personality of another.

The simplest solution might be to deem all goods collective, the right to their use being vested in the community as a whole. But, of itself, that may be no solution. Should everyone have, for example, the untrammelled right to consume public property? But how should the state decide on the allocation of shares? And how should the international community deal with the radioactive dust which falls on one country when another explodes hydrogen bombs?

The alternative is to deem all goods private, and hope that people do not feel strongly about the spillovers. Thus, the enjoyment obtained from the view of a neighbour's garden may be obtained without having to pay for the privilege. And the neighbour may not be annoyed. Many delights in life are, in fact, obtained for nothing and life would be very intolerable if we had to pay for all pleasure. What would we think and feel about a world in which everyone put a high hedge around his garden and all girls wore yashmaks and maxis? Tolerance of goods not paid for also extends to some bads which are received without payment. For most of the post-war period the Japanese have been more tolerant of smoke than the British. Evidently, the differences in tolerance are related to the hierarchy of wants. The Japanese have been prepared to put up with smoke in order to satisfy their higher wants. The British, having earlier solved the material problems of the nation, have sought to satisfy their desires for a healthy environment.

But when bads become intolerable then there will be private or collective attempts to eliminate them. Thus in the case of road accidents motorists may agree to compensate each other for injuries if the injured party can prove his claim. Or a householder may buy some waste land adjoining his house in order to prevent an ugly block of flats being built there. He may even pay the builder to build elsewhere. There are, however, more complex situations. Supposing the motorist fails in his claim for damages and, because of his injuries, cannot work. Should he therefore be allowed to starve? Not if the state is obliged to guarantee a minimum income.

In the bewildering assortment of options there will be a tendency to look for the least costly solution (a theme echoed and amplified in Chapter 14). Meanwhile we can classify some mechanisms for want satisfaction.

Mechanisms for want satisfaction

Looking at the kinds of wants, and the goods which satisfy those wants, forces us to realize that the arrangements for obtaining those goods can also be complex. We can for simplicity list them and briefly consider their merits.

Self-sufficiency

By self-sufficiency individuals can presumably satisfy their wants though they may do so in an inefficient manner. Indeed, in most cases self-sufficiency is inefficient. Who but the egoist can satisfy his own need for congenial company?

Theft

Robbery can be a means of supplementing resources and imperialism may be its highest expression. But it is impossible to maintain a stable society when 'life is nasty, brutish and short'. Safety of personal possessions, including life, necessitates law and order and defence and involves making agreements with others.

Charity

Suppose we wish to see other people as well fed and decently clothed as ourselves. We could give them the means to purchase food and clothing. Charity has always been a means of satisfying wants though it may not always be successful. Giving a poor man money may allow him to buy alcohol whilst giving him food might hurt his self-respect.

Trade

This is the commonest method of satisfying wants when a person's own resources are insufficient. Such trade may be state or private, formal or informal, simple or elaborate. It can range from children swapping toys to millionaires buying diamonds.

Trade requires markets – means whereby buyers and sellers can make offers. Such markets may be physical locations – the schoolyard, the corner shop or the high street – but physical location and physical contact are not essential as long as communications can be established. The telephone links buyers and sellers in different countries and people can reply to newspaper advertisements in complete anonymity.

Collectivization

Some of the wants we have examined cannot be satisfied by any of the methods we have so far considered. How can anyone buy a well-educated society? Slavery is not permitted in democratic societies and if someone provides education for others, how can he be sure that they will not migrate? Whilst if he gives them money they may spend it on alcohol. How can a community ensure that its countryside is preserved from speculative builders? These kinds of problem seem to require different solutions from those so far presented. They require an institutional arrangement different from charity or the market.

Collectivization can imply compulsory consumption or an opportunity to reject the collective good. Fluoride in drinking-water cannot be avoided without at the same time abstaining from drinking water. On the other hand, for many collective goods their level of supply suggests that most people regard the costs of additional units as exceeding the costs of alternative private goods. Thus most people are willing to pay for a collective police force but still put locks on their doors. Similarly the provision of a public fire protection service is not a sufficient safeguard against fire and most people still check the safety of electrical and gas appliances and coal fires.

Collectivization need not imply the invocation of the State. Most communities abound in clubs – voluntary societies – through which citizens provide a limited number of people with collective goods. Golf clubs, football clubs, mothers' meetings and youth clubs are examples of such private institutions designed to provide collective goods such as friendship.

Summary

We began from the proposition that wants are central to economic choice and consequently attempted to classify wants. We came to the conclusion that there was a hierarchy of wants – some wants had to be satisfied before others could be contemplated. From a classification of wants we were led to a classification of the goods which satisfy those wants. Here we distinguished between private and collective goods. Finally, and inevitably, we were led to an analysis of the means by which goods can be brought into contact with wants.

Questions

1 What is the economic problem?

2 What is the hierarchy of wants?

3 Is Westminster Abbey a collective good?

4 'Medical care is a personal-consumption good and should not be made into a collective good.' Discuss.

Chapter 3
Production

All our wants cannot be satisfied unless the means are available and Andrew Marvell's rebuke to his coy mistress for her assumption that time and space were unlimited is as relevant to all other human activities as it is to love-making. There just simply are not enough resources to satisfy all our needs. Why study the movement of national income, population or foreign trade in a world of abundance? Consider Figure 5. It depicts the amounts of two goods, which can be produced, beer and cheese, or beer and education – it does not matter whether one is a private good and the other a collective good

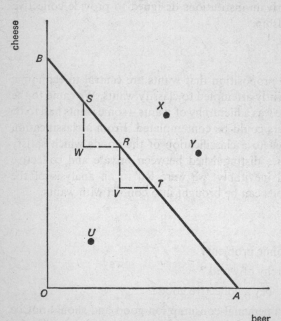

Figure 5 The production-possibility curve

since resources will be necessary to produce both. With total resources available either OA of beer or OB of cheese can be produced. We might also suppose that various combinations of beer and cheese can also be produced and that the total number of combinations, the set of outputs of beer and cheese, which can be produced lie within the area AOB or on the frontier AB. The line AB is the frontier of production possibilities – *the production-possibilities curve*: it is impossible to produce beyond it at, say, X or Y because there are not the resources available to do so. Within AOB, therefore, is the set of all attainable combinations of beer and cheese that can be produced. Beyond AB lies the set of unattainable production combinations.

It would be possible to produce *within* the frontier, say at U, but that would imply leaving some resources idle or in more general terms that resources were being used inefficiently. Even though the community's resources could take it on to the frontier, the actual output-combination produced may be that given by the point U because managers behave stupidly or workers are lazy, or because the institutional arrangements in society are such as to prevent the frontier being attained. Many countries, in fact, seem to be capable of producing more than they do. A glance at Figure 1 reveals that the United Kingdom has had over the post-war period unemployed labour which could presumably have been put to producing more goods, were the institutional arrangements for employing labour efficient. Just why idle resources do occur is a question which Part Four seeks to resolve.

But assuming that a community is on the frontier, say at R, what would be the implication of moving to either S or T? From Figure 5 we can see that such a move would mean a change in the amounts of beer and cheese produced and available for consumption. A move to S would give rise to more cheese and less beer whilst a move to T would mean more beer and less cheese. However, the interesting point about these switches of production is that they always result in a constant rate of transformation of one commodity into the other. Because line AB has a constant slope then the resources that are capable of producing one pint of beer will always be capable of producing, say, one pound of cheese.

We can express this point a little differently. Starting anywhere on the frontier the cost of obtaining an extra bottle of beer or pound of cheese is the cheese or beer foregone. This cost in terms of the alternative foregone is known as *opportunity cost*. For the economist, cost is not the money spent on goods and services but the other goods and services that have been rejected.[1]

In terms of Figure 5 the giving up of *TV* of beer enables the community to obtain *RV* of cheese, and giving up an additional *RW* of beer can result in the acquisition of *SW* of cheese. Since the slope of *AB* is constant then the opportunity cost of cheese in terms of beer is always constant (the ratios *RV/TV* and *SW/RW* are equal).

Increasing cost

Constant costs are not found in all situations. It is in fact more usual to find increasing costs. Thus in Figure 6 the production-possibility curve is concave to the origin which means that in order to obtain additional units of beer successively more units of cheese must be sacrificed: hence *CD* is longer than *AB* even though the lengths *BC* and *DE* are equal. Why should this be so?

If we think about constant costs we come to the conclusion that it

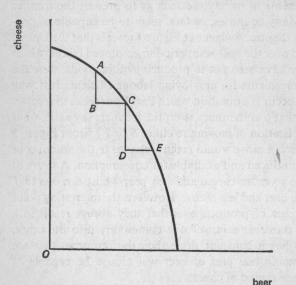

Figure 6

1. Strictly speaking it is the benefits derived from consuming goods and services that are compared. This is gone into in some detail in Chapter 12.

implies either that resources are equally efficient in all activities or that the proportions in which resources are employed are the same in all activities. Let us consider each of these assumptions in turn. It is unlikely that men employed in breweries will be equally efficient in producing cheese. If the community decides to give up beer in order to have more cheese, then it may find that after a while the cost of obtaining more cheese rises as the more skilful brewery workers move into cheese production, and the losses of beer become cumulatively greater.

It is, however, unnecessary to assume that resources differ in efficiency. Suppose that under ideal conditions beer requires three men and two units of natural resources for hop production, whereas cheese requires two men and five units of natural resources (cows and land), then whenever we switch from beer to cheese we always have more men than we need (plus 1) and too few natural resources (minus 3), and though we attempt to substitute men for natural resources there is a limit to substitution. This problem lies at the basis of the celebrated 'law' of diminishing returns. But let us examine this law in the context of the general laws of production.

Laws of production

Economists are interested in the efficiency with which resources are transformed into goods. This is partly a question of engineering, partly one of picking out the most efficient combinations – those that lie on the frontier – and then selecting the one which gives the desired combination of goods, given the prices of resources and the community's desires. For the moment, however, let us look at the engineering issue.

Economists tend to express the nature of the production process – the transformation of resources into goods – by means of a simple equation

$$Q = f(x_1, x_2, ..., x_n; T). \hspace{4cm} 1$$

This shorthand expression says that output, Q, is a function, f, of the inputs $(x_1, ..., x_n)$ and the prevailing state of technology or 'know-how', T. Both inputs and output are flows per unit of time. It may be that x_1 is a machine and we have therefore to imagine that so much of the machine is used up in each period. Accountants refer to this 'using-up' as depreciation and one of the accountant's difficult tasks is to measure this depreciation.

The most important item in the equation is the f-sign – or function – which tells us that there exists a systematic relationship between inputs and output. But what kind of systematic relationship exists? We can distinguish three general questions.

1 What happens to output as all inputs are increased by the same proportion?

2 Can the proportions in which inputs are employed be varied?

3 What happens to output when only some of the inputs are increased?

To the first question one is tempted to answer that if all inputs are increased by the same percentage then output will increase by this same percentage. But this sentence contains a trap for the unwary. 'Doubling' should not be confused with 'duplication'. It is always possible to double output by having two factories (instead of one) of the same size. But that is not what doubling means in this context. Rather, it refers to the *scale* of operations, that is, to an increase in the sizes of the inputs rather than to an increase in the number of inputs of constant size. We are interested in what happens when there is a *morphological change* – of what happens if ants became ten times their normal size, or the Soviet Union six times its present size. What then happens if all inputs are increased in scale by the same percentage? The answer to this question does not seem to be clear-cut. If all the dimensions of a blast furnace are increased by the same percentage then the volume (and hence output) increases by a greater percentage. If all the dimensions of a plough are increased by the same percentage then the motive power to pull it through the soil may have to be increased by a greater percentage. The problem is whether or not constant returns to scale exist.

If the scale of each input is increased by some proportion, k, then *constant returns to scale* prevail if output rises by the same proportion k.

In practice increasing or decreasing returns to scale may occur because of the existence of fixed factors. If all the inputs of a factory are increased tenfold we should expect to find workers eighteen metres high. The fact that we do not puts obstacles in the way of a ready acceptance of the notion of constant returns to scale. The ability to vary the proportions in which resources can be used is also something over which there is disagreement. Taxis and taxi-drivers seem to be available only in the proportion of one-to-one. But this may be an illusion since it is possible to have one driver for day duties and one for night duties. Variable proportions seem more likely if we allow enough time to transform equipment. Bulldozers can be converted into spades if we decide not to replace worn-out bulldozers. If then we allow for variations in proportions what happens to output as only one input is increased in amount? This is the question answered by the celebrated *law of diminishing returns*.

The law of diminishing returns

We begin with a definition and the conditions under which the law is said to operate:

If the input of units of one resource increases while the input of other resources remains unchanged then beyond a certain point output can only increase at a diminishing rate.

Conditions:

1 Other inputs must be held constant, otherwise the problem is one of returns to scale.

2 The state of technical knowledge must not change.

3 The proportions in which resources can be combined must be capable of variation.

4 All units of the variable resource are homogeneous.

The workings of the law are illustrated by Table 7. We assume that there exists an acre of land which is to be cultivated by an ever-increasing number of men. One man can produce eight bushels of wheat whilst two men can produce twenty-two bushels. In addition to the total product there are two other measures of output change which need to be observed. The first, *average product*, is self-explanatory. The second, *marginal product*, is a new concept and may be defined as the contribution which *each additional man* makes to total output. Generalizing, we may say: marginal product is the addition to total product caused by the addition of one more unit of the variable resources.

Table 7

Men (a)	Total output (b)	Average product (b/a)	Marginal product
0	0	0	0
1	8	8	8
2	22	11	14
3	37	12·33	15
4	50	12·50	13
5	60	12	10
6	68	11·33	8
7	74	10·57	6
8	80	10	6
9	85	9·44	5
10	90	9·00	5
11	88	8	−2
12	84	7	−4
13	78	6	−6

If we plot the data contained in Table 7 we can obtain Figure 7,[2] which brings out three interesting stages in the operations of diminishing returns.

Stage 1. There is an increase in the product due to the increase in the number of men employed. This is because the area to be cultivated is large in relation to the number of men. Indeed, rather than attempt to cultivate the whole area the men might decide to farm a small portion. The first stage ends with the average product being at its maximum. Note that when the average product reaches its maximum, the marginal product – the increase in output due to an increase by one unit of the variable input labour – cuts the average product curve from above.

Stage 2. This comprises the section in which both the average and marginal product are falling though the total product is increasing. The second stage ends when the marginal product of labour is zero.

Stage 3. This is the opposite of stage 1, as there are now too many men, whereas in stage 1 there was too much land. Stage 3 is unlikely to occur in practice except by accident or ignorance.

2. The use of a (discrete) arithmetic example causes the peak of average product not to coincide with the marginal intersection, and the total curve to fall before marginal product becomes negative.

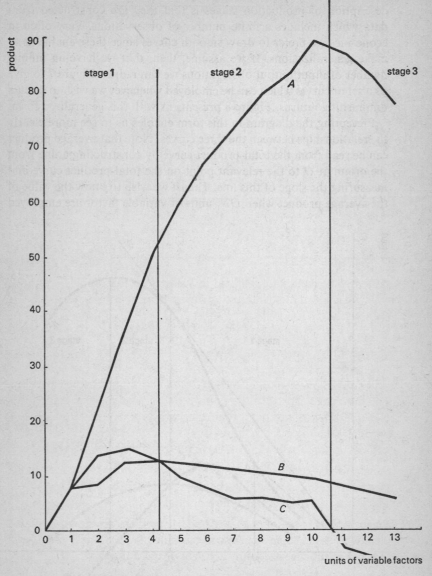

Figure 7 (a) Total-product curve. (b) Average-product curve.
(c) Marginal-product curve

The reason for the curves in Figure 7 not fitting perfectly to the description of production stages is that they are constructed from data which includes a finite number of observations. Very often in economics we prefer to draw smooth curves since these enable us to make generalizations. If we assume, then, that we have an infinite number of input/output observations we can redraw Figure 7 to give us a set of curves which can be employed whenever we wish to discuss diminishing returns. Figure 8 presents us with this generalized form.

Presenting the diagram in this form enables us to see more clearly the relationships between the three curves. Note that average product can be read from the total-product curve by constructing a line from the origin at O to the relevant point on the total-product curve and measuring the slope of this line. Thus if we wish to know the value of the average product when ON_1 units of variable factor are employed

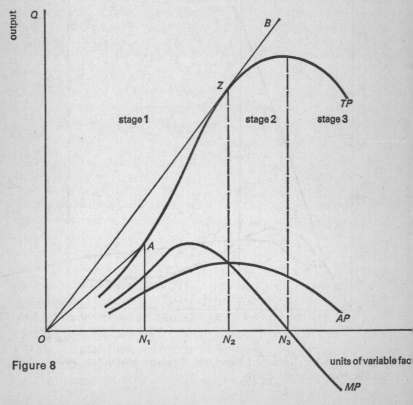

Figure 8

54 Production

the tan of angle AON_1 gives the answer AN_1/ON_1 (equals total output divided by the number of variable units employed). Stage 1 ends, therefore, when the slope of such a line to the origin is at a maximum, i.e. when it is tangential to the total-product curve (OB is tangential to TP at point Z).

Marginal product, on the other hand, is given by the slope of the total-product curve itself, i.e. this slope is measured by a small change in output divided by a small change in the number of units of variable factor employed $\Delta Q/\Delta N$. Knowing this enables us to note the features of the ending of stage 1, direct from the total-product curve. Stage 1 ends at point Z on the total-product curve and at this point the slope of the line OB equals the slope of the total-product curve – average product equals marginal product.

Finally, we can also note the feature of the end of stage 2 direct from the total-product curve. Stage 2 ends when ON_3 units of factor are employed. At this level of employment the total-product curve reaches its maximum point and then turns downwards, i.e. at an employment level ON_3 the slope of TP is zero – marginal product is zero.

These mechanics are not very stimulating in themselves but their applications can yield some fascinating results. Two interesting and important applications of the diminishing-returns principle are: the distinctions between farming and factory production techniques; and the problem of overpopulation.

Farm and factory

An understanding of the nature of the production function and the law of diminishing returns helps us to understand a phenomenon which intrigued economists who witnessed the emergence of the Industrial Revolution. They drew a distinction between agriculture, which they believed was subject to decreasing returns, and manufacturing, which they thought was subject to increasing returns. What was the reasoning behind this distinction? The principal source of energy in agriculture is the sun and two consequences follow from this dependence. First, the flow of solar energy cannot be varied by man because the stock inherent in the sun lies beyond his reach. Secondly, the flow of solar energy to the earth varies with the movement of the earth round the sun: only along the equator does the flow tend to remain constant.

It follows from the variation in sunlight that man cannot alter the nature of the interdependence of the various agricultural activities. Sowing must precede reaping: sowing and reaping cannot be reversed in time sequence nor can they be carried on simultaneously. So increasing the number of men on the land may not have much effect on output because of the fixity of solar energy and the land receiving that energy. More men may simply mean more idle men.

Contrast agriculture with manufacturing. In manufacturing, the energy sources are coal and oil – fossil fuels whose stocks lie embedded in the earth and since the stocks are accessible and can be mined, then the flow of the energy input can be varied. As a result the various processes that go together to make a manufacturing product can be carried on almost simultaneously. In the car industry, tyres, batteries, wheels, bodies and upholstery are being simultaneously produced. It is in fact possible to see all the stages in the production of a motor car in one period of time – a possibility denied to the agricultural economist.

What made possible the simultaneous production of all parts, and the possibility of doubling all inputs and producing more than double the output? The switch to fossil fuels was one cause. The other was the level of demand. As the level of demand for manufacturing goods rose it became possible to increase the degree of specialization of production at each stage. Some workers, as Adam Smith observed, would specialize in producing pin heads whilst others would specialize in sharpening the points of pins. This specialization led to an increase in efficiency and output at each stage. Hence the famous dictum of Adam Smith: *the division of labour is limited by the extent of the market*. And the classic example was the cotton industry. As demand rose the interdependent stages of production – spinning, weaving and finishing – became detached and separate producing units were established.[3]

Optimum population size and diminishing returns

One of the more obvious applications of the law of diminishing returns is to the question: how many people can be supported by a country's resources? The amount of resources available combined with the

3. Note that it is the industry and not the firm which is subject to increasing returns. The firm will ultimately encounter diminishing returns for two reasons. First, individual technical units – boilers and so forth – will exhibit diminishing returns. Secondly, the firm as a whole will face diminishing returns because management (the decision-making unit) will be a fixed factor.

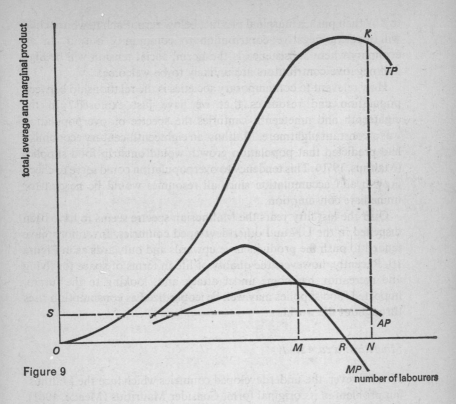

Figure 9

population and a given technology serve to determine a country's standard of living. Is it, then, possible to talk of an *optimum* population size? If so, then this optimum must be defined with reference to a subsistence living standard. Thus, given that subsistence is guaranteed, an optimum population size might be defined as one which maximizes output per head, i.e. average product. In terms of Figure 9, this population level would be *OM*.

An alternative definition might be in terms of the maximum population that a country can support. This optimum would be reached when, on an equal sharing of community output, each worker receives a subsistence reward. If subsistence is less than maximum average product then population size will be greater than *OM* in Figure 9. However, a country which accepts this definition of 'optimum' may be courting social disaster. Suppose, for example, that the subsistence level for each person is *OS* in Figure 9. Permitting population to rise

Optimum Population Size and Diminishing Returns 57

to ON then pushes marginal product below zero. Each newborn child will make a negative contribution to community output. In an economy where subsistence is the norm, social tension will be high and negative contributors are unlikely to be welcome.

How relevant to contemporary societies is the relationship between population and resources that we have just explored? In the eighteenth and nineteenth centuries the spectre of overpopulation was a constant nightmare. Malthus, an eighteenth-century economist, had predicted that population growth would outstrip food supplies (Malthus, 1970). This tendency to overpopulation could serve to check growth and accumulation since all resources would be needed for immediate consumption.

Over the last fifty years the Malthusian spectre seems to have been dispelled in the UK and other developed countries. Inventions have tended to push the product curve upwards and outwards as in Figure 10. Recently, however, the quality of life in terms of space for living and recreation has come under attack and, looking to the future, imported food supplies may well be jeopardized as consumption rises throughout the world.

Mauritius: a case study

It is, however, the underdeveloped countries which face the Malthusian problem in its original form. Consider Mauritius (Meade, 1961), a small island in the Indian Ocean, which is virtually a one-commodity economy producing sugar. During the post-war period her population has expanded enormously, largely as a result of the reduction in the incidence of malaria. Migration is difficult since many countries now have immigration controls and so Mauritius is almost in the situation of having a population of ON as in Figure 9. For such countries population control is inevitable but there may still have to be an abandonment of a wage system (that is, of paying workers according to their marginal product as in Figure 9), and a move towards giving everyone some share of the total product.

Marginal-product doctrine: a preview

In previous sections we have looked at the problem of overpopulation and the wage system. As we shall see later in Part Seven contemporary economic analysis tends to suggest that resources are paid in a wage system according to the value of the marginal product. In other words, if all men are alike then all men will be paid at the same rate as the last man employed since to pay more would be to incur losses. Now we have just seen that this doctrine breaks down when what a man might be paid would be less than the cost of his subsistence. This then is a criticism of the applicability of the doctrine. It says that in certain circumstances *men must be paid more than the marginal product.*

Later in Part Seven we shall encounter a body of theory that suggests that *men are paid less than their marginal product.* Briefly, the argument stresses the point that men are paid a subsistence wage whose value may be dictated by sociological factors, and that the difference between subsistence and the value of men's work constitutes a surplus or profit which goes partially to finance production before output emerges, and partly to the controllers of industry as their consumption. This theory raises many questions concerning the surplus which is necessary to finance production and development and these issues will be dealt with in Part Seven (notably Chapter 26). In the meantime it should be borne in mind that nothing has been said about the financing of production.

Immigration

The law of diminishing returns is also useful in considering the problem of immigration. In 1968 the British Government passed an Act which proposed stricter control of the entry of Commonwealth immigrants into the UK. This Act occasioned a great deal of controversy both before and after its passage. Supporters of the Act pointed to the outbreaks of racial violence in America and to the social tensions in areas where immigrants have settled in Britain, notably London and the Midlands. On the other hand critics of the Act said that it discriminated against people from certain countries and that Britain should be free to all who wish to enter.

Although the question of immigration is fraught with ethical and political issues the economist can present some light on the problem. An influx of people operates to increase both the labour force and the consuming public. The question is which is the stronger force? Immigrants provide a source of immediate labour from adults but they also bring dependents. In attempting to acclimatize themselves and to ensure the care of their dependents, immigrants draw on the available private and social services such as housing, education and health. Moreover, since they often reside in working-class areas they may aggravate the existing problems of slum clearance, and the poor educational and health services that are available in such areas. On the other hand, they provide a willing labour force to cover shortages in transport and health services though this may prevent new thinking on the provision of these services by, for example, operating one-man buses and eliminating many unskilled jobs through mechanization. What therefore needs to be known is how important are these opposing forces, as well as the tastes of the population regarding the goal of a multi-racial society.

Automation

Inventions are changes in technical knowledge which result either in the production of new commodities or new methods of producing existing goods. In the case of the latter, where it becomes possible to produce a commodity with fewer resources than previously, economists distinguish between three kinds of inventions:

1 Labour-saving inventions, where there is a saving in the amount of labour required to produce a commodity;

2 Capital-saving inventions which reduce the amount of capital needed to produce a good;

3 Neutral inventions which have no bias towards capital saving or labour saving but result in an overall reduction in the amounts of all factors required.

Most interest has been shown in the existence and strength of labour-saving inventions because they reduce the demands for labour. Indeed in the post-war period a particular form of labour-saving invention has been called automation because it is thought to dispense not merely with muscular strength but also with intelligence. Through the use of electronic devices it is possible to create machines which adjust and correct for errors and obviate the need for human adjustment. Now suppose that over the next few decades we had automation on a mass scale, what would happen to the demand for labour?

Figure 10a shows the vertical displacement of the total-product curve as a result of a labour-saving invention. So output OP requires

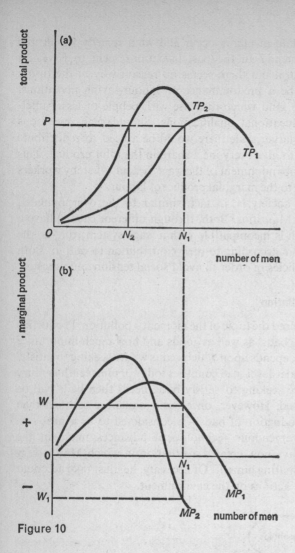

Figure 10

N_1N_2 fewer workers. In Figure 10b the effect on the marginal-product curve is shown. The MP curve is pulled towards the left. Now suppose that the labour force before the change was ON_1 and was paid at the wage rate OW. After the invention the labour force could only find employment at a wage of minus OW_1: in other words, workers would have to pay for the privilege of having a job!

Optimum Population Size and Diminishing Returns 61

Could such a state of affairs occur and what remedy should the economist recommend? In the past inventions seem to have, on balance, been neutral but there seems no reason why in the future there should not be a predominance of labour-saving inventions, particularly of the kind which dispense with people of lesser intelligence or low educational qualifications. Should such inventions occur on a much larger scale there would be a need to redistribute property in order to give everyone a share in the total product. This would require the abandonment of the wage system, whereby workers are paid according to the marginal product of labour.

The automated society is, in fact, similar to the overpopulated economy, such as Mauritius. Both, through different causes, have a labour force which is incompatible with a wage system; that is, the payment of workers according to their contribution to output. Both require similar policies in order to avoid social tension and unrest.

Production and pollution

So far we have ignored the topic of the moment – pollution. Productive processes produce 'bads' as well as goods and how much importance we attach to bads depends upon which wants we are seeking to satisfy. When, as in the underdeveloped countries today or nineteenth-century Britain, people are seeking to satisfy basic needs then bads will be ignored or tolerated. However, once basic wants are satisfied then pollution – the production of bads – is considered to be a problem. Moreover, the tremendous technological advances made in the Western World have now created a situation in which Man is very capable of exterminating himself. Of necessity, he must take acccount of the effect of his actions on the environment.

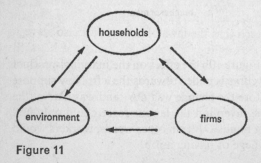

Figure 11

The production function, which was introduced at the beginning of this chapter, must be modified to take account of pollutants:

$$(Q_1, Q_2) = f(x_1, x_2, ..., x_n; T). \qquad 2$$

What we have done in equation 2 is to distinguish goods, Q_1, from bads, Q_2, which are jointly produced in the production process.

Figure 11 shows the typical system of production in an economy. This system is an *open system* in the sense that the production process delivers output to agents outside itself. Households demand goods and services from the production units, called firms, and households supply the firms with resources. In addition, both firms and households derive resources from the environment and deposit other materials (bads) into the environment. The environment is then conceived of as the repository of all free resources, that is resources not owned by anyone and which are initially in excess supply. Eventually, however, this state of affairs disappears. As economies progress, and production increases, the environment becomes depleted of resources which are useful.

The bads that are produced in advanced economies are in fact extraordinarily varied and complex: households may produce rubbish (paper, plastic containers), sewage, smoke and too many people! Firms may produce rubbish, noxious chemicals, scrap dumps, etc. How bads are reduced involves consideration of social institutions and rules of conduct that people develop. The citizens of a community may either tax or fine polluters; or cultivate good manners, implying that it is a social offence to have smoky garden fires and radios playing too loudly.

Summary

We have examined the determinants of production and in doing so have implied limits to the consumption possibilities of a community. We might also have added that the laws of production also serve to limit the consumption possibilities of the individual since his skills dictate his output. But we observed in Chapter 1 that it was possible for a country (and presumably an individual) to go beyond their production possibilities through trade, and for them to enlarge their production possibilities through accumulation and growth. These two topics – trade and growth – are the subject matter of the subsequent chapters.

Questions

1 What is the production-possibilities curve?

2 What arguments could you produce against the idea of constant returns to scale?

3 'But for the law of diminishing returns all the world's food could be grown in a flower pot.' Comment.

4 What are the main features of the three stages of production?

5 What relationships between the average and marginal products arise as output increases?

6 Is the concept of an optimum population ambiguous?

7 What effect will inventions have on the production function and the demand for labour?

8 Why have economists tended to ignore the production of 'bads'?

9 Scotia has 1500 miners seeking employment in the three pits still in operation. The total output of each pit depends upon the number of miners employed as follows:

Miners employed	Total output (thousand tons)		
	Pit A	Pit B	Pit C
300	95	85	85
400	120	100	90
500	130	110	125
600	138	118	150
700	146	122	170
800	153	125	180
900	160	128	189
1000	165	130	195

What is the greatest output of coal that can be raised with an optimum distribution of the 1500 miners between the three pits?

10 If towns produce something called 'urbanism' and nations produce something called 'nationalism' what factors limit the size of towns and nations?

Chapter 4
Exchange and Trade

In the previous chapter we indicated that a country could not consume beyond its productive potential, as illustrated by its production-possibility curve. But we normally observe countries, and even individuals, consuming goods for which they do not have productive potential. The UK imports bananas, timber and oil in quantities which are larger than she might be able to produce. Teachers of economics possess motor cars even though they might lack the ability to produce such complicated pieces of machinery. Evidently then it is possible to escape the confines of the production-possibility curve through trade.

Trade arises for a variety of reasons and the simple explanation, put forward by David Ricardo (1772–1825) in the nineteenth century, is that trade arises because of differences in opportunity cost or *comparative advantage*.

Countries, and even individuals and regions, will produce and sell those goods and services in which they have a relative (comparative) advantage. They buy those goods and services in which they have a relative (comparative) disadvantage.

We can illustrate this thesis by means of a simple arithmetic example. Suppose that we have two countries which can produce differing amounts of food and clothing with their resources. Country 1, we may suppose, can produce *either* 600 units of food *or* 500 units of clothing *or* any combination of food and clothing as long as it is prepared to give up six units of food for five units of clothing. In contrast, Country 2 can produce *either* 1100 units of food or 600 units of clothing *or* any combination of food and clothing as long as it is prepared to give up eleven units of food for six units of clothing. These production possibilities are set out in Table 8 below.

These production possibilities can also be illustrated by means of the production-possibility diagrams we introduced in the previous chapter (Figure 12).

Table 8

| | Production possibilities | |
	Food	Clothing
Country 1	600	500
Country 2	1100	600

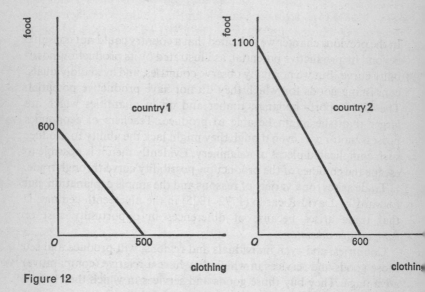

Figure 12

Three points should be noted. First, Country 2 can produce more of both food and clothing than can Country 1. Country 2 has an absolute advantage in the production of both goods. Secondly, the slopes of the production-possibility curves are constant: in Country 1 six units of food always cost five units of clothing, and in Country 2 eleven units of food always cost six units of clothing. Thirdly, though Country 2 has an absolute advantage in the production of both goods she has a relative advantage only in the production of food since one unit of food costs only 0·54 units of cloth, while in Country 1 one unit of food costs 0·83 units of cloth. Hence we can establish the following proposition:

Although Country 2 has an *absolute advantage* in the production of both goods she has a *comparative advantage* only in the production of food and so she may be prepared to trade with Country 1. Trade may be mutually beneficial.

The existence of different opportunity costs within each country means that it is possible for each country to gain through trade. If Country 1 could trade clothing with Country 2 at some rate which would give her more than six units of food for each five units of clothing, and if Country 2 could trade food with Country 1 at a rate which would give her more than six units of clothing for each eleven units of food, both countries would be better off. What this implies is that the rate at which they must trade goods should be different from the rates at which they trade domestically.

In Figure 13 we assume that both countries are willing to trade at a rate of three units of food for two units of clothing. This allows Country 1 to specialize in producing 500 units of clothing and exchanging some 200 units of clothing for 300 units of food. Country 2 specializes in producing 1100 units of food and exchanges 300 units for 200 units of clothing. The production and consumption possibilities before and after trade are set out in Table 9.

What Figure 13 and Table 9 indicate is that through trade both countries can consume more clothing and no less food than before trade so that there is an overall gain from trade.

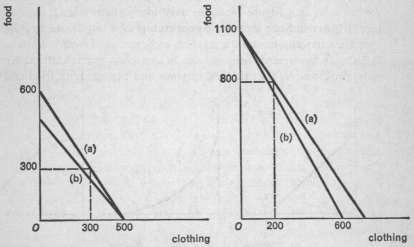

Figure 13 (a) Post-trade consumption possibilities
(b) Pre-trade consumption possibilities

Table 9 Specialization and the gains from trade

	Opportunity cost	Food production	Food consumption	Clothing production	Clothing consumption
before trade situation					
Country 1	6:5	300	300	250	250
Country 2	11:6	800	800	164	164
total		1100	1100	414	414
after trade situation					
Country 1	3:2	0	300	500	300
Country 2	3:2	1100	800	0	200
total		1100	1100	500	500

Increasing cost: increasing specialization

For the purpose of illustrating the gains from trade we used the production-possibility curve with a constant slope. We could, however, have chosen different shapes as Figures 14b and 14c suggest.

The question naturally arises: which is the more realistic? From the previous chapter, where we discussed the law of diminishing returns, we can infer that Figure 14c is the most likely shape since it exhibits increasing cost. Such increasing opportunity cost implies incomplete specialization and casual observation indicates that most countries, regions and people do not indulge in complete specialization. We note, for example, that the UK imports and exports both food and

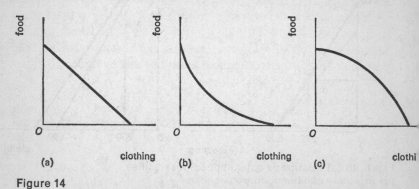

Figure 14

manufactures. Figure 14b illustrates the case of decreasing opportunity cost, a state of affairs most unlikely to be widespread.

Trade between countries: trade between people

The proposition that trade can be mutually beneficial applies to individuals as well as nations. A professor may be a good gardener, yet still find it advantageous to hire a gardener. Indeed, the internal characteristics of most countries exhibit trading between numerous individuals. Such specialization and trading can give rise to increased efficiency and greater consumption.

There is, however, one qualification to the extension of the analysis of trade to individuals. When we examine production and trading between people we become more conscious of the problems raised by collective goods. Suppose, for example, that we have two individuals, Smith and Jones, and that the goods are DDT (to kill malaria mosquitoes) and beer. If Smith specializes in the production of DDT he may find Jones refusing to buy it because he feels that there is no risk of malaria, Smith having sprayed the area with DDT. Trade therefore breaks down. Either both produce DDT or neither produces it. But if both produce it there is a loss of efficiency and if neither produces it then they may both die. What is therefore required is some extra mechanism whereby Jones and Smith combine to produce DDT: this may take the form of Jones being forced to buy some from Smith.

Another aspect of the trading model that we worked through concerns the distribution of the total output between countries. We assumed that each country was capable of producing something the other wanted and that trading guaranteed a minimum subsistence living standard. But if we look around we see people and countries who, through lack of resources, cannot survive even by trading. The problem of needs therefore cannot always be met by trade.

The pattern of trade

Armed with our insight into the causes of trade we can now look at the actual pattern of world trade depicted in Table 10.

What Table 10 suggests is that:

1 The less developed countries tend to trade more with the developed

Table 10 The pattern of world trade, 1970 (millions of US dollars)

Exports by	Exports to			
	World	Developed countries	Industrial countries	Industrial Europe
world	278 433			
developed countries	225 340	173 023	152 857	89 586
industrial countries	207 402	159 741	140 714	84 876
industrial Europe	109 320	9093	81 105	64 680
other Europe	9778	7199	6674	39 430
less developed	53 133	41 760	38 550	16 448
planned economies	n.a.	7288	5935	3828

Exports by	Exports to				
	UK	USA	EEC	Less developed	Oil countries
UK	—	2263	4209	4381	775
USA	2537	—	8423	12 977	1680
EEC	3691	63 956	—	11 968	1816
less developed	4576	9881	14 617	—	1748
oil countries	1496	1906	5114	1028	—

Source: International Monetary Fund (1971)

countries than with each other. The developed countries tend to trade more with each other than with the developing countries.

These two basic patterns form the basis of many discussions of imperialism and the arguments for industrialization of the less developed countries. The facts have a historical foundation in that many of the less developed countries were formerly colonies of the developed countries of Europe. Hence, so the arguments run, the underdeveloped countries were, and are, dependent upon the growth of the developed countries. They were, and are, exploited. The only way therefore to break this dependence would be through industrialization. However, not all today's developed countries were colonial powers. Some, like Japan, were still underdeveloped at the time of the extensive and intensive colonization of the world in the nineteenth century, but with the weakening of the ties between the former imperial powers and their dependents, other developed countries have begun to establish trading links with the former colonies, e.g. Japan with the Asian and African countries.

2 Since the developed countries tend to specialize in manufactures and the less developed concentrate on agricultural and mineral products, there exist two clearly defined trade patterns with two possibly different explanations of such trade. The trade between the developed economies of the temperate zones and the less developed economies of the tropics may have geographical origins. It may be possible to grow bananas in greenhouses in Scotland, but oil either exists or does not exist in Scotland. Oil and other mineral products are the free gifts of nature and their location owes nothing to human ingenuity. Although bananas could be grown in Scotland, it seems foolish to ignore the relatively lower production costs afforded to the tropical countries by nature. On the other hand, most manufactured goods are footloose in the sense that they are not rigidly tied to par-ticular climatic or geological conditions. Most manufacturing coun-tries produce motor cars so why do they exchange them? Why does the UK import German Volkswagen cars and Germany import Vauxhall Vivas? The explanation of trade between manufacturing countries, therefore, seems complex, and certainly different from that put forward for trade between manufacturers and primary producers. Perhaps it lies in the 'know-how'. One country happens to discover a certain manufacturing process before others. Perhaps it is all due to tastes.

3 The notable exception to the generalization that developed countries tend to trade more with each other than with the less developed has been the UK. The UK has always had extensive trading relations with her former colonies but these have been eroded in recent years and UK trade with Western Europe has been growing rapidly.

4 Continental countries such as the USA and Russia and China contain within their boundaries large developed and undeveloped areas and large manufacturing and agricultural regions. Generaliza-tions 2 and 3 may therefore apply to their internal trade as much as to their external trade.

5 Countries tend to trade more with their neighbours than with *distant countries*. Transport costs and harmonious relationships are important in explaining these facts.

6 *The corn and steel world.* We have emphasized the distinction be-tween industrial and agricultural regions and countries. Can we use the distinction to depict the development of industrialization and

world trade? The answer is yes. Suppose we have two sectors: one producing corn and the other producing steel, where corn and steel stand for all agricultural and industrial goods. If we ignore the importance of land then we can assume that corn is produced by men and steel, and steel is produced by men and steel. So we have:

Corn sector: men + steel → corn,
Steel sector: men + steel → steel.

Steel and corn are both traded and the prices of both goods will contain a wage component and a profit component.

Corn output: wages + profits,
Steel output: wages + profits.

Generalizing for the national or international economy we have:

Total output = corn + steel
     = consumption good + capital good
     = wages + profits.

If we now assume that workers do not save and neglect the consumption of the capitalists then savings out of profits must equal the amount spent on capital goods (i.e. investment). Hence the distribution of income is important for the development of the industrial sector. The development of the industrial sector requires the existence of an agricultural surplus which must not be consumed by those employed in the agricultural sector nor must it be wasted in the industrial sector. How the surplus is obtained for industrialization is partially a matter of prices and in the past of exploitation, military might and cunning.

The simple model we have used will be elaborated in Chapter 38 into a growth model. Before that however we shall stress the problems of ensuring harmony between the sectors. Steel is not used for immediate consumption but to produce corn in the future. Hence the production of steel depends upon expectations and if those expectations are wrong then there will be repercussions on consumption. In the last two hundred years fluctuations in domestic economies have arisen through fluctuations in capital-goods industries and fluctuations in the world economy have been due to fluctuations in the industrial countries.

The causes of comparative advantage

Table 10 has enabled us to go a little way behind David Ricardo's assertion that trade is based upon comparative advantages. We can now enumerate some of the causes of such advantages and disadvantages. In some cases there are initial resource disparities – the presence of precious minerals or possession of a favourable climate. In other cases it is know-how, technical knowledge or plentiful labour.

Summary

Countries, regions and people can consume more than their productive potential by trade. Such trade is based upon differences in comparative advantage. Countries, regions and people will produce and sell those goods in which they have a comparative advantage and buy those in which they have a comparative disadvantage in producing. Underlying the comparative advantages are such factors as initial endowments of natural resources, climate and technical knowledge.

Questions

1 'It is comparative and not absolute advantage that accounts for trade.' Discuss.

2 Is it true that a country can only gain from trade if another country loses?

3 America has an absolute advantage in the production of most goods as compared with the UK. Why then does she find it advantageous to trade with the UK?

4 Why have successive post-war governments attempted to introduce regional policies which interfere with the doctrine that each region should specialize in the production of those goods in which each has a comparative advantage?

5 'Bananas must be grown where the temperature is 80°F and there is adequate rainfall.' 'Bananas will be grown where the opportunity cost is lowest.' Comment on these two statements.

Chapter 5
Money and Trade

We used money in Chapter 1 to measure the national income which was, in turn, used as a measure of economic well-being. We said that it was necessary to use money because it was the only way of adding one motor car to one ice cream to one loaf. But in subsequent chapters money disappeared; we found no use for it. Production was carried on without the use of money; exchange and trade were carried on without the use of money. So evidently we do not need money or, if we do, it seems to be only for the limited objective of calculating the national income. Yet we do use money extensively in society and at least one international problem seems to revolve around the use of money. Is money important or is it a mere veil behind which the real action takes place?

From a barter economy to a money economy

Let us begin by considering the structure and behaviour of a world without money, of a barter world. We may suppose that Smith has some butter which he wishes to swap for some bread. Hence he must search for someone who has bread to offer in exchange for butter. There are, in short, costs of searching and negotiating a sale, there is a loss of time which could be spent doing something else and there is the uncertainty that there may be no one offering bread for butter and so Smith might have better spent his time making some bread. Collectively, we can refer to these various costs as *transaction costs*. These costs increase as we increase the number of goods traded. Thus, suppose that we endow each individual with one commodity, some of which he wishes to trade. The number of exchanges and exchange calculations will increase with the number of goods. Supposing that there are three individuals called Smith, Jones and Robinson trading three goods – bread, butter and wine, respectively – then we have three exchange calculations to be made – bread : butter; bread : wine; and butter : wine.

Adding another commodity, clothing, we have – bread : butter; bread : wine; bread : clothing; butter : wine; butter : clothing and wine : clothing. The addition of another good has added another three exchange calculations – transaction costs have increased more than proportionately to the increase in goods.

We can now begin to grasp the difficulties of trading in a modern community which does not have money. Assuming that everyone of the fifty-five million inhabitants of the UK had one good to trade then each would have to calculate how many combinations of two goods there are in a set of fifty-five million goods and then negotiate exchange rates. The mind boggles at the calculation even though it can be done:

The number of combinations of two goods $= \frac{1}{2}n(n-1)$,

where n is the number of goods.

Clans, clubs and tribes

It seems clear that faced with such severe transaction costs individuals would attempt to overcome the limitations of barter. One solution would be to form a club, clan or tribe (the family would be one such example of a club). Within the club specialization could take place and then the goods produced could be shared out. But there are limitations placed upon the size of such clubs by the problems of coordination and control. We could envisage some complicated control system, such as is shown in Figure 15, where one man controls four men and a hierarchical pyramid is built up. However, as the club grows there could arise distortion of information and people might attempt to short-cut the organizational structure and thereby create more confusion. Growth could therefore lead to inefficiency and breakdown.

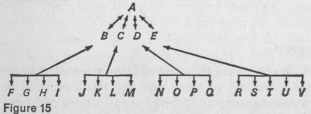

Figure 15

Trading posts and fairs

A second method of overcoming the limitations of barter would be to create trading posts or fairs – such were the origins of the towns. These could reduce transaction costs by bringing people together at a central place on specified days and times. Yet even these might not always be convenient – not everyone might be able to get to them on the appointed day.

Middlemen or merchants

A third method of overcoming some of the disadvantages of barter would be for some individuals to reduce their consumption (for a while) in order to build up stocks of trade goods. Consider Figure 16. M is the middleman. Now suppose A wants some bread and is willing to offer butter. He may not know B is willing to trade bread for butter and rather than undertake the risk and inconvenience of looking for B he may sell his butter to M in exchange for some bread. M will offer A a rate of exchange less favourable than he might eventually get from B and the differences in the exchange rates, say three butter for one bread instead of two butter for one bread, would compensate M for reducing his consumption and holding stocks. By a process of buying cheap and selling dear M could establish a livelihood. Moreover, by virtue of his pivotal position in the complex network of production, trade and consumption, the middleman could become an important person in such a society – a fact attested by even a casual reading of economic history.

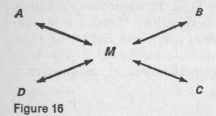

Figure 16

The money economy

Clans and clubs, trading posts, fairs, and middlemen are all means of overcoming the limitations of barter and still retain elements of usefulness in a modern economy. Yet they are as nothing compared with the introduction of a monetary system – a club which decides to use money. The effect is to impose a common unit of account and a universal medium of exchange. All goods are measured in terms of money and money buys everything. The implications of the transformation can be seen in the case of three goods – bread, wine and clothing – if we dub clothing the money commodity. Instead of three pairwise exchange rates we have bread : clothing (money), wine : clothing (money), that is, two. Thus a money economy involves a move to fewer calculations: from $\frac{1}{2}n(n-1)$ to $n-1$ or from 2^n-n-1 to $n-1$.[1] Furthermore, the functions of money also embrace its use as a store of value, as a command over goods and services in the future.

Some further implications

Although the introduction of a money economy brings numerous benefits – increased specialization leading to increased dexterity and hence output – it does impose some disadvantages. For in a monetary economy *money buys goods and goods buy money but goods do not buy goods*. Hence it follows that if there is a disturbance to such an economy the condition that all trade requires money can create difficulties. Suppose, for example, as in the 'thirties, there is a tremendous fall in the demand for workers, then those unemployed cannot buy goods until they obtain jobs which yield money, they cannot directly barter labour services for bread. This problem of monetary disturbances is dealt with more fully in Part Eight and until that point in the narrative we shall assume that there are no complications caused by money.

The money commodity

Most of the gains from the introduction of money result from the establishment of the system rather than the choice of commodity to be the unit of account and medium of exchange. But once such a

1. We can now bring together some of our equations. In the simple barter system of direct trading we had $\frac{1}{2}n(n-1)$. In the club system which embraced both direct and indirect trading (i.e. through a controller or without his intervention) the equation becomes 2^n-n-1. Finally, in the monetary system we had $n-1$. These three equations describe the intra-organizational linkages that we meet in an economy or its subsets.

system has been introduced men will seek out more useful commodities to serve as money. For example, it would clearly be wasteful to use foodstuffs as money. The attributes of a good money commodity have come to be recognized as:

Portability;
Durability;
Divisibility;
Homogeneity.

Given these characteristics, men began to experiment with furs, wampum, gold, and other precious metals. But all this takes us away from our immediate problems, and what men have come to use as money is the subject of Chapter 29. Meanwhile the next chapter takes up the problems of production and trading over time.

Summary

A monetary system exists because money can fulfil many important functions in society. These functions are as a medium of exchange, a unit of account and a store of value, and the effect of these functions is to reduce the transaction costs of trading. The benefits of a monetary system transcend the particular type of commodity used as money, though once a monetary system has been introduced men have searched for more efficient ways of producing the money commodity.

Questions

1 What are transaction costs?

2 Why is the distinction between a monetary system and a money commodity important?

3 How does a monetary system reduce transaction costs?

4 'Specialization is limited by the size of the market.' 'Specialization is dictated by the presence or absence of money.' Comment on these two statements.

5 Why do we never observe pure money economies but rather impure money economies in which clubs, trading posts and middlemen co-exist with money?

Chapter 6
Production and Trading over Time

How much should a football manager pay for a player? Should the government expand the polytechnics rather than the universities? How can we explain the growth of the UK national income over the last two centuries? What factors should a person take into consideration when deciding to buy a house? What have these questions got in common?

The football game

Suppose we begin with the football manager's problem. We may suppose that our manager's team is in the running for the Football League Championship. The purchase of another star player could make success probable and ensure entry into the lucrative European football competitions. We may now suppose that the player he has in mind will only be released if his present club is paid £350 000, so what should the manager do? He estimates that the player has a playing life of seven years and that he will then retire. So there will be no resale price, at the end of seven years, to a club in a lower division. If there are any gains to be made they must be achieved within seven years. But what are the gains that might make the player a worthwhile buy? Briefly they are the extra receipts that might flow from his crowd-pulling power and from his ability to obtain for the club the Football League Championship and major European honours, which would of course bring even greater gate receipts.

Our manager assumes that the player will be an instant success and expects him to bring in £75 000 a year over the seven years. Hence the outlook is as follows:

Season	1	2	3	4	5	6	7
outlay	350 000	—	—	—	—	—	—
receipt	75 000	75 000	75 000	75 000	75 000	75 000	75 000

In seven years the player is expected to bring in £525 000 which is greater than £350 000 so it looks as though the deal should be clinched. But wait a minute! What could the club earn on £350 000 if it was put into a building society or stocks and shares? And is it really correct to assume that £75 000 earned in the seventh season is equivalent to £75 000 earned in the first season? Suppose that the player gets injured or suspended in the later season? Shouldn't the manager allow for such contingencies? Evidently like is not being compared with like, and some method of comparing sums at different points of time must be devised.

Discounting

The process of comparing sums of money, or more generally benefits, at different points of time is known as *discounting*. Suppose an individual is faced with the choice of either spending £100 today or lending this amount to someone else in return for a higher sum one year hence. What future amount would he demand as an inducement to make the loan? If he demanded £105 one year hence we could say that he attaches equal values to £100 today and £105 next year; that is, he values £105 next year as equivalent to £100 today. In other words, his valuation of current income is 5 per cent greater than his valuation of next year's income and he is only prepared, therefore, to forego present consumption (to lend) if the rate of return from doing so is at least 5 per cent. Thus the rate of interest is a means of relating present and future benefits and the discounting process is no more than the reverse of the compound-interest technique. In our example we have an individual only prepared to forego £100 today in return for £105 next year:

£100 (today) = £105 (next year) = $100(1 + 0.05)$.

This compound-interest expression can now be turned on its head to perform a discounting-function:

£105 (next year) = £100 (today) = $\dfrac{105}{(1 + 0.05)}$.

The dim and distant future

The further into the future are the potential benefits of deferred consumption the lower will be the value placed on these benefits. In our example £105 next year was worth £100 currently, but £105 in, say, five years' time is worth much less than £100 currently. People do tend to prefer present benefits to future benefits largely because of the uncertainty attaching to future events. Hence there will be an undervaluation of an income sum five years distant as compared with a sum to be received in only a year's time. The greater the time span between the present and the receipt of a future sum of income, the more heavily is that sum discounted.

To clarify the point made in the above paragraph let us again proceed via the principle of compound interest and then reverse the process. Again, let us assume that currently £100 is to be loaned to a borrower, and the lender demands a five per cent rate of interest. The table below shows the annual sums to which the original £100 accumulates over a span of t years.

Table 11

Initial sum (£)	Years' end	Accumulated sum at year's end (£) (5 per cent p.a)
100	1	$100 + 0 \cdot 05 \times 100 = 100(1 + 0 \cdot 05)$ $= 105$
100	2	$100(1 + 0 \cdot 05) + 0 \cdot 05 \times 100(1 + 0 \cdot 05)$ $= 100(1 + 0 \cdot 05)(1 + 0 \cdot 05)$ $= 100(1 + 0 \cdot 05)^2$ $= 110 \cdot 3$
100	3	$100(1 + 0 \cdot 05)^2 + 0 \cdot 05 \times 100(1 + 0 \cdot 05)^2$ $= 100(1 + 0 \cdot 05)^2(1 + 0 \cdot 05)$ $= 100(1 + 0 \cdot 05)^3$ $= 115 \cdot 8$
100	4	$100(1 + 0 \cdot 05)^3 + 0 \cdot 05 \times 100(1 + 0 \cdot 05)^3$ $= 100(1 + 0 \cdot 05)^3(1 + 0 \cdot 05)$ $= 100(1 + 0 \cdot 05)^4$ $= 121 \cdot 6$
$\vdots$	$\vdots$	$\vdots$
100	t	$100(1 + 0 \cdot 5)^{t-1} + 0 \cdot 05 \times 100(1 + 0 \cdot 05)^{t-1}$ $= 100(1 + 0 \cdot 05)^t$

I.E. – 5

We can now collapse Table 11 into a general formula for the future value of the benefit derived from foregone current consumption

$$A = P(1+r)^t,$$ **1**

where A is the future value, P is the initial sum (i.e. the amount of current consumption given up), r is the rate of interest and t is the number of years in the time span.

Now, returning to our primary task of calculating present values of future benefits, i.e. discounting, we can simply rearrange equation **1** as

$$P = \frac{A}{(1+r)^t}.$$ **2**

Equation **2** permits a simple calculation of the present value of a known future sum of income for a given rate of discount.

It is important to note that **1** and **2** are *general* expressions. Since a given amount of foregone consumption has alternative uses, each of which will yield a different level of future benefits, the present value of a future benefit could differ considerably from the amount of current consumption foregone (investment) in order to yield that benefit. Investment is thus likely to take place when the difference is positive, i.e. when the benefits (in present value terms) from investment outweigh the costs. For example, suppose a machine costs £C and when operational will yield its owner £a per annum for t years. Furthermore, suppose that if £C is used for any other purpose the best it can yield is i per cent per annum. Since i per cent represents the opportunity cost of tying up each £1 in the machine, it is used as the discount rate and the present value, P, of the future income stream, $a_1, \ldots, a_t$, is calculated as follows:

$$P = \frac{a_1}{1+i} + \frac{a_2}{(1+i)^2} + \frac{a_3}{(1+i)^3} + \ldots + \frac{a_t}{(1+i)^t}.$$

Now, as long as the present value of the income stream is greater than (or at least equal to) the initial opportunity cost ($P > C$) it is worthwhile investing in the machine.

The method of investment appraisal outlined above is termed the *net present value* method. An alternative route to the same answer is to calculate the *internal rate of return*. As its name suggests this method concentrates upon the *rate* of benefit rather than upon the net benefit

in absolute terms. Using the same example again we can restate the
appraisal problem by the rate of return method as follows:

$$C = \frac{a_1}{1+r} + \frac{a_2}{(1+r)^2} + \frac{a_3}{(1+r)^3} + \ldots + \frac{a_t}{(1+r)^t}.$$

In this expression C and a are known, therefore the object is to find
the value of r which satisfies the equation, i.e. to find the value of r
which will make the income stream at least equal to the initial opportunity cost. Thus, r represents the minimum rate of return at which
the machine is a worthwhile investment in terms of costs and benefits.
Once r is known it can be compared to i, the best alternative rate of
return, and as long as $r > i$, the machine is the best investment.

The easy way

But we are not all mathematicians and provided we understand the
rudiments of compounding and discounting then there is no sense in
getting involved in laborious arithmetic. We can use simple tables
provided for us by mathematicians.

Table 12 gives present values for a sample of years and discount
rates. Each column shows how much £1 received at the end of various
years in the future is worth today. For example, at 10 per cent £1
received two years hence is worth £0·826 today. Since £1 can be
multiplied up to any amount we could have obtained the present value

Table 12 Present value of £1: What £1 at the end of a specified future
year is worth today at different rates of discount

End of year	Discount rate (*per cent*)					
	2½	5	7½	10	12½	15
1	0·976	0·952	0·930	0·909	0·889	0·870
2	0·952	0·907	0·865	0·826	0·790	0·756
3	0·929	0·864	0·805	0·751	0·702	0·658
4	0·906	0·823	0·749	0·683	0·624	0·572
5	0·884	0·784	0·697	0·621	0·555	0·497
6	0·862	0·746	0·648	0·564	0·493	0·432
7	0·841	0·711	0·603	0·513	0·438	0·376
8	0·821	0·677	0·561	0·467	0·390	0·327
9	0·801	0·645	0·522	0·424	0·346	0·284
10	0·781	0·614	0·485	0·386	0·308	0·247

Table 13 Future value of £1: What £1 would accumulate to at the end of a specified future year at various interest rates

End of year	Interest rate (*per cent*)					
	2½	5	7½	10	12½	15
1	1·025	1·050	1·075	1·100	1·125	1·150
2	1·050	1·103	1·156	1·210	1·266	1·323
3	1·077	1·158	1·242	1·331	1·424	1·521
4	1·104	1·216	1·336	1·464	1·602	1·749
5	1·131	1·276	1·436	1·610	1·802	2·011
6	1·160	1·340	1·543	1·772	2·027	2·313
7	1·189	1·407	1·659	1·949	2·281	2·660
8	1·218	1·478	1·784	2·144	2·566	3·059
9	1·249	1·551	1·917	2·358	2·887	3·518
10	1·280	1·629	2·061	2·594	3·247	4·046

of £100, received two years hence discounted at 10 per cent, as £82·6. Turning the information round we could say £0·826 today would grow to £1 in two years' time at 10 per cent of rate interest. Table 13 is a table of compound interest which shows what sums will grow to in the future at different rates of interest.

The football game again

We can now see how our football manager must deal with the problem of time. *Either*, his discount factor must make the sum of the present benefits greater than the outlay (as in the net present value method) *or* he must choose a discount factor which makes the sum of benefits equal to the outlay (the internal rate of return method) and then see if that discount rate is greater than the rate of interest he could get if he lent the money to someone else. Does a football manager think like this? Not explicitly nor so precisely although he is aware of the problem of cash flows at different points of time. Whatever he does, he must deal with time.

The education problem[1]

Let us look now at another area where the discounting approach has been used to yield some interesting conclusions. The Minister for

1. Based on Morris and Ziderman (1971).

Education has a problem. Should he (or she) expand the universities or the polytechnics? Is a Ph.D. worth more to society than a B.Sc.? Is a B.Sc. worth more than an HNC? Suppose that we accept that what people are paid represents their worth to society, then we could obtain the earnings figures for various types of educated person as in Figure 17, and on the basis of this information both individuals and the state could make decisions. Thus an individual could assume that when he attains various ages he could earn what people of that age and with particular qualifications are currently earning. Similarly, a Minister of Education could look at the earnings figures and decide that those with the highest earnings yield the greatest benefits to society and therefore their numbers should be expanded. But what about costs? Part of the costs are what each type of educated person would have earned had he stopped at the previous level of education, since the earnings would represent the opportunity cost to the individual. The other part of the cost represents the resources used in providing the extra education. We can use the earnings of different people to make *incremental* comparisons of the benefits of extra education. Or we can compare the earnings of higher educated people with those of the less educated: that is, we can make a *base line comparison*.

The next problem is the time dimension. Figure 17 depicts the age–earning profiles for people at different educational levels, and from this it can be seen that highly-educated people earn more than those with less education. It also shows that their higher earnings come after periods of training, so might it be possible for those with the least education to invest some of their earnings and thereby obtain higher earnings at a later date? What we have to do therefore is to put earnings and costs on the same basis by discounting them. This has been done in Table 14. What seems to emerge from this is that investment by the state in higher degrees does not seem worthwhile unless a zero discount rate is adopted – and that would imply that the community is indifferent between present and future benefits. For the individual, of course, the benefits would still exist provided the state subsidized part of the costs. Recent government policy suggests that this will not be the case in the future. Of course data such as that in Table 14 should be handled with care. We do not know to what extent earnings reflect innate ability, motivation and purpose. And do we, should we, readily accept earnings data as measuring the worth of poets and nurses?

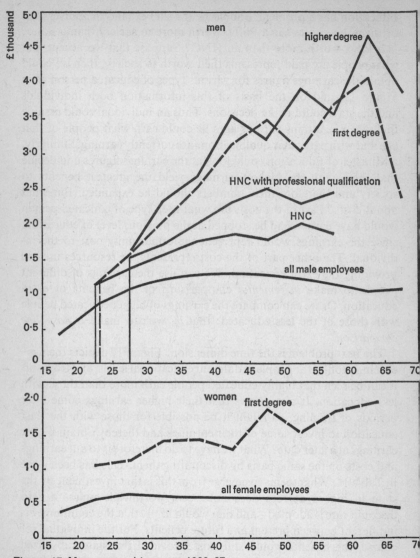

Figure 17 Mean annual income, 1966–67
Source: Morris and Ziderman (1971)

Table 14 Comparisons of present values at age 15 of benefits net of costs (including research) between educational levels at various discount rates (£), 1966–67

	0%	4%	6%	8%	10%	12%	16%
Males							
incremental comparison							
A-level/non-qualified	17 950	3158	1188	−144	−743	−1005	−1308
ONC/non-qualified	9278	1592	761	−40	−322	−473	−614
HNC/ONC	18 410	5335	3156	2000	1310	893	444
HNC-PQ/HNC	8338	3062	1814	1073	633	370	113
first degree/A-level	46 084	10 392	4763	1880	373	−425	−1079
master's/first degree	1282	1876	2250	−2314	−2229	−2078	−1723
doctorate/first degree	3163	−3218	−3760	−3754	−3516	−3198	−2546
base-line comparison							
A-level/non-qualified	17 950	3158	1188	−144	−743	−1005	−1308
ONC/non-qualified	9278	1592	761	−40	−322	−473	−614
HNC/non-qualified	27 788	6927	3917	1960	988	420	−170
HNC-PQ/ non-qualified	26 126	9989	5731	3033	1621	790	−57
first degree/ non-qualified	64 034	13 549	5951	1735	−370	−1481	−2384
master's degree/ non-qualified	65 315	11 673	3700	−579	−2599	−3558	−4109
doctorate/ non-qualified	67 196	10 331	2191	−2019	−3886	−4678	−4932
Females							
first degree/ non-qualified	25 133	4497	1195	−546	−1480	−1980	−2361
first degree/A-level	7974	749	−384	−941	−1210	−1325	−1360

Derived from earnings survey (except: no qualification, A-level and ONC) and DES cost data
Source: Morris and Ziderman (1971)

There is also the problem of the formative years – of parents, nursery schools and the class-structured educational system of the UK. Faced with such imponderables can it be easy to decide what discount rate, what measure of present and future benefits a society should adopt? We return to this issue in Chapter 21 and in Part Nine.

The larger issue

We can now turn to the larger issue of the growth of the UK economy. In an earlier chapter we saw that specialization and trade could increase the production and consumption possibilities at a point in time. But the principle also holds regarding such possibilities over time. Consumption possibilities can be increased over the long run as a result of the production of *capital goods*. The growth in the UK national income over the last 150 years has owed much to an increase in productive resources, particularly in durable capital goods such as plant and machinery.

Investment and opportunity cost

Of course a community's decision to produce capital goods requires, as always, the acceptance of an opportunity cost. At some time in the middle of the eighteenth century, possibly earlier, there began to emerge a sizeable surplus of community income over customary consumption. This surplus could have been used to increase current consumption, but instead it was used to increase future consumption, i.e. it was used for investment purposes. Instead of being channelled into producing more goods by customary production techniques, the surplus was used to divert resources into production methods which could lead, in the long run, to even greater output. These production methods were initially time-consuming, which is why their benefits could only accrue over a lengthy time period, and for this reason they have been labelled 'roundabout' methods of production.

Roundabout production techniques are not confined solely to the UK's experience. Indeed the principle has been employed by all societies although the scale of operations may differ. It is true that the long-run output of manufactured products can be increased if some short-run output is sacrificed to the production of conveyor belts and heavy lifting gear; and it is equally true that primitive hunters can increase their long-run meat consumption by giving up a day's chase in order to make animal traps. The costs and benefits of roundabout production methods are represented by Figure 18, which is of course our familiar production-possibilities curve with re-labelled axes. If the community devotes all its current resources to the production of goods for current consumption, *OB* goods can be produced and consumed. However, if some resources were used to produce capital

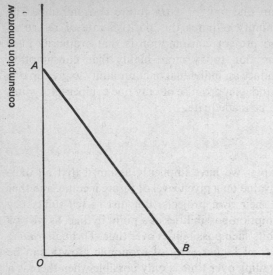

Figure 18   consumption today

goods instead of consumption goods it is possible for the community's future (tomorrow) consumption to be increased by more than its present (today) reduction in consumption, i.e. *OA* is greater than *OB*. In other words the benefits from roundabout production methods outweigh the opportunity cost involved, a unit of foregone consumption today yields more than one extra consumption unit tomorrow.

Whether or not future benefits will actually be pursued depends not only upon the possibilities of converting present consumption into future consumption, but also upon the community's willingness to do so, i.e. upon the community's relative *preferences* for present and future consumption. When the opportunity cost of future consumption in terms of present consumption matches the relative preferences of the community, then some capital goods are likely to be produced.

'Tomorrow is another day'

In the case of the community represented by Figure 18, production possibilities and community preferences could well coincide since the slope of *AB* is greater than 1, i.e. a unit of foregone present consumption yields more than one unit of extra future consumption. The reason why a community requires this positive rate of return as inducement to forego present consumption is that ordinarily individuals value consumption today more highly than consumption tomorrow. Thus to induce an individual or community to give up one unit of consumption today, a promise of only one compensatory unit tomorrow is likely to be inadequate.

Trading over time

Throughout this chapter we have implicitly assumed that all individuals put the same value on a given level of future income, and that all investors finance their own projects. But just as self-sufficiency severely limits consumption possibilities at a point in time, as we saw in Chapter 3, so it limits such possibilities over time. Through *trading* over time the benefits of higher rates of economic growth can be realized. However, trading over time is only possible when there is a divergence between the evaluations made of present and future income by different groups in the community. When time preferences for income diverge some individuals are net lenders at a given rate of interest, and others are net borrowers. In this way investments can be financed out of borrowed funds.

Suppose, for example, that two individuals A and B differ in their relative abilities to transform present consumption into future consumption in the following way: A is able to produce two extra units of future consumption by giving up a unit of current consumption, whereas if B foregoes a unit today he can produce five units for tomorrow in return. Figure 19 shows the two production-possibilities curves. The preferences for current consumption compared with future consumption will determine whereabouts on his frontier each individual settles.

As with international trade in Chapter 4, we can demonstrate that both individuals can benefit by trading. In this case it is trading through time. If A concentrates all his efforts on producing for today's consumption and B concentrates all his efforts on producing for tomorrow (using his resources for producing capital rather than consumer goods) then for the community of two $(A+B)$ they are each concentrating on the activity where they have a comparative advantage. The trade comes when A loans consumer goods *today* in exchange for a greater increase in consumption *tomorrow* than he individually could have managed. In our example they will both gain at any terms of trade between 1 : 2 and 1 : 5. In Figures 20a and 20b they trade to their mutual benefit at 1 : 3.

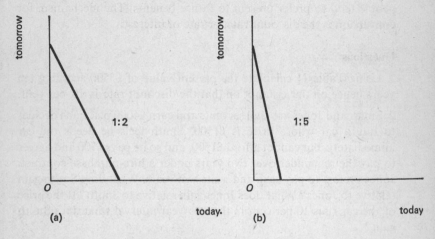

Figure 19 (a) *A*'s production-possibility curve.
(b) *B*'s production-possibility curve

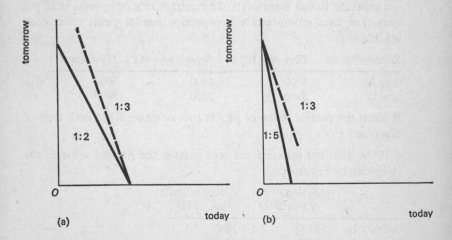

Figure 20

Summary

Many decisions involve the valuation of future benefits and some technique must be devised for the purpose. The procedure is known as discounting which means reducing the value of future benefits in order to compare them with present benefits. Reduction is necessary because people tend to prefer present to future benefits. The mechanism for conversion is the discount rate, or rate of interest.

Questions

1 Using Table 11 calculate the present value of £5500 accruing ten years hence on the assumption that the discount rate is 10 per cent.

2 Smith and Jones are civil servants and earn £4000 p.a. Each decides to buy a car whose price is £1500. Smith feels he needs the car immediately, but cannot afford £1500, and so he pays £700 and agrees to pay the remainder over two years under a hire-purchase contract. Jones prefers to pay cash and waits two years. What does Smith gain relative to Jones? What does Jones gain relative to Smith? If the price of the car rises 10 per cent in the two-year interval what does Smith gain?

3 A cotton mill has a choice of investing in two different types of spinning frames. Type A costs £10 000 but uses half as much yarn as type B which costs £8000. Both have the same output capacity and are expected to last three years. The market rate of interest is 10 per cent. The firm estimates the prospective annual yields from each machine as:

Spinning frame	First year (£)	Second year (£)	Third year (£)
type A	5000	6500	6000
type B	3000	3500	3000

What is the present value of profits (net revenue) from each type of machine?

4 If the discount rate is 5 per cent what is the present value of the following two prospects:

	Return at end of year 1 (£)	Return at end of year 2 (£)
decision 1	4500	3800
decision 2	3800	4500

(a) Which decision would you take?
(b) Why are the present values not identical?

5 For £1000 a man may become a partner in a firm and will receive the following returns over three years:

year	1	2	3
returns	£200	£400	£600

Alternatively he may place his money in a bank which will give him a rate of interest of 10 per cent. Which course of action would you advise him to take?

6 Set out the steps you would take in deciding whether to obtain a television set (a) by outright purchase; (b) hire-purchase agreement or (c) rental.

7 *Investment appraisal: a short case study situation report*
Imagine that in January 1973 you become Minister of Technology and are faced with the following situation. In January 1971 your predecessor gave the go-ahead for the 'Sweet Dream' supersonic transport aeroplane. In January 1971 the estimates upon which the viability of the project depended were:

development costs: £50m in 1971
                   £150m in 1972
                   £30m in 1973,
tooling up costs: £70m in 1973
                   £100m in 1974.

After 1974 there would be no further development or tooling up costs. Production and sales would commence in 1975. The cost per aeroplane of direct labour and raw materials was estimated (in 1971 after making allowances for inflation and wage claims) as £4 million per aeroplane. You could produce 200 aeroplanes per year. Sales forecasts are, at each of the two possible prices:

1975	1976	1977	1978	1979
100	100	100	100	100 at £6m each
200	200	200	200	200 at £5m each

After 1979 a rival supersonic transport is expected to come into service, and you expect to sell no more planes.

When you arrive at your new post in January 1973, you discover that costs have escalated steeply. You have already spent £200 million in 1971 and £400 million in 1972 on development. In 1973, unless you cancel the project now, you must spend £200 million to complete its development. New estimates of the tooling-up costs are £100 million in 1973 and £200 million in 1974. Estimates of direct labour and raw material costs are unchanged, as is your forecast of how many aeroplanes you could sell in each year. For the last ten years it has been government policy to apply a discount rate of 10 per cent to all projects.

Should you cancel the project? Should you have cancelled the project at some time in the past? If you go ahead with the project, what price should you charge?

Part Two
Markets, Demand and Supply

The notion of exchange leads on naturally to the idea of markets as arrangements whereby exchange is effected. A market need not be a physical location. It is any arrangement for bringing buyers and sellers together, and in these days of the teleprinter and television the market for a particular good or service could conceivably be the whole world. A market is not the only method of allocating goods and services since a central planner could achieve the same result. One of the longest-standing debates in economics has been over which is the more efficient method. Consider Figure 21 which is a simplified sketch of a market economy. Households sell resources – labour power, land, machinery – to firms which make payments to households, which constitute the latter's income. Households use their income to purchase goods from firms and the expenditure of households constitutes the income of firms. Figure 21 depicts two markets – a factor market and a goods market. In reality there are millions of markets because there are differing requirements of households and firms. All these markets enable households and firms to find out what is available, and how successfully the things that are available meet their needs.

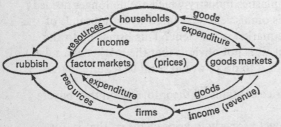

Figure 21

What happens when households want more of something? Prices are the links between households and firms, between demands and supplies, and they move in response to the relative strengths of demands and supplies. If demand rises relative to supply then prices will tend to rise. If demand falls relative to supply the prices will tend to fall. Prices are signals. Like the column of mercury in a thermometer, prices rise under the pressure of demand relative to supply. We can now see why money is useful. By serving as a unit of account and a medium of exchange, money improves the means of comparing exchange values and eliminates the need for complex tables of exchange rates.

Planning

Contrast this state of affairs with that arrived at under a central planner. Suppose the planner has to decide whether to use plastics or steel in the production of motor cars. How can he make his decision? He will have certain technical information at his disposal which may tell him that plastics are unsuitable for engine parts, that a steel car may withstand the impact of a crash better than a plastic one; plastic furnishings are probably better than steel ones. But how should he evaluate this evidence? If he listens to experts they may be biased in favour of either steel or plastics for aesthetic reasons or because they have friends in either industry. Even when the central planner has made up his mind there will still be problems.

Suppose the central planner decides to have all cars made of steel. He must then consider the implications of less steel being available for the construction industry, the engineering industry and so on. He may need to import steel in which case the effect on the balance of payments needs to be explored. And what should be done with the resources in the plastics industry which are no longer needed? Unless the planner is omniscient he is faced with thousands of problems. But is the market omniscient? This brings us to the core of disagreement. It is not obvious that the market can solve problems quickly; for it to do so would seem to require that:

The movement of price contains all the information that buyers and sellers require;
Buyers and sellers react properly to price changes; that is, for

example, that buyers cut down their demands when prices rise and suppliers increase supplies when prices rise.

When we look at any real market it may not be obvious what is *the price* and what that price is doing. For any good there may be as many different prices as there are sellers. If we wait for a change then it may be that some prices are raised and some are lowered because different sellers hold different views about the future, so an average of all prices might leave the buyer with the impression that prices were going to stay unchanged. Because of the existence of a range of prices we may find the reactions of buyers and sellers to be different from what we might expect. As we shall see in Part Eight there is a body of thought associated with the work of Keynes which believes that the usual market model postulated assumes away the information-sorting stage and hence arrives at what appear to be irrefutable conclusions. Before then, however, we shall indicate in Chapters 14 and 19 some of the problems that arise when there is ignorance and the abuse of power. We should, however, note that some mini-experiments have been conducted by psychologists into the relative merits of centralized and decentralized systems. There are also indications in some of the unrest and uprisings in post-war Eastern Europe that in some respects complete centralization may be less efficient than a system which uses markets. But even these events and their interpretation are surrounded in ideological smoke which makes firm conclusions difficult.

Some disadvantages of the market

There are, however, three obvious disadvantages that can be noted in the market system.

Unemployment. The market seems to be associated with the periodically unemployed resources and to the extent that living standards depend upon income from work then the market is inefficient.

Morals and income distribution. A market system says, in effect: 'put your money where your mouth is'. In other words, it displays a distrust of the planning model because of the possibilities of inefficiency, seduction and flattery inherent in it. But the aphorism could lead to a lack of moral responsibility particularly if the distribution of income in a market system leads to poverty.

Rubbish. The final point to note is that production processes produce *Bads* as well as *Goods* and an uncontrolled market system may not lead to their elimination.

General versus partial equilibrium analysis

Turning from the issues of political economy, we may note that there are two methods of analysing market systems. One known as *general equilibrium analysis* emphasizes the interdependence of markets whilst the other – *partial equilibrium analysis* – studies particular markets. Although general equilibrium analysis seems to be realistic it suffers from serious defects. In particular, by concentrating on interdependence it suggests simultaneous determination of prices and quantities in all markets which slurs over the problems of money and transaction costs. Only in a dictatorship might simultaneous determination of all prices be feasible. By way of contrast the partial equilibrium approach studies the exchange of money for goods and services in particular markets, and it provides two important insights. First, all markets may not be in simultaneous equilibrium with each other and there will be spillovers. Secondly, markets may respond at different speeds to disturbances. The partial equilibrium approach will be used in Parts Three to Seven and some aspects of general equilibrium analysis will be found in Part Eight.

Chapter 7
Demand

On one side of the market stand the buyers whose decisions to purchase serve to influence prices and thereby allocate resources. Demand by buyers in the market refers to the amount of a commodity which they are willing and able to purchase. It is *effective demand* and not mere wishful thinking or desire that constitutes demand. Furthermore, we can also distinguish between *ex ante*, or intended demand, and *ex post* demand or what is actually bought.

The individual's demand curve

We can express the general forces influencing the demand of an individual for a commodity by a shorthand statement of the form:

$$D_a = f(P_a, P_b, ..., P_z; Y; T; r; u). \qquad 1$$

where D_a is the quantity of a commodity a demanded per period of time; P_a is the price of a; Y is money income; T is tastes; $P_b, ..., P_z$ are the prices of other goods; r is the rate of interest which is relevant in the case of durable goods; and u is a term which summarizes all the unknown influences. Though equation 1 may be thought of as a convenient summary of the forces influencing demand we need to justify the variables we have included and the precise way in which demand is influenced by each of the variables in the right-hand bracket. What we shall now do is to take each of the variables in turn.

Income

Figure 22 shows the three possible relationships between income and the quantity demand of some commodity. Curve 1 shows the quantity demanded rising with income until the income level b is reached. Thereafter the quantity demanded does not change as income rises.

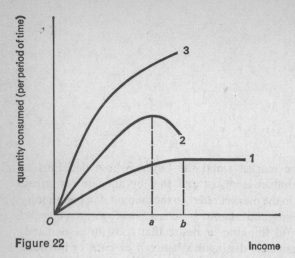

Figure 22

Curve 2 shows demand rising as income rises to *a* and falling thereafter. Curve 3 shows quantity demanded continually rising with income. Tables 15 and 16 throw some light on the relationship between demand and income. The information does, however, refer to households rather than individuals and though we might demur at the idea of operating with households rather than individuals, we can regard, for convenience, households as single-minded decision units. How such single-mindedness arises lies outside the scope of our analysis.

1 The proportion of income spent on certain goods *falls* as income rises. This proposition does of course correspond to what might be inferred from the notion of a hierarchy of wants or, as the statisticians term it, Engel's law. Once basic necessities have been satisfied then any increases in income are spent on other goods. Tables 15 and 16 seem to confirm these ideas. For all households, housing, food and, in a modern society, transport form the bulk of expenditure but Table 16 also shows that as incomes rise, expenditure on some of these items becomes a smaller relative proportion of total expenditure. There are, however, some odd features of Table 16 which do not seem to be reconcilable with casual observation. For example, we might expect the proportion of income spent on housing to remain constant since rich people do not live in council houses or 'two-up and two-down' but migrate to detached houses in stockbroker belts and perhaps retain a town house. And might there not be a switch from

Table 15 Household expenditure 1974

	Average weekly expenditure of all households	
	£	%
housing	6·36	13·8
fuel, light and power	2·42	5·2
food	11·29	24·5
drink and tobacco	3·87	8·4
clothing and footwear	4·19	9·1
household durables	3·62	7·8
other goods	3·53	7·7
transport and vehicles	6·19	13·4
services	4·44	9·6
miscellaneous	0·22	0·5
Total	46·13	100·0

Table 16 Household total weekly expenditure on goods and services by income size, 1974 (per cent)

	Under £12	£30 but under £35	£50 but under £60	£60 but under £80	£120 or more
housing	16·8	16·2	13·11	15·2	13·1
fuel, light and power	11·8	6·9	5·2	4·4	3·4
food	32·5	29·1	26·1	22·6	18·7
drink and tobacco	5·8	5·1	8·9	8·3	8·1
clothing and footwear	6·7	8·0	9·2	9·4	9·3
household durables	4·1	5·4	6·8	9·9	9·4
transport	5·3	9·3	13·6	14·9	16·5
services	8·2	8·4	9·0	9·5	13·9
other	8·5	8·0	8·1	8·4	8·0

Source: *Family Expenditure Survey*, 1974, HMSO 1975

'neck end' to steak and from open hearth to central heating? Our data might conceal such differences because it is aggregated over many goods and because many subsidies might be ignored. For example, the rich obtain tax concessions on mortgages particularly where the mortgage is tied to a life assurance policy. And in fact what

The Individual's Demand Curve 101

we do find is that mortgage payments and insurance policies are excluded from the expenditure figures and they do show a rise as income rises.

2 The proportion of income spent on some goods *rises* as income rises. Household durables, clothing, transport and vehicles, and services are good examples of this proposition.

Price of the good

A relationship in which economists express a great deal of interest is that which exists between changes in the quantity of a good demanded and changes in its price, other things (tastes, income, the prices of other goods, etc.) being held constant. This is because they regard price changes as a signal for the re-allocation of resources. The belief that demand rises as price falls, and demand falls as price rises, seems to have a firm basis in everyday experience, though the precise circumstances under which it will be found to be true will be a matter for exploration in Chapter 11. For the moment however we will assume that the relationship be taken on trust or casual observation.

Table 17 is a demand schedule showing the numbers of cans of beans demanded at differing prices and the price–quantity information it contains can be plotted on a graph as in Figure 23. Price is measured on the vertical axis and the numbers of cans demanded (quantity demanded) are plotted on the horizontal axis. Each point on the graph represents the coordinates of a price–quantity combination and a line joining such points, the locus D, is called a *demand curve*.

Table 17 A demand schedule

Price per can (pence)	Cans of beans demanded (per unit of time)
15	2
14	5
13	8
12	12
11	15
10	18

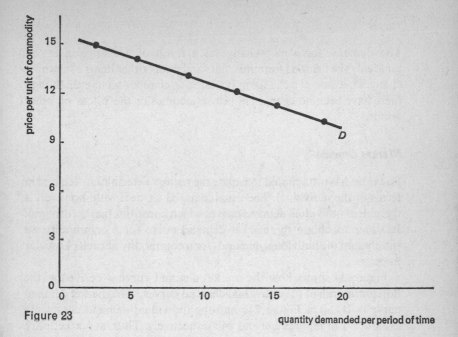

Figure 23

quantity demanded per period of time

The prices of other goods

If the prices of closely-related goods fall then one of three possible changes in the demand for commodity *a* may occur:

1 If the price of commodity *b* falls then the demand for *a* may fall. If the price of *b* rises then the demand for *a* may rise. The repercussions on the demand for *a* of changes in the price of *b* arise because *a* and *b* are substitutes, that is, they are both goods which can satisfy the same want, e.g. butter and margarine.

2 If the price of *b* falls then the demand for *a* may rise. If the price of *b* rises then the demand for *a* may fall. The repercussions on the demand for *a* of changes in the price of *b* arise because *a* and *b* are complements, that is, *a* and *b* are jointly demanded in order to satisfy the same want, e.g. milk and cornflakes.

3 Intermediate between the cases of substitute and complementary relations may be a situation where changes in the price of *b* have no effect on the demand for *a*.

The Individual's Demand Curve 103

Tastes

The demand for *a* may change as a result of a change in tastes. Suddenly the demand for minis, hats and many other items of clothing changes because of a change in tastes. Such changes occur even though there have been no changes in prices, incomes or the prices of other goods.

Market demand

So far we have attempted to isolate the factors determining demand in terms of the individual. The usual material we deal with, however, is the sum of individual demand curves which constitute market demand. In order to obtain the market demand curve for a commodity we simply sum the individual demands for a commodity at each particular price.

Figure 24 shows how the market demand curve is derived as the horizontal sum of the individual demand curves.[1] The market demand curve is D_{A+B} in Figure 24c and the individual demand curves are D_A and D_B in Figures 24a and 24b respectively. Thus, at market price OP_3 consumers demand Ox_2 of the commodity where $Ox_2 = Oa_2 + Ob_2$. For prices higher than OP_2, A's demand constitutes the market demand; for example, at OP_2 quantity $Ox_1 = Oa_1$. The demand curve of consumer B becomes effective at a price just below OP_2 (at OP_2, B's demand is zero). Hence the market demand curve

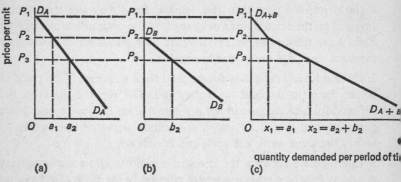

Figure 24

1. For simplicity, straight-line demand *curves* are assumed.

104 Demand

is kinked at price OP_2. When the number of consumers is large, so that each individual demand is small in relation to total demand, such kinks can be ironed out and the price–quantity relation becomes a smooth curve.

Market demand is influenced by:

The size and composition of the population;
The distribution of income within the population;
The influences discussed previously under the individual's demand curve.

The preceding analysis enables us to distinguish between changes in demand whenever there is a change in the price of that commodity, and changes in demand when there is no change in the price of that commodity.

Whenever the price of a commodity changes we can visualize a movement along the demand curve to buy either more or less of the commodity. Such movements are sometimes referred to as *extensions* or *contractions of demand* or *movements along demand curves*. On the other hand, we may sometimes encounter situations where the demand for a commodity changes even though price does not change. Such situations may be visualized as involving a shift of the demand curve. Figure 25 illustrates both possibilities. When the price falls from P_1 to P_2 there is a movement along the demand curve from A to B.

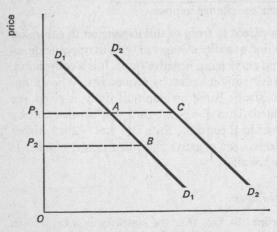

Figure 25 Quantity demanded per period of time

Now contrast this state of affairs with that which occurs when at price OP_1 there is an increase in demand from A to C. This involves a shift of demand as a result of either:

An increase in income – more can be bought at the existing price;
A change in tastes;
A fall in the price of a complementary good;
A rise in the price of a substitute good.

The demand elasticities

Whenever any of the variables on the right-hand side of the equation changes, a change in demand occurs. One of the great interests of economists is how much does demand respond to changes in the variables. We shall now consider three measures of response:

Price-elasticity of demand;
Cross-price elasticity of demand;
Income-elasticity of demand.

Price elasticity of demand

The response of demand for a commodity to a change in price is termed the *price-elasticity of demand* and its formulation is as follows:

$$e = -\frac{\text{the percentage change in quantity demanded}}{\text{the percentage change in price}}.$$

A minus sign is often placed in front of this expression to neutralize the effect of the price and quantity changes moving in opposite directions when the demand curve has a negative slope. It is a convention, although not one consistently adopted by economists. When a numerical measure of elasticity, based on empirical study, is given, the negative sign is retained. Thus $e = -2$ means that if price *falls* by 1 per cent demand rises by 2 per cent. Note also that -2 is a higher elasticity than -1 despite the negative sign; that is, the number is more important than the sign.

Absolutes versus percentages

We must now underline the fact that the elasticity is measured in terms of proportional changes in price and quantity rather than absolute changes. The reason for this is that absolute changes can give different measures of response depending upon what units of measurement are adopted. For example, suppose we compare the demand schedules for butter for an individual consumer using two different sets of measurements, as follows:

Table 18

Price of butter		Quantity of butter demanded per annum	
Pounds (£)	Francs (F)	Weight (lb)	Weight (kg)
1·00	500	50	22·50
0·90	450	55	24·75
0·80	400	65	29·25
0·70	350	70	31·50
0·60	300	75	33·75
0·50	250	80	36·00

Now suppose that our Englishman decides to calculate his price-elasticity of demand for butter when its price falls from 400 to 350 francs (we are assuming that £1 = 500F) on the assumption that elasticity is measured by

$$\frac{\text{Change in demand}}{\text{Change in price}}.$$

If he does the calculation in francs and kilograms, his result will be

$$e = \frac{2 \cdot 25}{50} = 0 \cdot 045.$$

On the other hand, if he does the calculation in English units of measurement, his result will be

$$e = \frac{5 \cdot 0}{0 \cdot 10} = 50.$$

The difference in the results is due to the fact that the units of measurement do affect the elasticity and in order to remove their influence the calculations must be in percentages. Thus

$$\text{French} \quad e = \frac{(2 \cdot 25 / 29 \cdot 25) \times 100}{(50 / 400) \times 100} = \frac{0 \cdot 09}{1 \cdot 17} \times \frac{8}{1} = 0 \cdot 615,$$

English $\quad e = \dfrac{(5/65)}{(0 \cdot 10/0 \cdot 80)} \qquad = \dfrac{1}{13} \times 8 \quad = 0 \cdot 615.$

There is one further problem to consider at this stage – for a given price the elasticity measure differs according to whether the original price was higher or lower than the new one. In the above example we considered a price *fall* from 400F to 350F which meant that the original price was 400F and the original quantity was 29·25 kilograms. Suppose, however, that we had considered a change in the opposite direction taking 350F and 31·50 kg as the original price and quantity. In this case a sharp rise of 50F would have yielded the following measure of elasticity:

$$e = \frac{(2 \cdot 25/31 \cdot 50) \times 100}{(50/350) \times 100} = \frac{2 \cdot 25}{31 \cdot 50} \times \frac{350}{50} = 0 \cdot 5.$$

In order to avoid such discrepancies when dealing with numerical elasticities we calculate an average measure, thus accounting for both the original and new levels of price and quantity, as follows:

$$e = \frac{\text{change in quantity demanded}}{\tfrac{1}{2}\,(\text{old quantity} + \text{new quantity})} \div \frac{\text{change in price}}{\tfrac{1}{2}\,(\text{old price} + \text{new price})}.$$

Applying this formula to our numerical example yields

$$e = \frac{2 \cdot 25}{\tfrac{1}{2}\,(29 \cdot 25 + 31 \cdot 50)} \div \frac{50}{\tfrac{1}{2}\,(400 + 350)} = 0 \cdot 55.$$

Elasticity and the slope of the demand curve

By grasping at the outset that elasticity refers to proportionate rather than absolute changes in price and quantity we can avoid the error of confusing elasticity with the *slope* of the demand curve. Let us take a closer look at the elasticity formula, representing it in symbols:

$$e = -\frac{\Delta Q/Q}{\Delta P/P},$$

where Q represents the original quantity, P represents the original price, and the changes in price and quantity are represented by ΔP and ΔQ respectively. Rearranging the symbols we have:

$$e = -\frac{\Delta Q}{Q}\left(\frac{P}{\Delta P}\right) \quad \text{or} \quad e = \frac{\Delta Q}{\Delta P}\left(\frac{P}{Q}\right).$$

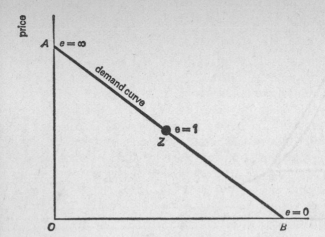

Figure 26   **quantity demanded per period of time**

This latter formula is the most useful since it shows elasticity to depend upon two things: *the ratio of the changes in quantity and price* multiplied by *the ratio of the original price and quantity*. In other words, this formula reminds us that price-elasticity of demand does not depend solely upon the slope of the demand curve.

To further emphasize the point made in the previous paragraph let us consider a straight-line demand curve. We shall see that although the slope of the demand curve does not change at each point on the curve, *elasticity does vary along the demand curve*. In Figure 26 the demand curve has been extended to meet the price axis at A and the quantity axis at B. The demand curve is a straight line and so $\Delta Q/\Delta P$ is a constant (since $\Delta P/\Delta Q$ is a constant). But elasticity is not constant because P/Q changes at each point on the demand curve:

1 As P approaches A, quantity Q approaches zero and P/Q approaches infinity. Thus price-elasticity of demand approaches infinity as the demand curve approaches the vertical axis.

2 As Q approaches B, price P approaches zero and P/Q approaches zero. Thus price-elasticity of demand approaches zero as the demand curve approaches the horizontal axis.

3 At the mid-point Z of the demand curve, price-elasticity of demand is equal to unity. We shall explain this more fully a little later.

Elasticity and the Slope of the Demand Curve 109

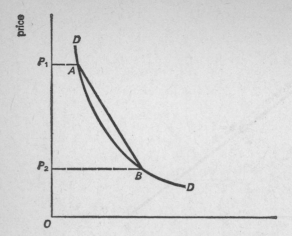

Figure 27   quantity demanded per period of time

What happens when the demand curve is not a straight line? Again the P/Q ratio is different at each point along the curve. But in this case the ratio $\Delta Q/\Delta P$ is also changing along the curve since the slope of the demand curve is different at each point. This means that our formula of elasticity gives an inaccurate measure when a discrete price/quantity change is taken along such a curve. At best our formula can only give an approximation to the true measure of elasticity, by providing an estimate of the average of the elasticities between any two points on the demand curve as shown in Figure 27. In this we depict a price change fr ɔm OP_1 to OP_2. Our elasticity formula gives only an approximation to the elasticity measure since $\Delta Q/\Delta P$ is the reciprocal of the slope $\Delta P/\Delta Q$ of the *chord AB*.

It should be clear that the greater the price change considered the greater will be the elasticity error. To reduce the error very small changes in price and quantity must be considered. In fact we really need a measure of the elasticity for each *point* on the demand curve since elasticity differs at every point. It is this measure, *point-elasticity*, that economists usually refer to in their theoretical discussions, as opposed to the *arc-elasticity* which is the measure that we have adopted so far in this chapter. From now on, therefore, elasticity will always mean point-elasticity unless we state otherwise.

How is point-elasticity calculated? In Chapter 13 we derive point-

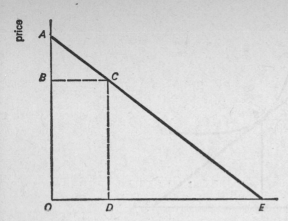

Figure 28   quantity demanded per period of time

elasticity with the use of the basic calculus, but meanwhile we can content ourselves with the use of similar triangles. Consider the straight-line demand curve in Figure 28 which meets the price axis at A and the quantity axis at E. Let us calculate elasticity at price $B (= DC)$ using our earlier formula,

$$e = - \frac{\Delta Q}{\Delta P} \left(\frac{P}{Q} \right).$$

The ratio $\Delta Q/\Delta P$ is constant along AE and, hence, is equal to DE/DC. The price P is equal to DC and Q equals OD. Thus,

$$e = - \frac{DE}{DC} \cdot \frac{DC}{OD} = \frac{DE}{OD}.$$

But $OD = BC$ so that $e = DE/BC$ and since ABC and CDE are similar triangles,

$$e = - \frac{DE}{BC} = \frac{CD}{AB} = \frac{CE}{AC}.$$

Repeating this for any point on the demand curve gives us the same answer – that elasticity is measured by the ratio of the distance from the point to where the curve meets the quantity axis (CE), to the distance from the point to where the curve meets the price axis (AC). This explains why $e = 1$ at the mid-point Z in Figure 26.

Elasticity and the Slope of the Demand Curve 111

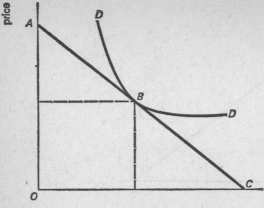

Figure 29 quantity demanded per period of time

Returning to the case of non-linear demand curves we can use this new formulation to calculate point-elasticity, for at each point we can treat the curve as a straight line since the slope of the curve equals the slope of the tangent to the curve at that point. We can calculate price-elasticity of demand at point B on the demand curve in Figure 29 by the ratio BC/AB.

Three special cases

Before leaving price-elasticity of demand, let us consider three special cases:

Demand is perfectly elastic;
Demand is perfectly inelastic;
Elasticity of demand is unity at all points on the demand curve.

Figure 30 shows all three cases. We have already seen that $e = \infty$ when a downward sloping demand curve meets the price axis. Figure 30a shows a demand curve where this is true at all points. Consumers are prepared to buy any amount at a unit price of OP^* but nothing at all at a price just above this level. Extensive use of this case is made in our later discussion of a market structure named *perfect competition* (Chapter 17).

Figure 30b shows another extreme case – where demand is perfectly inelastic, it does not respond at all to price changes. Consumers are

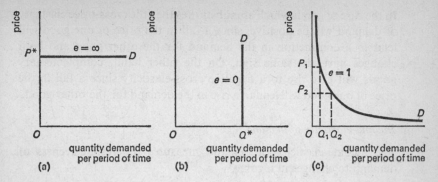

Figure 30

willing to pay any price for the quantity OQ^*. Such a case would exist in the cases of essentials of life, for example, water or heroin (in the case of an addict).

The third case, Figure 30c is where elasticity is unity at all points. This means that every proportional price change is exactly matched by a proportional change in quantity demanded. Expenditure in such a case is constant and the curve is therefore a *rectangular hyperbola* – the area of any rectangle drawn from any point on the curve to the axes is always the same $(OP_1. OQ_1 = OP_2. OQ_2$ and so on). We make extensive use of this curve when considering the problem of farm incomes in Chapter 10.

We have spent a long time in considering the concept of price-elasticity. Our efforts will be justified because it is the most important elasticity concept in a world in which prices operate, and the most complex. The other elasticity measures will be dealt with more briefly.

Cross-price elasticity of demand

This measures the response of demand for one good arising from a change in the price of another good.

$$e_x = \frac{\text{percentage change in the quantity demand of good } A}{\text{percentage change in the price of good } B}$$

$$= \frac{\Delta Q_A}{Q_A} \div \frac{\Delta P_B}{P_B} = \frac{\Delta Q_A}{\Delta P_B} \left(\frac{P_B}{Q_A} \right).$$

2

Elasticity and the Slope of the Demand Curve 113

In the case of goods which are substitutes then the cross-price elasticity of demand will be positive, since a fall in the price of one good will lead to a contraction in the demand for the other good and both changes have the same sign. On the other hand, complementary goods will give rise to a negative cross-elasticity since a fall in the price of one good will lead to a rise in the demand for the other good.

Income-elasticity of demand

The income-elasticity of demand measures the responsiveness of demand to changes in income,

$$e_y = \frac{\text{percentage change in quantity demanded of } A}{\text{percentage change in income}}. \qquad 3$$

For most goods an increase in income leads to an increased demand (i.e. a shift in the demand curve rather than a movement along the curve) and income-elasticities will be positive. For some goods, *inferior goods*, an increase in income can however lead to a downward shift in demand. Income-elasticity of demand may vary considerably as income varies through a wide range. Consider the case of housing. At low levels of income housing may account for a considerable proportion of income. As income rises this proportion may fall as households increase the range of goods they consume. But at very high levels of income the proportion of income spent on housing may rise as householders switch into Georgian and Tudor mansions.

Taste-elasticity of demand

If we look back to equation 1 we observe that we have an elasticity of demand for every variable except tastes. Is there, then, an elasticity measure for tastes? The answer is *no* because tastes are a qualitative phenomenon which are not amenable to measurement. There are some things which can be done with numbers and some things which cannot.

As a conclusion to the whole of the elasticities section, let us summarize some of the more important points in the form of Tables 19–21.

Revenue

So far we have looked at the concept of elastity of demand from the point of view of the consumers of a commodity. But we can also use

Table 19 Price-elasticity of demand

The e measure	What it means	Technical term
$e = 0$	Q does not change in response to changes in P	perfectly inelastic
$e > 0$ but < 1	Q changes by a smaller percentage than P changes	relatively (i.e. relative to 1) inelastic
$e = 1$	Q changes by exactly the same percentage as P changes	unit elasticity
$e > 1$ but $< \infty$	Q changes by a larger percentage than P changes	relatively elastic
$e = \infty$	consumers are willing to buy all they can obtain at the given price but are unwilling to buy any at a slightly higher price	perfectly elastic

Table 20 Cross-price elasticity of demand

The e measure	What it means
$e_x < 0$	the two goods are complements
$e_x > 0$	the two goods are substitutes
e_x has a *high* positive value	the two goods are *close* substitutes
e_x has a *low* positive value	the two goods are *not* very close substitutes

Table 21 Income-elasticity of demand

The e measure	What it means
$e_y = 0$	Q does not change in response to changes in Y
$e_y > 0$	as Y changes (proportionately) Q changes in the same direction – *normal good*
$e_y < 0$	as Y changes (proportionately) Q changes in the opposite direction – *inferior good*
$e_y > 0$ but < 1	the proportionate changes in Y and Q are in the same direction but Q change is less than the Y change
$e_y > 1$	the proportionate changes in Y and Q are in the same direction but the the Q change is greater than the Y change

Elasticity and the Slope of the Demand Curve 115

it to illustrate some of the problems facing producers. Consumer outlay is the revenue of the producers and, hence, variations in consumers' outlay also mean variations in producers' incomes. *Total revenue* is easily read off from the demand curve since it is defined as price times quantity. *Average revenue* (*AR*) is similarly straightforward, being total revenue divided by quantity purchased and, hence, equal to price. However, to reach his output decision, a producer must know (for reasons fully explored in later chapters) his *marginal revenue* (*MR*) which is defined as *the change in total revenue resulting from a unit change in quantity sold.* Table 22 illustrates this concept.

Column (*4*) shows the values of marginal revenue calculated as the

Table 22 The derivation of marginal revenue

Quantity bought and sold	Price per unit (average revenue)	Total revenue	Marginal revenue
(*1*)	(*2*)	(*3*)	(*4*)
0	100	0	
			+90
1	90	90	
			+70
2	80	160	
			+50
3	70	210	
			+30
4	60	240	
			+10
5	50	250	
			−10
6	40	240	
			−30
7	30	210	
			−50
8	20	160	
			−70
9	10	90	
			−90
10	0	0	

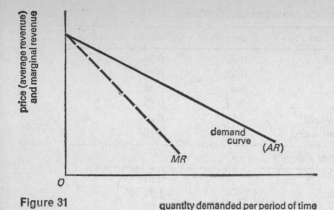

Figure 31   quantity demanded per period of time

changes in total revenue which can be observed in column (*3*). Note that as the number of units bought increases, marginal revenue declines, and that marginal revenue is less than price (average revenue). Figure 31 shows these points more clearly. Both observations result from the fact that the demand curve slopes downwards from left to right – an extra unit of output reduces the price of all units. It should be clear that marginal revenue varies with the price-elasticity of demand since a change in total revenue means a change in consumer expenditure, the size of which is measured by the elasticity of demand. An interesting case which we can appreciate without knowledge of further techniques is where demand is perfectly elastic (Figure 30a). Since each unit sells at the same price, marginal revenue must equal price (average revenue).

Empirical measures of elasticities

From the National Food Survey Committee Report for 1974 it is possible to obtain empirical estimates of income- and price-elasticities of demand. Two estimates of income-elasticities for each good are supplied. That the expenditure-elasticity is greater than the quantity elasticity indicates the extent to which consumers are buying a better quality product as their incomes rise. It is interesting that the elasticities for margarine confirm the commonplace view that it is an inferior good. This observation also applied to white bread though not to brown.

Table 23 Empirical measures of elasticities

Income-elasticities 1974	Expenditure	Quantity purchased
cheese, natural	0·39	0·36
pork	0·38	0·28
beef and veal	0·40	0·38
butter	0·14	0·15
bread, white sliced	−0·30	−0·29
bread, white unsliced	0·09	0·10

Price-elasticities 1969–74	
beef and veal	−0·81
mutton and lamb	−1·21
pork	−1·21
all carcase meat	−0·68
eggs	−0·07
potatoes	−0·18
bread	−0·18
butter	−0·40

Source: *Household Food Consumption and Expenditure*, 1974, HMSO, 1976

Table 24 Own- and cross-elasticities of demand for meat and poultry, 1967–74

	Elasticity with respect to the price of			
	Beef and veal	Mutton and lamb	Pork	Poultry
beef and veal	−1·07	0·22	0·15	0·05
mutton and lamb	0·44	−1·43	0·12	0·25
pork	0·48	0·18	−1·35	−0·12
poultry	0·20	0·53	−0·16	−1·20

In the case of the income-elasticities, as the value of the elasticity falls the broader is the category as is shown by the values for all meats as opposed to beef or pork. Notice also that the signs of the elasticities for bread are negative which suggests that people may reduce the quantity of bread bought when income rises though the fact that their expenditure rises may indicate a rising demand for 'real bread'.

All the price-elasticities are negative and consultation of the fuller list of elasticities in *Household Food Consumption and Expenditure* would reveal an absence of positive elasticities. This does not mean that they do not exist or that economists should not speculate on the implications of positive price-elasticities in order to check their reasoning about negative elasticities. In the eighteenth century, an economist and statistician, Sir Robert Giffen, thought he had come across an example in Ireland where, apparently, peasants reduced their consumption of potatoes when their price fell and bought more when their price rose.

Cross-elasticity of demand

The price-elasticities we have looked at were *own*-price elasticities: that is, the elasticity of demand in response to a change in the price of the good. What may be more relevant however is the effect on the demand for a commodity if the price of another commodity changes, i.e. the cross-elasticity. In Table 23 are shown some cross-elasticities and we leave the reader to consider whether complements and substitutes exist.

Statistics: a warning

The elasticity values we have quoted have been obtained from samples of household expenditures. They may therefore not be accurate measures of the whole population's response to price changes. When the reader has studied statistical theory he should consult the original sources of our data in order to examine the measure of the errors of the computations. Meanwhile, in this context we can remember that real world demand curves have to be constructed – they are not a free gift of nature! Economists and statisticians must collect data and they can plot their information on graphs. Such graphs are termed *scatter diagrams* and an example is given in Figure 32.

If the data collected and plotted are about a commodity which is assumed to be 'normal' and the economist's theory is correct then the scatter points would fall in the pattern shown in Figure 32. A visual interpretation of this diagram shows the price/quantity relationship to be generally downward sloping from left to right. The actual demand curve is obtained by finding the straight line (or curve) which is the best fit to the scatter points (by the technique known as *least squares regression*).

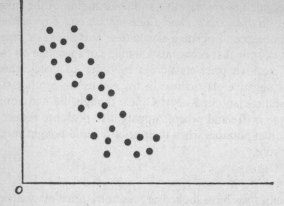

 price

Figure 32   quantity demanded per period of time

Summary

This chapter has explored the demand for goods, concentrating on the case of private goods. The forces influencing this demand were seen to be the price of the good; the prices of other goods; consumer income; and tastes. It was assumed that people would buy more of a good as its price fell and the extent to which such a response occurred was known as price-elasticity of demand. Other demand-elasticities were also analysed. Finally, it was found that there were exceptions to the belief that people would buy more of a good if its price fell or if their income rose.

Questions

1 Calculate the income-elasticities of demand for housing, transport, and services for different income changes from the data in Table 16.

2 If the price of *all* cars falls and an individual switches from buying a Volkswagen Golf to buying a Rover 3500, does this mean that Golfs are a Giffen good? Does this suggest that the conventional statistical measures of elasticities fail to indicate the great importance of Giffen goods?

3 Comment on the following proposition: if we observe a rise in the price of a good accompanied by a rise in the amount bought then the demand curve of that good must be upward sloping.

120 Demand

Chapter 8
Supply

The supply of a commodity may be defined as the amount of that commodity which producers are willing and able to offer for sale. The stress on ability indicates that it is effective supply that is important.

The determinants of supply

The determinants of supply can be summarized in a supply function or supply statement,

$$S_b = f(P_a, P_b, ..., P_z; P^f; O; T),$$

where P_b is the price of the good which is to be supplied, $P_b, ..., P_z$ are the prices of the other goods; P^f is the set of prices of the factors of production required to produce the good; O is the objective(s) of the producer and T is the state of technology.

Producer's objectives

For some goods the amount supplied will depend upon whether the suppliers are attempting to obtain a large money income or a non-monetary income. A producer interested in maximizing universal goodwill or the sales of his product might be found to be providing more of a commodity than one who looked at the money income to be obtained from the sale of his good. The latter might cease producing the good if he felt that he could obtain a larger income from selling something else whereas the saint, the universal fountain of good deeds, or the man who believes that everyone should eat Bono, would keep on providing goods long after Mister Five Per Cent had given up.

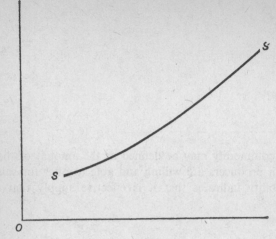

Figure 33   quantity supplied per unit of time

Price of the commodity

Other things being equal more of a commodity will be supplied if
the price rises as in Figure 33. This proposition follows naturally if
we assume that producers are interested in money incomes. Higher
rewards are necessary to induce producers to incur the higher costs of
increased outputs.

Prices of other goods

If the price of another good rises then this will be a signal to think
about not producing the existing good and to consider switching to
the good whose price has risen. Another way of expressing this
proposition is to say that as a result of the rise in the price of the other
good the opportunity cost of continuing in the present line of business
may be too high.

Prices of factors of production

Since factor prices contribute to production costs then a rise in factor
prices will cause an upward shift in production costs and hence in
the supply curve.

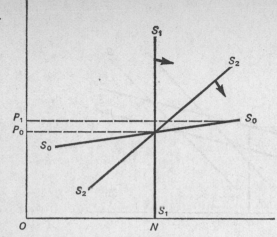

Figure 34

quantity supplied per unit of time

Technology

A change in technology brought about by an invention may lower costs and enable supply to be increased.

Shifts and movements along supply curves. The discussion so far means that care must be taken in distinguishing movements along, from shifts of, supply curves. Consider Figure 34. The initial supply curve is $S_1 S_1$. Let the initial price of the commodity be OP_0 at which price the supply will be ON. Now let the price rise to OP_1. Since the producers cannot immediately adapt their plant there will be no change in supply and ON will now be supplied at price OP_1. Gradually, producers will find ways of expanding output, by, for example, sub-contracting, shift-work or overtime working and they will expand output along $S_2 S_2$. Eventually, suppliers will fully adapt their plant by using known techniques which are more appropriate for the greater rates of output. This can be accomplished by recognizing that a greater output can be obtained by increasing the volume (capacity of the plant) and so enabling a movement along $S_0 S_0$. The distinction between the two supply curves $S_2 S_2$ and $S_0 S_0$ arises because in the case of the former a small plant can only increase a given output by increasing its *rate* of throughput, whereas the $S_0 S_0$ supply curve expresses the attempt to increase output by enlarging the volume of the plant as well as increasing the rate of throughput.

The Determinants of Supply 123

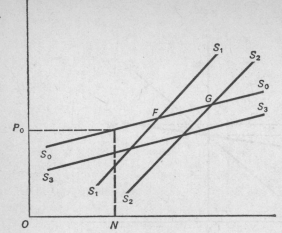

Figure 35   quantity supplied per unit of time

In Figure 35 we exhibit shifts of supply curves brought about by technical change. $S_3 S_3$ gives an overall increase in the supply of the commodity at all prices and lies below the curve $S_0 S_0$. On the other hand $S_1 S_1$ and $S_2 S_2$ yield improvements over certain ranges of prices. Thus the supply curve $S_1 S_1$ gives lower supply prices below F and higher supply prices above F. Likewise the supply curve $S_2 S_2$ yields higher supply prices above G.

Summary

In this chapter we looked briefly at the forces influencing the supply of goods. We took the view that supply would rise as price rose and that a price rise was necessary to overcome the tendency to rising costs caused by diminishing returns. Some causes of shifts in supply curves were also examined.

Questions

1 In the previous chapter we discussed the price-elasticity of demand. Attempt a definition of price-elasticity of supply. What will be the main determinants of supply elasticity?

2 What are the causes of shifts in supply curves?

124 Supply

Chapter 9
The Market

Introduction

With the information provided in the two previous chapters we can now continue the exploration of market behaviour which began in the introduction. Since the study of market behaviour has employed 90 per cent of economists' labours our discussion will be spread over two chapters. In this chapter we shall consider:

1 The implications of bringing the demand and supply curves together in a free market, i.e. one not subject to restrictions on entry or collusion by either buyers or sellers.

2 The possible results of interventions in markets.

3 Alternatives to the market.

4 Further mathematical properties of demand and supply curves. (This represents a more intensive exploration of the arguments of the section introduction using the simple technique of simultaneous equations.)

All the above subjects are discussed on the assumption that the demand and supply curves do not shift, i.e. only the price of the product changes. In the next chapter we shall look at situations where shifts occur.

Figure 36 brings the demand and supply curves for a commodity together. We notice three interesting features:

1 The two curves intersect once only because of the properties of the two curves. It might be possible for the curves to intersect more than once and in Chapter 35 we shall consider such a case, but for the moment let us ignore such oddities.

2 The two curves intersect at a *positive* price OP – if this were not so then the good would not be scarce. This price is termed the *equilibrium* price since it is the only one which balances the market.

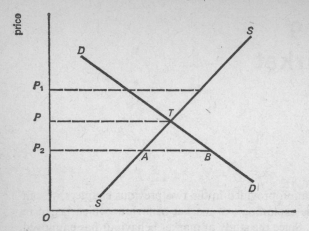

Figure 36   quantity per unit of time

3 The market equilibrium is stable. Suppose there was a displacement of price from OP to OP_1, then demand would contract and supply would extend. This would result in stocks piling up and in an endeavour to dispose of them producers would lower prices until the market was once more cleared at price OP. (Readers should now analyse the results from a change in price to OP_2.) Stability exists because the demand curve slopes downwards while the supply curve slopes upwards. If the slopes were reversed, equilibrium, following a displacement of price, would not occur.

The surpluses

Another unusual feature of the market situation is revealed by Figure 37. The price consumers pay for *all* units of the commodity is OP. Yet the price they would be prepared to give for individual units is given by points on the demand curve. Thus for the unit ON_1 consumers would be prepared to pay a price OP_1 but instead they get that unit for OP. This is a common occurrence since we normally find ourselves willing to pay more for some things than in fact we are asked. This state of affairs exists because it is rarely worthwhile for a producer to attempt to find out how much each person would in fact give for each unit he wished to consume, and it might be difficult for him to prevent a person who was prepared to pay a high price from

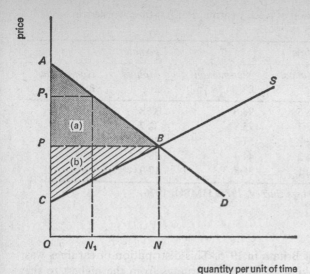

price

quantity per unit of time

Figure 37 (a) Consumer surplus. (b) Producer surplus or rent

getting it at a low price. There are costs of finding out what consumers will be prepared to pay. To get each consumer to pay exactly what he would be willing to pay, producers must be able to negotiate with each consumer separately and also be able to negotiate separately for every unit sold to each consumer. The difference that exists between the outlay which consumers are willing to pay, area $OABN$ under the demand curve, and what they have to pay, $OPBN$, is called *consumer surplus* and represents a gain to consumers equal to the area of the triangle APB. But this market result is mutually beneficial because there is also a difference between the revenue at which producers are willing to supply a good and the revenue they obtain; and this difference or gain is called the *producer surplus* or *rent*, represented by the triangle PBC in Figure 37.

Intervention in markets

One of the most interesting areas where it might be considered that government intervention should take place is the labour market. Since poverty often arises because of low wages it seems sensible to raise wages. Table 25 reveals the full-time earnings of male and female

Table 25 Distribution of weekly earnings of full-time workers in
Great Britain 1975

| | Male | | Female | |
	Manual £	Non-manual £	Manual £	Non-manual £
highest decile	56·5	98·6	37·8	60·1
upper quartile	47·7	75·8	32·7	44·4
median	39·8	57·9	28·2	35·0
lower quartile	34·2	44·4	23·3	28·3
lowest decile	30·1	35·8	17·9	23·5

Source: *New Earnings Survey, 1975*, HMSO, 1976

workers in Great Britain in 1975. This distribution of earnings was
obtained by ranking all workers' earnings from the highest to the
lowest. Hence the highest decile refers to the 10 per cent of workers
who have wages equal to or greater than (in the case of all male
manual workers) £56·5 per week, and the upper quartile refers to the
25 per cent of workers who have wages greater than or equal to £47·7.
The median is the wage of the worker whose earnings fall half-way
along the distribution. The lower quartile and lower decile are defined
in a similar way to the upper quartile and upper decile. The wage
surveys reveal that:

There is a considerable spread of wages;
The earnings of women are consistently lower than those of men;
The earnings of manual workers tend to be lower than those of non-
manual workers.

Now let us suppose that it is deemed undesirable for anyone to earn
less than £40 per week. In 1970 the Trades Union Congress (TUC)
passed a resolution which demanded that the minimum wage should
be £20 per week. What would be the effects of such a policy? We can
simplify the analysis by assuming as in Figure 38 that all units of labour
are homogeneous. Figure 38 then shows the demand for and supply of
homogeneous labour and indicates that the wage which will clear the
market is OW. Now suppose that OW is deemed to be too low and
the Government declares that no one shall work for less than OW_1.

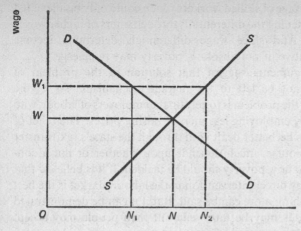

Figure 38   quantity per unit of time

The effect of a legal minimum wage of OW_1 is that ON_2 workers will try to get jobs but only ON_1 will be hired. Since ON_1 is less than ON then the effect of the minimum wage will be to reduce employment. Since there are now N_1N workers who previously had jobs without incomes, poverty has not been overcome despite the fact that workers who are employed receive higher wages. The effect of a minimum wage on employment will depend upon:

1 The elasticity of the employers' demand for labour. If the demand is relatively inelastic there may be a much reduced unemployment effect.

2 Whether or not higher wages lead to increased effort. If increased effort does result then the employers' demand will shift to the right.

It is conceivable that the distribution of receipts between employers and workers can be altered without any serious side effects; and that as a result of a wage increase morale might improve. But we do not know because no serious experiments on these hypotheses have been carried out. It may be that employers simply pass on wage increases in the form of price increases and governments cannot prevent them.

Once we relax the simplifying assumption of homogeneous labour then a further difficulty may arise. Since many skills are acquired through training and sacrifice of earnings then there may be resentment by higher paid workers at the loss of their differentials. So there could arise a shortage of skilled workers which could only be alleviated by employers widening the differentials through offers of higher wages to the skilled. And since wage differentials determine income differentials, relative, if not absolute, poverty may re-emerge.

The above arguments suggest that solution of the problem of poverty should not be left to the market mechanism. To let the market deal with the problem is to rely on the employers of labour, who may well react by employing less men or raising prices. The relief of poverty may thus be better dealt with through the state's tax/transfer mechanism. Of course, much depends upon whether or not a consensus exists as to how poverty should be tackled. If it is believed that raising incomes by direct intervention in the labour market is the best method then nothing more can be said. But if it can be demonstrated that other methods may be more efficient then people may accept them. The alternatives would seem to be:

1 Since unskilled workers earn less than skilled workers the state should subsidize training programmes.

2 Since poverty is linked to the number of dependents supported by one wage the state should introduce child allowances, tax reliefs and other low-income subsidies (on which see Chapter 42).

All such policies are, however, mere suggestions since we know so little about the actual effects of different policies. What we have done is to indicate the number of jobs that might be available after a wage rise and the redistribution of benefits that might then occur. These are the two predictive aspects of intervention that we considered in the previous section.

Housing, health and education

Now let us look at another method of dealing with poverty. Suppose the State decided that instead of raising wages it would try to keep down the prices of the commodities which the poor buy. The most essential of these commodities are housing, health and education. Let us take housing services as an example. Figure 39 represents the market situation for rented housing services. Price (rent) has been established at OP and ON units of housing services are supplied. Now suppose the government fixes the price at OP_1. From our previous analysis we can predict that there will be an excess demand for

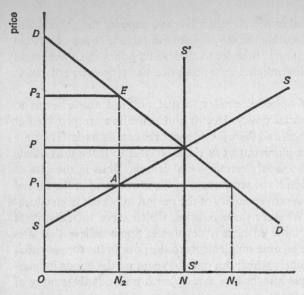

Figure 39   demand and supply per unit of time

housing. The supply of housing tends to be relatively fixed in the
short run (which may be a considerable time period in the case of
housing services) and we therefore depict the excess demand as
NN_1 ($S^1 S^1$ may be considered the short-run supply curve and SS the
long-run curve). Later, as houses fall into disrepair because rents are
insufficient to maintain them, or as houses arc taken out of the controlled market by such loopholes as exist in the law, the supply of
housing contracts to $P_1 A$ and excess demand rises to $N_1 N_2$. Hence the
conclusion follows that intervention has resulted in a shortage of
housing.

But now let us look at who gets the available houses, ON_2. Having
decided to interfere with market processes the state must take
responsibility for allocation. Clearly in a situation of excess demand
there might be several possible rationing rules. The state may operate
a 'first-come, first-served' rule, or the state may decide that only
those who would have been willing to pay a price OP_2 or more should
get the houses. In the case of this group their consumer surplus
would be $P_1 DEA$ instead of the $P_2 DE$ they would have obtained if
they had had to pay OP_2. Notice also that the producer surplus would

have been reduced to $SP_1 A$. As a final case, suppose the government was intent on allocating the ON_2 houses available to those who could only pay OP_1 or more; in order to achieve its policy the government would have to discriminate on a non-price basis by such criteria as social need.

Some kind of objective similar to that outlined above seems to underlie much social policy. Health and education are provided at below market prices and there is evidence of excess demand. The state then expects its administrators of these services to make it available only to those who satisfy certain social criteria. Thus in the case of health the criterion is the seriousness of the illness, and in the case of education it is the proven ability of the person to benefit from educational courses. Whether these policies, which serve to redistribute income, are the most efficient is debatable. Some believe that it is better to provide income supplements to the poor in the form of non-transferable vouchers which can only be spent on the goods in question. These people also believe that by such methods the supply of such goods would be made greater whereas the other procedure implies that supply cannot readily be expanded and ignores the possibility that it might contract. They would also argue that in order to discriminate against the rich the state is forced to lower the quality of the service – 'who would go and live in a council house' and 'why wait six months for an operation' are expressions symptomatic of a lowering of quality. As in all issues of social policy we still do not know which are the most efficient methods. For some purposes, as when consumers are ignorant or short-sighted, the policies pursued may be the most efficient. But they do run the risk of making people dependent upon others and may not educate people into thinking for themselves. State policy is of course full of paradoxes when it comes to the question 'does the consumer know what he wants?'. It insists, for example, on compulsory education but not compulsory chest X-ray examinations.

Rationing

What was suggested in the previous paragraph was that there are occasions when governments believe that physical rationing is better than rationing by prices. This presumption is even applied to the allocation of private goods under certain circumstances. In the

Second World War the UK government introduced food rationing. Each person was allowed weekly fixed quantities of particular foodstuffs (sugar, butter, bacon, etc.). This rationing system worked tolerably well because the state was dealing with basic wants and these were reasonably homogeneous for all people. Hence the physiological needs together with the ethical climate ('we are all in this together') combined to make food rationing work. At a later stage the coalition government introduced rationing for tinned foodstuffs (fruit and meat) and clothing. For both these groups it was recognized that peoples' tastes varied. So each person was given a fixed quantity of D coupons (for tinned foods) and clothing coupons which he could spend as he wished.

This war-time experience suggests that where needs are fairly simple and homogeneous a physical rationing system might work. Black markets, in which rationed goods were sold at higher prices but without coupons, did develop but they were never extensive enough to cause the system to break down.

The market for blood

One of the most interesting commodities to be allocated by non-pricing methods in the UK is blood for transfusion purposes. Surgeons demand blood for numerous operations and blood is collected from donors by the National Blood Transfusion Service. The collection of blood and its use is remarkable both for the absence of the use of a price mechanism by which to reward donors and ration supplies to users; and for the absence of a central planning dictator who would forecast demands and command supplies from suitable people. On the supply side the only instrument used is moral persuasion, and on the demand side professional responsibility presumably safeguards against abuse and wastage.

It has been argued by some observers that there is a shortage of blood and that we should therefore pay people to supply blood – that is, we should introduce the price system. This raises several issues which you should seek to verify. First, what evidence would you seek to indicate that there is a shortage of blood? Secondly, what effect would the introduction of a pricing system have upon voluntary blood donors? Finally, should the National Health Service intensify its advertising to make people aware of their moral responsibilities instead of introducing money rewards? These questions are left for the reader to consider.

The case for pricing is that it appeals to a strong motive in society. The case against is that it would result in undesirables offering their blood, and that it would destroy tender but important attributes of people – love and compassion. The other aspect of the problem is the question of the control of the *use* of blood. Should the patients or the hospitals be charged for the use of blood?

The case of blood transfusion is an example of a non-market mechanism for allocating a scarce resource. Perhaps we should not call it a non-market mechanism but a market without money prices. It is an example of a charity market where people obtain satisfaction from the act of giving.

Allocation by non-profit institutions

Blood is a special case but it serves to introduce other interesting cases of allocation by non-profit-making private institutions. Sometimes a price is charged but it is less than that which could be obtained in a free market; sometimes no price is charged but another condition of qualification is imposed.

The price of tickets for the FA Cup Final is an example of prices charged which are below those which could be obtained in a free market. Each year a thriving black market operates in which tickets are sold for prices well above their nominal stated prices. Why does the Football Association not fix high prices? Why do they forego extra income? The usual argument is that the FA believes that the club fans who have loyally supported their teams throughout the season, perhaps standing on the terraces in rain and snow, should not be 'exploited'. Why should the rich man who seldom goes to a match be able to outbid the poor man for a ticket? The FA therefore operates as a charity and then seeks to prevent a black market emerging by controlling the issue of tickets.[1] Unfortunately the costs of enforcing the charity seem to be much higher than the FA realizes.

People sometimes prefer that some resources should be allocated

1. Charities allocate resources outside the market and the number and variety of charities is endless. Indeed the law provides no definition of a charity, but prefers to test each claim (for tax exemption purposes) to charitable status on its merits.

according to merit and not income. University entrance is decided not by Mammon but by Jove; if a person possesses riches but no wisdom he cannot get in.

Do these examples contradict economic behaviour? The answer is No! Economics does not say how a man should maximize his welfare nor does it state that in pursuing his happiness a man should ignore the happiness of others. 'No man is an island' said John Donne, and most men, including economists, accept the truth of his dictum.

Simultaneous equations: a useful digression

In the section introduction we suggested that the major difficulties confronting the central planner concerned the collection and the analysis of information. This we said involved the solution of vast numbers of equations. Now the mention of the word equations invites the use of mathematical techniques – a thought which sometimes prompts consternation and dismay. Indeed many people feel that the introduction of mathematics into economics makes the subject more difficult than it is, and also makes the subject impersonal.

Both the arguments against the use of mathematics fall to the ground if it can be shown that the use of mathematics illuminates the subject. In this section we shall use mathematics to explore the problem of market determination. The mathematics used will be the technique of simultaneous equations which is taught in O-level mathematics courses. We are all fairly familiar with the type of question which says: 'If two knives and three forks cost 45p and five knives and three forks cost 66p, what is the price of a knife and what is the price of a fork?' It is this type of mathematical reasoning that underlies the type of problem which we shall consider. From our earlier discussions we may recall two propositions:

1 As the price of a commodity falls more of the commodity is demanded.
2 As the price of a commodity rises more of the commodity is supplied.

Both these propositions have been demonstrated with the use of graphs, as in Figures 40 and 41. Both graphs express a unique relationship between price and quantity (demanded or supplied). Such relations are called *functions*. An earlier example of such a unique relation was the production function of Chapter 3).

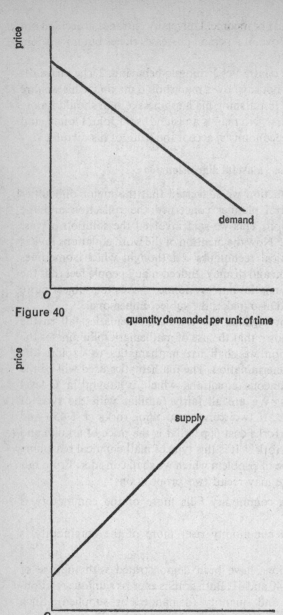

price

demand

O

Figure 40

quantity demanded per unit of time

price

supply

O

Figure 41

quantity supplied per unit of time

We shall explore the mathematics of functions more fully in Chapter 13 but we can note one or two points now. First, observe that the functions in Figures 40 and 41 are of the form:

$$q = f(p)$$

where q represents quantity and p represents price. The variable on the left-hand side is termed the *dependent variable* and the variable on the right-hand side the *independent variable*. Thus our present function tells us that the quantity depends upon price rather than the other way round. We should note, secondly, that it is mathematical convention to plot the dependent variable on the vertical axis and the independent variable along the horizontal axis. Although economists usually follow the same convention, demand and supply analysis is a confusing exception thanks to a habit handed down from Alfred Marshall (1842–1924). As we have seen, price (the independent variable) is usually plotted on the vertical axis and quantity (the dependent variable) on the horizontal axis. In order to avoid confusion, and also to demonstrate that the economics is unchanged as more formal mathematics is adopted, let us redraw the demand and supply functions in the conventional manner of mathematicians.

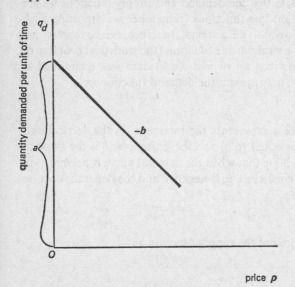

Figure 42 The demand function $q_d = a - bp$

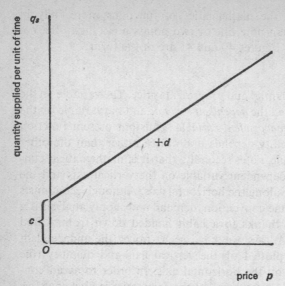

Figure 43 The supply function $q_s = c + dp$

Finally, we can note that the demand and supply functions we are employing are straight-line functions (remember we are using such functions for simplicity only). Each one, therefore, can be represented by the equation for a straight-line function (the statistical problem of fitting a straight line to a set of real world data was mentioned in Chapter 7). Thus we may present the demand function as

$$q_d = a + bp, \qquad\qquad\qquad 1$$

where the parameter a represents the intercept on the vertical axis (when p is zero, q_d is equal to a) and the parameter b is the slope of the demand curve.[2] Note that when the demand curve is normal as in Figure 42 the slope coefficient, b, is negative and the demand function is then

$$q_d = a - bp.$$

Similarly, we may present the supply function as

$$q_s = c + dp, \qquad\qquad\qquad 2$$

2. For those who may have forgotten, a parameter is a constant once its value has been specified for a particular function.

where the parameter c is the intercept on the vertical axis and the parameter d represents the slope of the supply function. Note that when the supply curve is normal, quantity supplied will be negative when the price is zero and the slope coefficient, d, will be positive (see Figure 43).

We can now return to our original task of illustrating the concept of market equilibrium with the use of simultaneous equations. We have, so far, two equations, 1 and 2, and three unknowns q_d, q_s, and p. Thus to complete the system of equations we must include the equilibrium condition,

$$q_d = q_s. \hspace{4cm} 3$$

Our model is now completed and we can solve for $q_d (= q_s)$ and p.

$$q_d = a + bp,$$

$$q_s = c + dp,$$

$$q_d = q_s.$$

Thus $a + bp = c + dp$,

and taking the a to the right-hand side and dp to the left-hand side

$$bp - dp = c - a,$$

or $\quad p(b - d) = c - a.$

Dividing both sides by $b - d$ gives,

$$p = \frac{c - a}{b - d}.$$

Presenting the solution in this form, usually termed the *reduced form* of the model, enables us to see at a glance that market price, p, is determined by the parameters of the demand and supply functions. In the case of the market for a normal good, b is negative, d is positive and a is greater than c. Thus $b - d$ is negative and $c - a$ is negative, yielding $(c - a)/(b - d)$ as positive, i.e. market price is positive.

Let us now try a numerical example:

$$q_d = 710 - 15p,$$

$$q_s = -10 + 10p.$$

Setting $q_d = q_s$ we have

$$710 - 15p = -10 + 10p,$$

or $$710 + 10 = 10p + 15p,$$

hence $$720 = 25p,$$

and $$28 \cdot 8 = p.$$

Equilibrium price is 28·8. To find equilibrium quantity we may feed this value of price into either the demand function or the supply function since $q_d = q_s$.

$$q_d = 710 - 15(28 \cdot 8)$$

$$= 710 - 432$$

$$= 278,$$

$$q_s = -10 + 10(28 \cdot 8)$$

$$= -10 + 288$$

$$= 278.$$

Perhaps we should finally note that the mechanics of market analysis can also be employed by the planner. We must recall that the derivation of equilibrium prices and quantities have been obtained on the assumption that both demand and supply statements are available. A major task of any central planner would be to gather this information unless he assumed that everyone would enjoy what he wanted or what he thought they would want. The cost of collecting such information could be enormous. He would have to ask everyone what they wanted at different hypothetical prices for different goods, and he would have to add all the answers together to obtain a general market demand table. From this table or schedule he would then have to obtain a general demand statement. Similarly he would have to perform the same tasks for the production side of his economy. It is these prior costs of information (which can be colossal) which, added to the computer problems of solving millions of equations, make wholesale central planning seem difficult.

Summary

In this chapter we looked at the market as a means of allocating resources. We found that there are circumstances in which the market gives results which society wishes to reject. The implications of interference in the market system were considered. It should not be assumed that interference is not warranted. What man has put together he can pull apart. The real issues are: what is the most efficient method of interference, and which method will give the least adverse effects?

Questions

1 What implications follow from the fact that demand curves intersect supply curves from above, and slope downwards from left to right, whereas supply curves slope upwards from left to right?

2 Can a consumer get more than he pays for?

3 If instead of giving workers a minimum wage we give them a minimum income subsidy will they work? Why do economists tend to accept interference with people's willingness to work rather than interference with the employers' willingness to hire them?

4 The government is anxious to curb inflation and the TUC agrees to cooperate if a minimum wage of £30 per week is introduced together with a price freeze on all goods and services. Assuming the government accepts, what consequences might follow?

5 'If rationing of the necessities of life was considered the best way of controlling demand and allocating resources in war-time, there is surely good reason to do so in peacetime'. Discuss.

6 Comment on the relative merits of conscription and mercenaries (use of price mechanism) as methods of raising armies.

7 Why do we see queues forming at bus stops at peak periods? Why don't we see some people jumping the queue by offering to pay more? Are queues ever more efficient for rationing resources than prices? What goods and services are usually rationed by queues?

8 Why are city centres dominated by industry and commerce, and suburbs dominated by residential housing?

9 Traffic signals allocate road space and prices allocate some goods. Why don't we use prices to allocate road space at junctions?

I.E.–8

10 In discussing low pay it was suggested that instead of raising wages it might be more efficient to increase family allowances, etc. Since these are subsidies, what might their possible effects be upon people's willingness to work? Illustrate by means of a diagram.

11 The Government has a choice of policies for combating the housing problems of the poor. Either it can:
(a) give them money to buy houses;
(b) give them vouchers to be spent only on houses;
(c) provide them with houses.
Comment on the relative merits of these schemes.

12 By what non-price measures might a Government increase the supply of non-toxic blood?

13 In the absence of a system of rationing by price how should the National Health Service decide whether
(a) resources should be devoted to geriatric wards or to spina bifida treatment;
(b) Mr Smith should be supplied with a kidney machine instead of Mr Jones?

14 'If the government gives income subsidies to poor farmers this will remove rural poverty but promote labour immobility'. Discuss.

15 How does the market determine the optimum length of life for a motor car?

16 Calculate the equilibrium prices and quantities from the following market information:
(a) $q_d = 35 - 8p$,
 $q_s = -5 + 2p$,
(b) $q_d = 10 - 2p$,
 $q_s = 4 + 4p$,
(c) $q_d = 16 - 8p$,
 $q_s = 4 + 2p$.

17 Our previous questions devoted to the solution of simultaneous equations were confined to systems of *linear* equations; that is, demand and supply statements which yield straight lines. However, textbooks and casual observation suggest that perhaps we should analyse *curves*. The solutions of systems of curves involves the use of quadratic equations of the form $ax^2 + bx + c = 0$ as opposed to the linear equation, $ax + b = 0$. For the solution we can use the formula:

$$x = \frac{-b \pm \sqrt{(b^2 - 4ac)}}{2a}.$$

The $\pm$ indicates there will be two roots (solutions) and we reject the negative one. Why?

Now try the following:

(a) $q_d = 100 - p^2$,
    $q_s = p + 5p$,

(b) $q_d = 10 - 2p$,
    $q_s = 5p^2$;

Chapter 10
The Market Continued

The previous chapter was concerned with examining situations where demand and supply curves remain fixed but where there might be the possibilities of outside intervention. This chapter examines the more usual cases of markets where demand and supply curves shift. As we have seen in Chapters 7 and 8, shifts in demand may come about through changes in income, tastes and other prices; shifts in supply may occur through changes in factor prices, technology and the firm's objective. When the demand curve shifts to the right a condition of excess demand occurs and this excess demand is removed by a variety of methods. If the market is knowledgeable about the shift in demand and considers that supply cannot be immediately increased, then price will rise from OP to OP_1 as in Figure 44. What Figure

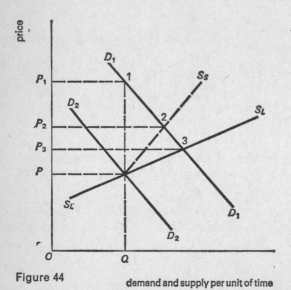

Figure 44   demand and supply per unit of time

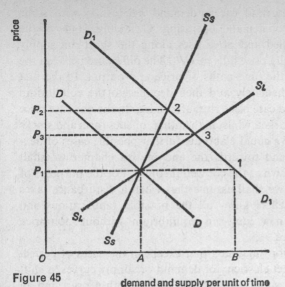

Figure 45   demand and supply per unit of time

44 shows is that in the immediate short run supply is fixed at OQ. After a period there will be an extension in supply along a short-run supply curve such as $S_S S_S$ which yields a price OP_2. Eventually price will fall to OP_3 as supply extends along the long-run supply curve $S_L S_L$.

We have distinguished three responses of supply to a change in demand and these distinctions are important in analysing market behaviour. They are:

1 Immediate supply response – possibly zero unless there is a run-down or build-up of stocks (the latter occurs if there is a *fall* in demand);

2 Short-run supply response – a rise or fall in supply brought about by overtime working or short-time working (for a fall in demand) of existing plant and equipment;

3 Long-run supply response – a rise or fall due to the building of more plant and equipment or the withdrawal of resources from the market.

The alternative extreme possibility is that for a while buyers and sellers are a little uncertain about the shift in demand or are uncertain as to whether the shift is permanent or temporary. Hence as in Figure

45 price does not rise and excess demand AB results with some non-price rationing of demand operating. Gradually, some of the uncertainty is dispelled and price rises along the short-run supply curve $S_S S_S$. Eventually price falls to OP_3. The difference between the two patterns lies in the time paths of price and output. In the first case, price rises immediately and then declines to the equilibrium whereas in the second case price rises after a lag. In the one case price moves to clear the market, whilst in the other, queues form and stocks may be run down. We could elaborate further possible cases of flex-price and fix-price and towards the end of this chapter we shall consider the case known as the cobweb theorem. For the purposes of subsequent analysis we shall assume that when a disturbance takes place, buyers and sellers know all the possible ramifications and move towards the new long-run equilibrium without non-price rationing taking place.

The previous section suggested that except in the cases of perfect inelasticity and perfect elasticity of demand or supply curves, a shift in either demand or supply would give rise to both a price and an output effect. Thus, if the supply was perfectly inelastic then an

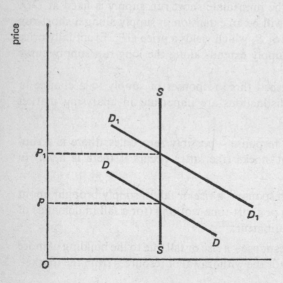

demand and supply per unit of time

Figure 46 Pure price effect

146 The Market Continued

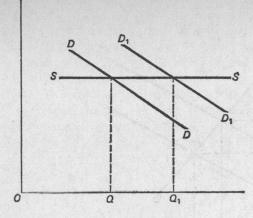

Figure 47 Pure quantity effect

increase in demand would simply raise price; there would be no change in supply. Similarly, if supply was perfectly price-elastic then an increase in demand would simply cause an extension of supply. These two cases are shown in Figures 46 and 47.

The effect of a tax or subsidy

We can now use this analysis to consider the effects of a tax being levied upon each unit produced of a commodity. The imposition of such a tax will cause the supply curve to be shifted upwards and to the left. This happens because producers now require, for each quantity they were previously prepared to produce, a higher price in order to cover the tax. By the supply curve shifting vertically upwards in this manner, producers receive the same revenue per unit as previously, but now *net* of tax.

The introduction of the tax should not, however, alter the position of the demand curve since its position is fixed by tastes and income. The new supply curve therefore slides up the demand curve. But what will be the equilibrium price and quantity sold after the tax? As Figure 48 indicates, the equilibrium will be governed by the price-elasticities of demand and supply. The tax increase is JK (which is equal to AE) but as the figure indicates the price increase is only CE.

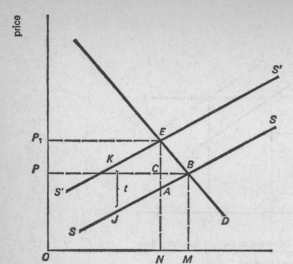

Figure 48

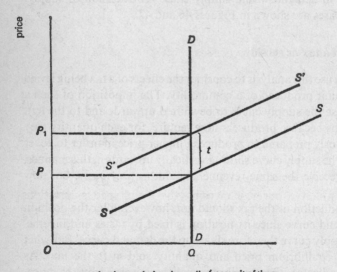

Figure 49

148 The Market Continued

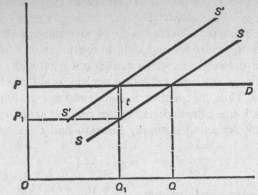

Figure 50

Consumers reduce the amount they consume by *NM* (which is equal to *BC*) but they cannot completely escape the tax and therefore pay *CE* per unit. The remaining portion of the tax increase, *AC* per unit, is borne by the producers.

To impress upon ourselves the importance of the relative price elasticities of demand and supply in determining the effects of a unit tax let us consider two of the special cases previously referred to. In Figure 49 the demand curve is perfectly inelastic, i.e. consumers want the same quantity irrespective of the price and in this case the price rises (*OP* to *OP₁*) by the full amount of the tax. In Figure 50 the demand curve is perfectly elastic and the producers bear the full burden of the tax in reduced sales (*OQ* to *OQ₁*) and in a reduced net price (the amount the producer receives per unit) of *OP₁*.

Some algebra

Let us now derive our results using the simultaneous equations technique of the previous chapter. Remember that in the no-tax situation the reduced form of the market model was,

$$p = (c-a/b-d).$$

What happens to the model when a unit tax is introduced? Since the tax does not affect demand, the demand function remains as

$$q_d = a + bp.$$

However, as we have seen, the tax *does* affect the supply function. Note that the price, p, in the supply function is a supply price, *i.e.* the quantity that the producer is *willing* to supply depends upon the return that he expects to receive for each unit. In the no-tax situation this return per unit is indeed the expected market price, but with the introduction of a unit tax any expected return per unit is reduced by the amount of the tax. Thus, the quantity that any producer is willing to supply now depends upon the expected return per unit *net of tax*. Representing the unit tax as t the supply function has, therefore, become

$$q_s = c + d(p - t).$$

We can now solve for price and quantity.

In equilibrium $q_d = q_s$,

thus $\quad a + bp = c + d(p - t),$

$$= c + dp - dt.$$

Rearranging gives $\quad bp - dp = c - a - dt,$

$$\text{or } \quad p(b - d) = c - a - dt,$$

and dividing both sides by $b - d$

$$p = \frac{c - a}{b - d} - \frac{d}{b - d}(t).$$

Putting the tax result against the no-tax result we can readily see the impact of the tax as:

No tax $\quad p = \dfrac{c - a}{b - d},$ 1

Unit tax $\quad p = \dfrac{c - a}{b - d} - \dfrac{d}{b - d}(t).$ 2

Equation **2** differs from **1** by the amount of $-\{d/(b-d)\}t$, thus p varies with t according to the expression $-\{d/(b-d)\}$. Now in the case of a normal good, d is positive, b is negative and $b - d$ is negative; thus $-d/(b-d)$ is positive (the tax raises the price).

Therefore p varies with t positively according to the relative slopes of the demand and supply curves (and not the intercept coefficients).

The tax conundrum

The distinction between movements along demand and supply curves and shifts of demand and supply curves is so important that it is worth working through another example which illustrates the pitfalls that arise when ambiguous words like 'rise' and 'fall', 'increase' and 'decrease' are used. Consider the following statement:

'A tax on a commodity causes the price to rise and demand to fall. The fall in demand will then restore price to its original level.'

Now let us take this quotation sentence by sentence. The first sentence tells us that as a result of the tax the supply curve will be shifted upwards and the result is a rise in price. So far so good, the first half of the first sentence is reiterating what we have discussed in the previous section. But will demand fall? Demand may contract if the demand curve is price-elastic, but if we encounter a zero price-elasticity then there need be no fall in demand. Let us, however, assume that the demand curve is price-elastic and demand contracts; what then can we make of the final sentence? Here we encounter the ambiguity of the phrase 'fall in demand'. We are given no indication or evidence to

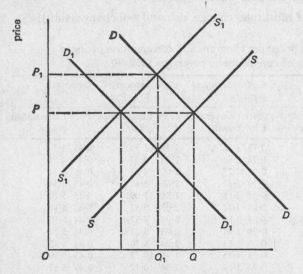

quantity demanded and supplied per unit of time

Figure 51

suggest that a tax can shift a demand curve to the left or right, nor are we told that there has been a change in tastes or fall in incomes. So there is no reason to suppose that price will fall to its original level. Figure 51 sketches out the conclusions reached in the previous paragraph. As a result of the tax the supply curve shifts from SS to $S_1 S_1$. At the new price OP_1 demand contracts along DD to OQ_1 from OQ. Price cannot fall to its original level unless the demand curve shifts to $D_1 D_1$.

Testing the theory

We are now in a position to make further applications of the theory of demand and supply. From previous discussions we know that the theory of demand makes certain predictions about the consumption of a good and certain key variables. These predictions are:

1 If price changes, demand will change (extend or contract) in the opposite direction;

2 If income increases, demand will normally increase (shift);

3 If tastes change, demand will change (shift);

4 If the prices of substitutes change, demand will change (shift);

Table 26 Average prices per kilogram and consumption per head in grams per week of non-alcoholic beverages 1959–70

Year	Tea		Coffee (bean and ground)		Coffee (instant)		Cocoa	
	Price £	Consumption grams	Price £	Consumption grams	Price £	Consumption grams	Price £	Consumption grams
1959	0·72	79·38	0·78	3·12	1·39	7·94	0·45	5·39
1960	0·71	79·38	0·75	2·83	2·18	3·97	0·45	4·54
1961	0·69	80·51	0·75	2·27	2·00	4·54	0·46	4·54
1962	0·68	79·10	0·79	2·83	1·89	5·67	0·45	4·54
1963	0·68	79·95	0·77	2·55	1·86	7·09	0·45	5·10
1964	0·68	76·26	0·84	3·12	2·03	6·52	0·42	5·10
1965	0·68	73·71	0·97	2·83	2·02	7·37	0·44	5·10
1966	0·68	74·84	0·98	2·83	2·05	8·22	0·44	5·39
1967	0·68	76·54	0·88	2·83	2·04	8·50	0·44	4·82
1968	0·67	73·71	0·94	4·25	1·96	10·77	0·43	5·10
1969	0·68	71·16	0·90	3·69	2·04	10·77	0·49	5·67
1970	0·71	73·43	1·08	2·55	2·08	11·90	0·51	5·67

Source: *Household Food Consumption and Expenditure*, Annual Reports of National Food Survey Committee

5 If the prices of complementary goods change, demand will change (shift).

Likewise the theory of supply predicts that when there are no monopolies or restrictions on markets, then;

1 If price increases, supply will increase (extend);
2 If technical know-how changes, then supply will increase (shift);
3 If the prices of factors of production change, then supply will change (shift).

'The cups that cheer but not inebriate' Cowper

Now let us test these predictions and the underlying reasoning by examining the case of the market for non-alcoholic beverages over the last decade. From Table 26 we obtain the following information for 1959–70

	Percentage change
Tea: change in price	−1·0
change in consumption	−7·5
Coffee (bean): change in price	+37·4
change in consumption	−18·2
Coffee (instant): change in price	+49·4
change in consumption	+50·0
Cocoa: change in price	+12·1
change in consumption	+5·3

The fact that the consumption of tea has fallen whilst the price of tea has fallen relative to the price of coffee contradicts our first prediction. We should have expected demand to extend as price fell. So presumably something else has altered. Clearly it is not the case that incomes have fallen; they have in fact risen. We can therefore reject the deduction that a fall in the price of tea was offset by a fall in incomes which reduced the consumption of tea. There remain three other possibilities. First, the price of some commodity complementary to tea such as milk or sugar has risen in price; second, that tastes have changed; thirdly, tea is an inferior good. Of the explanations the latter two seem the more plausible, but it would need to be tested. What still remains unexplained, however, is why the price of tea fell.

Was it due to an independent movement of the supply curve, or to the demand curve sliding down a given supply curve? Both possibilities are shown in Figures 52 and 53. We should note that we

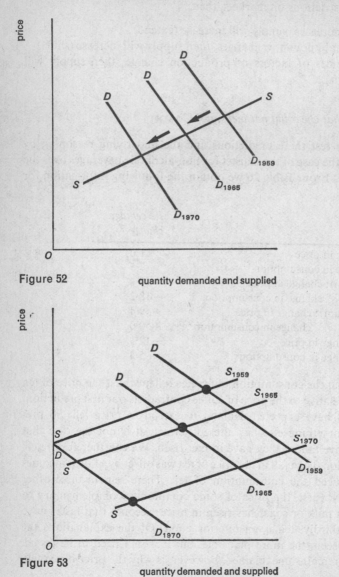

Figure 52   quantity demanded and supplied

Figure 53   quantity demanded and supplied

154 The Market Continued

cannot deduce from the data whether supply changes did take place. The price and consumption data reflect both demand and supply influences: this is the *identification problem* which can only be resolved by obtaining additional information.

So much for tea: what about coffee and cocoa? We leave the reader to puzzle out the behaviour of these two markets. And we also include in the questions at the end of this chapter further comparable problems.

Farmers' incomes

We have already seen that price-elasticity of demand determines consumers' expenditures and thus, producers' incomes. One of the most interesting applications of this linkage is to the case of farmers' incomes, which tend to be low in relation to other sector incomes and which also tend to fluctuate more than incomes in most other productive sectors.

Fluctuating incomes

Farm incomes tend to fluctuate because of variations in crop yields. There are often great differences between what farmers expect to sell and what they actually do sell when their crops have been harvested. Figure 54 demonstrates this point. The prevailing market demand

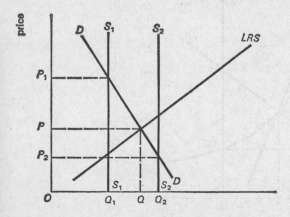

quantity demanded and supplied per unit of time

Figure 54

curve is *DD*. The long-run supply curve, upon which farmers base their output plans, is *LRS*. Farmers, therefore, intend to supply OQ units of produce and expect to sell it at a market price of OP per unit. Because of the perverseness of the weather their expectations are often not realized. For example, the actual short-run supply curve could be $S_1 S_1$ in the case of say, a drought; or $S_2 S_2$ if there is a bumper harvest. In the former case farm incomes are equal to $OP_1 . OQ_1$ and in the latter case they are equal to $OP_2 . OQ_2$.

Policy

Farmers, like other income earners, prefer stable incomes since the more certain income is, the easier it is to plan expenditures. Farmers would, therefore, like to face a demand curve for their product of unit elasticity. Is there any means by which governments can help to provide such stability? Figure 55 shows how it might be done.

Figure 55 depicts the same basic situation as Figure 54 but a demand curve of unit elasticity has been superimposed upon the earlier figure. This curve shows how governments can maintain stability in farm incomes by buying up surplus harvests and selling

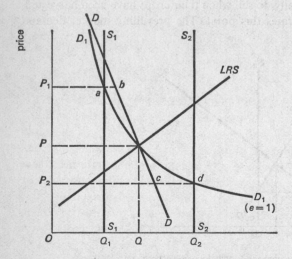

Figure 55

off stocks in times of bad harvests. For example, suppose that $S_2 S_2$ is again the unexpected short-run supply curve. The government maintains a price OP_2 by buying up what the market will not purchase – cd units – and farmers' incomes are equal to $OP_2 . OQ_2$ ($= OP . OQ$). Now suppose the unexpected short-run supply curve is $S_1 S_1$. This time there is a market shortage of ab and government again acts as a buffer against market forces by selling off an amount ab of its agricultural stocks, thus maintaining a price of P_1. In this case farmers' incomes are equal to $OP_1 . OQ_1$ which is again equal to $OP_2 . OQ_2$ and $OP . OQ$ because DD is a rectangular hyperbola. Thus, by making adjustments to the market process government is able to provide stability in farm incomes.

Low incomes

We now turn to the second observation – that farmers' incomes tend to be relatively low, and there are three major reasons for this. First, there is the fact that as real incomes grow, people do not demand proportionately more foodstuffs but spend relatively more on manufactured goods and therefore the income-elasticity of demand for foodstuffs is low. Secondly, the mobility of farmers out of agriculture and into other sectors tends to be low. And thirdly, farming tends to be dogged by low productivity.

Policy

What can the state do to alleviate the situation? Apart from measures to promote productivity the state can try to guarantee farmers a minimum income. (This raises the question of low wages and other problems dealt with in the previous chapter, but we shall now look at other issues.) In providing such a guarantee the state must face the problem of how to cope with any surpluses that might arise since these would threaten to pull down prices and incomes. These surpluses can be stored to cope with any shortages or they can be destroyed. Whatever policy is adopted, there is a cost in terms of the resources that could have been used elsewhere. Different procedures have been adopted in different countries and we shall consider those adopted by the UK (before entry to the EEC); and the EEC.

The UK system (prior to joining EEC). The UK traditionally pursued a cheap food policy by allowing food imports to enter without restrictions. To protect the livelihood of domestic farmers a deficiency payments scheme was employed whereby a guaranteed price was offered to home producers in the face of world competition. If the price received by the farmers in the market was less than the guaranteed price then the government made a cash payment to the farmers equal to the shortfall of price. The scheme is illustrated by Figure 56.

In Figure 56 the UK demand for foodstuffs is represented by the curve D_{UK} and the long run supply curve is S_{UK}. The world supply of foodstuffs is represented by S_W, i.e. the supply curve of the world to the UK is perfectly elastic. Left to itself the market process would establish equilibrium at OQ_3 and price OP_1. At this equilibrium domestic consumers would enjoy a consumers' surplus equal to the area of the triangle $ZP_1 H$. However, at this price UK farmers are only able to supply the amount OQ_1 yielding them an income of $OP_1 . OQ_1$.

Suppose, then, that the government decides to guarantee domestic farmers the income they would enjoy in the absence of a foreign supply. This guarantee could be provided by a price of OP_2 per unit sold, enabling home producers to supply OQ_2 and enjoy an income of

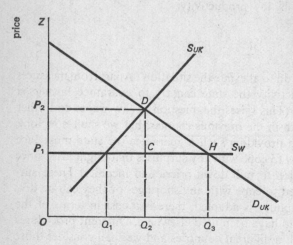

quantity demanded and supplied per unit of time

Figure 56

$OP_2 . OQ_2$. The result of the scheme is that consumers can still buy OQ_3 and enjoy the benefits of the low market price of OP_1. An amount of consumer surplus is, of course, transferred to producers in the form of deficiency payments but domestic consumers are still better off than they would be in the absence of a world supply – by an amount of consumers' surplus equal to area CHD.

The EEC system. Let us now contrast the UK scheme with the EEC method of trying to solve the problem. In essence the EEC policy is to remove foreign competition by imposing tariffs on relatively cheap imported foodstuffs in order to raise the domestic price level and give domestic farmers adequate remuneration. The scheme is illustrated in Figure 57 where S_W again represents world supply and D_{EEC} and S_{EEC} are the domestic demand and supply curves.

Free market forces would again establish equilibrium at price OP_1 and quantity OQ_3 giving rise to a consumers' surplus equal to area $ZP_1 H$. At this price farmers in the EEC are only able to supply OQ_1, giving them incomes of $OP_1 . OQ_1$. Suppose it is again decided to guarantee farmers an income of $OP_2 . OQ_2$. The EEC method of promoting domestic production of OQ_2 is to guarantee domestic producers a market price of OP_2 by the imposition of a tariff (equal to $P_2 - P_1$), and by a readiness to buy any surplus output. This has the

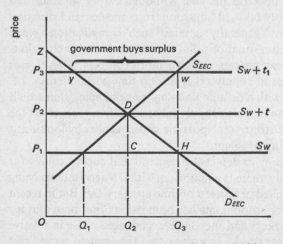

quantity demanded and supplied per unit of time

Figure 57

effect of shifting the world supply curve vertically to the position $S_W + t$. The result of this scheme is that the domestic consumption is reduced to OQ_2 and, while the transfer of $P_1 CDP_2$ is no greater than in the UK example, the EEC method results in an excess loss of consumers' surplus equal to area CHD. Consumers are thus left with a surplus of ZDP_2 (this excess loss is a pictorial representation of the relative misallocation of resources resulting from the EEC scheme). Furthermore, suppose that the EEC farmers demand and succeed in getting a higher income guarantee than UK farmers. Suppose, for example, that they are guaranteed an income of $OP_3 . OQ_3$. Such a guarantee requires the tariff to be raised to t_1 and the world supply curve shifted upwards to $S_W + t_1$. But at this higher price the EEC consumers will not purchase all that their farmers offer – there is an excess supply of yw. The only solution seems to be for the EEC authorities to buy up the surplus. But this raises further problems of how and for how long is the surplus to be stored; and what is the optimum way of financing the purchase and storage of the surplus?

Time

We turn now to some of the problems which result from explicitly incorporating time into the analysis. Although earlier we suggested the path which supply takes in adjusting from one demand situation to another, we have generally ignored such complications when comparing equilibrium situations. But there are some other situations where the adjustment process is much more complex. These cases arise when a change in supply takes a long time to take effect, i.e. when supply reacts with a definite time-lag. For example, what would happen in a situation in which supply takes some five years to hit the market? We can illustrate some possible consequences by looking at a manpower planning problem.

Figure 58a is meant to depict the demand and supply curves for accountants. Initially, there is equilibrium with ON accountants being demanded and supplied per period of time at salary OP. But in recent years the demand for accountants has been rising faster than that for other groups of workers and they have experienced a rise in relative pay. We can illustrate this by supposing that the demand curve shifts to the right, $D_1 D_1$, and pay rises to OP_1. Now let us look at the supply implications. Accountants cannot be produced overnight. There is a

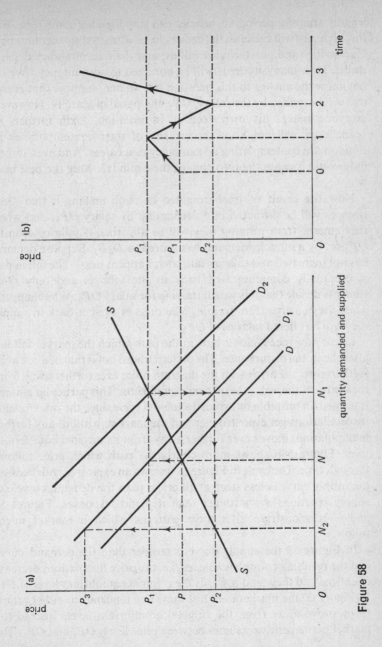

Figure 58

lengthy training period so salaries can stay high for some time. But this high pay will cause sixth formers to be attracted to accountancy. Universities and polytechnics will expand their accountancy departments. How many students will be attracted to accountancy? We do not know the answer to this question but we may suppose that everyone will be guided by the salary, OP_1, the signal of scarcity. However, everyone makes his own decision in isolation. Sixth formers in Manchester will not know how many of their contemporaries in London are contemplating accountancy as a career. And even if they did, would it cause them to change their minds? 'May the best man win.'

Now the result of uncoordinated decision making is that ON_1 trainees will be attracted into accounting by salary OP_1, and when they emerge from training they will be absorbed if salaries drop to OP_2 or, by a miracle, demand has shifted to D_2D_2. Suppose demand has not increased and salaries fall, what happens next? The fall in pay is eventually communicated back to the schools and only ON_2 students decide that it is worth training for salary OP_2. What happens when they emerge from training? Because of the cut-back in supply they will be offered salaries of OP_3.

Let us now take a closer look at the path which the market follows after the initial disturbance. The pattern traced out is that of a cobweb; furthermore, the arrows on the diagram point ever further away from the centre of the web – the original equilibrium. This particular pattern is termed an unstable or explosive *cobweb cycle* since the price/quantity oscillations get ever stronger and the market, without any further manipulation, moves ever further away from its original equilibrium level. Figure 58b shows more clearly the path which price follows through time. The cycle in Figure 58 follows an explosive path because the supply curve is less steep at all prices than the demand curve, i.e. supply reactions are stronger than demand responses. Figures 59 and 60 demonstrate alternative patterns which a market might follow.

In Figure 59 the supply curve is steeper than the demand curve and the resulting cobweb is *damped*, i.e. the price fluctuations decrease over time and they tend towards the original equilibrium level of OP. In Figure 60 the market does not show any tendency to either return to or move away from the original equilibrium level. Instead the market permanently oscillates between price levels OP_1 and OP_2. The

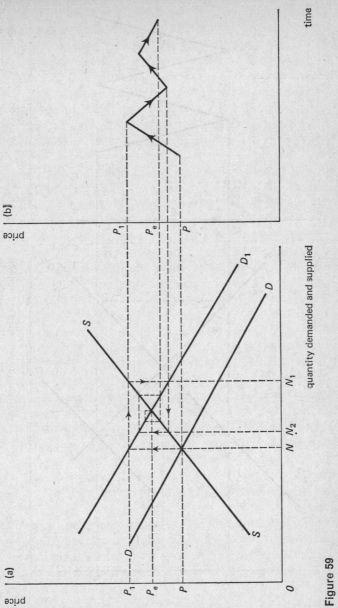

Figure 59

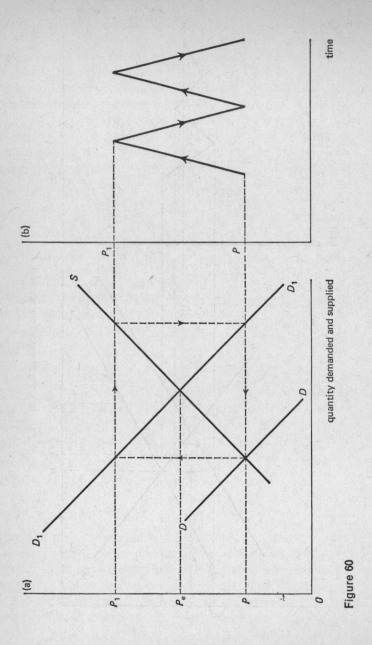

Figure 60

reason for this pattern is that the demand and supply curves have the same slopes at all prices.

We have considered the cobweb theorem in terms of manpower, but oscillations of price and quantity are typical also of many agricultural products. Thus a cycle in pig production (the hog cycle) can be traced through time series data for the UK back into the nineteenth century. A cycle can also be found in natural rubber production.

In a wider context we can observe that most economies exhibit fluctuations in all prices and quantities and this broad fluctuation has been given the name *trade cycle*. Economists have long been interested in the trade cycle and though trade-cycle analysis lies outside the scope of this volume we shall in Part Eight look at some of the possible contributory factors. In the meantime our discussion of damped, regular and explosive cycles can provide some insights. Throughout the nineteenth century fairly regular oscillations in economic activity occurred. Their existence suggests that the demand and supply curves had the same slope at all prices. That would, however, be difficult to imagine; could we really expect such a state of affairs to last for 150 years? If we reject the miracle, however, we are left with either damped or explosive cycles. Damped cycles would require for their continual occurrence a series of outside shocks to occur at regular intervals. Harvest conditions, the opening up of the New World and sudden bursts of inventions might be the sources of such shocks. Explosive cycles seem out of the question: the evidence seems to be against booms getting 'boomier' and slumps getting 'slumpier'. Yet it might be possible to envisage explosive cycles constrained by a ceiling (created by full employment of all resources) and a floor (caused by some outside factor).

Policy

We cannot forecast the future and so it would seem that the only way of coping with fluctuations of the cobweb variety is to reduce the delay in the response of supply. This is difficult in agriculture, though stockpiling might help, but in manpower planning the lag can be reduced by altering the nature of the education system from one which emphasizes early specialization to one which insists upon giving people a broad education.

Summary

In this chapter we have looked at market situations where demand and supply curves shift. This leads to a problem when examining data as to whether price and quantity changes have been due to demand or supply changes, or both. Shifting demand and supply curves also lead to problems when the state interferes in markets and add to the complications we noted in the previous chapter.

Questions

1 In 1973 the school-leaving age was raised from fifteen to sixteen years. What does economic theory predict would be the effects of such a change on the labour market? Do the following statistics refute the predictions of the theory? What additional information do you think is needed to produce a more satisfactory analysis of the raising of the school leaving age (ROSLA)?

Basic Statistics for Great Britain

Year	Number of school-leavers entering employment		Unemployment percentage (all workers)
	Youths (under 18)	Girls (under 18)	
1970	248 177	223 813	2·5
1971	242 122	220 409	3·4
1972	258 532	228 047	3·8
1973	140 532	107 047	2·6
1974	274 801	237 847	2·6
1975	not available		4·3

Average Weekly Earnings

Year	Boys (under 21)	Girls (under 18)	Men (over 21)	Women (over 18)
1970	13·60	9·46	28·91	13·98
1971	15·17	10·33	31·37	15·80
1972	17·73	11·83	36·20	18·34
1973	21·60	15·21	41·52	21·15
1974	26·13	19·31	49·12	27·05
1975	32·87	23·15	59·74	34·22

Source: Department of Employment *Gazette*.
Note: Employment figures are calculated on the basis of a count of National Insurance cards. This count was discontinued in 1974 and meant that low-wage earners such as boys and girls have become excluded from the survey.

2 What does the theory of supply imply about the response of supply of a commodity to:

(a) a change in the price of the commodity;
(b) a change in the technique of producing the commodity;
(c) a change in the price of resources used in producing the commodity?

Does the data below on milk refute the predictions formulated above?

3 What does the theory of demand predict will be the response in demand for a commodity of:

(a) a change in the price of the good;
(b) a change in incomes;
(c) a change in the price of substitutes;
(d) a change in tastes?

Does the following data relating to milk consumption refute the predictions established above?

Data for use in question 2

Year	Total sales from farms (million litres)	Number of dairy cows (thousands)	Yield per dairy cow (litres)	Price to farmer Pence per litre	Index 1955 = 100	Agricultural minimum wage index 1955 = 100	Price of feedstuffs index 1955 = 100	Retail price index (farmers' cost of living) 1955 = 100
1955	7515	2531	3069	3·14	100	100	100	100
1956	7592	2415	2991	3·52	102	105	105	105
1957	8242	2451	3273	3·30	98	113	107	110
1958	8528	2503	3387	3·19	95	118	100	114
1959	8024	2524	3273	3·30	97	125	94	117
1960	8174	2493	3341	3·30	97	129	98	117
1961	8869	2595	3478	3·08	92	133	98	118
1962	9328	2674	3546	3·08	91	138	96	123
1963	9419	2728	3569	3·08	90	146	100	128
1964	9092	2697	3500	3·19	95	152	103	130
1965	9047	2605	3546	3·52	102	159	104	135
1966	9401	2650	3637	3·52	103	166	106	142
1967	9274	2631	3614	3·52	106	186	106	147
1968	9733	2686	3705	3·63	107	192	109	151
1969	9833	2695	3705	3·63	108	206	113	159
1970	10 024	2742	3750	3·63	107	221	114	167
1971	10 260	2714	3864	3·85	115	246	128	179

Source: Milk Marketing Board, *Annual Reports and Accounts*

Milk consumption 1955–71

| Year | Retail price (pence per litre) | Index of price 1955 = 100 | Sales of full-price milk | | Index of retail prices 1955 = 100 |
			(million litres)	(litres per head)	
1955	4·93	100	5241	124·1	100
1956	5·17	105	5255	123·7	100
1957	5·50	112	5210	122·3	105
1958	5·72	116	5187	120·9	110
1959	5·72	116	5214	120·9	114
1960	5·72	116	5301	122·3	117
1961	5·72	116	5337	121·8	117
1962	5·83	118	5437	123·2	118
1963	6·05	123	5501	123·2	123
1964	6·16	125	5546	122·7	130
1965	6·60	134	5564	122·7	135
1966	6·82	138	5560	121·4	142
1967	6·97	142	5587	121·4	147
1968	7·33	149	5642	121·8	151
1969	7·61	154	5587	120·0	159
1970	7·88	160	5628	n.a.	167
1971	8·49	172	5596	n.a.	179

Source: Milk Marketing Board, *Annual Reports and Accounts*

4 Using the data given, attempt the following questions:

(a) What is the relationship between productivity and employment in coal mining?

(b) What is the connection between the degree of mechanization and labour productivity (output per manshift)? If you do not know go back and read the chapter on production.

(c) What would you predict the relationship between productivity, costs, prices and consumption of coal should be from the theory of demand and supply? What seems to be the observed relationship?

5 Suppose that in the initial market situation we have,

$q_d = 20 - 2p,$
$q_s = -4 + 3p.$

Calculate the equilibrium price and quantity demanded. Suppose that a tax of £2 per unit is placed upon the commodity, shifting the supply curve upwards,

Data for use in question 4: UK coal industry, 1963–70

Year	Number of coal mines	Saleable mined coal (million tonnes)	Undistributed stocks (million tonnes)	Wage-earners on colliery books (thousands)	Output per manshift (tonnes)	Degree of mechanization (per cent)	Total coal	(kilojoules)
1963–4	580	190·6	18·7	517·0	33·9	68·4	77·0	53·4
1964–5	545	187·0	20·0	491·0	35·4	75·0	77·5	51·5
1965–6	504	177·2	18·8	455·7	36·7	80·7	80·4	50·6
1966–7	442	167·4	20·6	419·4	37·2	85·7	80·7	48·2
1967–8	406	165·3	27·0	391·9	39·6	89·1	80·5	45·3
1968–9	359	155·5	25·3	336·3	43·2	91·8	82·5	45·0
1969–70	299	149·8	14·6	305·1	44·1	92·3	—	—

Source: *Digest of Energy Statistics*, National Coal Board, Reports and Accounts

$$q_s = -4+3(p-2) = -10+3p.$$

Calculate the equilibrium price and quantity after the imposition of the tax.

6 In the previous question we simplified the problem by expressing the tax rate numerically. In the following equation,

$$D = a-bp,$$
$$S = c+d(p-t),$$

the tax rate t can assume any value and therefore the supply equation is the general expression. Calculate the equilibrium price and quantity in terms of a, b, c, d and t.

7 Agricultural production is subject to climatic factors (r) and the supply and demand equations are

$$D = a+bp,$$
$$S = c+dp-r.$$

Calculate the equilibrium price and quantity in terms of a, b, c, d and r.

8 The market demand for a commodity increases over time as a result of increasing familiarity with the product. The market demand equation is

$$D = a-bp+t,$$

where t is a time variable which takes the values 0, 5, 8, 10 for the years 1, 2, 3, 4 respectively.

The supply of the commodity also increases overtime as a result of minor improvements in technology on the shop floor. The market supply equation is

$$S = c+dp+x,$$

where x is the time variable which takes the values 0, 3, 4, 5 for the years 1, 2, 3, 4 respectively.

Derive the equilibrium price and quantity for year 4.

9 What contribution can the economist make to the framing of education policy?

10 What is a tariff? What is a subsidy? Can tariffs and subsidies produce the same effects?

11 Suppose that the price of a good falls (due to a shift of the supply curve) but consumers are slow to react. Trace the resulting path to the new equilibrium.

12 Farmers' income can be maintained at a desired level either by tariffs on food imports or by direct subsidy. Compare the effects of these two policies on:
(a) the level of food imports;
(b) the level of food consumption;
(c) the price to the consumer.

13 A marketing consultant says to you: 'Economic theory ignores the fact that the market price has an information content. Rightly or wrongly people tend to judge a product's value by its price. Cheap cameras are not expected to be as good as expensive cameras. Prices in Woolworths are expected to be lower than in Harrods. If there are variations from the pattern of beliefs then people will refuse to buy. A consumer with little knowledge of the intrinsic value of a good expects the price to tell him something about its quality.' How would you reply?

14 How would you attempt to explain the variations in consumption given in the table below? Would you expect the concept of price-elasticity of demand to be of any assistance? What pieces of economic analysis would you use and why?

Changes in consumption and price and expenditure of canned fruit and chocolate biscuits.

		1959	1969	Percentage change
price per kilogram (pence)	canned peaches, pears and pineapples	18·48	18·28	−1
	chocolate biscuits	37·33	52·28	+40
consumption (grams per head per week)	canned peaches, etc.	74·84	69·74	−7
	chocolate biscuits	24·38	29·48	+21
expenditure (pence per head per week)	canned peaches, etc.	1·38	1·28	−7
	chocolate biscuits	0·91	1·54	+69

Source: *National Food Survey*

15 In a given year the price of wheat rose sharply because a drought reduced the wheat yield per acre and because millers increased their wheat stocks to protect themselves against expected future price increases. According to this statement the price of wheat rose because of:

(a) a shift in the supply curve and a movement along the demand curve,

(b) a shift in the demand curve and a movement along the supply curve,

(c) shifts in both the demand and supply curves,

(d) movements along both the demand and supply curves.

Which of these statements is true?

16 The statistics below continue the information on prices and consumption of beverages beyond that given in Table 26 of the text. Do the figures support the argument in the text?

	Tea		Coffee (bean)		Coffee (instant)		Cocoa	
	Price	Con- sumption	Price	Con- sumption	Price	Con- sumption	Price	Con- sumption
	(pence)	(grams)	(pence)	(grams)	(pence)	(grams)	(pence)	(grams)
1970	32·41	73·44	48·78	2·55	94·41	11·90	23·21	5·67
1971	34·37	67·70	52·01	2·83	109·99	12·46	24·47	4·53
1972	34·48	63·17	52·23	3·40	100·91	13·03	23·42	4·53
1973	35·53	61·19	59·92	2·55	111·33	13·31	23·26	4·25
1974	38·97	63·46	67·61	2·83	121·20	14·45	28·27	4·82

17 What do the following statistics reveal about the behaviour of buyers and sellers during the 1974 sugar shortage?

Sugar prices, purchases and consumption

	Average quantity purchased per person per week (a)	Percentage of households which bought sugar during their week of participation in the Survey	Average amount purchased at each transaction	Average number of transactions per buying household per week	Average price paid per lb
	oz	%	oz	no.	p
1973					
January–March	14·23	72	45·1	1·30	4·51
April–June	12·50	68	43·0	1·31	4·74
July–September	13·98	71	45·7	1·34	5·10
October–December	14·03	71	45·8	1·32	5·20
1974					
January–March	14·06	70	45·4	1·32	5·24
April–June	13·80	69	45·2	1·34	5·27
July	15·84	71	46·2	1·45	5·83
August	12·19	66	34·8	1·54	6·72
September	11·53	68	33·7	1·43	6·92
July–September	13·21	69	37·7	1·49	6·49
October	10·90	71	35·1	1·28	7·60
November	9·88	67	33·8	1·34	9·71
December	13·04	69	39·4	1·44	11·08
October–December	11·04	68	36·0	1·34	9·30

(a) Averaged over all households in the sample, including those which did not buy any sugar during their week of participation in the Survey.
Source: *Household Food Consumption*, 1974

Part Three
Utility and Cost

This is the high ground of economic analysis. This is where many of the great economists have established their reputations. In this century Nobel Prize winners, Samuelson, Hicks and Arrow, and the distinguished economist, Georgescu-Roegen, have fashioned and re-fashioned a beautiful, crystalline structure of logic. Before them, in the nineteenth century, the Englishmen, Jevons and Marshall, the Austrian, Menger, the Italian, Pareto, and the Swiss economist, Walras, hammered out a foundation from the rudiments created by Smith, Ricardo, Mill and Gossen. And before them, reaching out over the centuries, come the ideas of the great philosopher, Aristotle. Therein lies the attraction, for utility theory is about choice and choice lies at the centre of the human drama. It is that area of economic knowledge which reaches back into that core of human enquiry we call philosophy.

The starting point of theorizing was the attempt to transfer the ideas of the natural sciences to the social sciences. By analogy with 'attraction' and 'repulsion' it was assumed that satisfaction and dissatisfaction, utility and disutility as they came to be known, were capable of measurement. Unfortunately, the philosophical problems of measurement tended to be overlooked. There are, in fact, two methods of measurement. One method assumes that objects can be ordered according to some principle of 'greater or lesser' and this method is known as *ordinal measurement*. The second method assumes that we can say by how much one object is greater than another and this method is known as *cardinal measurement*. Now in order to proceed from ordinal to cardinal measurement the objects being compared must be capable of subsumption; that is, we must be able to consider them as qualitatively identical or homogeneous. For example, two pints of water are greater than one pint of water because we can pour them both into a pan, which will indicate that the addition of the second pint will cause the depth of water to be twice what it was previously. And we can have no doubts about our result because it is impossible to distinguish the two pints within the pan – they have merged.

Now it seemed obvious that the things measured by physicists – heat, light and sound – were homogeneous, for theorems based upon cardinal measurement seemed to provide both understanding and prediction. Could, therefore, satisfaction and dissatisfaction be regarded as qualitatively homogeneous with dissatisfaction being merely negative satisfaction?

At first sight the answer seemed to be in the affirmative. Man makes choices and he must, therefore, possess within himself the common denominator which renders all things comparable. But a moment's thought suggests that this observation is too simple. The satisfaction derived from a cigarette at work may be different from the satisfaction derived from smoking a cigarette at home. Furthermore, people make choices for reasons other than the satisfaction they might derive. They choose to do things out of a sense of duty, altruism or because they have been taught to do a job in a particular way.

What this suggests is that there may be severe limits to the role of measurement in economics. For what economists had hoped to do was to obtain homogeneous units of utility which could be measured by means of a measuring rod of money. But if utility is not homogeneous then measurement is not possible. Yet we need not despair. After all, there are limits to measurement in the natural sciences. What has to be discovered is the area of choice which is amenable to measurement. It may turn out to be quite small. The hopes of conducting cost benefit analyses of Channel Tunnels may be illusory, but attempts must be made.

Utility is obviously a subjective concept, but it is not so obvious that cost is a subjective concept. We are used to thinking of costs in an objective sense – units of money, tons of steel and so on – yet costs, at the moment a choice is made, represent the lost benefits that might have been obtained from the rejected courses of action. These costs are subjective – they are based upon guesses as to the possible benefits from different courses of action. The costs which are objective are the consequences of the decision, the aftermath which may bear no relationship to those costs which were expected. And because costs are subjective the problems of comparing benefits (are they qualitatively identical?) bedevils analysis.

Production involves the creation of benefits, so benefits and costs are linked to productive processes. In the theory of production we found a curve of diminishing marginal product which, though couched in objective terms, could also be thought of in decision-making situations as expected marginal products giving rise to expected benefits.

We conclude this brief survey of the foundations of the theory of value with a short reference to money and collective goods. The value of a quantity of money is what it can purchase and for the purposes of Parts One to Seven, it is assumed that the quantity of money is constant. In Part Eight we shall examine some of the problems that arise when the quantity of money is varied and its implications for value theory. We shall also, for the time being, ignore the problems of collective goods. In the case of collective goods an individual's willingness to pay for the goods may depend upon the willingness or unwillingness of others to also pay. Both money and collective goods involve a more fundamental problem – uncertainty. In many situations uncertainty is not a problem. Nobody goes into a bookshop and comes out with a sack of potatoes. Uncertainty can be ignored or its effects calculated and the measuring rod of money applied. Thus, workers in dangerous trades may command high wages. But there may be situations where measurement may not be possible because uncertainty is not homogeneous. The foundation stone of value theory has been utility, but once we grasp that the utilities derived from goods may not be homogeneous then we perceive that the true foundation stone of value theory is the structure of wants upon which a superstructure of utilities may be erected. If the superstructure can be erected then it may be possible to measure utilities with a measuring rod of money and then make inferences about the satisfaction of wants, but it is important to examine the nature of the foundation stone.

Chapter 11
Consumer Behaviour

Economic analysis would be simpler if we could take the nature of the demand curve with its prediction about the relationship between price and consumption as something given, as an observable fact. Unfortunately we cannot, for there are odd occasions when the normal relationship breaks down. For this reason another problem for the economist has been to derive the conditions under which the statement 'as price falls demand will rise' holds true. In the core of this chapter we shall adopt the approach known as the marginal utility theory. Some economists, however, prefer alternative theories and in the appendix we have outlined the alternatives. We have examined the relationship between the differing viewpoints but have adopted a narrative approach, in order to show how economists have refined an original theory by reducing the number of restrictive assumptions. This should prove worthwhile, since the evolution of any theory is a fascinating subject. However, for those who prefer one theory or the other, we have endeavoured to keep the continuity links separate.

Clearing the undergrowth

The simplest way of understanding the theory of choice is to observe its historical development. Economists noticed that as the prices of most goods fell people tended to buy more of these commodities, and when prices rose they bought less. The exceptions to this general tendency were twofold:

1 People sometimes bought more or less despite the absence of price changes.

2 People sometimes bought more as price rose.

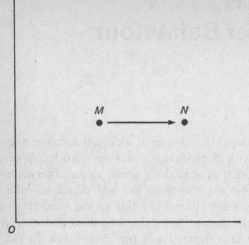

Figure 61   quantity demanded per unit of time

It was suggested that the causes of the observation 1 could be put down to:

Changes in tastes;
Changes in income;
Changes in wealth;
Changes in the prices of other goods.

In these circumstances, shifts in demand may occur even though price remains constant. This case is illustrated by Figure 61. Once the changes in 1 were eliminated, economists were left with a functional relationship between prices and quantities of a good. Causes of the behaviour described in 2 constitute a mixed bag:

Speculative purchases;
Snob purchases;
Other possible causes.

Speculative purchases did not create analytical difficulties for economists since they could be explained in terms of the general observation about price–demand relationships: if consumers expected a price rise then immediate purchases represented a kind of purchase at a lower price. Snob purchases were deemed possible as when, for example, diamonds are bought as their price rises but such demand reactions were considered to be rare and insignificant. There remained the final category of 'other possible causes' to be dealt with. One relationship which seemed to require explanation was the observation by the noted statistician, Sir Robert Giffen, that in the nineteenth century very poor families would buy more potatoes in response to a rise in their price. Further investigations failed to produce any more cases of so-called 'Giffen goods' but it is possible for such instances to occur and economists needed to provide an explanation for their occurrence. (Later in this chapter an explanation will be provided but in the meantime we shall continue the development of marginal-utility analysis.)

In the meantime, having clarified the causes of *shifts* in demand curves there remained the relationship between price and demand. This relationship could be either that of Figure 62 or Figure 63. The next step involved an *abstraction*. Instead of dealing with the discrete price and quantity changes that are the real-life observations and are shown in Figures 62 and 63, economists chose, for convenience, to assume perfect divisibility of prices and quantities in order to obtain smooth curves.

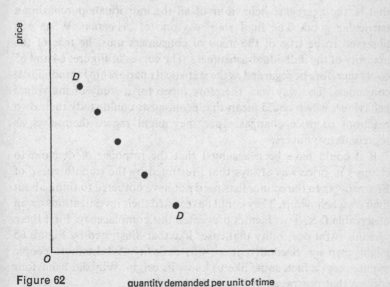

Figure 62   quantity demanded per unit of time

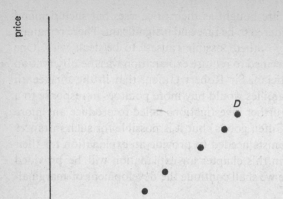

Figure 63   quantity demanded per unit of time

There was a further step. The statistical relationship revealed in Figures 64 and 65 was a relationship concerning *market behaviour*; that is, the aggregate behaviour of all the individuals purchasing a particular good. The final step was one of *deduction*. What was observed to be true of the mass of consumers must be true of the majority of the individual consumers. The curves of Figures 64 and 65 could therefore be regarded as the statistical relationship for individual consumers. The way was, therefore, open for a study of individual behaviour, which could mean that economists could study their own reactions to price changes, since they might regard themselves as representative buyers.

If it could have been assumed that the response of demand to changes in price was always that illustrated by the smooth curve of Figure 64, then the economists need not have bothered to think about their own behaviour. They could have rested their investigations on an observable fact. Two factors prevented this complacency. First there was the awful possibility that cases like that illustrated by Figure 65 might crop up. Secondly, there was curiosity. Whilst most people might accept a fact, some like to know its origin. Why did behaviour such as that portrayed in Figure 64 occur?

182 Consumer Behaviour

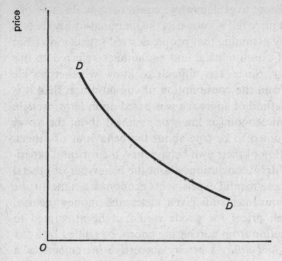

Figure 64   quantity demanded per unit of time

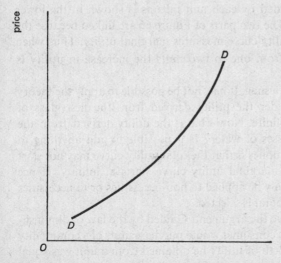

Figure 65   quantity demanded per unit of time

Marginal-utility theory

The first theory produced to explain why a consumer bought more of a commodity when its price fell is known as the marginal-utility theory. This theory began by assuming that people derived satisfaction from the consumption of commodities, and economists referred to this satisfaction as *utility*. Since it is difficult to know whether people derive satisfaction from the consumption of commodities, then it is apparent that the method of approach was based upon *introspection*. In other words, what economists knew or assumed about their own behaviour, they assumed to be true about the behaviour of others. From their observation of their own behaviour – their mental experiments – economists drew conclusions about the behaviour of others.

On the basis of these mental experiments economists came to the conclusion that a consumer with given tastes and money income, when faced by given prices for goods would, if he attempted to maximize his satisfaction from purchasing goods, be guided by a *law of diminishing marginal utility* whereby successive increments of a good would yield successively diminishing units of satisfaction.

What is important to note at this stage is that diminishing marginal utility is compatible with increasing total utility. As Figure 66 shows, total utility increases but at a diminishing rate. This implies that the additional utility added by each unit falls as is shown in the lower panel of Figure 66. The two parts of Figure 66 are linked because the slope of the total utility curve measures marginal utility. Thus when consumption rises from one to two units the increase in utility is AB.

There is, however, a snag. It may not be possible to apply the theory to necessities. Consider the utility derived from the first glass of water: it could be infinite. Now what is the utility derived from the first and second glasses of water? Is it possible to add anything to infinity? What this implies is that the total utility curve may not start at zero because the marginal utility curve starts at infinity. Hence utility analysis can only be applied to non-necessities or to necessities if a suitable starting point is selected.

We can now resume the argument. Guided by the law of diminishing marginal utility, a consumer would purchase units of a commodity until the money's worth of utility he obtained from a unit was equal to the price he paid for that good. That is, the price paid measured the

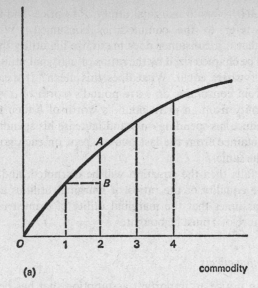

(a)   commodity

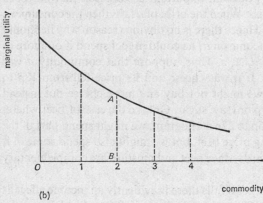

(b)   commodity

Figure 66

utility derived from the last unit. Price was conceived as a guide for
the consumer in allocating expenditure:

$$\frac{MU_a}{P_a} = \frac{MU_b}{P_b} = \ldots = \frac{MU_z}{P_z}. \qquad\qquad 1$$

Choice however involves the presence of at least two goods and the
more general expression for consumer behaviour is contained in

Marginal Utility Theory 185

equation **1** (where MU refers to marginal utility, P to price, and the subscripts $a, ..., z$ refer to the commodities consumed). What equation **1** says is that if a consumer does maximize his utility then his equilibrium will be characterized by the ratios of marginal utilities to prices being everywhere equal. What does this mean? It means that if the utility from consuming an extra pound's worth of a was greater than the utility from an extra pound's worth of b then the consumer would reduce his spending on b and increase his spending on a. The utility obtained from the last pound spent on each good must therefore be the same.

If the price of a falls then the equation will be disrupted, and in order to restore the equality of the ratios of marginal utilities and prices, the theory assumes that the marginal utility of a must fall, which means that more of a must be bought.

Income and substitution effects

At this stage we can notice an important assumption that has been slipped into the analysis. When the price of a falls then the consumer's *real* income has risen. Hence there is no obvious reason why he should spend his increased income on a; he could in fact spend it on more of the other goods $b, c, d, ..., z$. Thus, suppose that commodity a was either cheese or beef. If it was cheese and its price fell from 18p to 9p a kilogram, then we might not buy any more cheese but instead spend the saving of 9p on, say, sugar. Or take the case of beef where, if its price fell from 36p to 27p a kilogram, we might spend part of the saving of 9p on buying more beef, but we might also spend some of it on buying more mustard – since beef and mustard are complementary goods.

When the price of a good falls there is evidently an income effect as well as a substitution effect. The substitution effect arises because the money's worth of utility from purchasing extra units of the good whose price has fallen is greater than the money's worth of utility that could be got from spending on any other good. The income effect looks odd because it suggests that more utility may be obtained from spending on the goods whose prices have not fallen. Indeed the income effect goes further, for we saw in Chapter 7 that with a rise in income he might buy less of a good, so the income effect could work in the direction of persuading the consumer to buy more of the good (whose price has fallen), or less of the good and more of other goods.

In order to arrive at its prediction that as the price of a good falls more will be bought, the marginal-utility theory had to rule out cases where demand might fall as the price fell and where the consumption of other goods might rise. The method by which this was done was to assume that only a small part of total expenditure was spent on the good. This meant that the income effect of a price change would be small and would be weaker than the substitution effect. What this might be taken to mean is that in terms of the hierarchy of wants, discussed in Chapter 2, the marginal-utility theorists looked at the wants which were just being satisfied and at essential wants that required very little to satisfy them, e.g. salt. When, however, the amount spent on the good was a large fraction of income then the 'Giffen good' case might occur; i.e. demand falls as price falls.

Derivation of the demand curve

From equation **1** we can, by manipulation, obtain the following equation which holds for all pairs of goods:

$$\frac{MU_a}{MU_b} = \frac{P_a}{P_b}. \qquad\qquad 2$$

In effect this equation gives us a demand curve for it tells us that underlying a demand curve there is a marginal-utility curve with the prices and amounts of other goods being held constant. If the price of a falls then the marginal utility of a must fall if the denominators of both sides of the equation are to remain constant, and all income is to be spent both before and after the price change.

The paradox of value

The marginal-utility theory enables us to resolve the paradox of value. A problem that perplexed early economists was why water, which obviously is essential to maintain life, commanded a lower price than diamonds. The answer is seen to lie in the distinction between total and marginal utility. Although the total utility of water is considerably higher than that of diamonds, its marginal utility is much lower because it is more plentiful.

Sometimes the paradox of value is explained in that as we have more and more water we put it to less essential uses and thus we obtain a curve of diminishing marginal utility of water. We may use our first litre of water to slake our thirst, our second litre for washing and our fiftieth litre to wash down the car. But this approach may be misleading, for the different litres of water constitute different goods which satisfy different wants. The first litre of water possesses the technical properties of being able to sustain life, whilst the second possesses the characteristics of being a washing liquid. These characteristics serve to give rise to different goods which satisfy different wants; the fact that they are all characteristics possessed by water is irrelevant.

What we can think of is a curve of diminishing marginal utility for drinking water and a curve of diminishing marginal utility for washing water and so on. At some point the utility derived from an extra litre of drinking water will be lower than that derived from using water for washing and so an individual will reject any further drinking water. This suggests that *some* litres of washing water can be substituted for *some* litres of drinking water, but it is only some, for a person would not give up his first litre of drinking water for some more washing water. This is perhaps a fine point, for we usually envisage individuals operating in zones away from the boundaries of the hierarchy of wants. Yet there could be situations where people were moved from slums to a housing estate out of town and felt worse off because they ranked the delights of the countryside lower than the amenities of town centres. We should therefore guard against assuming that utilities are homogeneous.

In the indifference-curve approach (see appendix) the fundamental hierarchy of wants is concealed by the assumption that there can be indefinite substitution of one good for another, but it is difficult to see how anyone would be willing to give up their last drop of water for any extra amount of bread or a number of Rolls Royces.[1]

The labour theory of value

The third subject upon which marginal utility threw light was the labour theory of value. According to this latter theory commodities exchanged according to the amount of labour embodied in them so that if the price of a good fell, it could be presumed that either the

1. An alternative approach emphasizes that different goods possess different characteristics in different proportions.

amount of embodied labour in other goods had risen or the amount embodied in the good had fallen. The trouble was that this theory could not explain such goods as Old Masters whose price rose even though there was no change in labour embodiment. Moreover, as soon as other resources, land and capital, are introduced into the discussion, then the simple labour embodiment thesis suffers further complications, since it is possible to have goods with the same labour embodiment but different capital endowments selling at different prices.

Consumer surplus again

In Chapter 10 we drew attention to the fact that consumers frequently pay a price for goods which is less than that which they might be prepared to pay if they were subjected to an all-or-nothing offer. This gain we termed consumers' surplus and we illustrate it in Figure 67. Now it is evident that this gain is related to total utility and marginal utility. If each of the units of a commodity are homogeneous then a consumer will be prepared to pay a price for each unit which measures the utility derived from that unit. This is because all units are substitutable. Thus his total utility will be measured by the area *OPAB* although his expenditure is only *OFAB*.

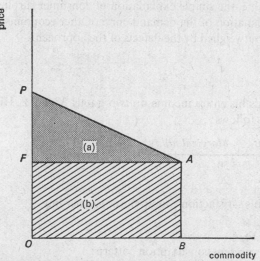

Figure 67 (a) Consumer surplus. (b) Total revenue

But note the difficulties.

1 It may not be possible to measure total utility if the utility derived from the first unit is infinite. This applies to necessities.

2 It may not be possible to measure total utility if the amount spent on the good is large because the income effect will cause the demand curve to shift. However, the next section will show one method of overcoming this problem (see points P, Q, S on Figure 72).

3 It may not be possible to add the utilities from different goods together.

4 It may not be possible to add the utilities derived by different people together unless they possess similar tastes. This means national income statistics may be misleading.

Conclusions

What has been said so far is a simple explanation of why demand tends to rise when price falls. In the subsequent sections alternative explanations are put forward which tend to be favoured by teachers. Any of the three methods can be employed, and preferences are largely dictated by one's system of philosophy. The advantages we see for a beginner in the marginal utility approach lie in the resolution of the paradox of value, the simple explanation of consumer surplus as well as in the explanation of the demand curve. Other economists see these benefits as outweighed by the defects of the approach.

Questions

1 A consumer spends his entire income on two goods X and Y. His present position is as follows:

	Price per unit	Marginal utility
X	10p	50
Y	6p	20

In order to increase his satisfaction should the consumer buy
(a) less X and more Y;
(b) more X and less Y;
(c) continue with his present consumption pattern;
(d) more X and the same amount of Y?

2 What is the paradox of value?

3 What is an inferior good? What is a Giffen good?

4 For a commodity like heroin, or even wine, the curve of marginal utility does not fall. Should we therefore abandon the theory or treat such goods as exceptional cases?

5 Comment on the following propositions:
(a) the theory of consumer behaviour assumes choice and ignores habit;
(b) the theory ignores uncertainty;
(c) the theory ignores advertising;
(d) the theory ignores the need to 'keep up with the Jones's'.

6 If the total utility derived from a good is at a maximum then the good is a free good and its marginal utility is zero. Do you agree?

7 A consumer with given tastes and money income confronted by two goods, A and B, whose prices are fixed will maximize his satisfaction when

(a) $\dfrac{MU_a}{MU_b} = \dfrac{P_a}{P_b}$, or (b) $\dfrac{MU_a}{P_a} = \dfrac{MU_b}{P_b}$, or (c) $\dfrac{P_b}{P_a} = \dfrac{MU_a}{MU_b}$.

Give reasons for your answer.

8 Comment on the following propositions:
(a) increments of utility derived from particular goods are both intrinsically measurable and practically measurable with the measuring rod of money;
(b) totals of utility derived from particular goods are intrinsically measurable provided you reckon them from a sensible starting point;
(c) totals of utility derived from particular goods are not practically measurable unless the amount spent on the good is small;
(d) totals of totals, i.e. total utility of income in general is not practically measurable.
(Derived from Robertson, 1952.)

9 If the effect of the fall in the price of a good is not to have repercussions on the purchases of other goods then the elasticity of the good whose price has fallen must be unity. Do you agree with this statement? Does it confine the usefulness of the theory? Could the theory be saved by assuming quasi-constancy of the marginal utility of money?

Appendix:
Other Approaches

In describing the marginal-utility approach to demand theory we drew attention to two important features:

1 *Introspection* – the belief that it was possible to say something about other people's behaviour from an examination of one's own.

2 *Income effect* – the suppression of changes in real income as a result of a price change.

In addition we should underline a third implicit assumption of the analysis:

3 *Cardinal measurement of utility* – the belief that units of utility or satisfaction are qualitatively identical (homogeneous) so that they could be added together.

In subsequent theories some or all of these aspects of marginal utility theory have been abandoned.

Indifference curve analysis

Instead of conducting a mental experiment some economists put forward the view that it was possible to conduct an experiment which could be observed by numerous people and from which it would be possible to infer something about the state of mind of the 'guinea pig'. Supposing, they said, that a person was presented with a basket of goods, say apples and oranges, and he was then asked how many oranges he would need to compensate him for the loss of one apple. It would be found that the number of oranges required varied but did increase as the number of apples diminished.

Table 27 illustrates the general proposition that an increasing number of oranges are needed to compensate a person for the loss of an apple. We now draw certain conclusions from this experiment.

Table 27 Apples and oranges

Apples	Oranges	Marginal rate of substitution of oranges for apples
10	3	—
9	4	1
8	6	2
7	9	3
6	13	4
5	18	5
4	25	7

First, it is possible to keep a person at the same level of satisfaction by varying the combination of goods he possesses. Secondly, it is not necessary to enquire how much utility a person gets from the addition of oranges but only whether he gets more or less satisfaction than previously. In other words, we can dispense with the *cardinal* measurement. We do not need to ask *how much* satisfaction is gained from another orange but whether his satisfaction is greater than, less than, or the same as previously. Thirdly, we vary the initial amounts of apples and oranges and so obtain a complete map of a person's

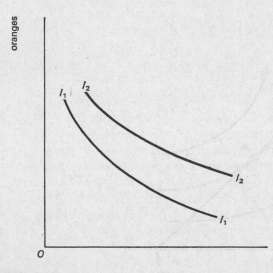

Figure 68

apples

preferences: that is, by experiment we can infer something about a person's mental state.

We can from information such as that presented in Table 27 draw up a map of a person's indifference between different combinations of apples and oranges and this has been done in Figure 68. Each curve represents those combinations which give the consumer the same level of satisfaction or between which he is indifferent: such curves are known as *indifference curves*. Now as between the combinations on curve I_1 and curve I_2 we can only say that those on the latter give more satisfaction than those on the former, but we need not enquire into how much more satisfaction.

The budget constraint

Armed with the consumer's indifference map we can now set out to find what combination of goods will be chosen when his income and the relative prices of the goods are given. Let us assume that in terms of Figure 69 a consumer has an income OB of Y and that he could spend the whole of that income on purchasing OA of X. By joining A and B we can establish the price at which one good will exchange for the other. This price will be given by the slope of the

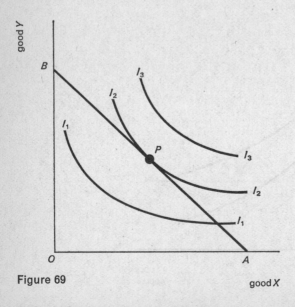

Figure 69

line *AB*. (The price of *B* in terms of *A* is given by the tangent of the angle *BAO* and the price of *A* is given by the tangent of the angle *ABO*.)

In the market, therefore, the consumer is confronted by the price line *AB* and if he is attempting to maximize his utility (satisfaction) he will attempt to locate himself on the line *AB*. He cannot go beyond that line since he is constrained by his income. Nor would he remain inside the triangle *AOB* since that would involve him in some needless loss of utility. But where will he go? The answer is that he will try to locate himself on his highest possible indifference curve, which is curve 2. He would then be at *P*. The slope of the indifference curve expresses, as we have seen, the marginal rate of substitution of one good for the other, and so we can express the consumer's equilibrium condition as:

$$MRS_{XY} = \frac{P_X}{P_Y}, \qquad\qquad 3$$

where *MRS* is the marginal rate of substitution and P_X and P_Y refer to the prices of goods *X* and *Y*.

Suppose the relative prices of the two goods remained constant but the consumer's income increased. Instead of *OA* of *X* or *OB* of *Y*

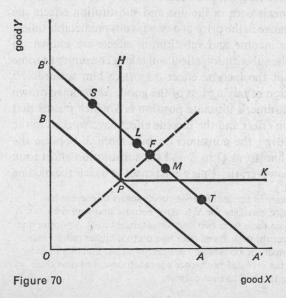

Figure 70   good *X*

(or some combination of X and Y along AB) he can now purchase OA' or OB' (or some combination along $A'B'$). What he will choose will depend upon tastes but we can, in fact, pick out three possible reactions as shown in Figure 70. They are:

1 Absolute increases in the consumption of both goods, e.g. F;

2 Absolute increase in the consumption of one goods but a *relative* decline in the consumption of the other, e.g. L or M;

3 Absolute fall in the consumption of one good, e.g. S or T.

Note that in Figure 70 the price lines AB and $A'B'$ are parallel and that HPK describes a right angle.

Now let us look at the case where the relative prices of X and Y change but the consumer's income remains unchanged. In Figure 71 the price of X has been assumed to fall relative to the price of Y but the consumer's income has been reduced so as to leave him on the same general level of utility or satisfaction as previously. We observe that he buys more of X, the precise amount he buys depending upon the curvature of the indifference curve, i.e. the willingness with which he is prepared to compensate for losses in Y by consuming more X. Originally the consumer was at P on line AB and after the price change he moves to Q on price line $A'B'$.[1]

Because of the coexistence of income and substitution effects the overall effect of a change in the price of a good is not predictable unless the strengths of the income and substitution effects are known. In terms of Figure 72 the substitution effect will take a consumer to some point such as Q but the income effect may take him towards R; that is, in the direction of buying less of the good. As we have drawn the diagram the consumer's ultimate position is S which means that both the substitution effect and the income effect have worked in the direction of persuading the consumer to buy more X because the income effect took him from Q to S and the substitution effect took him from P to Q. However, there may exist cases in which the income

1. Note that the curvature of the indifference curves seems to prevent his staying at P (i.e. the price elasticity for Y is zero) because that would be tantamount to saying that there were two price lines tangent to P. Any price line other than AB would cut through P and take him on to a higher indifference curve. This problem is really one created by geometry and our inability to show very small changes. In the revealed preference approach described next this is avoided by dropping the indifference curve.

effect not only works in the direction of buying less of the good whose price has fallen but is also sufficiently strong to outweigh the substitution effect: this is the phenomenon known as the Giffen good.

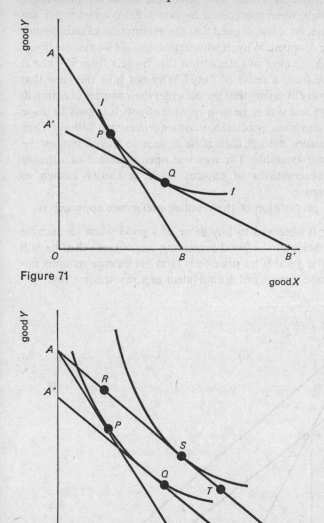

Figure 71

Figure 72

The final stage

The indifference-curve approach still left consumer theory encumbered with introspection, with inferences about an indifference map even though, when confronted by prices, the consumer did not dither but chose. So it was argued that the assumption of indifference states could be dropped. Why, it was argued, should we assume that a man chooses X because of satisfaction that he gets from it when it may be simply from a sense of duty? Why not take the view that utility is just a way of saying that people order their courses of action in particular ways and if they behave consistently with respect to those courses of action then predictable consequences will follow. Thus if a person prefers A to B then if he is seen to buy B it must be because A is not available. The way was open therefore to a theory based upon observations of choices made, a theory known as *revealed preference*.

The central proposition of the revealed-preference approach is:

If a consumer is observed to buy more of a good when his income increases (the price of the good remaining unchanged) then he will buy more of the good if its price falls (and his income remains unchanged) because a price fall is equivalent to a real income rise.

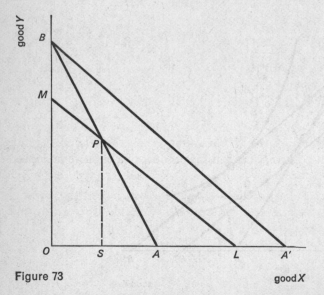

Figure 73

good *X*

This proposition is illustrated in Figure 73. The consumer is revealed to choose the combination of X and Y given by the point P when his income and the relative prices of X and Y are given. He could have, in fact, chosen any combination of X and Y within the triangle OAB but rejected all except that of P.

Suppose that the price of X falls; then he could move to any combination within the larger triangle $OA'B$ but the fact that he had already rejected some combinations suggests that he will in fact be considering only those which lie inside the triangle ABA'.

Before, however, ascertaining which combination he will choose, let us assume that whilst retaining the new relative prices we reduce his income so that he could still just purchase the combination P. In other words, through P we draw a price line LM parallel to BA'. Now which combination would he choose? We know that he would reject those lying along MP since those were previously revealed to have been rejected in favour of P. Hence he will either continue to purchase P or some combination along the line LP which would imply buying more of X. Hence when the substitution effect is examined without the income effect working the consumer will never buy less X. Another way of putting the point is to say that the substitution effect is non-positive.

The term 'non-positive'

We have used the term non-positive to indicate what happens to demand when price alters, because price and quantity move in opposite directions and the quantity change is an effect of the price change. Consider the two cases:

1 When price falls the price change is negative and the quantity change is zero or positive. The substitution effect is therefore negative or zero (non-positive) since it is the product of a negative multiplied by a positive or zero.

2 When price rises the price change is positive and the quantity change is negative or zero. The substitution effect is therefore negative or zero (non-positive).

Final thoughts on utility theory

In our presentation of consumer theory we have emphasized a movement away from introspection. However, this is not the most important feature of the development of the theory. Belief in utility is a matter of personal philosophy. What is important is the attempt to widen the area of measurement. This is most noticeable in the move from marginal utility theory to indifference analysis when the substitution effect was supplemented by the income effect. We could go further and analyse tastes in terms of education, sex and age and try to link these proxy variables to income. For example, men tend to earn more than women. We could also go on to consider whether in the case of goods satisfying more than one want it is possible to dissect those goods into their characteristics and identify those characteristics with different utilities, each of which can be measured. Thus, local rates attempt to identify and measure the various utilities attaching to houses in particular locations. We could consider whether rateable values attaching to different houses are based upon identifiable characteristics.

Questions

1 Will a rise in money income combined with a fall in the price of a commodity always lead to an increase in the demand for the commodity?

2 Does the theory of consumer behaviour predict that a 10 per cent rise in a person's income (all money prices remaining constant) will have the same effect on that person's behaviour as would a 10 per cent fall in all money prices (with money income held constant)?

3 Demonstrate that the substitution effect is non-positive.

4 The State can offer the poor subsidized housing *or* money. Which should the State offer if it wishes to ensure adequate housing of the poor? Which should the poor accept?

5 A rise in the price of milk leads to dairy farmers increasing their own consumption of milk and reducing the supply of milk to the market. Does this mean that milk is an inferior good?

6 Over time real incomes per head have risen but the numbers of domestic servants have fallen. Does this mean that domestic service is an inferior good?

Chapter 12
Costs and Supply: Economic Costs

In the last chapter we looked behind the demand curve to find the reasons for its shape and position and we found a theory of choice which is more widely known as a theory of utility. We now look behind the supply curve to find reasons for its shape and position. We shall find a theory of choice but it is not called utility theory: instead it parades under the title of the theory of costs. There is no reason why it should not be regarded as a part of utility theory except the historical accident which led economists to designate that part of choice theory connected with consumption to be known as utility theory, and that part concerned with production as cost theory. But for a household, decisions to produce and decisions to consume are just decisions based upon choice among alternative courses of action. Let us however begin our analysis with a definition:

Cost in economics means opportunity cost: it is the value placed on resources in their best alternative use.

Costs are benefits: costs are utilities

Definitions can be useful for examinations but their implications need to be fully explored if true understanding is to be achieved.

1 *Costs are rejected benefits.* Suppose that you are faced with the choice of going to a dance or watching television. If you decide to watch television then you must expect the benefits from watching television to outweigh those that might accrue from going to a dance.

2 *Costs involve comparisons of net benefits.* Suppose you have to choose between digging in the garden and going for a run in the car. Digging in the garden brings the benefits of flowers, vegetables, a place of solace and contemplation *and* the possibilities of a slipped disc. Should you then compare the benefits from the garden with the

pain yielded by a slipped disc? The answer is: No. You should look at the net pleasures from the run in the car and compare them with the net benefits from the garden. So your balance sheet might look like this:

	Utils	Disutils
garden	80	20
car run	60	40

Now the net benefits from gardening are not 60, i.e. $80-20$ but 40, i.e. $(80-20) - (60-40)$.

3 *Disutilities may not be negative utilities*. The previous analysis glosses over the point that utilities and disutilities may not be comparable. If it is illegitimate to compare them, what are the alternatives? One method is to ignore them and look solely at the ultimate benefits, i.e. $80-60$. This is a common approach in economics. Thus in Chapter 27 we shall look at how an individual allocates his time between work and leisure on the assumption that work yields only a benefit – income – which is compared with the benefits from leisure. Yet it must be apparent that many jobs yield disutility before they yield utility. The problem of disutility also occurs elsewhere in problems of time and leisure. Some writers, for example, assume that in buying washing machines and carpet cleaners, people are buying leisure whereas others would take the view that they are buying relief from dull, monotonous jobs. The problem may, in fact, be insoluble: utility and disutility may be inextricably mixed as are pain and pleasure. Throughout this book, however, we shall assume that it is net benefits, not gross benefits, that are compared.

4 It follows from what has been said so far that *maximizing utility means minimizing costs*; that is, the theory of costs is intimately linked with the theory of utility. Indeed it is another way of looking at the same problem. If the net benefits from digging in the garden were expected to be lower than going for a run in the car, then you would have said that the costs of digging were too high.

5 We can also see that the much bandied-about phrase *cost–benefit analysis* used in the evaluation of social projects, such as roads, railways and airports, means no more than a comparison of the benefits that might accrue from different courses of action. It could be called benefit–benefit analysis except that the rejected benefits are put under the heading 'costs'.

6 *Costs are subjective.* By 'subjective' we mean that the expected benefits from different courses of action are perceived and evaluated by the decision-maker and there may be no obvious objective criteria which an observer, an outsider, can point to as the factors influencing the decision-maker. This is important. It marks the difference between the businessman and his accountant. In making his decision the businessman will often be guided by intangibles, the 'feel of the market', those 'animal spirits' which prevent him from doing nothing. Contrast this with his accountant who regards as costs only those things which have bills of sale or receipts attached to them and who is forced to do so because the law requires him to measure income (the difference between receipts and costs) in an objective fashion by deducting the figures on one set of 'bits of paper' (receipts) from those on another set of 'bits of paper' (costs). But the businessman is not always guided by bits of paper: he may have only a hazy idea of the prices he will have to pay for resources at some future date and the receipts he will get at some future date.

7 Finally, we can now realize that *costs may be difficult to calculate.* Although we have drawn attention to the differences in the costing procedures of businessmen and accountants we can take the point further. For it is sometimes said that the decision-maker can enumerate his costs but not his benefits. This may not be so, for his costs are all the benefits that might accrue from any of the numerous courses of action that he might have taken and some of which he may have overlooked or neglected.

Costs and prices

Of course we normally expect costs, the foregone benefits, to be reflected in the prices paid for resources and in a world of perfect knowledge that would be true, because all the benefits from all courses of action would then be known. The subjective aspect of costs is strongest when decisions are 'once-and-for-all', for then there can be no recourse to past experience.

Durable goods and the classification of costs

There is, however, one large class of goods for which price does not automatically record costs. These are the durable or capital goods whose services are not instantly consumed. Now in the case of a house, a car or a fridge the immediate resale price may be as much as 90 per cent of the purchase price and it is the difference between purchase price and resale price which measures cost or, to be more precise, *acquisition cost*.

Supposing you bought a car for £1000 and could immediately sell it for £990, then the acquisition cost would be £10. If you then kept the car for a year without using it you might get £800 and the *retention cost* or *depreciation* of the car would not be the difference between £1000 and £800, but the difference between £1000 and the present value of £800 discounted to the date of initial purchase. Recall that £800 next year is not the same as £800 now.

It would be most unusual for you not to run the car and we may suppose that at the end of the year you could get £500 for it. The difference between the discounted value of £800 and £500 represents the *operating cost* though you would have to add in (appropriately discounted) expenditure on petrol, oil and maintenance. And you could be unlucky in that, though you assumed you would get £500 for it on resale, the makers decide to bring out a new model which causes the resale price of your car to drop to £300. You would then regard the difference between the present values of £500 and £300 as *obsolescence cost*. We can set out the cost calculations as follows:

	Expenditures (£)	
	Now	*End of one year*
purchase price	1000	
resale price	990	£800 or £500 or £300
Costs		
acquisition	10	
retention	272·8	(i.e. £1000 minus £800 discounted at 10 per cent for one year)
operating	272·7	(i.e. £800 minus £500 both discounted at 10 per cent for one year)
obsolescence	181·8	(i.e. £500 minus £300 both discounted at 10 per cent for one year)

We have also established a set of cost components which are sometimes given other names in economics and accounting and it is useful to remember them.

Table 28 Cost synonyms

acquisition cost	fixed cost	instantaneous or
	overhead cost	inescapable
	unavoidable cost	benefits
	supplementary cost	foregone
operating cost	variable cost	
	direct cost	avoidable or
	avoidable cost	escapable
	prime cost	benefits
	running cost	foregone
	retention cost	

Of the terms given above 'fixed' and 'variable' are fairly standard in the literature, though they do not always have the precision of 'acquisition' and 'operating' cost. We shall however use the terms 'fixed' and 'variable' so as to avoid confusion for readers of other books.

Bygones are bygones

The distinction between fixed and variable cost is important because once a car, house, fridge or record player has been acquired then that cost cannot influence future decisions. The cost of running the car immediately after it was purchased is not £1000 (the historical cost) but £990 which could be obtained on resale. Similarly the cost at the end of one year is not £1000 but the resale price of £800, £500 or £300.

The point we are trying to make is important. Once costs have been incurred they can be ignored until the decision has to be reconsidered (as, for example, when an asset needs replacing). The only situations when initial costs or historical costs become important is, paradoxically, when prices are changing. Suppose a machine costs £1000 and through its use earns £3000, then net income is £3000 discounted to the time of the decision minus £1000. Let us take a year. Suppose at the end of the year the machine needs replacing but its price has risen to £1500 then the income of the old machine should be regarded as £3000 (discounted) minus £1500. Failure to allow for rising prices can lead to inability to replace assets because too much income has been consumed. Accountants are forced, by law, to measure income on the basis of historical cost, but sensible ones set aside contingency funds.

Marginal cost

Having established a satisfactory definition of cost in terms of benefits foregone and drawn a distinction between fixed and variable costs we are now in a position to explore variable cost more fully. It is the cost that can be avoided that is relevant for decision-making and not the costs that have been incurred. Indeed, any consequences that have flowed from a previous decision may have no bearing on the next decision. Thus a previous decision may have committed a firm to a blast furnace of a certain size whilst the next decision may cause the firm to abandon iron-making. What is relevant and important therefore is the decision that has to be made and not the decision that has been made.

A producer will have to make a decision if there has been a change in demand or a technological change making for a possible reduction in the costs of continuing along the present programmes. Such a decision will therefore cause a change in output and the simplest concept we can established between cost and output change is marginal cost.

Marginal cost is the cost of increasing output by one unit.

Marginal cost is one of those concepts – along with marginal revenue, marginal utility and marginal product – which are fundamental in economics. All refer to small, incremental changes. In this case it is the change in cost associated with a change in output. Marginal cost can, however, be an ambiguous concept for there are a variety of methods of changing output and the output change can be effected quickly or slowly. We can set out some of the dimensions of marginal cost which need to be considered:

1 *The nature of the product.* In some cases the output of one good can only be increased if the output of another good is also increased. Joint products and joint costs are fairly common.

2 *Has the output to be increased quickly?*

3 *Is the increase in output to be permanent or temporary?*

4 *Does the decision include social as well as private benefits?*

Rate of output

Suppose we have a firm with given resources. We may suppose that within a given time period, say a year, it can produce 5200 units.

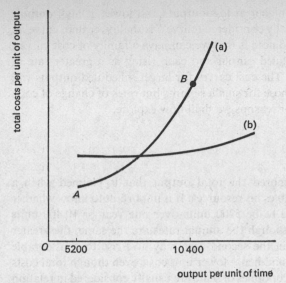

Figure 74

Now let us suppose that demand rises. How will the businessman react? If he decides to respond quickly then he may envisage a rise in costs. Thus if he hopes to produce 10 400 units in a year then overtime working or shift working may have to be introduced and workers will have to be paid higher rates of pay. Moreover, he may be forced to bid up the prices of raw materials, and bottlenecks may occur on the shop floor.

The expected behaviour of costs with respect to an increase in output from 5200 to 10 400 units a year can now be illustrated by means of Figure 74. In Figure 74 we show a cost curve for a plant capable of producing 5200 units in a year and we may envisage that the firm is producing at the point *A*, the lowest point on the cost curve, which is also a rate of 100 per week. Now when output rises the firm produces at *B* which indicates that costs rise as the rate of output rises. (Note that since these costs are expected costs they are discounted to the time of the decision.) Note that the effect of rate changes is to cause costs to rise steeply. Costs may not rise so steeply if the plant is underutilized or if there is planned reserve capacity to take into account that output may swing between 5200 and 10 400 units per year, but note that spare capacity involves a cost and so the cost curve will be higher at low outputs and lower at high outputs than the curve initially considered (curve b is shallower than curve a).

The final point to note is that we can have a family of cost curves, one for each scheduled output and each rising as a greater rate of output is imposed. The cost curves for larger scheduled outputs will initially be above those for smaller plants but rates of change of costs tend to be lower for reasons we shall now explore.

Volume of output

So far we have ignored the total output that is planned when a businessman assembles his resources. It is important to know whether output is scheduled to be 5200 units over one year or 10 400 units over two years. Although the annual rates are the same, the greater volume of output in the second case may give rise to considerable economies of scale and hence lower unit costs even though total costs are higher. These economies of scale are usually considered in relation to specific areas of the producer's production processes, e.g. Technical, Managerial, Marketing, Finance and Risk.

Technical. The commonest economy is that which comes from the relationship between the surface area and volume of a container, say a boiler or blast furnace. As the surface area is doubled the volume is more than doubled and there may be little need for stronger building materials.

Managerial. It may be possible by coordination and delegation to control the operations of large numbers of men. If one man can supervise ten men, then ten supervisors can control the work of one hundred men and one manager can coordinate the work of ten supervisors.

Marketing. By using sampling methods it may be possible to acquire considerable information about the requirements of large numbers of consumers.

Finance. It may be cheaper, in terms of brokers' fees, etc., to raise large sums of money.

Risk. With sampling methods it may be possible to exercise greater control over the quality of output.

Table 29 Printing costs for an initial printing order for a 256 page book

Number of copies printed (thousands)	Index of cost per copy including the cost of paper and binding	
	Hardback	Paperback
1	100	—
5	34	100
10	25	80
20	21	59
50	18	41
100	—	34
200	—	30

Source: Pratten (1971)

Set-up costs

Economies of scale arise because of 'lumpiness' in the production process. Some reductions in costs per unit arise only by using certain production techniques which are only worthwhile when the volume of output is increased. Even where set-up costs increase there may be no proportional increase of costs with output. Lecturing to eighty students may be expected to involve no greater problems than are encountered when lecturing to sixty or forty students. Indeed it might be possible to reduce lecturing costs appreciably by means of television. As an example of the possibilities of the reduction in unit costs following an initial set-up cost we cite data obtained by Pratten. What Table 29 reveals is that cost per unit falls for both hardback and paperback books the greater the volume or 'run' of books and that production of low runs of paperbacks has a pronounced effect on the unit cost.

Learning effects

Another source of cost reductions that occurs when it is expected to repeat a particular production run is learning effects. Adam Smith had noted in the eighteenth century that repetition brought with it increased dexterity and efficiency. Awkward operations become eliminated and workers 'filter' out the efficient methods of production.

Such learning effects cannot be known in advance though they can be guessed at. Indeed one of the most controversial areas in government planning concerns the price-fixing arrangements for government contracts. Failure to allow for learning effects may be why private contractors make large profits and governments become involved in acrimonious debates over their ability to cost defence projects. There is also the general point that where learning effects are prevalent then workers will prefer to be paid by the number of pieces they produce (i.e. piece-work) whereas employers will prefer to pay workers either on time-rates of wages (with stringent supervision) or on piece-rate price lists which pay a declining price per piece as the number of pieces produced increases in order to capture some of the gains from learning for themselves.

The effect on costs. The effect of increased volume on costs will be to cause the expected costs for any given rate of output to decline as in Figure 75; the unit total-cost curve rises at a diminishing rate.

The effect of rate and volume on costs

Now a common feature of most production processes is that the rate and volume of output increase together. This is because the length of

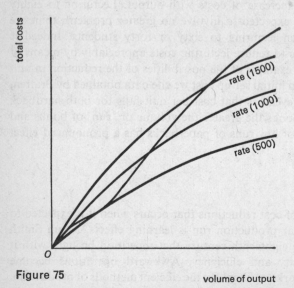

Figure 75

volume of output

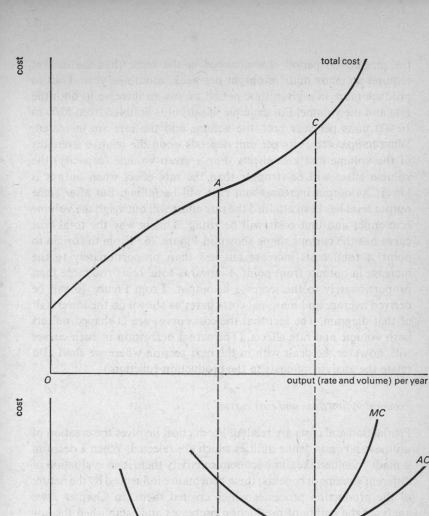

Figure 76

the production period is unchanged in the sense that the market requires so many units of output per week, month or year. Thus to produce more in a given time period means an increase in both the rate and the volume. For example, if output is doubled from 5200 to 10 400 units per year both the volume and the rate are increased. What happens to costs per unit depends upon the relative strengths of the volume and rate effects. For a given volume (capacity) the volume effect will be stronger than the rate effect when output is lower. As output increases unit cost will be falling. But after some output level has been attained the rate effect will outweigh the volume economies and unit costs will be rising. This is why the total cost curve has the curious shape shown in Figure 76.[1] From the origin to point A total costs increase but less than proportionately to the increase in output; from point A onwards total costs rise more than proportionately to the increase in output. From Figure 76 can be derived average and marginal cost curves as shown on the lower half of that diagram. The fact that the cost curves are U-shaped reflects both volume and rate effects. (The actual derivation of such curves will, however, be dealt with in the next section where we shall also relate the analysis of costs to the production function.)

Production functions and cost curves

Production and costs are related. Production involves the creation of utilities and costs define utilities which are rejected. When a decision is made to undertake some economic activity there is an evaluation of different streams of benefits; these benefits are influenced by the nature of the production processes which created them. In Chapter 3 we analysed the nature of production processes and established the law of diminishing returns: the notion that output grew at a diminishing rate as more and more of a variable factor was applied to a fixed factor. In that chapter output was thought of in physical terms, as actual rather than expected. What we must now do is to interpret the production function in a subjective rather than an objective manner.

In Table 30 we outline the expected outputs from applying differing numbers of men in a factory. From the information, and given the

1. The minimum point on the average cost curve occurs where the total cost curve begins to rise steeply beyond C. The minimum point on the marginal cost curve occurs at A where the total cost curve has an inflection point.

Table 30 Production and costs for a given production period

Units of variable factor	Units of fixed factor	Total output	Total variable cost	Total fixed cost	Total cost	Average variable cost	Average fixed cost	Average total cost	Marginal cost
0	10	0	0	50	50	—	—	—	—
1	10	5	5	50	55	1·00	10·00	11·00	1·00
2	10	12	10	50	60	0·83	4·16	4·99	0·71
3	10	24	15	50	65	0·62	2·04	2·66	0·42
4	10	39	20	50	70	0·51	1·28	1·79	0·33
5	10	50	25	50	75	0·50	1·00	1·50	0·36
6	10	59	30	50	80	0·51	0·85	1·36	0·56
7	10	67	35	50	85	0·52	0·74	1·26	0·63
8	10	75	40	50	90	0·53	0·67	1·20	0·63
9	10	80	45	50	95	0·56	0·63	1·19	1·00
10	10	84	50	50	100	0·60	0·60	1·20	1·25
11	10	86	55	50	105	0·64	0·58	1·22	2·50
12	10	87	60	50	110	0·69	0·58	1·27	5·00

expected wages of men and the price of the factory, we can obtain total costs, a variety of average costs and marginal costs. These cost categories are:

Average fixed cost (*AFC*), obtained by dividing total fixed cost by total output. Average fixed cost falls as the rate of output increases thereby confirming the commonplace saying that as output increases the overheads can be spread more easily. The average total cost curve is, of course, a vertical summation of the curves of average fixed cost and average variable cost and the reader might like to superimpose the relevant curves on to Figure 76 after reading the next section.

Average variable cost (*AVC*), obtained by dividing total variable cost by total output.

Average total cost (*ATC*), obtained by dividing total cost by total output.

Points to note about marginal cost are:

1 So long as marginal cost is below average variable or average total cost it is pulling average costs down. When marginal cost is equal to either average cost then that average cost is at a minimum level and when marginal cost is above either average cost then that average cost will be rising.

2 Marginal cost can be calculated as either the change in total cost or the change in total variable cost. Why? Because fixed cost will not be varying with output and so all changes in total cost must be changes in variable costs.

The old and the new

In a previous section it was suggested that with an expansion of output it would be more efficient to operate a new plant of larger capacity. This need not always be the case. What we usually observe is the coexistence of old and new plants sometimes in different firms but often within the same firm. Why should this be so? The answer lies in the unimportance of the sunk costs of old plant. Those costs have been incurred and can be forgotten and attention needs only be paid to running costs. The choice can therefore lie between the variable costs of old machines and the total costs (fixed plus variable) of new machines. As long as the running costs of old machines are lower than the total costs of new machines, old machines will be retained. But for an output expansion the firm will supplement its stock of old machines with new ones since these will be relatively cheaper.[2] Sometimes 'old' technologies may be retained for stand-by purposes: e.g. coal fired power stations may be built to cope with peak demands for electricity whilst nuclear stations may serve the off-peak.

Joint costs

So far we have assumed that only one product is being produced. Many firms, however, produce more than one product. Indeed the number of one-product firms is probably small. Even Guinness produce sweets and toffees; launderettes offer semi-dry or dry clothing as products. The reasons for multi-product firms are of course not hard to discover.

1 Technology – it may be impossible to produce mutton without wool.

2 Risk-avoidance – it may be more efficient to produce a range of goods rather than run the risk of putting all 'the eggs in one basket'.

Whenever firms produce more than one product accountants encounter the problem of allocating overheads. Remember the accountant's task is to attach costs to the various goods produced in order to meet the requirements of company law and the tax authorities. He has to try to ascertain the income obtained from various products and to do this he must deduct costs from revenues. Now economists say that the apportionment of costs cannot be carried out in any meaningful manner. Suppose, say, our sheep farmer has the following receipts and payments position:

Receipts		Payments	
sale of wool	£5000	wages	£2000
sale of mutton	£2000	materials	£1500
		buildings	£1000

Suppose that the farmer decides that half his outgoings shall be met from the sale of wool and half from the sale of mutton: then he

2. An alternative way of expressing this proposition is to say that a firm will use both old and new machines as long as the net present values of future earnings for the plants are equal. In calculating net present values the costs will be present values of operating and total costs respectively.

will discover that the production of mutton incurs a loss of £250 whereas wool production shows a profit of £2750. If he decides to stop producing mutton he will automatically cease producing wool. What should he do? His overall position is one of a £2500 profit so there is no reason why he should stop sheep farming. The correct solution seems therefore to be to cover all the overheads out of total revenue. In other words, the problem of overheads is really a marketing problem of trying to get the maximum revenue from the sale of each product.

Of course, not all joint costs are so rigidly fixed. Sometimes the proportions in which products are produced can be varied and therefore marginal costs can be ascertained. But there is still no case for allocating overheads. There is no case for adding to marginal cost (or more usually average variable cost) a percentage to cover the overheads if that procedure results in a loss because the overhead has been fixed too high. As long as revenue covers marginal cost and some contribution can be made to overheads then production should be continued unless it can be shown that another product will bring in greater profit.[3]

Collective goods

Joint consumption must be distinguished from joint production. In the case of jointly produced private goods the market can determine allocation issues as outlined in the previous paragraph; in the case of joint consumption, the collective goods case, the financing problems become more important since the good is made available to all consumers.

Private and social costs

The final classification of costs is into private and social. A chemical plant, let us say, discharges noxious effluent into a river which flows by the plant. The cost to the chemical plant is the cost of pumping the effluent into the river (or more precisely the benefits foregone by

3. Not all accountants adopt the policy of trying to allocate overheads by apportioning a percentage to costs in order to arrive at price. Some, more recently, have adopted the *direct costing* approach which is a form of marginal costing. By this method products are priced on the basis of (marginal) direct cost and each product makes whatever contribution it can to overheads.

pumping). If, however, the pollution reduces the incomes of others – fishermen and would-be bathers – then there are additional costs borne by others. The costs to the firm are *private costs* whereas the total costs of waste disposal are called *social costs*.

Evidently the distinction between private and social costs depends upon the system of cost enforcement in operation. If the chemical firm has to compensate those whose incomes fall or has to introduce a system of waste disposal which has no spillovers then private and social costs would equate.

Empirical aspects of costs

At various stages we have tried to relate our views on costs to the real world: most real-world studies of costs suggest that the U-shaped cost curve may not exist. Costs are usually depicted as either L-shaped or continually falling. Why should this be so?

1 Learning effects: the cost data show the effects of learning over time.

2 Volume effects: there may be changes in plant structure which give rise to economies of scale.

3 Wrong data. Accountancy data may contain biases because it was not designed to answer economists' questions.

4 Uncertainty: managers may build flexibility into plants. No one would build a steel firm to produce exactly 400 000 tonnes per year if demand was expected to fluctuate between 350 000 and 500 000 tonnes per year.

5 A different problem: the empirical results refer to the costs consequent upon decisions as recorded by the market but do not refer to the costs contemplated at the decision making stage.

Summary

Costs are the benefits foregone: the foregone utilities. As such they are subjective and may have no objective basis. When there is a change in tastes, income or the environment a decision will be made. This decision will involve a choice between various streams of discounted benefits and the highest valued stream of rejected benefits will constitute the costs of the decision.

The contemplated costs of a decision will vary with (a) the nature of the product; (b) how soon a decision has to be made; (c) the number of periods over which production will take place, i.e. the time horizon of the decision; (d) the presence or absence of technical change and (e) the social context within which decision-making takes place.

Costs are linked to production functions because it is productive processes that create utilities. But although production functions have an objectivity grounding in the inputs and products, often physical, that they involve, the production functions associated with costs are expected production functions. The empirical, or after-the-event, production functions show the consequences of decisions and may contain results different from those anticipated. As such they can only offer pointers to the likely outcomes of decisions based upon an extrapolation of past outcomes.

Questions

1 'Costs are utilities.' Explain.

2 What are the implications of viewing costs as subjective opportunity costs?

3 What is the relationship between production functions and costs?

4 'If I can get enough to cover my running costs, I can produce and forget about my overheads, even though I make a loss for the time being.' Comment on this statement.

5 'Fixed costs do not exist in the long run and are irrelevant in the short run.' Explain.

6 In this country some electric power stations are conventional, fired both by coal and oil, some are nuclear and some are hydro-electric. How would you use economic theory to explain the coexistence of different methods of production for a homogeneous commodity?

7 The following equations express the relationship between costs and output:

$C = 3Q,$

$C = 10+3Q,$

$C = 10+3Q^2,$

$C = 10+3Q^3+3Q^2,$

where C is total cost and Q is output. Insert values (from say 1 to 100) for Q and obtain values of C. What can you say about the nature of the cost curves? Which equation seems to express the relationship between costs and output as underlined by the law of diminishing returns?

Part Four
A Mathematical Interlude

In developing many of the arguments in this book we have had recourse to mathematical reasoning. We have not always provided rigorous proofs of our analysis, being content to illuminate our themes by juggling with shorthand symbols, yet often we have implied that more sophisticated techniques might be employed. Our aim here is to reproduce some of the major conclusions of the various chapters in a rather more elegant form. We are not about to plunge into the mainstream of pure mathematics but merely to *apply* some of the tools provided us by that branch of knowledge to the economic problems with which we have concerned ourselves. Economics is not mathematics and it is possible, although it may be difficult, to be a good 'non-mathematical' economist. Nevertheless, the language of mathematics provides us with both a shorthand to help us simplify mammoth problems to manageable proportions and a means of rigorously defining the models that we commonly employ in our economic analysis. Given these properties we would be extremely myopic not to make use of them. But for those so terrified by the title of this chapter as to resolve never again to deliberately open the book at this page, the chapter can be omitted without seriously damaging comprehension of basic economic theory. For those readers preparing the way for a more advanced study of economics we hope this chapter proves useful.

What mathematical concepts have we employed in our introduction to economic theory?

1 In the very first chapter we used the basic operations of *addition*, *subtraction*, *division* and *multiplication*. We also presented information in mathematical form, using the *table* as the basic format. Our tables presented *numbers* which in both absolute and relative (*percentage*) form conveyed information about prices,

incomes, quantities and time. Furthermore, we plotted some of our information on a *graph* which gave us a two-dimensional picture of the behaviour of some of our data.

2 In Chapter 2 we introduced the concept of a *set* and we discussed the relationships between sets of wants, resources and goods. The theory of sets and relations is an important branch of mathematics and the techniques of formally describing relationships (or non-relationships) between sets of things can be of use to the economist. But many of these techniques are complex and the level of economic analysis at which we are aiming does not warrant an exploration of them.

3 In Chapter 3 we introduced the all-important concept of a *function*, that is the relationship(s) between the associated values of two or more variables. The functional relationship described in Chapter 3 was that between output and resource inputs – we called this 'the production function'. But production functions are not the only examples of this type of relationship used in our analysis. Indeed, almost every problem we have posed was simplified by abstracting the functional relationships between the variables within the problem. In so doing we have analysed problems by using simple pictures (graphs) which tell us at a glance something about associated values of the variables we have plotted and, with a little more effort on our part, something about the effects on one variable of changes in the other(s). Because functions are so important in economics this chapter presents a more rigorous exposition of some issues previously discussed with the aid of graphs and by toying with symbols. The branch of mathematics which helps us in this direction is the *calculus*.

4 Another occasion on which we incorporated mathematics directly into the main text was in Chapters 10 and 11 where we employed the algebra of *simultaneous equations* to demonstrate the concept of market equilibrium. Little more need be said on this technique except to note that although it is a relatively simple one to employ, and probably one with which most readers are very familiar, its usage comes last in the logical ordering of our economic theory. This observation underlines again that economics is not mathematics and that our aim is to teach economics with the aid of mathematics and not the other way round. It should be clear

from this preamble that we are here presenting those areas of mathematics not explicitly used in the main text.

Functions

We commence with a tool employed on many occasions in our earlier chapters – the *function*. When two sets of things are functionally related then whatever values attach to the elements of one set, the values of the other set are uniquely determined. Consider the following diagram. In Figure 77 lots of cost–output combinations are plotted as a set of xy coordinates. As such, the diagram does not give us any precise information – for each x-value there are at least six y-values. Suppose, however, that we know that $y = x$, then we can immediately identify the xy coordinates which satisfy this equality. They are represented by rectangular shapes on the diagram and are seen to lie on a straight line. A similar exercise could be carried out for $y = \frac{1}{2}x$ (the relevant coordinates are represented by triangular shapes). Such unique xy relationships are functional relationships – in both cases y is a function of x, which we usually express as

$$y = f(x).\qquad\qquad\qquad 1$$

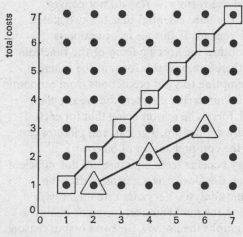

Figure 77 x output

It is important to note that although **1** may be read as 'y depends on x', the relationship does not imply causation. A function merely describes a relationship which exists, possibly by accident, between two variables and as such it can be expressed as **1** or as **2** without altering the nature of the relationship. When there is only one x such that $y = f(x)$ we can write

$$x = f^{-1}(y). \qquad\qquad\qquad 2$$

The variable which appears on the left-hand side of the expression we term the *dependent variable* and the variable on the right-hand side is termed the *independent variable*.[1]

The important thing to remember is that when two variables are functionally related the relation is neither vague nor haphazard but specific and predictable. We have suggested, so far, several such relationships which exist between economic variables. Three examples of such functions, in their general form, are listed below:

$Q = f(N)$: Output Q is a function of (depends upon) the number of resource units employed, N – *the production function.*
$U_x = f(X)$: The utility from consuming any commodity X, U_x, is a function of the amount of X consumed – *the utility function.*
$Q_D = f(P)$: Quantity demanded, Q_D, is a function of price P – *the demand function.*

But general expressions of the form $y = f(x)$ do not convey much information except the bare essential that the two stated variables are functionally related. If further information is required about the relationship the specific form of the function must be referred to and, therefore, it is this form of the function that we employ when attempting to yield predictions from economic theories. Yet only rarely in our earlier chapters did we stipulate our functions in algebraic form, the reason being that for each specific function we can draw a picture, a graph, and pictures can be a very useful guide to the comprehension of basics.

However, the expository benefits from a picture are not sufficient reason for total reliance on this device as a means of drawing conclusions from economic analysis. Very often we might wish to place more reliance upon the mathematical formulae behind a set of graphs than on the graphs themselves, for two obvious reasons.

1. A preliminary exploration of these concepts was made in Chapter 9.

Firstly, there is the mundane point that graphs are usually drawn by hand and require interpretation by the naked eye. Rigorous mathematical specification protects us from human error in the construction of graphs and the visual interpretation of the models which employ them. Secondly, a more important drawback to a total reliance on visual aids is that when more than three sets of variables are functionally related a picture becomes impossible to construct. When we had two variables in our function we drew a two-dimensional diagram; if we had three variables we would draw a three-dimensional diagram; but we cannot draw four-or-more-dimensional diagrams.

What mathematical specifications underlie the economic relationships we have met so far? While the variables in an economic problem could take on any functional relationship most of the *basic* economic principles can be expressed in one of three functional forms:

The *linear function*,
The *quadratic function*,
The *cubic function*.

These three are not so frightening as they may appear to anyone a little out of touch with mathematics. Each function can be expressed as an equation which is either linear, quadratic or cubic. Now these terms merely refer to the *degree* of the equation which is determined by the highest *power* (or exponent) of the known variable in the equation. Let us have a brief look at each separate function.

1 *Linear function.* Such a function is expressed in the form of the linear equation, i.e. an equation of the first degree – the highest power of the known variable is *one*.
Example. $y = 7x + 10$ is a linear equation. The known variable is x and its highest power is one – x can be written x^1. Generally we use the form

$$y = a + bx \hspace{4cm} 3$$

to express a linear function; where a and b are numerical constants. The graph of a linear function is a straight line with a representing the intercept on the y axis and b the slope of the line. To understand this, consider the relationships between y and x when x is zero.

The value of y in this case is given by a. Since a is a constant the relationship between different values of x and y is unaffected by it, i.e. y varies directly with x according to the constant b, thus b is the slope of the function. When b is positive the function slopes upwards to the right (a positive slope) since y increases as x increases; and when b is negative the function slopes downwards from left to right (a negative slope) since y decreases as x increases. Two linear functions are graphed below. Figure 78a is the function $y = a+bx = 4x-2$ (i.e. $a = -2$, $b = +4$). Figure 78b shows the function $y = a+bx = 2-4x$ (i.e. $a = +2$, $b = -4$).

Prime examples of linear functions are given by the straight line demand and supply curves of Chapter 9.

2 *Quadratic functions*. This type of function is expressed as a quadratic equation, i.e. an equation of the second degree – the highest power of the known variable is 2.
Example. $y = 7x^2 + 10x + 5$ is a quadratic equation. The known variable is x and its highest power is 2. Generally such a function is expressed by the form

$$y = ax^2 + bx + c. \qquad\qquad 4$$

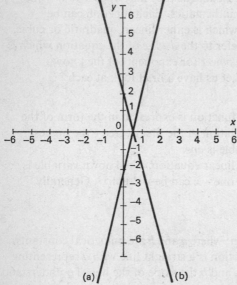

(a)   (b)

Figure 78

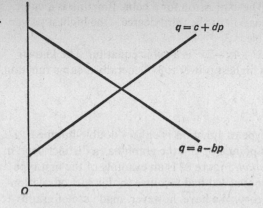

quantity demanded and supplied per unit of time

Figure 79

The graph of this type of function is either 'U-shaped' or 'hump-shaped' (it is a parabola). Thus, when we plotted an average-product curve in Chapter 3 and an average cost-curve in Chapter 12 we were drawing the graphs of two quadratic functions:

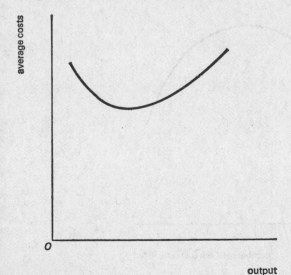

Figure 80 The average-cost curve $y(AC) = 12 + x^2 - 4x$

3 *Cubic functions.* The expression for a cubic function is a cubic equation, i.e. an equation of the third degree – the highest power of the known variable is 3.

Example. $y = 5 + 8x^3 + 4x - 2x^2$ is a cubic equation. The known variable is x and its highest power is 3. Generally a cubic function is expressed as

$$y = ax^3 + bx^2 + cx + d. \qquad\qquad 5$$

The graph of this type of function is either 'double-humped', i.e. it has distinct turning points, or else the graph has a distinct bend in it – a point of *inflection*. Figure 82 is an example of the first type of graph. We have not as yet had recourse to this sort of relation in our economic theory. We have, however, made use of graphs like Figure 83. If the y-axis of this graph were to represent total costs and the x-axis to represent output, Figure 83 would be an example of the total variable cost as constructed in Chapter 12.

These three functions, then, are the main ones employed so far. Have we made specific reference to any others? Perhaps we should

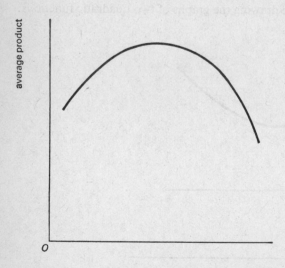

Figure 81 The average-product curve $y(AP) = 12 - x^2 + 4x$

mention one further type of function which has appeared twice
so far in our analysis – the *rectangular hyperbola*. Remember the
cases of the demand curve showing unit elasticity and the curve of
average fixed costs? The general expression for such a function is

$$y = \frac{k}{x}, \qquad\qquad 6$$

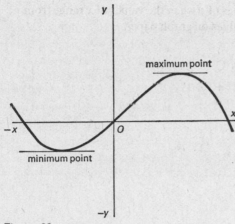

Figure 82

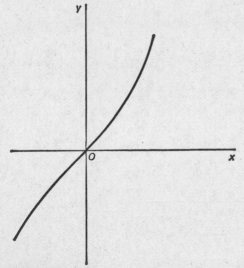

Figure 83

where k is a constant. As we know from our use of this function the area of any rectangle drawn under its curve is always constant regardless of the values of the x and y coordinates. We can see this by manipulation of **6** which may be rewritten as $yx = k$, telling us that the product of related x and y values (the area of the rectangle formed by the coordinates) is always a constant, k. Before proceeding to the next section, consider the following functions, calculate the values of y when the values of x range from -10 to $+10$ and plot the values on graph paper.

1 linear $y = x + 1$,

2 quadratic $y = x^2 + 2x + 3$,

5 cubic $y = x^3 + 3x^2 + 13x + 15$.

Chapter 13
The Calculus

Rates of change

The functions with which we have been dealing are smooth and *continuous* – their curves are free from breaks and kinks. From such functions we can readily calculate the related absolute values of the x, y variables. But how can we calculate the effect on one set of values resulting from some *change* in the other set? Time and again in our economic analysis we have referred to *a rate of change*, how something changes value in response to a change in some other thing.

Examples

1 In Chapter 3 we were concerned with how output might change in response to changes in man-hours employed – *marginal product*, i.e. the rate of change of output as employment changes.

2 In Chapter 11 we considered how utility might change in relation to changes in quantity consumed – *marginal utility*, i.e. the rate of change of utility as consumption changes.

3 In Chapter 12 we considered how costs might vary in response to output changes – *marginal cost*, i.e. the rate of change of cost as output changes.

These are just three examples of the concept of the *margin* and, therefore, three examples of our implicit use of the *calculus* which is that branch of mathematics employed to calculate rates of change of continuous functions. To fully appreciate the uses of this mathematical tool let us build up from a familiar diagram, Figure 7 of Chapter 3 which depicts a total-product curve. When we first used this diagram we said that the marginal product of an additional unit of resource is given by the slope[1] of the total-product curve between the two points

1. The terms 'slope' and 'gradient' are used to mean the same thing.

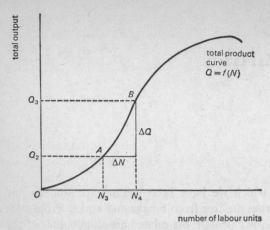

Figure 84 Total product curve $Q = f(N)$

(coordinates) at which the measurements are taken. This slope is defined as the ratio of change in total output to change in employment, or $\Delta Q/\Delta N$. Thus for a given change in employment, N_3 to N_4, marginal product is equal to Q_3 minus Q_2.

Marginal product, $\Delta Q/\Delta N = (Q_3 - Q_2)/(N_4 - N_3)$
$$= Q_3 - Q_2,$$
when $N_4 - N_3 = 1$.

In order to get this result we employed a little harmless trickery, a ploy we have resorted to often when analysing movements along curves. To enable our comprehension of the economics involved we depict a *discrete change* in the value of the two variables. It makes sense to discuss the effects of changes which could be perceived in reality – the farmer would be able to measure the output of an additional man-hour – and it helps exposition if the diagrammatic change can be seen with the naked eye. But we have represented the output/employment relationships as a smooth curve which means that a ratio such as $\Delta Q/\Delta N$ cannot be the slope of the curve between two points A and B since the curve has a different slope at each of the infinite number of intermediate points. Strictly speaking, the ratio $\Delta Q/\Delta N$ measures the slope of a line drawn between the points A and B, that is, the chord AB. Thus we are using the slope of this line as a proxy for the slope of the curve. In other words we are saying:

230 The Calculus

We have spaced the points A and B at a discrete distance in order to demonstrate an economic proposition; but since these points lie on a curve we are really assuming them to be an infinitesimally small distance apart so that a chord drawn between the two points approximates very closely to the slope of the curve.

The concept of the limit

If instead of *assuming* points A and B to be an infinitesimally small distance apart, we actually depicted them as such then what would we construct? The answer is a *point* on the total-product function (the total-product curve) since when two points are such a minute distance apart, to all intents and purposes they must coincide. This suggests that a marginal increment (marginal product, marginal utility, etc.) is actually given by the slope at a point on the total function (total-product curve, total-utility curve etc.). But how can a point on a curve have a gradient? What we really mean is that we measure the slope of a curve at a particular point by the slope of the *tangent* to the curve at that point. In Figure 85 the slope of the function $Q = f(N)$ at point A is given by the slope of the tangent Z and the slope at B by the slope of the tangent W.

Now, for expositional purposes, we 'blow up' points such as A (as we did in Figure 84) so that it appears not as a point but as a discrete distance AB on the curve although we assume the distance

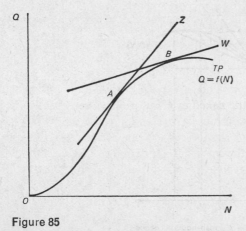

Figure 85

to be non-discrete. This seems a clumsy way of doing things: since we know that the marginal concept relates to points on the total function, is it not better to derive some useful formula which can always be applied, instead of continuing to explode diagrams in order to understand what we are doing?

The means whereby we discover such a short cut is to use the concept of the *limit*. To explain this idea we must persevere, for a little longer, with our diagrammatic methods, in particular with the manipulating of chords and tangents. Consider again a production function, $Q = f(N)$, which gives us a graph of the form previously employed and choose some point, A, on this function.

Suppose that we set ourselves the problem of finding marginal product using only the diagram when ON_1 man-hours are employed. Let us further suppose that we do not know that the slope of the function at point A (the point corresponding to N_1 labourers) is given by the slope of the tangent AZ. Is there some method which we might employ to lead us automatically to the discovery that the slope of AZ provides us with our answer? There is indeed such a method and it is described in the following paragraphs.

Our concern is with a rate of change in output at a point and we find it hard to conceive of such a thing when the number of man-hours employed is apparently not changing at that point. But if we take some large, observable increase in employment then we have no

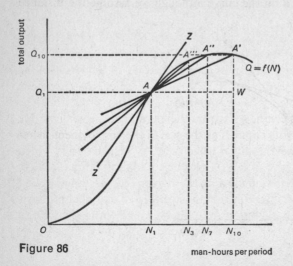

Figure 86

man-hours per period

intuitive difficulties, in fact we can easily calculate the corresponding change in output. Suppose we take the starting point as an increase in employment from ON_1 to ON_{10} which takes us from point A to point A' on the function $Q = f(N)$. We observe the corresponding change in output to be WA' ($= OQ_1$ to OQ_{10}). We can say that WA' is the product of the marginal increment in employment $(N_{10}–N_1)$. However, this increment in employment comprises several labour units and we are interested only in the output of the additional unit of labour. Thus the nearest approximation to what we want is given by the ratio WA'/AW (change in output/change in employment) which measures the slope of the chord AA' (the *tangent* of angle $A'AW$). This measure gives us an average of the marginal products for the ON_1 to ON_{10} labour units, the nearest we can get to marginal product for such a large discrete employment increment.

Suppose we now take a smaller increment in employment, say from ON_1 to ON_7. Again we can only obtain an average measure of marginal product, given by the gradient of the chord AA'', but this time our estimate is closer to the true measure (at point A) because the increment in employment is smaller. This fact is clearly shown on the diagram where the slope of the chord AA'' is seen to be steeper than the slope of the chord AA', that is, the gradient of AA'' is nearer to the slope of the curve at point A than is the slope of AA'. If we repeat this process, say for the employment increment ON_1 to ON_3, we obtain chord AA''', which gives us an even closer approximation to the slope at point A.

It should now be clear that what is happening as we reduce the size of the increment in employment is that the gradient of the chord between the relevant coordinates approaches ever more closely to the slope of the function at point A. In Figure 86 the chords have been deliberately continued through point A so that this process can be clearly observed. It can be seen from the figure that the original line through A to A' pivots about A as the size of the employment increment reduces, until eventually it has pivoted to the position in which it just touches the curve $Q = f(N)$ at point A. At this point the slope of the line, which is now no longer a *chord* but a *tangent* (tangent AZ), is exactly equal to the slope of the curve, that is, to marginal product. We can say, then, that the slope of the tangent AZ forms the limit to the slope of the chord AA as the increment in employment approaches zero.

The derivative

Let us now introduce some shorthand to reduce our reliance upon unwieldy diagrams. We may commence by restating the limit. Our analysis of the total-product function showed that, starting at point A on the curve, as the increment in employment (ΔN) gets ever smaller, i.e. approaches zero $(\to 0)$ the slope $\Delta Q/\Delta N$ (marginal product) approaches its limit (lim) which is the tangent to the total product curve at point A. In symbols

$$\lim_{\Delta N \to 0} \frac{\Delta Q}{\Delta N} = \text{slope of tangent to curve at } A.$$

In the language of the calculus this limit, this rate of change, is called the *derivative* of the function and its symbolic representation adopts the letter d (to denote infinitesimally small change) instead of the more general symbol Δ. Our analysis so far, then, has demonstrated that marginal product is the first derivative of the total product function, the rate of change of total product with respect to changes in employment. In symbols, we write

$$\frac{d}{dN}(Q) = \lim_{\Delta N \to 0} \frac{\Delta Q}{\Delta N},$$

and we usually adopt dQ/dN for $(d/dN)(Q)$ although sometimes $Q'(N)$ is used, i.e.

$$\frac{dQ}{dN} = \frac{d}{dN}(Q) = Q'(N).$$

Before taking a closer look at derivatives we should remind ourselves that the concept can be applied to many different functions. We have taken the total-product function and demonstrated marginal product as the first derivative of this function, but we could easily have used a total-utility function or a total-revenue function or any other total function and repeated the procedure to obtain the corresponding marginal measures. To entrench this general applicability in our minds it might be useful to revert briefly to our general expression $y = f(x)$ where y and x may be any two related variables. Our general expression then is

$$\frac{dy}{dx} = \lim_{\Delta x \to 0} \frac{\Delta y}{\Delta x}.$$

1

The rules of differentiation

So far we have related the marginal concept to the mathematical concept of a derivative. Now, the process of *differentiation* (i.e. the process which gives us the derivative) of a function is subject to certain rules. We are asking that these rules be accepted on trust. A mathematical proof underlies each one but such proofs are complex and not essential to our understanding of economics. Remember that we are primarily interested in applying mathematical tools to economic problems, and somewhat less interested in the tools themselves. However, in order to gain the trust we want, the first simple rule is elaborated below.

The general rule for power functions

How would we differentiate the simple functions that we have used several times already, $y = x^2$? The process follows our earlier description of the limit. Consider the definition of the first derivative as presented in **1**. If we spell out the right-hand side of this identity in more detail, the key to the process can be seen. Since y depends on x, so must Δy depend upon Δx. Thus we may write

$$\Delta x = (x + \Delta x) - x,$$

and $\quad \Delta y = f(x + \Delta x) - f(x),$

thus $\quad \dfrac{\Delta y}{\Delta x} = \dfrac{f(x + \Delta x) - f(x)}{\Delta x}.$ **2**

Substituting the right-hand side of **2** into our earlier definition **1**, we have

$$\frac{dy}{dx} = \lim_{\Delta x \to 0} \frac{f(x + \Delta x) - f(x)}{\Delta x}. \qquad \textbf{3}$$

Procedure

(a) General case, $y = f(x)$.

$$\frac{dy}{dx} = \lim_{\Delta x \to 0} \frac{f(x + \Delta x) - f(x)}{\Delta x}.$$

(b) Specific case, e.g. $y = x^2$.

$$\frac{dy}{dx} = \lim_{\Delta x \to 0} \frac{(x+\Delta x)^2 - x^2}{\Delta x},$$

$$= \lim_{\Delta x \to 0} \frac{x^2 + 2x\,\Delta x + (\Delta x)^2 - x^2}{\Delta x},$$

$$= \lim_{\Delta x \to 0} \frac{2x\,\Delta x + (\Delta x)^2}{\Delta x},$$

or $\quad \dfrac{dy}{dx} = \lim_{\Delta x \to 0} \left\{ \dfrac{2x\,\Delta x}{\Delta x} + \dfrac{(\Delta x)^2}{\Delta x} \right\}.$

If we now cancel the Δxs we are left with

$$\frac{dy}{dx} = \lim_{\Delta x \to 0} (2x + \Delta x). \qquad\qquad\qquad 4$$

What this final expression says is that at the limit, as Δx tends to zero, the whole expression $2x + \Delta x$ will approach $2x$, that is

$$\frac{dy}{dx} = \lim_{\Delta x \to 0} (2x + \Delta x),$$

$$= 2x.$$

The result of our process, then, is that the derivative of the function $y = x^2$ is $2x$. Substitute any other value for power 2 in the example we have just considered and the resultant derivative will always conform to the general rule:

If $y = x^n$, then $\dfrac{dy}{dx} = nx^{n-1}$, $\qquad\qquad\qquad 5$

and we can extend this rule to the function x *times* a constant: $y = ax^n$, where a is a constant, in which case

$$\frac{dy}{dx} = nax^{n-1} \qquad\qquad\qquad\qquad 6$$

(note that the first function, $y = x^n$, could be written as $y = 1x^n$ and its derivative as $dy/dx = n\,1\,x^{n-1}$).

Examples:

1 If $y = x^{10}$, then $\dfrac{dy}{dx} = 10x^9$.

2 $y = 4x^5$, $\frac{dy}{dx} = 20x^4$.

3 For practice, differentiate the following functions:

(a) $y = x^6$,

(b) $y = x^{150}$,

(c) $y = ax^{3/4}$,

(d) $y = 7x^{-7}$.

4 Suppose we have a variable-cost function

$$Cv = q^3,$$

where Cv is total variable costs and q is output. The derivative of this function is

$$\frac{dCv}{dq} = 3q^2,$$

which gives the rate of change of total variable costs (Cv) with respect to changes in output (q), in other words *marginal cost*. We can thus restate the definition of marginal cost as the first derivative of the total variable-cost function:

$$MC = \frac{dCv}{dq}.$$

But what about fixed costs? In our chapter on costs we said that marginal cost is the rate of change in *total* costs (fixed plus variable) as output changes by one very small unit. Remember, however, that we also pointed out that since fixed costs cannot vary with output (by definition) they do not enter into the calculation of marginal costs. Let us now try to express this point more rigorously in terms of the differentiation technique. To do so requires us to move on to our second and third rules, regarding the derivatives of constants and the differentiation of sums and differences, because a total-cost function takes the following form,

Total costs = total fixed costs + total variable costs, or in symbolic form,

$$C = a + q^3,$$

7

The Rules of Differentiation 237

where C represents total costs; a, fixed costs (a constant); and q, output (q^3 is variable costs).

The derivative of a constant

Since a derivative is a rate of change and since a constant cannot change, by definition the derivative of a constant must be zero. Fixed costs are thus independent of changes in the labour force, quantities of raw materials, etc., in other words, independent of the level of output. Given this constancy the rate of change of fixed costs in any set of circumstances must be zero, or put another way, the slope of the total fixed cost curve must be zero. This means that when calculating the rate of change of total cost with respect to a unit change in output, any constant term in the total function can be ignored. But before differentiating 7, we must consider a third rule.

Differentiation of sums and differences

The rule for differentiating a function containing additive terms is a simple extension of the general rule for differentiating power functions. This new rule merely demands that the separate derivatives be summed (or subtracted). Thus for any function:

$$y = x^n + x^m,$$

$$\frac{dy}{dx} = \frac{d}{dx}(x^n) + \frac{d}{dx}(x^m)$$

$$= nx^{n-1} + mx^{m-1},$$

or, for the function $y = u + v$,

where $u = f(x)$, $v = g(x)$,

$$\frac{dy}{dx} = \frac{du}{dx} + \frac{dv}{dx}. \qquad\qquad 8$$

Examples:

1 If $y = x^{25} + x^{13}$,

then $\dfrac{dy}{dx} = 25x^{24} + 13x^{12}$.

2 If $\qquad y = x^6 + 3x^2 - 4x^9$,

then $\qquad \dfrac{dy}{dx} = 6x^5 + 6x - 36x^8.$

3 $\quad C = a + q^3$

Now we can return to the problem of deriving marginal cost from the total cost function. We now know that $da/dq = 0$ and our third rule is that

$$\frac{dC}{dq} = \frac{d}{dq}(a) + \frac{d}{dq}(q^3).$$

$$= 0 + 3q^2$$

$$= 3q^2,$$

where dC/dq is the rate of change of total cost with respect to change in output, i.e. marginal cost. But we have already demonstrated that

$$\frac{dCv}{dq} = 3q^2,$$

so we may write $\quad MC = \dfrac{dC}{dq} = \dfrac{dCv}{dq},$

which expresses the familiar result that variable, and not fixed, costs affect the margin.

The product rule

The rule for differentiating a product is a little more complex than the other rules so far considered. By a product we mean a function of the form

$y = f(x)g(x),$

and to make the task easier we reform such a product into

$y = uv,$ $\qquad\qquad\qquad\qquad\qquad\qquad\qquad\qquad$ 9

where $u = f(x)$ and $v = g(x)$.

We now sum the product of the second term (v) and the derivative of the first (du/dx) and the product of the first term (u) and the derivative of the second (dv/dx);

$$\frac{dy}{dx} = v\frac{du}{dx} + u\frac{dv}{dx}.$$

Examples:[2]

1 If $y = (4x^2)(10x^5)$,

then $u = 4x^2$ and $du/dx = 8x$,

and $v = 10x^5$ and $dv/dx = 50x^4$.

Thus $\dfrac{dy}{dx} = (10x^5)(8x) + (4x^2)(50x^4)$,

$$= 80x^6 + 200x^6,$$

$$= 280x^6.$$

2 If $y = (6x+8)(7x^3)$,

then $u = 6x+8$ and $du/dx = 6$,

and $v = 7x^3$ and $dv/dx = 21x^2$.

Thus $\dfrac{dy}{dx} = (7x^3)(6) + (6x+8)(21x^2)$,

$$= 42x^3 + 126x^3 + 168x^2,$$

$$= 168x^3 + 168x^2.$$

Although the product rule has many applications in economics most of these uses can only be appreciated after a course of study at a higher level than our present aims. However, there is one important use to which we can put the rule at this stage. In Chapter 7 we first pointed out that marginal revenue must vary with price-elasticity of demand but we appealed more to intuition than rigour as a means of demonstrating this relationship. The product rule of differentiation allows us to show that our intuitive appeal was well-founded. Firstly let us reform the expression for price-elasticity of demand. In Chapter 7 we presented the form

$$e = -\frac{\Delta Q}{\Delta P}\left(\frac{P}{Q}\right).$$

2. It is often very useful to employ the product rule but note that when dealing with power functions the multiplication process can be completed before differentiating. Thus $y = (4x^2)(10x^5)$ is $40x^7$ and $dy/dx = 280x^6$.

Remember that this measure refers to point-elasticity,[3] elasticity at a point on the demand curve. Thus that part of the expression which relates to the slope of the demand curve, $-\Delta Q/\Delta P$ can now be more correctly presented as $-dQ/dP$. We now write

$$e = -\frac{dQ}{dP}\left(\frac{P}{Q}\right).$$

Now consider the concept of marginal revenue. Basic calculus tells us that marginal revenue MR is the first derivative of the total revenue function TR – marginal revenue is the rate of change of total revenue with respect to changes in output Q:

$$MR = \frac{dTR}{dQ}.\qquad\qquad\qquad\qquad\qquad\qquad\textbf{11}$$

However, we know that $TR = P.Q$ (where P represents price) so that finding MR involves differentiating a product:

$$TR = P.Q,$$

$$u = P \text{ and } du/dQ = dP/dQ,$$

$$v = Q \text{ and } dv/dQ = dQ/dQ = 1.$$

Differentiating gives

$$\frac{dTR}{dQ} = Q\,\frac{dP}{dQ}+P,$$

$$= P\left(1+\frac{Q}{P}\cdot\frac{dP}{dQ}\right).\qquad\qquad\qquad\textbf{12}$$

But does the expression within the bracket not seem familiar? In fact $Q/P.dP/dQ$ is no more than the reciprocal of the expression for price elasticity of demand:

$$-\frac{Q}{P}\cdot\frac{dP}{dQ} = -\frac{1}{P/Q.dQ/dP} = \frac{1}{e}.$$

We can now present **12** in a neater form. Replacing the negative sign:

$$MR = P(1-1/e).\qquad\qquad\qquad\qquad\qquad\textbf{13}$$

3. Recall how, in Chapter 7, we constructed a tangent to the demand curve in order to illustrate the concept of point elasticity.

Defining marginal revenue as in 13 we can see at a glance its relationship with price and with price-elasticity of demand. Marginal revenue is less than price by the amount of P/e: multiplying out the bracket in 13 gives $P - (P/e)$. Thus the larger is P/e the greater the difference between marginal revenue and price; and the smaller is P/e the smaller is the difference. This relationship is a very important discovery although its significance will only be fully appreciated in later chapters. In the meantime we can note that for a given P the size of P/e is determined by the size of e. Since the size of e has two limits, zero and infinity, what are the effects on marginal revenue as e approaches either of these limits?

1 As e approaches infinity P/e approaches zero and, therefore, at the limit marginal revenue equals price. Since e is infinite when the demand curve is horizontal then marginal revenue is equal to price for any producer when the demand curve for his product is horizontal.

2 As e approaches zero, P/e approaches infinity which means that at the limit marginal revenue 'disappears', it ceases to have meaning. This would be the case when the demand curve for a product is vertical.

3 Equally interesting are the in-between values of e. Given 1 and 2 it follows that so long as e is less than infinity and greater than zero, marginal revenue is less than price – the demand curve slopes downwards from left to right.

4 When $e = 1$ then marginal revenue $= 0$.

The quotient rule

The rule for differentiating a quotient appears complex at first sight but with practice proves to be straightforward. When

$$y = \frac{f(x)}{g(x)},$$

we let such a relationship be represented as

$$y = \frac{u}{v},$$

where $u = f(x)$ and $v = g(x)$ and differentiate as follows:

$$\frac{dy}{dx} = \frac{v(du/dx) - u(dv/dx)}{v^2}.$$

Example:

If $y = \frac{3x^2}{5x^4}$,

then $u = 3x^2$ and $du/dx = 6x$,

and $v = 5x^4$ and $dv/dx = 20x^3$.

Thus $\frac{dy}{dx} = \frac{(5x^4)(6x) - (3x^2)(20x^3)}{(5x^4)^2}$,

$$= \frac{30x^5 - 60x^5}{25x^8},$$

$$= -\frac{30x^5}{25x^8} = \frac{-6}{5x^3} = \frac{-6x^{-3}}{5}.$$

An obvious use to which such a rule might be put is to tell us something about the rate of change of the average-cost function with respect to the rate of output change. Suppose we had the total-cost function 7:

$$C = a + q^3.$$

The corresponding average total-cost function AC would be

$$AC = \frac{a + q^3}{q},$$

since average total cost is total cost divided by output q. Now suppose we wanted to know how AC changes with respect to q:

$$\frac{dAC}{dq} = \frac{d}{dq} \frac{(a + q^3)}{q}.$$

$u = a + q^3$ and $du/dq = 3q^2$,

$v = q$ and $dv/dq = dq/dq = 1$.

$$\frac{dAC}{dq} = \frac{q(3q^2) - (a + q)^3 1}{q^2},$$

$$= \frac{3q^3 - a - q^3}{q^2}.$$

Questions

1 A farmer has a given acreage of land on which he can employ labourers. The relationship between total output and the level of employment is given by

$$Q = 100 + 20L - L^2,$$

where Q represents total output, and L the number of man-hours employed.
(a) What is the average-product function?
(b) What is labour's marginal product when five man-hours are employed?

2 A producer can make and sell q units of his commodity per week at a total cost (in £s) given by

$$TC = 3q^3 + 2q^2 + 10q + 45.$$

(a) What is the producer's average-cost function?
(b) What is the marginal cost when producing twenty units?

3 The market demand for coffee is given by

$$Q = 100 - P,$$

where Q is the quantity purchased, in thousands of kilograms per week, and P is the price per kilogram.
(a) What is the total-revenue function?
(b) What is the marginal-revenue function?
(c) If consumers decide to buy five times their normal amount, whatever the price (and they continue to purchase the increased amounts for some time), what is the value of marginal revenue when 20 000 kilograms of coffee is being bought?

Higher order derivatives

The list of rules we have presented should provide an aid to deeper understanding of economic principles. It is not a complete list but we feel it to be adequate for our present purpose. But our manipulation of functions of one variable is incomplete until we have considered second derivatives, i.e. the derivative of a first derivative.

Why should we wish to calculate the rate of change of a rate of change? In fact such a calculation has many uses in economics, one of which we can well appreciate at this level of analysis – the test for maxima, minima, and points of inflection. Earlier we described quadratic and cubic functions, noting that the graph of the former is either U-shaped or hump-shaped and the graph of the latter has a point of inflection. Our most usual examples of these types of functional relationships have been the marginal-cost (MC) curve and marginal-product (MP) curve, representing quadratic functions, and the total-cost (TC) curve, representing cubic functions. Much of our interest in these curves centres around their turning points, for example in Chapters 3 and 12 we saw that when the MC curve turns then MC is at a *minimum*, and when the MP curve turns then MP is at a *maximum*. Yet how can we be sure that this is always true? Do we always have to construct a graph or is there a test which will quickly tell us whether or not a function has a point of inflection or a turning point and if so whether that turning point is a maximum or minimum?

Maxima and minima

1 *Use of the first derivative:* The first test to discover whether a function has a maximum or minimum turning point is to ask 'does the function have a *stationary value*?' When the function has a maximum turning point the slope of the graph of the function changes from positive to negative as the function passes through the turning point. At the point itself, however, the slope is neither positive nor negative, but equal to zero (the graph of the function is horizontal at the turning point). We thus define a stationary value as that value ($\bar{x}$) of x in the function $y = f(x)$ for which $dy/dx = 0$.

A function with a minimum turning point will also have a stationary value since the slope of the function is negative before the turning point, positive after the point and equal to zero at the point itself. We have now arrived at the first test for a maximum or minimum turning point – does the function possess a stationary value? In other words, the existence of a stationary value is a *necessary condition* for a function to possess a turning point which is either a maximum *or* a minimum. Parts (a) of Figures 87 and 88 summarize this condition: When marginal product is at a maximum the marginal-product curve (MP) of Figure 87a has a slope equal to zero – output level $\bar{x}$ is the stationary value of the function $y = f(x)$; and when marginal cost is at a minimum the marginal-cost function (MC) of Figure 88a has a slope equal to zero (again a stationary value at $\bar{x}$).

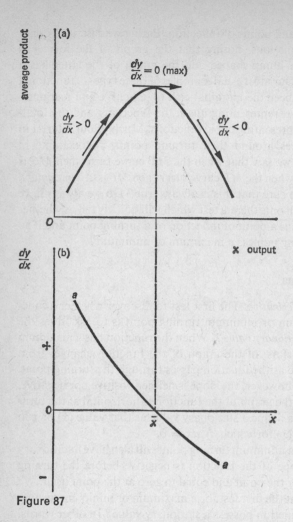

average product

(a)

$\dfrac{dy}{dx} = 0$ (max)

$\dfrac{dy}{dx} > 0$

$\dfrac{dy}{dx} < 0$

O

x output

$\dfrac{dy}{dx}$

(b)

a

+

0

$\bar{x}$

$\dot{x}$

−

a

Figure 87

2 *Use of the second derivative:* The necessary information, $dy/dx = 0$, does not enable us to distinguish between maximum and minimum turning points since both have stationary values. In order to make the distinction we require information about the gradient of the function before and after the turning point. Now, the first derivative gives us the information we require since dy/dx changes sign when the function passes through a turning point. But using the first derivative can often be a clumsy method of testing for maxima and minima, even when the

246 The Calculus

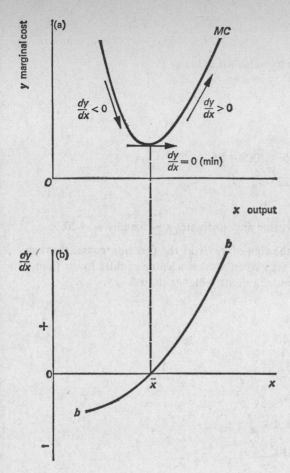

Figure 88

function is fairly straightforward. For example, suppose we attempt the following exercise:

$$y = x^2 - 10x + 5.$$

1 Find the turning point of this function.
2 Test whether this point is a maximum or minimum.
Proceed as follows:

1   $y = x^2 - 10x + 5,$

$$\frac{dy}{dx} = 2x - 10.$$

2 To find the stationary value set $dy/dx = 0$.

$$2x - 10 = 0,$$
$$2x = 10,$$
$$x = 5.$$

3 When $x = 5$, $y = 5^2 - 10(5) + 5$,

$$= 25 - 50 + 5,$$
$$= -20.$$

There is a stationary value at coordinates $x = 5$ and $y = -20$.

4 What happens to the sign of dy/dx as the function passes through $x = 5$? Consider the sign when x takes a value slightly lower than 5 and then when its value is slightly higher than 5.

When $x = 4.9$,

$$\frac{dy}{dx} = 2(4.9) - 10,$$
$$= 9.8 - 10,$$
$$= -0.2.$$

When $x = 5.1$,

$$\frac{dy}{dx} = 2(5.1) - 10,$$
$$= 10.2 - 10,$$
$$= +0.2.$$

The coordinates $(5, -20)$ give a minimum turning point since $dy/dx = 0$ and dy/dx changes sign from negative to positive as the function passes through the point.

There exists however a better tool for pursuing such tests – the second derivative. As mentioned earlier this is the slope of the first derivative function and it measures, therefore, the rate of change of dy/dx with respect to changes in x:

$$\frac{d^2y}{dx^2} = \frac{d}{dx}\left(\frac{dy}{dx}\right).$$

This is the notation for second derivatives. Note that since we could also differentiate **15** or indeed any derivative of the function $y = f(x)$ we may also form third, fourth etc., derivatives (d^3y/dx^3; d^4y/dx^4; ... gives the appropriate notations). The procedure for differentiating derivatives is precisely that followed for differentiating any function, hence:

$$y = 4x^3,$$

$$\frac{dy}{dx} = 12x^2,$$

$$\frac{d^2y}{dx^2} = 24x.$$

Now, the second derivative helps us with our present task since its sign differs according to whether the turning point is a maximum or a minimum. When the function has a maximum turning point, as in the case of the marginal product curve, the slope of the function $y = f(x)$ decreases as x increases, i.e. dy/dx falls as x increases. The graph of dy/dx, therefore, slopes downwards from left to right, as shown by curve aa in Figure 87b – note that this graph crosses the horizontal axis at $\bar{x}$, the stationary value.

The fact that dy/dx slopes downwards from left to right means that its gradient, the second derivative of $y = f(x)$, is negative. Thus we now have the *necessary and sufficient* condition for the existence of a maximum turning point:

$$\frac{dy}{dx} = 0; \text{ and } \frac{d^2y}{dx^2} < 0.$$

Consider, now, a function with a minimum turning point. In this case the gradient of the function changes from negative to positive as it passes through the minimum point. This means that the graph of dy/dx slopes upwards from left to right, as represented by bb in Figure 88b. Therefore, the gradient of dy/dx is *positive* and the necessary and sufficient condition for a minimum point to exist is:

$$\frac{dy}{dx} = 0; \text{ and } \frac{d^2y}{dx^2} > 0.$$

Summary

Necessary and sufficient condition

Turning point a maximum; $dy/dx = 0$; and $d^2y/dx^2 < 0$.

Turning point a minimum; $dy/dx = 0$; and $d^2y/dx^2 > 0$.

N.B. $dy/dx = 0$ is termed the *first order* condition and $dy^2/dx^2 \lessgtr 0$ the *second order* condition.

Using first and second order conditions we can now reconsider the earlier exercise.

$y = x^2 - 10x + 5$.

Procedure:

1 $dy/dx = 2x - 10$.

2 Set $dy/dx = 0$,

$\qquad 2x - 10 = 0$,

$\qquad\qquad x = 5$.

3 When $\quad x = 5, y = 5^2 - 10(5) + 5$,

$\qquad\qquad\qquad = -20$.

5 and -20 are the coordinates of the turning point. Is the point a maximum or a minimum?

$d^2y/dx^2 = 2$.

Thus when $dy/dx = 0$, $d^2y/dx^2 > 0$. The function has a minimum turning point at $x = 5$, $y = -20$.

Now let us try a more interesting example. A supplier faces a total cost function

$TC = 100x - 10x^2 + x^3$

where x is output. Find the output which minimizes average costs.

Procedure:

1 $AC = \dfrac{TC}{x}$,

$$= \frac{100x}{x} - \frac{10x^2}{x} + \frac{x^3}{x},$$

$$= 100 - 10x + x^2.$$

2 $\dfrac{dAC}{dx} = 2x - 10.$

3 Set $\dfrac{dAC}{dx} = 0,$

$$2x - 10 = 0,$$

$$x = \frac{10}{2} = 5.$$

The AC function has a turning point at $x = 5$. But before calling this output level that which minimizes costs we should make sure that the turning point is a minimum.

4 $d^2 AC/dx^2 = 2.$

Since $dAC/dx = 0$ and $d^2 AC/dx^2 > 0$, the turning point is indeed a minimum, and the output level which minimizes average costs is five units.

Points of inflection

Another use for the second derivative is the test for a point of inflection. But first let us consider a function which contains an inflectional point the test for which does not require more than the first derivative. It is interesting to consider this function first since, as we shall see, the necessary condition for the existence of its inflectional value does not distinguish this value from maxima and minima. Consider the function $y = f(x)$ illustrated in the following figure, Figure 89.

An inflectional point z exists at x-value $\bar{x}$. As can be seen, the slope of the function is zero at $\bar{x}$, i.e. x is a stationary value. How, then, can we distinguish this inflectional point from maxima and minima? In all three cases $dy/dx = 0$. But note that the slope of the function is positive before and after point z, i.e. unlike maxima and minima dy/dx does not change sign as the function passes through the point of inflection. Thus some points of inflection can be identified when $dy/dx = 0$ and is not changing sign.

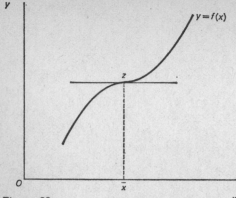

Figure 89

Example:

Test for a point of inflection in the function

$y = x^3 - 6x^2 + 12x.$

Procedure

1    $y = x^3 - 6x^2 + 12x,$

   $dy/dx = 3x^2 - 12x + 12.$

2 Set dy/dx equal to 0,

   $3x^2 - 12x + 12 = 0,$

then $x^2 - 4x + 4 = 0,$

   $(x - 2)(x - 2) = 0,$

   $x = 2.$

3 When $x = 2$, $y = 8 - 24 + 24,$

   $= 8.$

A stationary value exists at $x = 2$, $y = 8$.

4 Test the sign change in dy/dx as the function passes through $x = 2$.

252 The Calculus

(a) When $x = 1 \cdot 9$,

$$dy/dx = 3(1 \cdot 9^2) - 12(1 \cdot 9) + 12,$$
$$= 10 \cdot 83 - 22 \cdot 80 + 12,$$
$$= 0 \cdot 03.$$

When $x = 2 \cdot 1$,

(b) $$dy/dx = 3(2 \cdot 1^2) - 12(2 \cdot 1) + 12,$$
$$= 13 \cdot 23 - 25 \cdot 20 + 12,$$
$$= 0 \cdot 03.$$

Thus dy/dx is positive for both values of x and the point $(x = 2, y = 8)$ is a point of inflection.

Unfortunately, not all inflectional points are so easy to deal with. Consider now the function $y = f(x)$ which gives the graph shown in Figure 90a.

Point z in Figure 90a is a point of inflection but in this case there is no stationary value $- dy/dx \neq 0$. How, then, can we test for this sort of inflectional point? To do so we must consider the second derivative. In Figure 90b which depicts the graph of dy/dx, we can see that for x values below $\bar{x}$, dy/dx is falling and for values greater than $\bar{x}$, dy/dx is rising. This means that the dy/dx function has a stationary value at $x = \bar{x}$ and, therefore, d^2y/dx^2, the rate of change of dy/dx, is zero at $\bar{x}$.[4] Figure 90c, which depicts the graph of the second derivative, shows this clearly.

Thus the test for an inflectional point is that $d^2y/dx^2 = 0$ and is changing sign.

Example:

1 $y = x^3 - 12x^2 + 10$.

2 $dy/dx = 3x^2 - 24x$.

3 $d^2y/dx^2 = 6x - 24$,

$d^2y/dx^2 = 0$ when $x = 4$ and when $y = -118$,

when $x < 4$, $d^2y/dx^2 < 0$,

and when $x > 4$, $d^2y/dx^2 > 0$.

Therefore a point of inflection exists at $x = 4$, $y = -118$.

4. Point z is the minimum point on the graph of the first derivative.

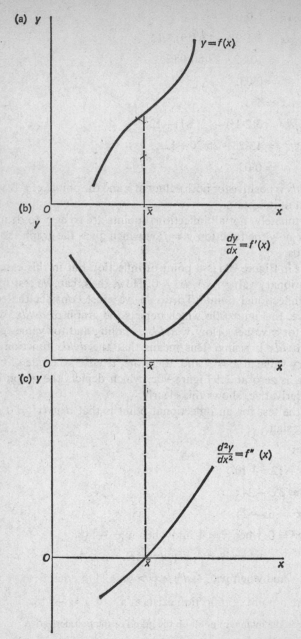

Figure 90

Questions

1 A producer faces the following total-cost function

$$TC = 150Q - 9Q^2 + \frac{3Q^3}{4}.$$

(a) What is the average-cost function?
(b) What is the marginal-cost function?
(c) What is the output level which minimizes average costs?

2 $Q = 50 + 60L - 5L^2$ is a farmer's production function showing the relationship between total output Q and number of labour units employed L.
(a) What is the average-product function?
(b) What is the marginal-product function?
(c) How many labour units should be employed to maximize total output?
(d) What is the value of average product at this level of employment?

3 Use the following total-cost function to show that marginal cost equals average cost when average cost is at minimum.

$$TC = 180 + 9q + 5q^2,$$

(TC represents total-cost and q represents output).

4 The market-demand function for commodity X is

$$P = 500 - 2Q.$$

How many units of X must be purchased to maximize total revenue?

5 Does the following total-cost function have a point of inflection?

$$TC = 80 + 6 - 4 + \frac{2Q^3}{3}.$$

Functions of several variables

So far we have confined our excursion into mathematics to problems relating only two variables, $y = f(x)$. Since many of the economic problems we have considered have concerned such a simple relationship the mathematics we have looked at so far suffices quite often.

But what of all those problems involving more than one independent variable, of the form

$$y = f(x_1, x_2, x_3, ..., x)_n.$$

What do we do in these cases? The mathematical technique involved is no more than what we have termed a 'simplifying' technique when facing such a function in economics. A good example of this is again provided by the production function.

In Chapter 3 we first introduced the concept of a production function, in the form

$$P = f(x_1, x_2, ..., x_n; T),$$

where P represents output, $x_1, ..., x_n$ are inputs, and T represents technology. Having expressed the function in this form we proceeded to analyse it by isolating the effects of only one independent variable, holding the values of the other variables constant (the infamous assumption of 'other things remaining unchanged'). This technique not only simplified the problem but also enabled us to consider the effects on production of changes in the magnitude of any single independent variable. As such the technique performed an invaluable service – an employer is often interested in the output effects of changes in his labour force, or in the amount of capital equipment used, or in the state of technology; but rarely does he need to calculate the output effects of all these changes occurring simultaneously.

The technique of isolating the effects of single independent variables has been repeated several times since we considered the production function. What, then, is the mathematical procedure involved? We have usually tried to begin the explanation of basic concepts with the aid of a graph and we can continue with this technique for three-dimensional diagrams (although they are often difficult to interpret) but when more than three variables are involved we can no longer rely on diagrams.

Consider the function $y = f(x, z)$. A diagram representing such a function is given by the 'quarter-igloo' picture below, the function being represented by the *surface* (instead of a curve) $y = f(x, z)$. The calculus, as we have seen, is concerned with the gradients of curves. If we are to contrive its use in the context of three (or more) variables we must somehow reduce the surface $y = f(x, z)$ (which is bulging out from the page) to more manageable proportions. We can do this

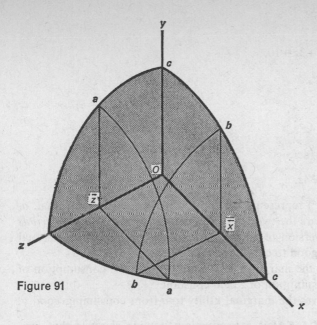

Figure 91

by measuring the gradient of 'slices' of the figure, that is, by holding
the value of one variable constant we can isolate the rate of change of
a second variable with respect to changes in the value of a third. For
example if z is held constant at $\bar{z}$, dy/dx is given by the gradient of the
curve aa (the curved edge of the slice $aa\bar{z}$); if x is held constant at $\bar{x}$,
dy/dz is given by the slope of curve bb.

The process of differentiating y with respect to x or z while holding
the value of the other variable constant is termed *partial* differentiation
and the symbol ∂ is adopted to distinguish it from the process of
differentiating the function $y = f(x)$. Thus the *partial derivative* of
y with respect to x is represented by $\partial y/\partial x$; and the partial derivative
of y with respect to z is given by $\partial y/\partial z$.

Although this new technique may appear on the surface to be
rather difficult, to find a partial derivative involves no rule that we
have not previously met. By treating the other variable(s) as
constant(s), finding $\partial y/\partial x$ is the same technique as deriving dy/dx
from $y = f(x)$. Generally, we can refer to: $y = x^n z^m$

then $\quad \partial y/\partial x = nx^{n-1} z^m$,

and $\quad \partial y/\partial z = mx^n z^{m-1}$

Functions of Several Variables 257

Examples:

1     $y = 4x^3 + 3z - 10,$

$\partial y / \partial x = 12x^2,$

$\partial y / \partial z = 3.$

2     $y = 5x^5 4z^2,$

$\partial y / \partial x = 25x^4 4z^2,$

$\partial y / \partial z = 10x^5 4z.$

3 $U^a = f(x^a, z^a)$ represents the utility function of an individual, a, where x and z are the two goods which a consumes. The two *partials* (a shorthand version of partial derivatives) represent the marginal utility of each good to consumer a.

(a) $\partial U^a / \partial x^a$ is the marginal utility of x to a as the consumption of x changes, consumption of z held constant.

(b) $\partial U^a / \partial z^a$ gives the marginal utility to a from consuming good z.

4 $P^y = f(L_a{}^y, L_b{}^y, K_a{}^y)$ is a production function showing that production, P, of good y is a function of three inputs; land, L_a, labour, L_b, and capital, K. The three partials represent the three marginal products.

(a) $\partial P^y / \partial L_a{}^y$ shows the rate of change in P^y with respect to change in $L_a{}^y$, the quantities of other inputs held constant, i.e. it gives the marginal product of land in the production of good y.

(b) $\partial P^y / \partial L_b{}^y$ gives the marginal product of labour in the production of good y.

(c) $\partial P^y / \partial K^y$ gives the marginal product of capital in producing y.

Questions

1 Mr McSmith consumes two commodities, x and y. The satisfaction (U) he gets from doing so is measured in utils and given by

$U = 10x^4 + 2y^3.$

(a) What is the marginal utility of x when five units of x are consumed?

(b) If his marginal utility from consuming y is equal to 384 utils, how many units of y has he consumed?

2 A producer employs labour, L, and capital, K, and together these factors produce a total output (Q tonnes) given by

$$Q = 20L^{1/2} \, 2K^{1/4}.$$

What is the marginal product of labour when five labour units work with a given amount of capital equipment?

3 Assuming the amount of labour to remain fixed what is the marginal product of capital function?

Some final remarks

A lot could be said on partial derivatives. For example, the astute reader will realize that higher order partials will also follow the pattern we outlined for the function $y = f(x)$. But we do not intend to pursue partials any further. Their use at this level of economic analysis is somewhat limited and our aim has been to introduce the concept rather than explore it in depth. Indeed, our treatment of partials echoes the whole tenor of this mathematical interlude. We have merely scratched the surface of the uses of mathematics in aiding the comprehension and solving of economic problems. Although we have underlined in some depth these mathematical tools which do help our analysis of basic economics, our primary aim has been to familiarize the reader with a lot of the language and some of the techniques which can be employed at a more sophisticated level of economic analysis. Perhaps we should reiterate, for the sake of those readers who like to read conclusions and summaries before they venture into the body of a chapter, that anyone reading this book in the hope of learning some basic economics, and no more, should find that the omission of this chapter leaves his comprehension of economic principles unimpaired. But for any reader using this text as a take-off to a higher level of economic analysis, this chapter should provide a useful introduction to some of the techniques he will later employ.

Part Five
The Social Institutions of Production

In the introduction to Part Two we looked at the relative merits of planning and the market as mechanisms for the allocation of resources and we put forward the tentative conclusion that we need both planning and the market in order to carry out different tasks. Which would be chosen – plan or market – would depend upon relative costs. In the intervening chapters we analysed the workings of markets. Now we return to the issue of planning, of which we can find many examples. Households are planning units: they produce children, a home, love and affection. There are also the giant corporations, such as ICI, Unilever and British Leyland, along whose corridors of power decisions are made which affect millions and in whose factories orders are issued which workers must obey or lose their jobs. Finally, there is the State which also produces what markets fail to provide and which can, through conscription, order its citizens to die so that such non-market goods as cultural heritage may be preserved.

There are in fact more planning units than markets – more firms than markets. It is the existence of these planners that we must now explain. Earlier economists sought to explain the workings of markets because for them markets were the novelty and were growing; now we look at the prior institutions whose persistence needs comment.

Chapter 14
The Social Institutions of Production

At the beginning of Part Two we drew a distinction between the plan and the market. Part Two then went on to discuss the market to the neglect of planning systems, but planning units do exist within markets and are called *firms*. We need to know why firms exist and to clarify the reasons for the choice of integration by administration, as opposed to integration by the market of various activities.

The single process

Let us begin with the single process of production whereby some resources are, by a qualitative change, converted into something desirable. Now, as we saw in Chapter 3, all processes seem to require the cooperation of at least two different factors of production – be they men and machines or men and natural resources. It is only when one factor can produce something without the cooperation of other factors of production that no problem arises. For the problem is: how can the individual contributions of factors be assessed so as to pay them rewards from the total output? There must be some method of supervision so as to measure the relative contributions of different factors and there must be some method of supervision to coordinate their activities. The market can play a part but it cannot perform the necessary supervision to ensure that factors perform their tasks with the necessary efficiency. The institutional arrangement which brings about the requisite supervision is called a *firm*. The firm is an institutional arrangement designed to cope with the collective goods problem that the existence of interdependence in the production function creates.

Consider the simple task of mending a boundary wall by two neighbours. The problem of 'how' can be handled by conferences. Whenever they hit a snag the neighbours can stop and discuss how the snag might be overcome. And since they constitute a small group they can check each other's efforts. But it is not always possible to hold conferences and in large groups supervision of each by all cannot be achieved, so there is a need to create a supervisor, a leviathan. It is the supervisor's task to monitor the work of each factor so as to determine rewards. When there is jointness in production and the rewards of factors depend upon their efficiency, then a supervision problem arises.

Contracts

There is then a supervision problem of monitoring the performances of the various factors of production. The easiest method is, of course, for someone to own all the factors of production, but slavery is forbidden and the outright purchase of other factors may be costly. So there arises a need to establish contracts to obtain the use of factors. Each resource owner is faced with a double problem:

1 Either he can hire all the resources he needs to produce a commodity *or* he can hire his resources to others;

2 Either he can pay all the resources he hires at a fixed rate *or* he can allow them an uncertain (or variable) share in an uncertain outcome. (These possibilities also confront any leasee of resources.)

The supervisor's reward

If a resource owner decides to hire other resources, then he seeks as his reward the residual – the difference between what he pays them and the value of the total product. The size of the residual will, in the first place, depend upon the vigour of his supervision and how it is implemented. In the case of labour the supervisor may need to know something about workers' motivation and the relative importance of monetary and non-monetary rewards.

The market can also help in determining supervisors' rewards. If they become abnormally large more people will set up as supervisors and rewards will decline. If some supervisors become lazy they will be eliminated because they will charge a higher price for what is produced than other supervisors. But within the limits set by the competition of others to become supervisors, there may exist a range of rewards – considerable differences in residuals.[1]

Fixed versus variable payments

The second issue is that of fixed or variable payments to resource owners by the supervisor. In a world of certainty the problem would not arise: it would make little difference whether the hirer of resources paid his factors on a fixed or variable basis. His costs would remain constant. For if he found it cheaper to pay his resources at a fixed rate then some resource owners would set up in opposition and bid up the fixed rate until it yielded the same result as the variable rate. But in the real world certainty does not exist and we find preferences for one or other form of contract. Here we consider a few examples.

1 Suppose the hirer of resources wishes to reduce the costs of supervision or finds it difficult to establish a rigorous system of supervision. Then he may attempt to transfer the costs of supervision to the owners of the resources he has hired. He may, for example, pay his workers on a piece-rate basis; that is, he may pay a fixed price for each unit they produce and nothing if they produce nothing. Such a policy is efficient if the output can be measured, its quality readily assessed and there are no breakdowns which prevent workers earning their livelihood. If none of these condition are present then the supervisor may be forced to pay workers on a time-rate basis and increase his control through the use of foremen.

2 A variation on simple piece rates and one that is tried when new processes are installed is to pay workers on a variable piece rate with the price falling per unit as output increases. The rationale for this policy is that not all the gains from improvements should go to workers, particularly those associated with learning by doing.

3 In agriculture tenancy agreements may specify who should own improvements (such as drainage schemes) installed by tenants, since landowners may claim them.

4 Situations where *all* resource owners take an uncertain share of an

1. The problem of the supervisor's reward (what is sometimes called profit) will be discussed in Chapter 17 under the heading 'normal profit' and in Chapter 18 where the inefficiency of monopolists leads to other resource owners capturing some of the residual. Profit is also discussed in Chapter 27.

uncertain outcome – profit sharing is feasible when the number of participants is small. When the group becomes large it may be difficult to police each participant's effort and problems of free riders may emerge.

Workers' control represents an extension of the principle of profit sharing to the entire economy. Difficulties can arise. What happens if a worker leaves his firm? Does he take with him his right to a share in future income? If not might workers be reluctant to allow some income to be ploughed back to increase future income? Would workers risk putting all their eggs in one basket? What about the problem that arises when different enterprises differ in their profitability? Should some of the gains be passed on to others through price reductions? These are all important issues and involve a consideration of the role of ideology in the motivation of workers in socialist countries. Furthermore, they raise the question of whether any economy can institute some basic income (a social dividend) without encountering policing problems to prevent scrounging (social dividends are discussed in Chapter 42).

Resource owners may allow some of their rewards to be ploughed back provided they can be allowed to sell their right to future income. This requires the establishment of a market in property rights (the stock market) and the effectiveness of such a market will be discussed in the next chapter. In the meantime let us note that if shareholders cannot effectively police their property rights then the appointed managers may divert the residual to their own ends. There may therefore be little difference between a property sharing socialist firm and a badly controlled capitalist firm.

Bads as well as goods. The incentive to seek to supervise resources applies to the production of bads as well as goods. People will seek to control the production of smoke, road accidents and injuries in factories.

Consumption as well as production

We have emphasized the interdependence of factors in the production process and the need for cooperation of factors, but let us not forget the interdependence of consumers in the consumption process of collective goods. Where a good can be consumed equally by all then there must be a means of policing its consumption and financing. This was briefly discussed in Chapter 2 and will be re-examined in Part Nine.

Sequential processes

To speak of a single process is an abstraction. Most firms control a sequence of operations, e.g. spinning and weaving and so on. The reasons for such integration by administration rather than integration by the market also lie in the costs of using the market – primarily the costs of time and uncertainty. Thus, it would be possible for each man on a car assembly line to sell his product to the next man down the line but it would be extremely inconvenient. Uncertainty presents a problem since it may not always be possible to ensure further supplies of resources through the market.

What limits the size of firms?

Firms can grow by expansion of a single process, i.e. increasing the scale of a single process by increasing the scale of all inputs; by horizontal integration of a number of independent, identical single processes; by vertically integrating a series of sequential processes; or by some mixture of the various methods.

Finance

The obvious limitation to the size or rate of growth of firms is finance – the resources or the command over resources necessary for growth. This is apparent in the case of one-man or family firms where abstention from immediate consumption of all current income may be dictated by the absence of an ability to borrow against future income. Financial limitations explain why the exploitation of the scientific and technological discoveries of the Renaissance and the Industrial Revolution had to await the contractual arrangement known as limited liability which allowed small savers to invest without the risk of losing their entire wealth. (The problems created by limited liability are dealt with in Chapter 18.)

The will to grow

Finance is closely linked with the will to grow, especially in family firms. Alfred Marshall, the great English economist, likened firms to the trees of the forest, some of which were striving to grow whilst others were dying. In the case of family firms he felt that the initial stimulus and drive of the founder might be lost by his children and grandchildren who would dissipate his accumulated wealth. While joint-stock companies do not die, they could stagnate through loss of leadership.

Technology

There may be limits to the size of firms set by technology but these may be rare since it is always possible to duplicate technological equipment.

The market

The market may limit the growth of a firm by limiting the demand for its product. But this might be overcome by moving into another market. Multi-product firms are, of course, common and are an important method of overcoming the risks of specialization as well as the obstacles to growth. Market growth may, however, work in the opposite direction by enabling a firm to get rid of costly processes.

Management

Coordination. Within a firm some method must be found for co-ordinating the activities of various individuals. Consider Figure 92 in which *A* controls the work of *B* and *C*. Suppose *B* wishes to communicate with *C*: does he do so directly or must all messages go via *A*? If all messages must go to *A* or via *A* then *A* may suffer from information overload – he may suffer from having too much information to digest. Information overload raises the question: how many people can one individual control? As Figure 93 shows it is possible by elaborate pyramiding for one man or board of directors to control large numbers of workers. But note that as the span of control increases the number of vertical and horizontal links increases and with each additional link there arises a communication problem.[2]

2. The problem of coordination has a great deal in common with our discussion of barter and monetary economies in Chapter 5.

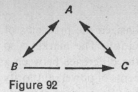
Figure 92

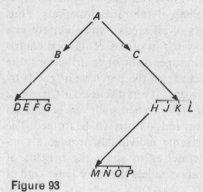
Figure 93

Communication. As the number of links in a communication channel increases so does the possibilities of loss of serial reproduction. Reproduction breaks down as in the fabled: 'Send reinforcements we are going to advance' which became 'Send three and fourpence we are going to a dance'.

Morale. Big organizations may be impersonal and suffer proportionately higher absentee rates, higher turnover rates and more strikes.

Uncertainty. Uncertainty in product markets and production processes may dictate the need for flexible management structures but these can lead to loss of control as independent decision-makers spring up all over the organization. Under conditions of certainty firms' controllers like to establish bureaucratic structures so as to ensure rational decision-making. Hence when faced with complex problems they may introduce committees as a kind of super controller. Unfortunately, committees have a habit of deliberating too long and seldom reaching conclusions. Another response is to bring in experts to whom control may be surrendered.

In our discussion of the firm we have emphasized the problems of communication, of the exchange of information. The market also exists to exchange information, so what is the difference between a firm and a market? What happens to the concepts of power, authority and status which are usually associated with people in organizations?

We begin with a bald statement. A firm is a market which emerges whenever there is failure in extremely decentralized markets. Thus market failures comprise spillovers of all kinds – the ability of one factor of production to obtain rewards in excess of its own contribution to output because there is no supervision of contributions; the ability of some consumers to benefit from the purchase of goods by others (the problem of collective goods that was discussed in Chapter 2 and will be looked at again in Part Nine). When spillovers occur then steps will be taken to eliminate them and so firms will be formed. The firm is an arrangement whereby some individuals arrange a contractual relationship between themselves to share the benefits of cooperation and exclude non-members unless they pay some kind of entrance fee.[3]

Our argument implies that the relationships between members of a firm or club are purely contractual and that there are no problems of power since power is merely an emotive word used to conceal the fact that an employer has the power to influence the behaviour of a worker, the worker having agreed to allow the employer to direct his activities in return for a share in the resulting product. In the ultimate the workman has the power to sack his employer by leaving him!

This is not what ordinary folk mean by power. What they refer to is the fact that the contractual relationships are strongly influenced by the distribution of wealth before the contract is agreed. Contracting parties may start as unequals. Thus, in Marx's analysis, workers possess only labour power and since the sources of labour power (their bodies) cannot be bought and sold because slavery is forbidden their only asset is a poor insurance against risk. Furthermore, Marx pointed out that power was a problem throughout the wider market known as capitalism because of the class structure of society which

3. Thus we can become members of the Heinz Beans Club or Firm by paying the entrance fee as indicated by the price of a tin of beans. In some cases there is a two-part fee – an initial charge and price per unit consumed.

gave possession of the means of production to one class. Within a firm power was personalized in the 'boss'; outside any firm it was depersonalized as the 'system'.

Households

Households are production and consumption units: they produce meals, a home, children, love and affection. However, households have certain peculiarities which have become accentuated in the course of economic development. The first important feature is their small size. Since Victorian times the household has become stripped down to a core or nucleus of parents and children. The tremendous emphasis upon individualism has reduced the roles of grandparents and spinster aunts that were a feature of nineteenth-century households. This individualism has been accompanied by disadvantages which make households dependent upon the environment in which they operate and often seriously dependent upon support from the State.

In market economies households acquire income from the sale of labour services which is then used to finance household activities. A characteristic of democratic societies is the prohibition on the sale of the sources of labour services: that is the buying and selling of people. Slavery is forbidden and this makes it difficult for households to finance their activities. No one, for example, can sell his children to someone else in return for their being educated or in return for the money to buy a house, a car or a Continental holiday. Planning tends therefore to be restricted to what current earnings permit, unless the household has ample non-human assets to sell.

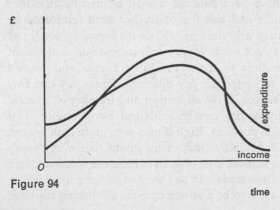

Figure 94

The typical household's life-time patterns of earnings and expenditure follow different paths as shown in Figure 94. Earnings tend to be low in the early years because of lack of skills. On the other hand, expenditures tend to be considerable – house purchase, and the maintenance of dependents such as wives and children. In the middle years earnings come to exceed expenditure as skills are acquired which lead to higher earnings, the children leave home and the house mortgage is paid off. Finally, there may be a stage in which earnings decline faster than expenditure and a second stage of low income may be encountered. Superimposed upon these trends may be major or minor dislocations caused by illness and accidents.

Within the household complex personal, social and economic changes have been taking place as a result of profound changes in society. The reduction in family size, assisted by the improvements in family planning, has reduced the amount of time spent by wives in motherhood. And the pulls and pressures on wives to seek a paid job outside the home have been helped by the emergence of labour-saving devices – the washing machine, the carpet cleaner, child nurseries, cafes and prepared foods. These forces have increased the potential lifetime earnings of wives but have, at the same time, increased tensions within the family and within society.

Two sources of tension can be detected. First, there is the problem of equal pay. Secondly, there is the problem of a wife's dependence upon her husband's earnings during motherhood. The two are not unrelated. As the length of time a woman can work in the labour market increases so does the demand for parity of pay with men. Traditionally men have been paid more than women because they were the breadwinners and this inequality has been reinforced by differences in education and training. Hence insistence on equal pay by the legislature may not work. It may only increase unemployment of women and pressures to make the jobs of men and women 'different' in order to keep their pay different. Equal pay can only work if there are changes in the education and training of women. Not all the disparity in pay can be explained by ignorance. This brings us to the second problem. Even if men earn more than women in order to maintain a family there is no doubt that many men's wages are too low to achieve that objective. Here the solution might be to increase child allowances – to pay women to bring up children. There does, in fact, seem to be a strong case for abolishing marriage tax allowances and treating married couples without children as two single people. The only case for giving marriage allowances seems to be to prevent people from falling into sin – but few believe in sin nowadays. What needs to be done is to get the property laws and tax laws into line with the changes that are taking place in the nature and behaviour of families.

Questions

1 What are the implications of the technology of the production process for the organization of production?

2 Is the Soviet Union a firm? Is Tony Jacklin a firm? Is Leeds United a firm?

3 How would you account for the fact that the spinning and weaving of wool are carried out in the same firms whereas the spinning and weaving of worsteds are usually carried out in separate firms?

4 (a) How would you account for the existence of slavery in America in the nineteenth century?
(b) What was the difference between slavery and serfdom?
(c) How would you account for the abolition of serfdom in Europe in the eighteenth and nineteenth centuries?

Chapter 15
The Corporation

Of all the institutions that modern man has devised for the production of goods and services, none has attracted as much attention as the corporation. Households seldom warrant attention except for the problem cases and the political deliberations of the state are usually considered to be a bore. But the affairs of ICI, Courtaulds, AEI or the even larger General Motors compel attention. And although they are confined in their activities to manufacturing, there are signs that their mode of operation and structure are spreading to other sectors, notably transport and services. Moreover, governments frequently call in 'corporation men' to advise on the structure and functioning of government departments. Even the planned economies seem to find much of value in the capitalist corporation and Lenin found Taylor's *Scientific Management* to be an instructive manual.

Main features

The essence of the modern corporation is its reliance for financing activities on the principle of limited liability of the owners for the debts of the firm. In other words if a man loans £100 to a corporation and the corporation incurs debts of £1 million the total liability of the individual is confined to £100 and is not extended to embrace all his assets (which may total, say, £30 000) in order to pay off the corporation debts. As a result of this principle of limited liability it is possible for large numbers of small savers to invest their accumulations in risky enterprises without endangering their livelihoods. And it is also possible for people with ideas and drive, but no money, to acquire finance. The institution which brings them together is the capital market, or, as it is more usually known, the stock market.

Though the concept of limited liability goes back to at least Roman times, it is nowadays felt to be the product of the nineteenth-century need for massive financing of scientific and industrial discoveries. There was a period in the seventeenth century of experimentation with limited liability, or joint-stock financing, but the disastrous fiascos of John Law's schemes in France and America led to its suppression. Indeed the founder of economics, Adam Smith, was opposed to the joint-stock company and many of his strictures underline contemporary criticisms and fears of corporate activity.

As a result of its method of financing, the corporation has been endowed with a legal existence distinct from its owners. The firm can own property, sue and be sued under its own name. It must appoint a board of directors, and accounts must be presented each year to a meeting of shareholders. The principle of limited liability has also given rise to several important market features of which the sheer size of corporations is important. Whether size be measured in terms of sales, number of employees or amount of money invested in the firm, many modern corporations are gigantic. The book value of ICI is over £1500 million, the turnover of IBM is larger than the national income of many states: for example Portugal.

The large size of the modern corporation has led to an emphasis upon the need for antennae which collect information from the environment and transmit it to the information-digesting organs whose efficiency must be continuously tested. The rise of business schools and business degrees reflects the problems posed by size and the quest for efficiency.

Size leads to problems between owners and operators, between shareholders and directors. Legally the shareholders are the owners but so numerous are they, so trusting and often so ignorant, that machinery has had to be created in order to protect their interests. The efficiency of the legal machinery is, however, in doubt.

A further consequence of the method of financing corporations is the increasing diversity of activity within any one firm. A firm making a single product has a much greater chance of financial disaster than a firm making products for ten different markets. Shareholders, by diversifying their holdings, can reduce this financial risk, so if managers acted purely in the interests of shareholders, they would not bother to reduce the risk of bankruptcy by diversifying their activities. As managers are, however, interested in job security, they will tend to reduce the risk of losing their jobs due to adverse market conditions, by producing for several different markets. In fact some companies are so large that the only sense in which they operate as a single company is in regard to the stock market. The company may be split up into several divisions, each of which has a large degree of independence. The only aspects of policy for which they might be subject to central control might be in raising funds and deciding on investment projects. The reason for this devolution of control is the increasing complexity of operation and the problems of central office.

Modern corporations tend in fact to become self-perpetuating entities. A company will generate cash and look around for somewhere to spend it. It may expand within its own industry combining surplus cash with the technological know-how of the management. But if its own industry has exhausted all opportunities for profitable investment, then it will expand elsewhere either by breaking into new fields or taking over other firms. As such the corporation may come to be regarded as a financial unit rather than a production unit, as a conglomerate of various productive activities.

The capital market

A necessary condition for the emergence of the corporation has been the creation of a capital market in which claims on the assets of companies can be traded. The capital market consists, in fact, of two markets – a primary market and a secondary market.

The primary market, or new-issue market as it is often called, is the market in which the finance for new companies is raised or in which existing companies can raise additional finance. A long-standing problem of the new-issue market has been the costs involved in floating a loan. There appear to be substantial economies of scale involved in finance and they are such as to preclude smaller firms from gaining access to the market. Various attempts have been made to remedy this gap in the market notably by government-supported institutions which are prepared to consider the demands of the smaller and medium-sized companies.

It is however the secondary market that tends to attract the greater attention. This is usually known as the stock market since it deals in the existing claims on companies, such claims being large in relationship to the flow of new claims in the new-issue market. The stock market gives the investor security by allowing him to market his shares at any time and thus to avoid the dangers of being illiquid.

Of course there are still risks and it may be that an investor will not get the price for his shares that he desires but it does avoid his wealth being committed indefinitely.

In theory the market prices of existing assets are dictated by the earnings of companies. This relationship is two-fold. First, companies declare dividends out of their earnings and these dividends constitute the income of the shareholders. Secondly, companies may retain some of their earnings in order to maintain or enlarge their productive capacity and the retained earnings constitute a source of wealth for the shareholders. Should the company be sold then the shareholders (strictly speaking the equity holders) would have claims on the proceeds of such a sale.

In practice share prices tend to be governed by the expected earnings of companies and this means that there is often considerable speculation as to the future fortunes of companies. The main trouble with the stock market as a device for allocating funds is the lack of information. The only information a firm is legally obliged to provide for its shareholders is an account of its financial transactions, which are historical and in many cases misleading. A firm may in fact be bankrupt, and yet its accounts give little indication of any trouble. (The form and content of the accounts is discussed in the appendix to this chapter.) Only in that past performance is a guide to what is likely to happen in the future are financial accounts of any use to a potential shareholder. Other information about the prospects for a firm comes from press reports and rumours. The signing of a large contract, the reporting of a mineral find, a strike, are all reported in the press, and influence the share price. The apparent randomness of stock-market prices is really the randomness of information. Hence guessing the rise of a particular share involves guessing what everyone else will guess.

The aims of the firm

The capital market acts not merely as a means of allocating new finance and existing claims but also as a method of control. In theory the ability of a company to raise extra finance will be governed by its expected earnings, and inefficiency will be dealt with by take-over or elimination of the existing management. All in theory. If, however, the information available to the market is meagre and if the number of shareholders, both actual and potential, is too numerous to form an efficient coalition, then the way is open for the creation of a divergence of interest between the *de jure* owners, the shareholders, and the *de facto* owners, the managers.

In recent years there has arisen a theory of the managerial enterprise which postulates that firms may often pursue goals other than profit maximization. Profits must still be attained and dividends must still be paid, but there is a minimum earnings level which, because of the weaknesses of the capital market, becomes a maximum. Indeed, firms come to insulate themselves from the capital market by relying on retained earnings for growth.

What then do the directors pursue? The answer is dependent upon the nature of executive remuneration. If directors obtain a large portion of their income from stock options then they may also wish to maximize the wealth of the shareholders. But if executive salaries depend on the sales of the firm, or its size as measured in some other way, then managers may have other goals than profit. Many writers suggest that prestige is one main goal of managers. Williamson (1964) suggested in his book that managers maximize something called 'organizational slack', which is defined as the number of employees under the control of a particular manager. This leads to empire-building. The more employees responsible to a manager, the more prestige he enjoys. Other components of organizational slack are elegant head offices, glamorous secretaries, chauffeur-driven cars. Such firms suffer periodic crises, when the number of superfluous staff becomes so large that profits are eroded. When profits have fallen to a dangerously low level, the firm fires large numbers of workers. Profits rise, and the process is repeated. Baumol (1959) put forward the theory that firms maximize sales, subject to a constraint on profits. If profits are regarded as too low, the firm tries to increase them. If profits are high enough, the firm concentrates on maximizing sales. Marris (1964) suggested that firms maximize the rate of growth of profits, subject to earning at least a minimum rate of return on capital. The point here is that a firm can allow its profits to grow too fast, if the last units of profit earned require an extra injection of capital large in relation to the extra profits generated.

Currently, there are many theories of the managerial firm, all of which await testing. If however we are to pick out any salient features then there are two: the nature of the capital market, and the nature of the market for directors. The first involves an enquiry into the information possessed by the capital market and how it is used (e.g. for take-overs). The second raises the question: are directors appointed for their ability to make money? There is, as yet, little information on the nature of either market.

Satisficing behaviour

Apart from the separation of ownership from control, we must mention other reasons why firms do not maximize profits. So far we have discussed reasons why they might not wish to maximize profits, and we now consider reasons why they cannot. To maximize profits, a firm requires information about its cost and revenue functions. Even in principle, with a multi-product firm facing joint costs, the problem is complex. Such information is only provided, after the event, in the world of perfect competition: if a firm makes a mistake, it fails to survive. In a world of monopolistic competition, the firm can make mistakes and survive. Hence it faces a problem of information which may not exist, or be expensive to obtain. It would require the information in the first place. If information is not worth obtaining, by the time we have obtained it, it is too late. Hence firms cannot even in principle, maximize profits. In principle they could plan sales and output perfectly, but they can never plan the gathering of information perfectly.

In view of the impossibility of ever maximizing anything, some economists have suggested the use of 'satisficing models' rather than maximizing models. Firms aim to obtain satisfactory levels of various quantities, rather than optimal levels. The world can never be perfect: let it merely be good. By 'satisfactory' is presumably meant levels (of profits or sales) that ensure the survival of the firm. In a world of imperfect competition, if a firm fails to maximize profits, it might never know that it is not maximizing profits. The satisfying, as opposed to maximizing, approach, leads to different models of firm behaviour. Instead of searching endlessly for the optimum, firms simply adopt rules of thumb. Rather than deliberately equating marginal cost with marginal revenue, firms base prices on average total cost. Since this quantity is easy to measure, most firms in fact use this 'cost plus' method of pricing. They somehow estimate how many units they can sell, make a guess about average total cost for this level of output, and discover whether they can make a profit with this level of output if they add a certain percentage to average total costs to obtain the price. Such methods cannot ignore the relationship between price and quantity sold. If the firm makes a mistake about how many units it can sell at a particular price, it revises the price in the light of this information. The percentage mark-up is to some extent arbitrary. A sophisticated variant of 'cost plus' pricing is 'rate of return' pricing, where the size of the mark-up is determined so as to allow the firm to achieve a certain rate of return on capital. If we require £100 of equipment to produce a good whose average total cost of production is £80, and we require a 10 per cent rate of return on capital, then it follows that we should charge £90 per unit. There is no guarantee that we can in fact sell enough units to ensure that the average total cost is £80. Unsatisfactory as these rules of thumb are, most firms use them frequently. It is only when these rules of thumb *prove* unsatisfactory that firms begin the search for new rules of thumb.

A corporate economy, a corporate world
A corporate economy

The great upsurge in technological progress and its translation into practical use, as a result of the capital market widening to permit the formation of the joint-stock company, has led Professor J. K. Galbraith to postulate the existence of a corporate as opposed to a market state. According to Galbraith there is now a very long time-lag between the emergence of a new idea and its fruition into consumer goods. Consequently careful planning has to be carried out at all stages of production and selling. This planning involves both fore-casting and coordinating activities and cannot be carried out by the market. It has to be carried out by the corporation.

In order to carry out its planning the corporation does, however, need the assistance of Government to ensure stability of the economy by providing a source of demand and by preventing inflation or recession. The corporation does attempt to manipulate consumer tastes through advertising. It is these aspects of the modern corpora-tion which give rise to fear that a corporate economy has emerged. For stability of the economy can be achieved by government spending and one of the largest components of government spending has been on defence. It is in the defence industries that the largest technological advances have been made and for whose justification it has often been asserted that there are important spillovers in the form, for example, of peaceful uses of atomic energy. It is also in the defence field that there has emerged, particularly in America, a complex association between military and industrial organizations which has, so it is alleged, threatened the political and social life of America. Such is the importance of the corporate–military complex that it dictates the pattern of independence of research and higher education. How true this is of the UK is a matter of conjecture, but it is certainly much less serious.

The importance of the corporation is confined to the manufacturing sector of the economy and there are areas where it is still not prevalent. Nevertheless, it can exercise a preponderant influence upon economic and social life. It is true that the ability of the corporation to brainwash the community has been much exaggerated and there are instances where advertising campaigns have failed; but it is perhaps in their ability to set the general tone, the prevailing sentiments of society, that corporate activities can be most pervasive.

What can be done to control the influence of the corporation? First, it might be possible to tax advertising so as to curb the excesses and it would be useful to develop and expand the knowledge consumers possess as to the technical properties of products. Secondly, in those cases where the corporation's power rests on the existence of indivisibilities (that is, lumpiness in production processes) then consideration should be given to state control and possibly ownership. Thirdly, changes in tax and company laws designed to encourage distribution of profit and greater disclosure of information to shareholders should be introduced. Fourthly, relaxation of trade barriers in order to increase competition could be considered, though its effectiveness would need to be judged in the light of the impact of the corporation upon international trade.

A corporate world

Another major feature of contemporary society has been the emergence of the multinational corporation. International companies have existed in the past and foreign investment has often taken the form, not of loans to foreigners, but of investment by firms in foreign countries. It is alleged that the scale of such investment by companies now transcends any achievements of the past and there are several reasons for this.

First there is the thesis of the 'product cycle', which attempts to link the economic factors responsible for research and development with the comparative advantage of countries. According to this theory, producers in America can, at any point in time, be expected to engage in relatively more research and development than producers elsewhere, because income levels and the size of the market are higher in America than elsewhere and so the demand for new products is likely to be greater. In the early stages of producing and distributing new goods the production plants will be located in America. Later as consideration of costs of production becomes important there is a transference of production to locations outside America. The transference of new technologies to other countries could take place by licensing arrangement if the laws governing the sale and enforcement of patent rights could always be enforced. However, since the knowledge market is not always efficient there is often a tendency for the pioneer firms to own and control production in other countries.

A second reason that has been put forward for the spread of multinational corporations, particularly American-based companies, has been the tendency of countries to use dollars as the international currency. As a result, therefore, of the willingness of foreigners to hold dollars without demanding repayment in either goods or services or other currencies, it has been alleged that Americans were in the fifties and sixties able to invest in other countries on an enormous scale. There emerged what one writer has called 'the American Challenge' (Servan-Schreiber, 1969).

To these major reasons can be added other subsidiary causes such as the desire to control sources of raw materials (notably minerals), political motives governing security and defence, and the advantages to be derived from differences in the tax laws of various countries. International investment can be advantageous to the inhabitants of a country but it can bring dangers in terms of foreign control of domestic policies. As yet the rules and institutions for the control of such companies have not been developed.

Questions

1 If a firm gives money to charities is it furthering the interests of its owners?

2 'Because of the widespread distribution of shares it is possible for a minority to effectively control a firm.' Discuss.

3 'Diffusion of share ownership permits the directors to control firms.' Discuss.

Appendix: Accounting for Information and Control

Previously, we indicated that a firm was a planning unit and represented a suspension of the market system over some area of economic activity. But whereas the (perfect) market reveals its information to all participants, a planning unit need not be so forthcoming, either to its controllers or to its would-be controllers. So there arises a need for information systems for the purposes of control and decision-making.

Private firms

Households conduct their own systems of collecting information but we shall neglect them in order to discuss the affairs of sole traders, partnerships and corporations. We are, in fact, interested in the latter since they are institutions which may be legally controlled by people who do not actively run the firms. The typical corporation appears, at least to the layman, as a black box within which decisions are made. The outcome of these decisions is the hiring of productive resources, the production and sale of goods and the receipt of payment for those goods and services (see Figure 95). This black box is owned by a group of householders and, after payments have been made to the owners of other productive resources (e.g. labour), the difference between the receipts and payments (costs) constitutes the profit or income of the owners. It is the calculation of this income which,

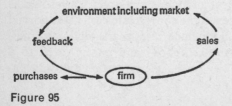

Figure 95

historically, has been the main task of the accountant. Accountants perform many tasks within the firm. As Figure 95 illustrates, a firm is an open system in the sense that, though it consists of a set of interdependent activities, these activities influence and respond to changes in its environment – be it the market or society at large. On the one hand, the accountant is involved in the decision of what to produce and how to produce – decisions concerning financial prospects of ventures and methods of financing activities. This is the field of management accounting which, because it involves subjective choice, is more closely identified with economics (in the context of this book Chapters 6, 12 and 19 are obvious sources of knowledge for accountants). The other division of accountancy is financial accountancy which is concerned with the effects of decisions. Obviously, this covers a wide field such as, for example, the effect of decisions and monitoring rules on work-force behaviour, but in this appendix we shall concentrate on the information for shareholders and 'outsiders'. The first piece of information is the balance sheet, which indicates the assets and liabilities of a firm. The second document is the profit-and-loss account, which indicates the difference between receipts and costs and how much of this difference is paid out in dividends, how much is retained in the firm, and so on. From these two documents a flow-of-funds statement can be obtained, which indicates the sources and uses of funds.

The balance sheet

The purpose of a balance sheet is to list and value the assets, liabilities and ownership structure of a firm. Assets are the property rights owned and used by the firm. Liabilities are claims on the assets of the firm by outsiders. The difference between assets and liabilities is the net assets (or equity) of the owners:

assets – liabilities = equity.

Assets are classified into current and long-term assets. Current assets are assets which a firm might expect to convert into cash in the normal course of events. These would include cash, marketable securities, stocks of finished and semi-finished goods and money owed to a firm. Long-term assets comprise land, buildings, plant and machinery. Liabilities of a firm are amounts of money it is liable to pay at some date in the future. These would include loans of any length, taxes and dividends not yet paid and goods not yet paid for.

We can now see some of the problems that confront the businessman. He has to decide on the 'mix' of fixed and current assets, and although his decision will be influenced by technology, it will also be influenced by factor prices and the businessman's view about his cash flows (receipts and payments over time). The equity of the firm refers to the rights of the owners, i.e. the shareholders. As stated above, equity is equal to assets minus liabilities: it can also be defined as how much the shareholders have subscribed in the past, by purchase of shares and retention of profit. In fact these two definitions come to the same thing. The reason for this identity is that any increase in assets not matched by a liability must be financed somehow, and it can only be financed from retained profits or issue of shares. Sometimes an increase in assets is not really financed anywhere. Suppose a firm's assets are increased because of a rise in land values: their equity as defined by assets minus liabilities increases. The increase in value is regarded by the accountant as a special kind of profit which is added to reserves on behalf of the shareholders.

The accuracy of the balance sheet

It is important to remember that the accuracy of the balance sheet depends upon certain accounting or recording conventions and the judgment of the accountant. Thus, unless an item has been purchased by the firm it will not usually appear in the balance sheet. Goodwill is not shown in the balance sheet even though it is important if a firm is considering selling a whole or part of its concern. Nor will the labour force appear in the accounts even though, as in the case of a football club, the workers may be a firm's most valuable asset. Finally we should observe that the balance sheet is a statement of stewardship and therefore records past transactions; it is not designed to show future worth nor the discounted present value of assets.

The profit-and-loss account

We have emphasized that what the owners of a firm are interested in is their profit and income. Now unless they propose to dispose of all their assets then their profit or income must be the change in equity between two periods. Indeed, income is a flow concept and is intended to measure the maximum value which the owners can consume during a period and still be as well off at the end of the period as they were at the beginning. Or putting it slightly differently, it is what the directors could distribute to the owners at the end of the financial year leaving the owner's equity the same as it was at the beginning of the financial year. Hence:

income = change in equity,
        = change in assets — change in liabilities.

The measurement of income

Most of the interesting and controversial problems of the accountant arise in the measurement of income, for let us remember that the income of the firm is the outcome of all the decisions made within the black box. Many of the problems of income measurement arise because the accountant is forced to follow certain rules laid down by the law under the Companies' Acts. Accounting income is defined as the difference between the historical costs of the net assets at the beginning and end of an accounting period (net of depreciation of fixed assets) after allowing for new capital. This definition of income differs from that given in the previous section (which was an economist's definition), in that it makes no allowance for changes in prices. Hence it is possible for a firm's profit or income to be greater or less than is warranted because there has been a failure to revalue assets at replacement prices.

Why do accountants cling to historical costs? Firstly, there are difficulties in finding an acceptable alternative. Secondly, there is the belief that historical cost is objective whereas replacement cost may be highly subjective for assets which have no obvious market price. Thus, whereas it might be possible to use indices of replacement prices for various types of machinery and equipment as prepared by the Economist Intelligence Unit there are many assets for which no such valuations exist.

There are two other features of the accountant's method of measuring income that are worth noting at this stage. First, he does not deduct from the income available to the owners an amount equivalent to what they could have earned in some other line of activity. This is important in the case of owner-managers. Secondly, and this is really another aspect of the first point, accountants do not usually deduct from accounting income (or profit) an amount equal to what the shareholders could have earned on their money in some other enterprise. Both points are of course aspects of the failure of the accountant to observe the importance of opportunity cost.

The funds-flow statement

The final statement which can be made available to the owners of a firm is the funds-flow statement which shows the sources and uses of funds. In recent years this statement has increased in importance. Historically the balance sheet was the most important statement but with the increased emphasis upon the measurement of income the profit-and-loss statement received more interest. Now with inflation and rising prices, attention has focused on the need to retain earnings in order to maintain assets intact, and this has in turn led to the need to explain what has been done with the retained earnings.

Table 31 Balance sheet with changes over the year (£000)

	1960	1961	Change over previous year	1962	Change over previous year
issued capital	594	791	+197	1205	+414
reserves	1227	1649	+422	1323	−326
capital plus reserves	1821	2440	+619	2528	+88
due bankers etc.	903	185	−718	394	+209
trade and other creditors	222	237	+15	283	+46
tax and dividend unpaid	277	251	−26	266	+15
external liabilities	1402	673	−729	943	+270
net fixed assets	500	577	+77	674	+97
stocks and work in progress	1679	1470	−209	1837	+367
debtors + cash	1044	1066	+22	960	−106
total assets	3223	3113	−110	3471	+358
net assets	1821	2440	+619	2528	+88

An example of accounting practice

In Tables 31, 32 and 33 we present the accounts of a particular firm, Hollis Brothers and ESA Limited. It is a medium-sized firm chosen at random from a set of firms whose accounts are reasonably easy to follow.

Table 32 Appropriation of income statement (£000)

	1961	1962
operating profit	407	457
less tax on current profit	168	195
less dividends	99	106
balance of profit (= internal cash flow)	140	156
of which depreciation	57	64
retained in reserves	83	92

Table 33 Sources and uses of funds statement (£000)

	1961	1962
sources: increase in balance-sheet external liabilities		
due to bankers	−718[a]	209[a]
due to trade creditors	15[a]	46[a]
tax and dividend unpaid	−26[a]	15[a]
increase in liabilities to owners:		
balance of profit (depreciation)	57	64
balance of profit (retained in reserves)	83	92
net receipts from issue of shares	538	0
total sources of funds	−51	426
uses: increase in balance-sheet assets		
value of stocks	−209[a]	367[a]
owed by debtors + cash	22[a]	−106[a]
net fixed assets + depreciation	134[a]	161[a]
(expenditure on fixed assets equals increase in fixed assets plus depreciation)		
other items:		
sundry expenditure out of revenues	0	4
total uses of funds	−53	426

[a] These items are changes in balance-sheet quantities

Table 31 presents the balance sheet. The item 'capital plus reserves' records the funds that the ordinary shareholders have contributed in the past, by retained profit and issue of shares. These 'external liabilities' record the amounts that the company owes to persons other than shareholders as well as the dividends due to shareholders. So at the end of 1960 it owed £1 821 000 to its shareholders and £1 402 000 to 'outsiders'. Hence its total liabilities were £3 223 000 which were exactly matched by its total assets of £3 223 000. Assets exactly match liabilities due to the principle of double-entry book-keeping whereby each transaction is recorded twice. Thus if a company borrows £1000 it simultaneously acquires assets and liabilities of £1000.

If external liabilities are subtracted from total assets we obtain net assets or net book value of the firm (as opposed to the market value of the firm). Net assets equal capital plus reserves. Book value may differ from market value for several reasons. First, market value will exceed book value if the firm has a monopolistic position. A monopolistic firm can obtain £1000 from its shareholders to finance a machine. Hence its net assets will rise by £1000. Its monopoly position allows it to earn extra profits, whose present value exceeds £1000. Secondly, in times of inflation the market value (i.e. resale value) of its assets may well exceed historical costs. Thirdly, if the assets of the firm suffer wear and tear to a greater degree than allowed for in depreciation, the market value of the firm may well be less than book value. The market value of the firm fluctuated during 1960 and reached £1 977 000 at its highest and £1 681 000 at its lowest. The price of its £0·25 ordinary shares fluctuated between £0·95 and £0·80. Table 32 is the Income Statement. 'Operating profit' is obtained by subtracting from profits, interest and directors' and auditors' fees. The tax refers to tax for which the firm will become liable later on. The balance of profit is split two ways; first to cover the depreciation of assets and secondly to cover retentions. Operating profit less taxes and depreciation yields the income of the shareholders. Although a portion of this profit is retained within the firm it still constitutes part of the income of the owners since it can be released and consumed by the selling of shares held.

Changes in the balance sheet plus the income statement can be used to construct a funds-flow statement. We shall do this for 1961 and 1962. Before doing so it is important to note that the firm was raising finance by the issue of shares during this period. The nominal value of shares sold in 1961 was £197 000 and this is recorded in the issued capital. The shares were in fact sold for considerably more and the surplus (£341 000) was added to reserves. In addition £83 000 profit recorded in the income statement was added to reserves. Retentions plus the surplus on the sale of shares almost match the increase in reserves. There were similar increases in reserves in 1962.

We can now discuss the funds-flow statement. The first three items refer to increases in external liabilities and these are followed by increases in liabilities to the shareholders in the form of retentions and surplus from reserves. Depreciation looks as though it ought to be a liability but is in fact a necessary means of keeping assets intact. The uses of funds represent changes in the assets of the firm and are related to the balance sheet.

Problems of communication and control

The information presented by companies to owners and hence to the capital market suffers from a number of deficiencies. The first is that the information appears at infrequent intervals, usually a year. Secondly, there is the technical nature of the language in which it is presented. Thirdly, there are the difficulties surrounding the assessment of the accountant's judgements in devising the information. Accounting information is not always objective; it can, in fact, be quite subjective. There is, for example, the difficulty of knowing at what price to value stocks.

Overriding these problems is the question of what kinds of information directors should provide? Many might like to disclose little on the grounds that to do so might invite a take-over bid, whilst what is provided relates to the past and says little about the future. One solution might be to make directors give firmer forecasts of expected earnings so as to enable shareholders to make more informed decisions.

The transition to national or social accounts

One way of looking at an economy is to see it as a set of productive institutions. We recognize some of these institutions as companies in the sense that we have just been discussing them. The other productive institutions are households and central and local government. If we wanted an account of what has been happening in the economy as a whole then it seems intuitively obvious that all we need to do is to add together (to consolidate) the accounts of all the productive institutions, companies, households and government. As the accounts of productive institutions are not drawn up with a view to national consolidation, a certain amount of rearrangement is necessary in order to facilitate this.

National income and expenditure

Economists are interested in those records that relate to the level and changes in the level of economic activity of a country; that is, the national accounts. These records constitute the best estimate of the total level of production in an economy and provide an index of the 'standard of living'.

Why should we bother ourselves about measuring the total of production, since knowing the total does not make the total greater? We will offer three justifications and then proceed with discussing the totalling.

1 A set of national accounts permits the monitoring of the economy that is necessary if one wishes to intervene and manipulate the economy in an effort to achieve policy aims. In particular, national accounts permit the comparative study of economic growth, income distribution and to some extent, welfare.

2 A study of the construction of national accounts and the underlying concepts will give a useful insight into our understanding of how economies work.

3 Some of the measures of total production developed in this chapter are used in later chapters. No measure should be used unless it is understood.

Production, income and expenditure

We will apply the useful technique of first discussing a very simple and apparently unrealistic model so that basic concepts can be easily explained. Once the basics have been discussed, further complexities will be introduced until we have a model that we can apply to the real world of the 1970s.

A first approach

Imagine a community that occupies an island. The community is economically closed, that is, no goods, services or people come to the island and none leave – as far as the community is concerned the rest of the world does not exist. Bread is the only commodity produced. The members of the community, having read the early chapters of this book, practice specialization – some grow the grain, others specialize in grinding the grain and yet others specialize in making bread. There is a fixed amount of money on the island which is used to facilitate all transactions.

Some people till the ground and grow grain. When it is harvested they sell it to the people who grind grain. Let us say they receive £100 for the grain. The income of the farmers is £100 which is their reward for their labour. They started with nothing but seeds and labour and made a product which sold for £100 – they added value of £100.

The millers pay £100 for the grain and then mill it into flour which they sell to the bakers for £250. The money the millers receive to compensate them for using their millstones and labour is £250 less the £100 they had to pay for the grain: thus their income is £150. The millers bought grain for £100 and sold the resultant flour for £250 – they have added value to the grain of £150. We note that like the farmers, the income of the millers (to compensate them for their labour and the use of their equipment) was identically and inevitably the same as the value added to the product.

The bakers spend £250 on flour and bake bread which they sell to farmers, millers and bakers for £500. The bakers' revenue from sales is £500, and their expenditure on inputs was £250 on flour. The payment to bakers to compensate them for providing labour and bakery equipment is thus £500 − £250 = £250. The value they added was also equal to £250.

Let us set out these transactions of our simple world in the form of Table 34.

The expenditure on the final product, bread, is £500. The value of production (value added) in the community is £500, the total of expenditure on the final product is £500 and the income received by productive factors is £500.

If now the community progresses to the point where they also make £1000 worth of whisky, then just like the bread sector the value of

Table 34

	Value added (£)	Income created (£)
farmers sell grain to millers for £100	100	100
millers sell flour to bakers for £250	150	150
bakers sell bread to farmers, millers and bakers for £500	250	250
total	500	500

Table 35

	Value added (£)	Income (£)
farmers sell grain to whisky makers (£200) and millers (£100)	300	300
whisky makers sell to distillers for £400	200	200
distillers sell to bottlers for £500	100	100
bottlers sell to farmers, whisky makers, distillers, bottlers, millers and bakers for £1000	500	500
millers sell flour to bakers for £250	150	150
bakers sell bread to farmers, whisky makers, distillers, bottlers, millers and bakers for £500	250	250
total	1500	1500

expenditure on whisky equals the value of the income created in the various stages of production and the total of value added.

The value of sales of the two final products, bread and whisky, is £500 and £1000. Total domestic production is £1500, the value of expenditure on final product is £1500 and the total income of productive factors is £1500. Conceptually we should get the same total for the value of production whether we total expenditure on final product, value added or the income of productive factors.

The total money changing hands is *not* the same as the value of production. In the bread–whisky example total money changing hands was £2950 = £(300 + 400 + 500 + 1000 + 250 + 500), but the value of production was £1500. When we added whisky-makers' sales to distillers (£400) and distillers' sales to bottlers (£500) we were 'double counting'. The £400 was already included in the £500 – the value added was £100 and *not* £500. In valuing total production we must avoid double counting.

A model including capital goods

Not only do we measure the total production of goods that households consume, as in the previous model, but we also include in our community production total the value of capital goods produced – the plant, machinery and tools which permit increased production of consumer goods in the future. Why include capital goods since the community gets no direct pleasure from capital goods? The answer is straightforward. The resources producing capital goods could have been producing bread, whisky and other consumer final products. The community must value the capital goods produced as highly as the consumer goods foregone or the production would not have taken place. Thus capital-goods production is part of what the community wants to produce and should be included in the production total.

In a community producing final products for consumers (bread, whisky, cars etc.) and capital goods, the value of domestic production is the total of value added during the production of consumer goods and capital goods, and is equal to the payments to productive factors,[1] which in turn is equal to the value of expenditure on consumer products plus the expenditure by firms on buying capital goods. (This latter expenditure is called the firm's gross domestic fixed capital formation – GDFCF.)

The introduction of capital goods has not altered the way in which we can calculate total domestic production by three methods:

1. The phrase 'payments to productive factors' sounds grand but rather vague – what exactly is meant? A firm buys parts and raw materials and then employs labour to work with machines and tools to convert the parts and raw materials into a product. The wages and salaries are the payments made to labour for its productive services. When the product is sold the profit belongs to the owners of the firm, the owners of the capital. The profits are the payments made to the owners of capital for the productive services rendered by that capital. Thus profits plus wages and salaries are the 'payments made to productive factors'.

Totalling value added (production);
Totalling the income of productive factors (income);
Totalling expenditure on the final product (demand).

A model including changes in stocks

We have gaily gone along implicitly assuming that everything produced would be purchased, thus ensuring the equality of value added and expenditure on final products. It is clear that goods produced in a period are available for consumption and thus the total of value added does measure the value of production. If some of the goods produced are not sold then expenditure does not equal production during the period. To ensure that we get the same answer whether we sum value added, expenditure on final product or payments to productive factors, it is normal practice to say that a rise of stocks is *inventory* investment and a constituent part of final expenditure. The extra goods in stocks are part of the production in the period and can be consumed in a later period. Expenditure on goods and services now has three constituent parts:

Consumers' expenditure;
GDFCF;
Inventory investment.

A closed economy including a government sector

If our simple closed economy organized a government then we can easily incorporate this in our analysis. The government raises revenue by taxing incomes (households' and firms') and borrowing. The money handed over in taxes and borrowing is simply a transfer of incomes. If the government spends this revenue on goods and services then this maintains total expenditure. If the government simply gives the money to the needy they have transferred income without increasing the production of any final good or service and without adding to final expenditure. All that the government has done is to reallocate income. The government buys education, health services etc. and gives them to the people. The expenditure on education and health services is equal to the value of education and health services produced, and the incomes of those paid to produce education and health services.

Transfers of income do not add to production and thus do not figure in estimates of total domestic production.

Our model now has households, firms, government and consumer and capital goods. Only one more elaboration is necessary – the opening of the economy to allow for economic transactions with other countries. Once the economy is open then our model resembles the UK or any other country.

A model of an open economy

1 In an economy whose only external transactions are imports and exports, exports constitute part of the expenditure on domestically produced goods and services and thus for expenditure to equal the value of production, the value of exported goods and services should be included in the total of final expenditure on domestic production. Expenditure equals the value of domestic production when the expenditure is on domestically produced goods and services, but part of the expenditure of government, firms and households is on imports (goods and services produced by other countries), thus the total of expenditure overstates the domestic production of goods and services by the amount of imports; so from total spending we deduct imports, to obtain expenditure on domestically produced final goods and services.

Total expenditure on domestically produced final goods and services
= consumer expenditure on final goods and services
+ government expenditure on final goods and services
+ GDFCF
+ inventory investment
+ exports of goods and services
− imports of goods and services.

2 An open economy is one which imports and exports goods and services and which sends abroad domestically earned income, and which receives income earned abroad. There are foreign-owned firms which produce in the UK and send home to the mother country some of the profits (the payments for the productive services of capital). Similarly foreign workers in the UK may send home some of their earnings. The situation is the exact reverse when UK firms and citizens abroad send to the UK all or part of their earnings.

If we add the repatriated earnings of Britons abroad to our total of payments (income) made to productive factors in the UK, and deduct from the total the repatriated earnings of foreigners in the UK we move from an estimate of *domestic* production to an estimate of *national* production. If we are interested in the level of production within the boundaries of the UK then it is estimates of domestic production that interest us.

Summary. We have shown that the value of *domestic* production can be arrived at in three ways which will all conceptually give the same answer. We can total value added at every stage in the production of final goods; we can total expenditure on domestically produced final goods; and finally we can total the incomes received by labour and the owners of capital for using their productive services to add value. The change to national production is simply achieved by adding to the domestic production total (arrived at by any of the three methods) the net foreign income from abroad (British earnings abroad repatriated *less* foreign earnings in Britain repatriated). Net foreign income from abroad is labelled 'net property income from abroad' in UK statistics.

The choice of prices used for valuation. If we estimate domestic production by adding up the value of all expenditure on final products we have valued production at market prices – we have used the actual prices that the purchaser paid. Now let us assume that in the next year all prices but one are unchanged and the quantity of final products purchased is also unchanged – the one change is that the tax on tobacco is raised, thus raising the price of tobacco products. The total of expenditure will rise simply because of the rise in the tax on tobacco. Similarly a subsidy will artificially lower the market price. To avoid the distorting effect of these expenditure taxes and subsidies and changes in them, we can deduct the total net revenue raised by these taxes from total expenditure with the result that we have expenditure valued at *factor costs*. (Net revenue from expenditure taxes = income from expenditure taxes *less* subsidies.)

If all prices this year are double those of last year then if total expenditure is double last year's we conclude that the quantity of production is unchanged. The doubling of expenditure is a mirage created by the higher prices. If each year we use the same set of prices when valuing expenditure, then we have expenditure at constant prices, and any rise in the total indicates that the quantity purchased has risen. In the succeding chapters we frequently use estimates at constant prices (those of 1963) so that quantity changes are clearly apparent.

The concepts of gross and net. When we discussed the inclusion of capital goods and stocks as part of the output of final products we observed that capital goods meant potentially higher production in the future. A point that we did not consider was that although new capital was being added some was wearing out and being thrown away. This is called capital consumption. If we add up total production without allowing for capital consumption we have estimates of *gross* production. If we deduct capital consumption from production we have *net* production available for distribution.

A summary of production measures. In Figure 96 below the following abbreviations are used:

GNP – gross national product   NDP – net domestic product
GDP – gross domestic product   MP – market prices used in valuation
NNP – net national product   FC – factor costs used in valuation.

The figure is taken from Wilfred Beckerman's very excellent introductory book on national income analysis (Beckerman, 1968).

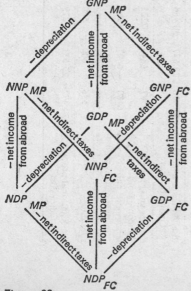

Figure 96

Table 36 Gross national product

	1961	1962	1963	1964	1965	1966	1967	1968	1969	1970	1971
expenditure											
consumers' expediture	17 835	18 923	20 130	21 516	22 891	24 247	25 422	27 245	28 849	31 216	34 504
public authorities' current expenditure on goods and services	4579	4910	5170	5498	6034	6564	7263	7718	8100	9022	10 278
gross domestic fixed capital formation	4675	4791	4994	5955	6404	6817	7379	8017	8323	9173	9923
value of physical increase in stocks and work in progress	317	53	191	642	395	264	218	214	372	371	31
total domestic expenditure at market prices	27 406	28 677	30 485	33 611	35 724	37 892	40 282	43 194	45 644	49 782	54 736
exports and property income from abroad	6587	6840	7225	7687	8311	8722	8957	10 817	12 223	13 897	15 585
less imports and property income paid abroad	−6480	−6607	−6964	−7896	−8176	−8436	−9040	−10 854	−11 553	−13 010	−14 331
less taxes on expenditure	−3627	−3879	−4027	−4437	−4962	−5585	−5968	−6906	−7833	−8426	−8697
subsidies	586	600	560	509	564	560	801	894	859	857	923
gross national product at factor cost	24 472	25 631	27 279	29 474	31 461	33 153	35 032	37 145	39 340	43 100	48 216

factor incomes

income from employment	16 407	17 306	18 195	19 717	21 291	22 786	23 706	25 340	27 037	30 235	33 491
income from self-employment	2122	2161	2220	2337	2530	2680	2840	3082	3299	3576	3941
gross trading profits of companies	3643	3595	4103	4544	4741	4446	4718	5061	4967	5161	5769
gross trading surplus of public corporations	639	745	840	924	988	1042	1132	1363	1452	1388	1441
gross trading surplus of other public enterprises	96	71	78	91	96	87	88	108	118	136	163
rent	1358	1476	1591	1727	1896	2068	2253	2466	2761	3085	3386
total domestic income before providing for depreciation and stock appreciation	24 265	25 354	27 027	29 340	31 542	33 109	34 737	37 420	39 634	43 581	48 191
less stock appreciation	−174	−147	−202	−298	−330	−313	−180	−639	−829	−975	−935
residual error	127	90	56	39	−136	−30	96	29	38	—	490
gross domestic product at factor cost	24 218	25 297	26 881	29 081	31 026	32 766	34 653	36 810	38 843	42 606	47 746
net property income from abroad	254	334	398	393	435	387	379	335	497	494	470
gross national product	24 472	25 631	27 279	29 474	31 461	33 153	35 032	37 145	39 340	43 100	48 216
less capital consumption	−2204	−2333	−2479	−2673	−2882	−3119	−3322	−3618	−3922	−4412	−5012
national income	22 268	23 298	24 800	26 801	28 579	30 034	31 710	33 527	35 418	38 688	43 204

Source: *National Income and Expenditure*, 1972, HMSO

Summary and conclusions

Gross national product and all the other measures are simply the total of a column of recorded and estimated figures. The figures included are those that we can measure and those that can be estimated reasonably accurately, thus they exclude the unpaid housework of women, home decorating and repairing etc. Within the limitations, the totals measure the value of production in a specified area during the course of one year. As the totals do not take into consideration many of the variables that add to or detract from the quality of life – beauty, peace, clean air, justice, freedom, lifeless rivers – they should not be seen as accurate measures of the standard of living or as an index of community welfare. However, a rise in gross domestic product is normally interpreted by many as indicating progress and a rise in living standards.

The demonstration of the conceptual identity of total expenditure on final products, total value added and the total income of productive factors will hopefully have added to your intuitive understanding of the anatomy of economies. Normally estimates are made using expenditure and income data only, as value added data is only available for years when there is a census of production.

The measures introduced in this chapter will be used repeatedly in subsequent chapters, ensuring at least some minimum reward for your diligence! You can test your understanding of the measures and concepts by considering Table 36. (Note that, whilst rent should not be shown separately if we follow the text of this book, it is traditional to show the payment for services rendered by land and buildings (rent) separately in the national accounts.)

Part Six
Market Structures

In this section we shall discuss the behaviour of firms in different market situations. Firms exist as we saw in Chapter 15 because of the costs of using the market; they are islands of conscious planning. But what are firms attempting to do? In a nutshell they are trying to maximize the utilities of their owners: maximizing utilities is a sufficiently broad concept to cover the activities of families, multinational corporations and the state. But sometimes it is suggested that firms attempt to maximize profits and it must be remembered that this assumption covers only a limited range of firms – it excludes, for example, hospitals and schools – and must be regarded as a proxy for utilities. Money is a universal medium of exchange and the maximization of money profits means that the owners of a firm can have a large income to spend on goods which yield them utility. Money profits can also be easily measured and monitored. Interest in profit maximizing therefore stems from the historical fact that some firms are interested in profits and profits can be measured and provide a means of measuring utilities.

Profit maximizing is, of course, subject to reservations and criticisms. In the first place it is sometimes alleged that firms cannot maximize profits. What this often means is that uncertainty makes it difficult for firms to maximize profits. A second argument is that firms do not attempt to maximize profits; that the directors of firms do not attempt to maximize the income of the owners, but pursue their own goals. This criticism draws attention to the problems of control. Because of the expansion of the capital market it is difficult for shareholders to combine to safeguard their interest. A third criticism is that profit maximization may be against the community's interest and thus draw attention to problems of monopoly.

We shall concentrate on market situations in which firms are attempting or supposed to be attempting to maximize profits. This embraces four trading situations:

Perfect competition
Pure monopoly
Oligopoly
Bilateral monopoly

In the trading situation known as perfect competition there are numerous buyers and sellers: so numerous that though each comes to the market with his own trading price, none can feel that his will be the clearing price. In pure monopoly there is only one seller and the important question is: how does the monopolist decide on his trading price. In oligopoly there are a few sellers. Will they conspire to announce a common price so that they can be regarded as a single seller? If so, how do they decide to divide the spoils?

Trading situations in which profits are the goal are common but they are not the only trading situations. Profit maximization does not appear to describe the behaviour of churches, youth clubs, charities and nationalized industries. And such organizations are involved in a considerable part of economic activity. Armchair reasoning suggests that such firms will obey the basic laws of demand and supply. When, for example, there is an increase in demand for their services they will increase their output. But how can we be sure that they are efficient? There is a difficulty once we move away from something as easily measurable as money profits. And because measurement is difficult, control is difficult. In this section of the book we emphasize the difficulties of defining the goals of nationalized industries and hence the difficulties of controlling them, but it is easy to multiply the list of difficult cases – universities, schools, hospitals, etc. A task that economists have not yet successfully solved is how to devise practical measuring rods of the utilities flowing from such firms – particularly when so many appear to be in monopoly situations.

Chapter 16
Organizational Behaviour

Our reply to the question 'why firms?' was centred upon reasons for the suppression of the market. Similar reasoning prevails when we discuss the question '*how* do firms behave?' Sometimes market suppression may extend to the control of households by one huge firm, the state, dictating how much of a commodity must be consumed and at what price. The costs of such an exercise are usually prohibitive and the most that any firm can expect to achieve is control of the price of its product, leaving the amounts purchased at various prices to be determined by consumer preferences.

Markets, as the section introduction suggested, can take various forms and the behaviour of firms within the varying market structures makes a fascinating study. However, before we embark upon it we must first note some of the more general responses of firms to their environment, whatever its nature. This is the aim of this short chapter.

The firm's objective

Our first task is to decide upon a common motivation for the firms we are to discuss. If we are to make a comparative analysis of firms' market responses then we must assume that they all pursue the same objective. As we saw in Chapter 15 firms may pursue several objectives depending on the desires of the decision-making unit. Fortunately there is one particular objective which most firms pursue although sometimes in a modified form. This common aim is the maximization of the firm's *net worth*, often referred to as 'profit maximization'.

Net worth

Let us now attempt to define the firm's objective more rigorously. At any point in time a firm holds many things of value, termed *assets*, which enable the firm to produce and sell its commodity. However, although the firm may be in possession of these things it does not necessarily own them all. Some of the things are owned by outsiders (individuals and institutions), having been leased to the firm or sold to it on credit, and these things are termed *liabilities*. Thus, the true value of the firm at any one time is the difference between the values of these two sets of things – the difference between the value of assets and the value of liabilities. The difference is the firm's net worth. A shorthand definition is given by identity 1 set out below, where W represents net worth; V^A represents the value of total assets; and V^L represents the value of total liabilities.

$$W \equiv V^A - V^L. \qquad\qquad 1$$

The accountant's breakdown of the composition of W is given in the firm's balance sheet. Remember from Chapter 15 that the accountant measures costs objectively so that the *true* measure of net worth, which is subjective, is not given by the balance sheet.

It is essential to realize that net worth is a *stock* concept – it relates to the true value of an enterprise at *only one point in time*. Whether or not net worth differs at a future point in time depends upon the activities of the firm in the intervening period. During this interval additions to, or subtractions from, the original net worth will determine the future value of net worth. Thus we can now refine our identity into the form of 2 below, where W_t represents net worth at time point t; W_{t-1} represents net worth at time point $t-1$ (i.e. the previous date at which net worth was calculated); and ΔW represents additions to, or subtractions from, net worth between $t-1$ and t.

$$W_t \equiv W_{t-1} + \Delta W, \qquad\qquad 2$$
$$\Delta W \equiv W_t - W_{t-1}.$$

Note that ΔW is a *flow* concept; it represents the flow of net returns to the firm from its original net worth stock. Clearly then, maximization of net worth also requires maximization of net returns between any two points in time. Consider the firm at time point $t-1$ with a given net worth stock of W_{t-1}. Its future plans are now geared to making W_t as large as possible, an objective which can only be realized by making ΔW as large as possible.

Profit as a residual

Before continuing to refine the firm's objective, let us take a closer look at the composition of ΔW. As the firm's net income, or surplus, for a given period, it represents the difference between the value of output for the period and the value of relevant inputs for the period. The alternative term for net income in the present context is the more often employed one of *profit*. Information regarding the firm's performance between two points in time would be given in the profit-and-loss account or 'income statement', but remember that this statement does not measure *true* present values (see Chapter 6). The disadvantage of using the term 'profit' instead of, say, 'net income' is that it does not readily convey the generality of the concept. We have tried to minimize the differences between the various social institutions of production and have acknowledged that the same rules govern the economic activities of them all. Thus a household is a firm and changing the label reflects other institutional arrangements within society rather than any significant differences in economic behaviour. 'Net income' is the better term to maintain this general applicability of economic concepts and it is difficult for those un-familiar with economics to imagine households aiming to maximize something labelled 'profit'. Yet we have adopted this term since most readers are familiar with it and with its relevance to something called a 'firm'.

We must note that 'profit' has not always meant the same thing in economic literature and we shall later devote a small chapter (Chapter 26) to the concept. In the meantime let us remember that *our* use of the term is to describe the net income[1] flow which can be enjoyed, for a given period, by *any* social institution of production. The precise definition will be easier recalled if we continue that habit of using shorthand expressions. In identity 3, then, P represents profit for the given period; R represents total revenue from all goods sold during the period; and C represents the total costs of producing all goods sold during the period.

$$P \equiv R - C. \qquad\qquad 3$$

1. Or, even more generally, 'net benefit', to remind us of the seemingly varied objectives previously referred to. All of these objectives can be collapsed into that of maximizing the utility of the firm's decision-maker(s), this utility being a function of many different things – money profit, sales, prestige, etc.

Present values

Finally, we note that the plans formulated for net-worth maximization are based upon *expected* costs and revenues. It is this fact, above all others, which emphasizes the subjective nature of net worth. Since decisions are made now, but costs and revenues are expected in the future, the latter flows must be discounted to obtain their *present values*. We can, therefore, even further refine the firm's motivation to that of maximizing the present value of future profits. Referring again to identity 2 the objective of the firm at time point W_{t-1} is to maximize the present value of W_t, i.e. to maximize the value of

W_{t-1} plus the present value of ΔW.

The object of the firm is to maximize its net present worth and this involves discounting future revenues and costs.

Long run and short run

At any time the firm's net worth is given, determined by past events; only future events can be influenced. Thus, for the most part, our study of the firm concerns its market plans. As we saw in Chapter 8, we can distinguish two planning periods – the short-run and the long-run. There is a third production period, the immediate, but this is not really a planning period. Rather, it is a point in time at which all the firm's data, including its net-worth value, is fixed. The short and long-run, however, do refer to planning periods in so far as the firm plans for efficient output operations and estimates the resultant present values of costs and revenues. For the short run, the period during which it is only possible to vary the amounts employed of a few productive resources (labour, raw materials, short-term loans, etc.), present value estimates can be made with some degree of confidence and success rates in achieving short-run targets may be quite high. But the amount of information on which long-run plans are based is necessarily scanty and consequently the planning exercise becomes much more hazardous.

Making the best of any circumstances

It should be made clear that any maximizing principle will be adhered to in both good times and bad times, in other words, the firm always aims to do the best it can in the circumstances. Thus in bad times, when costs outweigh revenues, the firm attempts to *minimize* its losses. In discounting terms we can say that the firm's objective is to maximize any *positive* present value of profit and to minimize any *negative* present value of profit. In some sets of circumstances the price–output choice which achieves the firm's objective will be a relatively simple one: there will be only one combination which guarantees maximum profit or minimum losses. In other circumstances the right price–output strategy may not be so clear-cut, facing the firm with a *range* of possibilities and a strong element of chance enters the decision-making process.

The golden rule

By 'circumstances' we refer to the type of market in which the firm sells its output; the conditions within that market at the time the firm plans its production and sales programmes; and the prevailing conditions at the time those plans are executed. Generally, as suggested earlier, one would expect any firm to achieve a higher success rate in attempting short-run targets than long-run ones but even the short run is subject to some uncertainty and circumstances may change from day to day. Is there, then, a rule, a guideline, for the firm to follow in order to ensure that it will always be doing the best it can in the circumstances? If such a rule exists then it must in some way combine both the revenue and costs side of the output problem since both sides together determine the firm's net income. Costs, we have seen, refer to foregone benefits. Revenue is determined by the nature of the demand curve for the firm's product since this determines how much the firm can sell and at what price. The nature of the demand curve is, in turn, determined by the characteristics of the market in which the firm sells its product and the position of the firm relative to that of the other firms selling in that market. Such considerations are the subject-matter of the following chapters.

A rule such as that suggested above does exist and it defines a precise relationship between costs and revenues to satisfy the objective. The rule is that the firm should always equate marginal cost with marginal revenue. We know well by now that *marginal cost* is the cost of an additional unit of output and *marginal revenue* is the in-

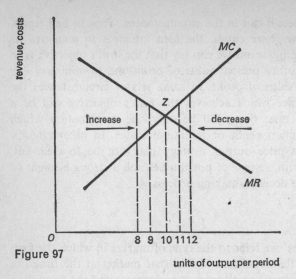

Figure 97

units of output per period

crease in revenue from an additional unit of output sold.[2] By adjusting output to equate these two marginal-values the firm will always ensure maximum income or minimum losses, depending on circumstances. Figure 97 should make this clear. MC represents the firm's marginal-cost curve and MR the firm's marginal-revenue curve. Now, assume the firm is currently producing eight units of output. If a ninth unit were to be produced the revenue the firm would receive from the sale of that unit would be greater than the cost of producing it. It is, therefore, in the firm's interest to produce the ninth unit. This is true, in fact, for any output level below ten units. However, if the firm is currently producing say eleven or twelve units then it is in the firm's interest to contract output by at least one unit. The resulting reduction in cost will outweigh the resulting loss in revenue. Only when ten units are produced (when $MC = MR$) should the firm maintain a constant rate of output. This reasoning holds even when the firm is making a loss since the size of the loss will then be minimized.

In Figure 97 only the upward sloping part of the marginal-cost curve was drawn because the maximizing rule only applies to output levels in the range referred to by this section of the curve. To be

2. For the sake of emphasizing the relevance of this rule to *all* social institutions of production the marginal-revenue curve may be interpreted as a curve of *marginal benefits*.

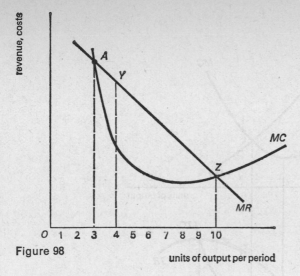

Figure 98

units of output per period

more precise, equating marginal cost and marginal revenue only maximizes the firm's profit flow if the marginal-cost curve is cutting the marginal-revenue curve from *below*. If production is maintained at a level at which the marginal-cost curve cuts the marginal-revenue curve from *above* the firm's profit flow is not being maximized since a unit increase in output will add more to revenue than costs. Figure 98 illustrates this point.

As can be seen from the diagram, for the firm to maintain output at a level of three units, where marginal cost equals marginal revenue when the former is falling (point *A*), is for it to forego the income which would be generated by the sale of the next seven units of output. Each additional unit from the fourth to the tenth adds more to revenue than it does to costs. Income is only being maximized when ten units are being produced, where marginal cost equals marginal revenue and the former is rising (point *Z* is also the point of inter-section in Figure 97). When the firm has reached this output level we say that it is in *equilibrium*; it cannot do any better in the existing circumstances.

Using total functions. Sometimes it is useful to represent equilibrium of the firm by the use of *total*-revenue and *total*-cost curves. Figure 99b presents such a situation and it includes a curve of total profits. The corresponding marginal curves are traced out in 99a.

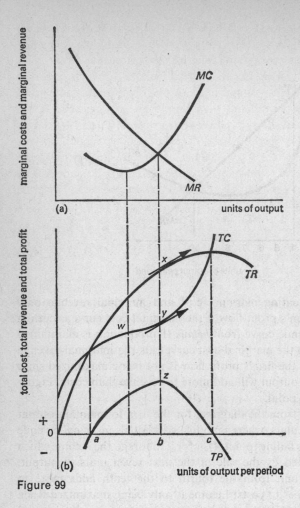

(a) — marginal costs and marginal revenue — units of output

(b) — total cost, total revenue and total profit — units of output per period

Figure 99

In Figure 99b *TC* is our familiar total-cost curve. *TR* is a total-revenue curve and we know by now that its slope measures marginal revenue.[3] *TP* is a total-profit curve derived as the locus of all the vertical distances (positive and negative) between the total-cost and total-revenue curves. Thus, when output is less than *Oa*, and total

3. Note that since the slope of *TR* flattens as output increases, marginal revenue is falling; and that since the slope of *TC* decreases up to point *W* and then increases, marginal costs are falling prior to the output level given by *W* and afterwards they rise.

revenue is less than total cost, total profit is negative (the *TP* curve falls below the horizontal axis). Total profit is again negative when intended output exceeds *c* units; and in between output levels *a* and *c* total profit is positive. It can be seen from the *TP* function that profit is greatest at output level *b*. At this level of output total profit is *bz*, equal to the greatest vertical distance, *xy*, between the *TR* and *TC* curves. It can also be seen that at this level of output *the slopes of the TR and TC curves are equal* – the curves are parallel at points *x* and *y*. In other words, at output level *b* marginal cost (given by the slope of *TC*) is equal to marginal revenue (given by the slope of *TR*) – *b* satisfies the golden rule. (Those readers who persevered with the 'mathematical interlude' should now turn to the appendix to the present chapter.)

When to shut down

In the analysis so far it has been suggested that by following the maximizing rule the firm's profit would be as great as possible under favourable market circumstances *or* the firm's losses would be as small as possible when the market situation is not favourable. This latter observation begs the question of why a profit-maximizing enterprise is prepared to remain in the industry when it is making a loss, albeit one which is being minimized? The firm's owners will only choose to keep their assets in their current use if the return from doing so is at least as great as could be obtained in their best alternative use. This necessary return is sometimes referred to as 'normal profit', a somewhat misleading term since it refers to one of the firm's costs. (Chapter 26 discusses the concept in more detail.) If the firm's owners are not currently receiving this minimum and yet their assets stay put, this must mean that future circumstances are expected to be so favourable as to render net returns over the long run at least as large as could be earned elsewhere. The firm may expect either a shift in market demand and hence a rise in market price, or a fall in costs of production; either of these two changes would reduce losses and possibly turn them into a surplus. Such optimism may be quite blind or it may be founded in the firm's ability to change market circumstances. Depending on the nature of the market, some firms may be able to influence the price at which their product sells, others may have no choice but to accept a market-determined price over which they, as individual enterprises, have no control. Similarly with respect to inputs, some firms may be able to influence the prices at which they buy their productive agents while others must accept such prices as given. This important concept of market power is the basis of the following two chapters.

Even when the future is viewed optimistically a firm is only able to ride a short-run loss if the condition is met that running (variable) costs are being covered. Since fixed costs must be met even if the firm shuts down, it is in the firm's interest to continue production as long as it is covering such items as wages and raw-material bills. Indeed, shutting down itself involves costs which may prevent the firm ever recommencing operations. Not only does shutting down require the employment of security patrols or alternative protective measures for idle plant, it may also mean other substantial opportunity costs such as foregone good-will, and loss of a market foothold as consumers switch to available substitutes. We are now prepared for a discussion of the response of firm to specific market situations. Before doing so let us remind ourselves of some of the general points made in this chapter.

Summary

1 We are assuming that over the long run firms attempt to maximize their *net worth*.

2 Net worth is a *stock* concept since it relates to a point in time. (Remember that the balance sheets of firms do not measure net worth, and that net worth must somehow be gleaned from the directors' statements about the future as well as past performances – see Chapter 15.)

3 The change in net worth between two points is determined by the amount of net revenue or profit earned by the firm during the interval. Thus, profit is a *flow* concept and is defined as the difference between the expected total revenue from the goods sold during the period and the expected total costs of producing all goods sold during the period.

4 It follows from the first three points that over the short run firms try to maximize their profit flows in present value terms (but remember that the income statements of firms do not measure these as such).

5 Maximizing profits is synonymous with minimizing losses when the market situation is not conducive to gains being made.

6 The profit-maximizing (loss-minimizing) guideline is *marginal revenue = marginal cost*. Output should not increase, in any given set of circumstances, beyond the level at which this equality is satisfied on the upward sloping section of the marginal-cost curve. When the firm is satisfying this conditon it is in short-run equilibrium.

7 Firms may be prepared to maintain production in the face of short-run losses as long as expectations are optimistic and variable costs are being covered.

8 The short-run decision concerns price whereas the long-run decision involves investment. Short and long run are linked by expectations which determine whether or not net present value is positive.

Questions

1 A University exists to promote teaching and research. How would you assess the efficiency of a University? Are teaching and research substitutes or complements? Can the golden rule be applied to these objectives?

2 How will a multi-plant firm or a multi-product firm ensure the efficiency of its different activities?

3 A newspaper produces 'news' and 'adverts'. What factors will determine the mix of 'news' and 'adverts'?

4 A firm donates annually to various charities. Is this compatible with the golden rule?

5 Can the golden rule be applied to the activities of the following:
(a) A hospital?
(b) A police station?

6 What is meant by net worth?

7 What are stocks and flows?

8(a) How will a businessman decide whether to work his plant on one or two shifts?
(b) When will a town and regional planner decide to build a new town instead of expanding an existing one?
(c) What factors determine the number of teams in the Football League?

(d) A group of firms decide to form a cartel. What factors will determine which plants are closed down or their output reduced or expanded?

Appendix: the calculus of the golden rule

Using the calculus we can now calculate, for given total-cost and total-revenue functions, the profit-maximizing level of output. We can employ one of two methods of calculation.

Method 1

Consider Figure 99 of this chapter. When profit is maximized the slope of the TP curve is zero, i.e. the first derivative of the total-profit function is zero. This fact enables us to find the profit-maximizing output level.

Procedure. Suppose we have the following total-revenue R and total-cost C functions:

$R = 300Q - 6Q^2$,
$C = 400 + 3Q^2 + 30Q$,

then total profit P is given by

$P = R - C$,
  $= (300Q - 6Q^2) - (400 + 3Q^2 + 30Q)$,
  $= 270Q - 9Q^2 - 400$.

Profit is maximized when $dP/dQ = 0$, (and when $d^2P/dQ^2 < 0$), i.e.

$d/dQ(270Q - 9Q^2 - 400) = 0$,
which gives $270 - 18Q = 0$,
  or $18Q = 270$.
  Thus $Q = 15$.

The profit-maximizing level of output is fifteen units. (Check that the second derivative is negative.)

Method 2

Profits are maximized when marginal revenue is equal to marginal cost and when the marginal-cost curve cuts the marginal-revenue curve from below, i.e. when the second derivative of the total-cost function is positive.

Procedure. Marginal revenue is given by dR/dQ and marginal cost by dC/dQ.

$$\frac{dR}{dQ} = 300 - 12Q,$$

and $\dfrac{dC}{dQ} = 6Q + 30.$

1 Let $\qquad \dfrac{dR}{dQ} = \dfrac{dC}{dQ},$

then $\quad 300 - 12Q = 6Q + 30,$
$$18Q = 270,$$
$$\text{and} \quad Q = 15.$$

2 $\dfrac{d^2R}{dQ^2} = -12,$

$\dfrac{d^2C}{dQ^2} = 6.$

Marginal cost equals marginal revenue when output is 15. Confirmation that this output maximizes profit is given by the fact that the second derivative of the total-revenue function is negative while the second derivative of the total-cost function is positive.

Perhaps as a final reminder we should work backwards through our example. What we have shown is that when output is fifteen units, profits are maximized since the first derivative of the total-profit function is then zero. Furthermore at this level of output marginal cost is equal to marginal revenue (and marginal costs are rising), i.e. when the first derivative of the total-profit function is zero, marginal cost equals marginal revenue. To summarize, we can present the rule in more general form:

$$P \equiv R - C,$$

where P represents profit; R represents total revenue; and C represents total costs. Using Q to denote quantity, $R = R(Q)$ and $C = C(Q)$, therefore $P = P(Q)$. When profit is maximized (the profit function is at a maximum) the first derivative of the profit function is zero and the second derivative is negative.

$$\frac{dP}{dQ} = 0, \left(\frac{d^2P}{dQ^2} < 0\right),$$

$$P = R - C,$$

$$\frac{dP}{dQ} = \frac{dR}{dQ} - \frac{dC}{dQ},$$

and when $\dfrac{dP}{dQ} = 0,$

$$\frac{dR}{dQ} = \frac{dC}{dQ},$$

i.e. marginal revenue equals marginal cost.

Chapter 17
Perfect Competition

We begin our survey of the structures of markets in which private goods and services are sold by considering *perfect competition*. There are two good reasons for commencing with this model. Firstly, the study of perfect competition provides the best possible synthesis of basic economic concepts. Secondly, this model epitomizes the idea of a free market, to which we have referred on several occasions, by considering a host of apparently complex economic relationships, stripping them of their irrelevancies and revealing their underlying, clockwork simplicity.

Not only does the perfectly competitive model make positive predictions but it also has enormous normative implications. The normative aspects of perfect competition were uppermost in the minds of the early writers on economics. For economic philosophers like Adam Smith, the destruction of monopoly privileges and the enlargement of the sphere of market competition was the means towards greater personal liberty as well as increased efficiency. Such considerations are just as important for the latter half of the twentieth century. Political freedom is dependent upon economic freedom and many economists are emphatic in their definition of which economic system best maximizes political freedom – competitive capitalism.[1]

But of all concepts, freedom is the most relative and it can only be defined according to the confines of personal experience. By 'economic freedom' economists usually refer to freedom to buy and sell goods and services. Absolute economic freedom prevails when any individual may buy (and sell) what he wants, where he wants and when he wants. To many this does not spell freedom but misery – many goods are socially harmful and how do those with nothing to sell survive? The normative debate hinges on such issues and concerns

1. A most cleverly argued exposition of this viewpoint is presented by Professor Milton Friedman of the University of Chicago (Friedman, 1962).

the 'proper' role of the State. We intend to consider this debate later but first we must study in some depth that theoretical state of the world which is the nearest thing devised by economists to the conditions for absolute economic freedom.

The assumptions of perfect competition

1 Producers aim to maximize their profits (as explained in the previous chapter) and consumers are interested in maximizing their utility.

2 There are a large number of actual and *potential* buyers and sellers.

3 All actual and potential buyers and sellers have perfect knowledge of all existing opportunities to buy and sell.

4 Although tastes differ, buyers are generally indifferent among all units of the commodity offered for sale, i.e. they view all units of the product as homogeneous.

5 Factors of production are perfectly mobile.

6 Productive processes are perfectly divisible, that is, constant returns to scale prevail.

7 Only pure private goods are bought and sold.

Having previously discussed the implications of maximizing behaviour we commence our analysis of these assumptions by considering the second one.

Equal distribution of market power

Our second assumption implies that the number of actual and potential sellers is so large that it has a twofold effect. Firstly, neither the output of any existing seller, nor the potential output of any individual seller outside the market is great enough, relative to industry output, to affect the market price of the product. Secondly, collusive agreements among existing sellers, buyers, or between both sides of the market, to exert an influence over price, are precluded by the massive costs of seeking out traders of a like mind and of policing any agreement once arrived at. We might also note that the existence of a large number of potential entrants, albeit an uncoordinated mass, substantiates the first effect by even further precluding collusion among existing firms. This latter point is explained in the next paragraph.

The attraction for new entrants

Part of the rationale behind the collusive checks also relates to our first assumption. Temporarily disregarding transaction costs, suppose the hundred or so producers in the sugarplum industry come to an agreement to restrict output in order to raise the price of sugar plums and hence raise their incomes. On our reasoning the industry would be swamped by hundreds of new producers entering the industry, *attracted by higher rewards than they could earn elsewhere*. The existing collusive arrangements would collapse as the price of sugar plums fell.

Why entrance is easy

New firms are able to enter the industry so easily because there are no barriers to prevent them. This demonstrates the importance of assumptions 5 and 6. The fifth assumption refers to the absence of restrictions on the mobility of any productive agent and is self-explanatory.[2] Assumption 6 is equally important regarding entry to the industry but perhaps requires further explanation. It is often the case that engineering technology or merely the confines of space necessitates the use of 'lumpy' inputs. For example transport systems require the construction of roads, railways and bridges. Such objects cannot be provided in little pieces, yet to provide more than one railway between London and Glasgow, or more than one bridge across the Humber estuary, may result in all of them running at a loss. Similarly, if cinemas can only be built in 200-seat sizes but there are 201 regular cinema-goers (at any price) in the locality then either two cinemas must be operated at well below their capacity, or there will always be at least one disappointed cinema-goer. In such situations, then, competition may be impossible and the product can only be provided under conditions of monopoly. We return to these questions in the following chapter and in our later discussion on the state.

2. Note for readers who do not find this obvious: restrictions could range from family or neighbourhood ties, or loss of pension rights, in the case of workers, to the existence of patent or licensing laws in the case of innovations.

When to enter

Not only can new firms easily enter the perfectly competitive market but our third assumption ensures that they always know exactly when the time is ripe for doing so. Perfect knowledge means that potential entrants know immediately of a change in market circumstances which will yield them better rewards than can be earned elsewhere.

A homogeneous product

The assumptions so far discussed also rule out collusive arrangements on the buyers' side of the market and the possibility of any concessionary price agreements between buyers and sellers. The assumption of perfect knowledge plays an extra role by linking up with assumption 4 to help further define the nature of the market. This makes reference to the tastes of consumers who regard all units of the industry's product as identical. Since we are also assuming perfect knowledge on both sides of the market all firms know their consumers' tastes and if one firm decides to produce a product slightly different to that of the other firms it can only be for a different market. In other words, product differentiation results in the market splitting up into several different competitive markets. A competitive market is therefore circumscribed by a gap in the chain of product substitutability.

The absence of spillovers

The final assumption is designed to rule out spillovers. No one receives extra benefits or suffers nuisances unless he purchases them. If Smith can benefit from Jones' possession of a radio and Jones can similarly benefit if Smith owns one then each will hope that the other buys a radio and refrain from purchasing one himself – neither enjoys the benefits of a radio. Spillovers may also create nuisances. These are equally ruled out by assumption 7. Factories cannot dump smoke on people unless they pay the latter for the privilege of doing so, or unless there are people of perverse tastes who want to purchase smoke.

The firm's short-run decision

The perfectly competitive firm is often referred to as a *price-taker/quantity adjuster*. The firm's course of action is dictated by forces outside its control, i.e. by the industry. It is industry supply matched against market demand which determines the price at which the individual firm can sell its output. Each firm must accept the market price as something given and unchangeable by individual action – the market is the 'price-maker'; each firm is a 'price-taker'. This means that although the market-demand curve slopes downwards (for reasons outlined in Chapter 7) the demand curve which faces the individual firm is horizontal, i.e. perfectly elastic. Since there is only one price which clears the market and every buyer (and seller) knows it, the firm can sell all it wants to at that price. If the firm charges a higher price, then no one buys its product: and what is the point of charging a price below that which is offered? Assuming the firm decides to produce, the only remaining decision is how much to produce in order to maximize profit. Given the circumstances of perfect competition this is very much a production engineering problem. The output decision is demonstrated by Figures 100a and 100b. For purposes of exposition the diagrams for firm and market have been laid side by side, but remember that the scale along the horizontal axis differs greatly in each case.

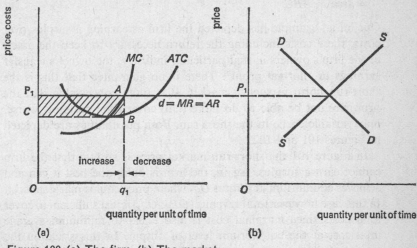

Figure 100 (a) The firm. (b) The market

The diagram shows the link between firm and industry and re-emphasizes the absence of a marketing problem. Market equilibrium is established at a price of OP_1 per unit of output. Remember that the firm can sell all it wants to at this price, as shown by the perfectly elastic demand curve d. As we saw in Chapter 7 this curve is also the firm's marginal-revenue curve since each additional unit sold yields the same revenue (i.e. the market price) as all previous units. Thus, given price OP_1 the firm produces and sells q_1 units of the product thereby equating price (marginal revenue) with marginal cost. As we saw in the previous chapter, Oq_1 is the short-run equilibrium output since even a very small change in the number of units produced and sold would prevent the firm from maximizing profit. The actual size of the profit generated by the sale of output Oq_1 is shown by the shaded area $P_1 ABC$ in Figure 100a. If this is not obvious recall identity **3** of the previous chapter:

$$P \equiv R - C.$$

In the example of Figure 100a total revenue R is equal to $OP_1 Oq_1$ (units sold multiplied by market price per unit); and C, total cost, is equal to $OC . Oq_1$ (units sold multiplied by average total costs of producing these units). Thus we may write

$$P = OP_1 . Oq_1 - OC . Oq_1,$$
$$= \text{area } P_1 ABC.$$

Our initial example has depicted the firm as earning a surplus over costs, these costs including the return necessary to keep the assets of the firm's owners in that particular industry; the owner's transfer earnings or 'normal profit'. There is no guarantee that this is the short-run norm in such a market. It is quite conceivable that the firm may not be able to do more than cover total costs or, worse, only variable costs, in the short run. Both possibilities are depicted in Figures 101 and 102.

In Figure 101 the short-run market price is so low that the firm cannot earn a surplus. Again, the firm is doing the best it can and achieves equilibrium at output Oq_2 where price equals marginal cost. In this case however total revenue ($OP_2 . Oq_2$) is just sufficient to cover total costs since marginal cost is also equal to minimum average total cost at the equilibrium level of output. In this situation the owners of the firm receive no surplus above the amount they require to induce them to stay in the industry. In Figure 102a the firm cannot cover total costs but *is* covering variable costs. Again the firm does the best it can which in the circumstances means minimizing losses to the size of the area P_3ABC.

Remember that the covering of variable costs induces the firm to remain in production but it will only remain in the industry when expectations of future circumstances are optimistic (see previous chapter). As the careful wording of assumption 3 suggests, we do not sup-

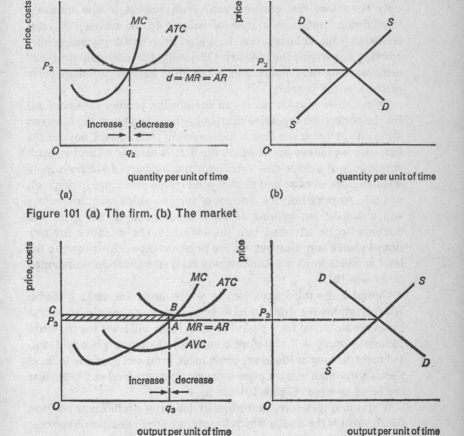

Figure 101 (a) The firm. (b) The market

Figure 102 (a) The firm. (b) The market

pose firms to possess perfect knowledge of *long-run* opportunities. From our earlier discussion of time and uncertainty (Chapter 5) the peculiar consequences of such an assumption should be clear. It is now time we took a closer look at the long run.

Long-run equilibrium of the firm and the industry

While it is possible to distinguish between short-run and long-run equilibrium for the individual firm, equilibrium of the industry can only be a long-run phenomenon. With respect to the industry, 'equilibrium' refers to a state of balance in the number of firms comprising the industry, that is, a state in which firms are neither entering nor leaving the industry. Obviously, the individual firm only achieves long-run equilibrium when this state is simultaneously reached by the industry.

Of the three possible short-run equilibrium positions we depicted for the perfectly competitive firm, only one is tenable in the long run – the one in which the firm is just covering total costs. Consider the first case we looked at, in which the firm is earning a surplus. Such surpluses will attract new firms into the industry. Industry supply will therefore increase and market price (given no change in demand) will fall. As price falls the amount of surplus which each firm enjoys will diminish; but as long as some profit remains new firms will continue to be attracted into the industry. The incentive for new firms to enter only disappears when price has been driven down to the level at which firms are just covering costs (the situation represented by Figure 101).

Consider the third situation, in which firms are making losses. If expectations turn out to have been unduly optimistic and these losses are sustained for a period of time, firms will leave the industry. Industry supply will therefore contract and market price will rise. However, as long as losses are being made firms will continue to leave the industry until market price is driven up to the level at which costs are being covered (Figure 101 again).

It appears, therefore, that the only long-run equilibrium position for the firm is the one in which it operates at minimum average cost and the owners of the enterprise do not earn any profit, any surplus over and above the amount required to induce them to remain in the industry.

Supply curves

Our analysis of equilibrium behaviour gives some interesting clues about the nature of the supply curves of both the firm and the industry under perfectly competitive conditions. The industry-supply curve is particularly interesting but let us begin with the short run and try to build up slowly the long-run supply picture.

Short-run supply curve of the firm. The task of constructing the firm's short-run supply curve is made relatively simple by the nature of the market. As we saw in Chapter 8 a firm's supply curve shows how much a firm is willing or intends to supply at different market prices. As such the supply curve is an *ex ante* concept relating to output *plans* based on information concerning *expected* market prices. Now, given a set of expected market prices, we can immediately predict the output plans of the perfectly competitive firm since we know that such a firm will always aim at equating price with marginal cost. In other words, once information regarding costs has been collected and the firm's marginal-cost curve is constructed we have the firm's supply curve uniquely determined. The firm's supply curve is that section of the marginal-cost curve which lies above the curve of average variable costs, since the firm will not produce unless variable costs are being covered. Figure 103 illustrates this conclusion for a given set of costs.

Figure 103a illustrates the firm's cost structure, AVC being the curve of average variable costs and MC the marginal-cost curve.

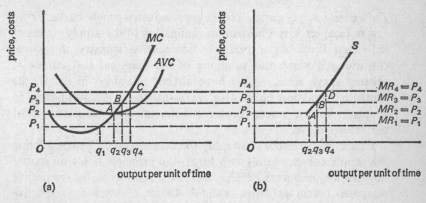

Figure 103

Figure 103b represents the firm's supply curve, point A corresponding to point A in (a). When the price is as low as OP_1 the best that the firm can possibly do is to produce Oq_1 units of output. Such an output would not yield sufficient revenue to cover variable costs and so the firm would not plan to produce anything at this price. Only when the price rises to OP_2 is the firm prepared to commence production, producing Oq_2 to equate marginal cost with price. Thus point A is the first point on the firm's supply curve showing that at a price of OP_2 the firm would plan to sell Oq_2 units. For any price above OP_2 the firm is always prepared to produce, hence, at price P_3, planned output is Oq_3 giving point B on the supply curve; and at price OP_4 planned output is Oq_4 giving point C on the supply curve. Thus the marginal cost curve from point A upwards is also the firm's supply curve.

The industry-supply curve

To construct the industry-supply curve we must underline the important distinction between *ex ante* and *ex post* supply curves. The *ex ante* supply curve refers to the intentions of the firms in the industry to produce certain quantities at given levels of market price, i.e. any point on the supply curve relates a market price to the quantity which the industry *intends to supply* at that price. The *ex post* supply curve relates to what the industry *actually does supply* in response to market prices.

The ex ante supply curve. The *ex ante* industry-supply curve, as we saw in Chapter 8, is a horizontal summation of the supply curves of individual firms. In a perfectly competitive industry this curve constitutes a horizontal summing of the marginal cost curves of existing firms, since, as we have already explained in detail, the firm's marginal-cost curve also represents the firm's willingness to supply at various prices. Figure 104 illustrates the construction of the *ex ante* curve.

Figure 104 attempts to simplify the demonstration by considering the supply curves of only two firms; the principle holds no matter how many producers. MC_A and MC_B represents the respective marginal-cost curves of firms A and B. A^* and B^* refer to the respective points of minimum average variable costs. Now, at a market price

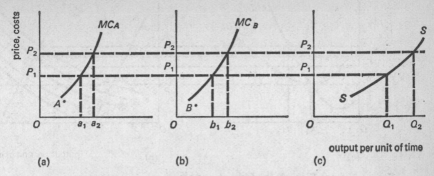

Figure 104 (a) Firm A. (b) Firm B. (c) Intended market supply

of OP_1 firm A would intend to sell a_1 and firm B would intend to sell b_1 – both aiming to equate marginal cost with price. Intended market supply would thus be $a_1 + b_1$ ($= OQ_1$). At a higher price of OP_2 firm A would intend to produce a_2 and firm B b_2 giving a total of $a_2 + b_2$ ($= OQ_2$) intended units for the market. The market curve, SS, would be flatter the greater the number of firms.

The ex post curve. A supply curve for the industry such as that drawn above never materializes *ex post* since not only do existing firms respond to price rises but so do potential firms, i.e. firms as yet outside the industry. As we saw earlier, as soon as price rises above the level of average total costs so that each firm earns a surplus, then new firms will enter the industry attracted by rewards which are higher than they can earn elsewhere. This will mean that existing firms will be intending to increase supply according to their marginal-cost curves but at the same time the *industry*-supply curve will also be shifting to the right as more units come onto the market, supplied by new entrants. Thus existing firms never realize their original expectations and intentions since market price moves from the level on which they based their original output plans, that is, *the* ex post *industry-supply curve does not coincide with the* ex ante *supply curve.*

The actual shape of the *ex post* industry-supply curve depends upon the availability of resources to the industry. If the supply curve of resources to the industry is perfectly elastic then the *ex post* supply curve of the industry's output will also be perfectly elastic; if the resources-supply curve is upward sloping then so will be the industry product-supply curve. In the former case cost conditions

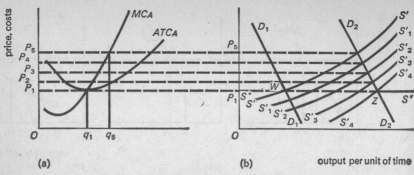

Figure 105 (a) Firm A. (b) Market supply

within the industry are unchanged as the size of the industry and its output expand, whereas in the latter case resource prices rise as the industry expands causing an upward shift in the firm's cost curves. The two cases are illustrated in Figure 105.

Case 1 Constant costs. There are of course many firms already in the industry but we are looking at one, firm A, for simplicity. At the existing market price of OP_1 firm A will intend to supply Oq_1 units to maximize income. Suppose now that market price rises (as the result of a shift in demand to $D_2 D_2$) to OP_5. At this high price firm A wants to produce Oq_1 and hence earn a surplus over production costs. But at the same time this potential surplus is an incentive to new firms to enter the industry. Now, as new firms do enter, market supply increases, i.e. the market-supply curve $S' S'$ shifts to the right. Thus firm A never actually does produce quantity Oq_5 since market price OP_5 does not hold sufficiently long enough for A to realize its output plans. As long as existing firms can earn the surplus, new firms will enter the industry. Consequently market supply continues to shift to the right, as shown by the movement from $S_1' S_1'$ to $S_2' S_2'$ to $S_3' S_3'$ in Figure 105 until market price is re-established at its original level of OP_1. Once price has returned to this level the incentive to new firms to enter the industry is removed. Points W and Z must, therefore, lie on the *ex post* supply-curve of the industry. Any tendency for market price to diverge from a level of OP_1, whether it be a rise or fall in price, is completely offset by a change in the number of firms in the industry and hence in the number of product units supplied to the market. If market

330 Perfect Competition

price rises from OP_1 new firms enter the industry and market supply is increased. If market price falls below OP_1 (e.g. as a result of a *fall* in demand) then firms leave the industry and the resulting supply contraction drives up the price of OP_1 again. The industry long-run supply curve is thus perfectly elastic.

Case 2 Rising costs. In the above analysis we implicitly assumed that as new firms entered the industry nothing happened to existing cost conditions, i.e. the increased pressure of demand on productive resources did not cause a rise in resource prices. This could only mean that the demand of the industry for resources was extremely small in relation to the total demand for resources. In other words, we were assuming that the supply of resources was perfectly elastic. In Figure 106 we consider the case where the supply curve of re-sources is upward-sloping so that any increased demand for the use of productive resources by the industry results in a rise in the price of resources.

Again, we assume that initially market price is at OP_1, at which level firm A intends to produce Oq_1 and that this initial price is disturbed as the result of a rise in demand causing market price to rise to OP_1. At this new price firm A intends to supply Oq_3 thereby earning a profit. This potential profit attracts new entrants which causes the industry-supply curve to shift to the right and depresses the market price below OP_3. However, this time price does not fall to its original level since the incentive for firms to enter the industry

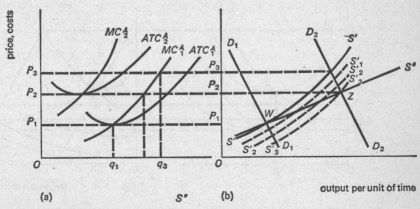

Figure 106 (a) Firm A. (b) Market supply

is removed at a much earlier stage as a result of a rise in the price of resources (due to the resultant demand pressure in the resource market) causing a rise in total costs. This rise in total costs, depicted by the vertical shift in the cost curves, means that the firm's surplus is eroded much earlier than it was in the first example. Market price settles at a new level which is higher than the original one but not as high as it would have been in the absence of new entrants to the industry. In our example the price settles at OP_2; and W and Z are both points on the upward sloping *ex post* industry-supply curve.

Case 3 Falling costs. Can there be a third case of falling costs? Our first reaction might be to dismiss such a possibility on the grounds that if firms regard a downward-sloping cost curve as a planning curve monopoly must inevitably result. This is where the distinction between *ex ante* and *ex post* becomes all important. If decreasing costs are to be compatible with perfect competition the downward-sloping supply curve can only be an *ex post* phenomenon – each individual firm continues to plan on the basis of its short-run marginal-cost curve. A falling industry-supply curve is illustrated in Figure 107 where W and Z represents two points on the curve.

The notion that an increase in output can be associated with falling costs goes back into the nineteenth century. In that period economists believed that agriculture was subject to diminishing returns (increasing costs) whereas manufacturing experienced increasing returns (diminishing costs). There is, of course, a grain of truth in this

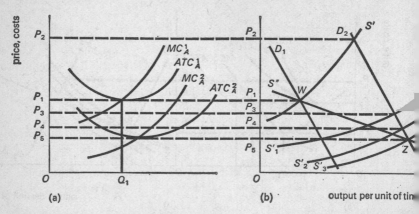

Figure 107 (a) Firm *A.* (b) Market supply

332 Perfect Competition

assertion. The dependence of agriculture upon climate means that its different operations cannot be operated simultaneously: they must be operated in sequence. In manufacturing there is no dependence on climate, and operations can be carried out in parallel *and* round the clock. There is less of a possibility of the co-existence of fixed factors in one operation and excess factors in another in manufacturing. There is also the possibility of more homogeneity of resources in manufacturing than when recourse has to be made to land.

Even if manufacturing industry was subject to increasing returns was it still possible to reconcile this with the existence of competition? Suppose one firm, by accident, received a lucky start, might it not quickly reap the scale economies, sliding down its average cost curve, buying up its competitors and creating a state of monopoly? Two sorts of answers were produced to deal with this problem. First, it was argued that the scope for increasing returns was extremely limited – in particular, firms would rapidly hit the bottleneck of a fixed management factor. This was an attempt to limit internal economies of scale. Secondly, it was allowed that all firms together might experience falling costs even though each individually was powerless to affect prices and costs. This was a reference to *external* economies of scale. Suppose that the industry expands in response to a price rise from an increase in market demand (Figure 107). As expansion takes place a reorganization of existing factor markets and of existing production functions may occur. This reorganization may reduce costs for *all* firms.[3]

3. This point is a very tricky one. If the reader can accept that 'somehow' reorganization takes place, all well and good. If not, then finding an example is exceedingly difficult. The following might suffice. Suppose that as a result of the initial expansion of market opportunities labour resources consider it worthwhile investing in new skills. This investment was not previously worthwhile since the scope for utilizing such skills was non-existent. Labour resources then offer these skills equally to all firms in the industry. As a consequence each firm reorganizes at the same time and costs for *all* fall by the same amount. The cost reductions are external to the firm but internal to the industry.

The notion of economies unattainable by an individual firm but attainable by the industry (the collection of firms) has led some writers to suggest that subsidies should be granted to such industries to allow these benefits to be realized. This proposal is an alternative to the creation of 'natural' monopolies which may internalize any benefits (as discussed in the following chapter).

Summary

In concluding this preliminary discussion of perfect competition we should remind ourselves of its social and political implications. We have tried to explore the conditions under which no productive institution enjoys an unequal share of market power and have found them to be most stringent; so stringent as to require modification if meant to provide us with a policy blue-print. The trouble with modified versions is that they tend to open the floodgates to a host of institutional problems which unrelentingly dog our efforts to construct the 'good society'.

The model yields two potential benefits – over the long run all firms produce at full capacity (minimum average cost) and consumers face a price per unit for a commodity which is just equal to the cost to any firm of producing that unit (marginal cost). Society would appear to receive maximum gains from the use of its resources and these gains are maintained by the checks of the market system which enforce firms to operate with maximum competence at all times in order to survive.

Against the potential benefits we must weigh the fact that there are many goods whose benefits would not be enjoyed in such a system. This is either because no one can obtain sole property rights to the goods – the case of collective goods; or because the production of the goods involves indivisibilities. As we saw in Chapter 2 alternative arrangements to the market have to be made for the allocation of resources to particular goods like education, typhoid vaccinations, national defence, blood etc. Furthermore, the competitive system is neutral and impersonal in doling out its rewards. A society accepting the free market system, because of its alleged efficiency *vis-à-vis* private goods, would be required simultaneously to accept the resultant distribution of incomes. Few societies have been prepared to go this far and alternative distributional arrangements have been devised.

The choice for society is not whether to embrace or to reject perfect competition. Rather, the important problem is how to devise a system which gleans the best features of the perfectly competitive model while avoiding the worst. Depending on the political and social values of the society concerned the adopted compromise may closely resemble the pure model of perfect competition or look more like the model of power which we discuss in the following chapters.

Questions

1 'The assumptions of perfect competition can be reduced to one: the demand curve facing the individual producer must be perfectly elastic.' Explain.

2 Why does the firm's marginal revenue equal its average revenue under perfect competition?

3 'The important thing is not whether the existing number of firms in an industry is few or many but the conditions of entry of new firms into the industry.' Comment.

4 Is freedom of entry to an industry a necessary and sufficient condition for production at minimum average cost in long-run equilibrium?

5 If all firms in a perfectly competitive industry have U-shaped cost curves can the industry-supply curve be upward-sloping?

6 Would a firm operating in a perfectly competitive market be likely to:
(a) advertise its own product?
(b) combine with other firms to advertise the industry's product?
(c) hold stocks of finished goods?

7 A tax is levied on every unit produced by each firm in a perfectly competitive industry. What would be the effects on:
(a) the output of each firm?
(b) the output of the industry?
Show how cost conditions in the industry determine whether in the long run the price of the product changes by more than, less than, or the same amount as, the tax.

8 Distinguish the short- and long-run consequences for the perfectly competitive firm and industry of imposing a lump sum tax on the profit of each firm.

9 There are 400 firms of equal size in a perfectly competitive industry. The market supply and demand functions are

$Q^D = 4000 - 10P,$
$Q^S = 1600 + 20P,$

where Q^D and Q^S respectively refer to quantity demanded and supplied and P represents market price.

(a) What is the equilibrium price?

(b) How much does each firm produce at the equilibrium price?

(c) What is each firm's marginal cost of producing this amount?

(d) If each firm were producing 12 units what must market price be?

10 A perfectly competitive industry is in equilibrium at a market price of £4 per unit when 1800 units are supplied. Each firm faces the total cost function,

$$TC = q^3 - 4{\cdot}5q^2 + 4q.$$

How many firms are in the industry?

11 The market for sweet chestnuts is perfectly competitive and there are 750 producers, each facing the same cost function. Each grower can produce q tonnes per annum at a total cost given by the function

$$TC = \tfrac{1}{4}q^2 + 10q + 20.$$

The market demand for sweet chestnuts is given by the function

$$Q^D = 20\,000 - 100P,$$

where Q^D represents demand and P the market price. How much will the industry supply and what will be the equilibrium market price?

12 A firm in a perfectly competitive industry faces the following total cost function:

$$TC = 250q - 20q^2 + 2q^3,$$

where q represents output.

(a) What is the marginal cost function?

(b) What output would minimize marginal costs?

(c) What is the firm's long-run equilibrium output?

(d) What price is consistent with this long-run output level?

Chapter 18
Monopoly

We turn now to the opposite end of the market spectrum, to where competition does not exist. But where, one might ask, was the competition in the previous case? There was no price cutting on the part of individual firms; no advertising; no intrigue with some rivals in order to plot the downfall of others (collusive price cuts, buying up scarce factor supplies etc.). It was precisely because competition was so 'perfect' that such activities were not undertaken. Remember that in such a market the individual firm wields no market power, it cannot influence the market price in any way. All firms are thus inward-looking and passive; taking the market price as given, they concentrate upon maximizing profits at that price. The most that any one firm can do to try and guarantee long-run existence is to keep an ever-watchful eye on costs of production – if it fails to do this then there is no possible price increase to save it.

In vivid contrast to this picture is the one in which all market power is concentrated in one source. Imagine a market in which there is only one seller; constrained only by the tastes and incomes of consumers this single enterprise has direct control over market price and can flood or starve the market of supplies according to its whims and objectives. If we further postulate that no new firms may ever enter the industry then, assuming no drastic changes in demand conditions, the position of the single seller appears impregnable, no rivals within the industry and no potential rivals without. Such a situation is usually described as *pure monopoly*, one firm constitutes the industry and that firm's demand curve is the market demand curve (downward-sloping), i.e. the firm can fix output or price, but not both simultaneously.

Why monopoly?

Monopoly can arise through a variety of causes:

1 *Natural causes.* Some monopolies may arise either through the possession of land containing particular minerals, spa water or a desirable location. Other monopolies may reflect freakish ability – Maria Callas's voice; George Best's feet.

2 *Licensing.* The state may permit certain monopolies to exist or create them through its licensing laws. Typical of these are laws which restrict the number of pubs and newsagents within a given area; allow only the Post Office to deliver mail or the Central Electricity Generating Board to produce electricity; allow trade unions the right to strike and permit certain people to call themselves members of a profession. Let us consider the last two. It is extremely doubtful whether trade unions would be able to raise the wages of their members were they not able to picket and harass employers.[1] The right to strike and its associated weaponry of boycott, social ostracism of non-unionists and non-strikers and sympathetic strikes by other unions are very powerful weapons with which to lever up wages. Why then does the state permit unions? The answer seems to be the failure of the state to accept that income determination and income distribution should be functions of the state and should not be left to the vagaries of the market. In the absence of state intervention what happens is that the state permits unions to exercise some kind of countervailing power against employers. Unfortunately, unions may do relatively little for workers who are not union members, or for those who do not work, e.g. retirement pensioners.

Slightly more sophisticated than the trade unions of manual and white-collar workers are the professions – doctors, architects, barristers, solicitors and accountants. Such groups are permitted to use particular titles in notifying the public that their services are available. Others can carry out similar services but they are not permitted to use the titles granted by the state. A man might practise medicine but if he has not been dubbed a doctor he may be considered a 'quack'. What is the reasoning behind professional licensing? The

1. Unions had this ability to harass employers in the days before trade-union legislation was passed because the law was not rigorously enforced. For a good account see Aspinall (1949).

answer seems to be to protect the health, safety and morals of the public against incompetents and sharks. The public is not knowledgeable, consumer sovereignty is a myth. The state therefore allows the public to delegate decisions concerning health, safety and morals to others and indicates who the 'others' might be. The professions can however sometimes behave like unionists or indeed any monopolies. They may control entry to the profession by insisting upon lengthy training, high entrance fees and high failure rates in examinations.

3 *Indivisibilities*. Indivisibilities are due to 'lumpiness' or discontinuities in the production process. It is impossible to have half a bridge, road or canal. One cinema in a town may earn its owner a handsome return; two cinemas would impoverish both owners if the demand was great enough for one cinema but insufficient for two. Indivisibilities are associated with economies of scale. If demand reaches a particular level then new techniques of production – mass production, buying – may be employed. Instead of constant returns to scale there may be increasing returns. We have two possibilities:
(a) Perfect divisibility – each production process can be replicated. If one plant can produce 500 units then two plants can each produce 500 units.
(b) Increasing returns – one plant can produce 500 units. With the finance available to produce 1000 units build a new plant using different production processes and 1500 units might be produced.

The kind of market structure resulting from indivisibilities depends upon demand. If demand for the product is low then only one firm may exist in the industry. However as demand increases other large firms enter and when a few firms co-exist in an industry the market structure is termed an *oligopoly*.

 How important are indivisibilities and the related economics of scale? Clearly there is no point in going into detail on the nature and implications of indivisibilities if they are unimportant. Surprisingly little work has been done on this subject.

Private sector indivisibilities

Work has been carried out by Pratten and some of his results are tabulated in Table 37. These indicate that the importance of economies of scale vary from industry to industry. In some industries

Table 37 Minimum efficient scale of new plant (MES) and economies of scale

Industry	MES as a percentage UK output in 1969	Percentage increase in total costs per unit at 50% of MES compared with the MES level
oil	10	5
ethylene	25	9
dyes	100	22
synthetic fibres	33	5
beer	3	9
soap and detergent	20	2·5
cement	10	9
bricks	0·5	25
motor cars	25	6
diesel engines	10	4
domestic electric appliances	20	8
newspapers	30	720
book printing (hardback)	2	small
book publishing	100	36

Source: Pratten (1971)

the optimum scale of plant may be small and even where economies exist the differences between optimal and smaller sized plants, as judged by the shape of the marginal-cost curve of the latter, may be small. In other words, the rate effect of an increase of output on costs may be so small as to allow a non-optimum plant to compete with the optimum.

Public sector indivisibilities

The public sector contains large numbers of examples of indivisibilities such as bridges, roads, canals, railways, health services and law and order. A peculiarity of these indivisibilities is that they have considerable spillover effects. A police force, army or fire service available for Smith tends to protect his next-door neighbour by its presence, because of these spillovers. These particular goods and services tend to be in the public sector. We shall therefore defer discussion until Chapter 40.

The closed monopoly

Let us concentrate, then, upon the polar case of absolute market power; when one firm has complete control of market supply of a product. In this case 'the firm' is synonymous with 'the industry', the firm's demand curve is the market demand curve for the product; and elasticity of demand for the firm's product is the same as market elasticity of demand. The firm is therefore the price-maker: faced with a downward sloping curve it sets price at that level which will maximize profits.

Profit, as we have seen, is maximized at the price–output combination which equates marginal cost with marginal revenue. But in the special case we are now considering, marginal revenue is not equal to price as it is in perfect competition. Marginal revenue is in fact less than price since the demand curve facing the firm is downward-sloping. Each unit increase in output can only be sold if the price asked for that unit is less than the price asked for any previous unit placed on the market; but if one unit is offered at this lower price then all units must also be offered at this price (since all units are homogeneous); thus the change in total revenue created by the unit increase in supply is less than the price received for that unit, e.g.[2]

50 units can be sold at 10p each; $TR^{(50)} = 500p$.

51 units can be sold at 9·95p each; $TR^{(51)} = 507\cdot45p$

$$MR = TR^{(51)} - TR^{(50)} = 507\cdot45p - 500p$$
$$= 7\cdot45p.$$

The change in total revenue created by a unit increase in sales (MR) is only 7·45p which is less than the new price of 9·95p.

Given that the marginal curve lies below the average revenue (demand) curve we may now proceed, in the usual fashion, to depict the equilibrium position of the firm. In order to do this we assume, for the time being, perfect knowledge on the buying side of the market – all potential consumers are aware of the existence of the product, the selling points at which it may be obtained, and the price at which it is being offered. (We are also assuming, as always, that the product is perfectly divisible, and can be offered for sale in minute

2. The relationship between total revenue and marginal revenue was fully analysed in Chapter 7.

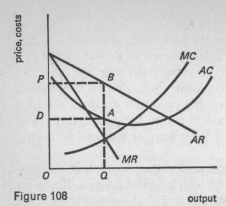

Figure 108   output

units – the price–quantity demanded relationship is a smooth curve.)
Equilibrium is shown in Figure 108. In this situation the firm is
enjoying a surplus of total revenue over total cost by selling output
OQ at price *OP*, thus equating marginal cost with marginal revenue.

The monopolist's demand curve

We have constructed the monopolist's demand curve as downward-
sloping. Can we say any more about its nature? There are two cases
which create difficulties for our analysis:

Demand for the monopolist's product is perfectly inelastic;
The monopolist's demand curve exhibits unit elasticity.

In the first case it is impossible, given our basic assumptions, to
identify the optimum levels of price and output. If elasticity is zero
at all prices then the monopolist can raise his price indefinitely and
thus forever increase his revenue. Thus, the only way for us to
depict an optimum position is to assume either a finite limit to
price – there is some price above which consumers will not buy any
– or that above some price demand becomes price elastic.

The second case is rather more interesting: it suggests that the
monopolist would produce no more than one unit of output. Since
the monopolist receives the same revenue regardless of price and the
quantity sold and since the total cost of two units exceeds the total
cost of producing one, then maximum profit is obtained from
producing one unit. We must consider such a situation as a curiosity

342 Monopoly

rather than a norm in a market economy. Its analysis does, however, have interesting implications for that model which assumes the monopolist to be sole controller of the supply of *all* goods and services. Under such circumstances the demand curve would again show unit elasticity since all consumer outlay would be spent on the monopolist's (composite) product. However, in this model the inducement to produce only one unit of output is tempered by the fact that consumer expenditure is determined by factor incomes and if the monopolist's output is kept so low in one period then factor incomes will be correspondingly low and demand for the product in the ensuing period will plunge dramatically. Thus, discovering the optimal input–output balance is a severe problem for such a monopolist; and it is a problem epitomized by the central planning model of state control of all resources.

We can expect, then, that the normal monopolist's demand curve will be neither of the two cases described above. More precision than this is impossible except to say that, assuming marginal costs to be positive, a monopolist will never operate along that section of his demand curve where price-elasticity is less than unity. Remember (Chapter 7) that when price-elasticity of demand is less than one, marginal revenue is negative and, therefore, if the monopolist were to operate along such a section of his demand curve he could always increase his revenue by reducing output.

The nature of the monopolist's supply curve

For any firm in a perfectly competitive market, marginal revenue is the same as average revenue. Since the optimizer equates marginal cost with marginal revenue there is a unique relationship between any price and the quantity the firm is willing to supply at that price. This unique relationship (supply curve) is traced out by the marginal-cost curve (as we saw in Chapter 17). When we turn to monopoly this price–quantity relationship is no longer determinate. Because the demand curve is downward-sloping, MR is no longer the same as AR. The monopolist himself sets the price and this is no longer equal to marginal cost (although MR is still equated with marginal cost).

In each set of circumstances, therefore, there is only a supply *point*, only one price–quantity position, and it follows that different

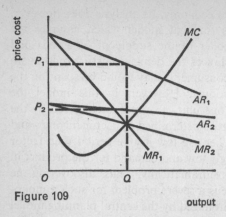

Figure 109

quantities may be associated with one price and different prices may be associated with one quantity. This means that we cannot construct an *ex ante* supply curve since we cannot determine precisely how much the monopolist is willing to supply at each price. The marginal-cost curve still provides necessary information but this alone is not sufficient to determine quantity: we must also know the demand curve. The importance of this problem will be more obvious when we eventually discuss the economy in macro terms (in the meantime think how you might construct an *aggregate* supply curve, i.e. one which relates to a whole economy).

Figure 109 demonstrates the lack of a unique price–quantity relationship under conditions of monopoly. Both the marginal-revenue curves MR_1 and MR_2 intersect the marginal-cost curve at the same point. The optimum output is therefore the same, Q, but the prices obtained, OP_1 and OP_2, are greatly different.

The measurement of monopoly power

From the condition that profit maximization requires the equating of marginal revenue and marginal cost we can obtain a simple measure of monopoly power. Under perfect competition marginal revenue is equal to price and so price is equal to marginal cost. Under monopoly, price is greater than marginal revenue and hence marginal cost. So a measure of monopoly might be:

$$\frac{\text{price} - \text{marginal cost}}{\text{price}} = \text{degree of monopoly.}$$

344 Monopoly

Under perfect competition the degree of monopoly would be zero. In Chapter 20 we shall consider the usefulness of this formula.

Economies of scale *versus* organizational behaviour

It is not our intention at this stage to present a detailed comparison of perfect competition and monopoly, but one observation is sufficiently straightforward to be made now. The so-called 'classical' comparison of the equilibrium positions for the industry in the two cases observes that price is higher and output is lower under monopoly relative to their respective levels under perfect competition. We shall see that the classical case against monopoly is watertight, but useless as a policy guide.

The classical comparison is made in Figure 110. The perfectly competitive equilibrium is given by the intersection of the market-demand curve and the market-supply curve (summation of marginal costs). Output is OQ_c and price OP_c. Suppose now that the industry is 'monopolized' so that equilibrium is determined by the intersection of the marginal cost and marginal-revenue curves. Output is now OQ_m and the price is OP_m; output has fallen and price has risen. Note that for our comparison to be legitimate we must compare like with like, which is why we assumed the industry to be monopolized, to enable us to compare the 'before-and-after' pictures. The assumptions about the nature of perfect competition are so rigorous that monopoly is bound to appear in an unfavourable light. Since our assump-

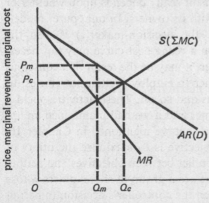

Figure 110   output

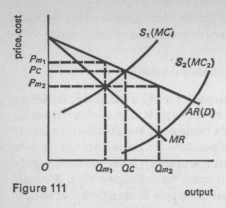

Figure 111

tions do not permit economies of scale then the issue is pre-judged. If, on the other hand, we were to relax our assumptions and allow for the possibility of scale economies, then monopolization could well result in a lower price and a higher output as a result of falling costs, as shown by Figure 111.

In Figure 111 the economies of scale which help to create the monopoly situation succeed in pushing the marginal-cost curve down to the level of S_2. Output rises from OQ_c to OQ_{m_2} and price falls from OP_c to OP_{m_2} instead of being OQ_{m_1} and OP_{m_1}. It is often claimed, however, that in spite of initial economies of scale a monopoly may become inefficient over the long run as a result of organizational slackness in the absence of market incentives to continually minimize costs. The strength of this argument really depends upon whether or not control of the firm resides with its owners. In our 'pure' models we have always assumed that the decision-maker(s) is also the owner(s) and on this assumption a rising cost curve may not necessarily reflect inefficiencies. Rather, it may be the result of a conscious decision on the part of the owner to employ prettier secretaries, to play more golf in the afternoons and so on. These activities yield a stream of net benefits to the owner and if we had maintained an approach to the theory of the firm that we mentioned in Chapter 16, namely, to assume the firm's objective is to maximize the utility of the owner, there would be no conflict between objectives and action. However, when the firm's owners are a group of shareholders whose aim is to maximize dividends then the controller's decision to permit longer tea-breaks and less office scrutiny conflicts with the owners' de-

346 Monopoly

sires. This is the 'X-inefficiency' model. The monopolist is considered inefficient because the market provides no incentive for him to be efficient or else the shareholders are either ignorant or apathetic.

Price discrimination

So far in our analysis we have imagined the monopolist to set only one price for his output. But if he could sell some of his output at that price and *some at a higher price* (for the same outlay) would he not be much better off? It seems so intuitively obvious that he would be better off that the question appears trivial. But is it not true that this apparent triviality stems from the fact that we tend to take for granted the downward-sloping demand curve? Perhaps we should remind ourselves of some of its consequences.

The market demand curve for a private good is a horizontal summation of the demand curves of individual consumers. Thus for a given set of incomes and tastes the producer knows how much he can charge for each quantity he puts on the market. When he offers each quantity at a single price (*per unit*) he foregoes potential revenue since all but the last unit offered is valued by consumers at a higher price.

In the situation depicted by Figure 112 the producer offers quantity OQ_4 at a price of A per unit. But all except the Q_4th unit is valued at a higher price, e.g. unit OQ_3 could be sold at price C; unit OQ_2 at price E, unit OQ_1 at price OG, and so on. Thus con-

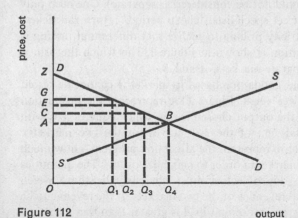

Figure 112

output

sumers enjoy a surplus (money-worth of utility) of ZAB – an amount of satisfaction they receive without paying for it. If each unit could be individually priced, total revenue for the producer would be $OZBQ_4$ instead of $OABQ_4$.

For the producer to realize the extra revenue he would need to know the marginal utility schedules of all his consumers and be able to negotiate with each individual buyer. Furthermore, each individual buyer must be willing to buy units of the product one at a time or at least be willing to negotiate a price for each separate unit purchased. Thus the firm may be torn between finding the one price that will clear the market and the set of prices that will both clear the market and extract consumers' surpluses. The opportunity cost of searching for the latter prices could be too high since it would take an immense amount of time to discover the full nature of each individual's demand curve. Since expected receipts would be inadequate to warrant acceptance of such costs the producer settles for the market price and the resultant consumer surplus.

Nevertheless, the principle still holds and although the producer is not able to treat each individual buyer as a separate market, he may at least be able to isolate two or more individual buyers, or groups of buyers, charge a different price to each and hence 'tap' some of the consumer surplus enjoyed by some of the consumers when only one price is charged. The necessary condition for such a policy to be effective is that price-elasticity of demand for the product should differ in each of the separate markets (if this were not so then the two markets could not be considered as separate). One need only think of Harley Street specialists, 'cheap period' return rail tickets or 'off-peak' electricity pricing to realize that differential pricing is possible. The situation is shown in Figure 113 in which the firm is faced with two separate markets, A and B.

It is essential that goods purchased in market A cannot be resold in market B and vice versa. Figure 113c represents the production decision: as usual the output chosen is that which equates MC with MR (the horizontal sum of the MR curves for the two markets). Figures 113a and 113b represent the allocation problem – how much to allocate to each market in order to maximize profit? The quantities which will satisfy this objective must obviously be those which equate the marginal revenues of the two markets. If the revenue to be gained from selling one more unit in A is greater than that to be lost

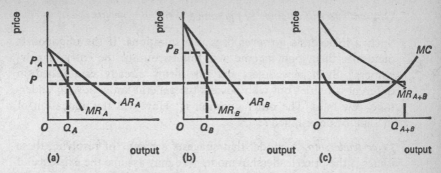

Figure 113 (a) Market *A*. (b) Market *B*

by selling one unit less in *B* then the firm will transfer a unit from *B* into *A*. If marginal revenues are equal then no further re-allocation can affect total profit. The prices charged in the two markets are OP_A and OP_B.

Oligopoly

Between perfect competition and pure monopoly lies the problem area of competition among a few sellers, or, as it is called, oligopoly.

The essence of oligopoly behaviour is that each firm knows that a change in his behaviour will have perceptible effects on his rivals' sales and profits. If *A* cuts his price *B* will be forced to follow suit or increase his advertising or do something to prevent a fall in sales. Interdependent, not independent, behaviour is the characteristic of oligopoly. Competition between a few sellers is supposed to be the dominant form of competition in mature market economies. In the late eighteenth and throughout the nineteenth century market behaviour of most industries approximated to that of perfect competition. In the late twentieth century the existence of independent, competitive behaviour has given way to interdependent behaviour. In the newer industries such as chemicals, size gives access to enormous economies of scale and few firms can gain a foothold. As for the older industries the comparative absence of innovation combined with stagnation and, sometimes, decline has produced monopolistic behaviour. Oligopoly behaviour suggests instability; a result which seems to be at odds with observed behaviour. Oligopolists do not always appear to be scrapping. This suggests the hypothesis:

Oligopoly 349

Oligopolists will attempt to maximize their joint profits.

Such a hypothesis however begs two questions. If the oligopolists maximize their joint income, will this encourage the entry of newcomers? Such newcomers may be firms already established in different activities but who possess the general know-how to undertake new lines. The other question is: How will the allocation of income be determined?

Price-leadership. A model that suggests a means of resolving these issues is the price-leadership model. We may assume the existence of a *dominant firm* who sets the industry market price and leaves all the other firms to produce as much as they can at that price, leaving the remainder of the market to be absorbed by the dominant firm. The price set will be chosen to deter new entrants as in the case of the pure monopolist. The idyllic situation of joint profit-maximization can, however, be destroyed by greed and technological change. To all members of the oligopolistic clique it must be particularly tempting to undercut the market price through quantity discounts and secret rebates, and this temptation will be stronger when any firm finds a cheaper method of production. *The problem of joint profit-maximization is therefore one of enforcement.*

Appendix: price discrimination

In Chapter 13 we derived the relationship between marginal revenue and price as $MR = P - (P/e)$, where e represents price-elasticity of demand. It follows from this definition that to equate the marginal revenue in any two markets (where $0 < e < \infty$ holds in each case) requires a different price to be charged in each when the elasticities differ. Furthermore the price must be highest in the market where price-elasticity of demand is lowest:

Market 1 $MR_1 = P_1 - \dfrac{P_1}{e_1}$,

Market 2 $MR_2 = P_2 - \dfrac{P_2}{e_2}$.

If $\quad MR_1 = MR_2$,

then $P_1 - \dfrac{P_1}{e_1} = P_2 - \dfrac{P_2}{e_2}$.

If $\quad e_1 > e_2$,

then $P_1 < P_2$.

Summary

Monopoly is the power to influence price or output. It arises through the existence of discontinuities of production possibilities which may be due to natural or legal causes. Though monopoly will give rise to a falling demand curve the monopolist will operate where his demand is price-elastic. Problems arise on the supply side because it is difficult to associate a unique output with a given marginal revenue. Whether a monopolist will be inefficient may turn upon his willingness to exploit any economies of scale available to him. Finally, a monopolist may obtain higher profit if he can divide his customers into separate markets.

Questions

1 'The firm under perfect competition can sell as much as it wants at the going price. Should the same firm find itself in a monopoly position it would be faced with a downward-sloping demand curve and could only increase sales by reducing prices. Therefore monopolistic control benefits consumers.' Discuss.

2 'The demand curve of a monopolist is elastic.' Examine this statement.

3 Why are most markets imperfect?

4 What problems are raised by the concept of a monopolist's supply curve?

5 If in a market all firms charged the same price what conclusion would you draw?

6 How would you attempt to establish whether an industry was monopolistic?

7 Milk can be produced either for liquid consumption or for manufacture into cheese, butter, cream, milk powder, etc. What factors will determine the relative amounts of milk sold for different uses?

What factors will determine changes in relative amounts of milk sold for different uses? Are your predictions refuted by the following data? Given that a litre of milk for liquid consumption always sells for more than a litre of milk for manufacture why do farmers ever sell milk to manufacturers?

| Year | Liquid milk sales | | Milk for manufacture | |
	Average price per litre (pence)	Million litres	Average price per litre (pence)	Million litres
1955	3·33	6105	1·67	1414
1960	3·22	6255	1·95	1923
1965	3·40	6646	2·04	2400
1970	3·55	6664	1·92	3359

Source: Milk Marketing Board, *Annual Reports and Accounts*

8 'The monopoly problem is not that monopolists charge high prices but that they misallocate resources.' Discuss.

9 Which world would you prefer to live in:

A world of perfect competition;
A world of pure monopoly?

10 A firm has a choice between:
(a) selling its product at a price based on factory costs and allowing the consumer to pay transport charges; *or*
(b) selling its product at a uniform price (which includes transport costs) to all customers irrespective of where they live.
What factors will determine the pricing policy it adopts?

11 A monopolist has the following revenue and cost functions

$$P = 8 - Q,$$

and $TC = 2Q,$

where P and Q refer to price and quantity respectively and TC represent total cost.

What is the monopolist's profit-maximizing price and output?
What is his total profit?

12 A monopolist faces a demand curve given by the function

$P = 50 - 2Q,$

and his total cost function is

$TC = 25 + 10Q.$

What are his optimum levels of output and profit?

13 The demand curve for a monopolist's product is given by

$P = 560 - 100Q,$

where P is the price in £s and Q the quantity demanded. The monopolist's fixed costs are £350 and his variable costs are given by the function

$TVC = £(20x^2 + 80x).$

Find:
The monopolist's optimum output;
The size of his maximum profit;
The price-elasticity of demand for his product.

Chapter 19
Accounting for Ignorance

In the two previous chapters we have examined the behaviour of the competitive firm and the pure monopolist under the assumption that the market clearing price was known. This yielded some important insights but also left out some more interesting ones. It would, for example, be helpful to know how the market clearing price was reached. After all, what competition was there under perfect competition? The competitive firm could only obey the market price. Hints of what might happen if the market price was not known came when we considered the displacement of price and output by demand. Then we looked at short- and long-run adjustments. But they were only hints and the analysis was in fact considerably more simplified than in Chapter 10 where we allowed the businessman, for a while, to misunderstand the market signals. In fact, what we did in the chapters on competition and monopoly was to assume that the businessman knew what the new market clearing price would be. This is the technique of *comparative statics* whereby one equilibrium is compared with another. It does not however indicate how businessmen move from one equilibrium to the other.

How does a businessman find the market price? He may have a rough idea of possible prices and associated outputs. He may believe that at successively lower prices more might be demanded. But which will be the market price? In the end he may simply pick a price and act *as if* that were the market clearing price: hence the state of affairs depicted in Figure 114 where he selects market price OP and then on the basis of estimated costs decides to produce OQ. The diagram is not unlike those presented for perfect competition in Chapter 17, but with a difference. There the firm was given the market clearing price and forced to accept it. Here the firm does not know the market clearing price but is forced to pick one, act as if that was the market clearing price, and seek to produce as efficiently

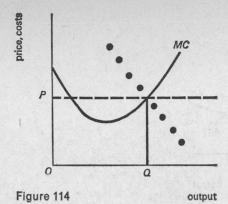

Figure 114   output

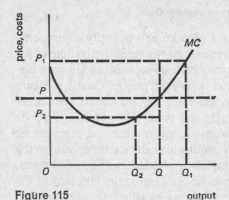

Figure 115   output

as possible at that price. In both situations the firm is a price-taker
but the reasoning behind the behaviour is different in the two market
situations. In one the firm is allowed to play in a game of blind-man's-
bluff whereas in the other the bluff has been called.

Suppose that the market clearing price is not OP but OP_1 as in
Figure 115. Here the effect of a higher than anticipated price is to
cause pressure to raise prices or allow a queue (QQ_1) to form. Or
suppose the clearing price is lower such as OP_2 then there will be a
build up of stocks ($Q_2 Q$) with a consequent pressure to lower prices.
By a process of trial and error the real market clearing price is
arrived at.[1]

1. The process of trial and error is the same process that a central planner
would indulge in. We are back to the introduction to Part Three.

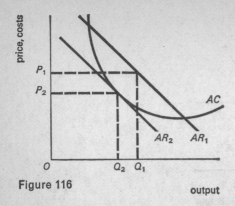

Figure 116

output

Ignorant competitors and ignorant monopolists

The preceding analysis in terms of price and quantity adjustments is applicable to both competitive and non-competitive trading situations. A firm may discover that it is a monopolist and it may discover that its monopoly position is only temporary. Consider Figure 116. The monopolist begins by assuming that he faces a market demand curve AR_1 and accordingly sets price OP_1 and sells OQ_1. At that price the discrepancy between average revenue and average cost creates an abnormal monopoly profit which attracts others and so the monopolist stands to find his sales are whittled away by newcomers. His demand curve is pushed back to AR_2 and at the tangency of the average-revenue and average-cost curves he sells OQ_2 at price OP_2: he earns only normal profit.

Strategies for monopolists

The case of the ignorant monopolist is interesting but not very helpful. The usual case is where a monopolist has a temporary advantage which he tries to sustain and where there are limits to his behaviour arising from interference from the state or the self-interest of other would-be producers. At some level of earnings the community may cry: 'Exploitation'. At some level of earnings someone will be prepared to provide a second cinema, a second bridge or even a fifth of anything. The monopolist has therefore to attempt a strategy which will protect his position. He can do this

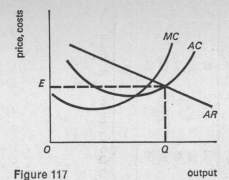

Figure 117

through choosing a price for his product which will restrict entry. He may, therefore, guarantee his earnings over the long run by threatening potential rivals with a price war if they enter, or holding price below the level which maximizes income in order to deter potential entrants as in Figure 117.

The monopolist in Figure 117 situation may set his price as low as E without experiencing a loss. At price E total revenue ($OQ . OE$) is equal to total cost ($OQ . OE$). Does this mean that we have changed the firm's objectives? Not necessarily: maximizing net worth in present value terms may require the firm to refrain from maximizing short-run income in order to maximize long-run profit. In other words, the firm may still be doing the best it can under the (expected) circumstances. If the firm anticipates new entrants when it maximizes short-run profit, i.e. a loss in revenue due to a reduced market share, it may well refrain from short-run maximization in order to maximize over the long-run period.

For example, consider the case of an established monopolist, firm A, planning output and sales for the five year period *year* 1 to *year* 5 inclusive. Suppose the firm anticipates that earning maximum profit of £100 in any one year will attract firm B into the market. The effect of B's entrance is anticipated to reduce A's annual revenue and hence A's profit. Firm A, therefore, intends to produce an annual output which will not yield maximum (annual) profit and in this way 'scare off' firm B. By following this strategy, A is still maximizing net worth (in present value terms) in the light of anticipated circumstances (see Table 38).

Thus by keeping annual income below £100 (the maximum level

Table 38

Year	Without potential entrants		If firm B enters at end of year 1		If A deters B by not maximizing annual income	
	A's anticipated maximum profit £	Present value at 10% discount rate £	A's anticipated income[1] £	Present value at 10% discount rate £	A's anticipated income £	Present value at 10% discount rate £
1	100	91	100	91	50	46
2	100	83	70	58·10	80	66
3	100	75	60	45·00	85	64
4	100	68	55	37·40	95	65
5	100	62	50	31·00	95	59
Total present value	—	379	—	262·50	—	300

1. A's anticipated income falls over the five-year period because firm B is expected to grow relative to A which has already exhausted most of the scale economies during the period.

which could be gained in any one year) firm A expects to earn income over the five-year period in excess of the level which could be earned if B was to enter the industry. A is still 'maximizing' under the expected circumstances, although this no longer requires the equating of MR with MC for any short-run output period.

Some accounting

The introduction of ignorance into our economic analysis enables us to appreciate many business procedures such as break-even charts and full-cost pricing. Typically these are rule-of-thumb procedures designed to give reasonable answers to problems. The economist's description of the pricing and production process is precise and technical. It differs from the way of the businessman and his accountant. Typically they think in terms of direct costs plus a percentage mark up to cover overheads yielding price. This reveals two differences from the economist's description. First, there is a preoccupation with overheads (fixed costs). Secondly, there is an apparent exclusion of demand forces. The accountant tends to regard his total variable costs as a linear function of output; that is, the cost of two units is twice that of one unit, the cost of three is thrice that of one, and so on. To his variable costs the accountant adds a figure to represent the proportion of overheads which sales of the product have to cover. The relationship between variable costs, fixed cost and total cost are shown in Figure 118. The next assumption that is commonly made is that the firm can sell as many units

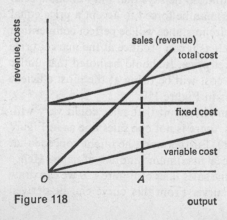

Figure 118

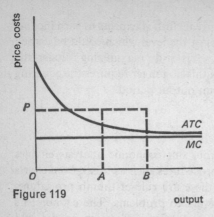

Figure 119

as it can produce at a constant price; this yields a linear total-revenue curve as in Figure 118.

The resulting intersection of total revenue and total costs as shown in Figure 118 yields what is known as a *break-even chart*. The break-even point *A* reveals the optimum output policy to lie to the right of output level *OA*. Figure 118 reveals a reason why many accountants have great difficulty in accepting the concept of marginal cost. If we derive the marginal- and average-cost curves from Figure 118 then we obtain the results shown in Figure 119. Since marginal cost is below average cost the accountant cannot understand how overheads can be covered. Hence he imposes a price *OP* and produces *OB*.

The economist does not say that the businessman should charge a price equal to marginal cost. Indeed he says that only under special circumstances will the businessman be forced to accept a price equal to marginal-cost policy. This circumstance will be perfect competition where the firm can sell as much as it can produce at the market price but has no influence on market price. It should be noted that under perfect competition marginal cost will be rising at the most efficient output and not be constant as in Figure 119.

If pressed the accountant might admit that sales could vary with price charged. In other words, there is not one sales line as in Figure 118 but many as in Figure 120. Furthermore, he might concede that at each price there would be a maximum amount of sales. Hence through particular points on the sales lines of Figure 120 we can draw the locus of a total-revenue curve. From this curve can be derived

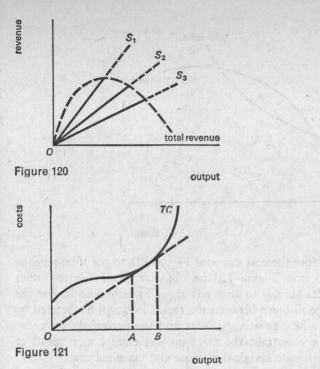

Figure 120

Figure 121

average- and marginal-revenue curves and, as in economic analysis, the accountant will be interested in the falling sections of average- and marginal-revenue curves.

The accountant's assumption that total costs are a linear function of output is probably a simplification brought about by considering only small deviations from some planned capacity output and the effect of certain accounting practices. If a firm has been built with the objective of producing, say, one million tonnes of steel per year then a risk factor of 10 per cent may be built into the plant design which would allow for outputs 10 per cent greater or less than one million tonnes to be produced without much change in costs. So in Figure 121 the effective output range AB can be produced at approximately constant average costs. The second group of reasons which may produce constant cost arises through, for example, the accountant's treatment of depreciation as a constant charge rather than allowing depreciation charges to vary with the degree of utilization of plant.

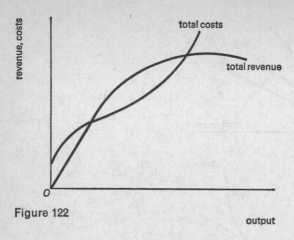

Figure 122

If we introduce the cost curve of Figure 121 to the total-revenue curve derived from Figure 120 we obtain a general price–output decision model similar to that envisaged by economists. For the accountant the distance between the two curves will be dictated by the mark-up added to average costs and the percentage for overheads; for the economist the mark-up will emerge as a result of attempting to equate marginal revenue and marginal cost.

Conclusions and implications

In this chapter we have sought to incorporate into the theories of the firm and market behaviour the assumption that firms are ignorant of the market clearing price. One consequence of this inclusion into the analysis is the conclusion that firms will tend to be price-setters. Further conclusions that might follow are that advertising and non-price competition might be efficient methods of marketing goods. Instead of juggling with prices it might be more sensible to tell people that certain goods exist. Moreover, in the case of the monopolist, ignorance and uncertainty might lead to strategies designed to reduce the flow of new entrants attracted by high profit.

The final aspect of ignorance and uncertainty that we touched upon was the accountant's rules for pricing and costing. Since a firm is an organization designed to seek information that the market does not instantly reveal we need to know whether those rules are consistent with what economic analysis would suggest. We found that some were.

Questions

1 What is the shape of the demand curve of a competitive firm under uncertainty? Why will such a firm tend to treat price as given?

2 Would you expect to find any differences between the behaviour of an ignorant competitor and an ignorant monopolist?

3 Can the accountant's break-even chart be reconciled with the economist's theory of pricing?

4 (For accountants) Is the accountant's standard costing procedure and analysis of variance compatible with the golden rule?

5 A businessman says that he bases his selling price upon his estimated average direct costs (which he assumes to be constant) plus a percentage addition to cover his overheads and profit. Using the relationship between price, marginal cost and price-elasticity of demand (mentioned in the Mathematical Interlude) show how the businessman's pricing procedure is compatible with the golden rule.

Chapter 20
The Regulation of Monopoly

Monopoly may give rise to a misallocation of resources or improve the allocation of resources by the attainment of economies of scale. Faced, therefore, with the monopoly problem the state may:

Seek to destroy the monopoly;
Acquiesce in its existence;
Nationalize the monopoly;
Regulate the prices or income of the monopoly by taxes or tariffs.

Which policy is adopted depends upon the likely effects of the monopoly so we must consider:

The case against monopoly;
The case for monopoly;
Some general issues;
The measurement of monopoly power;
Some methods of regulating monopolies;
Public policy towards monopoly;
Some cases.

The problems of public ownership of monopolies will be dealt with in the next chapter.

The static case against monopoly

The traditional case against monopoly is that it leads to an inefficient allocation of resources. By restricting entry to particular trades, resources are forced to work elsewhere for lower rewards whilst those employed by the monopolist can enjoy higher rewards. Consumers, as well as resources owners, are also deprived of the ability to obtain and enjoy more of the goods they demand through the restrictive practices of the monopolist. The traditional argument against monopoly and for perfect competition is often set out in technical language as follows:

1 Under perfect competition the price a consumer pays for a good measures the satisfaction he obtains from the last unit he consumes.

2 Under perfect competition the marginal revenue (= price) a producer receives from the sale of a good measures the costs incurred in producing the last unit of that good.

3 The same price is available both to producers and consumers.

4 From these propositions it follows that:
Marginal utility — price — marginal cost.
In other words the price consumers pay for a good measures the satisfaction obtained from the last unit consumed and the cost of providing that unit (or in the language of Chapter 12 the benefit he would have obtained from something else).

5 Under monopoly price does not equal marginal cost and so marginal cost does not measure the value to consumers of using resources in a monopoly activity.

The case for monopoly
Research and development

The model of perfect competition does, however, assume that consumers know what they want and that producers will always be rewarded for introducing new products. Consumers may not know what they want, and firms may be reluctant to introduce new products because of a fear that numerous imitations will appear and prevent the rewards of innovation being obtained. Competition therefore seems to stifle initiative. What kind of solution is possible? One solution is that the state should protect inventors by granting patent rights: patents would ensure an adequate return to inventors. But care needs to be taken in granting patent rights lest a loosely worded patent prevents desirable developments by others. Another solution is to allow firms to develop their own patent system through monopoly practices.

Stability

Under competition there are price fluctuations which lead to uncertainty, and are bad for trade. Such an argument underlines many monopoly regulations which seek to promote orderly markets; but as we have seen in Chapter 10 such price-fixing arrangements are not always successful in, for example, agricultural commodity markets. Moreover, general economic instability is more efficiently attained from state regulation of total demand (on which see Part Eight).

General issues

The trouble with the monopoly versus competition debate is that it is apt to produce doctrinaire answers to uninteresting problems. Competition is never perfect and monopoly is rarely absolute. What needs to be considered is the various implications of differing market structures for industry and performance. Consumers are interested in two things:

Being able to purchase goods at the lowest price possible;
Having new goods made available to them.

The two requirements need not always occur within the same market structure. Instead we may have the following cycle of events:

Stage 1 *Product competition*. A firm or small group of firms initiates a new product which gives them above average earnings. Because of novelty such firms have a monopoly position.

Stage 2 *Price competition*. Novelty is followed by imitation. How soon it occurs after product innovation determines the emergence of price competition.

Stage 3 *Monopoly or oligopoly*. If the market is such that economies of scale can be obtained then elimination of firms may take place until one or a few are left.

Stage 4 *Product competition once more*. This may occur within the industry or in another industry and depends upon the outcome of stage 3. It is a repeat of the first stage and arises because of the irresistible urge of some producers to be doing something and doing something better than their rivals.

The classification of stages poses some interesting questions.

1 Economists tend to concentrate on ensuring price competition. Is this because they are lazy or because their tools of analysis are weak? History might record a bit of both reasons.

2 Monopoly may be the result of being successful. The outcome of stage 3 may involve invention and innovation. An entrepreneur may find a cheap way of mass producing an item and in doing so may annihilate his rivals. Should he be punished for being too energetic?

3 Should economists concern themselves with the question: does *perfect* competition exist? Or should they ask: is there any competition? Should they look at the intensity of competition between existing producers? Should they look at the degree of freedom of entry to an industry? These are questions that often get overlooked.

Structure, conduct and performance

To summarize our discussion so far, we need to examine the structure, conduct and performance of firms in different markets. Structure refers to the number of firms in an industry, the distribution of output between these firms and the ease or difficulties of entry and exit into markets. But how can structure be described and measured? Conduct refers to the behaviour of firms in markets – the setting of prices and outputs. Performance refers to the outcomes of structure and conduct and the significance for economic welfare of the outcomes of behaviour. We should be able to derive hypotheses concerning conduct and performance from market structures. Market structure should give some indication of monopoly power.

The measurement of monopoly power

The case against monopoly is, first and foremost, that it misallocates resources. What is therefore required is some measure of monopoly power. Practical men need practical tools and it has been suggested that monopoly power may be measured by:

Price–cost ratios;
Cross-elasticity of demand;
Return on capital;
Concentration ratios.

All have been used on occasions though criticisms have been made of their use.

Price–cost ratio

This is simply the measure of the degree of monopoly we encountered in the previous chapter;

$$\text{degree of monopoly} = \frac{\text{price} - \text{marginal cost}}{\text{price}}.$$

The reasoning behind this formula is as follows. Under perfect competition price is equal to marginal cost and so according to the formula the degree of monopoly is zero. However, under monopoly, price will be greater than marginal cost and so the fraction on the right-hand side of the equation will have a numerator which is not zero. There are, however, problems involved in the use of such an index. But consider the following problems which the user of such an index might encounter.

The monopolist may attain economies of scale not available to the competitive firm.

The monopolist may become lazy or allow the owners of factors of production to obtain higher earnings (e.g. unionized labour) and so his cost curves rise and there is no apparent gap between price and marginal cost.

The measure is relative and takes no account of the absolute size of the market such that it fails to distinguish between Joe Bloggs' corner shop and ICI.

The measure provides no indication of potential competition.

The data by which to calculate the degree of monopoly power seldom exist.

Cross-elasticity of demand

Cross-elasticity of demand measures the effect on the sales of one firm of a change in the price of another commodity. If *A* raises his price and loses all his customers to *B* then the cross-elasticity of demand is high and the situation is one of perfect competition. If *A* can raise his price without loss of sales to *B* then the cross-elasticity of demand is low and monopoly obtains. Unfortunately this measure breaks down when oligopoly exists. If *A* increases his price *B* may increase or keep his price constant or may vary his advertising. We do not know what he will do. Cross-elasticity of demand is therefore a measuring rod with a beginning and an end but with no middle.

Return on capital

Under perfect competition a firm earns a return on the owner's capital, which is a cost and equal to the market rate of return; a surplus does not exist. Does the existence of a surplus denote the existence of monopoly? The answer is 'not necessarily'.

The monopolist may earn no surplus because he is inefficient.

Income as recorded by the accountant may ignore some of the businessman's costs: to the extent that costs are measured as historical costs then in periods of inflation costs are too low.

The existence of a surplus may be due to risk taking, innovation or short period abrupt changes in demand. These causes of surplus must not be confused with monopoly reasons for the existence of a surplus.

Concentration ratios

A concentration ratio measures the percentage of output or employment provided by the largest three, four, six or twelve firms in an industry. The hypothesis is that the greater the degree of concentration the greater will be the tendency for prices to diverge from costs and for there to be inefficiency. Concentration ratios, it would seem, permit of inference about immeasurable or undisclosed variables and as such the concentration ratio seems to be a useful measure. Unfortunately it suffers from several problems:

(a) It is difficult to define an industry or, more accurately, a market. The statistician tends to record industries nationally whereas many markets may be local, such as beer. The statistician may lump together non-competing groups as in the case of clothing for men and women or he may separate the competition of many industries such as plastics and wood, oil and coal. Statistics may ignore foreign competition.

(b) The concentration ratio may remain constant even though the firms involved may change or their relative strengths may change.

Table 39 Levels of concentration in British manufacturing industry (four-firm concentration ratios)

Frequency distribution	1958		1963	
	Number of industries	Employment %	Number of industries	Employment %
over 70%	11	3·4	14	5·1
30–70%	45	39·1	49	46·2
under 30%	61	57·5	54	48·7

Source: Sawyer (1971)

(c) The statisticians may continually revise their classifications and so preclude comparisons over time.

(d) Concentration ratios do not measure the concentration of finance.

Despite their limitations concentration ratios still attract the attention of economists and can, with supplementary material and findings, provide some useful indications of what is happening to the structure of industry. Table 39 above reveals that concentration, as measured by the percentage of an industry's labour force employed by the four largest firms, has been increasing in recent years. More than 50 per cent of the employment in the manufacturing sector is nowadays accounted for by industries in which the four-firm ratio exceeds 30 per cent. Sawyer, from whose work these figures were derived, suggested that some 72 per cent of the variation in the levels of concentration between industries could be accounted for by economies of scale, though this might be somewhat excessive due to the problem involved in detecting and measuring economies of scale. According to Utton, mergers were responsible for some 40 per cent of the change in the overall concentration in manufacturing industry (Utton, 1971).

Some methods of regulating monopolies

Assuming that a monopoly is deemed to be bad how should it be dealt with? If compulsory break-up or nationalization is considered impractical then it might be possible to cope with a monopoly either through taxing the surplus income or by imposing price controls. We can now examine the implications of such policies.

Taxing surplus

A method of coping with a monopolist's excess income would be to impose a lump sum tax on the monopolist. Such a tax would be, in effect, a fixed charge and would not therefore affect the monopolist's price and output policy. Unfortunately, care would have to be taken in setting such a tax since the supplies of all resources are ultimately variable and if a resource owner fails to earn at least what he can earn elsewhere he will eventually move. As an alternative, a tax can be placed on each unit of output produced. Since this has the effect of raising the marginal-cost curve it could lead to a reduction in output and rise in price.

Price control

The other method of regulating monopoly behaviour is through imposing a price ceiling or a ceiling on the rate of return on capital. For simplicity we shall consider the imposition of a price ceiling. Supposing as in Figure 123 a monopolist is charging a price OP and selling OQ units. A government might then insist upon a maximum price of OP_1, which would be equivalent to marginal-cost pricing and the monopolist would be forced to sell as many units as possible at the ruling price OP_1, so that average revenue and marginal

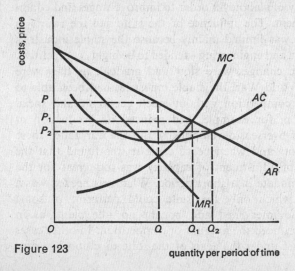

Figure 123   quantity per period of time

revenue became equal. Such a policy would result in lower price and increased output. Indeed a government might go further and attempt to set a price equal to average cost – price OP_2 forcing the monopolist to produce OQ_2.

The trouble with price or earnings ceilings in practice is that there is little attempt to explore the nature of the monopolist's cost conditions. What might occur is that a ceiling is imposed and the monopolist's costs rise to yield the socially acceptable return on capital. Instead of the shareholders getting higher incomes, the directors and workers obtain higher returns in the form of pretty secretaries and bigger tea breaks.

The public control of monopoly

British attitudes towards the monopoly problem exhibit a history of pragmatism rather than the application of doctrinaire convictions. In the nineteenth century the monopoly issue was governed by the common-law principles governing restraint of trade. All covenants in restraint of trade were deemed to be void and contrary to public policy unless it could be shown that such contracts were reasonable both to the parties concerned and the public. The only major modification to the common law came through a succession of parliamentary acts which allowed trade unions to exist and to withdraw (control the supply of) labour in order to improve wages and conditions of employment. The influence of the state and the courts in economic activity was limited mainly because the staple industries – textiles, coal, iron and engineering – tended to be highly competitive.

When economic changes were slow and gradual, as they were before the First World War, the staple industries had been able to adjust to foreign competition without much economic and social dislocation. Cotton, for example, had reduced its production of yarn as a result of overseas developments. But the war halted these delicate adjustments and when peace came it was found that the required amount of adjustment of capacity was too great for the market to accommodate in a short period. What was needed was a major operation which only the state could perform. In some instances the state intervened and bought up idle plant, as in textiles, and this reduced the amount of competition. In other cases firms came together under the aegis of the state to rationalize production. The general effect was therefore a movement towards a favourable attitude towards monopoly.

Although government controls during the Second World War favoured closer cooperation between businessmen, there was a shift of opinion towards competition in the late forties and early fifties. One impetus to this were the Anglo-American productivity teams which seemed to suggest that the the efficiency of American industry was due to its highly competitive nature. A second was the belief that Keynesian policies could remove unemployment and that monopoly price regulation was therefore unnecessary. A third factor was the coming to power of a Labour Government which favoured public but not private monopoly.

The Monopolies and Restrictive Practices (Control and Inquiry) Act, 1948

This – the first piece of post-war legislation dealing with monopolies – set up the Monopolies and Restrictive Practices Commission with powers of investigation into alleged monopolies. These powers could be invoked by the President of the Board of Trade. The Commission was required to consider:

Whether or not a monopoly situation existed;
Whether, if a monopoly existed, its working was in the public interest.

The Commission's report and recommendations were presented to the President of the Board of Trade to decide whether action was necessary.

The Restrictive Trade Practices Act, 1956

By 1955 the Commission had encountered a great many restrictive practices of the type usually made by trade associations. It therefore produced a general report which led to the passing of the above Act which provided for the registering of all agreements and for their prohibition if found contrary to the public interest. The Act was notable for two important features:

1 It made the firm or cartel responsible for proving that its policies were not contrary to the public interest. This marked a departure

The Public Control of Monopoly 373

from the traditional legal position that a defendant was innocent until proved guilty.

2 The Act defined certain 'gateways' and a 'tailpiece' through which a firm might plead that its actions were in the public interest. These gateways and the tailpiece were:

Protection and benefit of consumers

1 That the restriction is reasonably necessary to protect the public against injury;

2 That the removal of the restriction would deny to the public specific and substantial benefits.

Countervailing power

3 That the restriction is reasonably necessary to counteract measures taken by a person not party to the agreement with a view to restricting trade.

4 That the restriction is reasonably necessary to enable fair terms to be negotiated with a large supplier or purchaser.

Unemployment

5 That the removal of the restriction would be likely to have a serious and persistent adverse effect on unemployment in an area.

Exports

6 That the removal of the restriction would be likely to cause a reduction in export business.

Tailpiece

7 That the restriction was reasonably required for the purpose of supporting other restrictions in the agreement which were in the public interest.

Resale Prices Act, 1964

The 1956 Restrictive Trade Practices Act abolished collective resale price maintenance. The *Resale Prices Act*, 1964, was designed to outlaw individual resale price maintenance except for certain exempted goods. Each case for exemption was to be examined by the Restrictive Practices Court.

Merger references, 1965

During the late fifties and sixties the UK experienced a merger movement. The effect was to cause the President of the Board of Trade to refer mergers to the Monopolies Commission.

The Restrictive Trade Practices Act, 1968

Following the 1956 Act many industries replaced their resale price agreements with *information agreements* whereby firms could exchange information on such matters as costs and prices but not commit themselves to any particular action upon receipt of the information such as charging a common price. From the point of view of the general public, information agreements have advantages and disadvantages. The main advantage is that inter-firm comparisons of efficiency are a means of raising the overall level of efficiency in an industry and should result in lower prices. The chief disadvantage is that it is tempting for the efficient firms to sit back and obtain large profits whilst acquiescing in the desire of the more inefficient firms for price fixing.

Under the Act information agreements on prices have to be registered with the Board of Trade and the Board can require the registration of other agreements. Once registered, the agreements are subject to some procedural surveillance as under the 1956 Act with the notable point that a new gateway – that the agreement is permissible if it does not restrict competition – has been added under the 1968 Act.

Fair Trading Act, 1973

This piece of legislation codified and amended the Monopolies and Mergers Acts of 1948 and 1965 and the Restrictive Trade Practices Act, 1956. Its provisions include:

1 The establishment of a Director General of Fair Trading with the responsibility for protecting consumers. The Director also takes over the functions of the Registrar of Restrictive Trading Agreements established under the 1956 Act.

2 The Director can make references to a Consumer Protection Advisory Committee.

3 The Monopolies and Mergers Commission has been retained and its powers have been widened to embrace: regional monopolies; statutory monopolies including nationalized industries; and restrictive labour practices; but narrowed by the transfer of services (other than professional services which are exempt) to the Director of Fair Trading.

4 The criterion for a monopoly reference is reduced from at least one-third to one-quarter of market output.

5 The definition of 'public interest' is intended to have particular reference to competition and employment.

Some cases

To catalogue all the cases of state intervention in monopolistic arrangements would be tedious and dull. It seems much more useful to pick out a handful of cases as illustrating points which have been made in the previous chapters. Most of the cases are drawn from the reports of the Monopolies Commission and the Restrictive Practices Court. Some, however, are taken from other sources.

The Yarn Spinners' Agreement, 1959

The Yarn Spinners' Agreement was one of the first to be considered by the Restrictive Practices Court and it produced the important conclusion that the state is responsible for full employment.

The cotton industry in the fifties consisted of three major sections – spinning, weaving and finishing. The spinning section comprised a large number of firms which had agreed minimum prices for spun yarn. The weaving section contained a much larger number of highly competitive firms which because of their numbers were unable to collude. Finally, the finishing section consisted of a few firms dominated by the Calico Printers' Association (CPA).

During a recession prices would fall sharply in the competitive weaving section, moderately in the finishing section and hardly at all in the spinning section. The difference between the two monopolistic sections – spinning and finishing – lay in the fact that it was much easier for a single monopolist like CPA to respond to changing demand than it was for the spinners' cartel to reach agreement amongst its members. The upshot was that the brunt of the adjustment to changing demand conditions had to be borne by the weavers.

The arguments produced by the spinners were that their Agreement produced stability in the industry and prevented cut-throat competition. Unfortunately, and contrary to the spinners' arguments, the lack of price-flexibility probably increased unemployment and short-time working. Moreover, it was argued that even if the abolition of the Agreement increased unemployment the responsibility for full employment lay with the state.

In conclusion it should be noted that although the Court decided against the Agreement the (then) Conservative Government passed the Cotton (Reorganization) Act, 1959, which allowed the state to purchase and destroy spindles. Although the state accepted the notion of competition the Reorganization Act recognized that where there was considerable excess capacity competition might take a long time to effect its removal. Only the state could bring about the necessary surgical operation.

The Net Book Agreement, 1959

This is a very interesting agreement for economists because the first book ever to be published under an agreement which specified its resale price was Alfred Marshall's classic *Principles of Economics*.

The argument for the Agreement was that it enabled the public to obtain cultural and technical books at reasonable prices and that it permitted the public to browse through such books at their leisure in specialist bookshops. If the Agreement was discarded, it was argued, supermarkets would stock and sell fast-moving lines such as fiction and cut the price on such books. Since the extra income earned on the fast-moving lines served to subsidize the specialist bookseller for the cost of stocking slow moving lines and providing pleasant surroundings, abandonment of the agreement would force the specialist to discontinue stocking cultural books and thereby impoverish the public.

The Court seems to have accepted this argument. Their judgement was a mistake. If the community feels that technical and cultural books should be made available to certain groups of people, e.g.

Table 40 Total sales of colour film in the UK 1964

Company	By value (%)	By area (%)
Kodak	76·76	75·19
Ilford	3·59	4·84
Agfa	9·69	8·41
Gevaert	2·14	2·87
Gratispool	3·28	5·69
Bank (Ferrania colour)	1·5	1·32
Hannimex	2·00	1·00
David Williams	0·48	0·19
other	0·55	0·33
	100·00	100·00
	£5646	854 million square metres

students, then the community should give such groups income subsidies or vouchers with which to purchase such books. The vouchers would ensure that they were only used to buy books and the specialist bookseller could then obtain cash for the vouchers from the state.

The moral of the Net Book Agreement is: read all your books in the bookshop and ask the assistant for a chair.

Colour film, 1966

The Monopolies Commission's investigation of the colour-film market was a good example of the behaviour of a dominant firm. Kodak was responsible for 77 per cent of the sales by value and 75 per cent of the area of colour film in the UK market. Kodak dominated the market partly as a result of economies of scale engendered by inventions, partly through the existence of a tariff which reduced foreign competition and partly through exclusive dealing with retailers. We can now consider the implications of these features of the market.

Kodak became the dominant firm because of its greater economic efficiency and presumably set a market price which would restrain foreign competition. The other firms in the industry would accept this price and produce, given their costs, as much as they could. Kodak restricted the sales of its colour films to appointed dealers, mainly chemists' shops and photographic dealers. It refused to sell to Woolworths' or mail order houses on the grounds that it was necessary to ensure that retailers gave advice to consumers. This seems to be nonsense and one suspects that Kodak was frightened of the pressure that large buyers might exert. The Monopolies Commission recommended among other things:

1 The abolition of the tariff;
2 A reduction in the price of Kodak film;
3 A reduction in the discount that Kodak allowed retailers;
4 Kodak should permit any retailer to stock film.

Kodak agreed to implement items 2, 3 and 4, one effect of this being that the only other British-owned colour-film producer, Ilford, was eliminated because it was a high-cost producer. The president of the Board of Trade did not accept the need to change the tariff.

We're football crazy, 1963

In 1963 the Courts decided in the case of *Eastham versus Newcastle United Football Club* that the retain and transfer system of controlling the movement of footballers between clubs was in restraint of trade. Was the law right in reversing the verdict reached in *Kingaby versus Aston Villa* and ending the alleged wage slavery?

The retain and transfer system was devised by the Football League at its inception in 1893. The League emerged as a result of dissatisfaction with the main football competition of those days, the Football Cup Competition (more commonly known as the FA Cup Competition). As the official historian of the League noted, the early rounds of the FA Cup were unprofitable for the better clubs and they had to wait for the later rounds of the Cup in order to obtain keen matches and good 'gates' (receipts). Here we notice an important feature of football and indeed of all sports. A football club is not a firm: it cannot produce a football match without the cooperation of another club. A football club is a factor of production and like all factors of production it requires the cooperation of other factors to produce the product known as the match or game. This was the argument we hammered out in Chapter 14. What the football clubs were trying to do was to internalize the externality – the dependence of their efforts upon the efforts of others.

We need to analyse the thing called a football match. It depends upon the cooperation of two teams and the quality of the product depends upon how well matched the teams are. It is the uncertainty of the result that intrigues and attracts the crowds and, as the clubs noted, when results were certain then gate receipts were low. How then could the clubs ensure that match results would be uncertain? One solution might have been market forces. Let some teams become successful and their gates would fall. Then the successful clubs might wish to sell players to other clubs in order to equalize competition. But how long would it take to achieve the desired equality? And might there not be permanent disruptive forces? We may note that not all teams have the same supporter potential. The big industrial towns have qualitatively and quantitatively a different catchment area from the smaller and non-industrial towns. But need that matter? The answer would seem to depend upon how many clubs of the same calibre would be needed to provide a list of fixtures that would render all commercially viable.

The justification for the Football League is that it is the firm or cartel. The League laid down the rules but allowed its members some autonomy in order to preserve local pride and hence gates. And among the rules it created the retain and transfer system in order to produce an equal distribution of playing skills. Once a player had signed for a club he could not leave that club without the permission of the directors. Permission could be withheld or the club could negotiate a transfer fee for its most important asset – the player. It was a system from which poorer clubs could also benefit by discovering and selling players. Finally, the retention system permitted the clubs to impose a maximum wage. Thus the rules of the Football League were an attempt to answer the question: how should a firm allocate its resources amongst a given number of plants in order to produce the most profitable output? It was a question that we raised in Chapter 16, and in sport we find a variety of methods with differing results being pursued. For example:

1 All players should belong to the clubs in the area in which they are born or where they reside. Territorial rules are common in amateur sports, and vestiges can still be found in cricket.

2 All players should be centrally owned and controlled and allocated to teams so as to equalize skills, and switched from club to club if necessary. Such a procedure seems to operate in speedway.

The retain and transfer system became a bone of contention between players and clubs. The League and clubs, however, justified it on the grounds that it served to equalize the distribution of playing skills and, in 1913, the League's defence was upheld in the case of *Kingaby versus Aston Villa*. Between 1913 and 1963, however, there came changes in the law, changes in the nature of football competition, and in the general economic environment. The changes in the law concerned verdicts in cases which had many similarities to football. For example, in the case of *Kolok versus Kores* a no-poaching agreement between two manufacturing chemists was declared void. Within football there was the introduction of European competitions which tended to pull the more skilful players to a smaller number of domestic clubs. So the situation became ripe for the Court's decision in *Eastham versus Newcastle United* against the buying and selling of players under the retain and transfer system. But was the decision a sensible one? Might it be necessary to have restrictive rules in order to make football an entertainment industry? After all, the International Federation, to which most countries affiliate, still has a rule preventing free movement of players between clubs and between countries.

Summary

Monopoly policy in the UK has been largely pragmatic because of the different results that monopoly can produce. Most of the measures of monopoly are difficult to use and can give rise to conflicting interpretations whilst the legislation and cases considered have sometimes been curiously inconclusive.

Questions

1 Industrial concentration ratios measure the percentage of total sales in an industry accruing to a given number of firms in an industry. It is sometimes used as a measure of monopoly power. Between 1905 and 1970 the concentration ratio for the top twenty firms in the chain-mail industry rose from 39 per cent to 70 per cent. Simultaneously the number of firms fell from 350 to 130.

(a) What can you say about the trend in monopoly power?

(b) What would you expect to be the effect of these trends on the price of chain-mail?

(c) Is the industry becoming more competitive or oligopolistic?

2 Is a four-firm industry less competitive than a six-firm industry?

3 What is meant by 'monopoly profits' and how would you seek to measure them?

4 What might be the effects of trying to regulate the prices or profits of monopolists?

5 Under UK law the Restrictive Practices Court starts from the presumption that restrictive trading agreements are against the public interest. In dealing with mergers and with unitary monopoly power the Monopolies Commission starts with no such presumption. Consider whether there is any justification for this difference.

6 What might be the effects of trying to regulate the prices or the profits of monopolists?

7 Comment on the following:

(a) Authors should be paid a fee for each occasion on which a library issues one of their books.

(b) With the abandonment of price maintenance the poor shopper has great difficulty in finding out who provides the cheapest after-sales service for her washing machine. Resale price maintenance saved the shoppers' time.

8 If there is only room for one firm in an industry should the state auction the property right?

9 Compare the effect of (a) lump sum taxes and (b) taxes per unit of output upon the price, output and profit of a monopolist.

10 A monopolist faces the following demand and total cost functions

$$P = 50 - 2Q,$$

$$TC = 25 + 10Q,$$

where P refers to price, Q represents quantity and TC refers to total costs.

(a) Calculate marginal revenue, marginal cost and total profit.

(b) Suppose the monopolist is required to charge a price equal to marginal cost. What will be his output and his profit? Compare your answer to the profit-maximizing price and output.

(c) Suppose the government imposes a tax of £4 per unit. What will happen to price, output and profits?

(d) Suppose instead of a unit tax the government imposes a lump sum tax of £36. What will happen to price, output and profits?

11 In 1969 the Monopolies' Commission reported on the supply of beer. Some of the major findings were:

(a) In 1967 the brewers owned about 78 per cent of the public houses and 36 per cent of the 25 000 off-licensed retailed premises.

(b) The free retail trade buys most of its beer direct from the brewers who also sell direct to one another, i.e. the wholesale trade is largely in the hands of the brewers.

(c) Breweries allow their pubs to stock the beers of other breweries but only so long as it pays them to do so. A brewer takes a whole-saling margin on the beers of other brewers and he may obtain agreements from other brewers to sell his beer in their pubs.

(d) The prices charged by brewers to tied outlets (those owned by the breweries) differ from those charged to the free houses. Some examples are given below:

Brand	Sold by	Bottled by	Price (per dozen half-pint bottles)	
			Tied trade (new pence)	Free trade (new pence)
Newcastle Strong	S & N	S & N	62	62
Brown	Allied		—	62
	Whitbread		64	62
Mackeson Stout	Whitbread	Whitbread	57	57
	S & N		76	70
	Allied		77	70
Double Diamond	Allied	Allied	69	69
	S & N		72	69
	Whitbread		74	69

(a) Why do brewers want to own public houses?

(b) Does the consumer benefit from brewery ownership of public houses?

(c) In recent years there have been several mergers among breweries. What do you think are the major reasons for this development?

(d) Do consumers benefit from brewery mergers?

Chapter 21
Public Ownership

A radical solution to the monopoly problem is public ownership whereby the assets of an industry are owned and controlled by the state. Public enterprises exist in most countries and in the UK comprise the various departments of state, local authority undertakings and the so-called nationalized industries (coal, steel, railways, for example). The distinction between central and local government activities is primarily one of decentralization embodying the political belief that it is wise to allow local affairs to be run by local people. The distinction between industries run as departments of state (health, education, and defence) and the nationalized industries is institutional and historical. The nationalized industries were, for the most part, established in a specific historical period, were found to be more commercial in their operations than other public enterprises (i.e. their goods were more nearly private goods – see Chapter 2) and so their day-to-day operations have not been so closely controlled by Parliament, nor have their employees been dubbed civil servants.

In addition to the variety of institutional arrangements we can also note the variety of reasons advanced for public ownership, not all of which have been purely economic. Thus, Marxists have argued for the ownership of the means of production on the grounds that it would prevent exploitation and promote the end of capitalism. Within the Labour Party opinion has sometimes been voiced that private capitalism is immoral and panders to the acquisitive spirit in men. Amongst the particularly economic motives, however, we can single out the following:

Externalities. The belief that it is only under public ownership that the public welfare can be increased by allowing for the indirect social benefits which private producers ignore.

Economies of scale. The belief that it is only through public ownership that the necessary concentration of production into large-scale units can be achieved so as to obtain economies of scale, and that it is only through public ownership that small, inefficient plants can be eliminated.

The commanding heights of the economy. The belief that only if certain key industries are publicly owned can economic growth be increased.

Workers' participation. The belief that public control permits of worker participation in the running of firms.

Method of acquisition

Whilst many public enterprises were established initially by the state, some were taken over after first being in private hands. For example, coal, iron and steel, and railways were originally run by private producers. In the UK the traditional method of acquisition has been through the purchase of the assets of the industry. It is important therefore that public agencies can be more efficient than private agencies.

Operating rules

The mere establishment or acquisition of firms by the state still leaves unanswered the question: how shall they be operated? We can distinguish two possibilities. First, the public firms can be run as if they were private firms – they could be required to maximize profit – but that would suggest that the nature of ownership should be ignored. The alternative could be that the managers should behave 'responsibly', but that would require some specification of the characteristics of 'responsible' behaviour. It is the attempt to steer between these two principles that gives rise to considerable discussion and disagreement. We shall now look at two specific areas of decision-making – pricing and investment – and consider the problems that arise in trying to establish rules.

Pricing policy

The nationalized industries could give away their products for nothing. They could 'sell at zero prices'. After all, why not? Defence, law and order, education, roads and, to a large extent, health are examples of industries in the public sector which do not bother to set prices for their products. Why then set a price?

Consider, however, what would happen if the goods were given away. Demand would increase and there would be excess demand. There might be no deficiency of supply if the government increase the resources made available to the industries. That, however, would imply a willingness on the part of the government to increase taxes and a willingness on the part of the public to pay those taxes and accept a reduction in the amounts of other goods they might consume. However, resources are not free, prices cannot always be zero and raising taxes and allocating tax revenues is always an acrimonious affair. So if any industry can cover its costs then it prevents the industry's policies becoming the subject of political debate.[1]

How should prices be fixed? One solution that has been put forward is *marginal-cost pricing*. This means that consumers should pay a price equal to the cost of supplying them with the last unit of the commodity they require. In other words, price would reflect the value of the alternatives foregone and if the price consumers pay is equal to the benefit they derive from the last unit, then price will reflect both expected benefits and rejected benefits. There are, however, objections to such a policy which we shall now consider.

Indivisibilities

We encountered indivisibilities in Chapter 18 where conditions of production were found, on occasions, to be such that only a few technically efficient production units might be necessary to satisfy market demand and, given that state of affairs, it would be impossible to satisfy the marginal-cost pricing rule. To be precise, indivisibilities which arise because of lumpiness or discontinuities in production processes, may make it possible to increase output at a marginal cost less than the average cost of producing the industry's output. Thus, a choice has to be made between average-cost pricing which denies some consumers the chance of obtaining the product *or* marginal-cost pricing which results in total receipts being less than

1. This anticipates the argument of Chapter 42 on the efficiency of the political process. In the meantime, note the right-wing value judgement: physical rationing is bad – on which see Chapter 9.

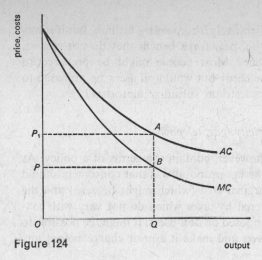

Figure 124

total costs. The choices are illustrated in Figure 124. The market demand is supposed to be OQ. If marginal-cost pricing is applied then the price to consumers is OP and losses of $PP_1 AB$ are incurred. If average-cost pricing is used then price is OP_1 and total revenue is equal to total costs. As Figure 124 reveals the dilemma arises because equipment is underutilized and average variable as well as average total costs may not be covered.

That total costs are not covered may be regarded as unimportant. After all, some of the costs are acquisition or fixed costs and they have been incurred; they are bygones. But what about replacement or the decision to build another plant? In these circumstances the community has no guidelines. Of course, the problem may be illusory. There may be few industries in which the productive processes are so lumpy as to exclude the possibilities of numerous production units. This is simply an empirical problem. But even if the problem is illusory it is such a fascinating problem that it is tempting for economists to try to answer it.

Taxes. We could argue that the overheads should be covered through taxes, since as long as no one is deprived of the use of the public facility no one's happiness is diminished. If anyone is willing to pay marginal cost then no obstacles should be put in their way. But who will pay the taxes? Presumably not the people who consume the good, otherwise they might as well pay their taxes (prices) in a more orthodox and less administratively inconvenient fashion. But if some-one else, some other group, pays for a benefit they do not receive, where is the social justice? Most people might be prepared to redistribute income to the needy but would oil users be prepared to subsidize coal users or pedestrians subsidize motorists?

The two-part tariff: electricity, gas, telephones

The tax proposal does, however, contain the germs of a policy. As originally propounded, the tax proposal was that consumers should pay a price equal to marginal cost (which might be zero) and the fixed cost should be covered by taxes which do not vary with con-sumption and might be imposed on non-users. It might be possible to impose the tax on the users and make it a prior charge before any units are consumed.

Electricity, gas and telephones are examples of services where two-part pricing is employed. In each case there is a daily variation in demand and, in the case of gas and electricity, a pronounced seasonal cycle. Plant must be capable of meeting the peak demand with the result that at other times plant is idle. Hence a fixed charge is imposed to cover plant installation and a variable charge is made to cover the degree of utilization of the plant.

Externalities

Our discussion of indivisibilities raised the problem of externalities by asking the question: should those who benefit pay? For an aspect of the pricing of the services of public agencies is the difficulty (or alleged difficulty) of deciding who are the beneficiaries. There are, it is alleged, considerable spillovers and it is difficult to identify the people who benefit. Hence the costs of a service should be borne out of general taxation. Free health and free education are obvious examples.

It should be possible to distinguish between *general* and *specific* benefits. In the case of general benefits subsidization would seem de-sirable, but many benefits are specific, e.g. rural transport, rural electrification, the slow run-down of an industry. And for these particular targets specific subsidies could be given. Indeed, if specific targets can be identified then it might be more sensible to give the subsidies to individuals – the poor.

Subjective versus objective cost

So far we have regarded marginal cost as objective and quantifiable. Unfortunately that may not be true. Recollection of Chapter 12 reminds us that it is the estimated marginal cost that is crucial and it would be easy for the public planner to say that he was attempting to equate price with marginal cost and that he was a little unfortunate in incurring a loss. What we are now emphasizing is that inefficiency of the kind encountered in our analysis of private monopoly can occur because there is no external check. If there is no community check through government upon the planners then social benefits may be less than the public planner's private benefits.

In a market the price-equal-to-marginal-cost rule is made steadfast by the existence of competition. If there is any divergence of price from marginal cost then firms will either make profits or go bankrupt. If firms make profits then these profits will be eliminated by newcomers. And it is the pressure of competition which keeps costs down to a minimum. What pressures are there in Whitehall or the Town Hall?

Investment

We have set out at length the criteria for investment appraisal in Chapter 6. What we emphasized there was the importance of taking account of the timing of cash flows: that is, that we could not assume that £100 three years hence was the equivalent of £100 today. We have also indicated that there were two possible methods of investment appraisal – (1) the net present value approach and (2) the internal rate of return approach.

From the point of view of the public planner the investment criteria raise particular difficulties. First, there is the problem that the estimated benefits may comprise benefits to which it may be difficult to give a monetary value. How, for example, can a value be put on the preservation of a piece of the countryside? Secondly, there is the question of what discount factor should be employed. Should the market discount rate be used? Perhaps not, since public enterprise might be subject to less risk and so a different discount rate might be used. Moreover, the public planner might be expected to use a low discount rate in order to permit projects that will benefit future generations to be carried out.

Pricing policy, investment policy and methods of finance are inextricably linked. For the moment let us consider methods of financing public enterprises. There are, basically, three methods of finance:

Borrowing on the open market;
Borrowing from the government;
Self-financing out of profits.

The three methods of financing involve problems of efficiency as well as equity. Thus it can be argued that the first method – resort to the open capital market – should always be carried out. The reasoning behind this argument is that only if a nationalized industry goes to the open market will there be any means of testing the soundness of the investment policy. Moreover, it is a method which allows resources to be withdrawn from producing consumer goods and transferred to, say, building power stations in a manner which involves the least burden on the community. Those people who are willing to purchase the shares of the nationalized industries are the people who refrain from current consumption and release resources to be used in the building of capital goods such as gas pipelines, atomic energy stations, etc.

The argument that says 'go to the market' assumes too readily that the capital market really is competent to judge the soundness of investment projects. There may be a temptation for private individuals not to release resources for the future. They may take the view that the future should take care of itself. They might only be willing to release resources if offered high interest payments. Whether individuals do adopt this attitude to community problems and whether they are right to do so are difficult questions to answer. If we devote current resources to future ends might we not make life 'soft' for our children and grandchildren? Should we use resources freely and lavishly in order to stimulate research and progress into the creation of new goods and materials?

The questions raised in the last paragraph are probably insoluble and account for the other two approaches being tried. Borrowing from the government may take the form of the government issuing bonds and the receipts being then handed over to the nationalized industries. Alternatively, theo gvernment may simply tax its citizens and hand over the proceeds to the directors of the nationalized industries. Neither method is completely satisfactory.

Taxation as a method of financing throws the whole problem of determining the wisdom of investment projects on to the Government. Taxation has however one redeeming feature. Taxes can be so constructed that those who can least afford to pay can be exempted from payment.

The third method – self-financing – appears to be an excellent method of financing capital projects. After all, if the industries are forced to find their own funds will they not seek to finance only the most sensible investment programmes? Unfortunately, this method breaks down if the industries are monopolies, for the directors will simply raise prices. Since the demand for products may be price-inelastic then raising prices will simply mean raising profits. And since the price increases will bear heaviest on those who can least afford them, they will represent a form of regressive tax.

Legislation for public ownership: a digression
The financial and economic obligations of the nationalized industries, Cmd 1337, 1961

In this White Paper the Government attempted to introduce a new financial framework for the industries:

The industries were required to break even over a five-year period;

The industries were to make greater provision for replacement of assets by earning sufficient to cover the difference between historical cost and replacement cost;

Financial targets were set for each industry.

Nationalized industries: a review of economic and financial objectives, Cmd 3437, 1967

This White Paper reflected the general upsurge of interest into efficient methods of investment appraisal, i.e. discounting.

Discount rates were set for the nationalized industries which were supposed to be similar to those in the private sector (though slightly lower because the nationalized industries are subject to less risk).

Some wider issues

The methods of ensuring efficiency in publicly owned industries have not been solved. Even in the case of the so-called nationalized industries which would seem to produce ordinary commercial goods there is still no evidence of rules having been found. The reason is that such industries have attempted to satisfy the demands of social justice (income distribution) as well as commercial criteria. Unfortunately it has not always been clear how justice and efficiency should be reconciled. Is it, for example, efficient to ask the coal industry to keep uneconomic pits open in order to give miners an income when the alternatives of giving them unemployment pay and retraining for new jobs have not been comprehensively attempted? Is it true that there are considerable spillovers from these industries? If these and other relevant questions do not find satisfactory answers then the correct policy might be to run the industries on private commercial lines leaving the social problems to be tackled through the introduction of specific subsidies.

Questions

1 Comment on the relative merits of public regulation and public ownership of a monopoly.

2 What are the main deficiencies of the marginal-cost pricing rule?

3 If the electricity industry is subject to increasing returns can it charge a price equal to marginal cost and still cover fixed costs?

4 What economic arguments can you advance for postal services being a government monopoly?

5 'Since the public sector invests in large numbers of projects it can afford to ignore the risk attaching to investments since risks will cancel out: the same policy could not of course be pursued by an individual.' Comment.

6 Transylvania's Railway Board is incurring a deficit on its rural passenger services. It can:
(a) close the services;
(b) raise fares on the services;
(c) cross-subsidize the services by raising the fares on main-line passenger and goods traffic;

(d) ask the State to cross-subsidize the services by raising taxes on the community.
Comment on the relative merits of these policies.

7 'London Transport should reduce fares in order to reduce road congestion.' 'London Transport should raise fares in order to cover costs.'
Comment on these two statements.

8 'The railway system confers benefits for which it cannot charge whilst road transport inflicts damages for which it cannot be made to pay.' Discuss.

9 The Post Office operates different price systems for mail and telephones. For letters a uniform price is charged irrespective of distance whereas telephone charges vary according to distance and the time at which phone calls are made. How would you justify these different price systems?

10 The Widget Corporation, a nationalized firm, is seeking to raise the price of widgets. Its arguments are:
(a) recent wage and raw-material price rises;
(b) British widget prices are below world prices;
(c) The Widget Corporation is importing widgets to cope with shortages and selling them at the lower British prices.
The price rise is opposed because:
(a) The prices of widget users' products will rise and intensify inflationary processes;
(b) The price of UK exports will rise and the balance of payments will deteriorate.
Carefully evaluate the above arguments. What policy recommendations would you make?

11 'Competition between gas and electricity should be banned as it has led to a waste of resources.' Comment.

12 On what grounds could a government justify earning a smaller rate of profit in nationalized industries than is available elsewhere in the economy?

13 'The aims of pricing policy in the nationalized industries should be that the consumer should pay the true cost of providing the goods and services he consumes' (*Nationalized Industries: Review of*

Financial and Economic Objectives, 1967). Discuss, paying particular attention to the phrase, 'true cost'.

14 'I suggest that the only price a public enterprise or nationalized industry can be expected to set is what we may as well call a *just price – a price which is set with some regard for its effect on the distribution of wealth* as well as for its effect on the allocation of resources' (J. de V. Graaf, 1967). Discuss.

15 Which of the following methods of financing the BBC do you consider to be the most efficient:
(a) a general subsidy out of taxes such as is used to finance overseas broadcasts;
(b) a pay-as-you-view or pay-as-you-listen system;
(c) continue the present licence system but increase the licence fees?

16 What criteria should the state use in compensating the owners of assets which it wishes to acquire?

17 Nationalization merely increases the size of the National Debt, it does not increase National Wealth, nor does it redistribute income. Do you agree with this statement? What does nationalization do?

18 *Bonks*, the students' weekly magazine at the University of Scunthorpe is incurring a weekly deficit of £100. The Students' Union calls in a business consultant to advise on a viable policy and he suggests doubling the price per copy from 5p to 10p. The left wing on the Union executive are outraged and state that *Bonks* should be made freely available to all students and that financing should be made effective by means of a general subsidy from Union funds. The right wing denounces the left wing's proposal as irresponsible. One or two voices express the view that a subsidy of 5p should be paid on every 25 copies sold above a minimum of 1000. Oliver asked for free lunches. In desperation the President of the Union turns to the staff of the Economics Department for help. The staff reply that they are only there for the beer, but recommend one of their students, YOU, to advise the President. *Required:* A memorandum outlining the relative merits of the proposals and some policy recommendations.

Part Seven
The Theory of Distribution:
A Preliminary Survey

In this section we enter one of the most disputed parts of economics. Many economists feel in fact that economics has no theory of distribution, only a few ill-assorted ideas. Let us therefore begin with some observations.

1 The general problem of any community is to decide how much of its production to devote to immediate needs (consumption) and how much to devote to future needs (savings leading to investment and the provision of greater consumption at a later date).

2 Arising out of this problem is how shall the community's decisions on the division of the product between immediate and future needs be implemented? Here we can distinguish between two methods. The first is the central planning approach and the second is the market procedure.

3 In the central planning procedure ethical considerations will enter immediately into the distribution of what is available whereas in the market system ethical considerations may tend to be neglected. Thus a market system will tend to reward a worker (the owner of labour services) according to his ability and will ignore the number of his dependents.

4 If a market economy produces rewards which fail to satisfy the broader considerations of fairness and needs it will convulse and explode into revolution unless some secondary mechanism is set up to correct disparities. The usual corrective is to redistribute some income through the tax regime.

5 A question that naturally arises is: why if market economies may fail to satisfy ethical standards is there a tendency to retain them instead of abandoning them completely? The answer is that it is believed that a market is the most efficient method of

allocating resources. The compromise of market plus government-regulated tax redistribution is regarded as a means of reconciling equity and efficiency and coping with the essential tension inherent in a market economy.

6 A final point concerns the use of the surplus over immediate needs. In a central planned economy the use of the surplus is controlled either by the dictator or by a committee representative (and presumably elected) of the people. On the other hand, in a market economy everyone can either decide how to divide and use his income into present and future use *or* he can hand over the use of the surplus to a private group of citizens known as capitalists.

7 We can now see that the sources of dispute about distribution theory are twofold. First, there is the feeling that nothing can be said about the ethical problems determining the rewards available to individuals. Secondly, there is the problem of seeing how the market solution is reconciled with a tax transfer scheme.

Chapter 22
The Global Problem
of Distribution

Nineteenth-century capitalism

We begin with John Maynard Keynes' brilliant analysis of the workings of nineteenth-century European capitalism contained in his book, *The Economic Consequences of the Peace* (Keynes, 1971a).

The psychology of society

Europe was so organized socially and economically as to secure the maximum accumulation of capital. While there was some continuous improvement in the daily conditions of life of the mass of the population, Society was so framed as to throw a great part of the increased income into the control of the class least likely to consume it. The new rich of the nineteenth century were not brought up to large expenditures, and preferred the power which investment gave them to the pleasures of immediate consumption. In fact, it was precisely the *inequality* of the distribution of wealth which made possible those vast accumulations of fixed wealth and of capital improvement which distinguished that age from all others. Herein lay, in fact, the main justification of the Capitalist System. If the rich had spent their new wealth on their own enjoyments, the world would long ago have found such a régime intolerable. But like bees they saved and accumulated, not less to the advantage of the whole community because they themselves held narrower ends in prospect.

The immense accumulations of fixed capital which, to the great benefit of mankind, were built up during the half century before the war, could never come about in a Society where wealth was divided equitably. The railways of the world, which that age built as a monument to posterity, were, not less than the Pyramids of Egypt, the work of labour which was not free to consume in immediate enjoyment the full equivalent of its efforts.

Thus this remarkable system depended for its growth on a double bluff or deception. On the one hand the labouring classes accepted from ignorance or powerlessness, or were compelled, persuaded, or cajoled by custom, convention, authority, and the well-established order of Society into accepting, a situation in which they could call their own very little of the cake, that they and Nature and the capitalists were co-operating to produce. And on the other hand the capitalist classes were allowed to call the best part of the cake theirs and were theoretically free to consume it, on the tacit underlying condition that they consumed very little of it in practice. The duty of 'saving' became nine-tenths of virtue and the growth of the cake the object of true religion. There grew round the non-consumption of the cake all those instincts of puritanism which in other ages has withdrawn itself from the world and has neglected the arts of production as well as those of enjoyment. And so the cake increased; but to what end was not clearly contemplated. Individuals would be exhorted not so much to abstain as to defer, and to cultivate the pleasures of security and anticipation. Saving was for old age or for your children; but this was only in theory – the virtue of the cake was that it was never to be consumed, neither by you nor by your children after you.

In writing thus I do not necessarily disparage the practices of that generation. In the unconscious recesses of its being Society knew what it was about. The cake was really very small in proportion to the appetites of consumption, and no one, if it were shared all round, would be much the better off by the cutting of it. Society was working not for the small pleasures of to-day but for the future security and improvement of the race, – in fact for 'progress'. If only the cake were not cut but was allowed to grow in the geometrical proportion predicted by Malthus of population, but not less true of compound interest, perhaps a day might come when there would at last be enough to go round, and when posterity could enter into the enjoyment of *our* labours. In that day overwork, overcrowding, and underfeeding would come to an end, and men, secure of the comforts and necessities of the body, could proceed to the nobler exercises of their faculties. One geometrical ratio might cancel another, and the nineteenth century was able to forget the fertility of the species in a contemplation of the dizzy virtues of compound interest.

There were two pitfalls in this prospect: lest, population still outstripping accumulation, our self-denials promote not happiness but numbers; and lest the cake be after all consumed, prematurely, in war, the consumer of all such hopes.

But these thoughts lead too far from my present purpose. I seek only to point out that the principle of accumulation based on inequality was a vital part of the pre-war order of Society and of progress as we then understood it, and to emphasize that this principle depended on unstable psychological conditions, which it may be impossible to re-create. It was not natural for a population, of whom so few enjoyed the comforts of life, to accumulate so hugely. The war has disclosed the possibility of consumption to all and the vanity of abstinence to many. Thus the bluff is discovered; the labouring classes may be no longer willing to forgo so largely, and the capitalist classes, no longer confident of the future, may seek to enjoy more fully their liberties of consumption so long as they last, and thus precipitate the hour of their confiscation.

Keynes and Marx

The analysis by Keynes is somewhat similar to that put forward by Marx. According to Marx, what the capitalists accumulated arose out of the exploitation of workers. A worker might work ten hours but be paid for only eight hours, eight hours' work being sufficient to bring him his subsistence. The two hours' extra work was pocketed by the capitalist and was known as *surplus value*. Marx used the highly emotive term exploitation to describe what happened under capitalism, yet it is clear that the process was little different from that described by Keynes. We still need to know why the workers were willing to accept the system. Why didn't they overthrow it?

Various attempts were made throughout the nineteenth century to alter society but most attempts failed. Marx, writing in the middle of the period, was probably more impressed by the methods used to condition the working classes to accept the system. Keynes writing after the events could see only a general pattern of acceptance. Perhaps this is the difference in their treatments of the period. For Keynes the system was not overthrown because people had lived in hope and accepted the possibilities for the future. For Marx, ignorance and powerlessness might hold back the working class for a while, but:

Along with the constantly diminishing number of magnates of capital, who usurp and monopolize all advantages of the process of transformation, grows the mass of misery, oppression, slavery, degradation, exploitation; but with this too grows the revolt of the working class, a class always increasing in numbers, and disciplined, united, organized by the very mechanism of the process of capitalist production itself. The monopoly of capital becomes a fetter upon the mode of production, which has sprung up and flourished along with, and under it. Centralization of the means of production and socialization of labour at last reach a point where they become incompatible with their capitalist integument. This integument is burst asunder. The knell of capitalist private property sounds. The expropriators are expropriated (Marx, 1867).

The end of capitalism

The society described by Keynes was a capitalist society whose virtue was that it seemed to provide the means whereby society could accumulate enough in order to rid itself forever of the difficulties of providing a material basis for civilization. He did in fact foresee that at some future point in time the basic economic problem would be solved. In 'Economic possibilities for our grandchildren' (Keynes, 1931a) he predicted a time when it would be no longer necessary to accumulate for the future, and avarice would no longer be a virtue. Indeed he wondered whether such a golden age would be so golden. 'To use the language of to-day – must we not expect a general "nervous breakdown"?' Did Keynes foresee the hippies and drop-outs?

We can in fact pick out several forces which have been sapping the capitalist system.

Trade unions. Even though the 'cake' was small it was always possible for certain groups to increase their share of the total product. In the nineteenth century, unions of skilled workers were able to maintain a privileged position *vis-à-vis* the unskilled. But this sectional interest prompted retaliation around the turn of the century from unions of unskilled workers.

Capital accumulation. The strongest force at work was possibly capital accumulation. By the turn of the century the compound interest of capital accumulation began to overtake the compound interest of population increase and even unskilled labour was becoming scarce relative to capital. It was this labour scarcity which seemed to account for the emergence of unskilled workers' unions.

Automation. Throughout the nineteenth century capital accumulation was probably complementary to population increase. Capital was, by and large, labour-using rather than labour-saving. More recently, however, capital accumulation seems to be labour-saving and brings with it the spectre of unemployment and poverty. Such automation raises the question of whether the control of the nation's surplus should still reside in private hands.

Divorce of ownership from control. The question of who should control the nation's surplus becomes most acute when it is realized that there has been a divorce of ownership from control in industry. In the nineteenth century the distinction between those who controlled the nation's surplus and those who owned it was blurred by the existence of the owner-manager. However, with the emergence of the joint-stock company the distinction became apparent and there grew up a rentier class who looked after the surplus and an entrepreneurial group who used it. What function did the rentiers serve that could not be served by the community at large, through the organs of the State? This has become the crucial issue with the emergence of the corporate economy.

Too few collective goods. The nineteenth-century system was designed to produce private goods, but in the mid-twentieth century the demands seem to be for collective goods – health, education – and stricter control of the bads which seem to be jointly produced with private goods. Some economists maintain that it is possible to control the production of the bads within a capitalist system and that it is also possible to produce collective goods in such a system. These propositions are disputable (as we shall see in Chapters 40 and 43) and their rejection would lead to the abandonment of a system of production and distribution which has dominated and controlled man's methods of obtaining a livelihood for many centuries.

The vote. The most powerful influence on capitalism has been the introduction of universal suffrage. In the market men are unequal because of the unequal distribution of income and wealth, but the principle of 'one man–one vote' has produced a means whereby political democracy can bring about economic democracy. The workings of the market depend upon an institutional framework and who can doubt that that framework has been severely modified by the ballot box?

Postscript

We have concentrated in this chapter on the global problem of distribution. This is the problem as a man from Mars might see it, but at the factory or market level we encounter the familiar demand

and supply analysis. We have now to go on to analyse the effects of differing demand and supply conditions on the prices of productive resources and how such prices determine incomes. Let us not forget that the results obtained in local markets cannot differ too greatly from that which an overall determination might produce, lest there be a social revolution.

Chapter 23
The Demand for Productive Resources

The brief discussion of the global problem of distribution presented in the previous chapter left unexplained the way in which resources are allocated among different uses. Allocation problems are typically problems in demand and supply analysis. In this and the next chapter we shall examine how demand and supply determine the rewards of factors of production. We begin with demand.

Derived demand

The demand for a factor of production by an employer is a derived demand, i.e. it is dependent upon the demand for the commodity which the resource assists in producing. The precise nature of the derived demand depends to a large extent upon the objectives of the employer. We are assuming that our employer, the firm, is aiming to maximize net income or profit and just as we were able to establish a rule for achieving this goal with respect to sales of final output, so we can establish an equivalent rule with respect to purchases of inputs. As we shall see, the nature of a firm's demand for productive resources depends upon prevailing conditions in both product and factor markets.

An equally important determinant of resource demand is the technical aspects of the firm's production process, i.e. the nature of the firm's production function. Whatever the characteristics of the markets in which the firm sells its product and buys its resources, its demand for resources must be partly determined by the engineering techniques it employs in production. As we saw in Chapter 3 the proportions in which resources are used in production processes can be varied or fixed; each case will give rise to different patterns of resource demand. For the most part of our analysis we shall concentrate upon the variable proportions case. The case of fixed proportions creates some technical difficulties best left for discussion at a more advanced theoretical level, and since we are interested here in the discovery of general laws of efficiency relating to the use of productive resources, the case of variable proportions suits our purpose.

Consider first the technical features of resource demand, since these are independent of the nature of markets. We have said that resources-demand depends to a large extent upon an input–output relationship, but as we saw in Chapter 3 this relationship may not be one to one. Indeed, over the short run (the period we are mainly concerned with in this chapter) output targets are dogged by diminishing returns. Output rises but at an ever-decreasing rate in response to increased resource employment since only some, and not all, inputs are readily available in increased amounts in the short run. We shall continue the technique of isolating one factor of production and considering its employment, given that the employment of other resources remains fixed.

The efficiency rule. In our earlier analysis of diminishing returns we constructed three curves: the total-product curve; the average-product curve; and the marginal-product curve. For the firm the most important guide to the employment of a factor is the marginal product of that factor. It is the marginal-product curve which shows the contribution made to total output by each additional unit of a factor of production. Since we are assuming the employer to be a profit-maximizer, such marginal output contributions are of prime importance in the employers' input–output calculations. The important decisions are always marginal decisions – in this case whether or not it is worthwhile employing an additional resource unit – and the answer must partly lie in the nature of the marginal-product curve.

To be more precise it is the *downward sloping section* of the marginal-product curve which is of importance to the employer, for reasons outlined in Chapter 16, but now viewed from a different angle. Applying the profit-maximizing output rule to *employment* decisions we can say that an employer should continue hiring resource units until the potential gain from hiring an additional unit is just equal to the cost of hiring that unit, i.e. until the marginal cost of employment is equal to the marginal benefit. For present

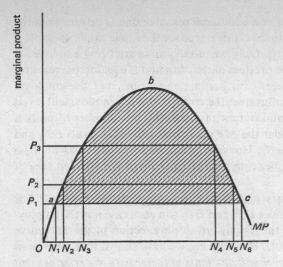

Figure 125   units of resource employed

purposes it is convenient to assume that the marginal cost of employment is constant (i.e. the supply curve of resources to the firm is horizontal at a given factor price) in order to isolate the importance of the marginal-product curve. In Chapter 27 we shall consider the implications of a rising marginal-cost curve of employment.

We illustrate the employment efficiency guide by Figure 125 and assume initially that resource units are paid in kind, an assumption we adopted in our earlier discussion of the overpopulation problem (see Chapter 3).

In Figure 125 MP represents the marginal-product curve for a factor of production. Consider first a price of OP_1 for each unit of factor. (Perhaps it is easiest for the reader to think in terms of agricultural labourers being paid in bushels of corn; in our case OP_1 bushels is the price of each labourer.) Which employment level will the employer desire at this price? The maximizing rule appears to be satisfied at two output levels, ON_1 and ON_6: which should the firm choose?

The problem is akin to that met earlier with respect to the two points on the marginal-cost curve which appeared to satisfy the output rule; and the answer to the employment question is similar to the one advanced there. ON_1 is ruled out because the potential gain from employing one additional resource unit is greater than the resource price OP_1. Indeed, this is true for the whole range of employment levels up to ON_6. Only when ON_6 units are being employed is the rule satisfied – the product of the N_6th unit is equal to the resource price. If the point needs further emphasis, note that the employer enjoys an output surplus over the costs of hire for employment levels ON_1 to ON_6. The total output produced by this number of units is equal to the area under the MP curve between input levels ON_1 and ON_6, i.e. area $N_1 abcN_6$. However, total employment costs of these units is only $N_1 acN_6$ leaving a surplus output of abc (shaded area of the diagram).

The above analysis also holds for other resource prices. For example, consider prices OP_2 and OP_3 – in each case it is the employment level given by the downward-sloping section of the MP curve which satisfies our rule. So far, then, we have shown that *for a given factor price an employer will hire units of factor until the price per unit is equal to marginal physical product.*

Recall, however, that the firm only produces when variable costs are covered: and the equivalence on the purchasing side of the firm's operations is to buy factors only when average product is greater than, or at least equal to, marginal product. To buy units of a factor when marginal product is greater than average product means

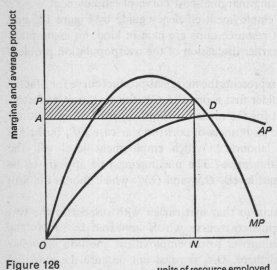

Figure 126

units of resource employed

that the amount produced is inadequate to cover employment costs – some factor units cannot be paid for. Figure 126 depicts the consequences of buying factor units when average product (AP) is less than marginal product (MP) and the size of loss made on the purchasing operations is shown by the shaded area. The employer is using ON units of factor at a price of OP per unit. Total output is $ON . OA$ and total costs of employment are $ON . OP$.

It should now be clear that when a firm can obtain all its factor units at the same price the firm's demand curve for that factor is the section of the marginal-product curve which lies below the average-product curve. In Figure 126 the demand curve commences at D.

Marginal revenue product

The analysis so far has assumed payments in kind so it must now be refined to take account of the existence of money. In a money economy most factors of production receive monetary payments as opposed to rewards in kind. Furthermore, in a money economy each employer is not interested merely in the *physical* output of each additional unit of resource but also in the *monetary value* of that output, i.e. how much revenue the employer can earn from selling the output of the additional unit of resource. This value is often referred to as *marginal revenue product* and is illustrated in Figure 127. Average revenue product (ARP) is also shown in the diagram.

In Figure 127a TRP is the total-revenue-product curve. It is the money value of the total-physical-product curve and as such it is shaped by the law of diminishing returns. Suppose employment of factor of production x is increased by one unit, say from N_1 to N_2, total revenue product increases by ab, i.e. marginal revenue product, the revenue to be gained from the sale of the output of the extra unit, is ab. For an increase in employment from N_2 to N_3, the resultant increase in revenue (marginal revenue product) is cd. If we repeated the exercise for all additions to employment we could trace out the marginal-revenue-product curve (MRP) as shown in Figure 127b.

Since this curve shows the money value of the marginal-physical-product curve, the downward-sloping section below ARP represents the resource-demand curve for an employer in a money economy. When the firm's product market is perfectly competitive, calculation

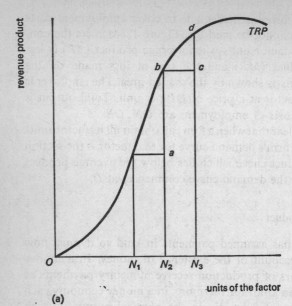

(a)

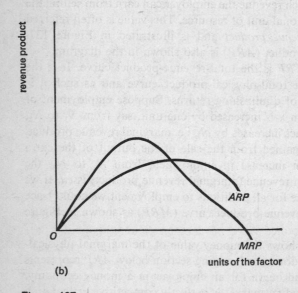

(b)

Figure 127

408 The Demand for Productive Resources

of marginal revenue product is very straightforward: since each extra unit of output sells at the same price as previous units, marginal revenue product equals marginal physical product multiplied by price per unit. When the firm's product market is monopolistic, calculations are more complicated since each additional unit of output results in a fall in product price (the demand curve for the product slopes downwards from left to right).

Does the demand curve always have a downward slope?

The fact that the marginal-product curve of a factor of production slopes downwards seems to prejudge the issue of whether an employer will always buy more of a factor when its price falls. But this is not the case. In Chapter 11 we saw that a consumer might buy less of a good as the price falls, given the existence of superior substitutes. The same may be true in the case of an employer's demand for resources. So far we have looked at an individual resource in isolation, but firms combine several resources and our efficiency rule must be extended to consider these other resources. The rule is the equivalent of the equi-marginal rule which we met in our earlier analysis of consumer behaviour. In the present case the employer maximizes the benefit from his outlay by spending on resources 1, 2, 3,..., N until

$$\frac{MRP_1}{P_1} = \frac{MRP_2}{P_2} = \frac{MRP_3}{P_3} = \cdots = \frac{MRP_N}{P_N},$$

where MRP refers to marginal revenue product, P indicates factor price and the subscripts 1 to N refer to specific factors.

Note that when more than one factor of production is variable the marginal-revenue-product curve of a factor ceases to be the firm's demand curve for that factor. A change in the price of one factor may lead to a substitution of that factor for the now relatively dearer factor(s) without a parallel change in output. This means that an employer's demand curve for a factor will be more elastic than the marginal-revenue-product curve: given the equi-marginal rule, the precise nature of an employer's demand response to a change in the price of any one factor of production will depend upon the ease with which factors can be substituted for one another within the firm's production function. In other words, the employer's response to a price change is determined by the relative strengths of the income, or in this context *output*, and the substitution effects.

Substitution effect. The fall in the price of one factor relative to the price of the other factors induces a substitution of the relatively cheaper factor for the one now relatively dearer.

Output effect. This is analogous to the income effect of consumer theory. The fall in the price of one productive resource means that costs have fallen and output can be profitably expanded. Three possibilities can be considered for implementing this increase in output:

Hire more of all factors;
Hire more of the factor whose price has fallen;
Hire more of the factors whose prices have not fallen.

The first possibility arises when factors can only be employed in fixed proportions or when there are limits to factor substitution. The second case, buying more of the new relatively cheaper factor, is consistent with the rules of optimizing behaviour. It is, however, the third case which is most interesting since it raises the question of whether an upward-sloping demand curve is possible – we encountered such a possibility in the earlier chapter on consumer behaviour.

It was assumed, in the case of the consumer, that his income was fixed so that a fall in the price of one good was equivalent to an increase in his income. He could therefore spend this increased income either on the good whose price had fallen or on the goods whose price had not fallen. The firm, however, is in a different position since, assuming a perfect capital market, its spending is not restricted by a given budget but by the benefit of buying more of a factor in relation to the cost (price of that factor). If the firm faces a perfect capital market it can borrow funds with which to buy factors as long as the expected revenue from using those factors exceeds their costs. This being so there is no reason why a firm should spend any of the increased income (resulting from a fall in one factor's price) on a factor whose price has not fallen. If it was previously not worthwhile buying more of that factor then there is no conceivable reason why more should be bought when its price has risen (relative to that of the factor whose price has fallen).

We can now see why the theory of consumer behaviour can give odd results. The theory gives the consumer a fixed income, and does not permit him to borrow because he possesses no assets nor buys any assets with which he can earn an income. If, however, we switch from a consumer to a household which obtains income by the sale of labour services then the rigid constraint would seem to disappear since the household could enter the capital market and borrow against future income. By borrowing, households may avoid having to buy some inferior goods, but the amount that they can borrow is limited by their prospects – they buy middle-price cars but not Rolls-Royces.

Differences in ease of access to the capital market of households and firms (corporations, partnerships) may be a reasonable assumption, given the problems that arise if a household goes bankrupt – the assets (labour services) of such a bankrupt cannot be owned by another person in a democratic society. There may be no restrictions on a person working harder or longer and income (work) may be dictated by consumption.

The price-elasticity of derived demand

We have established that more of a factor will be bought if its price falls and it now remains for us to consider the factors determining the strength of the response of demand to a change in price, i.e. the elasticity of derived demand.

1 The price-elasticity of demand for the product. If a particular factor of production, say labour, pushes up its price then production costs and the product price may rise. If consumers cannot switch to another product then the producer will be under no compulsion to resist the demand of a resource owner for a price increase and the price-elasticity of demand for the factor will be low.

2 Substitutability of factors. If an employer can easily substitute one factor for another then the price-elasticity of demand for those factors will be high.

3 Elasticity of supply of factors. If one factor has only one use then it may find that its earnings may be reduced because other resource owners obtain increased rewards at the expense of it. Thus if a

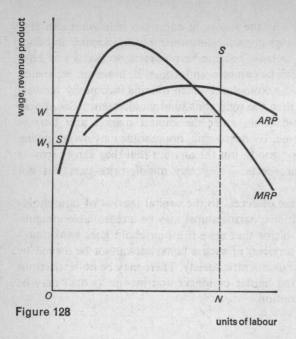

Figure 128

units of labour

group of workers are immobile it may be possible for the owners of capital to reduce wages, below the marginal product of labour, down to the supply price as in Figure 128 where the wage is pushed down from OW to OW_1.

4 The percentage of total costs. Supposing labour costs are 10 per cent of total costs, then a 10 per cent increase in wages will add only 1 per cent to total costs and hence to prices. So the effect on product demand may be slight.

Shifts in derived demand

Since demand for a productive factor is a derived demand, shifts in the demand curve for the final product will, other things being equal, induce shifts in the demand curve for the factor. Using the illustration of perfect competition in both product and factor markets, suppose the demand curve for the product shifts to the right resulting in a rise in product price. This means a rise in marginal revenue product – marginal physical product is unchanged but price has risen – and the marginal-revenue-product curve shifts to the right.

Product price changes, however, are not the sole cause of shifts in the derived demand curve. Even when product price has not changed, marginal-revenue product can still rise or fall as a result of changes in marginal physical product. Some technological change may cause a factor's productivity to rise (or fall) and the marginal-revenue-product curve to shift to the right (or left). There will eventually be a product price reaction to the change in productivity and this will create yet another shift in the marginal-revenue-product curve.

Finally, a change in the price of other factors will cause a shift in the marginal-revenue-product curve. (Ask yourself why.)

The industry's derived demand

When we constructed the market-demand curve for a product as the horizontal summation of individual demand curves there was no *a priori* reason why market demand *ex post* should differ from *ex ante* market demand. This is not the case when we attempt to construct an industry's derived-demand curve for a factor of production. Since we can construct an *ex ante* industry-supply curve for the product as the horizontal summation of marginal-cost curves, we can similarly construct an intended derived-demand curve – a horizontal summation of individual marginal-revenue-product curves. Such a curve would show how many factor units all firms in the industry intended to buy at various factor prices. Constructing an *ex post* derived-demand curve for the industry, however, is not so simple. As the price of a productive factor falls the individual firm's demand curve shows the firm to buy more units of the factor *on the assumption that the output of all other firms remains constant*. But if factor price falls to one firm it falls to all and, therefore, every firm wants to employ more units. As a result, output of final product rises and, final demand being unchanged, its price falls. This price fall means that marginal revenue product falls for each employer and individual derived demand curves shift to the left. Thus, *ex post*, each employer buys less of the factor than he intended and the resultant industry-demand curve is steeper than the *ex ante* industry-demand curve.

Figure 129 depicts the construction of an *ex post* derived-demand curve for an individual firm. Horizontally summing all such curves gives the industry situation.

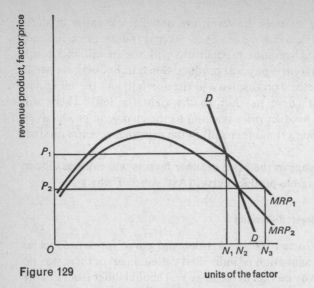

Figure 129

units of the factor

The original price in Figure 129 is OP_1. At this price the firm intends to hire ON_1 units of the factor, MRP_1 being the firm's original demand curve. Price now falls to OP_2 and the employer intends to hire ON_3 factor units. However, since the price has fallen to all employers, all hire more, produce more and product price falls. The resultant fall in marginal revenue product shifts the firm's factor-demand curve to the left, MRP_2, and, *ex post*, the firm hires ON_2 factor units instead of the intended ON_3 units. Repeating the analysis for all factor-price changes yields an *ex post* derived-demand curve DD.

Summary

This chapter has not distinguished among different factors of production but has presented a general theory of what determines the demand for productive resources in a market system. The two major determinants were seen to be the price of the factor and its contribution to the employer's revenue, i.e. marginal revenue product. The demand for a factor of production is a derived demand and the nature of the demand curve for a factor depends upon the nature of the demand for the final product as well as the technical conditions of production.

Questions

1 (a) Does a hump-shaped marginal-revenue-product curve imply a U-shaped marginal cost curve?

(b) A perfectly competitive firm employs only one variable factor of production. How could we distinguish its factor-demand curve from its supply curve of final output?

2 What happens to the firm's marginal-revenue-product curve if the market-demand curve for the final product shifts to the left?

3 What determines the elasticity of the *ex post* industry demand curve for a factor of production?

4 If the price of factor A used by a firm falls while the price of factor B remains constant, will the firm adjust its use of factors so that the ratio of the marginal-product of A to the marginal product of B falls?

5 A firm can freely vary the amount of factor X employed but the quantity available of other factors is fixed. The firm's product sells in a perfectly competitive market at a price of £2 per unit. The firm's production function is given by

$$Q = 20 + 24X - X^2.$$

(a) Give an algebraic expression for average product.

(b) Derive the marginal-product function.

(c) How many units of X must be employed to maximize total output?

(d) If the unit price of X is £8 how many units will the firm hire?

(e) The price of final output falls to £1 per unit. How many units of X will the firm hire now?

6 A farmer employs two factors of production – labour and land. His production function is given by

$$Q = 6AB - 10A^2 - 2B^2,$$

where A represents the number of men employed per acre and B represents the number of acres of land.

(a) Derive the two marginal-product functions.

(b) If labour's hiring-price is equal to that of land's, how many men per acre should the farmer employ?

7 'If, as we argued in the previous chapter, the distribution of income is of supreme importance to any society, then it is the demand for goods which is the derived demand and not that for factors.' Discuss.

Chapter 24
The Demand and Supply of Factors of Production

We can now bring demand and supply together in order to determine factor rewards. Demand is one determinant of factor rewards but without any indication of supply conditions it is but one blade of a pair of scissors. The simplest case of factor-price determination is where the supply of the productive resources is fixed and the resource has no production costs. Figure 130 shows the situation where ON units of a factor are available irrespective of the price per unit. The supply of the factor is therefore completely price-inelastic. In this instance the price of the factor, OP, is determined by the demand for the factor DD; and total return to the factor is $OPTN$.

The example shown in Figure 130 illustrates the theory of rent as propounded by David Ricardo (1772–1823). According to Ricardo,

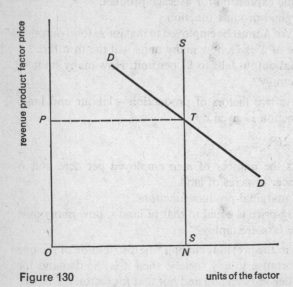

Figure 130   units of the factor

rent was the return to the owner of land. Since land was the gift of nature, it had no cost of production, it was fixed in supply, and so the return to land was demand-determined. In his general view of economic development Ricardo envisaged that as the demand for land shifted to the right, then the rents of landowners would rise.

The theory of rent, originally applied to land, was eventually extended to any factor of production in short supply. People with special abilities, footballers and opera singers, can earn rents. The generalized concept of *economic rent* is defined as *the amount of return to a factor over and above what is necessary to induce that factor to undertake its prevailing employment.* In other words, economic rent is a surplus over supply price (the entrepreneur's 'supernormal profit' is an example of economic rent). Thus, in Figure 130 the whole return is rent since the factor has no supply price.

Variable supply

Cases of resources which are fixed in supply are not the rule. Usually there is some variation in supply because resources have more than one possible use. When competing demands occur then the rewards of factors are not solely determined by demand; there is a supply-determined component, as well as a demand-determined component.

In Figure 131 we assume a price for the productive resources of *OP*. The area below the supply curve *SS* represents the supply-determined component. It is the amount which is determined by the opportunity cost – what the factor could earn elsewhere. Sometimes it is known as the *transfer earnings* of the factor. The other area is the rent element. One way of looking at the situation depicted in Figure 131 is to suppose that the horizontal axis refers to men willing to work at various rates of pay. We may suppose that the:

First man is willing to work for £20 per week;
Second man is willing to work for £22 per week;
⋮
Eighth man is willing to work for £25 per week;
⋮
Last man is willing to work for £30 per week.

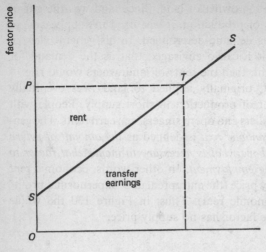

Figure 131   units of resource

As the diagram suggests that all men receive the same pay it follows that all receive £30, but for all but the last man his pay of £30 contains his transfer earnings and a rent. Thus:

First man has transfer earnings of £20 and a rent of £10;
Second man has transfer earnings of £22 and a rent of £8;
⋮
Eighth man has transfer earnings of £25 and a rent of £5;
⋮
Last man has transfer earnings of £30 and no rent.

Note that the marginal man, the last man employed, receives no rent.

Why pay rent?

A question that naturally arises out of the preceding section is: why should an employer pay all the men £30? Why doesn't he pay the first man £20, the second £22 and so on? We have met part of the answer before – there are search costs in finding out what each potential employee's transfer earnings are. The full answer, however, is a little more complex. The potential employee may not know accurately what his transfer earnings are, but is determined not to tell the employer what he thinks they are. Thus to find an employee's transfer earnings the employer cannot ask his potential employee because it is in the potential employee's interest not to divulge the information even if he knows it accurately.

The other main part of the answer lies in the particular nature of *labour* as opposed to some inanimate factor of production. If the potential employees band together and offer to work only for £30 then the employer has the choice of an optimum sized labour force or *no* labour force. By banding together every potential employee stands to gain, except the last man, the man with transfer earnings of £30.

An interesting feature of this analysis is that for the first time we have dropped the assumption of homogeneous factors of production. Some workers have different tastes or abilities from others and thus have higher transfer earnings. We have now established an important point:

When a factor is fixed in supply and has only one use then its reward will be demand-determined. It will obtain a rent. If, however, the factor has alternative uses then its reward will be dictated by its transfer earnings.

In his early exposition of rent theory Ricardo assumed that land had only one use – the production of corn. Hence he was able to say that the price of land was high because the price of corn was high, that it was the strong demand for corn which led to an intense demand for land. For Ricardo, rent did not enter into production costs but was determined by demand. If the land had alternative uses, then the opportunity cost of using the land for some other purpose would have entered into the determination of the price of corn.

Quasi-rent

In the short run resources are fixed and immobile. The decisions which have been made concerning their use were made in the past and so the costs have been incurred: 'bygones are bygones'. It follows therefore that in the short run any earnings of resources may be likened to a rent: they were called by Marshall 'quasi-rents'.

Questions

1 A professional footballer currently earning £200 per week faces the following employment opportunities.

Occupation	Weekly earnings
garage mechanic	£20
school teacher	£25
sports writer	£40
sales executive	£65

How much economic rent is he enjoying?

2 Distinguish between the effects (short-run and long-run) on factor supply of a unit tax on:
(a) A factor whose supply curve is perfectly elastic;
(b) A factor earning pure economic rent;
(c) A factor earning quasi-rent.

3 Colliery spoil heaps (which can provide road materials), scrap metals and antique furniture are examples of free gifts, not of Nature, but of the past. Does the reward to their owners constitute a rent?

4 Oil is discovered in the Irish Sea. Should the Government allocate quotas at a fixed price to producers or should it auction sites? What would be the effects of different pricing procedures?

5 A university professor is employed as a consultant by the Kruger Arms Company. His university claims that his fees constitute a rent to the Chair and as such should be surrendered to it. What do you think of the university's behaviour? Suppose the professor had worked as a consultant to the government and was awarded a knighthood. What should his university do? What do you think the professor will do? What do you think are the implications of this problem for the conduct of university teaching and research?

6 'The price of cinema seats is high because the demand for cinema seats is high.' 'The price of cinema seats is high because the price of land is high.' Comment on these two statements.

Chapter 25
Interest

We have referred to interest rates in Chapter 6 and so our discussion will be brief. The rate of interest is the price paid for a loan; it is the means by which future benefits can be compared with present benefits. The price will be paid by a borrower because he expects to use the loan in such a productive manner as to be capable of repaying both the principal and the interest charge. A lender will demand interest because he is being asked to forego current consumption. All this was spelled out in great detail in Chapter 6.

The rate of interest in a planned society

The rate of interest is determined in a market economy through the interplay of demand and supply, but even in a planned society there would still be a need for a rate of interest to express the relative preference for present and future benefits.

Monetary and real theories of the rate of interest

The rate of interest with which we have been concerned has been a real rate of interest determined by the forces of productivity (demand) and thrift (supply). Since the world we live in is one which uses money we can refer to a money rate of interest, although care needs to be exercised at this point. If money is but a veil over or lubricant to the economy and if the economy is in equilibrium then the money rate of interest will be equal to the real rate of interest. In other words, the money rate of interest will be mirroring the real intentions of the community. Each person in the community will be deciding how much money to hold, how many goods to consume and how many claims on future consumption benefits to hold. In equilibrium the plans of all individuals with regard to money holdings, current consumption and future consumption will be reconciled.

What happens if there is a discrepancy between the money and real rates of interest? This question has to be asked because it is always possible for the monetary authorities to vary the money supply and it is always possible for individuals to vary their money holdings. Suppose the authorities increase the money supply and so depress the money rate of interest below the real rate, encouraging spending and raising prices. The rise in prices would then lead to a rise in the demand for money and so pull the money rate up. In addition, if the initial reduction in the money rate of interest increased investment (a rise in the capital stock) then the real rate of interest will fall towards the money rate.

The analysis of the previous paragraph has however been complicated by a clash between those who stressed that the rate of interest is determined by the demand and supply of loanable funds and those who emphasized the view that the rate of interest was determined by the demand for and supply of money. The loanable funds theory tends to stress the *flow* of funds whilst liquidity preference emphasizes the stock of money.[1] If a short period is taken then the flow approximates to a stock. The crucial issue is – to which market should attention be directed when there is disequilibrium? The previous paragraph evaded this issue by looking at the initial and end positions when the plans of all individuals concerning money, goods and bonds (claims on the future) are in equilibrium. In the short run, when, for example, there is a monetary expansion, markets may be in disequilibrium and the marginal benefits from holding money, goods and bonds may be varying. In such circumstances, it may be the return in one market which may be crucial because, temporarily, it stands above the others. Thus in a severe slump, when people are pessimistic about the future, they may prefer to hold money rather than bonds and so it would not be inappropriate to speak of the rate of interest being determined by the demand for, and supply of, money. This is to be contrasted with the situation in a boom in which investment opportunities are extensive, and it would be fitting to think of the rate of interest being determined by productivity and thrift.

1. For liquidity preference theory see Chapter 29.

Questions

1 How do you think that the rate of interest is determined in Russia?

2 How is the rate of interest determined by the nationalized industries?

3 Why do economists attach importance to a real and a money rate of interest?

Chapter 26
Profit

In everyday usage profit refers to the difference between the receipts and the costs of firms and it is this profit which businessmen are supposed to seek to maximize. This surplus does, however, differ from what economists have tended to call profit, for the following reasons.

1 Commercial profit may include the transfer earnings of the businessman. Frequently, and particularly in the case of the owner-managed firm, the owner(s) may fail to deduct from the surplus the amount which he (they) might have earned in some other line of activity. The reason for transfer earnings appearing in the commercial profit is because they are not considered in everyday usage to be costs. *Commercial profits will often include transfer earnings.*

2 There will also be a tendency to overlook the opportunity cost of the owner's capital. This can arise in the case of the self-proprietor who not only fails to exclude transfer earnings but neglects to allow for the interest he could have earned on his capital had he invested it elsewhere. For example, suppose a man invests £5000 in a shop and in a particular year he incurs expenditures of £2000 and receives £3000 from the sale of his output. From the £1000 surplus he should deduct his transfer earnings and an amount equivalent to that which he would have obtained had he invested his £5000 elsewhere. *Commercial profit will therefore tend to include foregone interest receipts.*

3 Finally, commercial profit will often include rent elements such as might arise when something owned by the firm is in scarce supply relative to the demands of other institutions and individuals; the substitution of an alternative by these other institutions etc. is difficult.

When the elements of transfer earnings, interest and rent are deducted there may be left a residual difference between revenue and costs and the explanation of the possible occurrences of discrepancies has been put down to a variety of causes.

Ricardian theory (1817–?)[1]

David Ricardo began by explaining the origins of a surplus in an agrarian economy. He assumed that corn (a synonym for all agricultural products) was used to produce corn with the assistance of labour and land. Since corn took a year to produce workers were supported during the interval between sowing and reaping by advances of corn from a wage fund owned by capitalists. The basic features of this society can now be gleaned from Figure 132.

Along the horizontal axis is measured the number of workers

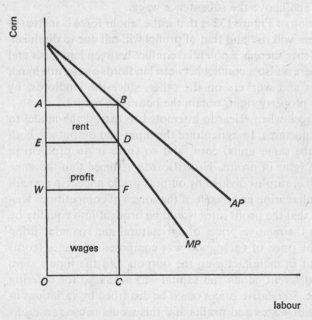

Figure 132

1. The absence of a concluding date indicates that in economics old theories seldom die nor do they fade away.

employed on a given amount of land and along the vertical axis is measured the output of corn. The curves AP and MP describe the average and marginal products of labour respectively. Hence total output is measured by the rectangle $OABC$. Now rent, the return to landowners, is assumed to be determined by the marginal productivity principle. Since land is given and has no costs its return must be determined by demand. So rent is determined by the demand for land at the margin and is measured by the difference between the AP and MP curves. The total return to land is, therefore, $ABDE$.

Ricardo did not extend the marginal productivity to labour which would have meant that labour's share was $OEDC$. Instead, he assumed that wages were determined by subsistence – in part, due to population pressure and, in part, due to convention. In Figure 132 the subsistence wage is OW and the wage share is $OWFC$. Hence the share of profits is $WEDF$. Profits are therefore a surplus or residual over and above the subsistence wage.

An implication of Figure 132 is that if the labour force is increased the share of rent will rise and that of profits will fall due to diminishing returns. Hence there is a potential conflict between landlords and capitalists. There is also a conflict between landlords on the one hand, and capitalists and workers on the other, since the landlords, by virtue of their property right, obtain the bounty of nature.

Problems arose when Ricardo attempted to extend the model to embrace manufactures. In agriculture the input and output are both measured in the same units, corn, and so there is no problem in measuring the value of profits. Now Ricardo assumed that the same rate of profit (i.e. surplus divided by output) would prevail in agriculture and manufacturing as a result of the forces of competition. Ricardo assumed that the profit rates would be brought into equality by movements in the relative prices of agricultural and manufacturing goods since the price of each good was composed of wages (corn) and profit. But in manufacturing the outputs and the inputs were composed of different goods and capital was advanced for differing lengths of time. So relative prices could be disturbed by variations in relative shares of wages and profits and this would cause variations in the valuation of output and destroy the invariance of output to changes in shares that occurred in agriculture.

As a first step Ricardo assumed that relative prices reflected relative labour costs but this did not provide a precise enough relationship between relative prices and profit rates. He then sought to establish an invariant standard by postulating the existence of a standard or average commodity which he called 'gold' but he was unable to define its properties. The trouble was that he wanted to have an absolute measure of value in the same way as there is an absolute measure of length. But in the social sciences values cannot be determined in this fashion but shift with changes in prices occasioned by changes in incomes. Nevertheless the notion that goods did not exchange in proportion to their labour costs was to point out the importance of distribution and to provide Marx with his political economy.

Marxian theory (1867–?)

In Ricardo's theory two things were left unexplained. First, there was the surplus. Second, there was the wage rate. The two were not unconnected since the surplus was what was left once the wage was determined. But what determined the wage? Ricardo assumed that subsistence plus some conventional or moral element was involved.

Marx resolved the problem of the surplus through his theory of exploitation. The worker worked ten hours but needed only the product of eight hours' work to provide for himself and his family. The capitalist pocketed the remaining two hours' work. This seemed to make sense in an industrial economy. For the characteristic of the late eighteenth and early nineteenth centuries was the massive increase in hours of work and the tremendous struggles to limit the length of the working day. These struggles were also intensified by the great expansion of employment of women and young children which meant that the working man had only to provide for himself.

The surplus was not spent in riotous living. As Keynes noted, the capitalists were allowed some of the cake but on condition that they did not consume it. The surplus was ploughed back because each capitalist feared being overtaken by his rivals. But if capitalists spent the surplus on building bigger and better factories might not that increase the demand for labour and raise real wages?

Wages might be held down by population expansion – the Malthusian terror. Marx did not like that idea. If wages were determined by biology what price socialism? So in Marx's theory wages were held down by a reserve army of unemployed created by the tendency of capitalists to buy labour-saving machines.

Marx also encountered Ricardo's problem of relating values to prices. But let us set out the basic information.

Let u be total value of a commodity (or if aggregation is done, all commodities), c be constant capital (machines used up in one period which do not create a surplus but merely transmit their own value to the final product), v be variable capital (labour) and s be surplus value created by labour. Then:

$$u = c + v + s.$$

This is no more than an accounting statement which says that the total value of a commodity can be broken down into the costs of machines, labour costs and a surplus or mark-up. It is similar to the accounting conventions discussed in Chapter 22.

Now follow three crucial definitions:

The rate of surplus value or exploitation,

$$s' = s/v.$$

The rate of profit,

$$p' = s/c + v.$$

The organic composition of capital or capital–labour ratio,

$$q = c/v.$$

Marx assumed that organic compositions of capital would be dictated by technologies and would not be equal in all industries. But he did assume a tendency for rates of surplus value and rates of profit to be equalized through competition. This, it is alleged, constitutes a contradiction for all three ratios are related. Thus:

$$p' = \frac{s}{c+v} = \frac{s/v}{c/v+v/v} = \frac{s'}{1+q}.$$

Hence if all p' and all s' are everywhere equal then all q must everywhere be equal. So if organic compositions of capital are allowed to differ then rates of surplus values and profits must be allowed to differ and that could mean that constant capital was the source of surplus value. Worse still it might be that land, an element of constant capital, was responsible for surplus value.

Marx sought to resolve the problem between values and prices by assuming that prices diverged from values in a systematic manner and was related to some average organic composition of capital. This was Marx's solution to the problem of an invariable standard.

Before concluding this section it is worth noting that Marx linked up the discussion of real forces with monetary forces by pointing out that exploitation takes place in a monetary economy where capitalists spend sums of money in order to obtain larger sums of money. Hence the process of exploitation was intimately related to the control of finance since that ensured control over all other means of production.

Neoclassical theory (1870-?)

By the 1870s Ricardian theory, based as it was on an agrarian economy, had become untenable whilst Marx's theory was unpalatable. Almost simultaneously there arose in various countries a group of theorists who sought to explain the problems of distribution along more satisfactory lines. These theorists – amongst whom were Jevons, Marshall, Walras, Menger, Böhm-Bawerk and Wicksell – were called neoclassical economists because they adopted certain elements from classical theory, particularly Ricardo's theory of rent, and gave them an emphasis which they had not previously been given.

The production function of Ricardian theory was conceived of as a fund concept. There was a fund of corn which was used as seed and wages and could therefore be reduced to a sum of consumption goods. In the hands of some neoclassical writers the production function came to be regarded as a stock of machines, as something physical. Hence they would write:

$$P = f(L, K),$$

where P measured output, L measured labour and K measured capital or machines.

The next step was to say that the return to capitalists who owned the K was dictated by the productivity of the machines at the margin. In effect, neoclassical theory gave to capitalists a property right and then said all owners of resources received a reward based on the marginal productivity of those resources. Neoclassical theorists extended to wages and profits the same principle that Ricardo had used to explain rent – the marginal-productivity principle. Furthermore, they suggested that the sum of all factor payments would just equal total output (or the value of total output) if all production functions exhibited constant returns to scale and contained no indivisibilities. This technical condition would be obtained under perfect competition and though the world was not perfect, it was sufficiently perfect for the total factor payments to equal total output; monopoly was relatively unimportant. But was this a legitimate extension of Ricardian theory? Land was given; the supply could not easily be increased. Therefore to say that the same principle applied to labour and capital was to suggest that their supplies were given and hence their rewards were demand-determined. We shall return to this point a little lower down and, in the meantime, we shall subject neoclassical theory to the same criticism as Ricardian and Marxian theory.

The problem is: in what units is K measured? One method is to discount all the future earnings of all machines by the procedure we adopted in Chapter 6. But where does the discount rate come from? At the level of the individual firm the discount rate is given by the market but it cannot be given for an entire economy. So the procedure takes as given that which has also to be determined. Of course, if all machines could readily be transformed into one type of machine or all industries had the same capital–labour ratio there would be no problem. We would be back in Ricardo's agrarian economy because the factors and the surplus would be measured in the same units.

If the supplies of machines are not given what determines their variability? One answer was that capitalists are rewarded for *waiting*. This seems to make sense when we look back at Ricardo's theory. Capitalists were rewarded for waiting a year for the harvest. They abstained from consuming. But in an industrial economy the periods of waiting are of different lengths and so need to be reduced to some common base. This gives rise to the search for an *average period of production* and to the hypothesis that the period of production, which measures the capital intensity of production, would expand and contract as the rate of interest (the cost of borrowing) varied. But is the period of production of a motor car two thousand years because some of the iron used in its construction was first mined in the Iron Age? And how do you average periods of different lengths? Do we have to assume that they are all of the same length?

The relationship between capital intensity and the rate of interest is ambiguous. Neoclassical theory tended to assume that if the rate of interest fell there would be a switch to capital intensive methods. But consider the following possibilities. A society can choose between method A which uses seven units of labour two periods before the final product is produced and method B which uses six units of labour one period before final output is produced and two units of labour three periods earlier. If the rate of interest is zero or close to zero or if the rate of interest is greater than 100 per cent then A will be cheaper than B whilst for intervening rates B is the cheapest method.[2] So the rich man does not have to be paid interest in order for society to have a particular method of production. More to the point, trade unions can raise wages without affecting methods of production. Of course, if we live in the twilight zone neoclassical theory holds but we cannot test this hypothesis because there are no agreed units of measurement. Casual observation, faith (?), suggests that abstinence brings great gains in the future but that does not imply that the distribution of gains should be so unequal.

The final strand in neoclassical analysis was the distinction between risk and uncertainty. Risks are events whose outcome is measurable in terms of probabilities whilst uncertainty defies measurement. Profit, it was then argued, was the reward for uncertainty-bearing. So workers as well as landlords can obtain profits. But the uncertainty theory contains snares. Only in a highly mobile society where people are rising and falling according to their ability to cope with uncertainty would the theory be plausible. But most of the people at the top seem to be able to bear risks not because they are genetically better endowed but because they are financially well endowed. Furthermore, if uncertainty was so pervasive it would destroy the marginal productivity doctrine since it is difficult to measure uncertainty and it defies causal explanation.

The usefulness of neoclassical theory

All of which is not to say that neoclassical theory is not useful. It is, for the following reasons:

1 At the level of individual markets the theory explains the reward of a factor in terms of the demand for the factor as measured by its productivity.

2. This example is taken from Merton (1972, pp. 230–45).

2 It decomposes a factor's reward into:

(a) a current reward consisting of two elements

(i) the payment necessary to keep a factor in its current employment – *transfer earnings*;

(ii) a possible surplus above transfer earnings – *rent*.

(b) and in terms of the initial outlay incurred in creating the factor its reward can be considered to consist of

(i) the *interest* on the original outlay: that is, the payment necessary to transfer resources from possible consumption in the past to increase consumption in the future;

(ii) the *profit* or loss arising from the decision to invest in resources in a particular activity whose outcome is clouded in uncertainty.

3 It extends the concept of capital to human beings and gives interesting insights into the problems of poverty and inequality.

Some disadvantages of neoclassical theory

But even at the level of individual markets the theory runs into difficulties.

1 The productivity of a factor depends upon the productivity of other factors. There is a monitoring problem as we observed in Chapter 14. If there is a collective goods problem then the only theory of distribution would seem to be one of equal shares.

2 The marginal-productivity theory is not a complete theory unless factor supplies are given. If factor supplies are variable then their variability might be explained in terms of alternative productivities. But this explanation raises monitoring problems once more. For if all workers belong to a trade union who can tell how efficiently and diligently each could work?

3 Uncertainty defies measurement and belongs to that collection of intangibles which beset economics.

4 If capital is durable then there may arise short-run problems of ensuring the full utilization of machines if demand forecasts are wrong. This is important at the aggregate level as we shall see in Part Eight, for though in the short run we do not have to bother about the measurement of capital – it is given – we do worry about the effects of unemployment on incomes, particularly wages.

5 If capital is not malleable it may not come in sizes which ensure its long-run utilization and could result in a failure to provide the machines. Confronted by lumpiness the neoclassical market solution seems to be monopoly which may lead to restricted output and employment.

6 Neoclassical theory regards income distribution as an aspect of the theory of price. The prices of factors are dictated by the prices of products. But one price – the wage – cannot be allowed to fall below subsistence or else market capitalism collapses into feudalism or a Welfare State which dictates that irrespective of productivity men must be guaranteed a certain income. If the market has to be supplemented then neoclassical economics should explain the levels of supplement.

At the macro level neoclassical economics does not seem to give sensible interpretations of 'aggregate capital', 'the general level of prices', 'the general level of wages' or 'the general rate of profit'. It is at its best in explaining relative prices but the substratum upon which relative prices float seems to elude it. Of course we could all delude ourselves that we live in a world of relative prices. But economists do tend to speak in aggregates and politicians expect them to do so. Unfortunately, complications arise. In the next section we shall find two explanations of the general level of prices – one would seem to follow quite sensibly from the discussion of this chapter in terms of the wage plus profit. The other explanation seems to involve the quantity of money. In another part we shall speak of economic growth and assume that capital can somehow be aggregated or that we can speak of additions to a capital stock without getting too deeply involved in measurement.

Conclusions

We set out to explain profit and this proved difficult without an account of how economists have, in the past, thought of it. We saw that it seemed to signify some surplus over and above subsistence and that this was some reward for waiting or risk taking. But when it came to the aggregate level problems of measurement arose. Many of the difficulties are caused by a dispute about appropriate rewards and might be solved by income redistribution. But this would also require some discussion of needs and economists tend to fight shy of this subject.

We lack a theory of distribution. Somehow we need to explain either the general level of wages or the general rate of profit. If we want to explain the wage level then perhaps we should look at what the poor want – what the rich have. Hence Europeans, Asians and Africans want what Americans have. And Americans want those things which their businessmen feel they should have in order to keep the economy going. The pressure to maximize profits and accumulate results in new goods being created and new wants stimulated. Sometimes the advertising pressures fail but the general effect is to awaken new desires and stimulate wage pressures.

Questions

1 In a Ricardian world is everything determined by supply conditions or does demand determine the amount of land used?

2 What problems did Ricardo encounter when he tried to extend his theory of profit to manufactures?

3 What are the main differences in the theories of wage determination of Ricardo, Marx and neoclassical writers?

4 'Marginal productivity theory is rent theory applied to all factors.' Discuss.

5 How did neoclassical writers explain the determinants of the supplies of factors?

6 'The measurement of capital is a red herring which gets in the way of a sensible discussion of income distribution.' Discuss.

7 'Ricardian and Marxian theories apply to capitalist societies whereas neoclassical theory applies to socialist societies.' Discuss.

8 What is meant by uncertainty? How can a businessman be expected to maximize the outcome of something which defies discussion?

9 Into what useful categories can the reward of a factor be divided?

10 'Factor payments are determined by technology since it is technology which determines how quickly marginal products diminish.' Discuss.

11 What happens to the rate of profit in:
(a) Ricardo's agricultural model when population increases;
(b) Marx's model when the organic composition of capital increases;
(c) The neoclassical model when the number of machines increases?

12 Are accountants Marxists?

13 'The neoclassical economists confused the return to capital as property with capital as a factor of production on a par with labour.' Discuss.

Chapter 27
Labour

Most people obtain their livelihood through the sale of labour services and this is the reason why we have a separate chapter on the rewards of labour. What workers obtain is called a wage and consists, as we have seen in previous chapters, of a mixture of transfer earnings, rent, interest and profit or, for simplicity, wage plus surplus, and this total payment presumably reflects and affects the allocation of labour between different jobs. Two questions arise: can the labour market be regarded like all other markets? Can labour services be treated like all other commodities and, if so, what are the consequences? It is because the welfare of people matters, and because economists believe that the labour market differs from other markets, that economists pay particular attention to the workings of the labour market.

Economists have tended to regard the labour market as somehow different from other markets for a variety of reasons:

1 *Personality*. Since the owner of labour services cannot detach himself from his services but must accompany them, a worker will be interested in the non-monetary aspects of employment. Workers will look to the pleasantness or otherwise of working conditions as a source of benefit from work.

2 *Human capital*. Since it is impossible, except in slave societies, to secure absolute control of the assets embodied in people, investment in education and training becomes the responsibility of the individual or his parents, or, in many societies, the state.

The first peculiarity of labour markets means that the simple statement that workers are interested in money wages must be qualified. Sometimes workers will be prepared to forego some money income in return for pleasant social conditions of work. This qualification can be incorporated into the traditional analysis by saying that workers are interested in the *net advantages* of jobs, where net advantages refers to both the monetary and the non-monetary aspects of jobs.

The second peculiarity of labour is important since it serves to determine mobility of labour. The man who invests in machinery can own the machinery and so be sure he gets whatever return accrues to his investment. The individual who invests in another individual cannot get this assurance. The distribution of wealth within the community therefore serves to determine who acquires particular skills and the monopoly of the rich can only be broken either by charity or by the state financing the education of the able poor. An interesting side effect of the distribution of finance for investment in human capital is that those who enjoy high wages usually enjoy good working conditions: monetary and non-monetary aspects of jobs do not always offset each other and the university professor enjoys high wages and pleasant conditions of work which the dustman does not.

The demand for labour

The demand for labour has been dealt with as part of the general explanation of the demand for factors of production in Chapter 23.

The supply of labour

The phrase 'supply of labour' can refer to many things. Either it can refer to the long-run supply of labour, when it is customary to ask whether the population and the proportion of the population seeking jobs (the source of labour supply) responds to changes in wages. Or it can refer to the question: will people work harder or longer as a result of a wage increase? Finally, the 'supply of labour' may be used as a peg on which to hang a discussion of the efficiency of changes in relative wages as an allocator of labour between different occupations, industries or regions. The first problem, population, has been looked at in Chapter 3, and will be re-examined in Chapter 43 and so need not detain us. The second issue, hours of work or effort, will be the subject of this section whilst the mobility of labour will form the basis of analysis in a succeeding section.

A problem that is of perennial interest to economists and politicians is whether with a given population the supply of labour (as in Figure 133) falls off as wages rise. Does absenteeism increase? Do

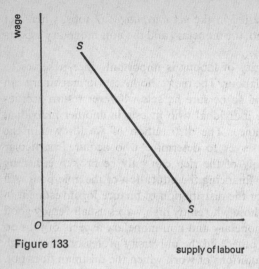

Figure 133

supply of labour

workers 'take their time' as wages increase? Have the British become indolent as they have become richer? Apart from its obvious political significance we can see that the question is important with respect to labour because a person is both a consumer of goods as well as a supplier of labour services. Since time is needed to consume goods and supply labour services there is an obvious tug of war created by an increase in wages. As the wage rises a worker can now purchase the same quantities of goods as previously for a smaller expenditure of time and effort. Hence if leisure is desirable and work irksome he may spend his increase in income on leisure. On the other hand, he will now observe that the price of leisure has risen relative to that of work and so he may be prepared to work longer (or harder).

The contradictory effects of a wage rise can be seen in Figure 134 which uses the revealed preference technique. Along the vertical axis is measured income and along the horizontal axis is measured hours available. We assume that the individual has available a total number of hours of ON and that if he devoted all those hours to work he would obtain income OA. Hence the slope of the line NA expresses the wage per unit of time. Of course, he would not normally work ON hours and we may assume that he decides to work MN hours and obtain OB income and enjoy OM leisure. Suppose now that the wage rate rises and the wage line rotates to NC. By working the same number of

438 Labour

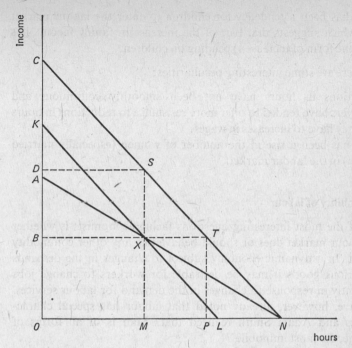

Figure 134

hours he could obtain income OD. Alternatively, he could seek to obtain the same income as previously but reduce his working hours and enjoy more leisure, MP. By drawing a line through X parallel to NC we can isolate the substitution effect due to the wage change. This substitution effect will induce him to work more hours. Why? Because the points along XK were previously not available to him whereas the points along XL had been rejected. Hence, unless the elasticity of supply is zero the substitution effect will cause him to work longer. The income effect will cause him to move from a point on NA to one on NC but where he will go will depend on the sign of the income effect.

Armchair reasoning cannot tell us whether the substitution effect will take on different values but the empirical evidence does indicate that it can. Thus:

There has been a secular decline in hours of work;

There has been a tendency for children to enter the labour market later which suggests that part of the increase in family income has taken the form of increased spending on children.

But there are some interesting peculiarities:

Reductions in hours have not been smoothly continuous and employers have tended to offer more resistance to reductions in hours than they have to increases in wages;
There has been a rise in the number of women (especially married women) in the labour market.

The mobility of labour

One of the most interesting questions facing economists is whether the labour market does or should behave like any other commodity market. In a dynamic economy subject to changes in the demands for various goods it may be desirable for workers to change jobs frequently in response to changes in the demand for labour services. We have, however, already noted that labour has special characteristics and Adam Smith realized that 'Man is of all forms of baggage, the most immobile'.

'Mobility' relates to many different sorts of movement: occupational mobility which refers to movement between job types and skill levels; social mobility which refers to movement between different social classes; and geographical mobility which refers to physical movement between areas. The economist is interested in all of these types of mobility in so far as they all affect the allocation of resources, but perhaps he is more interested in the spatial aspects because of the long-standing problem of regional economic balance. Moreover it is with respect to spatial distribution that labour has proved most immobile. People may be reluctant to move jobs for a variety of reasons: uncertainty about future demand for their skills; the breaking of strong social ties developed within a factory and local community; loss of pension rights etc. Moreover, the economist's analysis of mobility is hampered by the fact that when labour does move it may not always be in response to a price change, i.e. a change in wage rates, but in response to, say, the prospect of a pleasanter working and social environment.

If labour is immobile then appropriate government policies need to be clearly specified. Such policies may include taking work (i.e. capital) to the workers and establishing training schemes financed by the state. As a first step in deciding appropriate policies it is clearly important to ascertain how much labour mobility there is and what are its causes. One of the simplest sources of information is the Social Survey study of labour mobility in Great Britain between 1953 and 1963. Information from this survey is presented in Tables 41 and 42.

Table 41 suggests that over the period there was a considerable movement of people to the south of England and little movement into the north and west of the British Isles. Northern Ireland and Scotland were areas into which people may have gone as tourists but seldom as residents. In fact the movement of people to the south was a movement of people from the north and west. What caused these movements? Table 42 indicates that the majority of people moved in order to obtain better housing, but wages do not appear to be an obvious cause of movement though this may be due to the manner and type of questions asked of the movers. Many of these apparently 'social reasons' may have been conditional upon getting higher wages and many of the movers may have not been moving very far (perhaps to another part of the town) and so their replies can throw

Table 41 Percentage of people living in a region who were born there

Northern	81·8
North East	79·7
North Midland	78·3
Eastern	46·4
London	59·3
South East	50·3
South West	53·9
Wales	72·9
Midland	82·8
North West	79·2
Scotland	82·0
N. Ireland	90·2

Source: *Labour Mobility in Great Britain, 1953–63*,
Social Survey, London, 1966. Table 4

Table 42 Main reason given by men and women for moving

	Both sexes (%)
marriage (including prospective marriage)	11
had to – slum/redevelopment	6
had to – given notice	3
wanted – better/modern accommodation	24
wanted – different size dwelling	15
wanted – home of their own	8
work reasons	17
to be near relatives/friends	6
better surroundings	7
rents, rates, etc. too high	1
other vague answers	2
number on which percentage based	10 456

Source: *Labour Mobility in Great Britain, 1953–63*, Table 16

little light upon the broad geographical movements revealed in Table 41.

Examination of the geographical distribution of earnings and unemployment helps to explain the causes of this movement. Unfortunately the regions chosen by the Social Survey do not always correspond to those adopted by the Department of Employment and Productivity (e.g. Eastern is divided between East Anglia and Yorkshire and Humberside). Nevertheless, inspection of the available data suggests that the north and west parts of the country were areas of high unemployment and low wages, whereas the south was characterized by a strong demand for labour and high earnings. Perhaps it is just a statistical coincidence that people are moving to the areas of higher wages but it is a coincidence that seems to be in line with what economists predict.

Migration and unemployment

Another interesting insight into the mobility of labour is revealed by Figure 135 and Tables 43–44 which relate to the migration of people from Scotland either to England or to overseas countries. Both flows

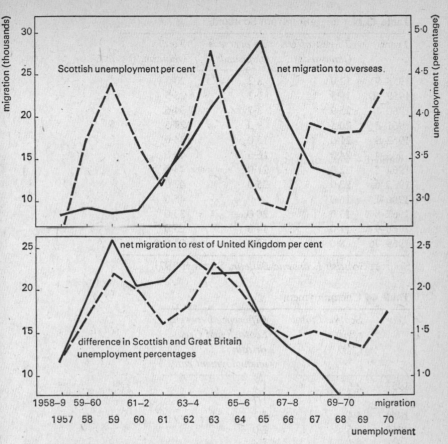

Figure 135 Migration and unemployment
Source: Scottish Economic Bulletin, Summer 1971

seem to be related to the relative prosperity of Scotland though the link is strongest for the shorter moves to England.

Trade unions

Trade unions are associations of workers seeking to improve their wages and conditions of employment and also, through pressure on governments, the social lives of their members. Unions, as Table 45 reveals, organize some 40 per cent of the labour force. This is a

Table 43 Net migration from Scotland

Years	To rest of UK (thousands)	To overseas (thousands)	Total (thousands)
1958–9	12·0	8·3	20·3
1959–60	19·3	9·2	28·5
1960–1	25·9	8·7	34·6
1961–2	20·5	9·0	29·5
1962–3	21·0	13·0	34·0
1963–4	24·0	16·6	40·6
1964–5	22·0	21·0	43·0
1965–6	22·0	25·0	47·0
1966–7	16·0	29·0	45·0
1967–8	13·0	20·0	33·0
1968–9	11·0	14·0	25·0
1969–70	8·0	13·0	21·0

Source: *Scottish Economic Bulletin*, Summer 1971

Table 44 Unemployment

Year	Scotland total register (%)	Difference between Scottish and Great Britain unemployment rates
1957	2·6	1·2
1958	3·8	1·7
1959	4·4	2·7
1960	3·6	2·0
1961	3·1	1·6
1962	3·8	1·8
1963	4·8	2·3
1964	3·6	2·0
1965	3·0	1·6
1966	2·9	1·4
1967	3·9	1·5
1968	3·8	1·4
1969	3·7	1·3
1970	4·3	1·7

Source: *Scottish Economic Bulletin*, Summer 1971

Table 45 Trade union membership, 1892–1970

Annual averages	Number of trade unions	Total membership (thousands)	Membership as a percentage of labour force
1892–1913	1292	2187	14·0
1914–20	1280	5934	33·0
1921–38	1126	5193	28·0
1939–45	963	7440	36·7
1946–70	669	9682	42·0

Source: *British Labour Statistics: Historical Abstract* 1886–1968, Department of Employment Gazette

considerable number which is enhanced by the fact that union leaders frequently sit on committees which fix the wages of unorganized groups of workers.

A further feature of Table 45 is that there has been an increasing tendency to concentrate trade unionists into fewer unions with the result that there are fewer centres of decision-making.

Methods of raising wages

In a particular industry

Unions can raise wages but if the demand for labour is elastic with respect to wages then there will be a fall in the demand for union labour; even if demand is completely wage inelastic there may be pressure on the union wage from outsiders attracted by the higher wages. Hence unions will normally try to control the supply of labour in order to raise wages. In Figure 136 the wage and employment levels in the absence of unions would be OW and ON respectively. Suppose that as a result of union pressure, the wage increases from W to W_1. Demand would shrink to W_1A resulting in unemployment of CB. To relieve the pressure on the wage which tends to pull it down to W a union could attempt by apprenticeship restrictions and closed-shop policies to shift the supply curve upwards through A so that the new supply curve would be the line W_1AS_1.

In the case analysed in the previous paragraph the undesirable effects (unemployment) of a wage increase might deter a union from pressing a wage claim. There is, however, one situation where a union might be able to raise wages without creating unemployment:

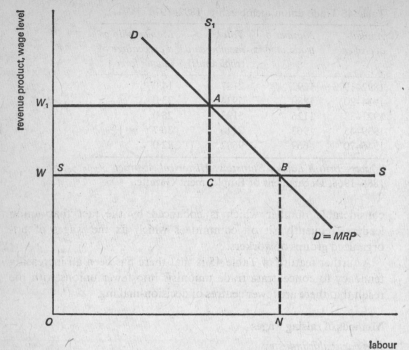

Figure 136

that situation is when the employer is a monopolist, i.e. a buyer who can influence price. This situation is depicted in Figure 137. In this diagram $S(AC)$ refers to the supply curve of labour which is also the employer's average cost curve of employment – the average cost of employment is the firm's wages bill divided by the number of workers employed, i.e. the wage per worker. The $S(MC)$ curve is the employer's *marginal*-cost curve of employment. Marginal cost is greater than average cost since the employment cost of the additional worker is the wage he must receive *plus* the increase on the wages bill as a result of paying all other workers the new, higher, wage rate. Now, if the employer equates the marginal cost of employment with the marginal product he will employ ON workers but pay no more than the average cost of employment since the desired supply is forthcoming at that wage rate. In this particular case, then, labour is not paid a wage equal to marginal product: this particular case is often described as one of exploitation, though not of the Marxian type.

446 Labour

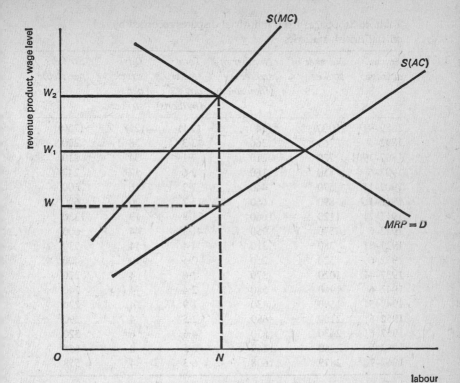

Figure 137

If now a union insists upon a wage OW_1 it can increase wages and employment. In effect a union makes the average and marginal cost of labour equal. A union could therefore push wages up to OW_2 without employment falling. The level of incidence of monopsony is not known. Nor do we know much about the effects of unionism though some writers believe that unions have their greatest impact on wages in their early years which would seem to suggest that non-union labour markets are monopsonistic.

All industries

The effect of unions on the general level of wages may be:

To increase labour's share of the national income; *or*
To leave the share unchanged because employers raise prices; *or*

Table 46 Stoppages from industrial disputes recorded by official British statistics

Annual averages	Number of strikes	Number of strikers (thousands)	Total striker days (millions)	Days struck per striker	Strikers per strike
1889–91[1]	(1050)	(340)	(7·1)	(21)	(250)
1892–6	760	360	13·3	38	270
1897–1901	720	210	7·1	34	210
1902–6	410	160	2·6	17	240
1907–11	570	440	7·2	16	600
1912–16	890	660	13·2	20	600
1917–21	1120	1660	31·8	19	1330
1922–6	570	950	41·8	44	1600
1927–31	380	310	4·4	14	730
1932–6	520	250	2·5	10	400
1937–41	1020	370	1·6	4	270
1942–6	1960	580	2·4	4	240
1947–51	1590	430	1·9	4	220
1952–6	2100	680	2·5	4	290
1957–61	2630	830	4·6	6	320
1962–6	2260	1460	2·5	2	650
1967–70[2]	2879	1608	6·3	4	558

1. Three years only (reports probably less complete than in later years)
2. Four years only
Source: Turner (1969), with addition of data for 1969 and 1970 from DEP Gazette

To raise the wages of those in jobs but not those who are made redundant.

Strikes. One of the most spectacular methods of attempting to alter the conditions of employment of workers is through the use of the strike. Presented in Table 46 are several measures of strike activity. Since these give rise to differing interpretations the reader is left to draw his own conclusions. Note that the terms *strikes* and *strikers* also refer to lockouts, and include workers 'indirectly involved' at the establishment where the stoppages occurred.

Summary

The labour market exhibits some peculiarities resulting from the characteristics of labour. Nevertheless, some pieces of economic analysis are useful, notably the distinction between income and substitution effects in the response of labour supply to changes in wages. Unions however create difficulties because there is little empirical evidence on their effects.

Questions

1 Why are teachers with degrees paid more than teachers who do not possess a degree?

2 'Time is the fundamental unit of cost in individual allocative decisions with respect to both labour and consumption' (H. G. Johnson). Explain.

3 'If married women go out to work then wages will fall and so families will be worse off.' Carefully explain the circumstances under which this prediction will (a) be refuted, and (b) be confirmed.

4 There exist uniform salary scales for teachers. If there was a shortage of mathematics teachers relative to chemistry teachers how would the educational system respond?

5 An increase in hourly wage-rates increases the opportunity cost of leisure in terms of other goods, and an increase in the tax on beer increases the opportunity cost of beer. Why is it possible to predict the direction of the effect on the demand for beer with more confidence than the direction of the demand for leisure?

6 The car industry is currently producing 2 million cars a year at an average price of £1000 per car. A union leader suggests that if the price of cars was reduced to £950 then sales would rise to 2½ million and employment would increase. Moreover, profits would not be reduced from their level of £200 million. The employers argued that the union leader had over-estimated the price elasticity and even if the union estimate was correct then, though sales might rise, employment would fall.

(a) What was the union's estimate of the price-elasticity of demand for cars?

(b) Why should the employers argue that employment might fall even though sales might rise?

(c) What assumption was the union making about the level of average costs for the outputs of 2 million and $2\frac{1}{2}$ million cars?

7 Will a sharp fall in attendance at theatres have a greater effect on the earnings of the actors than on the earnings of the electricians and joiners responsible for the stage settings?

8 What economic criteria should be employed in determining the pay of the Armed Forces?

9 What might be the economic consequences of a national minimum wage?

10 In the nineteenth century, unemployed cutlery workers were paid a 'wage' by their union. This 'wage' was obtained from a levy on those members who were working. In this way the union helped to keep wages up. Explain the circumstances under which this policy would have been preferable to one of allowing the wage to fall until all union members were employed.

11 The State compels employers to pay lump sums to workers who are made redundant. What effect will this action have on wages?

12 A union has an agreement with an employer whereby the ratio of apprentices to journeymen is fixed. The employer complains that the agreement is too restrictive whilst the union claims it is not, because the employer has not taken up his full quota of apprentices. What additional information would you require before agreeing with either the union or the employer? This question is based upon a disagreement between the London Typographical Society (now a constituent of the National Graphical Association) and the Newspaper Proprietors' Association as reported in the Report of the Royal Commission on the Press 1962.

13 'The concept of marginal productivity has no meaning in the public sector, not so much because the government does not sell its output, so that an increment of output cannot be valued in monetary terms – we would get round that by using some weighted bundle of physical indicators – but because governments are not profit-maximizers and hence can produce any output of public services that Parliament approves' (M. Blaug). Comment on this statement and

examine the effect of public sector wage fixing on private sector wage fixing and employment.

14 'Profit maximization is the best protection against racial discrimination.' Discuss.

15 'Although we do not allow Asians to enter the UK freely we allow their goods to enter our markets and that is just as bad.' Is it? In what circumstances would the free entry of textiles, radios and cameras have the same effects on the wages of UK workers as the free entry of Asians?

Part Eight
Money, Output and Growth

The subject matter of this part of the book is not in dispute though its interpretation has been a matter of serious contention for three decades. It is concerned with how the activities of various sectors or markets are coordinated and why it is that economies, as a whole rather than in parts, are subject to fluctuations in output, employment, prices and growth rates.

In previous chapters we assumed that decision making involved individuals attempting to maximize something called utility and that utility could be measured by a measuring rod of money. This theory of value in its varying forms – marginal utility, indifference analysis and revealed preference – was then applied to many situations where decisions were made and, in a slightly different form, was applied to the determination of factor rewards and so provided a theory of distribution. It did, however, tend to rest upon the assumption of a constant marginal utility of money income. It is true that the indifference and revealed preference approaches could incorporate income effects but only by excluding the possibilities of moving across the hierarchy of wants. Now the marginal utility of money income could vary either as a result of a fall in price or as a result of an increase in the quantity of money and both changes could break the relationship between utilities and prices.

David Hume (1711–76) and the Quantity Theory of Money

The notion that changes in the quantity of money could disturb the decision-making process was severely qualified by David Hume. What Hume suggested was that changes in the quantity of money could have a disturbing influence in the short run, but that in the long run money was neutral. What neutrality meant was that changes in the quantity of money would not cause changes in relative prices and the allocation of resources. This was an important insight because it removed any difficulties associated with changes in the measuring rod of money. A doubling of the quantity of money simply meant a doubling of the general level of prices and a halving of the value of money. A simple linear relationship was established between money and the price level. The task of monetary economics seemed, therefore, to be one of devising suitable index numbers to measure changes in the general level of prices and this involved finding representative bundles of goods and choosing between the arithmetic, geometric and harmonic means.

There was, of course, the problem of the short run effects of changes in the quantity of money. But this problem could not be analysed until the problem of market coordination had been resolved. Until, that is, economics had worked out the implications of disturbances in a barter economy. Similarly, the long run problems of introducing money into an economy where factor supplies and technical change were taking place seemed to require the prior analysis of a barter economy undergoing growth.

Leon Walras (1834–1910) and General Equilibrium

The first economist to provide an explicit statement of market coordination was Leon Walras in his classic, *Elements of Pure Economics*. He showed the interaction of markets by means of simultaneous equations. The problem was: how was this set of simultaneous equations resolved so that all the plans of economic agents were reconciled? Walras presented a simple story in which the solution was achieved by an auctioneer. He imagined that everyone came to a central market with a list of prices at which they were prepared to buy and sell goods. They would hand their lists to the auctioneer who would shout out the prospective demands, supplies and prices. If the market was not cleared then everyone would retire from the market and revise his plans. The process would continue until the market was cleared.

Walras's story was a simplification. It assumed a degree of centralization which is not normally encountered in economies. It assumed away the existence of money by assuming that every good was money. It allowed most of the interesting activity to take place 'off stage' where individuals made and revised their plans. Walras was well aware that his story was a simplification and that economic activity was often attended by crises but he was not able to show how equilibrium was reached in the real world.

Nevertheless, Walras's portrayal of the interconnections of market activities was an achievement and in more recent times the system of simultaneous equations has been used to throw light upon a variety of interesting questions. In this connection the use of matrix algebra and the development of high speed computers has reduced the time in which rough conclusions can be reached.

Alfred Marshall (1842–1924) and Partial Equilibrium Analysis

Alfred Marshall was well aware that all economic activity could be represented by a set of simultaneous equations but that such equations did not describe how an economy achieved equilibrium. Marshall was interested in the workings of a dynamic economy. He visualized an economy growing through time as a result of innovations and changes in factor supplies. This economy tended to a stable full employment equilibrium and all markets were linked together by the existence of money. Any disturbances of demand or supply would be damped down by the activities of speculators, who, using money, could switch between markets and buy up excess supplies of goods or release stocks to damp down excess demands. Of course, not all fluctuations could be erased and there was some unemployment of resources due to frictions in the workings of the economy.

Within the context of the dynamic economy Marshall chose to analyse the effects of disturbances in one market on the assumption that the repercussions on other markets would be minimal. This was the technique of *partial equilibrium* analysis which we used in Parts Two to Seven. Marshall divided the responses of market to a disturbance into two stages – the short run equilibrium and the long run equilibrium. In the short run supply was fixed and demand was the main determinant of price. Changes in demand led to changes in price, though Marshall did concede that in severe slumps price might not fall to the level of running costs. In the long run the major determinant of price was supply and changes in demand led to changes in the amount of investment and disinvestment.

The short run, however, dominated the scene and the long run equilibrium was a kind of never-never land. This carried the implication that prices might not measure marginal utilities and marginal products. Marginal utilities could only be measured for those goods on which only a small portion of income was spent. Marginal utilities could not be measured in the case of comparisons of the present and the future because of uncertainty. Marginal utilities from work and leisure could not be easily measured because the utility from leisure and the disutility from work were not strictly comparable. Prices might not measure costs if there were increasing returns.

John Maynard Keynes (1883–1946) and General Disequilibrium

What Keynes did was to take over the Marshallian short run equilibrium model and apply it to the whole economy. And whereas Marshall emphasized supply side problems, Keynes looked at the difficulties caused by demand. He analysed the total demand for goods and services, how it was influenced by expectations and how it determined not only the general level of prices but also the volume of output and employment.

Keynes's analysis contained problems and weaknesses. In a highly decentralized economy it will be the case that not all decisions take place simultaneously. There will be lags in reactions and these lags will be of different lengths. Marshall's analysis contained lags but they were confined to one industry and only occurred on the supply side. Keynes was aware of the existence of lags and in his *Treatise on Money* (1930) and in the years before the *General Theory* he had experimented with theories containing lags but found it difficult to say anything useful with lag or period analysis. In his *General Theory* he switched to the technique of *comparative statics*. What this amounted to was taking snapshots of an economy at various points of time. At one point the economy was in equilibrium and was then subjected to a disturbance and the consequences would be examined at a later time. The disturbances were variations in demand. Unfortunately, the technique meant that it was often difficult to see how the path to equilibrium was reached since everything appeared to happen instantaneously and it was also difficult to see how one short run was succeeded by another to produce a long run disequilibrium.

Although the *General Theory* is a general theory in the sense that it embraces both situations of unemployment and full employment, its basic message was that aggregate demand was often insufficient to guarantee full employment. This message seemed plausible in the thirties. The failure of market forces implied a failure of value theory; the prices that were supposed to clear the market did not exist and the prices that guided buyers were different from those influencing suppliers. On the one hand, wage earners based their supplies of labour services not on real wages over which they had no control but on money wages which were amenable to bargaining. On the other hand, employers based their demands for labour services on real wages because they had some control over product prices as well as money wages. On the one hand, lenders might be influenced by comparisons of present and future income, but could just as easily decide to hold command over future goods in the form of money as in the form of stocks and shares; there could be a reluctance to lend. On the other hand, borrowers based their investment decisions on extremely fragile assumptions about future profits. Value theory, which appeared to be set on a firm foundation by Walras, was qualified by Marshall and appeared to have been destroyed by Keynes. Moreover there was a strand in the *General Theory* which appeared to suggest that unemployment might persist forever; there might be secular stagnation. Wages might not fall because of trade union resistance or because social security benefits established a floor below which wages might not fall and even if they did fall then demand might also fall because wages were a source of income and hence demand. And even if the money rate of interest were pushed down businessmen might still be reluctant to borrow whilst lenders might consider the convenience of money more attractive than the uncertainty attaching to stocks and shares.

Although Keynes did not set out an explanation of how crisis might occur – there was, for example, no attempt at a detailed analysis of the upper turning point of business fluctuations – the *General Theory* can be read as giving support to the view that slumps are caused by real forces, principally a collapse of investment opportunities, and that changes in the money supply were not responsible for slumps. Money was a veil behind which real forces operated. In a slump, pumping money into an economy would do no good, it would just be held. In a boom, attempting to hold back the supply of money would do no good since businessmen would find some way of getting finance. The money supply expands and contracts in response to the demands of industry. It is just this thesis which Milton Friedman has attacked. He has suggested that major fluctuations in activity are the result of changes in the money supply. He does not deny that real forces do cause fluctuations but he believes that a mild recession in the thirties was converted into major catastrophe by a reduction in the money supply. The implications of Friedman's views are far reaching; they affect not merely theory but policy. Hence we need to take a look at the inter-war years.

A monetary theory of history

Presented here is a point of view which contrasts sharply with that to be found in the newspapers, the history books and the television utterances of politicians and commentators. Consider, for example, the history of the UK, the USA, indeed of the world since 1914. The UK came out of the First World War with her major industries – coal and iron, textiles and engineering – ill-adapted to the changed patterns of demands and supplies. Before the war these industries had been adapting to overseas competition, but the war suspended the adjustment with the result that a much greater adaptation was needed afterwards.

The process of adjustment could have been eased by the lowering of export prices, for the foreign demands for UK goods might have been presumed to have some price-elasticity. Economists distinguished between two methods whereby these prices could be reduced: bankers and politicians were apt to see only one. Since UK goods had to be sold at foreign prices then *either* the initial UK price could have been altered *or* the conversion rate (exchange rate) whereby UK prices were translated into foreign prices could have been altered. That sounds a little complicated though an example should dispel the confusion. Assuming a conversion rate of $2 equalling £1, then a good priced at £1 on the home market would sell for $2 in America. If it were desired to lower UK prices to sell more this could be done *either* by lowering the domestic price to 50p and then, by conversion, selling at $1 in America *or* by altering the conversion rate from $2 equals £1, to $1 equals £1.

Both methods might be expected to yield the same result yet in the real world the paths to the final result are apt to give rise to the unexpected. To achieve the first result it would have been necessary to reduce the amount of money in the UK economy so as to press prices downwards: this is a process known as *deflation* and assumes that there is some link between the quantity of money and the level of prices and that prices are flexible. The other method, the alteration of the conversion rate, is known as *devaluation* and also assumes some control of money supply lest the alteration of the conversion rate be nullified by rising domestic prices.

In an ideal world either method of lowering the foreign price of domestic goods would work and the choice might be decided by a flip of a coin. But the world in 1919 was not ideal and the decision of the UK government to pursue a deflationary policy was to have profound implications. It meant that the brunt of the adjustment had to be borne by those in the export trades, leaving those in domestic trades to escape unscathed. Social justice was therefore involved and *the economic consequences of Mr Churchill* (Keynes, 1931b) were the General Strike of 1926, the destruction of the first and second Labour Governments and the eventual devaluation of the pound sterling in 1931. Although organized labour was defeated in the battles of 1924, 1926 and 1931, it won the war. Deflation implied that wages bend to the dictates of a fixed ratio between pounds and other currencies, to the dictates of a Gold Standard, but in the end it was the Gold Standard that gave way to a Labour Standard: wages did not bend.

What of the rest of the world? In Germany there was inflation, prices rose dramatically, as the figures of Table 47 adequately indicate.

In America the twenties were the golden years of the motor car, jazz and prohibition. Apart from minor recessions in 1921, 1923, 1925 and 1927 the period was one of unprecedented prosperity. By 1927, however, there were signs that the boom was coming to an end: agriculture was in trouble and construction was entering the downswing of its long cycle of seventeen years. Yet the long

Table 47 Index of wholesale prices: 1913 = 1

1920	13·7
1921	14·3
1922	101·0
1923 January	2875
August	944 041
November	750 000 million

Source: Stolper (1967)

spell of prosperity served to allow the Stock Market to develop its own fantasies until the euphoria broke in 1929. Then there occurred a most momentous decision. The governors of the Federal Reserve Banks began to reduce the money supply and thereby intensified the crisis.

The rest of the world imported a slump from America. During the twenties loans from America propped up Europe but with the domestic crisis they were withdrawn. The reduction in industrial activity in Europe and the USA caused a fall in the demand for raw materials and foodstuffs and so the primary producers were embroiled in a world slump.

The world after the Second World War produced some variations on what had gone before. The difficulties of adaptation of the UK economy continued and were intensified by the loss of many overseas assets which had been sold to pay for the war. Europe was also exhausted. America emerged clearly as the greatest political-economic unit in the world. The world after the war was one that feared another Great Slump and so interest rates – the cost of borrowing – were kept low by cheap money policies so as to stimulate spending. Cheap money policies, the pent-up demands of people starved by war, and the great technological advances of thirty years conspired to produce a great technological boom.

The Second World War was a total war in the sense that there was extensive rationing and price control. The apparatus of controls and associated queues continued into the peace and so it was some time before people began to appreciate that they were living in an inflationary situation. Characteristic of the fifties and sixties was creeping rather than galloping inflation.

The UK commenced the peace with a cheap money policy and

in 1949 a Labour Government, having absorbed the experiences of its pre-war ancestors, devalued the pound so that, at least until the mid-fifties, the problem of exports and economic adjustments were eased. However, the lack of control over the money supply, created by the adoption of a Labour Standard and policies aimed at maintaining full employment, led to upward pressure on wages and prices and hence to difficulties in selling goods in foreign markets. Consequently, successive Conservative Governments of the late fifties and sixties attempted to solve the economy's problems by deflationary policies. Meanwhile the rest of the world prospered until the Vietnam War created inflationary pressures in America. The inflation was then exported to the rest of the world.

The tendency to worldwide inflation as a result of the Vietnam War was superimposed upon an expansion of the public sector. Looking back to 1945 it is difficult to realize the structural changes that have taken place in most industrial economies. At the end of the Second World War most of them were predominantly market economies with a small public sector devoted to defence and a few odds and ends. And it was envisaged that this structure would continue with the additional requirement that the public sector engage in occasional bouts of contra-cyclical spending so as to iron out booms and slumps. But this view of the future failed to anticipate the big expansion of the public sector.

The public sector grew because of the high dependency ratio of too many young and old relative to the working population. It also grew because people wanted a better environment – better towns, roads and leisure facilities. Unfortunately, the British economy was unable to provide these collective goods and the desired amounts of private goods and the financing of the public sector was often done by printing money.

Contemporary Analysis

Keynesian theory came under attack because it rested upon a number of debatable assumptions and predictions. First, it assumed that in the short run consumer spending is a stable function of current income but this was subsequently refuted (see Chapter 33). Secondly, it assumed that spending on capital goods is highly volatile but later research has softened the force of this argument (see Chapter 34).

Thirdly, it assumed that the demand for money is highly unstable and this assertion has been rejected (see Chapter 28). Fourthly, it assumed that the contraction in the money supply in the thirties was in response to a lack of demand for money brought about by a collapse of real forces rather than postulating that the cut-back in the money supply caused the collapse in spending. Fifthly, it assumed that workers took little interest in real wages (see Chapter 37). Sixthly, it assumed that governments could steer economies along stable full employment paths by the use of discretionary monetary and fiscal policies (see Chapter 38). Now we are more aware that the short run cannot be divorced from the long run. But despite its failings Keynesian theory was a bold attempt to explain and suggest remedies for the slump of the thirties. And it was the first theory to bring real and monetary forces together in an analytical framework of great power and elegance.

Today our problems are different. Inflation as well as unemployment exists. Economic growth has become a problem. The optimum size of the public sector has become a problem. The distribution of income and wealth has become a problem. And the economic consequences of a declining population threaten to become a problem.

Chapter 28
The Demand for Money[1]

People presumably hold money because it is useful to do so, because it represents a general command over goods and services. The existence of and the general acceptability of money, as a medium of exchange and a store of value, has permitted an enormous extension of the division of labour and a consequent increase in output. Indeed, so important and useful is money that even in the greatest of all inflations – often called hyper-inflation because of the exceptionally rapid rise in prices involved – people have still found it desirable to use money even though its value in terms of goods and services has been falling. For example, during the German inflation of the twenties, the Hungarian inflation of the forties, and the Latin American inflation of the fifties and sixties, people still accepted the idea of being paid in a currency whose value depreciated with each second that ticked away. Such is the usefulness of money.

Why do people use and hold money?

Money is apparently useful, but why? Answers were given in Chapter 5 and so we will merely recapitulate since our primary task is to examine more deeply the implications of the use of money.

Time and uncertainty

Most people are paid weekly or monthly but spend their income continuously so money is presumably held because of a lack of synchronization of payments and receipts. Such an answer could be wrong. If everyone possessed perfect foresight then all contracts concerning future payments and receipts could be arranged upon a given day. And from that day to eternity money need never be used.

1. Before reading this chapter it may be useful to re-read Chapter 5.

The techniques of transactions are therefore not sufficient to explain the existence of money. We could, and some do, contrive to lend out our money as soon as we get it, earn interest and recover our funds as and when we need them, but it is often inconvenient to do so. There are costs involved in getting rid of money. There is a loss of leisure in continuously going to the market. Money cannot always be disposed of in driblets.

The existence of money is incompatible with perfect foresight, but is compatible with our having a high degree of knowledge about the future. We may know with reasonable certainty the size of next year's national income, but we may not know the detailed manner of its attainment. Money will be held even when *general expectations* are likely to be fulfilled because it takes time to make up our minds about what we want to do.

We need not, of course, hold money since it yields no income. We could hold the alternative form of government debt – bonds. But if interest rates vary then the resale price of bonds will vary in the opposite direction. Hence, we may hold money because of the *specific uncertainty* attaching to the future price of apparently risk-free government bonds.

The quantity theory of money

Because it serves as a universal medium of exchange, money becomes the basic unit of account and this enables economists to speak of a general level of prices. In a barter economy, where money does not exist, the price of one good is measured in terms of the amount of another good for which it can be exchanged; that is, relative prices exist. However, it becomes impossible to speak of a general price level, or price level which is an average of two prices, unless one of the commodities is so generally acceptable that it becomes in fact money. Two sheep may exchange for one cow and it might therefore be possible to measure all prices in terms of cows or sheep, but that presupposes that cows or sheep act as money.

By virtue of its use as a unit of account there is established a link between money and the general level of prices. What is the nature of this link? This is the starting point of the quantity theory of money. In its simplest form the quantity theory postulates a strict proportionality between the quantity of money and the level of prices: if the quantity of money rises, for example, by 10 per cent, then the price level will rise by 10 per cent. It is doubtful if anyone holds the theory in this strict form and most economists would recognize that there are occasions when changes in the quantity of money exert no influence on prices and may in fact be accompanied by an increase in output. Perhaps the crucial feature of a quantity theory of money is, however, the amount of money that is required to effect transactions. Since the quantity theory emphasizes the role of money as a medium of exchange it points to the importance of the amount of money required to carry out exchanges. We might envisage a situation in which a single note could perform all the transactions desired by a community if it passed from hand to hand at a very high speed. There are of course limitations on the speed at which money can be turned over, such as the amount of time needed to decide whether to make a purchase, and it becomes imperative to know just how stable or unstable is the speed at which transactions are performed. This speed of turnover is known as the *transactions velocity of circulation of money* (V_T).

We are now in a position to set out the quantity theory of money in the form in which it was formulated by the great American economist, Irving Fisher (1867–1947). In equation **1** M refers to the stock of nominal money, V_T is the transactions velocity of circulation of money, P_T is the transactions price level and T is the total number of transactions to be carried out.

$$MV_T = P_T T \qquad\qquad\qquad\qquad\qquad\qquad 1$$

The stock of nominal money (M)

The definition of money becomes important in so far as any definition determines whether the stock of money can be regarded as something that is given (that is, determined from outside the equational system) or whether the stock of money is something that changes in response to changes in the other variables. Suppose, for example, that money is defined as a particular commodity, say gold, then the distribution of that amount of money available would move automatically in response to its price, and the amount of gold available in any one country would depend upon its international distribution and the relative price levels in different countries (this issue is taken up in Chapter 35, where the gold standard is discussed). On the other hand, money might consist of something, say paper, the amount of which was arbitrarily fixed by the state and which might bear no relationship to events elsewhere. The amount of money also needs to be defined carefully so as to make it clear whether it includes privately produced money such as that provided by the commercial banks or whether it is provided solely by the state, or whether the state has control over private production as well. For the sake of exposition, money will be taken to mean state notes and coin plus bank deposits. (These issues will be dealt with in the next chapter.)

The total number of transactions (T)

This is determined by the amount of resources available to an economy, the efficiency with which they are used, and the degree of integration of the economy. On this last point it should be noted that in a highly developed market economy the number of transactions will be greater than in a centrally planned economy.

Once a monetary economy has been established and full employment exists it is usually assumed that changes in M do not cause changes in T; that is, M and T are independent.

The price level (P_T)

The price level is the average price at which all transactions are made, though other price levels, e.g. wholesale, or consumer goods, can and are sometimes used.

It follows from what has been said that $P_T T$ is the money value of all transactions, each transaction taking place at some average price represented by P_T.

The transactions velocity of circulation (V_T)

This represents the crucial element in the theory since *if* it is allowed to vary passively in response to the movement of the other variables in the equation then that equation becomes an identity and therefore only a means of classifying material rather than a means of predicting responses. The Fisher version of quantity theory stresses spending and therefore V *appears* to be determined by such institutional arrangements as payments systems (weekly, monthly, etc.) rather than acts of choice. We are now in a position to understand the quantity theory.

If V is assumed to be constant and if T is independent of M then an increase in M will cause an increase in P and a decrease in M will cause a fall in P.

The Cambridge approach

An alternative approach to the role of money in an economy does not ask what dictates the speed with which money changes hands but why people hold money when it obviously cannot be consumed like cakes and ale. This approach, the Cambridge approach, seeks to bring monetary theory into the fold of value theory by asking why is there a demand for money: why do people apparently 'consume' money?

$$M = P_R KR \hspace{4cm} 2$$

The Cambridge approach is summarized in equation 2: M is the stock of money, P_R is the average price level of real output, R is the national income on constant prices (that is, the real national income) and K is the ratio of the money stock to income. Although K might be regarded as the reciprocal of V in the quantity theory there are several subtle differences between the two approaches which need to be recognized before any attempt is made to reconcile the two systems of thought.

1 The quantity theory stresses the spending of money whilst the Cambridge approach emphasizes that money is a temporary abode of purchasing power or store of value. It is therefore conceivable that the definition of M in the two equations may differ: in the Cambridge approach M might include antiques.

2 The quantity theory looks at payments schemes whereas the Cambridge approach has regard to utility, uncertainty and the costs and returns from holding money (see page 469).

3 The quantity approach concentrates on all transactions while the Cambridge approach narrows analysis down to income transactions for which data are usually more available. The number of transac-

tions, T, may in fact rise or fall because of a change in the number of hands through which goods pass before they reach the final consumer.

4 The quantity theory adopts a flow approach to monetary phenomena whereas the Cambridge theory is a stock approach.

Given the clarification of the differences in the two approaches we can now state the prediction from the Cambridge approach.
If K is a constant or a stable function, and R is given then an increase in M will lead to a rise in P_R and a fall in M will lead to a fall in P_R. If R is not at the full employment level then an increase in M can lead to an increase in R. If M is a constant and R is given P_R may still change if people decide to hold less or more money, that is, if K changes.

Money, the rate of interest, and the price level

The fact that money is used both as a medium of exchange and store of value means there is an automatic link between money and the rate of interest. Money is an asset which yields benefits in the present and in the future. Indeed it is the most accepted form of asset because it is the most acceptable medium of exchange. The term *liquidity* is used to signify the ease with which an asset can be converted at its full value into money. Money itself is obviously the most liquid of all assets and is held because of its liquidity. With money one can readily purchase goods and services in the present and in the future. However, if people have a positive rate of time preference (see Chapter 6), and prices are expected to remain unchanged, they will value the liquidity of a certain sum of money today more highly than the liquidity of the same sum in the future. To induce people to hold less money today – part with liquidity – they must be compensated for their reduced valuation of future liquidity. This compensation is provided by the rate of interest. The rate of interest is the 'reward' for parting with liquidity, and in this sense it is the price of money.

The implications of the previous paragraph are profound. In the first place, the contention of that paragraph is that the rate of interest is not a purely real phenomenon. The demand for and supply of money enters into the determination of the rate of interest as well as the so-called real forces of productivity and thrift. How all these forces enter into the determination of the rate of interest and how disturbances produced by variations in them are resolved lies outside the scope of our analysis. At this stage we can only suggest that since most people obtain their incomes in the form of money they have a threefold decision as to what to do with that money. Either they can hold the money, spend it on consumption goods, or buy a new asset such as a machine (or a claim on a firm) or government bond.

The second implication of the establishment of a link between money and the rate of interest is that the inclusion of money into an economy simultaneously determines both the price level and the rate of interest. Earlier we saw that the use of money as a unit of account enabled a move from relative prices to the absolute price level. We have seen that the rate of interest is influenced by money, but to say that both the rate of interest and the price level are simultaneously determined once a money economy is established does jump over the difficult problem of 'how'. This we cannot pretend to answer at this stage of your career, though we can illustrate what the problem is. The demand for money approach says that the amount of money held will be governed by the benefits from, and costs of, holding money.[2]

$$\frac{mu_1}{p_1} = \frac{mu_2}{p_2} = \ldots = \frac{mu_n}{p_n} = \frac{mu_m}{r}. \qquad\qquad 3$$

Though we cannot say anything about how money is introduced into a barter economy we can indicate the effects of a further increase in the quantity of money into an existing money economy by using the Cambridge approach modified to include the rate of interest as in equation 3. Here we take the case of an individual who is maximizing his satisfaction by consuming various goods including money services, the price of money being the rate of interest. Suppose he receives an increase in the amount of money he holds and suppose initially prices of all goods are fixed, then the marginal utility of money (mu_m) will fall and this will result in disequilibrium. He will want to spend some of his money on goods so that the marginal utilities of other goods ($mu_1, \ldots, mu_n$) will fall.

2. These benefits and costs cannot be evaluated until current and future prices are known and these depend upon the existence of money. Here there is a chicken and egg problem which is usually dodged by assuming simultaneous determination of the amount of money and prices.

If all individuals in the community receive an increase in the quantity of money they are holding then we must allow for the possibility that because other goods are scarce then their prices $(p_1, ..., p_n)$ will rise as people spend more. However, for any given initial decline in the marginal utility of money, the more the prices of other goods rise the less the marginal utility of the same goods must fall before equilibrium is re-established. Similarly if a part of the increase in the supply of money is not held directly but is placed in the money market the short-term rate of interest will be reduced and some of the equilibrium adjustment will occur on the right-hand side of the equation.[3]

Price and output effects

The quantity theory of money emphasizes the existence of a link between the quantity of money and the price level, but if there are unemployed resources then there may be an output effect and no price effect. We can therefore distinguish three possible effects:

1 *Pure price effect* which is most likely to occur when there is full employment.

2 *Pure output effect*. Most likely when there are unemployed resources.

3 *Mixed price/output effect*. A probable occurrence because of the existence of *some* unemployed resources or because of price rigidities due to lack of information or monopolies. If there is an increase in money then unemployed resources can be employed but there may

3. Equation 3 sums up the difference between the monetarists and the Keynesians. The former stress the direct effect of a change in the marginal utility of money on the demand for all other goods whereas the latter stress the indirect effect via the rate of interest. The former believe that small changes in the quantity of money held lead to relatively large changes in the marginal utility of money so that small changes in the rate of interest are insufficient to re-establish equilibrium. The monetary changes thus spill over directly into the goods market. The Keynesians, on the other hand, believe that large changes in the supply of money lead to only small changes in the marginal utility of money so that small changes in the rate of interest are sufficient to restore equilibrium, the adjustment coming wholly on the right hand side of the equation. The influence of money supply changes on the demand for goods is limited to the indirect effects of the rate-of-interest change.

be bottlenecks in terms of scarce skilled labour and so some prices rise. If the money supply is reduced some prices may not fall but output may fall and result in unemployment.

Inflation: a first examination

One central policy issue that emerges from the quantity theory of money is that if a community wishes to control its price level then it might need to control its quantity of money.

The quantity theory seems to imply that inflation – a state of rising prices in which people's expectations are disturbed – is due to increasing the quantity of money. More money is available and so people spend more, but because more goods are not available then prices rise. Inflation can, therefore, be thought of as too much money chasing too few goods. However, might not inflation be due to costs rising as a result of greedy unions or avaricious businessmen? The quantity theory seems to deny the possibility of cost-push inflation or disguises the importance by saying that if unions push up prices then the Government must increase money demand to prevent unemployment. However, that is to confuse the real cause of price changes with an apparent cause.

The liquidity trap

The case of people holding on to ever increasing amounts of money irrespective of its apparent lack of usefulness has been the subject of controversy since the publication of *The General Theory of Employment, Interest and Money* (Keynes, 1936). What Keynes did was to argue that in conditions of severe unemployment V or K would become highly variable and as a result the link between money and the rate of interest would be broken. In this situation very large increases in the quantity of money held have such a negligible effect on the marginal utility of money that they are held without offsetting variations in the other variables in equation 3. The situation envisaged by Keynes can be illustrated by means of Figure 138.

Keynes divided the reasons for holding money into three:

1 The transaction motive; $\Big\}$ = M_1 demand
2 The precautionary motive;
3 The speculative motive. $\Big\}$ = M_2 demand.

The first was the demand for money for transactions purposes. The second was the demand for security in the form of a given quantity of ready purchasing power. The third was the demand for money for speculative purposes. The first two were a function of the level of income, YY, and the third a function of the rate of interest, LL. The total demand for money (M_D) is the sum of the transactions, precautionary and speculative demands.

$$M_D = M_1 + M_2.$$

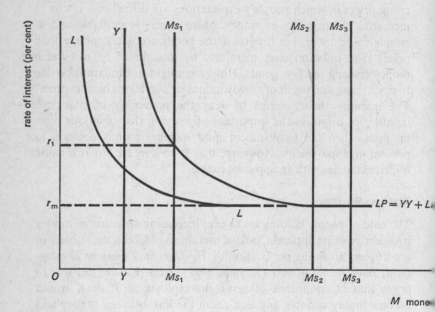

Figure 138

In Figure 138 the total demand is found from the horizontal summation of YY and LL and is depicted by the curve LP. Now the supply of money is assumed to be given independently of the rate of interest and is assumed to be M_{S1}. Given the demand for money, LP, and the supply of money the rate of interest is r_1. What is interesting is the long horizontal section of the demand curve where the price-elasticity of demand for money is infinite at a positive rate of interest with the result that increases in the money supply would have no

472 The Demand for Money

effect on the rate of interest. Thus increasing the money supply from M_{S2} to M_{S3} leaves the rate of interest unchanged. Why should this be so?

At extremely low rates of interest the returns on money (its convenience yield) and on government bonds become so close that money and bonds approach the state of being perfect substitutes so far as the rate of return is concerned. If people find themselves with additional money they will be reluctant to buy bonds since not only will the return on them be low, but additional purchases of them might further depress the return. Moreover, and this is an important element in Keynes's thinking, the lower the return the more people will be speculating on a future rise in interest rates and the more they will fear a capital loss from bond holding. To understand this it is essential to grasp that the price of bonds and their actual yield move in opposite directions. A Government $2\frac{1}{2}$ per cent Consol[4] which is sold in £100 nominal units will yield £2.50 per year if a person pays £100 for it. Suppose however that $2\frac{1}{2}$ per cent Consols are selling for £50, then the yield or actual return will be 5 per cent or £5.00 per year. This is because by spending £100 a person can obtain £200 of nominal units of Consols each giving £2.50 per year. For irredeemable fixed-interest-bearing securities with a nominal denomination of £100 the actual yield or rate of interest is given by the formula:

$$\text{Actual yield} = \frac{£100}{\text{price of bond}} \times \text{fixed interest payment per year.}$$

The important implication from Keynes's conjecture is that if the liquidity trap (as it is called) exists, then increasing the supply of money will not lead to a fall in interest rates and thereby stimulate investment. This is because people will feel that the fall in the interest rate will give a yield less than that on money, and they will speculate that there will be a rise in interest rates which would cause them a capital loss. Hence increasing the supply of money would simply increase K (or in quantity theory terminology, lower V). People will therefore hold money and any attempt to increase the quantity of money in order to stimulate employment will only result in more money being trapped in people's hoardings: it will not be

4. Consol is the name given to an irredeemable fixed-interest-bearing government security.

spent. And in terms of equation 3 the marginal utility of money will remain constant.

Keynes's conjecture raises many interesting issues. First, there is the simple empirical question: what is the relationship between the quantity of money and the rate of interest? In Chapter 29 we shall supply some statistical information from which the reader can draw his own conclusions. The second question is: how is the increase in the quantity of money brought about? The topic will be discussed in the next chapter and will be dealt with again in Chapter 37. The third question is: how stable is the demand-for-money function? If the demand-for-money function (K or V) is highly unstable what are the stable functions upon which the State can act, in periods of crisis? One such alternative, the consumption function, is considered in Chapter 33.

Here we may note that a lot of empirical work has been done to determine whether the demand for money function is stable. Stability does not, of course, mean that velocity (V or K) does not change or is constant, but that variations in V are predictable in terms of other variables (sometimes called arguments) in the demand-for-money equation. The demand-for-money function is stable if demand varies in a predictable way as the level of income, the rate of interest and the expected price level vary.

The empirical studies have shown that the demand for money is stable. It is not so interest-elastic as to give rise to a liquidity trap nor to large fluctuations in velocity. It responds to the level of income and the price level.

The problems raised by money

We have raised two issues concerning the role of money in an economy. The first was the link between money and prices. The second was the link between money and interest rates. There is, however, a more general problem raised by the 'rules of the game' in a money economy. The chief characteristic of a barter economy is that all goods are exchangeable against each other. A barter economy cannot, however, be viable because of the problems created by time and uncertainty and so a monetary economy comes into being. In such an economy the direct exchange of goods for goods becomes replaced by the exchange of goods for money. In a barter economy the supply of one good necessarily implies the demand for something else, and so the total supply of goods can never differ from the total demand for goods. In a money economy the total demand and supply of goods can only be equal if the amount of money offered by buyers equals the amount demanded by sellers. In other words, money is treated as a mere lubricant, but if people hold money and vary the amount of money held then total demand for goods can differ from the total supply of goods. This is why we have looked at the reasons why people hold money.

Summary

In this chapter we began by looking at the implications of money and we sketched out the quantity theory of money which emphasized the link between the money supply and the price level. An alternative approach – the demand for money approach – was also considered.

It was concluded that the two approaches were not substitutes but complements, though the demand approach did serve to relate the demand for money to the demand for all goods. We then looked more closely at why people decide to hold money. Arising out of that discussion was the link between money and interest rates. From that discussion we were led on to consider how a change in money affects behaviour through interest rates. We also pointed out that changes in the quantity of money may affect output as well as prices. Finally, we cautioned against relying on a demand pull explanation of inflation.

Questions

1 'It is nonsense to say that people have a demand to hold money. They simply hold money because they receive their wages on a Friday and the shops are closed until Monday.' Comment.

2 'People hold money because of a lack of synchronization of payments and receipts.' Comment.

3 'If people had perfect knowledge then they would not hold money so the only reason for holding money must be the existence of uncertainty.' Discuss.

4 'It is ridiculous to hold non-interest-bearing money as long as interest is paid on other financial assets.' Discuss.

5 'The theory of the demand for money is but a special case of the general theory of choice.' Comment.

6 In what circumstances will an increase in the quantity of money lead to an increase in (a) the general level of prices and (b) the volume of output?

7 What factors determine the velocity of circulation of money?

8 One of the most subtle concepts in economics is enshrined in the symbol K. What do you think K expresses?

9 From the equation $MV_T = P_T T$ is it possible to deduce the value of M?

10 Express the effects of a change in the amount of money people possess in terms of the marginal utility approach.

11 What is meant by liquidity?

12

	Money supply M_3 (£m)	Housing completions index 1970 = 100:	Average house price (building society)
			£
1968	15 800	118·1	4344
1969	16 270	104·7	4640
1970	17 850	100·0	4975
1971	20 230	100·0	5631
1972	25 940	91·1	7374
1973 1st Quarter	27 320	89·0	9222
2nd Quarter	28 690	92·4	9639

	Average mortgage as % price	Average income of borrowers	Ratio house price to income
		£	
1968	72·6	1618	2·68
1969	71·0	1762	2·63
1970	72·2	1929	2·58
1971	72·9	2188	2·57
1972	70·4	2474	2·98
1973 1st Quarter	65·0	2770	3·33
2nd Quarter	62·8	2834	3·40

Source: *Construction Statistics*

Using the above data, comment on the behaviour of the housing market, paying particular attention to:

(a) the possible links between changes in the quantity of money, money incomes and house prices;

(b) the possible links between changes in the quantity of money and the supply of houses;

(c) the factors which might account for the willingness of house buyers to allow the ratio between house prices and family income to rise.

13 Which of the following statements gives the clearest statement of the functions of money?

(a) 'We can't afford to pay for the Channel Tunnel';

(b) 'I keep my money in stocks and shares';

(c) 'If I didn't keep cash in my pocket or a cheque book handy, I would always be running to the bank before I could buy a packet of cigarettes'.

Chapter 29
The Supply of Money

The gist of the previous chapter was that people preferred to live in a monetary economy rather than a barter economy because there were advantages attaching to the use of money. These advantages were summarized under the headings of economizing on time and coping with uncertainty. What we then went on to examine was the effects of a change in the amount of money (under the assumption that there was a stable demand for money). We indicated that an increase in the amount of money possessed by people would mean an imbalance in their holding of goods and (portfolio) holdings of money and other financial assets, and so they would attempt to increase their expenditure in order to re-establish the desired ratio between them. This effect of an increase in the amount of money on people's behaviour is called the *real balance effect* because with an unchanged price level, people find that the real value of the money held has increased as a result of the increase in the nominal amount.[1] The next step was to enquire what happened to prices and output. If all resources were fully employed then we predicted that the price level would rise: this is the prediction of the quantity theory of money. If, however, some resources were idle then output could increase. In one case the change in the quantity of money did not affect output whereas in the other situation it caused output to increase.

If the changes in the supply of money can have destabilizing effects on prices and/or output then it would seem desirable to control its production. We want to produce some money because, as we saw, the velocity of circulation of money cannot be speeded up indefinitely as national income grows, but we may not want haphazard pro-

1. The real balance effect was first evolved for a symmetrical case. Suppose people's money holdings remain constant while all prices fall. Then the real value of money holdings will rise and people will start spending. Our example is the case where prices do not change but the amount of money does.

duction at this stage and therefore we need to define clearly the money thing. This is an issue we have so far evaded. For in Chapter 28 we defined money as that which was generally acceptable as a medium of exchange and in settlement of debts: that was a *generic definition of money*. If everything is acceptable as money then we are in a barter world. Casual observation suggests that not everything is acceptable as money. Only governments and students seem willing to accept lectures on economics as an acceptable settlement of debts, so in the previous chapter we adopted a *specific* or *operational definition* of money which told us that people were only prepared to accept state notes and coins plus commercial bank deposits as money. We did not advance any arguments for this definition: this we must now do.

The money industry

Figure 139 provides some assistance both to the specific definition of money and the forms that money has taken over time.

Unit of account

Once a monetary economy has been established there is a unit of account against which all transactions are measured. But this unit of account need not be the actual money used in transactions. Thus, in the United Kingdom some prices are still quoted in terms of the 'guinea', even though there is no longer a corresponding unit of currency in circulation. The money of account can therefore be abstract rather than actual and concrete.

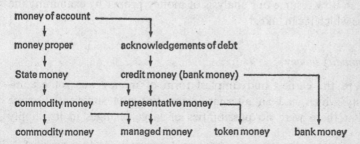

Figure 139 Based on a diagram in Keynes (1930)

Money proper

The actual money used in transactions may be referred to as *money proper* and since its production can be directly controlled by the state it can also be regarded as state money. The state is involved because of the need to provide a standard currency by which it may enforce contracts.

Acknowledgements of debt

Although state money proper (notes and coins) may be regarded as the legal or actual tender medium of exchange people have found it convenient to use debt acknowledgements as a form of money. Thus if Smith owes Jones £100 then Jones may give the IOU to Robinson in payment for goods leaving Robinson to collect £100 from Smith. In this manner people have been able to economize in the use of money proper. The most interesting development has however been the gradual transformation of some IOUs into a money akin to money proper. In the seventeenth century the goldsmiths, the forerunners of the modern commercial banks, began acting as safekeepers for people's gold coins. The receipts which they issued began to circulate as if they were money and from that historical accident those receipts (bank notes) came gradually to be money. Bank money has thus come to be sharply distinguished from other IOUs and we have now a situation where the state has delegated the production of some money proper to the commercial banks.

The forms of money proper

We can now resume our analysis of money proper by examining the forms which it can take.[2]

Commodity money

Perhaps the earliest and simplest form of money was some commodity which had an alternative use but was sufficiently scarce so that there were no possibilities of large changes in its supply

2. For an informative and somewhat unusual account of the development of different forms of money in an economy see Radford (1945).

disrupting trade. Gold has been perhaps the outstanding species of this large genus of commodity moneys. Coinage can be regarded as a means of ensuring homogeneity of commodity moneys though it was not essential to their development – think of the old prospectors settling debts with gold dust.

Token money

Commodity money is expensive to produce, using time and resources which might be put to alternative uses. And, as in all human activity, there has been a conscious attempt to reduce the costs of producing money, to release as many resources as possible from producing that which 'cannot be eaten, slept on or driven in'. So we have had the emergence of token moneys of which paper is the most outstanding example. These moneys – paper notes and 'worthless coins' – have a face value which is distinct from the intrinsic value of the commodities of which they are made. Thus, the face value of a paper note is greater than its production cost, and, in terms of the real resource cost of providing a nation's currency, society as a whole benefits from the substitution of low resource cost money commodities for high resource cost money commodities. Provided the monetary authorities exercise strict control over the production of 'paper' money, so as to avoid inflation, the resultant welfare gains accrue not only at the time the substitution is made but throughout all subsequent time periods. Consequently, virtually all countries today have a paper rather than a metallic national currency. Hence the disappearance of gold, at least off the stage, if not out of the theatre. In the United Kingdom money proper consists of coins and notes issued by the Bank of England on behalf of the state.

Since all countries other than those producing gold would benefit from the introduction of a unified world paper currency, and the final exclusion of gold from monetary affairs, one of the big questions in international monetary economics is: why do countries still hold back from taking this final step? There are several reasons, political as well as economic, but one of the major factors is the problem of deciding how to distribute the resultant welfare gains amongst the participating countries.

Managed money

Commodity money has a value in terms of its alternative use whilst token money appears to have none. The Bank of England one pound note bears the inscription: 'I promise to pay the Bearer on Demand the sum of One Pound' – a vestige of the times when such notes were convertible into gold of a specified amount. Nowadays the promise is empty, and all that the bearer can hope to obtain is perhaps a cleaner note. Nevertheless there are occasions when the state may undertake to manage the production of token money in such a way as to ensure a determinate value of the token money in terms of some objective standard. Thus, the state may allow inconvertible token money to circulate internally whilst agreeing to conversion at a fixed rate of exchange externally into other token moneys or commodity moneys. This aspect of management will, however, be ignored in this chapter and will be considered in Chapter 37.

Money and credit

We have drawn a distinction between money proper and acknowledgements of debt. Since what is a debt to one person is a credit to another we can speak of a distinction between money proper and credit. Our task in this section is to emphasize this distinction and, in particular, seek to answer the question: in what circumstances does credit become money proper?

Money, as we have argued, is that which is usually acceptable as a medium of exchange and as a means of settling debts. Credit, on the other hand, is the granting or extension, of purchasing power, or lending. It may involve the transfer of money proper or it may involve nothing more than a book-keeping entry which records the indebtedness of the borrower to the lender, though in the latter case the credit granted is likely to be backed by cash since it is usual for the lender to have a surplus of cash before he lends. Credit only becomes money proper (credit money) when it is acceptable as a universal means of settling debts. Such is the case when the public have perfect confidence in the credit-granting institutions' ability to always convert its credit into money proper of equivalent value.

Credit granted only becomes money when the liabilities of the credit-granting institution are generally acceptable in settlement of debts.

The creation of credit money

Historically, the central problem of money supply has been how to control the supply of credit money: that is, how to ensure that there is some link between money proper and the amount of debt money created. Bank deposits are money and the total of bank deposits far exceeds the supply of cash. Bankers have usually argued that there is no control problem since they only lend what is lent to them. This is the *cloakroom theory of banking* whereby banks are but cloakrooms supplying tickets for the money proper deposited with them. Credit money creation implies that the banks issue more tickets than they have money proper. The control problem is thus tied up with the process of credit granting by the banks. If it turns out that the granting of credit can also include the creation of credit then the banks and their critics may both be right and there is a money supply problem.

Fractional reserve banking

Fractional reserve banking implies the creation of credit money and for this reason the process of creation of credit money has traditionally been illustrated by examination of the operations of the commercial banks. We follow tradition but enter a caveat. The only reason for studying the commercial banks is that they were 'first on the scene'. All financial institutions have the potential to create credit money but only the commercial banks do. The banks' ability to create money has been made legitimate by the public's willingness to accept banks' liabilities as money over a long historical period. When a banker grants credit, he automatically creates money and incurs a liability and this liability appears in his accounts as a deposit of the customer who uses it to pay for goods and services. These bank deposits are regarded as equivalent to notes and coin and, as columns 1–3 of Tables 48 (a) and (b) reveal, form the larger part of the money supply.

The figures in Tables 48 (a) and (b) do, in fact, illustrate the magnitude of the 'money supply problem'. For whilst the supply of notes and coins is clearly in the hands of the state, the supply of credit money appears to be determined by private producers. Is it possible therefore for the state to control credit money?

Table 48a The UK money supply, 1952–1970[1]

Year	Notes and coins in circulation (£m) 1	Notes and coins held by banks (£m) 2	Bank deposits Current account (£m) 3	Bank deposits Deposit account (£m) 4	Total deposits (£m) 5	Money supply (£m) $M_1 = (1)+(3)$ 6	Money supply (£m) $M_2 = (1)+(5)$ 7	Ratio of M_2 to total domestic expenditure 8	Rate of interest 2½% consols 9	Index of retail prices 1963 = 100 10	Total domestic expenditure at market prices (£m) 11
1952	1370	304·9	4326	2308	6634	5696	8004	0·50	4·23	73·0	15 825
1953	1462	321·1	4367	2416	6783	5829	8245	0·48	4·08	75·0	17 014
1954	1551	339·1	4534	2473	7007	6085	8558	0·48	3·75	76·0	17 917
1955	1657	373·4	4492	2446	6938	6149	8595	0·44	4·17	80·0	19 459
1956	1765	395·2	4339	2374	6713	6104	8478	0·41	4·73	83·3	20 669
1957	1842	424·7	4314	2515	6829	6156	8671	0·40	4·98	86·9	21 850
1958	1905	438·7	4160	2844	7004	6065	8909	0·99	4·98	89·5	22 708
1959	1969	448·2	4476	2851	7327	6445	9296	0·38	4·82	90·1	24 082
1960	2062	467·5	4638	2937	7575	6700	9637	0·37	5·42	91·1	25 937
1961	2151	489·6	4589	3068	7657	6740	9808	0·35	6·20	94·1	27 406
1962	2161	508·4	4609	3186	7795	6770	9956	0·35	5·98	98·0	28 677
1963	2208	529·9	4928	3223	8151	7136	10 359	0·34	5·38	100·0	30 485
1964	2319	582·5	5313	3370	8683	7632	11 002	0·33	6·03	103·2	33 611
1965	2464	609·1	5361	3767	9128	7825	11 592	0·32	6·42	108·1	35 724
1966	2610	640·4	5468	4038	9506	8078	12 116	0·32	6·80	112·4	37 892
1967	2670	669·6	5621	4298	9917	8291	12 587	0·31	6·69	115·2	40 282
1968	2805	698·5	5917	4749	10 666	8722	13 471	0·31	7·39	120·6	43 194
1969	2912	758·4	5856	4958	10 814	8768	13 726	0·30	8·98	127·2	45 644
1970	3101	820·7	5975	5107	11 082	9076	14 183	0·28	9·23	135·3	49 782

1. Figures of deposits for London clearing banks plus Scottish and Northern Ireland banks only
Sources: *Annual Abstract of Statistics*, 1963 and 1971. *Financial Statistics*, 1971. *The British Economy: Key Statistics, 1900–1970. Monthly Digest of Statistics*, various dates

Table 48b The UK money supply, 1969–1976[1] (Figures in this table are not comparable with those in table 48a)

Year	Notes and coins in circulation with public £m (weekly average for December)	Notes and coins held by banks £m (weekly average for December)	Money stock M_2 £m (unadjusted figure for December)	Money stock M_3 £m (unadjusted figure for December)	Long-term rate of interest 2½% consol rate (annual average)	Index of retail prices 1962 = 100 (December)	Sterling–dollar exchange rate (London spot rate December)	Total domestic expenditure at market prices £m	Ratio of M_3 to total domestic expenditure
	1	2	3	4	5	6	7	8	9
1969	3046	904	8812	16 596	8·88	131·8	2·4007	45 938	0·36
1970	3296	903	9635	18 175	9·16	140·2	2·3937	50 372	0·36
1971	3526	882	11 088	20 541	9·05	153·4	2·5522	55 524	0·37
1972	4090	865	12 657	26 245	9·11	164·3	2·3481	62 654	0·41
1973	4438	1020	13 090	33 478	10·85	179·4	2·3235	73 301	0·45
1974	5166	1159	14 739	37 698	14·95	208·1	2·3495	85 571	0·44
1975	5934	1145	17 300	40 587	14·66	258·5	2·0233	104 315	0·39
1976	6017 (April)	1088 (April)	17 360 (April)	40 424 (April)	13·85 (April)	294·4 (April)	1·8410 (April)	—	—

1. Banking figures are for UK banking sector which comprises all banks in the UK together with the National Giro, the discount market and the Bank of England banking department.

M_2 = Notes and coins in circulation + UK private sector sterling sight deposits – 60% of items in transit between banks.

M_3 = M_2 + UK private sector sterling time deposits + UK public sector sterling sight and time deposits + UK residents' deposits in other currencies.

Sources: Monthly Digest of Statistics, Financial Statistics, Bank of England Quarterly Bulletin, all various cates.

Imagine a financial system in which all the banks are required to hold 100 per cent reserves of 'high-powered money' (another term for state money) against deposits. In such a world the banks can grant credit if they hold excess reserves but they cannot create credit money. More correctly, their ability to create credit money is identically equal to their holdings of high-powered money. Net credit money creation is impossible in a 100 per cent reserve banking system, but in a system in which banks are not compelled to hold 100 per cent reserves the production of net credit money becomes possible. All that is required for production to occur is that the public should not be able to distinguish, or should not wish to distinguish, between credit money backed by reserves and credit money not backed by reserves. All this requires is general acceptance of bank credit money as a medium of exchange.

In normal circumstances all bank deposits are accepted on an equal basis. It is the individual's credit worthiness, and not that of the bank, which is questioned. As long as each holder of bank deposits believes his credit balance is readily convertible into high-powered money all will be well. Given, therefore, the public's acceptance of credit money and the interest of the banks in making profits we can determine the amount of credit money which can be created since its production depends on the amount of high-powered money, the public's relative preference for bank deposits and the bank's cash reserve ratio.

Public confidence in the 'moneyness' of bank deposits is the foundation stone of fractional reserve banking and hence of the creation of bank credit money.

Credit money creation: some arithmetic

Let us now examine the process of producing bank money in some detail. We begin by emphasizing, because it is often forgotten, that commercial banks and other financial intermediaries are private firms intent on making profits. Commercial banks produce many services as well as creating credit money. Moreover, their profits are linked to the volume of services that they sell which are linked to the level of their deposits, so banks have an obvious interest in seeing their deposits grow by as much as possible.

Next, we make the simplifying assumption that there is only one banking firm (it could, of course, have many branches). This enables us to ignore the additional complexities which occur when there are movements of high-powered money between different banking firms. Simplicity is possible because the final result of the analysis will be the same regardless of the number of firms provided each expands his deposits at the same rate and provided they work to the same cash reserve ratio.

Now the public hold high-powered money (hereafter referred to as the public's cash holding) and non-interest-bearing bank deposits. In the previous chapter we analysed their total demand for money in terms of their desire to hold a portfolio of goods, services and assets which would yield maximum satisfaction (see equation 3 on page 469). People will be holding cash because it is the most liquid (the most marketable) of all assets. They will hold bank money because, though it yields no interest, it offers security against loss and provides access to some of the financial services offered by banks. Over time the ratio of deposits to cash in each individual's portfolio will vary as deposits become more or less attractive relative to cash and all other goods. In the short run this ratio will tend to be constant. This ratio is the *public's cash-deposit ratio* and we shall use the symbol α to denote it.

We can analyse the commercial banks' demand for cash (high-powered money) in similar fashion to the public's demand for cash. The banks' desire for profit leads them to attempt to minimize their holdings of non-income-yielding cash. Profit also depends on staying in business and this requires the maintenance of the public's confidence in their solvency, in their ability to meet all demands for cash. The banks could be sure of solvency by always holding 100 per cent reserves. This need not make banking unprofitable because banks would still be able to charge for their other services, but it would eliminate the extra profit to be earned from swtching out of cash into other assets. Table 48a shows that banks do, in fact, manage with less than 100 per cent reserves: the question is, how?

As long as the public believe in the 'moneyness' of bank deposits, the banks will find that the calls for cash will constitute only a small fraction of their total deposit liabilities. For most of the time their customers are content to receive and make payments with claims to bank deposits. In a credit money system credit transfers replace cash in many exchange transactions. Thus the banks can use their excess cash holdings to earn extra income and in doing so initiate *fractional reserve banking* and the creation of bank credit money. The cash reserves of the banks will be determined by the need to meet the 'normal' volume of cash withdrawals at any point of time. The ratio of cash to deposits which might be converted into cash gives us the bank's cash ratio, β.

The relationship between fractional reserve banking and the creation of credit money (deposits) by banks is illustrated in Table 49. For the purpose of the example the public's cash-deposit ratio (α) is assumed to be 0·5 and the cash-deposit ratio of the bank (β) to be 0·25. The total supply of cash (high-powered money) in the economy is £200. The table is deliberately extended over a fairly

Table 49 The process of bank deposit expansion (credit money creation)

Stage	The bank Assets[1] (£)	Liabilities (deposits) (£)	The public Cash holdings (£)
1	133 cash	133	67
2	133 cash	233	
	100 securities		67
3	100 cash	200	
	100 securities		100
4	100 cash	250	
	150 securities		100
5	83 cash		
	150 securities	233	117
6	83 cash		
	173 securities	258	125
7	75 cash		
	175 securities	250	125
.	.	.	.
.	.	.	.
.	.	.	.
n	67 cash	267	133
	200 securities		

1. For the purpose of this example, securities refer to all income-yielding assets held instead of cash. Figures do not add up exactly because of rounding

large number of stages so as to make as clear as possible the process of credit money creation.

The first stage shows the public to be in equilibrium with regard to their cash-deposit ratio, but the bank is in disequilibrium in that with a desired cash-reserve ratio of 0·25 it is holding excess cash. At this stage the bank's excess cash amounts to £100 and it will seek to convert this free cash into an income-yielding asset by buying £100 worth of securities. To pay for the securities the bank credits the accounts of the sellers with an amount equal to the value of their sales. The end result of this transaction is depicted in stage 2. The bank's assets have grown by the addition of £100 worth of securities and its liabilities (its deposits) have grown by the same amount.

Initially the public were in equilibrium with regard to their cash-deposit ratio, so at the end of stage 2 they must be in disequilibrium since their deposits have risen by £100 to £233·3, while their cash holdings have remained at £66·6. They will re-establish an equilibrium cash ratio by withdrawing cash from the bank. This decreases their deposit balances and increases their cash balances. Stage 3 depicts the public in equilibrium with deposits of £200 and cash balances of £100. Things are different for the bank. The bank's purchase of securities was intended to place it in an equilibrium position but after the purchase the bank still finds it has excess cash despite an increase in deposits. Stage 3 shows the bank to have free reserves of £50. And in stage 4 we see the bank attempting to reach equilibrium again by buying a further £50 of securities from the public. This increases the bank's portfolio of securities but throws the public into disequilibrium once more.

The growth of deposits and the persistence of free reserves at the bank are reconciled by the recognition of the public's willingness to hold additional deposits as deposits and not as cash. The moneyness of deposits means that while people will always withdraw cash from the bank to maintain their cash-deposit ratio they will not withdraw cash merely because their bank balance has increased. This is why the bank finds itself with excess cash even after it has made a purchase from the public equal in value to its free cash holding. The process only stops when both the public and the bank are in equilibrium. This is shown in the final line of Table 49. Total deposits stand at £267 and the bank's cash holding stands at one-quarter of this amount, namely £67, and the public's cash holding is one half of the value of the deposits, namely, £133. The sum of the two cash holdings is £200 which is the amount of cash in the economy. Initially the total of money was £200 (133 + 67). After the creation of credit money it is £400 (267 + 133).

In this example, the ability of banks to create credit money is determined by the public's demand for cash as opposed to credit money (the public's cash-deposit ratio), the bank's demand for cash (the bank's cash-deposit ratio) and the total amount of cash in the economy.

Credit money creation: some algebra

The determinants of the supply of credit money (the process of deposit expansion), can now be set down algebraically:

C = total amount of cash (high-powered money),
Cp = cash held by public,
Cb = cash held by commercial banks (cash reserves),
$C = Cp + Cb$,
D = total bank deposits (subject to cheque),
$\alpha = Cp/D$ = public's cash-deposit ratio,
$\beta = Cb/D$ = banks' cash-deposit ratio (reserve ratio),
then $C = \alpha D + \beta D$
$\quad\quad\quad = D(\alpha + \beta)$

therefore $D = \dfrac{C}{(\alpha + \beta)}$ 1

and $\quad \Delta D = \dfrac{\Delta C}{\Delta(\alpha + \beta)}$ 2

Equation 1 indicates that the total amount of credit creation depends upon the total amount of cash and the cash-deposit ratios of the public and the banks.

Equation 1 can be used to verify the final line of the numerical example of credit creation with C = £200. Substituting these values into equation 1 yields:

$$D = \frac{200}{(\frac{1}{2} + \frac{1}{4})} = \frac{200}{\frac{3}{4}}$$

$$= £266.6 = £267 \text{ (if we round up again).}$$

This answer accords with the final line of the table in our previous example.

The credit multiplier: some important qualifications

In practice the bank credit multiplier relationship is far more complex than the above example suggests. First, because the supply of cash is never under the absolute control of the monetary authorities but varies positively with the demand for it, more so in an 'open' trading economy than in a 'closed' economy. Secondly, the banks' cash-deposit, or cash-reserve ratio is set by the monetary authorities but this only establishes its lower limit since the banks are free to hold a higher ratio of cash to deposits. Bank cash reserves in excess of the required minimum are referred to as 'free reserves'. Whether or not the banks hold such reserves, and hence whether or not their cash-reserve ratio is variable, depends upon their portfolio behaviour. But given that it is a choice variable it is obviously inappropriate to treat it as fixed in the multiplier relationship. Instead in the extended version of the credit multiplier the fixed coefficient β is replaced by an expression which describes the determination of β as a result of the banks' portfolio behaviour.

Finally, similar considerations apply to the public's cash-deposit ratio. The public is not faced with a simple choice between bank deposits and cash but a much wider one encompassing cash, bank deposits (current and time) and the diverse financial assets offered by the many other financial institutions found in modern economies. Moreover, the choice problem is not constant since an important feature of the development of mature economies is *financial evolution*, the expansion of the range of financial institutions and the assets they offer to the public. Thus the public's cash deposit ratio, α, is not fixed but varies, both in the short-run and over time, as they alter the composition of their asset portfolios in response to changes in tastes, wealth and the relative yields on assets. Consequently, as with β, it is inappropriate to treat it as fixed. In the extended version of the credit multiplier relationship it is replaced by a detailed expression which describes the public's portfolio behaviour in determining the amounts of cash and bank deposits in their overall portfolio of assets.

Allowance for these factors does not rob the bank credit multiplier relationship of its predictive powers. Provided the monetary authorities can exercise control over the amount of high-powered money in the economy, albeit less than perfect, and provided the behavioural relationships describing the determination of α and β are well defined, stable and functions of a small number of variables, there exists a predictable and measurable relationship between high-powered money and bank deposits. From the point of view of monetary control the predictability and stability of relationships is far more important than their complexity.

Some economists have challenged this view on the grounds that the spectrum of liquid assets available to the public, which at one end of the spectrum are so liquid as to be close substitutes for cash, robs the concept of money and hence monetary policy, of any practical significance. They argue that small changes in the yields on liquid assets are sufficient to induce the public, and the banks, to hold more or less cash in their portfolio of assets. This in turn means that policy-induced changes in the supply of money are neutral in their impact on economic activity because small interest rate changes have a negligible impact on expenditure decisions, or so it is claimed.

This argument, however, is essentially spurious in that it neglects the fundamental characteristic of money, namely that it is the only financial asset which serves as a generally acceptable medium of exchange. It also neglects the fact that it is also the only financial asset which *all* financial institutions must hold as a necessary prerequisite for staying in business. The argument confuses variability of behaviour with predictability of behaviour.

Control of money supply: control of the economy

The bank credit multiplier relationship is the key by which the state can control the supply of money. Given the existence of a stable multiplier relationship, no matter how complex it might be, the principles of monetary control are simple. Despite their simplicity they have been hotly debated and at times veiled in a mist of confusion, and the mechanism of control has sometimes been ignored or rejected. The reasons for neglect will form the subject matter of another section. Meanwhile we will inform ourselves as to how the money supply can be controlled and, since money is presumed to have some influence on economic activity, how economic activity can be controlled.

We have seen that the principal creators of an effective substitute for money proper are the commercial banks. All other forms of credit have to be converted reasonably quickly into money proper. We have also noticed that the ability of banks to create credit money rests on the process of fractional reserve banking. Banks do not completely abandon money proper and there is a link between money proper and bank money. Hence the bank's cash-reserve ratio can provide a fulcrum for monetary control. All that is required for monetary control is for the state, or its delegate, the central bank, to control the supply of money proper (hence the term 'high-powered money').

What methods of control of money proper are available? There seem to be two. First, there is taxation or subsidization: that is, the monetary authority can demand from the commercial banks a certain sum of money proper or it can give them freely a sum of money proper. Secondly, the monetary authority can play the market game and exchange with the public and the commercial banks interest bearing assets for money proper: this is known as *open-market operations*.

Open-market operations are sales and purchases of government securities by the monetary authority.

In order to finance its own activities the state can either tax or borrow from the public.[3] If it borrows it sells interest-bearing securities to the public and these securities comprise what is known as the *National Debt*.[4] Since the public pay for the securities with money proper or, when they sell securities back to the state, are paid in money proper it follows that changes in the money supply will accompany the buying and selling of securities.

In the previous chapter we established a direct link between changes in the money supply and the general level of prices and/or

3. Further aspects of state borrowing and taxing are explored in the chapter on financing the state.
4. The National Debt is the paper legacy of government borrowing. It first grew into massive proportions as a result of the two world wars. It has continued to grow since as a result of the rapid expansion of the public sector and its residual demand for finance.

output. There may, however, be an indirect effect operating via interest rates.

What we have to show now is how the indirect effect operating through interest rates influences the level of spending, particularly investment spending. Traditionally the authorities operate on the short end of the money and capital market (i.e. they buy and sell securities soon to be redeemed). Hence we must indicate how changes in short-term interest rates cause changes in long-term interest rates which are presumed to be the more important influence on investment. Figure 140 indicates why this might be so. We suppose that the monetary authority is seeking to reduce the money supply and so sells securities to the banks. The effect of the transaction is to cause a fall in the cash reserves of the banks and to set in motion a contraction of bank deposits and cause short-term interest rates to rise. At the same time the banks and the public will find that not only are they short of cash but that they are also holding long-term securities whose interest payment is now lower, relative to that of the short-term securities. Consequently they will sell long-term securities which will lower their price and raise their interest rates and thus long- and short-term interest rates will move together. The rise in long-term rates will serve to check investment.

We have now established that open-market operations working via the bank credit multiplier process link changes in the supply of high-powered money (otherwise known as cash, base money or money proper) and changes in the total supply of money. The existence of a link between high-powered money and bank money is illustrated by the data in Table 48a and 48b, which show how the two have moved together since 1952. Two separate tables are needed because the reform of the banking system in 1971 led to the availability of additional banking data and changes in the coverage of some of the statistical series. These changes, while welcome in that they provide more useful and more accurate information, mean that the later data series are not directly comparable with the earlier information.

Figure 141 relates the total amount of high-powered money outstanding in the UK to the supply of money[5] – currency held by the public plus bank deposits. This clearly shows that a similar relationship has existed for the much longer period, 1881–1962. This evidence would seem to support the theory of control outlined in this section.

5. As of approximately 30 June in each year.

sale of short-term securities with relatively high
interest rate; increase in short-term rates

↓

fall in cash held by banks
and public, and rise in short-term securities held

↓

sale of long-term securities
fall in their price and rise in interest rates,

↓

check to investment.

Figure 140 Reduction of money supplies by open-market operations

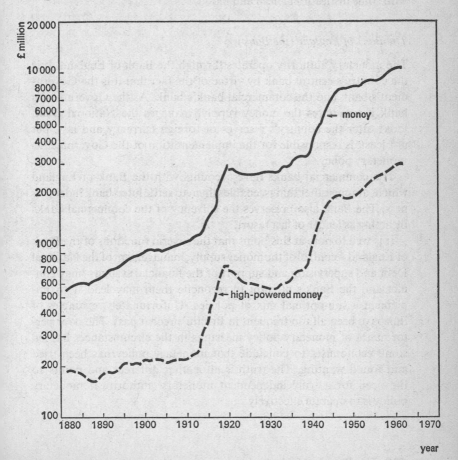

Figure 141

As to the link between changes in the money supply and economic activity – the subject matter of the previous chapter – we leave the reader to draw his own conclusions from the data in Tables 48(a) and (b). But note that statistical association is not causation.

The institutions of monetary control: a digression

In this section we shall describe the main institutions connected with monetary control in the UK. It is not essential and may be regarded as a break in the discussion between theory and practice. Some readers may however find it useful to cloak the bare bones of analysis with some institutional flesh and blood.

The Bank of England (the Bank)

The monetary authority operates through the Bank of England. It is the country's central bank by virtue of the fact that it is the Government's bank and the commercial bank's bank. As the Government's bank it supervises the money supply, manages the National Debt, looks after the country's reserves of foreign currency and last, but not least, is responsible for the implementation of the Government's monetary policy.

The commercial banks have accounts with the Bank of England which, among other things, enables them to settle inter-bank indebtedness. The Bank also preserves the solvency of the commercial banks by acting as lender of last resort.

It is well to note at this point that the several functions of the Bank of England – control of the money supply, management of the National Debt and supervision and support of the financial system – may conflict and the Bank's attempt to reconcile them may lead it to implement a sub-optimal mix of policies. Unfortunately, examples of this have been all too frequent in Britain's recent past. The poor performance of monetary policy measures in the circumstances has led some economists to conclude that monetary policy has been tried and found wanting. The truth is altogether different and points to the need for a truly independent monetary authority if monetary policy is to operate effectively.

Discount houses

The discount houses are a British oddity: they do not exist in other countries. Originally, they existed in connection with the predominance in the nineteenth century of commercial bills of exchange. These were promises to settle debts within a short period of time. Creditors who could not afford to wait until the specified date would sell their bills below redemption value to the discount houses (hence their name) who would hold them until maturity (redemption). Bills of exchange declined in importance, however, in the inter-war years and the discount houses found a new role. A monopolistic arrangement was devised so that they could make a profit through the extensive buying and selling of short-term Government securities, in particular the 91-day *Treasury Bills*. In this way the discount houses continue to occupy an important place in the monetary system.

Treasury bills

The Bank of England issues treasury bills each week by tender, to provide short-term finance for the Government. Because they are short-dated and backed by the Government they are highly marketable (liquid) and as such much prized by the banks. But by arrangement, the banks do not bid directly for their treasury bills at the weekly tender. Instead they buy from the discount houses. (This only applies to the banks' own needs, for in respect of their own customers they buy direct.) The discount houses in turn, acting as a syndicate, bid for the whole of each week's treasury bills issue. Until recently they bid at a common price. The arrangement suits all the parties – the Bank has an assured customer, the discount houses have an assured income and the commercial banks like it because they can lend any spare cash to the discount houses on a short-term basis. Money thus loaned is termed *money at call*.

In addition to the banks these are the main institutions of the monetary system. They are surrounded by a host of other financial institutions – insurance companies, hire-purchase finance companies, unit trusts, investment trusts, etc. – these are the *non-bank financial intermediaries* whose task is to increase the efficiency of the money and capital markets.

More recently there has been a rapid growth of so-called secondary banks and the development of a parallel money market in which they operate. These banks, many of which are foreign, or branches of British-owned overseas banks, do not seek to attract a large number of customers, and hence develop a wide branch network, but to attract large deposits. They deal in sterling and foreign currency deposits, especially dollars, and consequently have been largely responsible for the growth of the *Eurodollar* market. In contrast to traditional British banking customs and practices they sought business and enlarged their share of the market through keen interest rate competition. The success, as witnessed by their rapid growth, was largely at the expense of the UK clearing banks, and was one of the factors leading to the reform of UK banking in 1971.

Control of the money supply: practice

The policy of open-market operations directed to controlling the money supply has not been used efficiently in the post-war period. Instead a succession of directives, credit ceilings and numerous other instruments were used. Why was this? The first answer is the one with which we ended the previous section: the authorities believed that they could not control the money supply because of the existence of many perfect credit substitutes for money proper. If this argument were true then we would expect to find an inverse relationship between changes in the supply of high-powered money and the supply of effective money substitutes. As the authorities squeezed the supply of high-powered money so the supply of substitute moneys should have expanded. We have not tested the hypothesis, but leave this to the reader, though it should be noted that Figure 141 suggests some evidence to the contrary.[6]

The second answer to our question starts from the observation that the monetary authorities can control either the amount of securities held by the public (and thus the amount of high-powered money) *or* the price of those securities but not both. The public will have a demand curve for securities as in Figure 142.

In terms of Figure 142 if the authorities release OQ securities they will be sold at price OP and if they release OQ_1 they will be sold at price OP_1. Alternatively, if the authorities fix price OP they will sell

6. Figure 141 is not wholly conclusive since it leaves undisclosed the behaviour of the credit facilities of non-bank financial intermediaries.

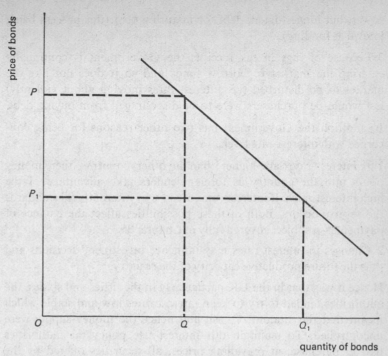

Figure 142

OQ and so on. A concomitant of price is the rate of interest: if the price of bonds rises then the rate of interest will fall, and if the price of bonds falls the rate of interest will rise. This can place the monetary authority in a dilemma since an attempt to reduce the money supply may move interest rates in an undesirable direction.

Why should the monetary authority be interested in the behaviour of interest rates? The answer lies partly in the existence of the National Debt. A government has several problems in managing the debt.

1 It has to ensure that the interest payments on the debt are kept as low as possible.

2 It has to control the conversion of securities into cash as each block of securities matures, otherwise there might be unwarranted increases in the money supply. One way of doing this is to offer

newer, but longer-dated, debt for maturing debt (this process being known as funding).

3 Because of lags in tax receipts the Government is continually entering the market to borrow funds and so it does not like the market to be disturbed (i.e. interest rates moving about violently) lest would-be purchasers were to be discouraged from buying debt.

In addition the Government has two other reasons for being concerned with interest-rate levels.

1 If interest rates are higher than in other countries then money pours into the country as foreign lenders take advantage of the high interest rates. If interest rates are low by international standards the reverse occurs. Both of these possibilities affect the balance of payments – a subject covered fully in Chapter 35.

2 Changes in interest rates may influence investment decisions and thus the future productive capacity of the country.

Hence it was that in the UK particularly in the fifties and sixties, the authorities tended to try to keep interest rates low and stable which meant that the amount of cash and hence the money supply were uncontrolled. To maintain this interest-rate policy the authorities had to purchase, at prevailing prices, all securities offered by the banks to raise cash. Thus, unable to control cash, the authorities had to resort to other methods of control such as:

Special deposits. All commercial banks were compelled to deposit an amount of their cash, some percentage of their total deposits, with the Bank of England (which was the monetary authority's banker). In effect this was a tax (though interest was paid on the cash) since, whilst the cash still belonged to banks, they could not include it in their cash reserves.

Directives. Direct requests were issued from the Bank of England to the commercial banks asking them to behave in a particular way, e.g. to lend more to exporters and less to private consumers.

Credit ceilings. A stronger restriction was to limit the annual growth of commercial bank lending to a percentage of the previous year's lending.

The trouble with these methods was not that they did not work – they did and can – but that they distort the workings of the financial system by only applying to commercial banks and by not reflecting the interplay of market forces.

Competition and credit control

The desire to establish a method of monetary control which was effective without interfering with the efficiency of the financial system led the Bank of England to introduce a new method of credit control in September 1971. It was heralded in May of that year by the issue of a consultative document with the title 'Competition and Credit Control'.[7]

The new arrangements involve two separate, but complementary, lines of change. One has to do with improving the efficiency of the financial system by promoting competition between the clearing banks[8] and the other financial institutions. Amongst other things this involves the abandonment of the monopolistic arrangement between the banks, the discount houses and the Bank of England referred to earlier. The other part was the new method of control. This is complementary to the other since it substitutes a market form of control, designed to influence *all* financial institutions, for the previous battery of direct controls which operated mainly on the banks.

The new method centres on the 'classic' technique of open-market operations. By making it the basis of the new control method the Bank signified its intention to no longer manage interest rates to the exclusion of the money supply. Equity in operation is achieved by setting a common 'reserve asset ratio' of $12\frac{1}{2}$ per cent for all banks and of 10 per cent for the finance houses. Whilst ostensibly fixed, these ratios, which provide the fulcrum of control, are in fact variable in an upwards direction by virtue of the fact that the Bank can request all institutions subject to reserve ratios to hold reserve assets in excess of the prescribed amounts. This is achieved through calls for special deposits.

How has Competition and Credit Control worked out in practice? The new control policy and banking reforms have only had a few

7. This was reprinted in the Bank of England *Quarterly Bulletin*, June 1971. Subsequent issues of the *Bulletin* should be consulted for other articles on the new method of credit control.
8. The clearing banks are those banks which use the London Clearing House to settle inter-bank debts. The clearing banks are also the major banks.

years in which to work but it is already clear that the new arrangements have failed. Although the arrangements were fine in principle they were rapidly overtaken by, and subsequently contributed to, events which made them unworkable in practice. At the same time as competition (and hence deposit expansion) was encouraged in the banking sector, long-standing controls over hire-purchase and related forms of credit were abolished under a separate reform package, and the two together served to fuel the economy's accelerating inflation. Inflation in turn led to additional upward pressure on interest rates. Further upward pressure on interest rates was provided by increases in the Government's borrowing requirement. The Bank, caught between the desire to restrain monetary expansion on the one hand and prevent interest rates rising on the other, reverted to its interventionist policies with respect to the behaviour of interest rates. Continued inflation and balance of payments difficulties led to the floating of sterling and increased government intervention in the economy first to deal with inflation and then with unemployment, as the economic situation deteriorated further and brought the emergence of a new state of affairs, *stagflation*. This was hardly the situation in which to introduce a bold new system of monetary control based on a free and competitive banking system and market-determined interest rates. The spirit of competition and credit control rapidly withered as the Bank and the commercial banks reverted to old ways and methods of control. Harsher critics might even go as far as to say that the Bank and the commercial banks, like individuals, have a preference for old ways of doing things, even when they are not the best!

Rules versus authority in money supply

Because of the difficulties in controlling the supply of money some writers have proposed that discretionary variations in the money supply should be abandoned in favour of specific rules. Despite the good intentions of central bankers they are not infallible, and their attempts to match the money supply with the needs of the community have often caused the supply to move in the wrong direction. However, with a rule – of the form that the money supply shall grow by x per cent per annum – such discretionary variations in the supply of money are no longer allowed.

The money supply would then behave in a regular and predictable way and a concomitant of this stability of supply is that the general price level, while free to vary in both an upwards and downwards direction, would do so in a gradual and predictable fashion. Just how it would vary in the long run would depend upon the annual percentage increase in the money supply as specified in the rule relative to the rate of growth of real output and the income-elasticity of demand for money. If, for example, the income-elasticity of demand for money is unity and the annual rate of increase of real output is 5 per cent a monetary rule of 5 per cent annual increase in the supply of money should lead to a stable general level of prices in the long run.

The success of the monetary rule would seem to depend on three things. Firstly, a link between money and real output. Secondly, that the country should be able to pursue an independent monetary policy. Thirdly, that other economic forces operate so as to lead to steady growth in output in the absence of de-stabilizing monetary actions. The second requires that if the country be small it should be able to operate floating exchange rates (on which see Chapter 35) whilst the first and third would seem to require a world of free competition.

Inside and outside money: a digression

In our analysis we have suggested that changes in the money supply can have price and output effects. In recessions we are interested in the output effects of money. (In situations of inflation the price effect assumes the greater importance, but, as yet, little attempt has been made to relate the issues discussed in this section to the problem of inflation.) Is it possible to stimulate an economy and restore full employment by monetary expansion alone? The answer appears to be in the affirmative though the mechanism by which it does so is still debatable.

One aspect of this debate is whether bank money has the same stimulating effect as state money. Usually the argument is couched in terms of definitions of *inside money* (i.e. bank money) and *outside money* (i.e. state money); that is, between money produced within and outside the market system. Some economists believe that a stimulating effect can only be achieved with state money because this is regarded by everyone as an asset to which there is no corresponding debt. (Remember the Bank of England's sole liability with respect to the note issue is to replace one note with another identical one.) With such money, changes in the real value of the amount outstanding represent equal changes in the *net wealth* of the private sector.

In contrast, it is argued that bank deposits cannot have a stimulating effect since the asset and debt components of the outstanding amount are fully recorded in the private sector, and hence cancel out. The net wealth effect in this case is zero. However, and this complicates the issue, this is only true in a perfectly competitive banking system in which banks only earn normal profits. In practice the ability to operate a bank involves a monopoly right to print money and make excess profits. When a bank creates deposits it exchanges the convenience of the cheque book for claims to real resources and in the process makes a profit. This profit is reflected in the bank's share price, and to the extent that the bank makes monopoly profit, its shareholders will experience changes in the real value of their wealth, which, from the point of view of the economy as a whole represents a change in the net wealth of the economy. In the case of an increase in the real value of the bank's monopoly profit the net wealth effect will be positive and demand will be stimulated. Whether or not this change is an accounting mirage is irrelevant if people act on the basis of it. Inside money, in this case, has the same stimulating effects as outside money.

Can we apply the same argument to government bonds? Here, it is argued, we cannot, since the interest payments on the bonds would represent an equivalent future tax liability. But since a similar argument ultimately applies to state money, which it is claimed the public treat as adding to net wealth, it may also be argued that bonds should be treated as adding to net wealth. This rests on conjecture, since it hinges on the fact that the issue of government bonds creates a debt which does not have to be redeemed until a later date. People may be aware that changes in the amount of debt outstanding affect the private sector's future tax liabilities, but do not act as though it were *their* liability.

Changes in the real value of the supply of inside money may or may not affect the net wealth of the private sector, and thus expenditure decisions, depending upon whether or not banks make monopoly profits. In the pure inside money case no such wealth effects result because changes in the real value of the banks' liabilities (the public's bank assets) are exactly matched by changes in the real value of bank assets (the public's liabilities to banks). Nothing corresponds to this valuation process for state money. When the state creates money it has a debt which it chooses to ignore and hence there is only an asset which makes people better off and which they might spend.

Summary

The thing which is acceptable as money has passed through many stages of evolution from commodity money to token, and in a parallel and not unconnected evolutionary strand instruments have developed for the acknowledgement of debts, one of which, bank debt, has come to be regarded as the same as money proper. The central problem of money supply, therefore, has been how to control the supply of bank money. The answer has been found in requiring banks to retain some money proper and their willingness, in the pursuit of profit to exchange their money proper for interest-bearing government securities.

Questions

1 Why is it useful to have a knowledge of the history of money?

2 What is (a) money proper; (b) commodity money and (c) token money?

3 What is the difference between inside and outside money?

4 Why must money be managed?

5 What is the difference between money proper, credit and credit money?

6 What are the main determinants of the commercial banks' ability to create credit money?

7 Describe the mechanism of open market operations. Why might open market operations be ineffective?

8 In what respects do the activities of banks differ from those of a building society?

9 A banker said to an economist: 'Every pound that I lend has been deposited with me by someone else. How do I create money?' What reply should an economist make?

10 'The case for decentralized private production of money is that it enables banks to cater for the needs of trade, but the same result can be achieved by centralized public production of money with private financial intermediaries improving the velocity of circulation.' Comment.

11 If banks were required to hold 100 per cent reserves would they survive?

12 What are the main determinants of the banks' demand for money proper?

13 What are the main determinants of the public's demand for money? (You may wish to tackle this question after revising the previous chapter.)

14 'The essence of monetary economics is the confrontation of a total demand for real money balances and a supply of nominal money balances.' Discuss.

Asset structure of UK deposit banks[1]

| | March 1971 | | March 1972 | |
	£ million	%	£ million	%
notes and coin	874	2·5	641	1·5
money at call and short notice	467	1·3	519	1·2
British Government treasury bills	435	1·2	560	1·3
other UK bills discounted	1461	4·2	1702	4·1
other bills	500	1·4	454	1·1
British Government stock	2171	6·2	2990	7·2
other securities	1271	4·6	1673	4·2
advances (loans)	26 452	77·0	32 061	77·2
acceptances	918	2·6	927	2·2
total	34 549	100%	41 527	100%

1. Includes all banks in UK plus National Giro and discount houses
Source: Bank of England *Quarterly Bulletin*, June 1972

15 Answer the following with reference to the above table:
(a) What is the cash ratio of the banks?
(b) If the Bank of England purchases £500 of securities, what is

likely to happen to deposits assuming that banks attempt to keep the proportions between assets unchanged?

(c) What are the main determinants of the asset structure revealed in the table?

16 'Fine in principle, unmarkable in practice.' Is this an apt description of the rise and fall of Competition and Credit Control?

17 If, as some economists argue, the Bank of England does not control the money supply, who does?

18 If the supply of money cannot be controlled but is demand-determined, why are periods of deflation associated with monetary contraction and not expansion?

19 What are Eurodollars and what is the Eurodollar market?

The following questions relate to the previous chapter, but use the data in Tables 48a and 48b on money supply in this chapter.

20 Plot the data on money supply divided by total domestic expenditure against the rate of interest.

Do you find any significant relationship is established? What does it mean to divide the money supply by total domestic expenditure?

21 Plot the time series of the following data.
(a) annual percentage change in the money supply;
(b) annual percentage change in total domestic expenditure;
(c) annual percentage change in retail prices;
(d) the level of unemployment (use the data from Chapter 37).

Do you find any significant relationships? Does it matter which definition of money supply is used?

Chapter 30
The Income–Expenditure Approach

Our analysis now takes a dramatic turn. In the previous chapters we have looked at the part played by money in economic activity. We found that monetary changes could affect prices and output. In the short run, output effects might predominate if there were unemployed resources, or if people suffered a 'money illusion' and believed that because they had more money in their pockets they were better off. But, ultimately, continuing increases in the money supply would lead to rising prices. This is the essence of the Quantity Theory of Money. In its simplest, its long run form, it assumes that demand and supply in the goods market yield full employment, leaving changes in the demand for and supply of money to determine the price level.

The dramatic turn comes from a reversal of assumptions. Suppose now we assume that the price level is given but that the volume of output and employment have to be determined. Now the analysis of this problem introduces the possibilities of unemployment and we need to distinguish between several kinds of unemployment.

Types of unemployment

1 *Frictional Unemployment* arises as people search for jobs. Because of desires for higher wages, better working conditions and because of changes in demands for goods and services there is a certain amount of unemployment in the labour market. This unemployment is the price paid for allowing people freedom of choice. If we wanted continuous full employment then we would have to have direction of labour on the scale operated in the Second World War. Frictional unemployment involves choice. It involves a choice between staying with an existing employer at a lower wage because the demand for his goods has fallen and he can only guarantee jobs at a lower wage *or* going to look for another job. It involves choice between taking the

first job offered *or* waiting until something better turns up. Frictional unemployment is the cost of attaining efficiency since it would always be possible to create an illusion of full employment by allowing everyone to work more slowly. How much frictional unemployment is required in an economy is debatable; it depends upon the mobility of labour, the speed with which new skills can be acquired, government training schemes, and so on. In the nineteenth century, frictional unemployment accounted for about six per cent of the labour force; since 1945 the average has been less than three per cent.

2 *Structural Unemployment* is a more severe form of frictional unemployment arising out of the collapse of demand for the goods and services of whole industries and regions, and the long time that elapses before workers find new jobs. In the twenties a great deal of British unemployment was structural, brought about by the huge fall in the export demand for coal, textiles, iron and steel and engineering goods. In the sixties most countries in Western Europe, including Britain, encountered difficulties in running down their coal industries, the demand for whose product had fallen as a result of cheap oil imports from the Middle East.

3 *Cyclical Unemployment* is associated with the existence of a trade cycle, that is a fairly regular fluctuation in the demand for goods and services. What causes this fluctuation is still something of a mystery. In the nineteenth century the cycle was of about seven years in duration, since 1945 there has been a shorter, less pronounced cycle of about four years.

4 *Involuntary Unemployment* is a term coined by J. M. Keynes to describe a situation where the unemployed would like to work at the prevailing wages in the market but cannot get jobs at those wages. This situation contrasts with voluntary unemployment which arises because workers regard working at the existing wages as inferior to leisure or working at home. Just why involuntary unemployment arises has been a matter of considerable controversy since the publication of Keynes's *General Theory*. Some writers have argued that it can only occur if wages are inflexible downwards and that this rigidity arises because of trade union monopoly wage policies, state-determined minimum wages or because social security benefits provide a floor below which wages cannot fall. Surely, these critics argue, if there are large numbers of workers seeking jobs then wages must fall

Types of Unemployment 509

until full employment (less frictional unemployment) is restored. Hence they argue that involuntary unemployment is just a variety of voluntary/frictional unemployment in which the market is taking a long time to adjust. On the other hand, its proponents argue that in a decentralized economy it is extremely difficult to get everyone to accept a wage cut in a slump. Suppose there is a fall in the demand for cars. Then in a centrally planned economy it would be possible overnight to cut the wages of everyone concerned with car production – assembly line operators, tyre producers, iron and steel workers, glass makers, etc. But in a decentralized system that is not possible. As a result, car workers resist a wage cut because they think everyone else should get a wage cut or because they think they can get better wages elsewhere. So they become unemployed and because they are unemployed they spend less and so other workers become unemployed. It may take time in a decentralized economy to make changes. And when changes take place there tends to be an over-reaction. Think of the cobweb cycle and accountants mentioned in Chapter 10. Involuntary unemployment creates general unemployment which may be intensified by mistakes in government policies.

Involuntary unemployment arises when there is a widespread deficiency of aggregate money demand. This deficiency may be due to a mismatch between the nominal supply of money and the general level of prices and money wages resulting in too low a stock of real money balances. Real wages may be correct but money wages and prices may be too high relative to the stock of money. Such a state of affairs could occur if the monetary authorities suddenly reduced the money supply. At the moment of reduction all relative prices might be correct in the sense of giving the right distribution of resources but because the money supply had been cut, individuals would want to increase their money balances and in doing so would cut their spending and create unemployment. Two solutions would then be possible. One would be to cut money prices and wages so as to induce people to spend. But this would be difficult in a decentralized economy. The other method would be to increase the money supply. Involuntary unemployment is therefore likely to be associated with massive changes in the money supply as in the thirties.

This lengthy discussion of the various types of unemployment is essential to an understanding of the income–expenditure approach, which has been closely identified with Keynesian analysis. The income–

expenditure approach is, however, more general: it is a demand and supply approach which suggests that prices and outputs can be analysed in terms of demand and supply. Thus, the income–expenditure approach can be applied to the quantity theory of money because changing the quantity of money can change prices. But whereas the quantity theory draws attention to prices the income–expenditure approach directs interest to the forces determining the *total* volume of output and employment and the price level.

The circular flow of income: a simple representation

The starting point of the income–expenditure approach is the recognition of the circular flow of income, spending and output. Production creates a flow of goods and services and generates incomes, and incomes are spent on the goods and services.

The income–expenditure approach requires some definitions.

Income is the total payments made by firms to the owners of resources (households) and comprises wages, interest, rent and profit payments during a given period.

Expenditure is the total spending by households and by firms on goods and sevices that they have bought and not re-sold by the end of the period.

Output is those goods and services produced during a period and valued at current prices.

As Figure 143 illustrates, resources are hired by firms from house-

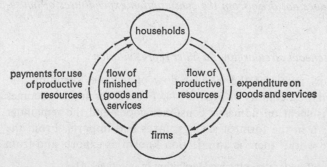

Figure 143 Solid lines indicate flows of goods and services. Broken lines indicate money flows

holds to produce goods and services and the owners of those resources are paid incomes which they spend on those goods and services.

Withdrawals from the circular flow

Figure 143 is a simplification of economic activity because it ignores the fact that not all income is automatically spent. Some income is withdrawn in the form of savings, some is taken in taxes and some is spent on imports, the effect of these withdrawals is to depress the demand for goods and services and to create unemployment of resources. Withdrawals tend to deny the possibilities of full employment.

A withdrawal is income which is not passed on in the circular flow and therefore reduces the magnitude of spending, income and output.

Injections into the circular flow

In addition to withdrawals from the circular flow there are injections into the circular flow. Exports constitute one form of injection since they are determined by the incomes of foreigners. Government spending can also form an injection of spending into the circular flow since governments can borrow or print money, as well as tax, to finance their activities. Finally, firms can borrow to finance their spending on capital goods.

An injection is an addition to the incomes of households that does not arise from the spending of firms, or it is an addition to the income of firms that does not arise from the consumption expenditures of households.[1]

The instantaneous circular flow: a fuller representation

We can now represent the circular flow of income, spending and output in more detail as in Figure 144. From households' incomes a portion is spent on domestic consumer goods and the remainder is withdrawn in the form of savings, taxes and imports. From the 'rest of the world' there is an injection known as exports and from

1. There are difficulties in producing a definition of injections. The definition breaks down if injections are a function of the rate of change of consumption, or if the constant term in a consumption function changes.

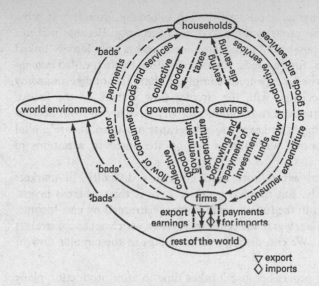

Figure 144 Solid lines indicate flows of goods and services. Broken lines indicate money flows. For simplicity it is assumed that only firms import and export and that the role of the government is to provide collective goods

government there is an injection known as government spending. Although firms are owned by households it is convenient to consider them as separate entities which are responsible for the injection known as investment.

Two further points can be noted. First, though the monetary flows are circular, the underlying physical flows are not circular since there are unilateral flows into the environment: these flows accord with the physical laws which state that there will be an increase in waste (a rise in entropy) following productive activity. Secondly, since all flows occur because of decisions made at a point of time or in the same period of time then we can refer to an *instantaneous* circular flow.

Autonomous expenditure and lags

The crucial feature of economic activity is that some components of spending are not determined by immediate circumstances. Investment, spending on capital goods, will be influenced by future profit prospects but those profits are cloaked in uncertainty. Because it is not induced by households' immediate needs and is only loosely linked to households' future needs, such expenditure is often called *autonomous* or *exogeneous* expenditure implying that it is not determined by events and decisions with the circular flow system. In the British economy fluctuations in economic activity have arisen from fluctuations in investment and exports, but because most exports are capital goods then booms and slumps can be attributed to variations in investment.

Autonomous expenditure need not cause difficulties if markets work efficiently. But the first point to note is that, whereas investment is linked to the future, savings are constrained by past income. There are, in fact, lags in the economic system which act as constraints on the future. We can distinguish three lags in the circular flow of income:

An *output lag* occurs because it takes time to alter production plans in response to changes in demand;

A *factor-payments lag* arises because some factor payments (e.g. dividends) are made at infrequent intervals;

An *income-consumption lag* may be unimportant for weekly wage-earners but of considerable importance for those who receive dividends.

Since households own firms we can regard the second and third lags as constituting one lag and thus we have an output lag and a spending lag. For simplicity we shall regard the output and spending lags as being of the same duration and concentrate attention upon the spending lag.

The existence of lags serves to link the past with the present and the future and to indicate the possibilities of disequilibrium. Planned investment, which is influenced by future profit expectations, may not be equal to planned current savings which are dictated by past income.

Equilibrium

Equilibrium in the circular flow requires that planned injections and withdrawals be equal. That is, that planned investment, which is based upon future profits, be equal to planned savings which is out of past income. More generally, we require that all planned injections be equal to all planned withdrawals. Thus, we require:

$$J_t = I_t + X_t + G_t \qquad \qquad 1$$
$$W_t = S_t + M_t + T_t \qquad \qquad 2$$
$$W_t = f(Y_{t-1}) \qquad \qquad 3$$
$$J_t = W_t$$

where J denotes injections, W is withdrawals, I is investment, X is exports, G is government expenditure, S is savings, M is imports, T is taxes and the subscripts t and $t-1$ refer to different time periods.

Equilibrium in flex price markets

The problem is how is equilibrium to be achieved? If all resource owners could be gathered together then reconciliation of different plans could soon be achieved. Resources would be allocated to the highest bidders. Prices would serve to ration resources. Something like this state of affairs occurs in an economy, particularly when it is operating at or near a full employment. Then, if planned investment threatens to exceed planned savings, the rate of interest rises to choke off excess demand for funds. If imports exceed exports then markets react to bring them into equilibrium. But it may take time for prices to rise and everyone to realize there is a disequilibrium.

Equilibrium in fix price markets

Suppose that there is considerable unemployment of resources; that is, there is general or involuntary unemployment. In such a situation a rise in planned investment need not lead to a rise in interest rates and other prices. In such a situation investment could be said to generate its own savings. Firms which had optimistic prospects about the future would borrow from the banks and buy resources. Their spending would not bid up prices because there is considerable unemployment. But they would create employment and incomes, as well as goods and services, and the incomes generated would provide the means to pay off bank loans. The point about an unemployment situation is that there need be no sacrifice of current consumption in order to release resources for use in the capital goods industries.

Money and monetary equilibrium

So far we have ignored the role of money in our analysis. Yet all our flows are measured in money terms and what is spent is money. The task of the monetary authorities is to provide enough money to lubricate the system and not to distort the intentions of households, firms and governments. Money must attempt to be neutral in the sense that the money rate of interest established by the monetary authorities must attempt to mirror the profit rate foreseen by entrepreneurs and households. If the money rate is below this profit rate then too much money will be created and there will be excess demand for resources. If it is above the profit rate then the plans of households and firms will be stifled. Yet there may be occasions when the authorities must behave vigorously and not passively. The problem is to decide when and how. The existence of lags means that adjustments take time.

Booms and slumps

We are now in a position to analyse fluctuations in economic activity. Starting in a slump we may find the stimulus to expansion coming from a variety of sources. First, falling prices may induce households to spend; the real value of money hoards will rise and promote spending. Secondly, under the stimulus of intense competition firms will have innovated, cut costs and prices, stimulated demand and be willing to hire resources to meet that demand. Thirdly, the monetary authorities may be worried by the severity of the slump and may therefore lower interest rates and engage in a cheap money policy.

Once the recovery gets under way, optimism breeds optimism, employment creates incomes which create spending which creates employment. But sooner or later an upper turning point is reached. Once resources are fully employed the continuing pressure of demand raises prices and rising prices change expectations. Business men begin to be worried that sales cannot continue at previous rates and so they start to cut back. Households also restrict purchases. The monetary authorities begin to fear that the boom is getting out of hand and raise interest rates. The slackening in spending leads to a slackening in investment, workers are laid off and the recession begins. But in a highly decentralized economy it takes time for everyone to accept the fall-off in demand. Prices and wages tend to be sticky and so employment and production bear the first brunt of the recession. Eventually prices and wages start to fall but it may take a long time before they fall sufficiently to start a recovery.

Summary

Changes in spending decisions produce fluctuations in economic activity and these decisions can be grouped under the headings of injections and withdrawals. Equilibrium requires that injections be equal to withdrawals and full employment and stable prices require that injections be sufficient to absorb the resources not needed to produce consumption goods. Disequilibrium arises because injections are strongly influenced by the future whereas withdrawals are constrained by the past. How disequilibrium is erased depends upon the nature of the economy. If there is full employment prices change, if there are unemployed resources output and employment change.

Questions

1 What is the circular flow of spending, income, and output?

2 Are the income–expenditure and quantity theories necessarily in conflict?

3 'If there is perfect foresight there are no lags in the circular flow and money does not exist.' Explain.

4 What are the causes of lags in the circular flow?

5 'The rate of interest reconciles savings and investment.' 'Changes in the level of income reconcile savings and investment.' Comment on these two statements.

6 What factors determine planned injections and planned withdrawals? What factors serve to reconcile injections and withdrawals?

7 'In the very short run prices are sticky and quantities adjust.' 'In the short run prices are flexible and quantities are sticky.' 'In the long run both prices and quantities are flexible.' Explain these statements.

8 If planned savings and planned investment are not equal does that mean that an economy is in disequilibrium?

Chapter 31
Income Determination: Aggregate Demand and Supply

In the previous chapter we sketched the circular flow of income, expenditure and output, and indicated the conditions for equilibrium in the circular flow. We also went into some detail as to the mechanisms responsible for maintaining equilibrium in the various components of the circular flow – investment, savings, exports, imports, taxes and government spending. We now arrest the process of disaggregation and examine from another angle the determination of equilibrium of the whole economy, of the total flow. What we shall emphasize is the influence of aggregate demand and aggregate supply.

There are, however, two ways of showing the influence of aggregate demand and supply. In one, prices are ignored; they can be taken as a constant on the grounds that either (1) we are taking only a very short-period analysis and in the short run buyers and sellers take prices as given and adjust quantities (incomes, employment and output) only, *or* (2) that various monopolies, such as trade unions, fix prices, *or* (3) that there are always unemployed resources which permit an increase in output without a change in prices. This particular version of aggregate demand and supply is known as the 45 degree model, so named because of the diagram used to illustrate its properties. In contrast, there is the demand and supply model in which prices and price changes are possible and explicit. The two models correspond to the two possible effects – price effect or output effect – of a change in demand and supply, that we stressed in Chapter 10. Which approach is used depends upon the problem at hand.

There are two models for analysing aggregate behaviour. One emphasizes output effects whilst the other stresses price effects.

The 45-degree approach

The basic features of a theory which assumes that price movements can be ignored, are depicted in Figure 145. Consider first the top half of the diagram. Along the horizontal axis is measured national income (Y) in constant prices (so it is national incomes in real terms). The vertical axis measures expenditures (E). Since we have assumed that injections (J) are autonomous (an alternative expression is exogeneous) and unrelated to income then in Figure 145 they can be illustrated by a line drawn parallel to the horizontal axis; OK measures the amount of injections. Consumer spending is, however, assumed to be related to income and to increases in income (though consumption rises less than proportionately as income increases). The line CC' expresses the functional relationship between consumption and income and OC measures an amount of consumption which is assumed to be constant (the subsistence amount). We have, in fact, assumed a consumption function of the form:

$$C_t = a + bY_t \qquad\qquad 1$$

where a is a subsistence constant and b is a positive constant but less than unity.

Together consumption and injections constitute total expenditure, E. More correctly, consumption expenditure on domestically produced goods and services plus injections constitute total expenditure. (The reason for the distinction between consumption expenditure and consumption expenditure on domestically produced goods and services will become clear later.)

Let us introduce a 45-degree line into the analysis. The 45-degree line need not be interpreted as a supply curve; it can simply be regarded as the line which traces out all those positions at which total expenditure is equal to total income. If it were thought of as a supply curve then it would indicate the minimum proceeds entrepreneurs required to produce a given output under the assumptions that factor prices, were constant and determined the slope of the 45-degree line, and the marginal productivities of factors were constant. The last condition is necessary to eliminate the possibility that marginal productivities might decline as output increased and so force up costs and product prices or result in a fall in factor prices to keep product prices constant.

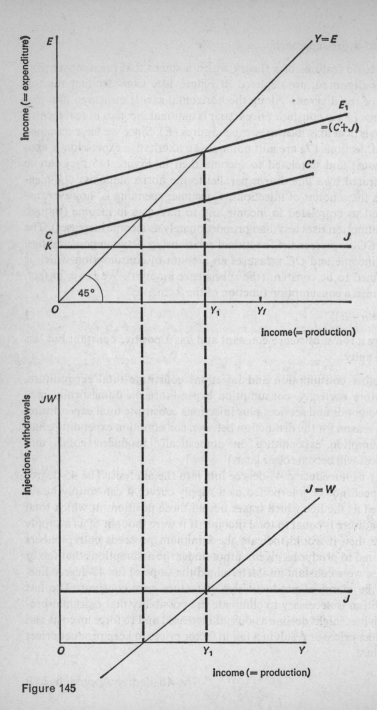

Figure 145

Injections–withdrawals diagram

From the 45-degree diagram can be derived another useful diagram. Since equilibrium depends upon the equality of injections and withdrawals we can obtain from the 45-degree diagram a withdrawals function which can be placed against the injection function. Thus in the lower half of Figure 145 we measure injections and withdrawals on the vertical axis and income along the horizontal axis. The assumption is made, for the time being, that savings are the only form of withdrawal. The withdrawals function is derived as follows: when consumption is equal to income (the break-even point) saving is zero and thus there are no withdrawals. Hence we can define a point on the horizontal axis through which the withdrawals function must pass. Further points on the withdrawals function are obtained by measuring the perpendicular distances between the 45-degree line and the consumption function for income and consumption magnitudes greater than the break-even point and also for magnitudes below the break-even point. The perpendicular distance measures the difference between income and consumption expenditure, i.e. withdrawals. Combining the withdrawals function thus derived with the injection function, as in the lower half of Figure 145, serves to determine the equilibrium level of income: the point where injections equal withdrawals, $J = W$. Note that the equilibrium level of income determined by the injections–withdrawals diagram is identical with that obtained from the equality of total internal expenditure and income, $E = Y$.

If we now allow for all withdrawals and not just savings, then the equilibrium level of income will be different by virtue of a shift in the withdrawals function but the analysis will be the same. Thus if income tax is paid and some consumer goods are imported then total withdrawals at each income level will be greater and the withdrawals function will be shifted upwards. With the same level of injections this will lead to a lower equilibrium level of income. It is for this reason that the consumption function in the upper half of Figure 145 is to be understood as referring to consumption expenditure on domestically produced goods. If it is taken to indicate total consumer expenditure then it must be adjusted for the level of imported consumer goods at each income level.

With this understanding of the 45-degree analysis it is easy to

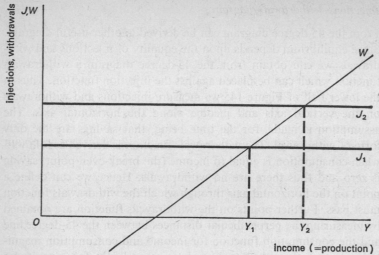

Figure 146

see that not only will national income vary as the withdrawals change but also as the level of injections changes. In Figure 146 is reproduced the lower half of Figure 145 and in the figure the result of a change in the level of injections on the equilibrium level of income is illustrated.

As the level of injections rises from J_1 to J_2 the equilibrium level of national income rises from OY_1 to OY_2.

Some algebra

The 45 degree model can also be expressed in algebra as follows:

$$M_D = M_S,$$ **1**

$$M_S = \overline{M}_S \, (= \text{a fixed supply}),$$ **2**

$$M_D = f(Y_t, r),$$ **3**

$$E_t = Y_t,$$ **4**

$$E_t = C_t + J_t,$$ **5**

$$C_t = a + bY_t : 0 < b < 1.$$ **6**

Equations **1**, **2**, **3** express the fact that money appears in the model and that the supply and demand for money are equal. Money is regarded, for the most part, as a mere lubricant of the system (though we saw earlier that money can be disruptive we are choosing for the moment to ignore that possibility) and we assume that the supply of money is always adequate. We can therefore forget about money and concentrate upon the other equations. The equation

$$E_t = Y_t$$

is the equilibrium of aggregate demand and supply and if equation **6** is substituted into equation **5** and the result inserted into **4** we obtain

$$Y_t = a + bY_t + J_t,\qquad\qquad\textbf{7}$$

which by manipulation yields

$$Y_t(1-b) = a + J_t\qquad\qquad\textbf{8}$$

$$Y_t = \frac{a+J_t}{(1-b)}.\qquad\qquad\textbf{9}$$

This is an extremely useful result which enables us to specify the equilibrium national income in terms of the parameters a and b and the autonomous injections, J. We have a compact solution model similar to that we derived for the market supply and demand model of Chapter 9.

Remember that at this stage of the analysis we are assuming that all consumption spending is on domestically produced goods and services. Recall that in Chapter 9 we had

$$q_d = a + bp,\qquad\qquad\textbf{10}$$

$$q_s = c + dp.\qquad\qquad\textbf{11}$$

If $\qquad q_d = q_s,\qquad\qquad\textbf{12}$

then $\quad a + bp = c + dp,\qquad\qquad\textbf{13}$

$$a - c = dp - bp,\qquad\qquad\textbf{14}$$

$$a - c = p(d-b),\qquad\qquad\textbf{15}$$

$$\frac{a-c}{d-b} = p.\qquad\qquad\textbf{16}$$

The condition $Y_t = E_t$ is analogous to $q_d = q_s$.

As an example of the use of equation **9** suppose that the following values of injection and consumption are known:

$C = 100 + 0.5\ Y_t,$
$J = 200,$

then the equilibrium value of national income is

$$Y_t = \frac{100 + 200}{(1 - 0.5)} = \frac{300}{0.5} = 600.$$

At the end of this chapter will be found more equilibrium income problems for the reader to solve.

The level of income

We have used the 45-degree diagram and some simple algebra to drive home the point that the level of income is determined by the amount of consumption expenditures plus injections. Hence we can go farther and deduce that if the level of expenditure is less than the full employment level of expenditure then output and income will be at lower levels. Thus if, as in Figure 145, the full employment level of income is OY_f but the actual or planned expenditure is OY_1 then the economy will be at the underemployment level of income OY_1. This level of income and spending will be stable because there is no mechanism to restore full employment. The unemployed resources which could produce $Y_1 Y_f$ income cannot obtain work because of our assumption of rigid prices.

In an economy with rigid prices it may be a coincidence that aggregate demand is sufficient to guarantee a full employment level of output and income.

Lags again

In deriving the equilibrium condition for the economy we neglected lags. This we must now remedy. If a consumption lag is introduced then it is no longer easy to produce a compact solution since we will have income expressed in the past as well as the current period values. Thus:

$$Y_t = C_t + J_t \qquad\qquad\qquad\qquad\qquad \textbf{17}$$
$$= (a + bY_{t-1}) + J_t. \qquad\qquad\qquad \textbf{18}$$
$$Y_t - bY_{t-1} = a + J_t. \qquad\qquad\qquad\qquad\qquad \textbf{19}$$

In equation **19** it is possible to simplify the expression on the left-hand side by assuming that income today is equal to income yesterday, i.e. $Y_t = Y_{t-1}$, but that removes the problems created by lags.

The introduction of lags into the analysis also means that we should be careful in our labelling of the 45 degree diagram. The vertical axis should be labelled E_t and the horizontal axis should be labelled Y_{t-1}. The 45-degree line then indicates equality of current expenditures and income generated in the previous period.

The price–quantity model

The alternative approach to the determination of equilibrium in the circular flow includes explicitly the price and wage levels as variables which we have so far ignored. Figure 147 shows an aggregate-supply curve. This is, in a sense, the summation of the supply curves of all firms in the economy. Like the supply curve of the individual firm it has a monetary dimension: it shows the minimum revenue (price times quantity) that all firms need to receive in order to maintain particular levels of output. 'Minimum revenue' is, of course, another name for supply price. Any earnings above this minimum supply price would constitute a rent, whilst earnings below a given supply price would result in a contraction of output. There is, therefore, a link between the aggregate-supply curve and the supply curve of individual firms.

The production function

The above aggregate-supply relationship can be expressed in a different way if we relate output to employment. We can, for simplicity, conceive of real output as being a function of inputs of labour and capital equipment,

$$O = f(L, K). \qquad\qquad\qquad\qquad\qquad \textbf{20}$$

Now as we recall from Chapter 3 the relationship between inputs and output is that in the short run, when the stock of capital equipment is fixed, output will expand first at an increasing rate and then

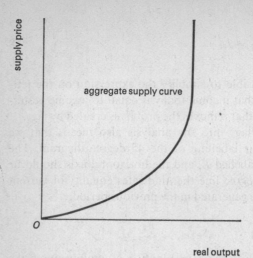

Figure 147

real output

a diminishing rate when additional labour is employed. The law of diminishing returns operates. Moreover, diminishing returns implies increasing costs and a rising supply price which is why the aggregate-supply curve rises as employment increases. Not only do costs, and hence supply price, increase more than proportionately as employment and output expand, but at the point of full employment working, it becomes physically impossible to increase real output any further and the aggregate-supply curve becomes perfectly inelastic.[1]

The money wage rate

Visually we can see some sort of relationship between the aggregate supply curve and the aggregate-production function of Figure 148, but what is the nature of the link? One curve is expressing *money returns* whilst the other expresses *physical returns*. The answer to our question is that supply in physical terms is linked to supply in money terms by means of the money wage rate. Assuming perfect competition the supply curve is the marginal-cost curve and if labour is the only variable factor then marginal-cost is wage cost, which is simply

1. It is possible for the aggregate-supply curve to take on varying shapes according to the assumptions made.

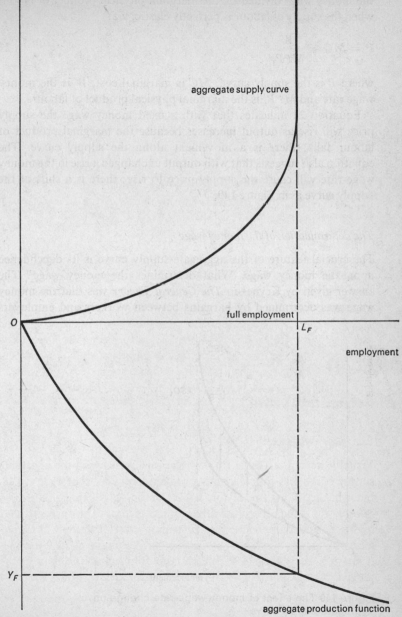

Figure 148

the money wage divided by the marginal physical product of labour when the supply of labour is perfectly elastic, viz:

$$P = MC = \frac{W}{MPP_L}$$ **21**

where P is the supply curve, MC is marginal cost, W is the money wage rate and MPP_L is the marginal physical product of labour.

Equation **21** indicates that with a fixed money wage the supply price will rise as output increases because the marginal product of labour falls: there is a movement along the supply curve. The equation also suggests that with output unchanged a rise in the money wage rate will cause the supply price to rise: there is a shift of the supply curve as in Figure 149.

The determination of the money wage

The crucial feature of the aggregate-supply curve is its dependence upon the money wage. What determines the money wage? The answer given by Keynes in *The General Theory* was that the money wage was determined by bargains between workers and employers

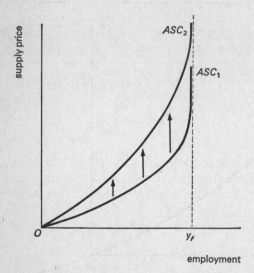

Figure 149 The effect of money wage-rate change on aggregate-supply curve

and that such bargains were about money wages because real wages (what wages could buy) lay outside their control. This still leaves the factors which influence employers and workers undetermined and some writers have sought to relate the money wage to the level of unemployment, but this is still an unresolved and controversial issue which we shall look at in Chapter 37.

The aggregate-demand curve

The aggregate-demand curve shows the community's intended money expenditure (effective demand) on goods and services at each employment level and wage rate. It is therefore a curve showing what producers expect to receive for goods and services as opposed to what they need to cover costs, or expected supply price, as indicated by the aggregate-supply curve.

In Figure 150 we employ the same basic diagram as Figure 147 but now we measure sales revenue as well as supply price on the vertical axis. The aggregate-demand curve which is shown is directly linked to the level of employment through the income-generating aspects of employment and production (as recounted in Chapter 30 where we discussed the circular flow).

What is the nature of the aggregate-demand curve? As drawn it is upward-sloping but with a slope of less than unity and an intersection on the vertical axis. The reason why the aggregate-demand curve is positive even when employment is zero is that the unemployed will still demand goods in order to survive and they will do so by dissaving, begging, borrowing or relying on state aid.[2]

Equilibrium

We can now examine the equilibrium, and stability of the equilibrium, of the aggregate demand and supply curves. Since the curves are analogous to the particular demand and supply curves of Chapter 9 the analysis is much the same.

For employment levels below OL_e the aggregate-supply curve is

2. In some texts the aggregate-demand curve is drawn with a diminishing rate of increase in slope. Consistency with the 45 degree analysis expenditure curve has caused us to reject that idea although it is applicable to both approaches.

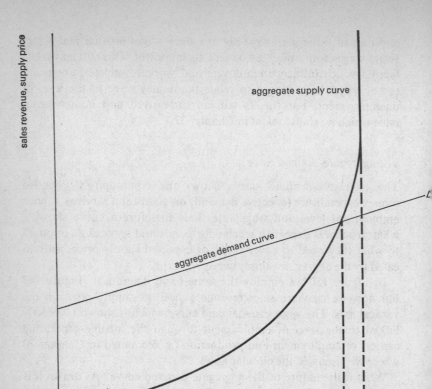

Figure 150

below the aggregate-demand curve, which means that the revenue firms actually *expect* from selling an additional amount of output is greater than the minimum revenue that they *need* if they are to produce the additional amount. In other words, total revenue is above total costs and the presence of quasi-rents (profits) will induce producers to expand output. In doing so they increase incomes and employment. As incomes increase, spending increases, and there is a movement along the aggregate-demand curve which parallels the movement along the aggregate-supply curve.

Ultimately the economy will converge on some point such as L_e. Such a point as L_e is an equilibrium point because it is a point at which there is zero excess demand. Beyond L_e supply is greater than demand, below L_e demand is greater than supply.

The level of employment for the economy as a whole is determined by the intersection of the aggregate-demand and aggregate-supply curves.

Will the point of intersection be one of full employment? A glance at Figure 150 reveals that this depends upon the strength of the depressing tendencies exerted by withdrawals. If the demand curve intersects the supply curve to the left of L_f, there will be unemployment. How can such a tendency be avoided? Clearly we would need to know what happens to the withdrawals. Some of these are savings – income not spent by households and firms – and if they are loaned to others then spending will be generated. Again if there is unemployment then might not prices fall so as to stimulate demand?

Unemployment and inflation

We can begin to appreciate the central message of the greatest economic treatise of the twentieth century – *The General Theory of Employment, Interest and Money* (Keynes, 1936). Keynes argued that there was no automatic tendency for a money economy to operate at full employment. Indeed there was a strong tendency for such an economy to operate at a less than full employment level. In later writings, he pointed out that even if the state managed to achieve full employment it might then encounter inflation through trade union pressure on wages and prices. So it looks as though economies are destined to lurch either into unemployment or inflation.

The argument can be appreciated by means of the aggregate demand and supply diagram of Figure 151. It was always a dubious assumption to accept the 45 degree approach of rigid prices. Whilst that approach could readily be used to analyse unemployment it was difficult to accept because of its postulate of rigid prices and neglect of supply forces. Surely they should have been brought into the analysis? In Figure 151 we assume that aggregate demand, D, is deficient and this causes $L_f - L_o$ unemployment. This situation can be resolved by allowing wages to fall and so permitting the aggregate-supply curve to shift to the right, to S_1. This gives the full employment level L_f determined by the intersection of D and S_1.

But wages are an important component of total incomes and hence

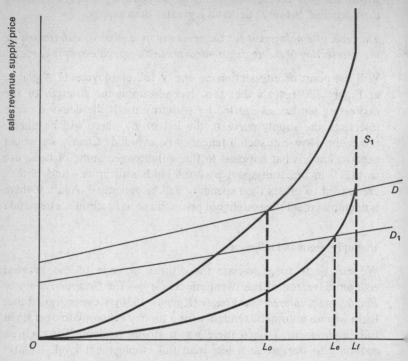

Figure 151

of spending, so if wages fall then spending will also fall. The aggregate-demand curve will shift downwards as does D_1. How far the curve will fall will depend upon a number of influences. If all else remains the same, the curve will fall until it cuts the new supply curve at the original employment level. All else is unlikely to remain the same. The wage cut may have an adverse effect on investment and thus on spending. However, if the money supply remains constant then falling prices and wages will give rise to a positive real balance effect and this may increase spending. Similarly, if exchange rates remain unaltered then falling export prices will make an increase in exports possible.

The important point is that at the aggregate level, wages are not merely a cost: they are also a source of income and spending.

The problem is: how can total demand be raised so as to keep the aggregate-demand curve at D? One answer is that the state can stimulate spending by injecting money into the system. But if people simply hold on to money (as we warned in Chapter 28) then demand will not rise.

The other problem is inflation. If the economy is at full employment then any additional demand may create rising prices, the symptom of inflation. If the excess demand persists and prices go on rising then trade unions may push for higher wages and in this way put further pressure on prices. Will the process continue? If the exchange rate does not alter, exports will fall and if the money supply does not alter then real balances will fall and people will attempt to restore them. But if the exchange rate is allowed to vary, if real balances are restored through higher money wages and if governments prefer printing money to taxation then inflation can persist.

Summary

In this chapter we set out to establish the determination of the equilibrium level of the national income – the size of the flows of income, spending and output which we discussed in the previous chapter. We discovered two approaches to the equilibrium national income. One approach ignored prices on the assumption that output could be increased without altering costs and prices. The other approach introduced supply problems in order to determine the price level in addition to the level of employment: this approach is much more complex though nearer to the spirit of the market analysis of earlier chapters.

We have now determined the level of income but a great deal of interest attaches to how income behaves as autonomous expenditures (injections) alter. This is the task of the next chapter.

Questions

1 What is the relationship between the analysis of this chapter and that to be found in Chapter 9?

2 Why do we have two approaches to the determination of the level of income?

3 Why might it be accidental that aggregate demand is sufficient to generate full employment? Suppose that consumption expenditures were insufficient to maintain full employment, then what mechanism might exist to ensure that total injections were equal to total withdrawals? What assumption has been made concerning the behaviour of injections in this chapter?

4 Why is the money wage level important?

5 How is the aggregate-supply curve constructed?

6 An economy has the following features:

$C = 150 + 0.3Y_t$
$J = 200$

Solve for the equilibrium level of national income. How would you interpret your result?

7 An economy has the following features

$C = 110 + 0.6Y_t$
$I = 100$
$X = 50$
$G = 60$
$W = 10 + 0.25Y$

where C is consumption, I is investment, X is exports, G is government spending, and W is withdrawals. Solve for the equilibrium level of national income. How would you interpret your solution?

8 What is the importance of the money wage rate in the analysis of aggregate demand and aggregate supply?

9 Is the 45-degree line a supply curve?

Chapter 32
The Multiplier

The previous chapter discussed the determinants of the equilibrium level of national income. In this chapter we shall consider the effects of changes in injections and withdrawals upon the level of income. Not much will be said about the path from one equilibrium to another. Instead we shall concentrate upon comparisons between the initial and equilibrium positions, beginning by looking at the origins of what is known as the *multiplier*.

The origins of the multiplier

In the midst of the greatest slump recorded by historians Mr Richard (now Professor, Lord) Kahn attempted to solve the following problem: If there exist unemployed resources in a country how effective would a public works policy be in removing the unemployment and how large must the government project be? Kahn assumed that the men who were employed on, say, road building would spend their wages and so create jobs for others, the latter would in turn spend and so the employment-creating process would snowball. This was the *employment multiplier*. But how large did the project have to be? At the time (1931) that Kahn was writing there were $2\frac{1}{2}$ million unemployed. So the question then became, did the Government have to employ all of them or only some of them? The example given above suggests that the Government did not have to employ everyone since some would be sucked into employment by the spending of the roadbuilders. But could the Government solve the problem by employing only one man? Suppose one man was paid £20 and spent it all, and the person who received the £20 spent it all and that in like fashion everyone spent everything they received, then full employment could be restored. However, as Kahn recognized, not all income is spent and so the effectiveness of the multiplier is dependent upon what is spent.

Kahn's was an employment multiplier. Later Keynes was to switch to an investment multiplier, thereby emphasizing that it was spending that was important. Next came the foreign trade multiplier which stressed the importance of fluctuations in exports and imports. More recently, all forms of spending have been embraced by a general multiplier which refers to all injections.

The mechanics of the multiplier

The essence of the multiplier is simplicity itself, but it has far-reaching implications. It rests on the interdependence of income and expenditure within the circular flow of income. It is because there is this interdependence that an increase in injections increases total incomes by more than the income increase of the people who receive the initial extra injections of expenditure. What happens is that the increased expenditure of the initial income recipients becomes additional income for others who in turn spend. The process continues in this fashion, period by period, but successive income increments rapidly diminish because of the positive level of withdrawals in each period. The process finally ends and equilibrium is re-established in the circular flow when desired withdrawals again equal desired injections. The final stage however is only reached over a very large number of periods but this need not bother us because the arithmetic of a convergent series takes us close to the final value within the space of a fairly short number of periods. For many purposes it is often convenient to treat the multiplier as instantaneous.

Why does the equality of desired injections and withdrawals signify the end of the multiplier process? The answer is that as long as desired injections and withdrawals are unequal then the circular flow of income will be in disequilibrium and the level of income will be changing. If desired injections are greater than desired withdrawals then the level of income will be rising. The opposite is true when withdrawals exceed injections.

An alternative way of thinking about the process is to note that while actual injections and actual withdrawals are always equal desired injections and withdrawals are only equal when income stops changing. We shall now bring out the main features of the multiplier process by means of a little algebra and some geometry.

Some algebra

The essence of the multiplier is that an increase in injections will lead to an increase in income. This can be expressed as:

$$k\Delta J_t = \Delta Y_t, \qquad\qquad 1$$

where ΔY_t is the increase in income, ΔJ_t is the increase in injections and k is the amount (the multiplier) by which injections must be multiplied to equal the resulting increase in income. On rearrangement equation 1 yields:

$$k = \frac{\Delta Y_t}{\Delta J_t}, \qquad\qquad 2$$

whence k is revealed as the multiplier. Using equations 1 and 2 we can derive an expression for the determination of the value of the multiplier. When the circular flow is in equilibrium, income (Y) equals expenditure (E),

$$E_t = Y_t, \qquad\qquad 3$$

where the subscript denotes the time period of the variables. We know that income arises as a result of domestic expenditure on consumption goods (Cd) and injections (J), so that:

$$Y_t = E_t = Cd_t + J_t. \qquad\qquad 4$$

Furthermore we know that income received is either spent on domestic consumption goods (Cd) or lost from the circular flow as a result of withdrawals, (W), so that

$$Y_t = Cd_t + W_t. \qquad\qquad 5$$

From equations 3, 4 and 5 we derive the equality of injections and withdrawals as follows:

$$J_t = Y_t - Cd_t,$$
$$W_t = Y_t - Cd_t,$$

therefore $\quad J_t = W_t. \qquad\qquad 6$

The marginal propensity to withdraw (mpw) is the term used to denote the relationship between a change in income and the change in withdrawals, the change in withdrawals gives rise to, symbolically,

$$\text{mpw} = w = \frac{\Delta W_t}{\Delta Y_t} \qquad\qquad 7$$

where w stands for the marginal propensity to withdraw. Equation 1 tells us that a change in injections will give rise to a change in income which is k times the change in injections,

$$\Delta Y_t = k\Delta J_t.$$

From equation 6 we know that in equilibrium, desired injections equal desired withdrawals, so that it follows that in equilibrium, the change in injections (ΔJ) must equal the change in withdrawals (ΔW), which allows us to rewrite equation 1 as

$$\Delta Y_t = k\Delta W_t. \qquad\qquad 8$$

But the change in withdrawals is merely the change in income times the marginal propensity to withdraw, so we also have

$$\Delta Y_t = kw\Delta Y_t, \qquad\qquad 9$$

which, on dividing both sides by w and rearranging, yields the following expression for the multiplier:

$$k = \frac{1}{w}. \qquad\qquad 10$$

The multiplier is equal to the reciprocal of the marginal propensity to withdraw.

The value of the multiplier varies inversely with the value of the marginal propensity to withdraw.

An example

We can illustrate our conclusion by means of an example. Suppose we have the following knowledge about an economy:

$$Y_t = C_t + J_t, \qquad\qquad 11$$

$$C_t = 0 + 0 \cdot 8 Y_t, \qquad\qquad 12$$

$J_t = 50.$ 13

Now let injections be increased by 50, then the increase in income
will be:

$\Delta Y_t = k\Delta J_t,$ 14

$\Delta Y_t = k.50;$ 15

but $k = \dfrac{1}{w} = \dfrac{1}{0\cdot 2},$ 16

because equation **12** tells us that $0\cdot8$ of every increase in income is
spent and therefore $0\cdot2$ of every increase in income is withdrawn.
So

$\Delta Y_t = \dfrac{1}{0\cdot2} \times 50 = 250.$ 17

Further examples will be found at the end of this chapter.

Some geometry

Since the value of the multiplier depends upon the value of the
marginal propensity to withdraw we can also illustrate the workings
of the multiplier by means of the 45-degree diagram we introduced in
Figure 145.

For simplicity we shall concentrate on the injections–withdrawals
diagram which is reproduced below. Initially, planned injections
and planned withdrawals are equal and yield income level OY.
Should injections increase by AB, this would result in a shift of the
injections curve upwards from J to J_1. The result is that the level of
income rises from Y to Y_1. The multiplier is the increase in income
(YY_1) divided by the increase in injections inducing the change
(AB); thus, the multiplier $k = YY_1/AB$. Notice in Figure 152 that
the steeper the withdrawals function, i.e. the higher the marginal
propensity to withdraw, the lower the value of the multiplier. A
change in the position, as well as the slope, of the withdrawals
function will also alter the equilibrium level of income.

Thrift a virtue?

One interesting point that arises from the preceding analysis is that
since savings are a withdrawal, thrift may be a vice and not a

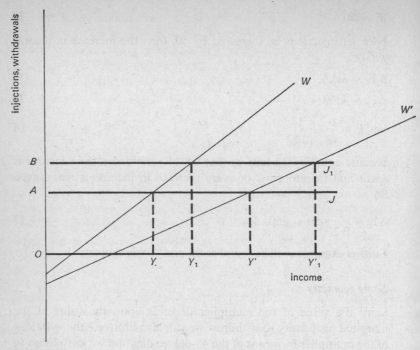

Figure 152

virtue. Unless the income not spent on consumer goods is spent on capital goods, then the result can be a lowering of the national income.

Policymakers need to know whether the withdrawals function is stable – meaning that it doesn't shift about in a random manner. Suppose, for example, that the amount of unemployed resources in an economy could produce £200 million worth of goods and that the anticipated marginal propensity to withdraw was 0·5, then an injection of £100 million would give full employment with price stability, e.g.

1   $k\Delta J = \Delta Y$; $\Delta J = \Delta Y/k$;

2   $\Delta Y = 200$;

$$\Delta J = \frac{200}{2} = 100.$$

If, however, the withdrawals function was unstable and shifted so as to give a marginal propensity to withdraw of 0·25 at the time of the injection, then inflation (rising prices) would occur. Alternatively, if the marginal propensity to withdraw rose to 0·75 then there would still be unemployed resources after the injection. It is important, therefore, to know whether the withdrawals function is stable.

Instantaneous versus period multiplier

The multiplier that we have just considered has been an *instantaneous multiplier*; that is, the multiplier process has worked itself out instantaneously or in a single period. This is in line with the early analysis of the circular flow in Chapter 30 where we assumed that there were no delays, or lags, in adjustments. But, as we noted there, it may be unreasonable to assume that everything takes place instantly and it may be more realistic to assume a time lag before equilibrium is attained.

Table 50 illustrates the workings of a multiplier process in which there are lags in the adjustment process; this is known as the *period multiplier*. It is assumed that there is not one single injection but a series of injections of 100 per period and that the marginal propensity to withdraw is one-half of the increase in income received in the previous period. In other words, consumption in one period is out of the previous period's income.

Table 50 Period multiplier

Number of periods	Initial injection	Additional receipts through successive expenditures of half of income receipts in preceding period

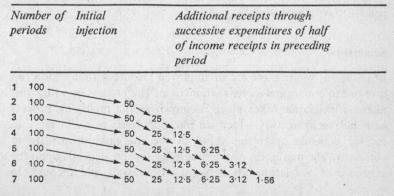

1	100						
2	100	50					
3	100	50	25				
4	100	50	25	12·5			
5	100	50	25	12·5	6·25		
6	100	50	25	12·5	6·25	3·12	
7	100	50	25	12·5	6·25	3·12	1·56

In the table the diagonal sums, as indicated by the arrows, represent the income generated by the primary injection. They approach

$$100. \ 1/0{\cdot}5 = 200 = 50 + 25 + 12{\cdot}5 + 6{\cdot}25 + 3{\cdot}125 + \ldots = 200$$

if continued long enough. The horizontal sums (in each row) represent the sum total of income generated in the period which corresponds to the injection plus the indirect contribution from the expenditures generated from the incomes received in previous periods. This sum also approaches 200 after a sufficient length of time.

Real versus money multipliers

The multiplier has been discussed in the context of unemployed resources, but what happens if there is full employment? The effect of an injection in a situation of full employment is to cause a rise in the general level of prices. We are back in the world of the quantity theory of money. In situations of less than perfect elasticity of resources (between the cases of full employment and mass unemployment) there may be both price and output effects. The multiplier of the previous sections was a *real multiplier* in the sense that there were unemployed resources. This was why we used the 45-degree line, or fix-price approach, but when we leave the fix-price world then the multiplier may be operating in a world where the general level of prices as well as output responds to changes in aggregate demand. In such situations we can use the aggregate demand and supply approach. And in such a world the value of the real output multiplier will fall below the magnitude of the reciprocal of the marginal propensity to withdraw ($1/w$).

Summary

In situations where there are unemployed resources an injection can give rise to a marginal increase in income. The process by which this increase in income takes place is known as the multiplier process and the mechanism by which an injection leads to an increase in income depends upon the value of the marginal propensity to withdraw. The usefulness of the multiplier process depends upon the existence of a relationship between withdrawals and income. In

Chapter 30 we identified three types of withdrawal – savings, imports and taxes. The relationship between savings (consumption) and income will be studied in the next chapter, and imports and income in Chapter 35. The multiplier process also fits into the context of the circular flow of income and expenditure which assumes that the injection components of expenditure are autonomous. We shall in subsequent chapters seek to see if autonomous expenditures, such as investment and exports, are autonomous.

Questions

1 In a closed economy, i.e. one which does not engage in foreign trade, spending on consumer goods is related to the national income by the following schedule:

National income (£m)	Consumption (£m)
0	15
20	30
40	45
60	60
80	75
100	90
120	105
140	120
160	135
180	150
200	165
220	180

If firms are investing at the rate of £10 million per year and the government is spending £15 million per year,

(a) What is the equilibrium level of national income?

(b) What is the average propensity to consume at the equilibrium level of income?

(c) Suppose that full employment yields a national income of £200 million, by how much must government expenditure be increased to reach full employment income?

2 In a closed economy with zero government expenditure and taxation the consumption function is

$C = 100 + 0.5Y,$

where C is consumers' outlay and Y is the gross national product.

(a) What is the marginal propensity to save?

(b) Suppose unemployment existed and national income was £12 million below full employment income. What increase in investment would eliminate unemployment?

3 Will an increase in withdrawals lead to a decrease in the level of national income and hence to a decrease in withdrawals?

4 What is indicated by changes in the *slope* and *position* of the withdrawals function?

5 An economy has the following features:

$C = 1000 + 0.75Y_t$
$J = 100$.

Let J be increased by 25. What would be the effect on national income?

Chapter 33
Households: Their Contribution to Aggregate Demand

Investigations into the determinants of consumption and saving have been a major field of activity since Keynes suggested that unemployment was a result of demand deficiency.[1] As consumption is a major component of aggregate demand, research was obviously necessary so that the resulting knowledge could be used to predict and manipulate the level of aggregate demand.[2] A second reason for examining the split between consumption and savings is that savings permit the diversion of resources from current consumption to capital accumulation upon which depends the future productive capacity of an economy. The third reason for examining the division between consumption and savings is that it strongly influences the distribution of income.

But having stressed the importance of households' decisions concerning savings we enter a caveat. The bulk of saving in a modern economy is undertaken by corporations and government and though they might be said to be acting on behalf of their owners – households – there is much evidence to suggest that control is not always rigorously exercised. In Chapter 15 we drew attention to the implications of the divorce of ownership from control in the modern corporation in determining the distribution of firms' profits. And later in Chapter 44 we shall draw a parallel in the case of government.

From micro to macro

We shall use the theory of household spending developed in earlier chapters to derive a theory of aggregate consumption. A theory of the

1. The terms 'household consumption', 'household consumption spending', 'consumption', and 'consumer spending' will be used as synonyms in this chapter and will refer to the amount that households spend on buying new goods and services.
2. In 1975 UK consumer spending accounted for 48 per cent of total demand.

determinants of how much one individual spends on one good will be used to derive a theory of how much all individuals spend on all goods.

In Chapters 7 and 11 we set out a theory of consumer's demand, which indicated that an individual derived utility from his consumption of goods and services. His choice is constrained by his income and the prices of goods and services. We then obtain the demand for any good as a function of all prices P, tastes t, his income Y:

$$d = f(P_a, ..., P_z, Y, t), \qquad\qquad 1$$

when the subscripts a to z refer to goods.

In Chapter 6 we noted that individuals could borrow and lend, so that they could consume more than their income 'today' and less that their income 'tomorrow', or vice-versa. Such a decision is influenced by the rate of interest r, and the individual's stock of assets A. So we can write:

$$d = f(P_{a_t}, ..., P_{z_t}, Y_t, t, A, r, P_{a_{t+1}}, ..., P_{z_{t+1}}, Y_{t+1}) \qquad\qquad 2$$

where the subscripts t, $t+1$ indicate the time periods.

In Chapter 27 we indicated that an individual's income depended upon the allocation of his time between work and leisure, and that this choice might depend on the wage rate. With fixed working weeks quite common, the individual's income-leisure choice may take the form of training for a different type of job. This implies that in the long run, income is determined as much by consumption as consumption is by income: an individual will choose a job and (where possible) hours of work, so as to obtain an optimal combination of income and leisure. However, in the short run, the individual is less free to choose his income, and he cannot, therefore choose his consumption.

As well as his choice of private goods, an individual will consume public goods, provided collectively. But the individual cannot, by himself choose his consumption of public goods, so in this chapter we ignore collective goods. The individual may however pay taxes to finance the provision of public goods if the government takes responsibility for their allocation, and his taxes reduce the amount of money he has left over to pay for private goods. In what follows, we use income to mean *disposable income* which is income after taxes have been paid.

What we have so far is a catalogue of all the factors which can influence a consumer's spending. As we are interested in total consumption, we can ignore relative prices, and hence concentrate on consumption as a function of individual incomes. Strictly speaking, this should be real incomes, which are money incomes corrected for price changes. We are mainly interested in consumption in relation to aggregate disposable income, and we shall hold the individual's stock of assets and rate of interest constant. We shall also assume that current prices are given. Hence we can write a relationship between consumption and current income,

$$c = d = f(y_t). \qquad\qquad 3$$

Aggregation

The final step is to aggregate the behaviour of all households into one macro household. This implies that though some households may be spending more than their current income they are offset by those who may be spending less. In addition, we shall be ignoring all internal transfers such as when parents give pocket money to their children. So we can write

$$D = F(Y_t), \qquad\qquad 4$$

or, replacing demand (D) by consumption (C) and inserting a suffix (d) to denote disposable income, we can write utility, U, as

$$U = G(C) = G\{F(Yd_t)\}, \qquad\qquad 5$$

or $$C = F(Yd_t), \qquad\qquad 6$$

which is known as the *consumption function*.[3] This states that consumption is a function of real disposable income.

Before going on to test this theory we should take stock of what we have done, for it does seem puzzling to reduce a theory of consumer behaviour to a dependence upon one variable, current income. Part of the reason for doing this lies in the costs of information. If we can obtain a good understanding of consumer behaviour with only one variable then we can reduce the amount of information we need to collect.

3. Thus the consumption function is related to the income–consumption curve of Chapter 11.

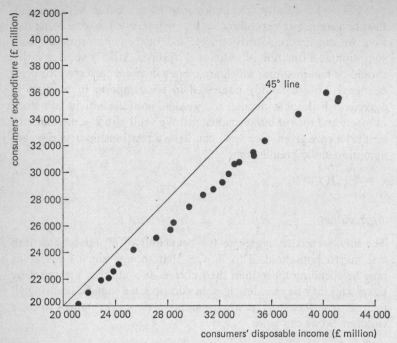

Figure 153

The consumption function

We now have a theory which states that consumption depends upon real disposable income and, thus, that changes in consumption depend upon changes in real disposable income. We can test this theory by simply looking at the historical data on consumption and disposable income. If we use the data in the statistical appendix we get the result shown in Figure 153.[4]

It looks as though we can use the level of disposable income to explain consumption. More light is thrown on the relationship if we calculate the *average propensity to consume* (*APC* = consumer spending/disposable income). The figures for the *APC* in each year

4. All the totals for spending and income are in constant price terms. The prices used are 1970 prices. Thus an income of £500 in 1955 will buy exactly the same bundle of goods as an income of £500 in 1963 or in 1973. This procedure reveals the *quantities* demanded and supplied.

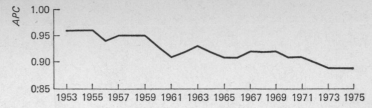

Figure 154

are shown in Figure 154 (row 3 of the statistical appendix). Whilst the overall trend was for the *APC* to fall from 1953 to 1975, there were quite marked fluctuations from one year to the next. In the short run it seems as though something has disturbed the relationship between consumer spending and disposable income.

We can further examine the relationship if we compare the changes in disposable income from year to year with a change in consumption from year to year. The question being asked is, 'if we know that disposable income is £1000 million higher than last year, can we predict how much higher consumer spending will be, compared with the previous year?' The answer can be found in rows 5, 6 and 7 of the data. Row 5 shows the amount by which consumer spending exceeded that of the previous year. Similarly, row 6 is the increase in real disposable income. If the change in disposable income perfectly explains the change in consumer spending then the fraction, change in consumer spending/change in disposable income, should be a constant. Figure 155 (based on row 7) shows the ratio for each of the years 1954 to 1975. What is immediately noticeable is that the fractions have not been constant, nor has there been a rising or falling trend. What we observe is apparently random fluctuations from year to year with values in the range 0·34 to 7·71. If disposable income rose by £1000 million from one year to the next then the first of these figures would predict a rise in consumer spending over the previous year of £340 millions whilst the other figure predicts a rise of £7710 millions – a difference between the estimates of £7320 millions. The ratios in row 7 are the estimates of the *marginal propensity to consume* (*MPC*) – that is, the fraction of an increase in income which is spent on consumption. What the fluctuations in the *MPC* from year to year clearly show is that we cannot explain the behaviour of household consumption solely in terms of current disposable income.

The Consumption Function 549

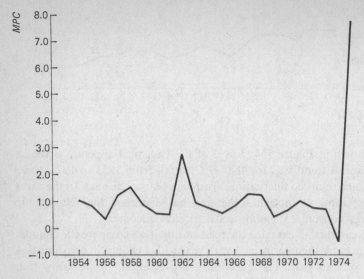

Figure 155

The theory with which we started, that the level of consumption spending depended solely on current disposable income, has been tested and found wanting. We must now go back and consider whether we need to add more variables from our original catalogue.

A statistical digression

The points in the scatter diagram in Figure 153 appear to fall very closely along a straight line. Using the statistical technique called regression, a straight line has been estimated which most closely fits the scatter diagram for the years 1954–75. The result is equation

$$C_t = 4017 + 0.785 \ Yd_t, \qquad\qquad 7$$

where C_t is consumption spending in period t and Yd_t is disposable income in period t. Thus we predict that when disposable income was £34 622 millions (as in 1970), household consumer spending in that year would be:

$$C_t = 4017 + 0.785 \ (34\ 622) = 31\ 195 \qquad\qquad 8$$

Since household consumption spending in 1970 was actually £31 472

550 Households: Their Contribution to Aggregate Demand

million, this estimate was £277 million too low.[5] We can go on to calculate that for the years 1954–75 these annual estimates were in error by £287 million on average. This is the average absolute error.[6]

A slightly more sophisticated theory of household consumption spending

A little introspection may lead to the formulation of a better theory to explain what determines household consumer spending.

Because our standard of living has been rising steadily over a long period of time (remember this has been the case for perhaps at least two hundred years in Britain – see Chapter 1) it may have become one of those things that we take for granted. We may make spending decisions on the implicit assumption that our real disposable income will rise by some 'average' amount, by an amount that we have come to expect. We may stick more or less to our spending plans even if for some reason disposable income only rises this year by very little. We are reluctant to lower our sights unless the low growth becomes the norm, and thus this year we only trim our spending plans slightly because of the shortfall of disposable income below the expected level. Thus, this year the increase in spending is unusually high *in relation* to the rise in disposable income, and the marginal propensity to consume is unusually high. Perhaps another year the rise in disposable income is unexpectedly large – in this year the rise in spending will be unusually low in relation to the unexpectedly high rise in income and *MPC* will be unusually low. This theory can be tested by plotting a time series for the *MPC* and another for the percentage rise in real disposable income and comparing them (Figure 156). The solid horizontal line in each time series shows the arithmetic mean for the series for the years 1954-75. What we can see fairly clearly is that for those years when real income growth was higher than average the *MPC* was normally lower than average, and that when income growth was lower than average, *MPC* was normally higher than average. With the aid of a little introspection we have produced a theory

5. Whilst an error of £277 million seems small in a total of £31 472 million it makes a big difference to the level of unemployment when demand changes by £277 million.
6. The reader should note that the efforts to estimate consumption functions that are made in this book represent a very elementary beginning to what is statistically and economically a very difficult undertaking.

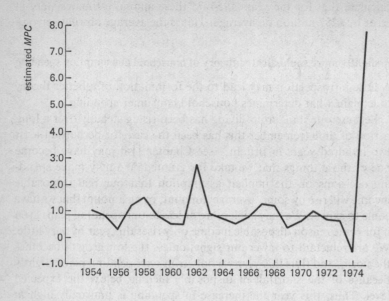

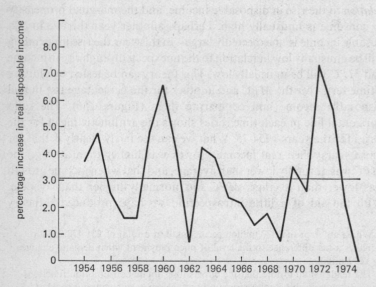

Figure 156 Variations in *MPC* and real disposable income

which seems to be validated by the available data. The formal development of this theory was carried out by Milton Friedman who called it the *permanent income hypothesis*.[7] Friedman suggested that people related their consumption to what they saw as their permanent income. Their conception of their permanent income was subject to continual revision in the light of their most recent experiences. If in a year their disposable income differed from their notion of their permanent income then they made some adjustment to their notional permanent income and thus to their consumption. But how do we 'get at' permanent income? It is not something that automatically reveals itself. The answer is by means of a lag analysis similar to that used in Chapter 30. We assume that permanent income will be reflected by previous consumption. Hence we can say that current consumption is determined by the interplay of current disposable income and past consumption. The theory can be summarised in the following equation:

$$C_t = a\beta + \alpha\beta Yd_t + (1-\beta)C_{t-1} \qquad\qquad 9$$

where a, α and β are parameters.[8]

By again using regression analysis we can estimate the value of the constants using the historical data for the period 1954–75 included in the statistical appendix. The result obtained is

$$C_t = 3534 + 0{\cdot}668\,Yd_t + 0{\cdot}149\,C_{t-1}. \qquad\qquad 10$$

Let us check how to use this result. As with our simple theory, let us try to predict consumer spending in 1970. Disposable income in that year was £34 622 million and consumer spending in the previous year was £30 715 million. Thus we predict that consumer spending in 1970 was

$$
\begin{aligned}
C_t &= 3534 + 0{\cdot}668\,(34\,622) + 0{\cdot}149\,(30\,715) \\
&= £31\,238 \text{ million} \qquad\qquad 11
\end{aligned}
$$

7. Friedman's theory (Friedman, 1957) is but one of several which attempt to cope with the problem under discussion by introducing past experience. In addition there are Duesenberry's relative income hypothesis, Modigliani and Brumberg's life cycle hypothesis, and Clower and Johnson's endogenous income hypothesis. What is common to all is the implicit reference to time preference and interest rates.
8. The formal derivation of this equation is to be found in the appendix to this chapter.

A Slightly More Sophisticated Theory 553

As consumer spending in 1970 was actually £31 472 million this is an error of only £234 million. The prediction error for 1970 using the first regression equation based on the simple theory was £277 million. Whilst the error for 1970 is smaller, the improvement over the whole period 1954–75 is even less impressive, with an average annual error of £279 million as compared with £287 million with the simple theory. The gain in accuracy seems small and obviously we have not got to the bottom of what determines the level of consumer spending. There are several things we can do. First, we can abandon the theories on the grounds that they are not good predictors but before we do that we would have to consider what constitutes a good theory. Since the data may contain errors of observation should we not say that the theory is in some sense all right? This question poses the further one of how we should lay down acceptable rules for testing and accepting theories. The second approach would be to attempt to obtain better data though even this strategy leads us back to a consideration of what constitutes a good test since we cannot expect error-free data. The third approach would be to disaggregate the data to see if there are any particular components of spending that need special treatment. This is what we shall do, but first we shall provide a diagrammatic exposition of the preceding analysis which some readers will find a useful generalization. Meanwhile we must note that, for the moment, not only is our consumer theory suspect but so is the entire apparatus of lagged analysis that we used in Chapter 30. For the moment it seems to be no better than a theory without lags unless we can assume that the lags are less than one year in duration.

Long- and short-run consumption functions

In the last section we investigated a complex consumption function which explicitly allowed for the fact that households take time to adjust to changed circumstances. The initial reaction of households to a change in income does not reflect their long-run normal pattern of behaviour. We can therefore distinguish between short- and long-run behaviour. The version of the permanent-income hypothesis that we investigated stated that households adjusted their consumption to changes in their permanent income (P_t). Thus,

$$C_t = a + \alpha P_t. \tag{12}$$

The fraction of any change in their permanent (long-run) income that they spend on consumption is α; that is, their long-run marginal propensity to consume is α. We estimated the long-run marginal propensity to consume to be 0·785.[9]

The short-run consumption function was estimated as equal to 0·668. Thus if disposable income rose by £1000 million, consumer spending would rise in the short run by £668 million, but in the long run when consumers had incorporated the income increase into what they perceived as their permanent income, they would increase their consumption by a further £117 million, making a total rise of £785 million.

We can show the difference between the short- and long-run marginal propensities diagrammatically by drawing short- and long-run consumptions functions as in Figure 157 opposite.

Let us assume that initially income is at a level OY_0 with aggregate consumption OC_0. Now we increase income to OY_1. In the short run the community only partially adjusts and raises consumption to OC'_0. When the community has had time to adjust fully, consumption rises to OC''_0, so that it bears its normal long-run relationship to income. We could analyse a fall in income below OY_0 in a similar way.

9. Thus from equation 8 on page 552

$$C_t = a\beta + \alpha\beta\,Yd_t + (1-\beta)C_{t-1},$$

we estimated

$$C_t = 3534 + 0·688Yd_t + 0·149C_{t-1}.$$

Thus $1-\beta = +0·149$
i.e. $\beta = +0·851$
and $\alpha\beta = +0·668$
hence $\alpha = +0·668/\beta$
Thus $\alpha = +0·688/+0·851,$
          $= +0·785.$

Using the regression equation we estimated consumption spending in 1970

$$C_t = 3534 + 0·668(34\,622) + 0·149(30\,715),$$
$$= £31\,238 \text{ million.}$$

Now assume that disposable income had risen £1000 million extra in 1970 to £35 622 million. Consumption would have then risen to

$$C_t = 3534 + 0·668(35\,622) + 0·149(30\,715),$$
$$= £31\,906 \text{ million,}$$

an immediate rise of £668 million which is the value of the short-run consumption function.

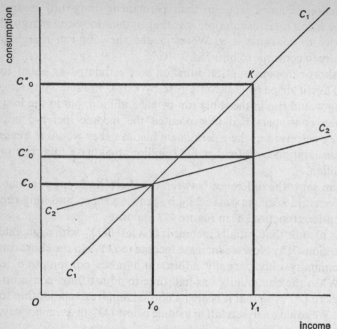

Figure 158

The line C_2C_2 is a short-run consumption function and C_1C_1 is the long-run consumption function. After full adjustment when consumption is at point K there will be another short-run consumption function C_3C_3 which cuts C_1C_1 at K in Figure 158.

The short-run marginal propensity to consume in Figure 158 is the short-run change in consumption divided by the change in income, i.e. $C_0C'_0/Y_0Y_1$, and the long-run MPC is $C_0C''_0/Y_0Y_1$.

The distinction between the short- and long-run consumption functions has implications for the workings of the multiplier. Although the value of the multiplier will depend upon all the withdrawals (saving, imports and taxes), the existence of short- and long-run consumption functions suggests that there may be short- and long-run import and tax functions, and thus there may be short- and long-run values to the overall multiplier.

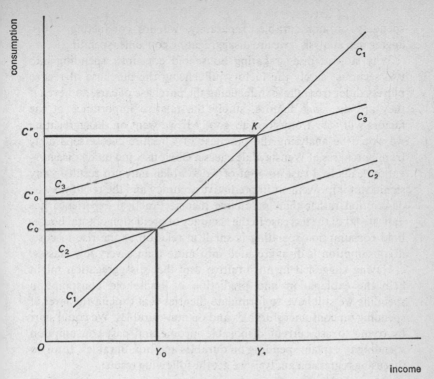

Figure 158

Further efforts to explain household consumer spending

Either we could try a little more introspection in an attempt to find any factors which affect household consumer spending, or we could try a fresh approach. Let us do the latter. The goods and services that households purchase vary very much in their characteristics. Some items are purchased frequently and are quickly consumed as with food, public transport, heat and light. Other items are purchased much less often and last for a long time as with record players, new cars, washing-machines, etc. – these are known as consumer durables. It seems intuitively reasonable to argue that the pattern of purchases of consumer durables will differ from the pattern for non-durables. If we pursue this line of inquiry, that is, trying to explain spending on durables and then trying to explain spending on non-durables separately, we are conducting a disaggregated analysis – we are disaggregating consumer spending.

Why stop at disaggregating household consumer spending into two sections; surely the factors influencing the purchase of record players differ from those influencing the purchase of cars, and even if they are the *same* factors, surely the relative importance of the factors will vary from good to good? If we went on disaggregating we would be analysing the purchase of Cheshire cheese separately from purchases of Wensleydale cheese. Obviously too much disaggregation leads to a vast amount of work which may not result in any significant improvement in predictive accuracy and the result may be description rather than predictive theory. Practical experience has indicated that the increase in the accuracy of prediction of total household consumption spending is small in relation to the rise in costs if consumption is disaggregated into more than a very few classes.

Having suggested in an intuitive way that disaggregation might help the explanation and prediction of household consumption spending we still have to formulate theories that explain the level of spending on consumer durables and on non-durables. We could start by trying to use current disposable income and past consumption spending to explain spending on durables and non-durables. If we do this using regression analysis we get the following result:

$$C_{D_t} = -1323 + 0\cdot100 Yd_t + 0\cdot151 C_{D_{t-1}}, \qquad \text{durables } 13$$

$$C_{ND_t} = 3329 + 0\cdot360 Yd_t + 0\cdot459 C_{ND_{t-1}}. \qquad \text{non-durables } 14$$

If we calculate the short- and long-run marginal propensities to consume of both durables (long-run $MPC = 0\cdot118$, short-run $MPC = 0\cdot100$) and non-durables (long-run $MPC = 0\cdot665$, short-run $MPC = 0\cdot360$) then we see that the way in which households respond to a change in their incomes differs as between durables and non-durables. Expenditure on non-durables increases much more slowly than spending on durables. This result has interesting policy as well as theoretical implications.

But we should be cautious. The equations may be imperfect, the data deficient and there are errors in the predictions of purchases of both durables and non-durables. We need more sophisticated theories and better data. Perhaps spending on durables depends on interest rates and hire-purchase conditions. The need to keep a balance in this book prevents us from going further both in theorizing and testing, but one point must be made very clearly. It is probably not possible to explain and predict consumption spending perfectly however much effort we put into our theorizing and statistical work. This is because the behaviour of groups is not entirely constant, and because there may be factors which are unpredictable such as hard winters, strikes, international crises, etc. Nevertheless, there is still considerable scope for theorizing and testing. Economics, as a quantitative subject, is yet in its infancy. We still need to establish the measurable area of the subject.

Household spending on new dwellings: a special case of a durable good

An important injection from the household sector which creates effective demand and thus employment is the purchase of *new* dwellings (flats, houses, etc.). It is obvious that the purchase of second-hand houses does not create employment for builders – it only constitutes a swapping of existing assets, though we should perhaps note, in passing, that the purchase of a second-hand house does create employment for estate agents, solicitors, surveyors, etc. These people provide a service and consumer spending on their services is included in the 'consumer spending on services' figures.

If we look at real personal investment in new dwellings (row 11 of the statistical appendix) and plot it as a time series, as in Figure 159, what is immediately noticeable is the surprising irregularity of the series.

As a simple test we could plot the time series for the data on disposable income, interest rates and purchases of new dwellings that are set out in the appendix. Having done that we need to recognize that the investment data may reflect supply as well as demand conditions. It may be influenced by severe weather conditions and by possible changes in productivity in building. We have, in short, an identification problem of the kind discussed in Chapter 10. The problem in relation to the historical data on new dwellings is too complex to unravel in this book.

Explaining consumption spending by investigating saving

So far we have concentrated on trying to explain consumer spending by framing questions and theories as though the sole concern of

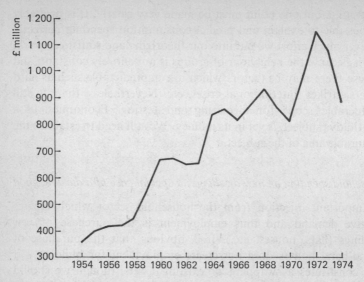

Figure 159 Personal investment in new
dwellings at 1970 prices

households was with current consumption. The implication has
almost been that savings are a residual, something that is not
adjusted deliberately. Yet savings decisions are just as deliberate as
consumption decisions. It may therefore be useful to explore the
behaviour of savings data in order to provide a check on our theories
of consumer behaviour. Unfortunately, savings data are unreliable.
They are not calculated directly, but are obtained as residuals from
the estimates of income and consumption. Hence any errors in the
calculations of consumption and income tend to be magnified in the
savings figures and corrections to savings data tend to be of much
larger magnitudes than those made to consumption and income
estimates.

Before we leave savings a comment is in order on the years 1974
and 1975 in the UK. In both these years the level of savings was
quite exceptionally high as a proportion of income. This sudden rise
came about at the same time as consumers' disposable income was
rising by much less than usual and when real interest rates were very
low (real interest rates = money rate of interest *less* the rate of price
increase). During these years the real value of savings was falling.

Both on grounds of income and interest rate we would have predicted a fall in savings: the observation of the exact opposite has surprised economists and has sent them back to look again at their theories.

Summary and conclusions

We have discussed in this chapter the behaviour of households as this affects the level of demand for new goods and services and, through production, the level of employment. Households were separated from a discussion of firms' and government's expenditures because households have some features that uniquely distinguish them from the other economic agencies. They act purely out of self-interest which one hopes governments do not, and their ability to borrow is much more constrained than that of firms.

Households were discussed as a group because the group seems to behave in a consistent, predictable way as the eccentricities of individual households are averaged out. Our discussion has had three aims. First, we discussed the erection and development of theories of household behaviour. Secondly, elementary ideas of testing were introduced. Finally, we tried to give some idea of the problems, both theoretical and statistical, which are particularly developed in more advanced courses.

We found that the principle factor controlling household spending on goods was disposable income and we went on to show that the power of the theory was increased by including past consumption as an explanatory variable. Later sections went on to suggest that the theories could be improved by a measure of disaggregation and by a consideration of savings. A consideration of savings suggests that interest rates might be influential in explaining consumption. No direct testing of the effects of interest rates was attempted though they were implicit in the permanent income hypothesis.

An important assumption made in our analysis was that households take time to adjust fully to changed circumstances. This assumption was one that we used in Part Two when we examined short- and long-run responses in particular markets. It testifies to the power of Marshall's partial equilibrium analysis with its stress on the time lags. This difference in responses implied that the long-run and short-run multipliers will take on different values and may be difficult to predict accurately. However, before accepting that conclusion we noted that the multiplier is also dependent upon the behaviour of imports and taxes and that their behaviour may offset any waywardness in the income-consumption multiplier. Moreover, the crudeness in our theories and data suggested that more work needed to be done on refining both.

Questions

1 It is suggested that the aggregate consumption function was derived from the micro behaviour of households in Chapters 6, 7, 11 and 27. Indicate how this is done.

2 If we aggregate all incomes and spending do we have to assume that all individuals have identical tastes and incomes in order to derive a meaningful theory of the consumption function?

3 What is the connection between the consumption function and the income–consumption curve of Chapter 11?

4 What is the connection between the analysis of Chapter 6 and Friedman's consumption function?

5 Does the empirical testing of the consumption function suggest the need for new theories or new facts?

6 Using the data in the statistical appendix, test for any possible relationship between investment in dwellings and the change from the previous year in household disposable income.

7 Can you explain the marked difference between the short and long run MPC for durables and non-durables?

8 In 1970 household disposable income was £34 622 million and in the previous year consumption spending was £30 715 million. Assume that disposable income rose by £1000 millions in 1971 and remained unchanged for six years. Using the consumption function

$$C_t = 3534 + 0{\cdot}688\,Yd_t + 0{\cdot}149\,C_{t-1},$$

calculate the level of consumption in 1971, 1972, 1973 and 1974.

9 How would you expect a change in future prices to affect current consumption?

Appendix: derivation of the permanent income equation

We can write that consumption in time period $t(C_t)$ depends upon permanent income in period $t(P_t)$:

$$C_t = a + \alpha P_t. \tag{1}$$

This is the type of equation that we found when we used actual current disposable income to explain current consumption. The change in permanent income is seen as a fraction (β) which is greater than zero and less than one of the differences between current disposable income and the previously perceived level of permanent income. That is,

$$P_t - P_{t-1} - \beta(Yd_t - P_{t-1}). \tag{2}$$

If we rearrange **2** we get

$$P_t = \beta Yd_t - \beta P_{t-1} + P_{t-1} \tag{3}$$

$$= \beta Yd_t + P_{t-1}(1-\beta). \tag{4}$$

Now we have an expression for the permanent income in time period $t(P_t)$ which we can substitute in equation **1**. Thus,

$$C_t = a + \alpha[\beta Yd_t + P_{t-1}(1-\beta)]. \tag{5}$$

Now if we can write equation **1** we can also write that consumption in an earlier time period depends upon permanent income in that earlier time period. Thus

$$C_{t-1} = a + \alpha P_{t-1}. \tag{6}$$

Rearranging **6** we get

$$C_{t-1} - a = \alpha P_{t-1},$$

and dividing both sides by α gives

$$(C_{t-1} - a)/\alpha = P_{t-1}. \tag{7}$$

We can substitute the expression for P_{t-1} in equation **7** into equation **5**, thus obtaining

$$C_t = a + \alpha[\beta Yd_t + ((C_{t-1} - a)/\alpha)(1-\beta)]$$
$$= a + \alpha\beta Yd_t + (C_{t-1} - a)(1-\beta)$$

$$= a+\alpha\beta Yd_t+C_{t-1}-\beta C_{t-1}-a+\alpha\beta$$
$$= (a-a+a\beta)+\alpha\beta Yd_t+C_{t-1}(1-\beta)$$
$$C_t = a\beta+\alpha\beta Yd_t+(1-\beta)C_{t-1}.$$
8

What we have finished with is an expression (a function) which says
that changes in current household consumption spending depend
upon changes in current disposable income and changes in past

Statistical appendix

Row Number	1954	1955	1956	1957	1958	1959	1960	1961
1 Consumers' expenditure at 1970 prices (£ million)	21 059	21 933	22 131	22 601	23 187	24 195	25 146	25 734
2 Personal disposable income at 1970 prices (£ million)	21 908	22 948	23 522	23 896	24 285	25 452	27 122	28 241
3 Average propensity to consume	0·96	0·96	0·94	0·95	0·95	0·95	0·93	0·91
4 Average propensity to save	0·04	0·04	0·06	0·05	0·05	0·05	0·07	0·09
5 Change in consumers' expenditure (row 1) from the previous year ($\triangle C$)	832	874	198	470	586	1008	951	588
6 Change in personal disposable income (row 2) from the previous year ($\triangle Yd$)	782	1040	574	374	389	1167	1670	1119
7 Marginal propensity to consume ($\triangle C/\triangle Yd$)	1·06	0·84	0·34	1·26	1·51	0·86	0·57	0·52
8 Percentage increase of disposable income (row 2) over the previous year	3·70	4·75	2·50	1·59	1·63	4·81	6·56	4·12
9 Consumers' expenditure on durable goods at 1970 prices (£ million)	1086	1196	1054	1181	1381	1630	1677	1613
10 Consumers' expenditure on non-durables at 1970 prices (£ million)	19 973	20 737	21 077	21 420	22 012	22 565	23 469	24 121
11 Personal investment in new dwellings at 1970 prices (£ million)	358	398	420	423	445	554	670	673
12 Building society interest rates on loans, annual average	4·58	4·66	5·31	5·98	6·13	5·98	5·89	6·28

Source: *National Income and Expenditure*, 1964–75, HMSO
     Annual Abstract of Statistics, various issues, HMSO

consumption spending. The equation was implied when we suggested that consumption depends upon current disposable income and our expectation about disposable income – our expectation was based on past disposable income received and this in turn influenced past consumption. Thus current consumption reflects current disposable income and past consumption.

1962	1963	1964	1965	1966	1967	1968	1969	1970	1971	1972	1973	1974	1975
26 279	27 427	28 330	28 760	29 301	29 869	30 598	30 715	31 472	32 396	34 344	35 894	35 521	35 413
28 437	29 644	30 789	31 507	32 182	32 616	33 198	33 452	34 622	35 537	38 140	40 300	41 130	41 116
0·92	0·93	0·92	0·91	0·91	0·92	0·92	0·92	0·91	0·91	0·90	0·89	0·86	0·86
0·08	0·07	0·08	0·09	0·09	0·08	0·08	0·08	0·09	0·09	0·10	0·11	0·14	0·14
545	1148	903	430	541	568	729	117	757	924	1948	1550	−373	−108
196	1207	1145	718	675	434	582	254	1170	915	2603	2160	830	−14
2·78	0·95	0·79	0·60	0·80	1·31	1·25	0·46	0·65	1·01	0·75	0·72	−0·45	7·71
0·69	4·24	3·86	2·33	2·14	1·35	1·78	0·76	3·50	2·64	7·32	5·66	2·06	−0·04
1691	1962	2141	2143	2106	2214	2369	2221	2401	2838	3376	3595	3089	2954
24 588	25 465	26 189	26 617	27 195	27 655	28 229	28 494	29 071	29 558	30 968	32 299	32 432	32 459
652	655	834	854	814	877	929	859	812	979	1142	1073	886	
6·61	6·27	6·16	6·63	6·98	7·20	7·46	8·07	8·58	8·59	8·26	9·59		

Chapter 34
Aggregate Demand: Investment by Firms

In this chapter we discuss the impact of firms' behaviour on aggregate demand. Like households or government (local and national) firms make both injections and withdrawals which contribute to the aggregate level of demand in the economy. Firms add to aggregate demand by demanding plant and machinery and other assets to be used to add to, and to maintain, the level of production, and they reduce aggregate demand to the extent that they have undistributed profits (business savings). As with households in the previous chapter, we consider the behaviour of firms as a group, not seeking to explain the exact behaviour of a particular firm but seeking to explain the behaviour of the typical firm and firms as a group. Again we justify this approach by a resort to the so-called 'law of averages', which suggests that the grouping will average out the behaviour of eccentric firms. But first we draw attention to two important distinctions. The first concerns the difference between gross and net investment whilst the second relates to the difference between stocks and flows.

Gross and net investment

Not all spending by firms constitutes addition to their capital stocks of buildings and machines. A great deal is concerned with replacing or maintaining existing equipment. This is referred to as replacement investment and will be carried out as long as it yields a greater return than can be obtained from doing something else. From the point of view of an entire community 'doing something else' would mean consuming more presently and allowing the capital stock to fall. Hence we must subtract replacement investment from gross investment in order to arrive at net investment. Net investment will tend to take place when profit expectations increase, when technical change arises, when machine costs fall and when labour costs rise.

Stocks and flows

At various points in this book we have drawn attention to the distinction between stocks and flows. *Stocks are quantities at a point of time whereas flows are quantities spread over a period of time.* Thus in a theory of demand and supply (Part Three) and in the theory of market structures (Part Five) – we used the distinction between stocks and flows as a means of distinguishing the short- and long-run responses of supply to changes in demand.

Ideas about stocks and flows are important in the theory of investment. Firms purchase capital goods (machines, buildings, etc.) which are a stock but which yield a flow of services over time. And the relationship between the stock and flow may be variable as, for example, when machines are worked on one, two or three shifts. There is also another flow – the time rate of demand for capital goods and it is this time rate which we refer to as investment.

Investment

We saw in Chapter 6 that investment is the spending of money now, in the hope of increased cash returns in the future. The decision by a firm to buy a new machine (or replace an old one) is an example of this. If p is the current price of a new machine, r the rate of interest, and R_t the expected return from operating the machine in year t. The purchase of the capital good will be worthwhile if,

$$p \leqslant \frac{R_1}{(1+r)} + \frac{R_2}{(1+r)^2} + \cdots \frac{R_n}{(1+r)_n} \qquad \mathbf{1}$$

where N is the life of the machine. Here R_t is the total operating profit the firm would obtain if it had the machine, less the profit the firm would have obtained without the machine, and R_N will include scrap at resale value. Indeed, N is one of the things the firm has to decide: many machines are sold or scrapped before the end of their potential working life, and the decision about when to get rid of a machine is an important part of the investment decision.

The expected stream of profits depends upon the physical productivity of the machine, its operating costs and the prices of raw material inputs and the wage rate. The stream of profits also depends on the expected level of the firm's sales in the future, and the prices of its outputs. For various reasons, unless the firm's operations are subject to strongly increasing returns to scale, as the number of machines increase, the returns R_t increase at a diminishing rate. The basic reasons for this are diminishing marginal physical product and/ or rising prices of cooperating factors, plus the fact that the demand curve for the firm's product may slope downwards, so that higher output can only be sold at a lower price. For this reason, the firm will buy capital goods until the present value of the net cash flow from the last machine bought just equals the price of that machine.

From the various factors influencing investment, economists have concentrated on two: the rate of interest and the rate of growth of output (the accelerator). We shall discuss the rate of interest first.

The rate of interest

Given the profit streams R_t as functions of the firm's capital stock K, if we knew the price of capital goods[1] and the rate of interest r, we would know how many capital goods the firm would wish to hold. Specifically, the present value of extra return from holding the last machine would just equal its price. This allows us to write,

$$D = f(p, r) \qquad\qquad 2$$

as the stock demand curve for capital goods. In Figure 160a we have drawn two such demand curves, one for a lower rate of interest r^1, and one for a higher rate of interest r. This indicates that at a lower rate of interest, the firm would wish to hold a larger capital stock, and also the lower the price of machines the more machines the firm would wish to hold at a given rate of interest.

What determines the price of machines? The obvious answer is supply and demand, but the problem here is that we have the demand for a stock of machines, whereas the supply curve of new machines is a flow. If the machine-producing industry produced 100 machines per week at a price of £1000 per machine, a price of £1000 would also induce a supply of 400 machines per month.

1. Because capital goods are heterogeneous there is an aggregation and valuation problem here. In what units do we measure the stock of capital? We could measure in terms of the future earnings streams but that would require prior knowledge of the interest rate, or we could measure in labour units. This is an aspect of the capital controversy which we dodge at this level.

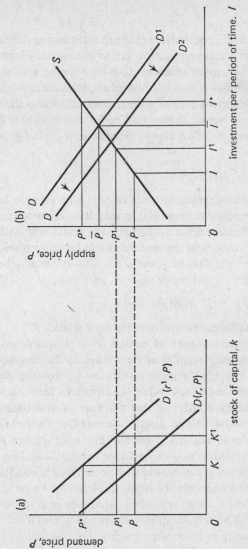

Figure 160 The demand for capital and the rate of investment. (a) The stock demand curve for capital; (b) The flow demand and supply curves for investment goods

Suppose the rate of interest is r, and firms are in equilibrium with a capital stock K, and the machine price is p. Then since firms are in equilibrium they are happy to hold the existing capital stock K. Here,

$K = D(r, p)$.

Since firms are in equilibrium they are maintaining the capital stock at K, hence net investment is zero. Gross investment I is just sufficient to maintain the capital stock at K. Now suppose that the industry supplying machines is also in equilibrium, then the amount of investment I, just sufficient to maintain a stock K, is *also* the amount of investment I per period that would be forthcoming at a flow supply price p. If $S(p)$ is the flow supply price of new capital goods, then in equilibrium,

$K = D(r, p) \qquad I = S(p)$.

Let us now try another equilibrium value (i.e. an exercise in comparative statics). Suppose the rate of interest fell suddenly to r^1, and stayed there. At each price, firms in the industry would now wish to hold a larger capital stock, and the stock demand function would shift outwards to $D(r^1, p)$. The new static equilibrium would be a capital stock K^1, with a capital goods price p^1, such that,

$K^1 = D(r^1, p^1) \qquad I^1 = S(p^1)$

and I^1 is just sufficient to maintain the capital stock K^1.

So far we have a theory of capital (or how many new machines firms will eventually acquire as they move to the new equilibrium). We have not, as yet, a theory of investment (or how rapidly firms will acquire the new machine). What is to prevent firms acquiring new machines instantaneously, so that the rate of investment jumps to infinity for an infinitesimal length of time? One factor is the supply price. If $D(r^1 p)$ is the stock demand curve, at a price p^* the firm would wish to hold its existing stock of capital K, and no more. But suppliers of capital goods would wish to supply I^*, which is far more than required to maintain the stock K. Hence we know that the new price will be less than p^*. However, at any price $\bar{p}$ less than p^*, the firm would wish to acquire more capital goods, and if firms in aggregate tried to acquire them very quickly, there would be excess flow demand in the market for new capital goods. One way out of this difficulty, used in some textbooks, is to say that $D(r^1, p)$ is the demand for capital goods, K is the existing stock, hence $D(r^1, p) - K$ is the demand for new capital goods. This is shown as DD^1 in Figure 160(b). Where DD^1 in Figure 160(b) intersects the supply curve S gives the new price and investment in the first instant after the interest rate has changed as $\bar{p}$ and $\bar{I}$. As the capital stock increases over time, so the distance $D(r^1, p) - K$ falls, the curve DD shifts down over time. Eventually, the new price p^1 is reached, with flow supply I^1 just sufficient to maintain the stock K^1.

This is pure nonsense, because the curve DD^1 is the demand for a stock (measured in so many machines) and the curve S is the supply of a flow (measured in so many machines per period). Suppose, for example, that at a price $\bar{p}$, the excess stock demand is 100 machines, and the flow supply at $\bar{p}$ is 100 machines per month. Change the units of measurement to weeks, and the flow supply is 25 per week. Stock demand is still 100. The nonsense arises from comparing two quantities that are measured in different units. Is 5 pears a larger quantity than 15 peas?

One solution to this problem, which does work, is to say that firms adjust their capital stock over a fixed period, or that there is a fixed period of production in the industry supplying the machines. In their case, the flow supply over the period now assumes the dimensions of a stock: if the period is one month, a flow supply of 25 per week for one month is a stock of 100. In this case from Figure 160(b), in the first period after the fall in the rate of interest from r to r^1, investment is $\bar{I}$. Since the capital stock at the end of this period is now larger, the stock demand curve DD for new machines shifts to the left, and investment falls slightly. Although the length of the period is somewhat arbitrary, we discuss below some of the factors determining it. We have, however, the following conclusion:

Starting from an initial equilibrium, the greater the fall in the rate of interest, the greater the amount of investment in each subsequent time period. However, for any new rate of interest, the rate of investment will fall over time, until it is just sufficient to maintain the stock of capital at its new equilibrium level.

The above analysis is extremely artificial. Periods of production are rarely fixed, and to state that adjustment to a new capital stock will take place over a fixed period begs the question – what determines the length of this period? The answer lies in what economists call *Adjust-*

ment Costs. Rome was not built in a day, and the reason was not just an inelastic supply of marble. As well as an optimal quantity of new machines, there is an optimal time-path over which they should be acquired. It may be possible to build a power station in six months, and it is possible in ten years. The average duration is five years. Why? To build it in much less than five years would cost much more than to build it in five years, to build it more slowly would cost so little less that it is better to build it in five years, and obtain its benefits. Careful planning and negotiations of contracts takes time, sites must be prepared, flow-charts drawn up, some tasks must be done before others. Various sub-contractors must be coordinated, men must be trained, executives have other urgent tasks as well as supervising the installation. All these factors, plus the inelastic supply of new capital goods, imply that investment occurs over a period of time, not instantaneously. A final point is that if a rise in demand pushes up the price of new capital goods so much that some firms expect it to fall subsequently they may delay their purchases until the price has fallen. These considerations allow us to talk of a marginal efficiency of investment schedule relating the amount of investment to the rate of interest.

We conclude that, other things being equal, the optimal capital stock and hence the flow demand for investment goods will rise as the rate of interest falls and fall as the rate of interest rises.

Future revenue

Now let us hold all factors constant except expected future revenue. The effect of an increase in expected revenue from an investment project will be to increase the present value of the revenue flow from the project and hence the net present value of the project. All projects which previously had a positive net present value will become more attractive, and some projects which had previously failed to yield a positive net present value will now become worthwhile. The effect of an increase in expected revenue is thus to shift the marginal efficiency curve to the right.

The effect of an increase in expected revenue is to shift the marginal efficiency curve to the right. All projects accepted and rejected will yield greater profits.

Costs

The next variable in the decision process to consider is the expected movement of costs. Again holding all other factors constant, a rise in the costs of equipment, labour, etc., either current or future, will reduce the net present value of projects. The effect will be to shift the marginal efficiency curves to the left. This will result in a lower equilibrium capital stock and a decline in the rate of interest.

In the absence of substitution effects between inputs an increase in costs, other things being equal, will shift the marginal efficiency curves to the left.

However, it is important to note that if a rise in all prices is expected in the future, the revenue flows as well as the cost flows will be increased and so will all the net present values of projects. The number of viable projects and the returns on investment will increase and this will show up as a rightward shift of the marginal efficiency curves.

Technology

Investment is strongly influenced by changes in technology, by inventions. New ideas change the costs of production and later the expected streams of revenues. Technological change presupposes investment – the diversion of resources from current consumption to the search for new ideas. And in its turn, technological change stimulates investment in the implementation of the new ideas.

The importance of expectations

We have discussed the importance of expected interest rates, expected demand and expected costs. Obviously expectations play a key role. If we are trying to predict demand, costs and interest rates we quickly find that this cannot be a precise exercise, and indeed the forecasts that we have will reflect partly the optimism/pessimism of the forecaster. In expectations the optimism/pessimism of the potential investor is vital, the more so as we know that optimism is a delicate and unstable commodity. The volatility of optimism/pessimism is clearly shown by the surveys of businessmen's expectations regularly carried out by the Confederation of British Industries. We conclude that the delicate balance of optimism/pessimism will seriously affect the number of projects estimated to be viable, independently of changes in the other variables.[2]

The rate of interest and the length of life of machines

Changes in the rate of interest exert a differential effect on investment decisions according to the length of life of the equipment. Machines which have a long life tend to exhibit greater variations in their present values as interest rates alter than do short-lived machines.

The rate of change of revenue: the acceleration principle

We now come to the second of the two major influences on investment, the rate of change of revenue. A change in the rate of increase of demand for the product of investment goods, and hence in sales revenue, will give rise to a phenomenon known as the *acceleration principle*. It is sometimes regarded as an alternative theory of investment to that which stresses the influence of the rate of interest, but this is misleading. The role of the rate of interest and the acceleration principle in determining the rate of investment are simply different aspects of the theory of investment.

In discussing the influence of the rate of interest on the rate of investment, the state of expectations concerning future sales (and costs) was assumed constant. When examining the acceleration principle these assumptions are reversed; the rate of interest is assumed constant and the focus of attention is the role of changes in expectations as proxied by the rate of change of sales, that is the acceleration principle represents an attempt, necessarily crude, to analyse the determination of business expectations. In the absence of a more realistic expectations formation hypothesis, the assumption is made that expectations as to future sales revenues are formed by reference to the rate of change of current output.

Holding prices and interest rates constant, the acceleration principle considers the demand for capital as a derived demand. With a given

2. The reader should consult the simple and lucid discussion of expectations in Keynes (1936, chapter 12).

capital-output ratio, demand for capital is proportional to output. Hence investment is proportional to the rate of change of output.

Let us say that to produce output of £100 per year it is necessary to have capital equipment costing £500, i.e. the capital-output ratio $v = 500/100 = 5$. Now let us assume that the demand for a firm's products rises by £1000 per annum. The firm meets the demand as a temporary measure by taking on extra labour to use with its current capital, but then begins to increase its capital stock, increasing it finally by £5000.

Let C_t be the purchases of a product in one year and C_{t-1} the purchases of the good in the previous year. The addition to the capital stock this year is I_t, that is, the net investment. Thus we can write

$$I_t = v(C_t - C_{t-1}),$$

£5000 = 5(1000).

So that the impact of the accelerator stands out sharply let us assume that no equipment wears out, and nothing except demand changes. Thus, each year, the only investment demand is net investment to accommodate the increased demand (see Table 51).

The important year is year 3. Final demand rises only by £500 and investment falls by five times that, namely £2500. Thus a small fluctuation in the rate of growth of consumer demand is magnified into a big absolute fluctuation in the demand for investment goods.

For the economy as a whole, output is produced by labour and capital goods, and a change in total output (Y) will, other things being equal, call forth a rise in the total capital stock. Thus,

$$I_t = v(Y_t - Y_{t-1}).$$

The impact of the accelerator depends upon the value of v, the capital/output ratio.[3]

The accelerator is a fairly crude device, and only works when output is increasing, since gross investment cannot usually be negative. In

3. The acceleration principle seems to explain the observation that fluctuations in the output and employment of the capital goods industries are greater than those of the consumption goods trades. But this observation needs to be tempered by the fact that we should not expect v to be constant. Moreover, the rate of interest must play a part in the investment decision unless the stock of money is increased so as to keep the rate of interest constant.

Table 51

Year	Change of demand from previous year	Net investment
1	1000	5000
2	1000	5000
3	500	2500
4	1000	5000

addition, it fails to take account of other factors in determining expectations, and it assumes away any capacity constraints in the investment industries. A better device is the *Capital Stock Adjustment* principle. This assumes that firms have a desired capital-output ratio, which may depend on interest rates and factor prices. They have expectations about the future levels of sales, which may be formed by the adaptive expectations mechanism discussed in Chapter 33. Finally, investment is a positive fraction of the difference between the actual capital stock and the desired capital stock (which is the expected level of sales multiplied by the desired capital-output ratio). This fraction reflects costs of adjustment and supply constraints in the capital goods industries.

Tastes and technology

From what we have written above, it would seem that the growth of output and the movement of the rate of interest are the main determinants of the level of investment. If the working population is growing slowly, then the rate of interest would have to fall continuously for positive net investment to occur. The reason for this is that continuous additions to the capital stock would diminish the marginal product of capital, and progressively inferior investment opportunities would have to be selected. Keynes was worried by this, and the under-consumptionist theory was that the rate of interest might (for reasons discussed in Chapter 26) never fall fast enough to equate the demand for investment by entrepreneurs with the supply of savings at full employment. The economy was doomed to long-run stagnation.

In this case, Keynes was proved wrong. Schumpeter had earlier suggested that technical progress was the main spur to investment, so that even with a static population, the marginal efficiency of investment curve need not move downwards over time. New inventions would offset the depressing effect of capital accumulation. Actually, technical progress often requires new machines (we call this 'embodied technical progress') even if it takes the form of new methods of producing existing goods. Technical progress creates new industries, and the capital goods used to produce output for declining industries often cannot be adapted to produce output for expanding industries. Here, as well as technical progress *per se*, changes in the composition of output due to changes in tastes as well as innovation, can maintain the demand for new capital goods. Suppose, for example, that output as measured by the national income statistics, is constant, and the rate of interest does not change. The accelerator would predict zero investment. Suppose, however, that the demand for beer is going up, and the demand for coffee is falling. Machines used for processing coffee cannot be used for brewing beer and hence net investment may be positive, since the process of physical decay will set a limit to the rate at which the capital stock in the coffee-producing industry can decline.

A summary of the theoretical conclusions about investment demand

We have theorized by holding all variables constant and considering the impact of changes in one variable. We considered each variable singly. Investment demand depends upon interest rates; future revenues; the current prices of capital goods; the price of second-hand capital goods; the state of, and change in, the available technology; factor prices; the rate of change of demand and expectations.

In real life all of the variables listed above are likely to be changing at the same time – they do not change one at a time. Any inspection of historical data for investment is thus bound to be very complex. Some of the complexity results from changing our study from the investment behaviour of a typical firm to the investment demand of firms as a group. If one firm expands it can probably do so without forcing up wages or producing such a big increase in national income that the demand for its product rises, thus requiring even more investment. If, however, many firms expand together they will affect national income and thus demand. They will force up labour costs by fighting over the existing pool of available labour, and so on.

Before we have a look at the historical data for the UK an important matter needs to be discussed.

The empirical evidence: an important matter

The historical data for firms' total investment spending (GDFCF) is not identically the same as their investment *demand*. What we observe is what they *did* spend and not what they *planned* to spend. If the capital goods industry was working at full capacity and couldn't increase the output of capital goods in the short run then investment plans would be thwarted unless firms could buy their capital goods abroad. The limitation on importing capital goods from abroad is that by and large buildings cannot be imported. Thus the data we have may show investment partially constrained by domestic capital goods capacity and the capacity of the building and construction industry in particular.

A further constraint may be applied by the nature of the capital market. For various institutional reasons a rise in the demand to borrow money in excess of the supply may not force up the rate of interest – some people wanting to borrow may be turned away empty-handed. In our perfect theoretical world the rate of interest

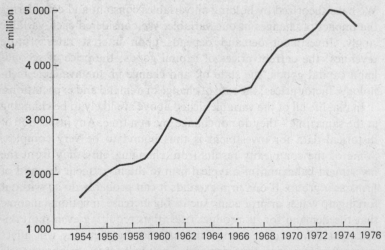

Figure 161 Firms' gross domestic fixed capital formation at 1970 prices

would simply have risen and we could have predicted the effect of this on the demand for investment goods. In the practical world the rate of interest often doesn't change and potential borrowers turn away empty-handed. Thus the investment *spending* of UK firms may be their investment demand constrained by the capital-goods-industries supply problems and imperfections of the money capital market. It may not be planned or *ex ante* investment that we observe but *ex post* investment.

The UK data for 1954–75 (at constant prices)

The following discussion of spending data is also in real terms – the effect of price changes has been removed.

Consider the data in row 1 of the statistical appendix to this chapter for firms' gross domestic fixed capital formation (GDFCF)[4] through time: Figure 161 comes from this.

A feature that is immediately apparent is that the growth of investment spending has been much more irregular than the growth of consumer spending, with periods of stagnation in 1961–3, 1965–7 and 1974–5. This irregularity might fit our discussions of the volatility of expectations and the fluctuations resulting from the accelerator actions. Whilst it was easy to write about the importance of expected future costs, expected interest rates and the balance of optimism/ pessimism it is much more difficult to find some quantifiable measure of these variables. At this level all we can hope to do is to inspect those variables and relationships that we can readily quantify. The statistical appendix sets out such readily available and easily understood data.

Changes in consumer spending

Let us begin our investigation by examining the link between investment and recent changes in demand which formed the accelerator. Rows 2 and 3 of the statistical appendix show the change in investment from the previous year and the change in real consumer

4. Firms' GDFCF = Private sector GDFCF *less* personal (household) investment in dwellings. 'Firms' is therefore the most accurate approximation available to all private productive institutions excluding households.

spending from the previous year. An increase in production can be obtained by bringing spare capacity into use and then by more intensive use of the capital stock and by using more labour, but the pressure tends, other things being equal, to lead to a rise in net present values and thus a rise of investment. Try using the analysis

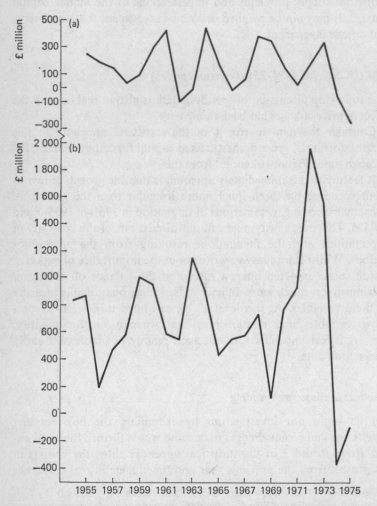

Figure 162 (a) Change in firms' gross domestic fixed capital formation from previous year at 1970 prices. (b) Change in consumers expenditure from the previous year at 1970 prices

of the first few pages of this chapter to explain why net present values rise.

Figure 162 shows the two time series.[5] Two features of the figure tend to confirm our theory. First, changes in consumer spending and changes in investment do seem to be related – the rise and fall of the two series have a similar pattern to each other. Secondly, a high increase in consumer spending is *followed* by a high level of investment – note how the peaks of the investment series tend to be a year after the peaks of the output changes. Investment seems to follow output (demand) change. What is also clear is that the magnitude of investment changes could not be predicted simply by looking at output changes in the previous period; for example, the big investment boom of 1968–9 followed a very small recovery in the rate of growth of consumer spending in 1966–8 (see Figure 162 to confirm this comment). There is lack of complete stability in the relationship of investment changes and demand changes because factors other than expected future revenue had changed.

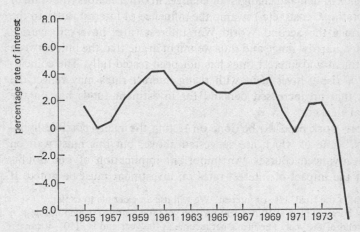

Figure 163 Perceived real rate of interest

5. An interesting feature, which Figure 162 makes clear, is that the years of falling investment growth coincide with the years of rising consumption spending growth and vice versa. This pattern helps reduce the fluctuations in the total demand from investment plus household consumption spending.

The rate of interest

Another variable that our theorizing suggested would be important was the real rate of interest at which firms could borrow or lend money.[6] The time series for the rate of interest shown in Figure 163 uses the data from the statistical appendix.

If we compare Figure 163 with the changes in investment spending in Figure 162 we notice that investment is booming when interest rates are rising, which is the reverse of what our theorizing leads us to expect. The answer may be a practical one. We suggest that as investment planning takes time, businessmen may use current rates of interest when appraising an investment project. Having decided to go ahead they may be reluctant to drop the plans even though interest rates have now changed. We are suggesting that low interest rates *this* year result in high investment *next* year even though interest rates have then risen. It could be that interest rate changes do not, in practice, influence investment decisions significantly, or that the influence of demand changes, or changes in other factors (the state of expectations, costs, etc.) swamp the influence of interest rates. In the UK since the Second World War interest rates have only varied within a narrow range and thus we might argue that the link between investment and interest rates has not been tested fully. The coincidence of rising investment with rising interest rates may reflect the effect that an increased demand for investment funds has on the capital market.

More work needs to be done on testing the many possible hypotheses, some of which are suggested above, but this must wait on more advanced courses. An important implication of our doubts about the impact of interest rates on investment must be noted. If

6. What is the 'real' rate of interest? We will use an example to explain.
A firm borrows £100 at 10 per cent for one year for a project which finishes at the end of the year. The firm's net income at the year end is £110 – it can just pay off the £100 loan and the 10 per cent interest. Now assume that all prices rose by 10 per cent during the year so that net income earned by the firm was £121. The firm pays off the loan and interest and has a balance of £11, that is £121 − 100 − 10 = £11. In the first case, when there was no inflation, if the firm did not have to pay interest on the loan it would have had £10 after the loan of £100 was repaid. Thus the effect of the price rise has been the same as a zero-interest-rate loan. A 10 per cent rise has made the 10 per cent nominal interest rate into a zero 'real' interest rate. The difference of £1 between £11 and £10 benefit results from the 10 per cent inflation.

interest rates and investment are unlinked or only weakly linked then governments should not try and stimulate investment by changing the level of interest rates: a more effective policy would seem to lie in influencing investment indirectly by increasing consumer demand for final products.

Company profits[7]

Since the role of profits was not discussed in the theoretical part of the chapter, why should it be introduced now? The reason is very practical. Recent econometric research has indicated that the inclusion of profits improves the predictive power of our theories. Let us try now to produce some theoretical foundation to support this observation. There are at least three reasons why changes in profits should be associated with changes in firms' investment in plant and machinery.

1 Firms may consider that rising (falling) profits indicate good (poor) future prospects and thus be encouraged to invest in more (less) plant and machinery. The effect here seems to be largely through the role of changes in profits in shaping optimism/pessimism.

2 If profits rise then firms can increase dividend payments, lend out the extra profits, or increase investment in plant and machinery. A manufacturing firm will probably have a 'mental block' against loaning money even if the return on the money was greatest in this use. Thus they are thrown back on more investment or higher dividends. Because of the way the Stock Exchange works, firms usually try and keep the growth of their dividends steady, thus the outlet for increased profits is at least partly in increased investment.[8]

7. 'Company' is almost identical with the 'firm' that we have discussed previously. The only reason that company profits and not firms' profits have been used is that the latter is not available and the former is known to be almost identically the same as firms' profits. We are using company profits as a proxy for firms' profits.
8. It is important to realize that retained profits are the major source of savings to finance firms' investment – the savings of households are a comparatively small source of saving for firms' investment. Additionally, approximately 8 per cent of company investment in the UK during 1967–74 was financed by Government investment grants.

3 It may be that investment is strongly related to changes in consumer demand (as seems to be the case) and that profits happen to be high when demand is growing rapidly. This argument says that the causation is from rising demand to rising investment, and that rising profits are a result of rising demand but not a cause of rising investment.

Row 5 of the statistical appendix gives gross company profits before tax on a constant price basis. The series is plotted in Figure 164. If we compare Figures 162(a) and 164 we note that the peaks of profits seem to occur slightly before the peaks of firms' fixed investment – a result that the above discussion leads us to expect for all three reasons. Tests of the three theories relating to profits are possible but are not attempted here.

Government investment incentives

Because the capital stock fixes the maximum level of production in an economy governments in many industrial countries try to encourage a high level of investment. This aim can be achieved by influencing any of the variables which determine investment spending, expected

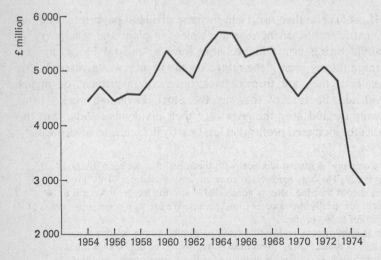

Figure 164 Gross company profit before tax and net of stock appreciation at 1970 prices

future sales, interest rates, etc. Perhaps the most important influence of governments on investment is the effect that their policies, and changes in these policies, have on the climate of optimism/pessimism in the business community.

The UK Government has tried two major types of policy since the early nineteen-fifties in order to raise the level of investment. The first type of policy has worked through the tax system. Firms' tax liabilities have been reduced when they have invested – broadly, the more they invested the lower was their tax liability. The more recent policy has been to give cash grants to firms investing. The general effect of both types of policy has been to lower the cost of investment. Some projects with negative net present values have been converted into projects with positive net present values as a result of the government subsidies.

The effect of the incentives in practice has been very complex to analyse. Recent research suggests that in the UK the incentives have been so complex and so frequently changing that firms have not adjusted their investment programmes in order to take advantage of the incentives.

Summary of firms' fixed capital formation

We have found that when we examine historical data, investment, changes in demand, interest rates and profits all vary in a similar pattern. Our theory suggests that the investment changes depend in part on variations of these factors. Some of the factors that we suggested in the theoretical part of the chapter as being important determinants of investment demand have not been considered in the statistical section – they cannot be suitably quantified, e.g. optimism/ pessimism and technical progress.

Recent econometric studies using regression analysis have indicated that investment can be explained by considering recent income level, change in income level, recent investment, recent interest rates, the recent changes of interest rates, recent profit levels and the recent change of profit levels. Because investment takes time – plant has to be ordered, buildings built and so on – all the explanatory variables are lagged, e.g. investment spending this year depends not on current profits but on profits last year.

Inventory investment

When we discussed the components of demand we discussed inventory investment, defining it as the value of the net physical *addition* to stocks of finished goods, raw materials and work in progress. The desire to add to stocks increases aggregate demand, and the ability to run down stocks means that in the short run demand can exceed production.

Firms hold stock because of the existence of uncertainty about production and demand and because distribution takes time. We must, however, be careful to avoid the idea that *all* inventory investment is deliberate. If demand falls short of the expected level then production will be excessive and stocks will build up, and if demand grows quicker than expected then stocks will be run down (negative inventory investment) or the rate of increase will be reduced. Thus, to some extent, stocks act as a buffer between production and demand. A simple theory of inventory investment for firms is needed. We would expect that as stocks are *necessary* (because of uncertainty and the existence of time) then when production rises so will the necessary level of stocks, other things being equal. Thus as the total production of firms in the economy grows so will stocks. This discussion sounds very like the discussion of the accelerator earlier in the chapter. Let us assume that the desired ratio of stocks to production is given, at, say 0·40. We can now say that the desired rise in stocks, i.e. the inventory investment, will be four-tenths of the rise in production. Thus:

$$\text{Inventory investment}_t = 0\cdot4\,(GDP_t - GDP_{t-1}).$$

With a numerical example we will be able to see that the violent fluctuations given by the accelerator will also occur when we have an inventory accelerator.

It is apparent from Table 52 that unless production grows each year by a constant amount then inventory investment will fluctuate violently.

If we examine UK company inventory investment as set out in Figure 165(a) then we see that inventory investment does indeed fluctuate very markedly. We suggested above that inventory investment was a function of the change in company sales – and that it would act as a buffer between supply and demand. Both

Table 52

Inventory investment	Rise of production	Total production
40	100	10 000
40	100	10 100
44	110	10 210
0	0	10 210
40	100	10 310

of these points can be examined using the remaining parts of Figure 165.

If there is a stable relationship between inventory investment and the rise in sales, then for each year if we divided inventory investment by the change in sales, we should obtain a constant. (In our example we assumed it to have a value of 0·40.) This ratio – the *marginal propensity to stock build* – has been calculated for UK companies for the years 1955–74 and is set out in Figure 165(b). It is clear that stock building is not just a simple function of increased output. Let us look at the changes in company sales. These are set out in Figure 165(c). If we examine parts (b) and (c) of the diagram together we see that as a rough generalization when company sales were rising particularly quickly (slowly) the marginal propensity to stock build was particularly low (high).

We may conclude from our very brief investigation of inventory investment that stocks are desired and are a function of output (the average of inventory investment in Figure 165(a) is strongly positive); that the marginal propensity to stock build fluctuates; and that the marginal propensity to stock build is an inverse function of the rate of increase of company sales.

Summary

In this chapter we have investigated the part of aggregate demand arising from private firms in the form of demand for fixed capital goods and inventory investment.

We have noted that the demand for investment goods need not necessarily imply that the demand will be fulfilled by the domestic

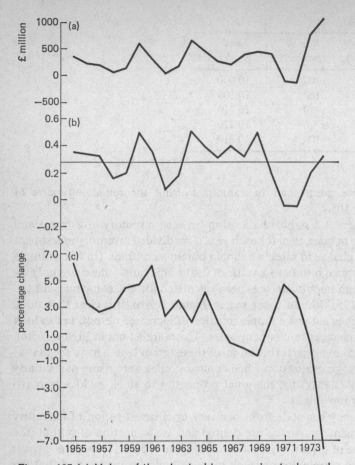

Figure 165 (a) Value of the physical increase in stocks and work in progress at current prices (company totals).
(b) Marginal propensity to build stocks by UK companies.
(c) Percentage change from the previous year in UK company sales

manufacturers. Some of the demand may be met by overseas producers in the form of imports.

In our theoretical discussion of fixed capital formation we saw how firms sought to maximize their net present value. Given this assumption we saw that firms' investment demand would vary with prospective revenue, costs, interest rates, optimism/pessimism, the

588 Aggregate Demand: Investment by Firms

second-hand value of capital goods, and the price of new capital goods and technical progress. These variables were used to discuss replacement, net investment and the principle of the accelerator.

Much of the theoretical discussion considered how a typical firm would react to change in the variables. When considering firms as a group we need to remember that the actions of the group may change the value of the variables which determine investment – this is not the case for an individual firm. Let us illustrate this point. The future prospects for a firm improve and the firm responds by increasing its capital stock to the new optimum level. Investment by a single firm has no noticeable effect on the rate of interest, wage levels, national income or any of the other variables. If all firms start to invest, the big rise in demand for funds may force up interest rates causing a reappraisal of projects, the increased demand for labour may force up national wage levels and the rise in the production of investment goods may significantly increase national income and thus demand. When we came to apply our theoretical models to UK historical data we found that, as expected, fixed capital formation fluctuated quite markedly. We also found that the relationships were rather complex and difficult to disentangle without resort to sophisticated regression analysis. The result of such analysis was referred to with its findings that confirmed our theories, and we mentioned that the level of company profits had also been found to add to a satisfactory explanation of investment behaviour.

Finally we briefly considered the importance and short-run instability of inventory investment. It was noted that an important feature of inventory investment was the import content, which meant that the violent fluctuations in inventory investment did not influence the UK quite as much as might at first be expected.

Questions

1 How do you think that you could try to estimate the value of v (the accelerator)? If you look at the Capital Account tables in the latest copy of *National Income & Expenditure*, HMSO, you may find some of the figures that you feel you will require.

2 Do you think that the value of v will be the same for each industry? If the value of v differs from industry to industry can we know the value of v for the whole economy?

3 What are the main factors influencing the level of replacement investment?

4 What influences the choice of machine when a firm thinks that an expansion of output is needed? Remember that there may be many possible processes available, each with its own machines and labour requirements.

5 Using the tables on inventory investment in the latest copy of *National Income & Expenditure*, HMSO, investigate the composition

Statistical appendix

Row number	1954	1955	1956	1957	1958	1959	1960	1961
1 Firms' GDFCF 1970 prices (£ million)	1573	1820	2005	2156	2196	2292	2597	3016
2 Change from the previous year of firms' GDFCF (row 1)		247	185	151	40	96	305	419
3 Change in consumers' expenditure from the previous year 1970 prices (£ million)		874	198	470	586	1008	951	588
4 Perceived real rate of interest (adjusted flat yield on 2½% consols)		1·61	0·08	0·50	2·12	3·12	4·14	4·19
5 Gross company profits before tax and net of stocks (£ million) appreciation at 1970 prices	4450	4698	4459	4563	4568	4887	5398	5081
6 Value of companies' physical increase in stocks and work in progress at current prices (£ million)	200	352	235	190	69	137	594	284
7 Growth in company output at current prices over the previous year (£ million)		1007	691	587	435	703	1178	792
8 Marginal propensity to stock build by UK companies (row 6/row 7)	average = 0·28	0·35	0·28	0·32	0·16	0·19	0·50	0·36
9 Percentage change from the previous year of UK company sales in 1970 prices		6·25	3·27	2·73	3·03	4·45	4·73	6·02

Source: *National Income and Expenditure*, various issues, HMSO

of inventory investment. If you find that raw materials form most of the fluctuations what implications does this have for employment in the UK?

6 Why are expectations so important in investment decisions?

7 Can we reasonably speak of a *flow* of investment expenditure when firms are adjusting their *stock* of capital to an optimum level?

1962	1963	1964	1965	1966	1967	1968	1969	1970	1971	1972	1973	1974	1975
2913	2906	3335	3509	3492	3567	3945	4289	4432	4458	4642	4976	4914	4669
-103	-7	429	174	-17	64	378	344	143	26	184	334	-62	-245
545	1148	903	430	541	568	729	117	757	924	1948	1550	-373	-108
2·86	2·87	3·27	2·59	2·58	3·23	3·24	3·68	1·32	-0·29	1·73	1·83	0·24	-682
4888	5433	5711	5684	5260	5361	5405	4892	4538	4840	5068	4811	3245	2908
38	171	654	457	267	206	389	437	396	-129	-149	764	1066	
499	959	1273	1169	851	516	1212	891	1907	2426	2722	3911	3466	
0·08	0·18	0·51	0·39	0·31	0·40	0·32	0·49	0·21	-0·05	-0·06	0·19	0·31	
2·25	3·46	1·87	4·03	1·88	0·33	-0·01	-0·69	1·94	4·62	3·68	0·13	-7·51	

Chapter 35
Aggregate Demand: Exports and Imports

This chapter is concerned with exports and imports and the part they play in determining the level of demand and employment in the economy.

The topics to be discussed are of very real importance to all countries whether their exports form a large or a small part of their total production. In the case of the UK where exports formed 30 per cent of total output in 1975, the importance is very obvious – exports are a major constituent of demand. In the case of countries where exports form a much smaller fraction of total production the significance is no less, because, as a result of policy constraints, governments normally try to influence the relative levels of exports and imports by changing the level of activity in the whole economy. An example of this latter type of policy has been provided by the US for whom international trading is a marginal item in aggregate demand and supply. (Approximately 5 per cent of US output is exported.) In the late 1960s the US, in an attempt to cure its balance-of-payments difficulties, thrust its domestic economy into a minor recession and then in 1971 disrupted the world economy.

A theoretical discussion of exporting and importing

Imagine a man in France who is wondering how to dispose of his income. We have discussed the motives and actions of such a man in the earlier chapters of the book, and we can draw on that work. The way in which he disposes of his income reflects his tastes, the size of his income, the price of the various goods and services available to him, the attributes possessed by these goods and services and their availability. The last mentioned factor is new to our discussions. By availability we imply that he wants to know whether the product is readily available, or whether he will have to go to some trouble to obtain it; will the product be delivered without delay; will he have to order the product and wait for it to be made for him, or is there a waiting list for the product?

The goods and services that the Frenchman sees as competing for his expenditure will be from all over the world. When planning to buy a car he considers the alternatives from the UK, Germany, Italy, Eastern Europe, US, France, Sweden and all other countries which make cars. For the vast majority of goods and services there will be a similarly long list of possible sources of supply to satisfy his wants.

Chapter 4 on trading – which discussed the theory of comparative advantage – dealt with a simple world where the products were homogeneous. In the real world many goods and services are differentiated.[1] The characteristics of a UK car may appeal to one Frenchman, whereas another may value particularly highly the characteristics of a German car. We thus see France importing cars from both Germany and the UK. For products that are not homogeneous the price charged is not the only variable considered, thus there is not one country that is the only world exporter of cars or machine tools or holidays. There are, of course, some products where price is the major criteria. Most primary products approximate to this form of product. A man who wants to buy rice buys it from the cheapest source. Why, then, do many countries – and not just one – export rice? Rice costs money to transport and the further it is transported the higher the charges. The cheapest rice in the world may be available on the other side of the world but transport costs raise the price until it cannot compete with a more expensive, but closer, country.

What we have said implies that for some products a country may both import and export. France imports cars from many countries and exports cars to the same countries plus other countries. This situation can arise because of the wide range of tastes that exist with respect to motor cars (a product with many variable attributes and characteristics).

1. You may wonder how there can be international trade in services. Exports and imports of services are called invisible exports and imports. A Briton holidaying in Spain is buying an invisible import, a French firm buying fire insurance from a British company is buying an invisible export; for the French it is an invisible import. Invisible trade is to be contrasted with visible trade, which is trade in physical goods which can be handled.

Let us summarize our discussion to this point. A potential purchaser sees commodities as having several dimensions:

Price;
Characteristics;
Availability.

The particular combination of the three factors that an individual chooses is personal to him. What we can say is that if any of the three factors changes there will be a substitution effect. Let us illustrate this last point. The Frenchman chooses from UK, German, Italian and French cars. If the price of German cars is lowered (with unchanged characteristics and availability) and the price, characteristics and availability of UK, Italian and French cars are unchanged then *some* Frenchmen will switch from UK, Italian and French to German cars. There will be similar substitution effects if there is a change in characteristics or availability. If it is the price that changes, there will also be an income effect as discussed in Chapter 11. The geographical source of the products you buy depends upon the price, characteristics and availability and relative changes in these three factors.

There is also a substitution effect between products. If the price of pleasure cruisers falls relative to the price of cars then there will be a shift of global demand from cars to cruisers, to be satisfied by one or many geographical sources. If the incomes of Frenchmen rise then we expect that their total demand for cars, boats, holidays and all other goods with positive income-elasticities will rise. If demand rises and the price, characteristics and availability of goods and services from all possible suppliers is unchanged then each of these suppliers expects their sales to rise. Thus when incomes rise in France sales of French, German, UK and Italian cars can be expected to rise, other things being equal.

All the above discussion about the French consumer applies equally to the French producer/manufacturer. When buying raw materials, semi-finished goods, machinery, etc. he surveys all the possible sources including overseas sources. He, like the consumer, purchases the 'best buy' for him, dependent upon consideration of prices, characteristics and availability, and when production rises, so too will the imports of inputs, other things being equal.

Some simple testing

Exports

We now have all the elements of a theory that we need in order to formulate some simple hypotheses for testing. The theory applies both to exports and imports, but let us look at exports first as a separate item. Consider UK exports. It has been implied that they depend upon the growth of income (demand) in other countries, the price of UK goods and services relative to prices in other countries, and the availability for export of goods in the UK relative to availability in other countries.

Relative prices

Let us look at the part of the theory that says that change in relative national price levels will change buying decisions; and turn to the statistical appendix on page 602. If we examine the fraction of UK products that was exported over the period 1954–75 (row 1) we get Figure 166(a). The change after 1967 is dramatic. The only factor that changed significantly in 1967 was the UK exchange rate.[2] The devaluation during 1967 meant that all UK exports suddenly became relatively cheaper than the exports of rival countries. Relative price levels certainly seem to be important.

Availability

Examining the availability variable, we ask of the UK, 'Did exports flag when domestic demand was growing very quickly?' The implication is that inadequate production meant that when domestic demand was growing quickly, part of the domestic demand was satisfied by reducing exports or reducing the rate of growth of exports. Figure 166 gives us two ways of checking the short run relationship between availability and exports. Parts (b) and (c) can be used to compare the changes in UK domestic demand with the changes of UK exports. If availability limits exports then we would expect low (high) domestic demand increases to go with high (low) export

2. A later section will show that world trade grew rapidly for all countries in 1968, but even so the growth was not so high that it could explain the UK export 'boom'.

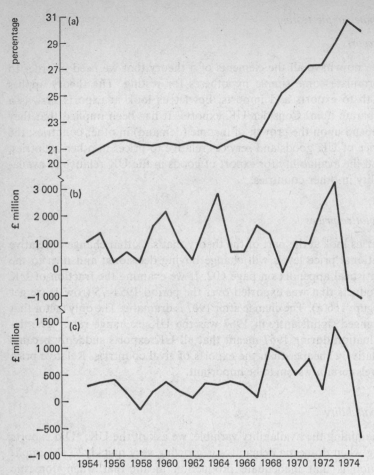

Figure 166 (a) Exports of goods and services as a percentage of UK gross domestic product at factor costs at 1970 prices. (b) Change in total UK domestic demand from the previous year at 1970 prices. (c) Change in UK exports of goods and services from the previous year at 1970 prices

increases. This relationship seems to exist in 1964–70, but in the other periods 1954–63 and 1972–5 exports seemed to rise (fall) most quickly when domestic demand was *rising* (*falling*) most quickly. We can draw no clear-cut conclusion – we cannot accept or reject the hypothesis. An additional test is to inspect parts (a) and

596 Aggregate Demand: Exports and Imports

(b) of Figure 166 and see whether the proportion of production exported falls (rises) when domestic demand is growing particularly quickly (slowly). For the periods 1955–8, 1968–71 and 1974–5 and in 1964 the relationship seems to hold. Our results on both tests indicate that there does not seem to be a reliable inverse relationship between the pressure of domestic demand and the growth of exports. This conforms with the results of the sophisticated econometric study by Ball, Eaton and Steuer (1966).

Growth of incomes in markets

We suggested that if incomes grow in a country then all the suppliers of non-inferior goods to that country should find their sales rising. If overseas markets grow then, other things being equal, UK exports should grow. We can examine the growth of the international market by examining the rise in total world exports. This is not quite the same as the growth of income in potential markets as trade has grown faster than income in recent years, largely as the result of the removal of artificial obstacles to international trade.

As the UK exports of goods are heavily concentrated on manu- factured goods (83 per cent of goods exported by the UK in 1975 were manufactures) we will examine the relationship between UK exports of manufactures and the exports of manufactures to UK ex- port markets by all other countries. This data is shown in Figure 167. The two time series in Figure 167 clearly show that when exports to UK export markets from UK rivals were growing quickly (slowly) then UK exports were also growing quickly (slowly). UK exports boom in a booming international market and slump in a depressed international market. Foreign demand changes influence UK exports.

Imports

Our general discussion of trade in the early part of the chapter suggested that exporting and importing are the same process viewed from two vantage points. A good is an export if it leaves your shores, but to the recipient it is an import. The results of tests of exporting hypotheses thus apply to importing hypotheses. In this section we will just look briefly at one aspect of UK importing. The theoretical discussion suggested that a rise of income will mean a rise in im- ports. There are two reasons for this:

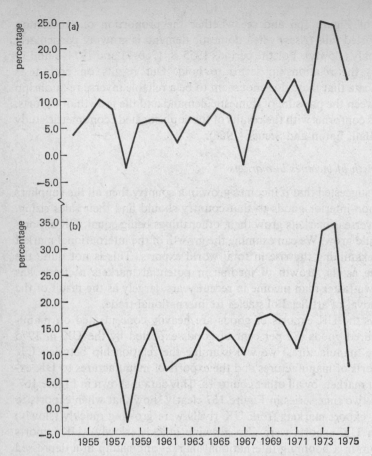

Figure 167 (a) Percentage growth over the previous year of UK manufactured exports (current prices). (b) Percentage growth over the previous year of non-UK manufactured exports to UK export markets

Consumers will spend more on foreign goods;
The rise in production will mean that producers' demand for imports of raw materials and semi-finished products will rise.

If we compare the rise in UK production (and thus income) with the rise in UK imports we get Figure 168 below.

It seems clear that rapid (slow) growth of imports occurs at the same time as rapid (slow) growth of domestic income. If we go

598 Aggregate Demand: Exports and Imports

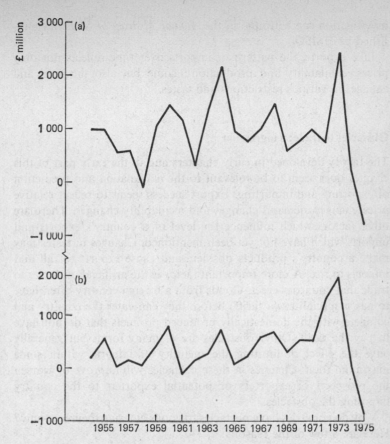

Figure 168 (a) Change from the previous year of UK gross domestic product at 1970 factor costs. (b) Change from the previous year of UK imports of goods and services at 1970 prices

further and look at which imports it is that increase when production is growing rapidly, we find that the surge of imports is concentrated in basic materials and manufactured goods, whilst the imports of food, beverages and tobacco, and fuel grow in a regular fashion, little affected by fluctuation in the rate of growth of output. Whether the surge of manufactured imports is in the form of inputs for industry or in finished goods for consumers we must leave for the reader to investigate in later courses. All the data that is needed for such an

A Theoretical Discussion of Exporting and Importing 599

investigation can be found in the *Annual Abstract of Statistics* published by HMSO.

Like exports, the pattern of imports over time reflects not only prices, availability and production/income but also the level and changes in various restrictions and tastes.

Obstacles to trade: a digression

The theory developed in early chapters and in the early part of this chapter does seem to be relevant to the explanation and prediction of exporting and importing. Export success seems to reflect relative price changes, demand changes and availability changes. There are other factors which influence the level of a country's exports and imports which have not yet been mentioned. Changes in tastes may make a country's products obsolete and cause exports to fall and imports to rise. A more important factor is the artificial obstacles to trade that countries erect. Goods from a foreign country often have to pay a special tax (a tariff) before they can enter the country and compete with the domestically produced products that do not have to pay the tariff. Other obstacles are of many forms but generally have the effect of limiting the quantity of imports within some maximum total. Changes in these obstacles will improve or worsen the prospects of exporters or potential exporters to the country imposing the obstacles.

Why do countries have obstacles to goods entering their economy? Here are a few of the reasons:

1 Whilst the world as a whole might gain from free trade it is possible for an individual country to do better by behaving like a monopolist so long as retaliation does not occur. By putting tariffs, subsidies and quotas on either imports or exports a country might be able to get more foreign goods for fewer domestically produced goods. Small importing countries and countries who are not a major export source of a product or products will not be able to obtain these monopoly gains.

2 Workers in one country can obtain higher real wages if cheaper substitutes are prevented from entering the domestic market. Thus Lancashire textile workers benefit from quotas on Asian textiles and

coal-miners benefit from tariffs on oil. But note that the argument does not depend merely on low wages abroad, but on low wage costs. Money wages may be lower in Hong Kong but if productivity is also lower then wage costs may be no different from those in Britain. To show that foreign workers get lower wages, they must also be shown to be as productive. Low wages can mean low productivity.

3 Tariffs may improve a country's balance of payments and may be quicker to bring about than price changes. We leave this till later but note that we do not say tariffs may always be more efficient – only that they may be more efficient in the short run. The danger with tariffs is that they can freeze a country's structure of production.

4 Tariffs may be useful in getting an industry going. Suppose a country such as Lesotho tries to develop a plastics industry. Since plastics firms can derive considerable economies of scale, a firm in Lesotho may be at a disadvantage compared with foreign firms until it has attained a certain size. By protecting the domestic market against foreign competition a local firm might attain the optimum size. Alternatively, it might settle for a quiet life producing inefficiently and protected from international competition.

5 The Government imposing the tariff may do so in order to raise revenue.

All discussion of importing and exporting has, so far, been carried out with no reference to the use of money. The question of whether the French car exporter wanted payment in francs or in pounds sterling for his exports was not asked. In the discussion of international relative price levels we referred to the fact that devaluation changes relative international price levels but did not explain how or why. The chapter which follows takes up this necessary discussion of the flows of, and markets for, foreign currencies: the foreign exchange market. The analysis used builds on the analysis of markets, supply, demand and equilibrium price, that have been covered in earlier chapters.

Summary and conclusions

We have shown that UK exports and imports did seem to respond to changes in demand and prices in the way that our theorizing suggested. Exports did rapidly increase after 1967 when the general price level moved in favour of the UK following the devaluation of November 1967, and they respond to changes in demand in export markets. We found conflicting evidence, however, for the view, sometimes expressed, that excessive growth of home demand had held back UK exports. We also showed for the UK that the rate of change of domestic production influenced the rate of increase of imports.

Statistical appendix

Row number	1954	1955	1956	1957	1958	1959	1960	1961
1 Exports of goods and services as a percentage of UK GDP at factor costs	20·6	21·1	21·6	21·7	21·4	21·3	21·5	21·4
2 Change in UK domestic demand from the previous year at 1970 prices (£ million)	1083	1395	302	686	277	1667	2186	1016
3 Change in UK exports of goods and services from the previous year, 1970 prices (£ million)	309	357	431	163	−105	179	375	220
4 Percentage growth over the previous year of non-UK manufactured exports to UK export markets, current prices	10·5	15·1	16·1	11·3	−2·7	10·0	15·0	7·1
5 Percentage growth over the previous year of UK exports of manufactures, current prices	3·8	6·9	10·4	8·6	2·2	5·9	6·6	6·5
6 Change from the previous year of UK imports of goods and services, 1970 prices (£ million)	192	547	17	150	67	407	788	−53
7 Change from the previous year of UK GDP at 1970 factor costs (£ million)	981	977	559	583	−76	1054	1452	1174
8 UK imports of goods and services as a percentage of GDP at factor costs	19·3	20·5	20·2	20·3	20·6	21·2	22·7	21·7

Sources: *National Income and Expenditure*, various issues, HMSO; *National Institute Economic*

Questions

1 What are the main determinants of the demands for imports and exports? What light is thrown on the relative importance of the determinants by the behaviour of UK exports and imports.

2 Using the statistical appendix to this chapter investigate the relationship between imports and relative prices, pre and post 1967. You may want to turn to the *Annual Abstract of Statistics* and the *National Income and Expenditure* for additional information.

3 Investigate the 'availability' hypothesis on exports by comparing the time series for the share of exports and the share of imports in national income.

1962	1963	1964	1965	1966	1967	1968	1969	1970	1971	1972	1973	1974	1975
21·5	21·6	21·2	21·7	22·1	21·8	23·4	25·3	26·1	27·3	27·4	29·0	30·8	29·9
387	1586	2845	685	770	1688	1296	−70	1058	1007	2417	3288	748	1055
117	305	328	381	329	100	1017	921	536	790	259	1413	945	−668
9·1	9·5	15·1	12·7	13·6	9·9	16·6	17·6	16·0	11·1	18·3	33·1	34·4	7·8
2·4	6·9	5·6	8·5	7·3	−0·2	8·8	13·8	10·0	14·1	7·8	25·1	24·4	14·0
152	271	718	84	210	592	687	298	529	526	1319	1722	30	−825
335	1368	2149	955	769	999	1463	579	784	987	758	2422	236	−769
21·9	21·9	22·5	22·2	22·3	23·2	24·0	24·4	25·2	25·8	28·3	30·5	30·4	29·1

review, various issues; *Annual Abstract of Statistics*, various issues, HMSO

Chapter 36
The Foreign Exchange Market and the Balance of Payments

In the previous chapter we ignored problems of how UK citizens with pound notes can buy cars from French firms which use francs as their currency. Additionally, we did not discuss how a UK firm which wants to set up a factory in France can acquire the francs to do this. In this chapter we are going to look at the flows of money that result from foreign trade and investment and at how currencies are traded one for another to allow this trade and investment.

Just as there are markets for apples and oranges, so there are markets for currencies with supplies and demands determining prices; for example, the price of sterling in terms of francs or marks in terms of dollars.

To simplify the exposition we shall concentrate on only two currencies (the pound sterling and the franc) and two economies, the UK and France; but it should be easy to see how this analysis can be extended to consider the relationship of more than two currencies to one another.

The demand for sterling

We can distinguish two reasons for Frenchmen wishing to buy sterling.

Consumption

Frenchmen wishing to buy holidays or cars in the UK have to pay with sterling and even if they pay with francs, the UK hoteliers or car salesmen will want to exchange the francs for pounds sterling so that they can conveniently spend their income within the UK. In either case, people with francs will want to exchange them for sterling – there is therefore a supply of francs and a demand for sterling. Let us

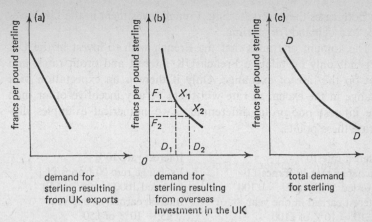

Figure 169

take an example in order to derive the demand curve for sterling resulting from exports-sales to Frenchmen. Suppose the 'price' of sterling is 10 francs per £1 – if a Frenchman goes to a foreign exchange dealer he can buy £1 with 10 francs. The UK cars that Frenchmen wish to buy are £1000 each; which is equivalent to 10 000 francs. At a price of 10 000 francs the French will buy a certain number of UK cars per period of time. Now if the exchange rate were not 10 but 20 francs per £1 then the French price of the £1000 cars would be 20 000 francs. Demand theory tells us that fewer cars (at an unchanged sterling price) will be bought at the higher franc price and thus the demand for sterling will be lower at 20 than at 10 francs per £1. The demand for sterling resulting from UK exports will thus be as in Figure 169(a).

Investment

Frenchmen may see that interest rates and profits are higher in the UK than in France. In order to receive the high rates of interest they have to lend money to individuals, firms, or other institutions in the UK. These institutions do not want francs and so the French have to buy sterling with their francs in order to lend. Thus, a demand for sterling arises. If UK industry is more profitable than French industry Frenchmen may want to benefit from this discrepancy by buying shares in UK companies, or even by starting a new firm in the UK.

The Demand for Sterling 605

In both cases they need sterling. French investment in the UK gives rise to a demand for sterling.

The amount of francs that the French wish to invest in the UK depends only on relative French/UK interest and profit rates, and not on the rate of exchange. Only if there is an expectation of a change in the exchange rate will there be any incentive other than the interest rate/profit differential. Two numerical examples illustrate these points.

Interest rate 10%	Interest rate 10%
Exchange rate 10 francs/£1	Exchange rate 20 francs/£1
Invested 1000 francs = £100	Invested 1000 francs = £50
Interest earned in one year	Interest earned in one year
£10 = 10% of £100	£5 = 10% of £50
Interest expressed in francs	Interest expressed in francs
100 francs = £10 times	100 francs = £5 times 20
10 francs/£1	francs/£1
Rate of interest	Rate of interest
$= \dfrac{100 \text{ francs}}{1000 \text{ francs}} = 10\%$	$= \dfrac{100 \text{ francs}}{1000 \text{ francs}} = 10\%$

In the first case, where the exchange rate was 10 francs per £1, if the exchange rate had changed at the end of the year from 10 to 20 francs per £1 then the £10 of interest would have converted into £10 × 20 francs per £1 = 200 francs return on an investment of 1000 francs. An extra profit has been made simply by buying sterling at 10 francs per £1 and selling at 20 francs per £1. It is apparent therefore that if the value of the pound is expected to rise then people will buy in anticipation. Conversely, if the value of the pound is expected to fall then people will sell sterling at the high price and then buy it back at the lower price. This buying and selling of currency in anticipation of a change in its value is called *speculation*. No profit is made if the anticipated change in exchange rate fails to occur.

If we assume for the moment that exchange rate changes are not anticipated then the number of francs that Frenchmen wish to invest in the UK either long-term or short-term depends on the interest/profit rates in the UK relative to France and all other countries where investments could be made. The volume of francs does not depend upon the level of the exchange rate. However, the sterling demanded does depend on the exchange rate, for example, if there are 1000 francs to be invested at an exchange rate of 10 francs per £1 the demand is for £100. If the exchange rate is 20 francs per £1 then the demand is for £50. The relationship results in the demand for sterling by French investors being a rectangular hyperbola, as in Figure 169(b).

The total demand for sterling in the course of a period of time is thus the demand arising from trade plus the demand arising from new investments made in the UK during that time period.

Flow versus stock

We have discussed investment as though our Frenchmen have a stock of funds and put them into the country which offers the greatest reward. This is certainly part of the truth. Additionally we need to remember that saving is a continuous process and thus, at any time there is a *stock* of francs which may or may not be used to buy sterling in order to hold UK assets, and in addition, there is a *flow* of savings also looking for outlets (forms of assets to hold) both in France and in other economies.

In summary we can say that, per period of time, the demand for sterling will result from both UK exports of goods and services, and overseas (French) desire to buy UK assets to hold in both the short run and the long run. The total demand for sterling is the sum of those demands. Thus Figure 169c is the horizontal summation of Figures 169a and 169b.[1]

The supply of sterling

The supply of sterling depends upon a variety of factors.

Importing

Let us say that a bottle of wine in France costs 10 francs. At the exchange rate of 10 francs per £1 a Briton would give £1 for a bottle.

1. The reader should note that we have here assumed that the supply of UK exports is perfectly elastic, that is, a fall in French demand for UK goods has no effect on prices within the UK. In the discussion of the supply of sterling we will similarly assume that the supply of French goods is perfectly elastic. Readers who wish to examine the consequences of dropping this simplifying assumption could read the early parts of Haberler (1969).

If the rate of exchange was 20 francs per £1 then the Briton has to give up 50p to buy a 10 franc bottle of wine. The price has fallen and he will buy more bottles of wine as a result. The sterling price is half what it was; if he more than doubles his purchases of bottles the supply of sterling will be greater than before the exchange rate change. If he doubles his purchases then supply of sterling is unchanged, and if he less than doubles his purchases the supply of sterling will fall. What happens to the supply of sterling after the exchange rate changes depends upon the price-elasticity of demand. Let us examine the supply of sterling resulting from UK imports in more detail. Figure 170 shows the UK demand for French wine at each of the sterling prices that the UK purchaser faces as the exchange rate varies.

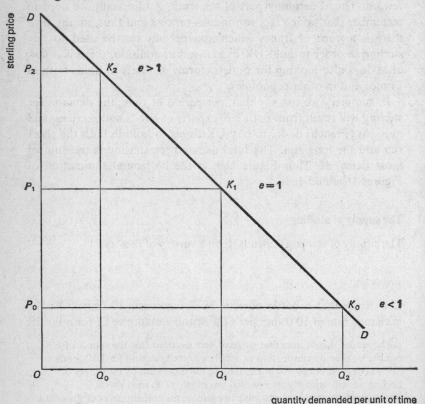

Figure 170

At the initial exchange rate the sterling price is OP_2 and the demand is OQ_0, thus the expenditure (and the supply of sterling) is price times quantity $= OP_2 \cdot OQ_0$ (represented by the area on the graph $OP_2K_2Q_0$). Now the number of francs per pound is raised and so the sterling price falls to, say, OP_1 with demand rising to OQ_1. Thus the supply of sterling is the area $OP_1K_1Q_1$. If the price elasticity of demand is greater than unity over the price range OP_2 to OP_1 then $OP_1K_1Q_1 > OP_2K_2Q_0$ and the supply of sterling has increased. Somewhere as we go down the demand curve the price-elasticity of demand will fall to unity and then to less than unity as we continue down the line. We see this if the number of francs per pound again rises making the sterling price of French wine even lower, the price falling to P_0. The total supply of sterling is now $OP_0K_0Q_2$ and is less than at OP_1 and the same as at OP_0. We can now draw Figure 171 which is a supply curve of sterling resulting from the UK purchases of French wine.

This supply curve is an unusual shape, depending as it does on elasticity of demand for imports. Such evidence as we have suggests that demand elasticities for imports are characteristically in the range 0·5 to 1·0, but values outside this range cannot be discounted. If they fall in this range then only the upper part of the curve will be observed with the supply curve sloping downwards from left to right.

Investment

The supply of sterling arising from UK desires to invest overseas either in the long run or the short run will be unaffected by the level of the exchange rates, but solely by relative interest/profit rates. The supply of sterling by people buying foreign currency for speculative purposes will depend not upon the level of the exchange rate but upon expectations of a change in that level. Thus if for simplicity we assume that no exchange rate change is expected then there will be no speculation and the supply of sterling resulting from UK investment overseas will be as in Figure 172(a) – the vertical line will shift if relative interest/profit rates change between the UK and other countries.

The total supply of sterling in a given time period is thus the horizontal summation of Figures 172(a) and 172(b), giving 172(c).

Now that we have discussed the supply and demand curves for

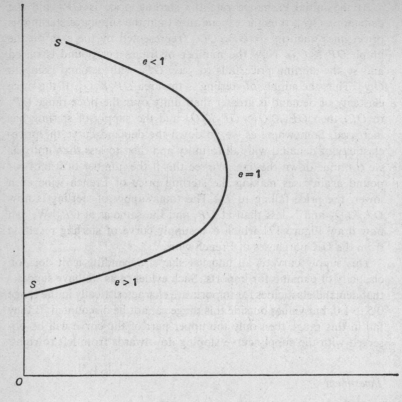

Figure 171

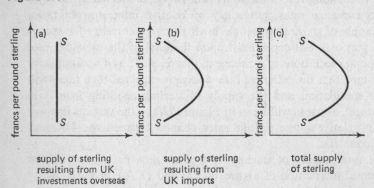

(a)
supply of sterling
resulting from UK
investments overseas

(b)
supply of sterling
resulting from
UK imports

(c)
total supply
of sterling

Figure 172

sterling (the flows) we can bring the two together in order to determine the equilibrium rate of exchange, the one at which the supply and the demand during a given time are equal.

Equilibrium rate of exchange

Figure 173(a) depicts a market for sterling in which the demand and supply curves have the customary shapes; the demand curve has a negative slope and the supply curve has a positive slope. The market is in equilibrium with OA pounds being supplied and demanded at exchange rate OH. Embodied in this equilibrium is the *purchasing power parity theory* which says that there is a connection between the exchange rate and the prices of traded goods in alternative currencies. Thus, if a good sells for £1 in Britain it must sell for 10 francs in France if the exchange rate is £1 for 10 francs.

Now suppose there is an increase in the demand for sterling. The demand curve shifts to the right and a new equilibrium is established at exchange rate OM. This accords with common sense: an increase in demand will tend to raise price. In international trade theory the move from OH to OM is referred to as an *appreciation* of sterling in terms of francs and a *devaluation* of the franc. Now consider the case shown in 173(b). The demand curve for sterling cuts a backward sloping segment of the supply curve. The equilibrium at A is therefore unstable. If the franc is devalued from OH to OM then the excess demand for sterling increases rather than decreases. Indeed the correct, although not so obvious policy, would be to appreciate the franc to OP. It is the possibilities of such perverse cases that have led some economists to suggest that balance of payments problems should be tackled by the use of tariffs.

The efficiency of the foreign exchange market can only be settled empirically. However, we should note that the perverse case rests upon the assumption that import demand elasticities are extremely low. As we have observed, a backward sloping supply curve of sterling can only be derived from a UK demand curve for French goods that has an elasticity less than unity. But it seems common sense to assume that as the franc falls in value, Britons will purchase more francs in order to buy the relatively cheaper French goods. Hence the supply curve of sterling would eventually twist round and assume an upward slope. It is also plausible to assume that at some adverse rate of ex-

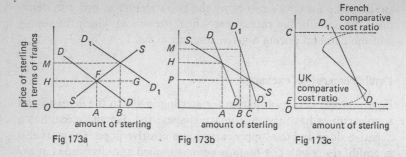

Fig 173a   Fig 173b   Fig 173c

change Frenchmen will consider it advantageous to substitute domestic goods for British goods. Therefore, we would expect the demand and supply curves for sterling to intersect at some exchange rate. Such a result is indicated in 173(c) and arises because at some exchange rate Frenchmen would decide to become self-sufficient; the exchange rate OC is dictated by France's comparative cost ratio. And a similar boundary is OE which is dictated by the UK comparative cost ratio.

Before concluding that devaluations can work it is useful to consider Figure 174 where the demand curve cuts the supply curve from below; the distinction between Figures 173(b) and 174 lies in the fact that in Figure 174 the demand curve is more elastic than the supply curve. Figure 174 yields a stable equilibrium in the sense that any arbitrary displacement from A will lead to a restoration of the equilibrium. In this example a shift of the demand curve to D_1D_1 will produce a new equilibrium at B and devaluation will work. So a backward sloping supply curve of a currency can be compatible with an efficiently working foreign exchange market.

We have three possible market situations and the question arises: which is the typical case. Early studies suggested that import demands were extremely low, and gave rise to 'elasticity pessimism' and the belief that devaluations will not work. Subsequent studies suggested that the low elasticities might have been due to the existence of tariffs. Our study of UK exports and imports after 1967 devaluation, in the previous chapter, suggested that elasticities might be high enough for devaluation to work. Finally, we should note that sometimes devaluations may not work because domestic money supplies are allowed to expand and people are able to buy the same amounts of imports. We must, therefore, examine the part played by money in exchange rate adjustments.

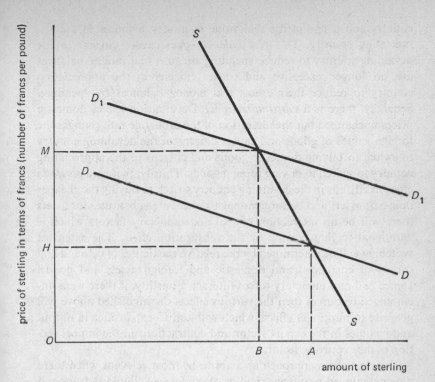

Figure 174

The role of money in exchange rate adjustments

So far we have analysed the workings of the foreign exchange market using the tools of demand and supply analysis and regarding money as just another commodity. Indeed, the elasticities approach tends to suggest that it is the real forces of demand and supply of goods that are important and that money is merely required as a medium of exchange. As such it tends to suppress the workings of monetary disturbances in the foreign exchange market. It is this deficiency we must now remedy.

When a devaluation occurs several consequences follow. First, there is a fall in the real value of money balances in the devaluing country and a rise in the real value of money balances in the appreciating country. This *real balance effect* causes citizens in the devaluing country to reduce spending because real money balances are no longer excessive and causes citizens in the appreciating country to reduce their excess real money balances by spending. Secondly, there is a *substitution effect*. Devaluation leaves domestic prices unchanged but the alteration of the exchange rate changes the foreign values of goods and causes citizens of the devaluing country to switch to buying domestic goods and citizens in the appreciating country to switch to buying foreign goods. Thirdly, there is a *portfolio effect* as citizens in the devaluing country switch to buying the cheaper domestic assets and because money balances are substitutes for assets there will be an interaction of real and monetary factors which is additional to that created by the substitution effect. The extent of switching will be determined by the relative elasticities of demand and supply of currencies and domestic and foreign assets and goods. Hence real and monetary forces interact. Fourthly, if there were unemployed resources then the various effects distinguished above will give rise to multiplier effects which will lead to expansions in output and incomes in the export sector and contractions in the import section of the exporting sector.

The elasticities approach appears to be most relevant when there are unemployed resources, rigid prices and wages, liquidity traps and constant supplies of currencies: that is, a Keynesian world. The emphasis upon monetary variables seems most appropriate when there is full employment and flexible prices; that is in a monetarist world. In the Keynesian world devaluation would lead via multiplier effects to full employment and an absence of balance of payments problems. In the monetarist world devaluation would lead via real balance effects to the elimination of balance of payments difficulties. But the real world is not always at the polar extremes and frequently the two models have to be combined for policy purposes. In an economy suffering from inflation and an adverse balance of payments, the first step may be to reduce the money supply which could lead to unemployment. The second step would be to devalue and switch the idle resources into the export sector.

The conclusion we reach therefore is that both the elasticities and monetary approaches to exchange rate adjustments are required. The elasticities approach emphasises flows of money and goods whilst the monetary approach reminds us that stocks of money, as well as other assets, may be large in relation to any net additions per period of time. Finally, we observe that a country has a choice between altering its money supply or its exchange rate in order to achieve a real balance effect – which policy is most efficient will be considered later.

Movements of curves

From the discussion above it will be apparent that shifts in the demand and supply curves for currencies will be a function of changes in national incomes, price levels, interest rates and real balance effects at any given exchange rate.

The analysis of the elasticities and monetary approaches to exchange rate adjustment serves to remind us that a complete understanding of economic activity requires a general equilibrium approach and that the elasticities analysis may be one of partial equilibrium. But it is impossible to construct a general equilibrium model which embraces *simultaneous* changes in prices and outputs. In this section we shall therefore derive a balance of payments equilibrium locus for different levels of real income and interest rates on the assumption that the price level is given. This is the Keynesian model and justification for its derivation is that it permits an extension of the widely used *IS-LM* general equilibrium model to an open economy. The complete *IS-LM* model will be found in Chapter 40. In the meantime it should be noted that it would be possible to derive an alternative model in which the price level was allowed to vary.

A first approximation to a general equilibrium analysis of the balance of payments.

In order to construct the balance of payments equilibrium locus we shall make the following assumptions.

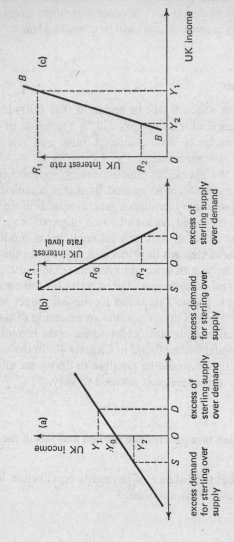

Figure 175

1 Exports of UK goods and services depend on foreign income levels.

2 Imports of goods and services into the UK depend on the level of UK income.

3 UK investment overseas depends on UK interest rates (assuming foreign interest rates constant).[3]

4 Foreign investment in the UK depends on UK interest rates (assuming foreign interest rates constant).

If overseas income is constant then UK exports are constant. If UK income rises, UK imports rise and, with UK exports constant, the supply of sterling rises with the demand for sterling constant, when only trade in goods and services is considered. At some income level the supply of sterling from imports equals the demand for sterling from exports – the *trade balance* is zero. At higher UK income levels exports are unchanged (demand for sterling is unchanged) but UK imports are higher (supply of sterling is higher) – there is a deficit on the *trade balance*. We can show this situation in Figure 175(a). At income level OY_0 the sterling value of exports equals the sterling value of imports (*zero trade balance*). At the higher level of income OY_1 imports have grown and exports are unchanged and thus the sterling value of imports exceed the sterling value of exports by OD (*a trade deficit*). Similarly at the low income level OY_2 exports exceed imports in sterling terms (*a trade surplus*) by OS.

If we now consider the *capital account*, the demand for sterling resulting from foreign investment in the UK set against the supply of sterling resulting from UK investment overseas, we can draw a diagram similar to Figure 175(a) except that the balance depends not on income but upon the UK interest rate (asuming the interest rates in other countries to be unchanging). In Figure 175(b) at interest rate OR_0 the demand for and supply of sterling as a result of foreign investment are equal – a zero balance on the *capital account*. At the higher interest rate OR_1 more funds are attracted into the UK and the flow of funds out of the UK is reduced due to the increased attraction. There is a surplus of OS on the capital account. Conversely at the lower interest rate OR_2 there is a deficit on the capital account equal to OD.

3. We are assuming for the sake of simplicity that interest rates and rates of profit move together and thus we need refer only to interest rates.

Now we can combine these two diagrams together to show the combinations of interest rate and income level which will ensure that the overall *balance of payments* is in equilibrium, that is, the balance on the trade account (or current account) *plus* the balance on the capital account equals zero. In Figure 175(a) at income level OY_1 the current account has a *deficit* of OD (the demand for sterling arising from exports is less than the supply of sterling resulting from UK imports by OD). If we turn to Figure 175(b) we can find a rate of interest at which there is an equal and opposite *surplus* on the capital account. Such an interest rate is OR_1 where OS in Figure 175(b) equals OD in Figure 175(a). Similarly we can choose any other income level in Figure 175(a) and find the interest rate in Figure 175(b) where the surplus on one account balances out the deficit on the other. The combinations of interest rate and income that ensure overall balance of payments equilibrium are shown in Figure 175(c) as the points on the line *BB*.

Balance of payments policy and control

We have seen earlier in the chapter that if relative interest rates, income levels or price levels change between countries then the supply and demand curves for currencies will move, other things being equal. If governments allow the curves to move, and new equilibrium prices to emerge quite freely, then these are called *freely floating exchange rates*. In this situation a balance of payments problem cannot exist because changes in the price of currencies will always ensure that demands and supplies are reconciled. Any excess supply or demand can only result from a failure of the exchange rate to adjust.

The actual processes that occur in the economy when the supply of or the demand for a country's currency are not equal on the foreign exchange market is quite complex as we have indicated in the earlier part of the chapter, the money supply changes, interest rates change, investment levels change with resulting multiplier effects on income and so on; all these changes inter-reacting on one another. But at this stage it is enough to have sketched their nature.

Now we shall look briefly at the possibility that a government will not let the exchange rate float freely for various policy reasons. We will examine the case of a country with a deficit on its balance of payments.

To some extent, given enough time the balance of payments will adjust itself, provided that the government can in the short run buy the excess sterling using its foreign currency reserves or borrowed funds. Some of this adjustment we have already met. If the flows of sterling out of the UK to buy foreign currency exceeds the flow into the country from those overseas buying UK imports and investing in the UK, then the supply of sterling (money) within the UK is declining. Earlier chapters have suggested that the effect of reduction in the money supply is to reduce prices and force up interest rates. The first result improves the competitive level of prices, raising exports and cutting imports; and the second attracts foreign investment into the UK thus increasing the demand for sterling.

The rise in interest rates will discourage domestic investment in plant and machinery and domestic consumption and this will, through the multiplier, reduce the level of income and thus the demand for imports. A related feature is that if the country's prices have been rising relative to foreign prices (perhaps the cause of the payments deficit) then exports will be reduced and imports increased, both reducing domestic demand and, through the multiplier, national income. Lower income means lower imports and possibly lower prices (see the chapter on inflation).

Over the last few years the money supply in the UK has grown so strongly that the monetary effect of the balance of payments deficit had no noticeable effect and thus automatic adjustment became too slow in practice and deliberate non-automatic policies were resorted to in order to restore equality between the demand for and supply of sterling on the foreign exchange market.

Balance of payments policies

If some change in the economic environment causes the supply and demand curves for a currency to shift, then at the initial equilibrium exchange rate the supply of currency will not equal the demand. This situation is shown in Figure 173, where the demand excess exceeds the supply by an amount *FG*.

If the government chooses to maintain the old exchange rate then it has a number of possible short- and long-run policies. All the policies must either have the effect of reducing the supply of, or increasing the demand for, the currency. How can this be done? We will list, and briefly discuss, a number of possible policies which may be used singly or together.

1 In the short run the UK government can use its reserves of foreign currency to buy up the excess sterling (to take an example), in the process providing the foreign currency that the sterling holders were trying to buy. This way of removing the sterling excess can only be used in the short run as the government will run out of reserves.

2 The government can deflate the economy. With this policy it reduces the level of demand for imports, or at least slows the rate of growth of imports relative to the rate of growth of exports. We have seen that a major determinant of imports is the level of income. Deflation reduces national income or slows its rate of growth. As the labour force normally grows continuously any fall in income or its rate of growth results in unemployment. The cost of this solution to a balance of payments problem is the output that could have been produced by the unemployed. An additional problem is that the solution may only be short run in that when the government allows income to grow again at its 'normal' rate, imports may again jump up to a level where the supply of sterling again exceeds the demand for it.

If the low level of activity in the economy reduces the level of UK prices or their rate of growth relative to other countries, then the benefit may be long lasting if UK prices continue at the reduced level relative to other economies even after the deflation ends.

The government can deflate the economy in a number of ways, by cutting government spending, by increasing taxation, by reducing the money supply or by increasing the rate of interest and thus discouraging investment, or by a combination of these and other possible policies.

The raising of interest rates may be introduced for reasons other than their deflationary effect – to increase the inflow of foreign investment.

3 We have already seen how a rise in UK interest rates will increase private lending to the UK and tend to reduce UK private investment overseas, thus increasing the demand for sterling and reducing its supply. This is again a short-run policy as, unless high interest rates are maintained, the loans will be repaid and not replaced. Foreign loans may allow some parts of the economy to go on spending in excess of their income but the high interest rates will tend to dis-

courage manufacturers from investing in plant and machinery, thus reducing future potential output.

4 Another possible solution which doesn't require a change of exchange rates is to borrow foreign currency with which to buy the excess sterling until such time as the 'good times' return. Again the policy will only work in the short run, it does not remove the cause of the initial imbalance in the exchange markets. It does, however, give you time for other policies to take effect which will alter the long-run position. Such borrowing has a natural limit; lenders must be sure that the loan and the interest can, and will, be repaid.

5 The fifth policy that we would mention relates to inflation as a cause of balance of payments crisis. If imports are rising and exports are falling because the price level is becoming uncompetitive, then a solution is to reduce or stop inflation. In the past deflation has been used and so have incomes policies. The new element not previously discussed is incomes policies where the rate of growth of incomes is acted upon directly by voluntary agreement or legislation. Whether such policies are a long-term or only a short-term cure for inflation and balance of payments difficulties is not clear to researchers.

There is a full discussion of inflation in Chapter 37, all we need to remember at this stage is that it may cause foreign exchange market disequilibrium and its removal or reduction will certainly effect that market. Finally, is there a cost to incomes policy? – many argue that there is, the chief of which is loss of freedom in wage negotiation.

6 The last policy that we would mention is that of physical controls. If tariffs are imposed on imports then their value falls. Similarly, subsidies on exports will boost them. On the capital account you may place various restrictions on investment overseas by your nationals.

These restrictive measures are not normally available to countries as most are bound by international agreements forbidding or discouraging the erection of obstacles to free trade and the free flows of capital.

Floating versus fixed rates of exchange

During the period from the Second World War until the early 1970s, the world's major trading nations were committed to a system of fixed exchange rates, but since then an increasing number of economies have allowed their currency to float.

The reasons are complex but what we will do is indicate at least some of the advantages that countries saw in fixed exchange rates.

Firstly, many countries saw the aim of a stable fixed exchange rate as highly desirable after the economic chaos of the 1930s. If the international community could agree on fixed exchange rates, then the beggar-my-neighbour devaluation policies of the 1930s could not reoccur. Eventually this desire became a political objective, almost a sign of political virility – 'what did you think of a country which couldn't even control its own balance of payments?' Unchanged currency values became a point of political honour. Attitudes have changed on this point somewhat.

Secondly, it was felt that free floating rates would fluctuate sufficiently widely that there would be uncertainty about currency values and that this would limit world trade which was seen to be a 'bad' thing. Recent world experience of floating seems to have allayed this fear.

Thirdly, it was felt that fixed exchange rates provided a useful and important discipline especially in relation to inflation. With fixed rates, inflation causes balance of payments crises, therefore stamp out inflation! With floating rates the rate just floats down as you inflate, therefore inflation would not apparently need to be so tightly checked as under fixed rates.

Paradoxically, one of the disadvantages of floating rates is that if the rate floats down then the cost of imports rises and if you are an economy like the UK with huge imports of food and raw materials which are not domestically available then your prices are forced up unavoidably and inflation is that much harder to control. The size of the downward float necessary to restore equilibrium will depend partly on the slopes of the currency supply and demand curves – they could be such that to restore equilibrium, a massive rise in import prices would occur. This is a situation, some argue, that the UK is in in 1977.

The breakdown of the fixed exchange rate system was caused by a number of factors although there is still not complete agreement over all the factors and their relative importance.

Two major factors developed throughout the post war period. Firstly, there was a very rapid and sustained growth in world trade which meant that the absolute magnitude of temporary balance of payments fluctuations tended to be bigger, thus requiring larger foreign currency reserves. But the reserves did not grow proportionately and the temporary disequilibrium could not readily be accommodated. The second feature was a change in the relationship of international prices. Price levels in countries tended to diverge by more than had previously been the case. In this situation balance of payments problems arose which required that both the surplus and the deficit countries made adjustments. Unfortunately, the pressure on surplus countries to adjust their policies was slight, and they tended not to make these changes. Thus all of the burden of adjustment fell on the deficit countries who, in a period of fixed exchange rates, used deflation, thus imposing slower growth and unemployment on their economies. Gradually these costs became less acceptable and floating conversely began to seem attractive.

Two other contributory factors leading to the breakdown of the fixed exchanges rate regime were the US involvement in Vietnam, which fuelled a world inflation, and the sudden sharp rise in world mineral oil prices which immediately made the value of oil imports rise very suddenly without a compensating increase in exports.

Thus continuing developments and sudden shocks found the fixed exchange rate system wanting and encouraged a number of countries to experiment with floating rates.

Summary and conclusions

We have seen that exports and imports of goods and services depend upon relative price level and income levels. We have suggested that the flow of international private lending and borrowing depends upon the relative interest rates and rates of profit.

We have investigated how trade in goods and services and private lending and borrowing across international frontiers leads to supplies and demands for currencies which are reconciled in the foreign exchange market at a price for each currency in terms of the other currencies – a price which, if the market is left free to float, will equate supply and demand.

If the exchange rate is fixed, and we looked at some reasons why this has seemed a reasonable policy, then any imbalance between demand and supply for a currency has had to be met in the short run by buying up the excess, and in the long run by adopting policies which would shift the supply and demand curves relative to one another so that they intersect at the desired rate.

The only other acceptable policy was of devaluation – a discrete change in the exchange rate to what was estimated to be the new equilibrium rate. The difficulties of this policy were that speculative pressure grew in anticipation of the discrete change and the chosen new exchange rate had to be estimated, and it might prove not to be at a level where currency demand and supply were equal.

All of these policies have costs as well as benefits. It may well be properly a political question just what costs are borne by whom in order to gain the desired balance of payments situation.

Two topics have not been mentioned and clearly should be. We have made no real mention of countries with a balance of payments *surplus*, where there is an excess demand for their currency at the current exchange rate. The analysis here is really the analysis that we have examined for a deficit country, but simply put into reverse, inflating rather than deflating, lowering interest rates, increasing money supplies and so on. The problem of a surplus is very much an embarrassment of riches not needing immediate action. If your exchange rate is not floating then you *have* to do something about a balance of payments deficit.

The second topic not mentioned is that of government spending overseas on military matters, diplomacy, etc. These currency flows occur as a result of government carrying out their policy aims and even in a deficit situation it does not follow that they should be cut in order to restore equilibrium. The effect of this government spending can be analysed using the balance of payments analysis developed in this chapter.

In an appendix to this chapter the balance of payments accounts of the UK for recent years are set out and explained.

This may have seemed a long and hard chapter, but we would justify it in terms of the importance of trade to many countries (the UK exports about one quarter of all it produces) and the profound effect on economies of balance of payments policies.

Appendix I: International Monetary Experience 1875–1975

In order to understand the relative merits of fixed and floating exchange rates it is necessary to examine international monetary history over the last century.

Gold standard

In the last quarter of the nineteenth century, world trade tended to operate on the basis of what was known as the *gold standard*. What this meant was that countries fixed the values of their currencies in terms of a given amount of gold and they adhered to these exchange rates. Because all currencies were tied to gold there was an international currency and the existence of the fixed ratios gave rise to all the advantages that stem from the introduction of a monetary system, such as easier communications and greater division of labour. Gold was the international currency though it was not always used in transactions. By virtue of Britain's importance in world trade there was a tendency to use sterling as the unit of account and medium of exchange. Thus, the system was sometimes referred to as a *gold exchange standard*.

The gold standard was a fixed exchange rate system – all currencies had their values fixed in terms of gold – and this provided a discipline and a check to currency debasement; and the system seemed to work, though it is not clear how and why it worked.

In theory, the system worked as follows. A country which experienced a deficit – an outflow of currency because it was importing too much and exporting too little – was required to deflate and reduce domestic demand. The outflow of currency implied less currency inside the country as the banking system contracted deposits because reserves were contracting. The fall in demand was supposed to lead to a fall in prices and costs which would make the goods of the country less expensive for foreigners to buy. At the same time the inflow of currency into other countries would cause an expansion of demand and a rise in prices making it dear to buy from them but easy to sell to. In short, the gold standard adjustment process was nothing more than the quantity theory of money with monetary flows between countries, or even regions, causing changes in prices and costs. Thus, a fixed exchange rate system rather similar to the gold standard system operates within countries. When the demand for coal declined in the sixties there was a fall in the exports of coal from Northumberland and Durham and there was a balance of payments problem.

We must now consider why the gold standard worked in the nineteenth century and failed in the twentieth century.

1 The first reason that can be put forward for its apparent success is that it was never called upon to operate. Most of the industrial countries kept in step with each other in the sense that their booms and slumps coincided. And even where their rates of growth differed, it was never serious enough to matter or was controlled by the use of tariffs.

2 The second reason that can be advanced is that imbalances were only temporary and were covered by capital flows. When a country had a balance of payments deficit it raised interest rates and this resulted in an inflow of short term capital.

3 The adjustment process overlooked the effects on the underdeveloped, primary-producing countries. When, for example, Britain had a deficit, there would be a fall in demand for agricultural goods and raw materials and a fall in the amount of capital flowing out to be invested in the underdeveloped world. Because of the high price inelasticities of demand and supply for their goods, primary producers were forced to deflate drastically and this, paradoxically, had the effect of turning the terms of trade in favour of Britain. Hence, the underdeveloped countries came to view the gold standard as a capitalist plot.

In the interwar years the gold standard broke down, and Britain discarded it in 1931. To understand why it broke down it is necessary to look at certain features of that troubled period. During the First World War many countries suffered major inflations and rates of inflation varied from country to country. After the war attempts to establish a fixed exchange rate system, a gold standard, ran into the difficulties of deciding what the new exchange rates should be. Many countries experimented with fluctuating exchange rates in an endeavour to find the right level, but these experiments were not successful because many of them were still experiencing inflation. As a consequence, exchange rates seemed to oscillate wildly and this was attributed to fundamental instability in the foreign exchange markets. It was seldom acknowledged that the instability stemmed from inflation. In the case of Britain the decision to return to the gold standard at the wrong rate created problems throughout the twenties.

The fundamental reaction to the gold standard came in the thirties and, in restrospect, for the wrong reasons. The decision of the American authorities to cut back their money supply and to call in loans led to a general reduction in currencies and left a situation in which the volume of international transactions could not be sustained by the volume of moneys internationally acceptable as proxies for gold. Just as the introduction of money results in improved communications and a greater division of labour, so its contraction results in chaos and a return to barter. These consequences were not understood at the time. The collapse of the gold standard was attributed to wage and price rigidities but these were the short-run responses to a traumatic shock. Beggar-my-neighbour policies of devaluation and tariffs merely intensified the problem because such policies had the effect of improving one country's balance of payments at the expense of others – there was not enough international money to go round. The collapse was due to ignorance and inexperience. What was wanted in the interwar years was for America to provide the gold exchange standard that Britain had offered in the nineteenth century.

The dollar standard

After the Second World War there was an attempt to return to a gold standard. The Bretton Woods Agreement of 1944 attempted to establish a regime of fixed exchange rates and laid down the conditions under which exchange rate adjustments could take place. Countries which did experience a 'fundamental disequilibrium' were permitted to realign their currencies and could borrow gold or dollars from a newly established International Monetary Fund to tide them over short-run difficulties. The Fund was financed by member countries. In addition to the IMF there was also established an International Bank for Reconstruction and Development (often referred to as the World Bank) which was intended to assist in the movement of long-term capital and to provide loans to developing countries.

Between 1950 and 1970 the system seemed to work, though the reasons for its success were not always obvious or desirable.

1 There were very few exchange rate variations. After an initial phase of difficulties which were sorted out by currency variations in the late forties, most countries accepted the fixed exchange rate discipline.

2 America provided enough liquidity, enough currency, to provide a gold exchange rate system. America did not produce too many dollars to induce a loss of foreign confidence nor so few as to cause severe domestic unemployment.

From the late sixties, however, problems began to arise and finally caused a collapse of the fixed exchange rate system.

1 The lowering of tariff barriers by countries exposed them to competition from the developing nations. Since the middle sixties, tariff reduction has virtually ceased. In the fifties the gold standard worked because tariffs provided some protection from necessary adjustments, but if tariffs are to be reduced can the gold exchange system survive the numerous and complex adjustments?

2 Towards the end of the sixties, American restraint broke down under the necessity of financing the Vietnam War and a domestic anti-poverty programme. The sharp expansion in the dollar supply caused a worldwide rise in prices and a loss of confidence in the dollar.

3 Surplus countries, such as Western Germany, were reluctant to allow their domestic price levels to rise or their currencies to be revalued.

4 The upsurge in oil prices which led to difficult financing and adjustment problems.

Today (1977) it is not clear how the international monetary system will evolve. The situation is very much like the 1920s with strong and weak currencies coexisting in an uneasy alliance. Some economists believe that there is nothing to worry about, a world of floating exchange rates has not proved disastrous. Some, however, maintain that sooner or later there will be a return to a fixed exchange rate system because people will prefer to make their transactions in terms of the currencies which fluctuate least. Others argue for a return to gold, but that might mean that South Africa would benefit from a revaluation of gold – an action which, on political grounds, many dislike. A fourth group would like to see the establishment of an international manmade currency provided by an international agency and not subject to the limitations of supply, as in the case of gold, or the vagaries of domestic policies, as is the case of the dollar.

Appendix II: Balance of Payments Accounts

Now that we know something of the factors affecting the supply of, and demand for, various currencies on the market for foreign exchange, we can go on to discuss the particular case of the UK balance of payments.

It has been demonstrated that there is a demand for sterling by foreigners in order to buy UK exports or to invest in the UK. The supply of sterling on the currency markets results from UK imports and overseas investment. In Table 53 a plus sign before a number indicates that under this heading the demand for sterling exceeded the supply of sterling by the amount indicated.

In 1975 the sterling value of UK visible imports exceeded visible exports by £3200 million. The negative sign means that the supply of sterling exceeded the demand.

In examining in detail the make-up of the table, the column headed 1975 is studied for ease of exposition. There are two entries which summarize the currency flows resulting from economic agents going about their business – trading, investing and finding a safe place to keep their currency (their money balances). The two entries are:

1 *Current Balance.* This figure of −£1702 million shows that the sterling value of UK visible and invisible imports exceeds the sterling value of the visible and invisible exports by £1702 million. Thus considering trade alone, the supply of sterling exceeded the demand by £1702 million.

2 *Investment and other capital flows.* This item shows the net demand for sterling resulting from the demand and supply of sterling arising from several activities:

Inter-government loans and repayment of loans;
UK subscriptions and loans to various international institutions, e.g. the International Development Association;
Private overseas investment in the UK and UK private overseas investment and borrowing;
Currency reserves kept in sterling in the UK by other countries and institutions;

International trade credit;
Other minor items.

In 1975 the net demand for sterling resulting from all these activities was −£410 million. You will notice that this figure is normally negative – normally the supply of sterling under this head exceeds the demand. The negatives largely result from the UK's traditional role as an exporter of private capital. The UK has a long history of considerable private investment overseas.

The balancing item of +£1020 million is the net total of errors and omissions arising throughout the accounts. As you would expect, the balancing item varies very much from year to year.

The summation of the current balance, investment and other capital flows and the balancing item £(−1702)+(−410)+(+1020) shows that the supply of sterling exceeded the demand by £1092 million. Another way to look at this is to say that at the existing rates of exchange, the foreign currency offered by people wanting to buy sterling was exceeded by the sterling holders' demand for that currency by £1092 million.

If supply exceeds demand in a normal market, the price of the commodity falls until the supply and demand are equalized. In currency markets, as we have seen, this need not happen so long as the government is prepared to buy up the excess currency. In 1975 the UK was pursuing two policies at the same time, namely, the pound sterling was floating and yet the rate of change was being controlled so that import prices should not be forced up too quickly. If there had been an entirely free float then we would expect that the exchange rate would have been at a level to ensure that the supply of, and demand for, sterling were equal. That they were not equal (supply exceeded demand by £1092 million) shows the extent to which the government limited the downward float of sterling.

The excess supply of sterling in 1975 was purchased by the government of the UK. It was financed from two sources, as shown in the table. Official reserves of foreign currency were used to buy £669 million of the surplus, and the remainder was purchased using foreign currency borrowing by the government of £423 million.

Table 53 Summary of balance of payments, £ million

	1964	1965	1966	1967	1968	1969	1970	1971	1972	1973	1974	1975
Current account												
visible trade	−500	−223	−66	−554	−667	−147	−12	+282	−702	−2332	−5264	−3200
invisibles	+145	+195	+166	+253	+392	+609	+747	+766	+833	+1490	+1614	+1498
current balance	−355	−27	+100	−301	−275	+462	+735	+1048	+131	−842	−3650	−1702
Currency flow and official financing												
current balance	−355	−27	+100	−301	−275	+462	+735	+1048	+131	−842	−3650	−1702
capital transfers	—	—	—	—	—	—	—	—	—	−59	−75	—
investment and other capital flows	−301	−326	−578	−600[1]	−1006[1]	−109	+572	+1895	−712	+907	+2797	−410
balancing item	−39	—	−69	+230	−129	+390	−20	+285	−684	+204	+363	+1020
total currency flow	−695	−353	−547	−671	−1410	+743	+1287	+3228	−1265	+210	−565	−1092
allocation of Special Drawing Rights (+)	—	—	—	—	—	—	+171	+125	+124	—	—	—
gold subscription to IMF (−)	—	—	−44	—	—	—	−38	—	—	—	—	—
total	−695	−353	−591	−671	−1410	+743	+1420	+3353	−1141	+210	−565	−1092
Financed as follows:												
net transactions with overseas monetary authorities[2]	+573	+599	+625[3]	+556[3]	+1296	−699	−1285	−1817	+449			
foreign currency borrowing by HM Government											+644	+423
official reserves (drawings on +/ additions to −)[2]	+22	−246	−34	+115	+114	−44	−125	−1536	+692	−210	−79	+669

1. Including EEA loss on forward commitments.
2. From July 1972 transactions with the IMF affecting the United Kingdom reserve position in the Fund are included as changes in the official reserves.
3. Including transfer from dollar portfolio to reserves.
Source: *United Kingdom Balance of Payments 1974*; and *Monthly Digest of Statistics*, June 1976

Questions

1 What determines the demand for, and supply of, foreign currencies? What conditions can give rise to a backward-sloping supply curve of a currency? What does such a backward-sloping curve imply concerning exchange rate variation?

2 Describe the workings of a world in which everyone produced his own money. What conditions would ensure its efficiency?

3 Do the operations of a fixed exchange rate system rest upon the quantity theory of money?

4 What are the main factors which determine the effectiveness of a floating exchange rate policy?

5 Why do monetary authorities sometimes believe that exchange rate flexibility is preferable to price flexibility?

6 'Balance of payments problems are monetary problems.' 'Balance of payments problems are problems of relative (domestic and foreign) prices.' Comment on the above statements and indicate whether they are reconcilable.

7 Countries have employed gold as an international money. What would be the implications of using bricks as the international standard?

8 Answer the following questions with reference to the table, which shows the number of hours required to produce one unit of goods *A-H*.

	A	B	C	D	E	F	G	H
country 1	50	50	50	50	50	50	50	50
country 2	100	90	80	70	60	50	40	30

(a) Which country has an absolute advantage in the production of which goods? Which country has a relative advantage?

(b) Suppose that in country 1 labour is paid £1 per hour and that in country 2 labour is paid $1 per hour. In addition let £1 exchange for $1. What goods will be traded? Suppose the exchange rate is altered so that £1 exchanges for $3 what goods will be traded? Suppose the exchange rate remains at £1 = $3 but that wages will fall to £0·50 per hour in country 1. What will be the effect on trade? What general conclusions can you deduce concerning the relationships between labour productivities, wage rates and exchange rates and trade?

9 Using the data contained in the import tables of the *Annual Abstract of Statistics*, HMSO, investigate the commodity pattern of UK imports through time. A useful set of divisions for this purpose is (a) food, beverages and tobacco, (b) basic materials, (c) fuels, (d) manufactured goods. Try, as a start, drawing time series for each of these divisions and comparing the results with the time series for the growth of UK demand (row 2 of the statistical appendix to the chapter).

10 A country wishes to encourage the growth of a large capital stock and so the government forces down the interest rate. The country's exchange rate is freely floating. What effects will the change in interest rates have on the exchange rate, income, imports and exports? You need to combine the analysis of several previous chapters to answer this question.

11 What happens to the balance of payments equilibrium line *BB* when, other things being equal (a) foreign interest rate levels rise, (b) the UK price level rises, (c) exchange rates change?

Chapter 37
Aggregate Supply and Inflation

Before we can consider inflation and the causes of inflation we need a working definition of inflation. Such a definition is '*a sustained rise in the general level of prices*', that is, a rise in some average or index of prices. Two things need to be emphasized about this definition. The first is that it defines inflation as a macroeconomic phenomenon and hence in terms of an average of all prices in the economy.[1] A rise in the price of a single commodity or even a group of commodities need not be inflationary if the commodities involved are only a small fraction of total output (or value of output), or if at the same time as they are increasing in price other commodities are falling in price. In the latter case the average of all prices could be constant or even falling. Variations in prices are a normal feature of a free market economy. The second point is that inflation need not be *open* as the definition implies, since inflation can exist without showing itself in changes in quoted prices. Such an inflation is termed *suppressed inflation*. In a situation of suppressed inflation upward pressure on prices is prevented from influencing quoted prices – this, of course, implies a controlled economy. Evidence of inflationary pressure reveals itself in other ways if prices are prevented from rising. Queues and rationing are one sign. Black market prices above quoted prices are another. Depreciation of the country's currency in internal black markets for foreign exchange would also indicate inflationary pressure.

In what follows, however, we will be concerned explicitly with the case of open inflation but the analysis of the mechanics of inflation, and its cure, apply to suppressed inflation as well.

1. To be meaningful the index would have to be a *weighted* average of all prices. Ideally the commodities in the index should also be the same over time, otherwise price changes could reflect quality changes, and not inflation or deflation.

The inflation problem

Why does inflation have a chapter all to itself? Why does it make the news and cause heated debate? Why does it cause governments to fall? What is wrong with inflation? Many books have been written for and against inflation but the short answer to the above questions is that inflation causes waste – the dissipation of scarce economic resources – and increases social conflict. Inflation is largely a problem in political economy. This is best illustrated by answering the question: *under what conditions would inflation not be a bad thing?* Inflation would not be a bad thing if:

1 People on fixed incomes – pensioners, students, etc. – could be compensated for the reduction in real incomes caused by inflation.

2 Freely floating exchange rates prevented balance-of-payments imbalances resulting from falling exports as the prices of export goods rose.

3 Inflation were slow and crawled rather than galloped. Creeping inflation permits anticipation of its effects.

4 The administrative costs of adjusting to inflation were low.

5 Expectations were fully realized and all processes of adjustment to inflation were instantaneous.

The last two reasons are the big giveaway. Even if a conscious attempt was made by society to alleviate *all* of the problems caused by inflation and the attempt was as successful as possible, inflation would still involve some direct hardship because of the time needed to implement offsets to the waste of resources. Society would be using resources purely to offset inflation. However, this by itself is not sufficient to warrant attempts to prevent inflation from starting, or to cure it if it does exist. The cure may be worse than the sickness, in which case effort should be concentrated on finding the best methods of offsetting the worse effects. So great is the dread of inflation in most mature economies that this is not often considered and a cure is always sought.

The causes of inflation

Many books have been written for and against inflation but many times more have been written on the subject of the causes of inflation. We are not so vain as to attempt to give what appears to be the definitive answer to the question, or to suggest that only economists are equipped to answer it, but we will outline what appear to be the basic economic features of all inflationary processes.

At root inflation is caused by an imbalance between demand and supply. Not demand and supply in the sense of a single demand-and-supply imbalance but in the macro sense of total or aggregate demand and supply. And not necessarily effective aggregate demand and supply! For at least in terms of prime causes, inflation may be the result of some group(s) in society trying to increase their share of total income, that is their real effective demands. This situation is a conflict situation in the sense of social conflict but then all inflation is the child of conflict.

An inflationary process resulting from conflict between social groups over their share in national income would soon bring its own cure if the money supply remained constant. One of the parties to the conflict would have to give way as the price level rose and employment fell. Why the caveat about maintaining the supply of money constant? Because inflation is a monetary phenomenon and rising prices can only continue to rise if the money is available to finance purchases at high prices. The basic quantity-theory equation reveals the role of money in inflationary processes:

$$MV_T = P_T T.$$

If the average price of transactions (P_T) is rising then either T is decreasing, or M and/or V_T rising or some combination of all three is occurring. Thus if M is constant and the price level rising V_T and/or T must also be changing. If transactions are falling then sooner or later so must employment and output fall. If the transactions velocity of circulation (V_T) is rising something must be happening to alter the demand for money to hold. Velocity of circulation is the inverse of the demand for money to hold and the demand for money to hold is determined by choice. People will choose to hold less money for a variety of reasons and the strongest is a rise in the opportunity cost of holding money, that is,

Expectations of rising prices (a falling in the value of money);
Rising interest rates; and
An increase in the money yield on other assets.

But if the opportunity cost of holding money continuously increases then there will be a flight from money and a collapse of the monetary exchange system – hyper-inflation. The fact that hyper-inflation coupled with a very low employment is a rare phenomenon, while creeping inflation and the co-existence of mild inflation and high levels of employment are not, leads to the inevitable conclusion that inflation also involves monetary expansion. All the hyper-inflations of which we have knowledge have not just involved monetary expansion but have also involved phenomenal increases in the supply of money.

As an example of inflation resulting from conflict over shares in national income and financed by increases in the supply of money we can look at the consequence of an attempt on the part of unions to increase the share of wages at the expense of profits. (This is often misleadingly referred to as cost-push inflation.) The stages of such an inflationary process are shown in Figure 176. In the diagram money income is measured on both axes, the horizontal axis showing the money value of the total wage bill, and the vertical axis showing the total value of profits. Since the sum of wages plus profits equals the money value of national income, the slope of any ray through the origin will indicate the distribution of the national income between wages and profits.

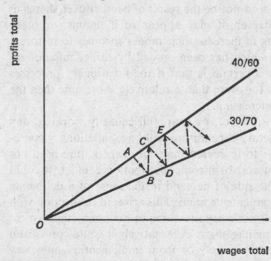

Figure 176

We start by assuming that equilibrium prevails with labour's share at 60 per cent, point A. If the unions then decide to push labour's share to 70 per cent and they are successful this takes the wage share to point B. Initially, the total money value of national income will remain unchanged and what is lost from profits will just equal what is gained by wages and so the line from A to B will have an angle of 45 degrees. Since profits are now reduced, employers will raise prices and precipitate a fall in employment. If, however, the government increases aggregate money demand to maintain the level of employment then the money value of national income will rise and the original division between wages and profits will be restored. This is shown in the move from B to C. At C the real national income is the same as at A but the general level of prices has risen. If unions attempt to re-establish the 70 per cent share then the process will repeat itself. In this model the money supply moves in response to the clash of unions and employers and the solution can only come through (a) a redistribution of income through taxes; (b) allowing unemployment to rise in order to weaken unions; or (c) effective legislation against monopolies of unions and employers. What all these policies do however suggest is that full employment and free collective bargaining may be incompatible with price stability.

Imbalance between aggregate supply and demand and the implied inflationary pressure need not be the result of conflict over shares in national income. However, it may appear so if unions, or other groups, are attempting to increase their money incomes to restore a real income position which has been eroded by earlier inflationary price rises. But what is certain is that if the inflationary processes have been in progress for more than a relatively short time then the money supply is also increasing.

Starting from a position of, or near, full capacity working, any increase in total monetary expenditure will have inflationary consequences. The stimulus to increased monetary expenditure need not come from the side of cost or income-distribution conflict. It could come directly from the side of demand in the sense of a deliberate attempt to increase aggregate demand. This arises in connection with government fiscal and monetary measures to maintain employment and growth—demand management. Alternatively it could come from lax control of the money supply or from implementing monetary expansion at the wrong time. But, as before, whatever the initial cause, continuation of the inflationary process would necessitate continued monetary expansion and involve expansionary wage and income pressure from groups as their real positions worsened. There would be a wage-price spiral. It is a feature of inflationary processes that if they continue for a long enough period the wage-price spiral will exhibit a tendency to accelerate as expectations start to play a role in the process. Once people come to anticipate inflation they will build the expected rate into their economic calculations and demands.

In Figure 177 below we describe an inflationary process which begins with an increase in total monetary demand, perhaps due to the Government trying to increase its real expenditure in advance of tax revenue. The starting point is at A where aggregate demand just equals aggregate supply. The price level is assumed to be constant and full employment to exist.

Aggregate monetary expenditure then increases as is shown by the movement of the aggregate demand curve from D_1 to D_2. If wages and money incomes remained unchanged all that would happen would be a rise in the price level as represented by the equilibrium at B where the money value of real output is higher. But if workers try to restore their real income position and wages increase, the aggregate supply curve will also move upwards. This move is represented by the curve Z_2 which is drawn so as to pass through the

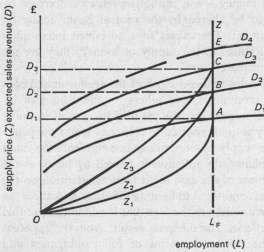

Figure 177

point B, but this does not imply that B is the new point of equilibrium. Why? Because with higher incomes money expenditure will increase and the aggregate demand curve shift to a higher point such as C. The increase in demand D_3–D_2 will be less than the increase D_2–D_1 because of leakages from the expenditure flow and reduced real consumption on the part of those with fixed money incomes.

So while the process will be repeated and wages, incomes and aggregate supply curve rise yet again, to be followed by further increases in aggregate demand, the process will eventually approach a new stable equilibrium position. However, if the initial cause of the spiral continues to operate (in this example, if the government continues to spend in excess of its revenue) then the process is being fuelled by increases in the supply of money and will show no tendency to converge on equilibrium.

Money not the prime mover

Sustained inflationary processes are inseparable from monetary expansion. Because of this many economists call increases in the supply of money the cause of inflation, but this is only a half truth. Money itself cannot be the prime mover; it is the fuel of inflation but not the vehicle. The domestic money supply is based on the cash base – high-powered money – and cannot increase or decrease by itself; rather it has to be altered by the central bank, acting on behalf of the government. The causes of a sustained inflationary process lie behind increases in the supply of money; they are the forces explaining the increase.

Recognition of this helps to dispel much of the argument and confusion generated by economists, and others, in discussions of inflation. Control of the money supply is the obvious way of stopping inflation. Note we say stop and not cure. If money is not the prime mover, control of the supply of money does not eliminate the cause of inflation. This explains why inflation is viewed by many as the major economic problem of the day, for it focuses attention on the fact that governments, committed to fighting inflation, still allow the money supply to increase despite the fact that it will add more fuel to the inflationary process. The dilemma results from the apparent incompatibility of the twin policy aims of full employment and stable prices.

Unemployment was a persistent problem of the nineteenth century and such a calamitous social disaster in the nineteen-twenties and thirties that it dominated economic and political thinking thereafter. Throughout the fifties and sixties it did, however, appear to have been conquered, but only at a price, namely inflation. At first this was regarded as a tolerable nuisance since it took the form of creeping inflation and not runaway inflation. But inflation is cumulative and by the end of the sixties price increases caused resentment. And with that resentment came a greater awareness of the relationship between unemployment and inflation.

Unemployment and inflation

To understand the dilemma of full employment and stable prices we need to understand how unemployment arises and the policies proposed for its solution. At any moment of time there are some unemployed workers. This unemployment arises from changes in demand due to changes in tastes, innovations, seasonal factors and changes in the money supply. Now if all these changes could be anticipated and if all workers could readily change jobs there would be no problems. But labour markets are not so well organized and the adjustment of supply to changes in demand is apt to be delayed.

Consider the reactions of an employer and his labour force to a fall in the demand for the product they produce. The employer will cut back output and in doing so will seek to reduce his labour force. In some cases he may retain his workers on a reduced work-week, but if the fall in demand is severe he will dismiss some workers. The problem is: why does he not offer them a lower rate of pay and thereby cut costs and prices and indirectly stimulate demand? From his point of view wage cuts may not be very useful if wages are only a small part of total costs. Moreover, a reduction in wages may result in a drop in morale. On the workers' side wage cuts may be resisted because it is feared they may be permanent. We do not know the reasons why wages tend to be sticky downwards but it seems to be a well attested fact that though wage contracts tend to be short in duration, attempts by employers to revise them seem to evoke resistance. Workers seem to prefer the risk of unemployment to the possibilities of employment at reduced wages.

For those who are unemployed the search for a job may begin

with the search for a new job at the old rate of pay. Some, of course, may immediately accept lower paid jobs in the hope of getting better paid jobs later; others may hold out for better paid jobs. The length of time spent in searching will be governed by the expected benefits from searching as opposed to the expected costs of searching, and costs will be strongly influenced by personal assets – savings, a wife working, etc.

An implication of the job loss is that income is reduced. The labour market is the market in which a person trades his labour services for money so as to purchase goods. In a barter economy or a smoothly functioning money economy we could ignore the importance of money and regard trade as the exchange of labour services for goods. But disruption forces our attention on the lack of money income. So we should expect consumer spending to fall. In the case of mass unemployment this fall in spending can have serious implications, particularly if, as in the thirties, it is accompanied by a fall in the money supply. Multiplier effects could lead to prolonged and severe recession, although nowadays with monetary-fiscal policies and unemployment benefits the severity of recessions is reduced. To restore full employment we can imagine a government increasing aggregate demand and employers hiring more labour as a consequence. And on the upswing real wages would rise for a variety of reasons, for example:

Morale could improve and productivity rise;
During the recession clusters of innovations could have occurred as a result of competitive pressure;
Idle plant will be re-employed;
There will be less hoarding of labour.

Real and money wages could therefore rise in the early part of the upswing, though we should expect real wages to fall at a later date as the benefits enumerated above begin to evaporate. In the downswing, money wages being stickier than prices and employers being slow to reduce their work forces could lead to real wages rising for a while. But eventually money wages might fall and so real and money wages would move down together. The historical evidence does, in fact, indicate that money and real wages move together through boom and slump.

Monetary injections designed to produce full employment may,

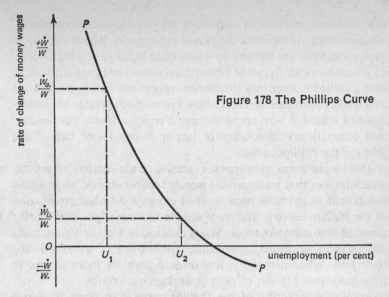

Figure 178 The Phillips Curve

The y-axis is labelled "rate of change of money wages" with markings $+\dfrac{\dot{W}}{W}$, $\dfrac{\dot{W}_a}{W}$, $\dfrac{\dot{W}_b}{W}$, O, and $-\dfrac{\dot{W}}{W}$. The x-axis is labelled "unemployment (per cent)" with points U_1 and U_2. The curve is labelled P at both ends.

however, give rise to inflation. This view is supported by the *Phillips Curve*, which seems to establish a link between the rate of change of money wages and the level of employment.[2]

The Phillips curve is an historical relationship and worked very well for the UK until the end of the 1960s. Figure 178 illustrates the curve as it was originally derived by A. W. Phillips. It shows an inverse relationship between the level of unemployment and the rate of change of money wages. This relationship can be interpreted in terms of excess demand for labour, and hence must assume that as excess demand for labour rises, unemployment falls. This assumption can be rationalized in a number of ways.

If we take a particular market for labour of a given type in a given area (e.g. plumbers in Manchester), there will be either excess demand (no unemployment) or excess supply (no vacancies). As aggregate demand rises in more and more individual (micro) labour markets, more men will be employed (if they were previously un-employed), or new vacancies will occur. When full employment for a particular skill in a particular locality is achieved, excess demand for labour pushes up money wage rates, as firms compete to attract scarce labour. When we aggregate labour markets together we get a Phillips curve. At a very low overall level of unemployment, U_1, a

2. So named after the empirical work done by Phillips (1958).

few unskilled workers in depressed regions may be unemployed, whereas in the prosperous regions some types of labour will be so scarce that firms are bidding up wages quite rapidly. At a higher level of unemployment, U_2, some labour markets will be in equilibrium, so that a skilled worker in a prosperous region can just find a job. At this level of aggregate demand, there will be much greater unemployment of unskilled workers in depressed regions. Hence the regional and occupational immobility of labour is one factor behind the shape of the Phillips curve.

This explanation presupposes passive trade union behaviour, which implies that trade unions merely 'rubber-stamp' wage agreements that would have been reached anyway. Another explanation of the Phillips curve is that trade unions are more 'pushfull' during times of low unemployment. When demand is high or rising, trade unions can force wage agreements, without fear of workers losing their jobs. When demand is low trade unions are more passive in their behaviour for fear of pricing workers out of jobs.

Another explanation of the Phillips curve is in terms of *search unemployment*. It is rarely optimal for an unemployed worker to take the first job offered him. In fact, an unemployed worker will adopt a *search strategy*. This involves balancing the expected benefits and costs (in terms of lost wages) of holding out for a better job, with the costs of accepting a job now, and hence foregoing the chance of better paid employment. This strategy involves the worker having a *reservation wage*: this is the minimum wage at which he would accept a job. He will revise this minimum wage downwards in the light of subsequent experience. Now if aggregate demand rises, money wages rise, and, if all workers do not realize that money wages are rising, on average, unemployed workers searching for jobs will accept a job sooner than they would have done. Consequently all *unanticipated* increases in money wage rates will reduce the number of people searching for jobs.

Obviously there is no single explanation of the Phillips curve, and the three above seem to be the most important elements. All three *suggest* that money wages will rise by more than the rate of productivity increase if unemployment is held below the natural rate $\overline{U}$.

What is meant by the *natural rate of unemployment*? The natural rate of unemployment, which is determined by labour mobility and job information is the rate of unemployment associated with stability of the general price level. It is given a special name because it is such a critical level of unemployment.

The name itself refers to the fact that price stability is regarded by many as a desirable or natural state of affairs, it does not imply that the level of unemployment is desirable or rigidly fixed.

To understand the natural level of unemployment more clearly, and better appreciate the bearing of the Phillips curve on the problem of inflation, it is helpful to translate the curve into one showing the relationship between the level of unemployment (excess demand) and the rate of change of prices. This is possible because wages make up a large fraction of manufacturing costs, so that changes in the general level of prices will closely mirror changes in money wages.

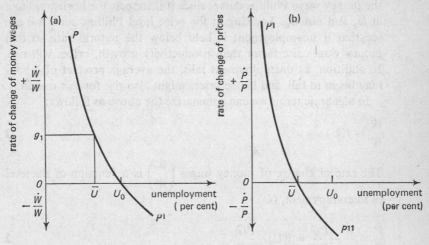

Figure 179 The Phillips Curve. (a) The money wage Phillips curve. (b) The price level Phillips curve

This is done in Figure 179. Part (a) is the same as before and shows the money wage Phillips curve, part (b) shows the alternative relationship, the price level Phillips curve. The difference in the two diagrams, other than the relabelling of the vertical axis in part (b), lies in the point of intersection of the Phillips curve with the horizontal axis. In part (a) the Phillips curve cuts the horizontal axis to the right of $\overline{U}$, the natural level of unemployment. Why? Because in going from changes in money wages to changes in prices it is necessary to allow for the existence of labour productivity growth. If the average rate of labour productivity is rising at say 3 per cent per annum then clearly money wages can rise at this rate without causing prices to rise. That is, stability of the general level of prices is consistent with rising money and real wages as long as the rate of increase in money wages does *not* exceed the average rate of productivity increase.

In part (a) let Og_1 indicate the rate of productivity growth, and hence the rate of change of money wages consistent with price stability. The level of unemployment associated with this rate of change in money wages is thus $\overline{U}$, the natural rate of unemployment, which, as long as productivity growth is positive, must lie to the left of U_O, the unemployment level associated with stable money wage. In part (b) the price level Phillips curve lies further to the left than the money wage Phillips curve, since it intersects the horizontal axis at $\overline{U}$, and not U_O. Looking at the price level Phillips curve we can see that if unemployment is held below the natural rate so that money wages rise faster than productivity growth, prices will rise. In addition, as unemployment falls, the average product of labour may begin to fall, and hence prices might also rise for this reason.

In algebraic terms we can summarize the above as follows:

$$\frac{\dot{W}}{W} = f(U) \tag{1}$$

The rate of change of money wages $\left(\dfrac{\dot{W}}{W}\right)$ is a function of the level of unemployment, (U).

$$\frac{\dot{P}}{P} = \frac{\dot{W}}{W} - \frac{\dot{PG}}{PG} = f(U) - \frac{\dot{PG}}{PG} \tag{2}$$

The rate of change of the general price level $\left(\dfrac{\dot{P}}{P}\right)$ depends upon the relationship between the rate of change of money wages and the rate of change of productivity $\left(\dfrac{\dot{PG}}{PG}\right)$.

When there is no productivity growth, the money wage and the price level Phillips curves are similar in that they will both intersect the horizontal axis at the same unemployment level.

Is this a complete summary of the money wage and price level

Phillips curves? Unfortunately, the answer is no. As already mentioned the Phillips curves worked well in the UK and in other mature economies until the late 1960s; thereafter things changed, and the curve appeared to 'breakdown'. Strictly speaking, a statistical relationship cannot 'breakdown', but it can cease to hold in the sense that it no longer accurately predicts the relationship in question. This is what has happened with the Phillips curve since the late 1960s, as the rates of change of money wages and prices associated with a particular level of unemployment have, at first gradually and then more rapidly, increased. In terms of the diagram, the points that make up the Phillips curve have moved to the right away from the original curve, and with this move has come the new economic phenomenon known as *stagflation*.

The explanation for this 'breakdown' lies in expectations. Consider a trade union, negotiating for higher wages. Let us suppose that if prices are expected to stay the same, the union feels that it can squeeze y per cent out of employers, without jeopardizing the jobs of many of its workers (i.e. by pricing the product out of the market). Now let the union believe that all prices are going to rise by x per cent, it will now feel that it can squeeze $x+y$ per cent out of the employers, before it begins to put the jobs of its workers at risk. Likewise, consider a worker searching for a job. If he expects wages in general to rise by x per cent, the expected rate of inflation, he is much less likely to accept a job at a given money wage, than if he expected prices to remain constant. Finally, suppose that firms expect all prices to rise x per cent. Then a firm wishing to attract workers will expect that it will have to offer wages x per cent higher than it would have done. Since in aggregate prices and money wages rise together, we can conclude that the Phillips curve will shift bodily upwards, if the expected rate of inflation rises.

That is, the original Phillips curve relationship, summarized by equation **1** above, is an incomplete specification of the true wage/ price unemployment relationship in that it fails to take account of the role of price expectations. It worked well for so long because the time periods for which it was derived were not periods of accelerating inflation, and hence price expectations were unimportant. But once inflation began to accelerate, as it did in the late 1960s, the original relationship ceased to hold. More precisely, the original relationship assumes that workers suffer from *money illusion*; that in wage negotiations they are only interested in the level of money wages and not in the real value of wages. This is pure nonsense as recent experience all too clearly demonstrates. Once inflation starts to accelerate and workers discover that increased money wages do not lead to increased real wages, they will begin to rectify matters by incorporating the expected rate of inflation into their money wage demands. As indicated above, unions and firms respond rationally to inflation.

In algebraic terms, the correct Phillips curve specification is:

$$\frac{\dot{W}}{W} = f(U) + \alpha\left(\frac{\dot{P}}{P}\right)^e, \text{ and } \frac{\dot{P}}{P} = f(U) + \alpha\left(\frac{\dot{P}}{P}\right)^e - \frac{P\dot{G}}{PG} \qquad 3$$

where $\left(\frac{\dot{P}}{P}\right)^e$ stands for the expected rate of inflation, and α is the coefficient of adjustment linking changes in money wages to the expected rate of inflation. If workers do not suffer from money illusions, and can fully adjust their money wages for the expected rate of inflation, α will be unity. In practice α is likely to be less than unity for a number of reasons. One of the most important of these is that starting from price stability, or even creeping inflation, it will take time for workers to adjust their expectations of inflation to the actual rate, as the actual rate continually accelerates.

What determines the expected rate of inflation? The obvious answer is previous inflation. We can now construct a scenario. Consider the curve E^O in Figure 180. Let wages be increasing at the same rate as productivity Og_1, hence prices would be constant. People would not expect inflation and the Phillips curve would stay constant at E^O. Now suppose that the government regards $\overline{U}$ as an unacceptably high level of unemployment, and by monetary and fiscal stimulus, succeeds in reducing unemployment to U_1. The proportionate rate of wage increase is now OB, hence prices increase by g_1B. The Phillips curve will now shift upwards, by an amount depending on how quickly people incorporate the experience of price inflation into their expectations, $(O < \alpha < 1)$. Suppose this gives the Phillips curve E^1 in the next period. If the government persists in maintaining unemployment at U_1, *validates* the rate of inflation by monetary expansion, wages would increase by OC in the following periods which would give price inflation of g_1C, and as people reacted to this, the Phillips curve would shift upwards even further.

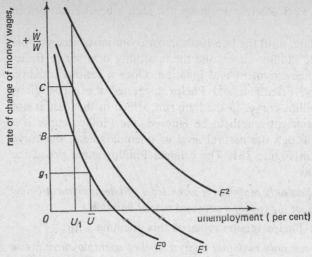

Figure 180 Price expectations and the 'breakdown' of the Phillips curve

The rate at which it will shift up will, again, depend on how rapidly expectations adjust.

If the government now becomes alarmed at the rate of inflation, it must allow the level of unemployment to rise. But as well as moving down a short run Phillips curve like E^2, it must bring the Phillips curve itself down. To achieve this it must reduce inflationary expectations and this can only be done by an actual rate of price increase of less than the expected rate. This would involve a level of unemployment in excess of $\overline{U}$, in Figure 181. Worse still, the deceleration of inflation implies a period of rising unemployment while price expectations are revised downwards. Only as inflationary expectations fall towards zero, and the Phillips curve shifts down towards E^0, can the government reflate demand slightly to allow the level of unemployment to fall to $\overline{U}$. Thus we see the tragedy of attempts by the government to use the Phillips curve to trade-off unemployment against inflation. The initial success of such a policy in bringing about less unemployment for only a little more inflation, rapidly evaporates and ultimately results in *both* higher unemployment and accelerating inflation. What makes this tragedy worse is that it could have been avoided, since some economists, notably Milton

Friedman and E. S. Phelps, predicted just such a breakdown before the event.

To recapitulate, until the late 1960s, most economists accepted the idea of a stable Phillips curve, and the feasibility of a stable trade-off between unemployment and inflation. Once a serious inflation got under way, Friedman and Phelps suggested the expectations augmented Phillips curve. In the long run, which in this case is not a period of sufficient length to be ignored, the Phillips curve is a vertical line through the natural level of unemployment, the curve labelled *PLR* in Figure 181. The original Phillips curve posed the policy dilemma:

A government can only maintain a given level of unemployment below the natural rate, at the cost of a constant rate of inflation.

The Friedman–Phelps version replaced this dilemma with:

A government can only maintain a given level of unemployment below the natural rate at the cost of a constantly accelerating rate of inflation.

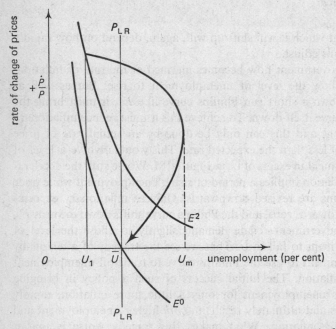

Figure 181 The reversal of price expectations and the level of unemployment

The only remaining question is: if the Phillips curve process is so unstable, why did it only explode after 1965? (See Table 54a, in which column 1 shows the actual rate of wage inflation and column 2 the rate predicted on the basis of a stable Phillips curve; and the data in Table 54b, which illustrates the emergence of stagflation.)

As far as the United States is concerned, the level of unemployment rarely fell below the natural level for long enough for expectations of inflation to take hold. The apparent breakdown in the Phillips curve appeared after 1965, when the US government resorted to the printing press as a means of financing its unpopular involvement in Vietnam and as a means of reducing domestic unemployment and poverty. The result was that excess monetary demand spilled over into foreign markets. Because most countries were on a fixed exchange rate system the spill-over of demand did not result in a fall in the foreign value of the dollar and a rise in the value of other currencies. Instead there was a rise in the general level of world prices. When all countries are on a fixed exchange rate system it is as if they were all regions of one country. The effect of the American inflation was subsequently aggravated in the UK by an expansion of the public sector and a freeing of credit markets, both of which were financed by an increase in the domestic money supply. Later, in 1973 and 1974, there was a sharp rise in world commodity prices – especially oil and wheat – which led to a redistribution of world income to certain primary producers and which many manufacturing countries attempted to avoid by still further depreciating their currencies.

Incomes policies

Eliminating inflation depends upon changing people's attitudes and their demands. One method is to increase unemployment but that may be socially unacceptable. A second method could be to introduce an incomes policy designed to control the rate of change of wages and prices. The little evidence we have (Table 55) does not suggest that incomes policies are successful in controlling wages and they may in fact distort the allocation of resources. But if the consensus favours an incomes policy then it will take precedence over any other policy.

It would be a miracle if an incomes policy were successful in curing inflation. When inflation results from the government seeking to set

Table 54a Actual and predicted money wage inflation rates (%), UK 1961–71

Year	1	2
1961	4·14	4·58
1962	4·28	3·03
1963	4·89	2·11
1964	5·22	3·85
1965	7·95	5·14
1966	3·20	4·58
1967	7·87	2·11
1968	5·30	1·82
1969	7·35	1·82
1970	13·69	1·65
1971	11·93	0·93

Source: Saunders (1973)

Table 54b

Year	Index of retail prices 1963 = 100	UK registered unemployed (monthly averages) thousands
1960	91·1	393·0
1961	94·1	377·0
1962	98·0	500·0
1963	100·0	612·0
1964	103·2	413·0
1965	108·1	359·9
1966	112·4	390·9
1967	115·2	558·8
1968	120·6	586·0
1969	127·2	580·9
1970	135·3	618·0
1971	148·0	792·1
1972	158·5	875·7
1973	173·1	618·8
1974	200·8	614·9
1975	249·5	977·6
1976		

Source: *Annual Abstract of Statistics*, various dates

too low a level of unemployment, and hence involves a race between monetary expansion and price expectations, economic forces will rapidly make a mockery of any attempt to control wages and prices by decree. An incomes policy has about the same chance of success as King Canute. But though an incomes policy cannot work if it is asked to do the impossible, it may still have its uses.

In the previous section we explained how the process of deflation required to reverse price expectations would involve, for a time, rising unemployment. Control of the money supply is a cure for inflation but it has its price. This is where there may be a role for a prices and incomes policy. It may be possible to speed up, and lessen the cost (in terms of unemployment), of a deflationary policy designed to eliminate inflation, if a prices and incomes policy is introduced at the same time as the deflationary measures. To the extent that the prices and incomes policy causes people to revise price expectations downwards more rapidly than they otherwise would, it increases the effectiveness of the deflationary measures. It must be stressed, however, that it is the combination of a prices and incomes policy with a deflationary package, rather than the prices and incomes policy as such, which provides the cure for inflation.

But in order to produce an efficient incomes policy the following issues would have to be resolved:

1 How can workers in each industry be prevented from capturing the whole of the productivity gains in their industry? If workers in industry A get a 10 per cent wage increase based on productivity and workers in B get 2 per cent, then if workers in A spend all their increased incomes on B goods this will drive up the price of B goods and cause wages in B to rise. Thus, overall wages would rise by more than the average increase in productivity.

2 Point 1 raises the question: what are the sources of productivity advance?

3 What should happen to profits? How should they be measured?

4 What part should taxes play in the incomes policy? In the UK income tax has served to reduce disposable income but because of its lack of progression it has increased income inequality. Low-paid workers have paid tax at the same rates as high-paid workers as inflation has driven all wages on to the higher tax rates.

Unemployment and Inflation 653

Table 55 Effects of incomes policies on the rate of wage inflation

Author	Data period	Dependent variable	Average annual impact of policies percentage points[1]
Brechling	1948–65	weekly rates	−1·8
Smith	1948–67	weekly rates	−1·1
		hourly rates	−0·3
Lipsey/Parkin	1948–67	weekly rates	−0·8
Parkin	1948–69	weekly rates	+0·01
Hines	1949–69	hourly rates	−0·2

1. Column 4 shows the actual change in wages in periods of incomes policy minus 'predicted' change on the basis of policy-off experience
Compiled by: Sumner (1973)

5 Can an incomes policy work without monetary policy?

6 What kind of exchange-rate policy does an incomes policy require?

Manpower policies

One point that does emerge out of the Phillips curve analysis is that reducing the level of unemployment may require supply-orientated policies, that is, policies designed to increase the mobility of labour by travel and training grants. This is important in the UK because unemployment tends to be uneven in its incidence. Policies which increase the overall level of demand merely create excess demand in London and the south-east. And in similar fashion policies designed to increase demand in the depressed regions merely cause their inhabitants to demand more goods (cars, washing-machines, etc.) from the regions of full employment.

Summary

An understanding of inflation must begin from an understanding of the supply and demand basis of all inflation and the role of the money supply in fuelling the inflationary process. An understanding of inflation must also begin from an appreciation of unemployment.

Appendix: inflation as a source of government revenue

'A government can live for a long time . . . by printing paper money. That is to say, it can by this means secure the command over real resources, resources just as real as those obtained by taxation. The method is condemned, but its efficiency, up to a point, must be admitted. A government can live by this means when it can live by no other. It is the form of taxation which the public finds hardest to evade and even the weakest government can enforce, when it can enforce nothing else.'

J. M. Keynes, *A Tract on Monetary Reform*
(Keynes 1923).

In the preceding chapter we argued that inflation was the 'child of conflict'. In particular, we emphasized two kinds of conflict as causes of inflation; conflict between groups in society over their shares in national income – the distribution of the national cake problem – and conflict at the level of macroeconomic policy between the goals of full employment and price stability. In this appendix we consider another, and no less important, source of conflict which can result in inflation, that between the public sector and the private sector of the economy. It may be thought that this is merely another instance of conflict involving the distribution of the national cake, in many ways it is, but because it involves the state directly and because the government, and the government alone, controls the printing presses, it has special features which justify a separate treatment.

The important issues involved in financing the state are discussed in detail in a subsequent chapter (Chapter 41). At this stage it is sufficient to note that the state has many legitimate economic functions to perform, and when a government is elected to office the electorate sanction its powers to raise revenue to finance its activities. If we ignore direct confiscation of resources, the state can raise revenue by loan finance (borrowing), taxation and the printing press. Democratically elected governments are only supposed to raise revenue by the first two of these methods, and the amount they can raise is, in principle at least, determined by the public. In the case of loan finance, by the amount the public is prepared to lend to the state, which depends upon the rate of interest the state is prepared to pay, and in the case of taxation, by the mandate the electorate grant to a government when it is elected. The 'voluntary' nature of these two methods of financing explains why the state may resort to the third method, use of the printing press or inflationary finance. An unfortunate attribute of this method is that it allows the state to 'tax' the public without approval of the revenue it raises.

Throughout recorded history, there are instances of states resorting to inflationary finance as a means of financing politically unpopular activities. This raises the question: Why, in view of all too well known dire consequences of inflation and inflationary financing, do governments still resort to it? The short answer is because, at least in its early stages, it appears to allow the state to gain something for nothing. The state can speed up the printing presses to gain command over additional resources while simultaneously, and vehemently, claiming that it disapproves of the resultant inflation and attributing blame for it elsewhere. Resort to inflationary finance may be the ultimate form of betrayal of the electorate by democratically elected government and, as noted by Lenin, if carried to excess the most effective way of destroying capitalism.

In mature economies, inflationary finance channels additional resources to the state in two ways. The first of these works through the system of direct taxation. In economies with progressive income tax systems, inflation increases government tax revenue, without the need for legislation, because as money incomes rise people move into higher tax brackets, and hence the yield from taxation rises more rapidly than incomes. This phenomenon is referred to as *fiscal drag*.

The second way which, in terms of the revenue it yields, is probably the more important, relies on the fact that inflation is a 'tax' on the holding of money. To explain this we need to refer to Figure 182.

Let M_D be the demand curve for real money balances, and in the absence of inflation, $\left(\dfrac{M}{P}\right)_1$ the quantity of real money balances held at interest rate r_1. Now suppose the government decides to raise additional revenue through inflation, and increases the supply of money at a rate which causes the price level to rise by $r_1 r_2$ per cent per annum. The amount of 'tax' revenue the government obtains by this means will depend upon whether or not the inflation is unanticipated or fully anticipated. In the latter case, r_1 will be the real rate of interest and r_2 the money rate of interest.

Consider first the case of a fully anticipated inflation. Suppose the

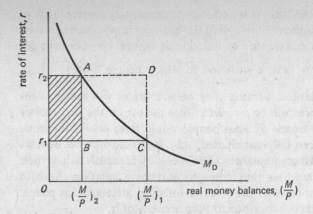

Figure 182 The demand for money and the welfare cost of inflationary finance

government announces that it is going to expand the money supply and that the price level will rise by $r_1 r_2$ per cent per annum if people act on the basis of this announcement. Then in this case, admittedly exceptional, people will try to minimize the incidence of the inflation tax by reducing their demand for real money balances to $\left(\dfrac{M}{P}\right)_2$. This is the level at which the higher opportunity cost of holding money just equals the marginal valuation of the benefits of the smaller quantity of real money balances. The amount of revenue the government obtains from this tax is then equivalent to the annual decrease in the real value of money holdings; that is the rectangle $r_1 r_2$ AB, which is the *tax base*, the amount of real balances held $\left(\dfrac{M}{P}\right)_2$, times the rate of tax $r_1 r_2$. The welfare cost of this form of taxation is similar to the *excess burden* of indirect taxation (see Chapter 41), and is represented by the area under the demand curve, $\left(\dfrac{M}{P}\right)_2 AC \left(\dfrac{M}{P}\right)_1$. It is the loss in welfare which individuals incur by making do with a smaller quantity of real money balances. It corresponds to the leisure forgone and additional real resources used by individuals as they seek ways to economize on the use of money.

If inflation is unanticipated the 'tax' yield is greater because the base on which the 'tax' is levied is correspondingly greater. This in turn implies that the welfare cost of the tax is correspondingly greater. If we assume the same rate of inflation as before, $r_1 r_2$ per cent per annum, but now have a situation in which people hold $\left(\dfrac{M}{P} \right)_1$ of real money balances, because they believe prices will remain constant, the tax yield will be $r_1 r_2 \, DC$. Since the tax on the real money balance held in excess of what people would have held if the same inflation had been fully anticipated, $ABCD$, exceeds the net benefits of the extra real money balances, ABC, people will rapidly reduce their real money balance as they come to anticipate inflation. As with wages, we again see that the costs of inflation are such that people rapidly adjust their behaviour to take account of it.

Whether anticipated or unanticipated this form of taxation contains the seeds of its own destruction. If it continues people will adjust to it and attempt to minimize their tax liability by reducing the base on which it operates, namely real money balances. As individuals reduce their real money holdings, the state, to maintain its revenue from this source, must continually increase the tax rate, the rate of inflation, by printing even more money. But the higher the rate of inflation the less money people hold and so the process accelerates. At the limit of severe hyper-inflation the public cry 'enough' and as money is abandoned altogether inflation ceases to be a source of government revenue. Usually, however, the political and economic consequences of hyper-inflation are such as to force governments to abandon inflationary finance before this stage is reached.

To conclude, inflation is a means whereby the state can raise revenue, but one which should be avoided if at all possible. Where it cannot be avoided, such as in some developing countries where, due to limited institutional arrangements and lack of suitable personnel, other forms of taxation cannot be fully utilized, it should be used with extreme caution. In such circumstances, if the rate of inflation can be kept fairly low, inflationary finance may not only be the sole way of raising additional revenues, it may even be the most efficient way. The problem with it, however, is that its very success may encourage abuse and lead to inefficiency.

Questions

1 How would you explain the existence of unemployment?

2 How would you expect real and money wages to move through boom and slump?

3 Outline a monetary theory of inflation.

4 What is the Phillips curve?

5 Consider the proposition that inflation constitutes a tax on money balances.

6 The conflict model of inflation suggests that inflation is explosive. Is it?

7 What is the case for an incomes policy?

8 In Transylvania there is a group of industries whose annual rate of productivity is less than 10 per cent and a group whose advance is greater than 10 per cent. What policies for wages, employment and prices would you recommend? (Hint: read Chapter 36 on fixed exchange rates.)

9 What is the natural rate of unemployment?

10 What policies should the government use to permanently reduce the natural level of unemployment?

11 How do price expectations affect:
(a) the rate of change of money wages;
(b) the rate of change of prices?

12 How can governments be prevented from causing inflation?

Chapter 38
Government Expenditure and Control of Aggregate Demand

The spending decisions of governments are really quite different from those of consumers or firms, affecting, as they do, the whole environment within which people live. In democracies we see the role of government as satisfying the aims and expectations of at least a majority of the electorate. The view is that governments are responsible both for the general level of economic activity (the maintenance of full employment) and for the efficient use of all the resources.

The first of these responsibilities – the level of employment – is seen to be a matter for government policy because of a belief (based on certain theoretical models of how economies work) that full and stable employment of resources will not automatically come about through the natural working of the economy. This is because interest rates may not be able to fall to a level low enough to stimulate an adequate level of investment; and because wages and prices are not sufficiently flexible. The complete theoretical explanation of why economies are not self-adjusting is complex, but central to the explanation are these factors of interest rate, wages and price flexibility.

The second government responsibility – for the efficient use of resources in maximizing community welfare at any given level of overall employment – rests largely on the existence of the externalities, spillovers. Thus, purely private markets tend to produce too little education, health care, old age pensions, social security provisions, national defence and so on. Conversely, they tend to over-produce pollution, violence, exploitation and inequality. Government action is necessary to increase the production of privately produced goods which are underproduced, and control, reduce or suppress those which are overproduced.

Government responsibility for ensuring the absence of under-production does not necessarily imply that the government must actually be the producer. It does not necessarily follow that health, education, roads and other services are produced by the state. The state may be able to ensure a proper level of provision by providing an appropriate legal framework or by financing the provision but not actually organizing the production. Whether the provision is private or public depends partly on the relative efficiency of state and private production and partly on the tastes and traditions of the community. Thus in the USA production of roads, education and medical care are much more in private hands than in the UK. But not all is provided by the state in the UK; for example, the state feels it proper that motorists should have a certain minimum insurance cover – this cover is a legal requirement, but the provision is through private insurance companies.

Just as there are alternatives as to who produces, state or private industry, there are alternative methods of financing. Expenditure may be financed by taxes, by borrowing, by printing money or by making charges. There are problems that will be taken up again in the chapters 'The Role of the State' and 'Financing the State'. The major policy aims of most economies are those set out below.

Full employment;
Efficient use of resources;
Economic growth;
Stable prices;
An equitable distribution of income;
A stable exchange rate – the rate of exchange between sterling and other currencies.

The exact meaning to be put on each of these aims is open to considerable variation – what is an equitable distribution of income, what is economic growth? A further difficulty is that the priority attached to each of the aims may vary from one elector to another and from one political party to another. The matter of priorities arises because theoretical consideration and our experience suggest that all the aims cannot be achieved simultaneously – the six aims are to some extent incompatible. It may be possible, however, to fail simultaneously to achieve any of the aims, as the UK has discovered several times!

Even when aims and the priority ordering are agreed there may still be a need to choose between the several policies which will lead to each aim being achieved. Rarely is there only one possible method (policy) of achieving a particular aim. Changes of government often result in economic-policy changes because the party newly in power orders the aims differently and chooses different policies to achieve particular aims.

It is noticeable that these major policy headings are intimately bound up with the level and rate of growth of overall demand. The connection with full employment is clear; growth may require and allow a rising level of demand; and the level of prices is influenced by the level and growth of demand as is the distribution of income and the balance of payments.

In the next section of this chapter we are going to look in some detail at the state's role and difficulties in managing the overall level of demand and only then go on to look at the government's spending pattern within the total – the spending pattern within the total reflecting the state's efforts to meet policy aims other than the overall level of demand.

Fiscal policy: short run

Historically, public opinion took the view that governments should, like private households and firms, balance their books. Such a point of view has much to commend itself. It meant that governments must present their spending programmes to the electorate for approval and financing. It limited expenditure to what could be raised through taxes and it was a safeguard against profligate spending, excessive concentration of power in the hands of governments and debasement of the currency. And when allied to Gladstone's dictum that, 'money should be left to fructify in the hands of the public', it asserted that it was the private market sector that was the main provider of goods and services.

Unfortunately, the balanced budget doctrine implied that governments should remain passive whenever there were slumps. As spending fell, taxes would fall and so government spending would fall. Thus, governments added to, and probably intensified through the workings of the multiplier, downswings and upswings of economic activity. Although this passive stance was criticized, and often ignored as a result of manipulation of the accounts, it was largely accepted in the nineteenth century. And, when, in the twenties and thirties, Keynes and others advocated deficit spending it was contrary to what came to be known as the '*Treasury view*'. Briefly, the Treasury view stated that every pound spent by the government would result in a reduction by one pound of private spending. The reasoning behind this thesis was that both the government and the private sector were competing for resources and, therefore, what one got the other lost. It seems strange to believe that some people could put forward such an idea when there was mass unemployment, though it may have contained a grain of truth if only skilled labour was considered. But as a result of Keynes's questioning of political orthodoxy, the doctrine that the budget should always balance was discarded. We shall, therefore, now consider the alternative methods of stabilizing an economy by varying government expenditures.

Alternative methods of stabilizing an economy

1 *Balancing the budget*

At first sight, and given our previous discussion, it might seem paradoxical that by balancing its budget a government can stabilize an economy, can inject spending so as to eliminate unemployment, or withdraw spending so as to curb inflation. But government spending and taxing are not offsetting activities. When a government spends it spends all its income. Whereas private households, as we have seen, do not spend all their income. Thus, if a government taxes a man's income by £1 the government receives £1 and the man loses £1. The government spends £1 whereas the average man would have spent, say £0·785 and saved £0·215 (see Chapter 33). The income transfer results in an increase in aggregate money demand from £0·785 to £1 following from which are multiplier effects. Algebraically, this can be expressed as below, where $C = 0·785$, the marginal propensity to consume.

government spending and generated private spending	$£1+C+C^2+C^3+ \ldots$
reduction in private spending as a result of taxation	$-C-C^2-C^3- \ldots$
net effect	$£1+0+0+0+ \ldots$

Thus a rise in government spending of £1 financed by a tax of £1 will always raise total demand by £1.

2 Government spending with a deficit

Instead of financing increased expenditure by raising taxes a government could borrow or print money. The relative merits of these two methods of finance will be considered in Chapter 42 since they constitute (along with taxation) methods of financing government expenditure in general, rather than varying such expenditure in order to promote economic stability. But we can, in the meantime, note two things. First, borrowing may be simply deferred taxation since interest payments have to be met. Secondly, printing money may be an extremely efficient method of injecting extra demand into an economy in a slump because it costs so little to produce and involves little administrative costs in its disposal.

3 A deficit without spending

Instead of increasing its spending, a government may hold it constant and allow private spending to increase by *reducing taxes*, thus meaning that the fall in tax income must be compensated for by an increase in borrowing or printing money.

An important distinction can, however, be drawn between raising private spending and raising government spending. Because government spends all its income a given increase in aggregate demand will require a larger budget deficit if it is accomplished by cutting taxes rather than by raising spending. This does not, however, mean that government spending should always be preferred to private spending since that would be to assume that households always preferred collective to private goods. Suppose, as in Figure 183, that the economy is at U inside the frontier of its production possibilities. Fiscal policy could move the economy to either E or P. A movement to E – either by a balanced budget increase or spending with a deficit – would imply an increase in the proportion of publicly produced goods relative to private goods. Alternatively, a move to P – a decrease in taxation would increase the proportion of private goods. Which path is chosen could depend upon the community's preferences for private and collective goods. Although unemploy-

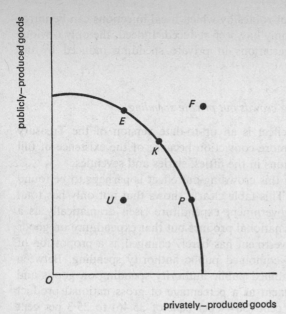

Figure 183

ment is a social evil a public works programme of digging holes may not be an efficient solution.

Controversial issues

Having outlined alternative short run methods of stabilizing an economy, we can now consider some of the objections to the use of fiscal policy.

Fiscal policy is inflexible

When fiscal methods of stabilization were first proposed the size of the public sector was small. Hence it seemed plausible to assume that public works programmes, such as roads, could be easily turned on and off. But as the size of the public sector has increased and its composition changed, it has become questionable whether public sector spending has a high degree of flexibility. It is not easy, for example, to turn on and off school building programmes. What this has meant is that the number of routes by which fiscal injections can be introduced into an economy has been reduced. Indeed, the only obvious route is through variations in private spending induced by tax changes.

Government spending crowds out private spending

The crowding-out effect is an up-to-date version of the Treasury view but it carries more conviction because of the existence of full employment conditions in the fifties, sixties and seventies.

Some evidence of this crowding-out effect is perhaps to be found in Table 56 below. This table clearly shows that not only has total central and local government expenditure risen dramatically as a proportion of gross national product but that expenditure on goods and services and investment has barely changed as a proportion of that rising total of combined public authority spending. Between 1961 and 1974 combined public authority spending on goods and services and investment as a percentage of gross national product rose from 20·0 per cent (56·44 per cent of 35·46) to 25·3 per cent (53·81 per cent of 47·13 per cent). These figures do not even include investment spending by public corporations.

Fiscal policy cannot be divorced from monetary policy

After the end of the Second World War a sharp controversy arose as to the relative efficiencies of monetary and fiscal policies. It was alleged by the Keynesians that in a slump, monetary policy was ineffective because of the possible existence of a liquidity trap. If the government attempted to put money into the economy by buying bonds it would bid up the prices of bonds and depress interest rates. But if a liquidity trap existed then interest rates would not fall below a certain level. Doubts, however, have been cast by the monetarists on the existence of a liquidity trap. Furthermore, the sharp distinction drawn between fiscal and monetary policies often led to a tendency to pursue conflicting policies. Fiscal policy was used to control aggregate demand in inflationary conditions whilst the money supply was left uncontrolled.

Table 56 Public expenditure

	1	2	3	4	5	6
	Combined public authority spending as a percentage of GNP$_{MP}$[1][2]	Percentage of combined public authority spending financed by borrowing and printing money[3]	Percentage of total P.A. spending formed by			
			Expenditure on goods and services and capital equipment	Subsidies, grants and transfers	Net lending to the private sector	Debt interest
1975						
1974	47·13	14·47	53·81	31·54	6·08	8·56
1973	41·83	12·22	55·48	30·42	5·25	8·86
1972	41·93	5·72	55·26	30·30	5·72	8·72
1971	40·85	6·27	55·51	29·28	6·27	8·94
1970	40·62	−0·74	55·45	29·77	5·07	9·71
1969	40·76	−1·54	54·36	30·45	5·08	10·11
1968	42·07	7·11	54·00	29·70	6·55	9·75
1967	41·37	11·21	55·25	27·47	7·90	9·38
1966	37·86	6·58	56·96	25·92	7·05	10·08
1965	37·09	8·80	56·44	26·38	7·09	10·08
1964	35·87	8·25	57·45	25·56	6·55	10·44
1963	35·80	7·17	57·19	26·81	5·11	10·89
1962	36·01	5·16	57·19	26·10	6·01	10·70
1961	35·46	7·49	56·44	25·65	6·60	11·31

1. All the figures in this table exclude public corporations GDFC.

2. Spending on goods and services, *plus* capital investment, *plus* subsidies, grants and transfers, excluding such payments between central and local authorities, *plus* debt interest paid, excluding such payments between local and central authorities, *plus* net public authority lending to the private sector.

3. Percentage of spending, as defined in column 1, financed by borrowing and printing money.

Source: *National Income and Expenditure, 1964–74*, HMSO.

Discretionary fiscal policy has been destabilizing

Over the last two decades it has been suggested that far from government fiscal policy stabilizing the economy it has made it even more unstable; booms and slumps have been exaggerated. This argument is based on the following assumptions.

1 The prediction of future levels of activity in the economy is at best a very imprecise art and at worst is little better than guessing.

2 Whilst we are fairly certain that we know the type of effect that a policy change will have on the level of economic activity we are very unsure about the exact *magnitudes* of the effect *ex ante*.

3 Policy changes take time to have effect and there may be a delay of months or even years before the effect of a policy change is apparent – you will remember that the multiplier effect goes through many stages before it is fully worked out.

These are the unavoidable handicaps which government suffers in its efforts to control the level of aggregate demand and activity. What is the nature of the problem facing government? As a result of the existence of lags in adjustment processes in various markets the level of activity in the economy fluctuates through time as in Figure 184. The solid line in the figure represents the course that the economy would take if governments did not intervene.

Governments see their objective as controlling the level of activity with a view to avoiding the periods of low activity and high unemployment such as *A*, *B* and *C* and the periods of 'overheating' and inflation such as *D*. When the economy is at time T_0 in Figure 184 forecasters begin to predict that soon the economy will begin to 'overheat' and that to avoid this the government must introduce policies to cut back aggregate spending. The government introduces policies to cut spending and when the rate of growth slows they congratulate themselves on their success. What they don't know is whether the slowing is a result of the policies or the natural course of the economy. When the policies really begin to act about time T_1 the effect is simply to accelerate the rate of decline that would have occurred so that the economy follows path *EF*. Even when the government realizes what is happening they can do little as they cannot arrest the working out of their initial policies and it takes time before new policies start to act. The consequence is that the economy de-

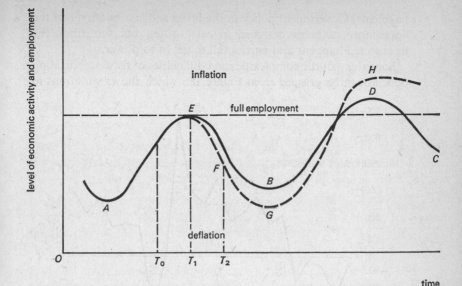

Figure 184

clines to G before the policies introduced at time T_2 act sufficiently strongly to arrest the decline. At G the government worries that the policies introduced at F to raise demand have not worked and because they do not correctly foresee the natural rise in the level of activity they introduce further reflationary measures causing the economy to follow path GH. Again the combination of ignorance, and the time lags in policy working and being perceived to work, result in a rise of activity above D to H. The effect of the two forms of ignorance and the lag in policy acting has been to accentuate the natural fluctuations and not to reduce them as was intended.

In the argument set out above we have assumed that governments know what to do but, through unavoidable ignorance, do it at the wrong time. Such governments might be described as idealistic. However, it is possible to argue that many governments are opportunistic; that is, political parties assume that the electorate has a short memory and that it is possible to obtain votes by pursuing popular policies for a short while. Thus, before an election, a government may boost its spending to create more jobs or cut taxes to boost private spending. After winning the election, it must cut spending to check inflation and the deterioration in the balance of

Controversial Issues 669

payments. Government policy in the fifties and sixties often had the appearance of being designed to catch votes, but sometimes the unexpected happens and parties fail to get in to power.

Something of the complexities and difficulties of fiscal stabilization policies can be grasped from Figure 185 which shows variations in

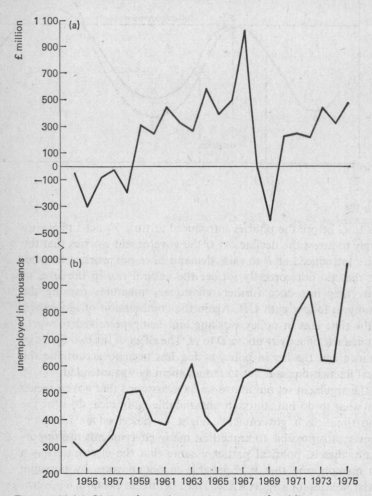

Figure 185 (a) Change from the previous year of public authorities expenditure on goods and services plus *GDFCF plus* public corporations *GDFCF*. (b) UK registered unemployed monthly averages

unemployment and variations in public authority and public corporation spending. What is noticeable is that some periods of rising or high unemployment, e.g. 1955–8 and 1968–70 coincided with unusually low increases in government expenditure and the *low* unemployment levels of 1960–61 and 1964–6 coincided with particularly high increases in government expenditure. Although the pattern of variation is far from perfect it does suggest that government spending may have contributed to, rather than prevented, some of the fluctuations in employment: before that conclusion can be reached, however, it would be necessary to examine what was happening to the components of private spending. Did governments reduce taxes rather than increase their spending in periods of high unemployment? Were governments relying on the power of automatic stabilizers? What effects did government repayment of loans – particularly to foreigners, since that might constitute a leakage – have on unemployment? We leave the reader to answer these questions, using the data at the end of this and other chapters.

Demand management in an open economy

Demand management is particularly difficult in open economies subject to changes in the rest of the world. In the case of the UK which exports approximately 30 per cent of its gross domestic product this is particularly true. If UK export fell by 10 per cent due to a world recession this is equivalent to a fall in the UK demand levels of 3 per cent which when magnified by an unmodified multiplier could, in turn, lead to a major UK recession. Similarly, the sudden, and big, increase in mineral oil prices in 1973 caused a severe shock to the domestic economies of the oil importing nations.

Non-discretionary behaviour and automatic stabilizers

Instability and political abuse can be reduced if non-discretionary fiscal policies are pursued. In other words, if instead of varying taxes in an attempt to steer the economy, certain *automatic stabilizers* were to come into operation then many of the problems we have so far considered would, it is alleged, disappear.

What is an automatic stabilizer? It is a corrective measure which automatically comes into operation whenever there is a change in the environment and thus it serves to reduce the impact of changes in the environment. It is rather like the thermostat on a central-heating system which when there is a fall in room temperature signals that it is necessary to increase the heating to maintain the room temperature at an even level. Examples of automatic stabilizers are the income tax and unemployment pay. The effect of income tax is most easily shown by a numerical example. Let us say that income tax is 30p in the pound. A man earning £10 pays £3 income tax. If his income rises by £1 his disposable income rises by only 70p as 30p is taken in tax – the impact of the rise is reduced. Similarly if the man's income falls to £9 he pays £2.70 tax and has a disposable income of £6.30. When income falls by £1 from £10 to £9 the man's disposable income only falls from £7 to £6.30 – the reduction in disposable income is less than the fall in pre-tax income. If the tax system is progressive the automatic stabilizing effect is even more marked. In the case of unemployment pay the higher is unemployment the greater is the sum of money handed out as unemployment pay – the fall in purchasing power is not as great as it would be without the unemployment pay.

Automatic stabilizers can be incorporated into the management of demand through rules, and rules can also be laid down concerning the variations of money supply through monetary policy proper. Such rules, it is alleged, would prevent instability arising out of arbitrary government actions. They would not necessarily remove fluctuations but only dampen them and they would not remove the need to improve the flexibility of prices and the desirability of improving the communicating efficiency of the market system.[2]

2. Automatic stabilizers are not some kind of economic magic which cures all economic ills. If automatic stabilizers are badly designed they may actually accentuate fluctuation. There is a design problem. A further difficulty is that every time you think that you have designed an improved automatic stabilizer you want to introduce it – if these introductions occur too often you may approach the situation existing with discretionary policies. A final difficulty is that with automatic stabilizers the government appears to be inactive – when unemployment rises the public expects to see government action, and reference to automatic stabilizers may not impress them.

Components of public sector spending: long run fiscal policy

So far we have viewed public sector spending as a total controlled in order to stabilize the economy and to pursue policies of inflation control, balance of payments equilibrium, economic growth and so on. We have been principally concerned with the public sector's demand for resources as an aggregate total. In this section we are going to look briefly at the pattern of spending within the totals, patterns that reveal government policy on education, health, industrial development, social security and many other areas of policy.

During the period since the Second World War and especially since the mid 1960s there has been a steady increase in the magnitude of public sector spending, as clearly shown in column 1 of Table 56, with combined public authority (central and local government but not

Table 57 UK public sector expenditure on goods and services, gross domestic fixed capital formation and inventories at 1970 prices (£ million)

	1964	1969	1974	Percentage growth 1964–74
defence	2895	2532	2645	−8·7
education	1624	2038	2446	+50·6
national health service	1639	1946	2369	+44·5
housing	701	940	984	+40·4
personal social services, social security, school meals, welfare foods	449	598	815	+81·5
roads and public lighting	575	744	701	+21·9
police, prisons, parliament, law courts	383	507	658	+71·8
water, sewage, refuse disposal, public health services	387	521	491	+26·9
finance, tax collection, records, registrations, surveys	212	285	332	+56·6
public corporations GDFCF	1522	1616	1651	+8·5
total of others not elsewhere specified	1081	1271	1608	+48·7
grand total	11 468	12 998	14 700	+28·2

Derived from: *National Income and Expenditure*, 1964–74, HMSO

Components Public Sector Spending: Long Run Fiscal Policy 673

public corporations) spending rising from 35 per cent of GNP in 1961 to 47 per cent in 1974. Much of this rise has been because of rising population, a rise in standards of provision in education, health and social security and extensions of government involvement into new areas such as industrial policy. Tables 57 and 58 show the relative importance of public sector spending and the pattern of use within that total for the 1960s and 1970s.

Parallel with the growth of public authority spending there has been a growth of public production such that in 1974 the public sector produced 29 per cent of GNP compared with only 24 per cent in 1954.

Now the result of this big expansion of the public sector has been that resources have been diverted from the private sector and an increasing proportion of all income is diverted through government hands; this is illustrated by Tables 56 and 57. Fewer resources are available for the private sector and the totals to be raised by taxation and borrowing as a percentage of total income have risen.

Several consequences have followed from the diversion of resources. First, because of the absence of sufficient resources to pro-

Table 58 UK public sector expenditure on grants, net loans and subsidies at 1970 prices (£ million)

	1964	1969	1974	Percentage growth 1964–74
social security benefits	2638	3624	4260	+61·4
housing	365	308	1441	+294·8
trade and industry[1]	39	905	882	+2161·5
education	389	535	608	+56·3
agriculture, forestry, fishing and food	355	306	598	+68·5
transport and communication	168	158	441	+162·5
total of others not elsewhere specified	101	205	219	+116·8
grand total	4055	6041	8450	+108·4

Derived from: *National Income and Expenditure*, 1964–74, HMSO

1. The sudden rise in this item is caused by the change in investment incentives from tax relief to grants.

duce both the desired levels of private and collective goods the attempt to produce the desired amount of collective goods resulted in a reduction in the amount of private goods. Secondly, the reduction in private goods resulted in a reduction in the outputs of capital goods and exports. Thirdly, the fall in the output of capital goods led to a drop in the rate of growth of the economy. Fourthly, the reduction in the output of exports caused balance of payments problems.

It could also be argued that the increased proportion of GNP spent by the public sector has meant that taxation has had to increase to levels where incentives are eroded at the margin which may have resulted in reduced risk-taking. Further, the particularly rapid recent growth of public sector spending has meant that this could no longer be tax financed and thus there has been resort to increased use of borrowing which has only been possible with high interest rates, another factor which would tend to reduce investment levels, other things being equal, and thus private sector economic growth. The recent growing resort to borrowing is clearly shown in column 2 of Table 56.

Summary and conclusion

We have discussed both the control of aggregate demand by governments and the contribution of governments to aggregate demand in the form of spending on goods and services and investment. The control of aggregate demand by fiscal means was discussed as a policy aimed at stabilizing the economy (smoothing out fluctuations) and at maintaining a level of employment higher than that which would arise from the free functioning of the economy. We also noted that the control of the level of aggregate demand would also have an impact on inflation, the balance of payments and the rate of growth.

Subsequently, we went on to show that fiscal control of the economy would be very difficult owing to time lags, and might well be destabilizing. Similarly, the control of economic activity by discrete monetary policy might also be destabilizing because of the existence of similar lags. A fuller discussion of monetary and fiscal policy for control can be found in the chapter 'Fitting the Pieces Together'. The role of automatic stabilizers was introduced and it was suggested that they might be superior to discretionary policies.

In the last part of the chapter we looked briefly at the total of government spending as the sum of expenditures made in pursuit of a whole range of economic and social policies intended to counteract the influence of spillovers, maldistribution of income and inadequate growth.

The final section led naturally to some tentative ideas that the growth of public sector demand could starve the private sector of resources necessary for investment and exports, and the problem of financing public sector spending could lead to undesirably high tax rates and borrowing requirements both of which might reduce the rate of growth of the private sector.

Questions

1 What is the balanced budget multiplier theorem?

2 What are the main weaknesses of discretionary behaviour?

3 What are automatic stabilizers?

Statistical appendix

	1954	1955	1956	1957	1958	1959	1960	1961
1 Public authority spending on goods and services plus public sector investment at 1970 prices (£ million)	9881	9573	9487	9459	9258	9572	9824	10 280
2 Change from the previous year of row 1	−47	−308	−86	−28	−201	314	252	456
3 Registered unemployment monthly averages in thousands	318	264	287	347	501	512	393	377

Source: *National Income and Expenditure*, various issues, HMSO
       Monthly Digest of Statistics, various issues, HMSO

4 What is the difference between monetary policy and fiscal policy?

5 What evidence would you look for to support the claims of successive governments that they tried to control the level of aggregate demand and employment?

6 Why may a government find that when it is trying to control employment it cannot disregard its other policy aims?

7 If full employment means inflation how can a government control the balance of payments?

8 What limitations are there on the growth of government expenditure?

9 What policies are open to a government which wishes to reduce unemployment? List the disadvantages of each policy given the usual list of government policy aims.

10 It is possible for governments to intervene to control aggregate demand without the action being 'too late'?

1962	1963	1964	1965	1966	1967	1968	1969	1970	1971	1972	1973	1974	1975
10 616	10 883	11 469	11 857	12 348	13 364	13 376	12 968	13 201	13 448	13 668	14 110	14 431	14 905
336	267	586	388	491	1016	12	−408	233	247	220	442	321	474
500	612	413	360	391	559	586	581	518	792	876	619	615	978

Chapter 39
Development and Growth

So we come back to our starting point, the causes of the wealth of
nations. Economists have tended to divide the subject into three parts.
First, there has been an exploration of the problems of the poorer
countries of the world. How can they increase their living standards?
Secondly, there has been an investigation of the factors which determine whether an economy can maintain a full employment equilibrium growth path. Once measures for combatting mass unemployment in the short run had been discovered, economists turned to the
problems of growth. The third region of exploration has been more
practical and has been concerned with the poor growth rate of the
UK compared with that of other European countries and America
and Japan. This practical problem has involved the three aspects of
economics; *positive* – what are the factors responsible for a poor
growth rate; *normative* – what ought to be done; *art* – how can it be
done. And because it has been concerned with raising the growth rate
the third problem has been as much a problem of development as of
growth.

Development economics

The chief characteristic of the poorer countries of the world is their
low standard of living. This can be measured by statistics of national
income per head although problems of measurement and interpretation
often fail to reveal the enormous disparities in living standards. Visual
evidence – poverty, starvation and disease – are often more reliable
indicators. And a more interesting method of indicating the differences between the developed and the developing countries is to compare the number of hours of labour required to purchase selected
commodities. Workers in poorer countries have a great deal of un-
wanted leisure but enjoy few other commodities – this is the substance

of the labour theory of value, how many units of labour are required to produce the goods that are wanted?

Development economics was the preoccupation of the classical economists, from Adam Smith to John Stuart Mill, from 1760 to 1870. The neoclassical economists showed a greater interest in the economics of the stationary state and it was not until after the problems of mass unemployment had been analysed that interest in development was renewed. So development economics is in its infancy – a product of old lessons rediscovered and new contexts giving rise to new problems. Because of its newness we can only indicate some of the issues.

Agriculture

Most of the developing countries are agricultural countries. Agriculture seems to yield low and unstable incomes which renders planning difficult. Instability of incomes might be overcome by diversifying crops and the creation of buffer stocks and international agreements to stabilize prices. But there are costs in such measures. Buffer stocks might prove unmanageable and international cartels tend to break down because of price cutting.

Another line of advance could be through reform of land tenure. In some countries plots are small and uneconomic, and in others there is a concentration of land in the hands of few landowners. Reform could, in the one case, lead to consolidation and the release of labour for other activities, but in the second case could lead to inefficiency if small plots are given to peasants. Reform involves the problem of compensation versus confiscation. If compensation is paid then there may be no gains from the redistribution of property, whilst confiscation might discourage foreign investment.

A third means of improving agriculture is through the development of new crops. The Green Revolution in Pakistan, stemming from the introduction of dwarf varieties of rice and wheat, is the most spectacular development in recent decades. But new crops involve research costs, new technologies and make heavy demands on fertilizers.

Population

Not all the developing countries are heavily populated. There are some parts of Africa and Latin America where population density is low. But a characteristic of many countries, particularly in South East Asia is overpopulation. Thus, India's population which was about 430 million in 1960 could reach 900 million by the turn of the century. The population explosion of developing countries has been mainly brought about by a reduction in mortality rates consequent upon improvements in public health measures to combat such diseases as malaria. In the long run birth rates may decline, as they have in the industrialized countries, but at present the only prospect of a substantial reduction in the birth rate seems to be a campaign of persuasion coupled with the availability of cheap contraceptives.

Foreign investment and foreign aid

Foreign investment and foreign aid can stimulate development by providing scarce resources. Both, however, can be subject to drawbacks. Much foreign aid has been tied-aid in which the donor stipulated the nature of the aid and its use and a great deal of aid has been given to secure political objectives. It is questionable whether such aid has secured its objectives. It tends to bolster up reactionary rulers and governments and identifies the donors with repression. Foreign investment has also been criticized for increasing the dependence of developing countries on the developed and creating a new form of imperialism. A great deal depends upon how much significance a country's inhabitants place upon independence and in this respect the citizens of poorer countries often behave in a similar fashion to those of the UK who resent American investment.

Development strategies

The task of development economies is to resolve the interplay of resources and ideas. Should development be balanced or unbalanced? Should equal consideration be given to all sectors of the economy? In the nineteenth century Britain filled its agricultural needs from abroad and America developed as an agricultural country. What part should the market play in development? Should import substitution be encouraged by means of tariffs? The temptation to use tariffs stems from the possibilities that foreign manufacturing industries enjoy considerable economies of scale and that it would be futile to expose infant industries to the unrestricted competition from foreign countries. Development economics supplies no easy answers to these questions and yet two-thirds of the world's population seek answers from economists.

Growth economics

Whereas development economics seems to be concerned with the radical transformation of a country's production possibilities curve, growth economics has been preoccupied with the more modest task of sustaining a line of advance already attained. Once economists thought they had solved the problem of mass unemployment, they turned their attention to growth. The theory at its simplest can be put as follows. In order to achieve equilibrium, planned injections must equal planned withdrawals or, in the language of the literature, planned investment must equal planned savings. Now if they are equal and the volume of investment is sufficient to absorb all the labour seeking jobs then a full employment equilibrium will be attained. This was the conclusion of previous chapters. So the growth problem emerges in two ways. First, it is not sufficient to solve the unemployment at a point of time because the labour force may be growing over time and creating future unemployment. Secondly, investment creates employment in the short run but adds to capacity in the long run. There is, therefore, a growth in productive potential in the long run which must be absorbed by increasing demand if the economy is not to sink back to a low level of utilization of its existing labour and equipment with a resulting failure to grow.

A fix-price growth model

The construction of a growth model to solve the basic dilemma presented in the previous section depends upon one's theory of markets. If one emphasizes that the long run emerges out of a succession of short-run disequilibria in which price movements are sluggish, then a fix-price model emerges.

Let us begin by assuming that the population, and hence the labour force, L, is growing at a constant rate, n. Thus:

$$n = \frac{L_{t+1} - L_t}{L_t}. \tag{1}$$

Between two periods (t and $t+1$) the labour force grows at the rate n. That is, the growth rate is such that L_{t+1} is equal in size to the labour force in the previous period plus some fraction (n) of its previous size.

$$L_{t+1} = L_t(1+n). \tag{2}$$

Now if labour is to be fully employed then there must be an increase in the demand for labour from period to period. Let us, therefore, suppose that labour and capital are employed in fixed proportions so that we can switch from looking at the demand for labour to looking at the determinants of the demand for capital. We may suppose that investment is governed by the desire to begin each period with a stock of capital appropriate for the level of demand in that period. Hence investment, which is, of course, the change in the capital stock will be given by

$$\Delta K_t = K_{t+1} - K_t. \tag{3}$$

But how in one period can we determine the capital requirement of the next period? If there exists a fixed or desired relationship between the capital stock and output, called the capital–output ratio, v (that is, the number of units of capital required to produce one unit of output), then K_{t+1} will be vY_{t+1} where Y is income – the determinant of demand. This does not seem very helpful since in any period we do not know next period's income (Y_{t+1}). However, if a certain rate of growth of income is expected then we can have an expected value for next period's income. One way of arriving at an expected value would be to project the past trend of demand. What we can state, however, is that investment is governed by the expected rate of increase in demand and the desired capital–output ratio.

$$\Delta K_t = K^*_{t+1} - K_t = I_t = v(Y^*_{t+1} - Y_t) \tag{4}$$

where the symbol * denotes desired values. The right-hand side of the expression is the accelerator which we encountered in Chapter

34 but here it is the expected change in demand rather than the past change in demand which is the influential factor.

Increasing income will stimulate investment but will also be associated with withdrawals. If we assume for simplicity that savings are the only form of withdrawal and that they are a constant fraction of income, s, where s is the marginal propensity to save, then we have:

$$S_t = sY_t. \qquad\qquad 5$$

We know that investment and savings are always equal, but that equilibrium only exists when desired savings and investment are equal, so our condition for stable equilibrium growth is the equality of desired savings and investment. We can, therefore, combine equations 4 and 5 as follows:

$$sY_t = v(Y^*_{t+1} - Y_t). \qquad\qquad 6$$

Equation 6 is more important than it might appear at first sight. To appreciate this we can divide both sides by Y_t and v to yield:

$$\frac{s}{v} = \frac{Y^*_{t+1} - Yt}{Y_t}. \qquad\qquad 7$$

The expression on the right-hand side is the expected growth of income, g^*. But if the economy is in growth equilibrium then the expected growth rate must be equal to the actual growth rate, g_a. So for an equilibrium growth path we have the proposition that:

$$\frac{s}{v} = g^* = g_a = \frac{Y_{t+1} - Y_t}{Y_t}. \qquad\qquad 8$$

The rate of growth, $g^* = g_a$, is equal to the savings propensity divided by the desired capital–output ratio. Equation 7 and 8 therefore tells us a great deal. We can, in fact, go a little further by designating s/v as dictating a warranted rate of growth, g_w.

At this stage a recapitulation should be useful. We have derived a variety of growth paths. One, the warranted rate of growth, refers to the potential growth rate as dictated by certain basic forces – savings and technology. A second growth rate refers to what is desired or expected. And a third growth rate refers to the actual or realized growth rate. Obviously, if an economy is on a stable equilibrium growth path then what is desired is equal to what is achieved and what is warranted:

$$g^* = g_a = g_w.$$ **9**

Equation **9** also implies that desired investment and savings are also equal and this may be accidental since the decisions to save and the decisions to invest are governed by different factors (recall the discussion of Chapter 30). The equilibrium growth path may in fact be highly unstable. If the expected rate does differ from the warranted rate then the economy will move further away from equilibrium since there are no forces to pull it back again.[1]

But there is another problem. If the labour force is growing at a rate different from the rate of growth of the capital stock then either there will be unemployment or there will be inflation. If the labour force grows faster than the capital stock there will be unemployment: if it grows at a slower rate there will be inflation. Both possibilities can lead to disequilibrium. Stable economic growth thus requires that the labour force should grow at the same rate as the warranted rate of growth and, in turn, at the desired rate of growth:

$$n = g_w = g^* = g_a.$$ **10**

The alarming picture of economic instability that we have drawn needs to be treated with caution. Real economies do not have a history of ever-increasing recessions nor do they soar upwards without restriction. And they do not exhibit smooth growth paths but cyclical variations around long-term upward trends. Within the context of the fix-price model it is possible to introduce modifications that go some way to meeting these objections.

1 An upper and a lower limit can be put on the tendency of the economy to shoot away in either direction by assuming the existence of a ceiling imposed by full employment of resources beyond which the economy cannot go and a floor created by investment which is not induced by recent changes in demand. Starting from the floor, an increase in investment could cause the economy to take off and move towards the ceiling. Once it hits the ceiling it bounces down again because the ceiling imposes a lower rate of increase of demand than previously and this causes investment to fall. The

1. The problem of instability is considered in Sen (1970).

economy then moves towards the floor. By making various assumptions about the strength of consumption and investment it is possible to develop cycles of varying strength, some of which may not reach the ceiling. But, of course, the difficulty with this type of amended model is to discover what determines the trend of non-induced investment.[2]

2 Another method of introducing some stability is to allow changes in the distribution of income between wage-earners and capitalists to dictate the amount of savings that are available. Savings could then be allowed to fluctuate between limits imposed by a subsistence wage and a minimum reward for risk with the actual amount of saving being the outcome of collective bargaining.

A flex-price model

Instead of a fix-price model we can produce a flex-price model in which prices always adjust to maintain full employment and a given growth rate. In such a model the central concept would be a production function embodying the inputs of labour and capital and those inputs would change according to changes in relative prices.

Technical progress

Technical progress needs to be considered in growth economics. Most studies of growth have suggested that mere capital accumulation only accounts for a small part of the observed rise in national income and the difference has been referred to as The Residual which has been accounted for in terms of new inventions which periodically become embodied in machines or in labour (e.g. education) or lies disembodied as a kind of organized knowledge in society.

2. The basic equation determining the cyclical behaviour of income about a trend is:

$$Y_t = aY_{t-1} + b(Y_{t-1} - Y_{t-2}) + A_t$$

where a is the marginal propensity to consume and b is the capital–output ratio and the equation is similar to equation 8 with the addition of autonomous investment, A_t. If a and b take on high values then a strong cycle develops.

The energy and raw materials crisis

The analysis has so far been conducted on the assumption that the problem was to ensure full employment of a growing labour force and that there was no problem of obtaining raw materials; land and natural resources did not constitute a problem. In recent years some writers have argued that the pursuit of economic growth will lead to catastrophe because the supplies of raw material are finite and in many cases are non-renewable. These writers deny that the price mechanism can solve the problem and lead to a stationary state. What they suggest is that the consumption of raw materials follows an exponential path so that at one moment of time there will appear to be plentiful supplies of materials and at the next moment, complete exhaustion. What doomsday writers deny is that the price mechanism can cope with intergenerational decisions concerning the allocation of resources. Since the people of the year 2200 have not yet been born how can they be expected to bid for resources against those now living? The price mechanism may allow parents to make decisions which will affect the welfare of their children and grandchildren, but it is difficult to believe that parents think much further ahead nor, for that matter, does the state.

Although there are difficulties in using the price mechanism to allocate resources over time, it is possible that the doomsday writers have exaggerated the problem. History records that increasing scarcity of particular resources has been accompanied by rising prices and that those rising prices have led to a search for substitutes. Thus, the increasing scarcity of fossil fuels will cause a switch to solar energy. And recycling of metals will take place on a more intensive scale. What might, however, be doubted is whether the world's resources are sufficient to support the world's population at the standards of living enjoyed by the advanced countries.

Population decline

So far we have analysed the determinants of a stable growth path for a developed country on the assumption that the task was to ensure full employment of a growing labour force. The causes of that growing labour force were not, however, analysed. It would have been possible to explain the growth of the labour force as a response to rising real incomes. That would have meant the incorporation of a

Malthusian explanation of changes in the population and the labour force into the model. But, until recently, economists have shown a reluctance to analyse population change. The reason lay in the co-existence of a falling birth rate and rising real incomes after 1870 which seemed to refute the Malthusian hypothesis. However, it is possible to put forward reasons for the apparent refutation. After 1870 the expenses of bringing up children rose; compulsory education raised the costs of children and delayed the time before a return could be expected; and the gradual emergence of state pensions may have reduced the necessity to have children as an insurance against old age. In the inter-war years the birth rate fell because of the slump – a Malthusian explanation. In the fifties and sixties there were baby booms – a consequence of economic booms. But these booms were superimposed upon a downward trend – the costs of children seemed to be persistently higher than the costs of other things.

In the middle of the 1970s the decline accelerated in the industrialized countries. Between 1963 and 1973 the annual birth rate fell by 44 per cent in West Germany, 25 per cent in the UK, 16 per cent in Italy, 9 per cent in France and Sweden. Nor is the decline confined to the market economies. In East Germany, over the same period, the annual birth rate fell 3·8 per cent. The causes of these declines have not yet been assessed. The introduction of the pill and abortion have played an important part and parents may be spending more on fewer children.

Whatever the fundamental reasons for the decline in the projected fall in total populations it is possible to trace out some of the implications. A falling population could mean less necessity to invest in order to maintain full employment. But a falling population will imply a changing age structure with more elderly dependants. This could mean a change in the patterns of investment and consumption. It could also mean an increase in the amount of income redistribution in the form of pensions, though this might be offset by the fall in transfer incomes to parents of children. It is possible, therefore, that population decline may not bring a fall in living standards if productivity and technical change remain constant or increase. If not, then the bulge in the age structure of the population will have to be carried, until the stationary population has been achieved, by a postponement of retirement and an influx of migrant labour to support the elderly in the transitional period.

The decline in the populations of the advanced countries constitutes one of the most interesting and fascinating problems of the next few decades. In the UK the decline in the birth rate has been most marked at the bottom of the social scale and this could have the effect of reducing inequality in society. But the international implications are much more compelling. It could bring about a redistribution of world population as workers from the poorer countries migrate to Europe, and it could bring about a collapse of vitality. For, perhaps, the gigantic boom of the last two hundred years has been a response to population pressure which once removed might produce an equally gigantic slump.

The UK economy 1945–1977

Although the growth models we have referred to are extremely abstract they do provide a framework in which the problems of the UK growth rate can be considered. Moreover, the basic ideas underlying these models have exerted an influence on policy since they constitute part of the Keynesian debate. The first thing to observe, however, is that Britain's growth rate of about 2·5 per cent has been good when compared with past performances. It is higher than in the golden period of the Victorian and Edwardian economies, 1870–1914, when it was about 2·2 per cent, and higher than in the early phases of the Industrial Revolution. But it has been poor when compared with those of other countries.

Some of the factors that have been put forward to account for the low growth rate are:

1 A lack of willingness to invest which has revealed itself both in the volume of investment and the unwillingness to invest in new lines of development.

2 The lack of willingness to invest has not been overcome by government subsidies to investment.

3 The lack of willingness to invest may have been due to a lack of labour. The UK has not been able to draw upon surplus labour in agriculture as did the Europeans and Americans nor has she allowed in migrant labour as did the Europeans.

4 A high level of consumption occurred because of a high dependency ratio of young and old relative to the working population. This high ratio was offset in Europe by migrant labour.

5 The high level of consumption was responsible for the expansion of the public sector, particularly health and education. Similar expansions in Europe were probably financed by migrant labour.

6 Because of the long period of unemployment and the absence of inflation in the inter-war years there has been a tendency to maintain full employment regardless of the costs and, as a result, declining industries have been run down too slowly and inflation has hampered efficiency.

7 Discretionary monetary and fiscal policies have rendered business planning difficult.

8 Despite the loss of overseas assets there has been a tendency to pursue policies more appropriate to a great power and to indulge in prestigious spending.

9 Foreigners work harder and enjoy more leisure whereas Britons work at a slower pace and enjoy less leisure.

10 British trade unions are stronger than in other countries and restrict the introduction of new ideas.

The catalogue of possible sources of weakness is, of course, endless.

Summary

Development economics is concerned with the transformation of an economy's production possibilities whereas growth economics has tended to examine the determinants of a steady state-growth path. No comprehensive theory of development exists because the problems facing poorer countries are so diverse. Growth theory has produced some simplified models based on either fix-prices or flex-prices which are capable of indicating the factors necessary for the attainment of a long-run equilibrium growth path. Some of the ideas embodied in these models are useful in explaining Britain's economic growth rate though they are too simplified to provide an adequate explanation.

Questions

1 What problems arise in making international comparisons of real income?

2 Discuss the extent to which aid can promote economic development.

3 'g determines the long-run growth path and v determines whether there will be fluctuations around that growth path.' Discuss.

4 Set out a framework for analysing Britain's recent economic growth problems.

Chapter 40
Fitting the Pieces Together

So far, with the exception of a brief preamble, our discussion of macroeconomic variables has proceeded in a piecemeal fashion. Each component has been looked at in splendid isolation. Yet all economic variables are linked together, to a greater or lesser degree, all are interdependent so that changes in one promote changes in others. This interdependence is especially marked in the case of the main macroeconomic variables: output, employment, investment, savings, consumption, exports, the stock of money, the general price level, the rate of interest, and the real and money wage rates.

We have, until now, avoided detailed consideration of the interdependence between these variables, for two reasons. First, because before trying to understand the new problems encountered in analysing interaction between variables in the economy as a whole even in relatively simple terms, it is necessary to have a thorough understanding of the component parts. This is provided by the preceding chapters. Secondly, to analyse the simultaneous interaction between some, let alone all, of the main macroeconomic variables requires the use of unfamiliar analytical frameworks and/or models.

Given the large number of variables we need to consider, and the unfamiliar problem of analysing the simultaneous interaction between them, how do we 'fit the pieces together'?

Several ways suggest themselves. One possibility is suggested by the great vision of Leon Walras, that an economic system can be described by a set of simultaneous equations. This approach has a number of desirable features. It can handle a large number of variables. It can be used to derive quantitative estimates of the degree of association between variables. It is rigorous, and thus provides a check against faulty reasoning, and, of importance to some, it is elegant. For these reasons such an approach is used by economists to construct large scale econometric models of the economy. This approach is not without faults, or critics, and some of these faults are considered later in the chapter. For the task in hand the approach, in its mathematical form, is too complex for an introductory text. What we will do later in this chapter is describe a graphical version of a simplified general equilibrium macroeconomic model.

Another, more cumbersome, way of examining the interdependence between a number of macroeconomic variables, is to set out the partial equilibrium analysis for each of the separate variables, or markets in which they occur, if possible in a composite diagram, and show how adjustment to a disturbance in one market leads to adjustments in variables in other markets. The drawback with this approach is that it becomes exceedingly difficult to analyse feedback effects between markets and variables, i.e. how adjustment in one market causes adjustment in other markets, which in turn lead to further changes in the first market, and so on. Despite this drawback the approach is useful on pedagogical grounds in that it helps to illustrate all the various channels of operation linking variables and markets together. For this reason we make use of this approach in this chapter as a step on the route to the general equilibrium model.

We commence with a third approach, which is less elegant than the other two approaches, but serves to delineate the dimension of the problem in hand and indicate some of the unresolved problems in macroeconomics. This is the flow chart approach (Figure 186) supplemented by a reiteration of the main points of the preceding chapters.

The grand vision and some unresolved problems

1 We began by postulating that people require money and proceeded to examine its method of production (Chapter 29). We noted that the production of money might be subject to monopolistic influences. Later (in Chapter 35) we observed that the amount of domestic money could be influenced by the behaviour of the international market for monies and the extent to which any one domestic money is chosen as the international money. Domestic and international money supplies are therefore linked.

2 The demand of people for money is twofold – firstly as a medium of exchange and, secondly, to serve as a store of value.

3 The use of money as a unit of account/medium of exchange establishes a link between money and the general level of prices. This raises two problems. First, what is the precise nature of the link: is there a stable relationship? Secondly, how do the 'real' forces of demand and supply of goods interact with this monetary phenomenon?

4 The existence of money as a store of value also means that there is a link between money and other (real) stores of value. Money becomes a capital good. Money, therefore, enters into the determination of the rate of interest.

5 For some writers, instability in the economy arises because of a mismatching of planned investment and planned savings. These are supposed to be brought together by the rate of interest. But money complicates the picture since it enters into the determination of the rate of interest. We have a problem: the 'real' forces of productivity and thrift indicate a flow determination of the rate of interest whereas the demand for and supply of money suggest a stock approach. (These two approaches echo the flow and stock versions of the demand for money.) Somehow stocks and flows have to be reconciled. The subject is still controversial.

6 Instability in an economy is supposed to arise because of the volatility of investment. This is only partly true and in the nineteenth century and in the first half of the inter-war years period, instability was caused by instability of exports. However, when Keynes wrote his *General Theory*, the UK was not on a fixed exchange rate and so balance of payments problems were corrected by depreciation or appreciation of the exchange rate. In the post-war period a fixed exchange rate regime has operated for the most part and so exports and imports have again been a source of instability.

7 The existence of money as a store of value blurs the distinction between money and other goods and financial assets. Some writers attach great weight to this and argue that it is impossible to define what is meant by money in terms of a distinct, measurable, set of assets. Hence they are able to argue that it is meaningless to attempt

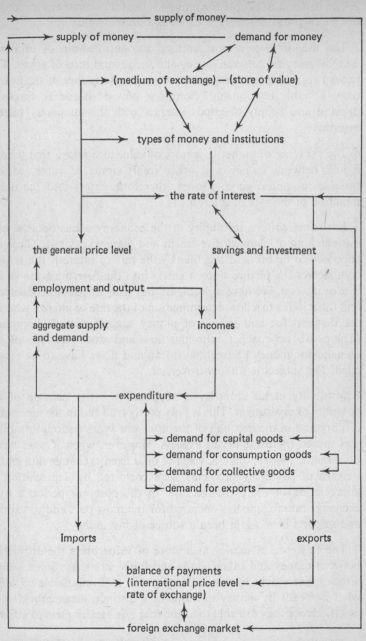

Figure 186

to establish a precise link between 'money', the price level and economic activity. Others, however, argue that it is possible and meaningful to define a set of assets as money, but nevertheless, doubt the existence of a stable link between money and the price level. This view is based on their belief in the instability of the velocity of circulation, due to the uneven and unpredictable development of financial institutions which speed up the flow of money. A third group also believes that money can be defined and argue that, because the demand for money function is a stable function of a few variables, variations in velocity can be predicted and hence a stable relationship exists between changes in the supply of money and the price level. All these views are amenable to empirical investigation, and the weight of recent evidence tends to favour the last mentioned group. Nevertheless, these issues continue to be controversial.

8 Turning to the real forces, we note that in the short run, the amounts of productive resources used depend upon the total demand for the goods and services produced by those resources.

9 Demand promotes production which leads to incomes and hence expenditure. There is a circular flow of expenditure (output-income-expenditure) though this is in part an illusion created by a failure to consider the problems caused by internal and external lags preventing a continuous matching of flows. The timeless equilibrium nature of the circular flow concept also distracts attention from other important aspects of the economic process, namely environmental pollution and natural resource depletion. Both of these alter the economy in an irreversible way so that the continuous sequence of economic activity can be thought of as following a linear path, rather than a circular course. (A preoccupation with money and national income accounting measures of welfare, should not cause an economist to lose sight of the physical side of economic activity, and the fact that this is governed by the laws of physics, not least those concerning waste.)

10 Attempts to create conditions of full employment of resources, by demand boosting policies, can lead to instability because of the existence of expectational based links between various components of demand and the price level and money wages. The short-run success of such policies may not only be replaced in the longer run by

the reoccurrence of the initial problem, but also have adverse repercussions on the balance of payments and the rate of growth.

11 The task of controlling the economy is in part a problem of seeing that the right amount of lubricant (money) is fed into the system. Failure to do so can result in the monetary system strangling an economy. Not only must the quality be right but so must be the rate at which it is fed in. Some argue, persuasively, that monetary policy is often destabilizing rather than stabilizing, because it leads to frequent and large changes in the rate of monetary expansion. If the money supply ceased to be subject to discretionary control and was expanded at a steady rate in line with some pre-selected target, it would enable the real forces in the economy to operate in a more stable fashion. Not surprisingly, such a view, which seeks to limit the economic powers of the state, is not without its critics. Lest the impression be created that money dominates all, it needs to be emphasized that the control problem is also one of improving the mobility of resources, and the responsiveness of economic agents to changes in tastes and technology. These in turn imply a need to improve the informational efficiency of both market and non-market institutions.

12 The failure to see the full interdependence of parts of the economy arises because of imperfections which act so as to put constraints on the variables.

The above discussion serves to show how the monetary and real sides of the economy are bound together. For equilibrium to exist between the aggregate demand and supply for 'real' goods and services there must simultaneously exist equilibrium in the market for money. An analogy drawn from Alfred Marshall's *Principles of Economics* may help to make this clear. Imagine a bowl containing a large number of billiard balls. Equilibrium prevails when all the balls are stationary and in this state all the balls will be interdependent in the sense that each ball will be in contact with several others. If one ball is removed from the bowl the equilibrium will be disturbed and all the balls will move, continuing to do so until a new equilibrium is established. The balls need not all move the same distance in the process of establishing the new equilibrium but they are all affected by the initial disturbance.

Further insight into some of the relationships listed above can be gained by building up a single model of macro-interdependence, along the lines suggested by the interdependences sketched out in Figure 187.

Starting from a position of equilibrium, in the sense of equality of aggregate supply and demand, we know that a change in the level of injections per time period will bring the multiplier into operation and lead to a new equilibrium income level. A certain volume of

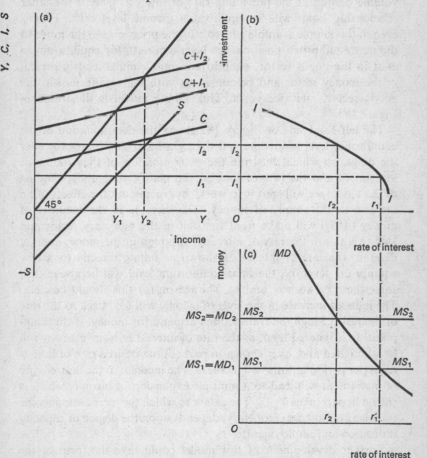

Figure 187 (a) This is drawn on the simplifying assumption that investment and savings are the only withdrawals. (b) and (c) differ from the figures drawn before in having the variables on the axes reversed

investment per time period will exist at the new equilibrium. Similarly, the rate of interest and the general price level will be at new equilibrium levels so that the supply of, and demand for money are equal. Now if the rate of interest has some influence on the volume of investment per time period, it also follows that in the new equilibrium the volume of investment which prevails must correspond to the volume desired at the prevailing rate of interest. Only if the latter relationship holds will an equilibrium income level exist. That is even in this simple example (the role of the price level in the move to the new equilibrium position has been ignored), for equilibrium to exist in the goods sector, equilibrium must simultaneously prevail in the money sector and be consistent with the equilibrium in the goods sector, and vice versa. This simple model is illustrated in Figure 187.

The left-hand side of Figure 187 shows the determination of the equilibrium level of income and the right-hand side brings together the diagrams which illustrate the determination of the volume of investment and the rate of interest. To clarify your understanding of the model we will 'put it to work' by tracing out the effects of an increase in the supply of money. The increase in the quantity of money (MS_2) will make itself first felt in the monetary sector and lead to a fall in the rate of interest. Although in the money market diagram the rate of interest is shown as falling directly to a new equilibrium level, r_2, the final equilibrium level will lie above this, somewhere between r_1 and r_2. The reason for this should be clear. The induced increase in the level of income will feed back to the rate of interest through the transactions demand for money. If this complication is ignored then, as the rate of interest falls, investment will be stimulated and, as is shown in part (b) the desired rate of investment per period of time will increase. The increase in the desired rate of investment will lead to a multiple expansion of income, which is shown in part (a) as $Y_1 Y_2$. The extent to which the increase in income is real, as opposed to monetary, depends upon the degree of capacity utilization and employment.

Further development of this model could take the form of the explicit introduction of the determination of the price level and its influence on the level of imports, exports and the rate of interest. Thus, changes in the supply of money would not only influence the level of income via the rate of interest but also through the impact of price level changes on the value and volume of imports and exports.

The interdependence of real and monetary variables: the general equilibrium model

The approach described in this section is a graphical version of a simplified general equilibrium macro model. The model is used extensively in more advanced treatments of macrotheory, and is termed the Hicks-Hansen model, in honour of the economists who first developed the model.[1] The model is alternatively, and more commonly, referred to as the *IS-LM* curve model. This latter title derives from the basic feature of the model that it combines the real macro variables, represented in the model by the investment and savings functions, (the *IS* curve), and the monetary variables represented by the supply and demand curves for money (the *LM* curve).

The essence of the general equilibrium approach, as applied in this kind of model, is that the economy can be described in terms of a set of markets, which together embrace all the main macroeconomic variables. Each market in turn is described by a demand equation, a supply equation and a market clearing (equilibrium) relationship. All the equations are then brought together and 'solved' simultaneously to determine equilibrium values for each of the macro variables, such that equilibrium values in one market are consistent with the simultaneous equilibrium of variables in the other markets.

The *IS-LM* curve model is a simplified general equilibrium model because it is based on the assumption that the economy can be adequately represented by four distinct markets: the goods (output) market, the labour (factor) market, the money market and the bond (securities) market. This degree of aggregation immediately reveals one weakness of the model, it ignores the breakdown of output into consumption and investment goods. It implies that total output can be described in terms of a single homogeneous commodity. This has the advantage of allowing the production side of the economy to be represented by an aggregate production function. This is a drastic

1. J. R. Hicks, 'Mr Keynes and the "Classics": a suggested interpretation', *Econometrica*, 1937.

assumption which may or may not be justified by the insights the model yields. Our view is that at this level of exposition it is a useful simplifying assumption. But it is one which should be borne in mind especially when using the model to analyse the impact and role of different economic policies.

Although the model is based on a four-market view of the economy, only two appear explicitly in the graphical representation of the model, the goods, and money markets. How is this trick achieved? The labour market is subsumed in the goods market because of the link between output and employment provided by the aggregate production function. As described in Chapter 31 and Figure 148, the use of an aggregate production function establishes a unique relationship between employment and output. This means that knowledge of the equilibrium value of either variable is sufficient to determine the equilibrium value of the other. Thus, since the goods market appears explicitly in the model, it is possible via the aggregate production function to determine the equilibrium level of employment associated with any level of real income (output). The other market which is not directly represented in the model is the bond market. The reason in this case is provided by one of the 'Laws' of general equilibrium analysis. This law, known as Walras's Law, states that in any interdependent system of equations or markets, if equilibrium prevails in all but one of the markets, it must necessarily exist in the remaining market. Since the model serves to determine the general equilibrium values of real output (goods market), the rate of interest (money market) and employment (labour market), it follows that when these three markets are in equilibrium the fourth market (bond or securities) is also in equilibrium at the same rate of interest. Hence it is unnecessary to represent this market in the model.

The validity of Walras's Law should be self-evident. In a money economy an excess supply of money necessarily implies an excess demand for commodities and an excess supply of commodities necessarily implies an excess demand for money. Thus, when one market is out of equilibrium, it means that at least one other market will be as well. Conversely, it follows that when all but one market are in equilibrium the remaining market must also be in equilibrium.

A possible cause for concern is why the bond market is selected to be the redundant market since Walras's Law is neutral as to which market is dropped. The reason, on the face of it, is quite straight-forward. In partial equilibrium analysis we can examine the determination of the rate of interest either in terms of the supply and demand for money (money market), or the supply and demand for loanable funds (bond market). So in a general equilibrium model when the determination of the rate of interest also involves interaction between real and monetary variables, the choice of redundant market is between money and bonds. By tradition the bond market is dropped. This deliberate decision reflects the fact that money links all markets together so that it makes sense to treat it explicitly in the construction of the model.

This is perfectly reasonable so long as it is recognized that in general equilibrium analysis we are concerned with the equilibrium values of variables. Thus when general equilibrium prevails in an economy the equilibrium value of the rate of interest must be the same in the money and bond markets. So long as the general equilibrium model is used to derive comparative static propositions all is well. However, this does reveal another weakness of the *IS-LM* curve model. It cannot be used to answer questions involving time, that is to analyse processes, such as the dynamics of adjustment from one equilibrium position to another. Out of equilibrium Walras's Law no longer holds, hence it is not possible to treat one market as redundant. Thus, for disequilibrium analysis both bond and money market processes need to be considered when analysing the behaviour of the rate of interest. Again this limitation of the *IS-LM* model does not make the model useless, as long as it is borne in mind and the model is not used to analyse problems involving disequilibrium processes. The appendix to this chapter describes some of the problems which arise when this limitation is ignored, and the model is 'asked' to do too much.

To construct the *IS-LM* model we have to set out the relationships which describe the real side of the model (the goods market), and the money side of the economy (the money market). The relationship for the two sides of the model are then solved to give two curves which plot the loci of combinations of the rate of interest and the level of real income which yield equilibrium in the respective markets. These two curves, the *IS* and *LM* curves, are then plotted on the same axes and their intersection point determines the unique pair of values for the rate of interest and the level of real income which allows the real and the money sides of the economy to be simultaneously in equilibrium.

Although the resultant diagram resembles the familiar supply and demand diagram, the differences are greater than the similarities. The *IS* and *LM* curves are not the graphical counterparts of behavioural relationships but the loci of equilibrium points established by the interaction of a larger number of behavioural relationships. The macroeconomic behavioural relationships of the economy lie 'behind' the *IS* and *LM* curves, and when using the model it is necessary to refer to them.

This feature of the model presents a minor difficulty in deriving the curves. Since all the relevant behavioural relationships have to be brought together to construct the curves, it is necessary to resort to composite diagrams and graphical devices for relating the different parts together. There are a number of ways of doing this and we use one which builds on the technique used earlier in this chapter. But you should remember that it is only one of several possible methods and do not be surprised if you find a different method used in other texts.

In Figure 188 we illustrate the derivation of the *IS* curve. Part (a) depicts the investment function. It shows, given the investment demand curve, *Id*, how the rate of investment per period of time increases as the rate of interest decreases. Part (c) of the diagram, simplifies part (a) of Figure 187 by merely reproducing the investment and savings schedules of the 45° model of income determination. The savings schedule is derived from the familiar short-run consumption function and shows that the level of savings increases with real income. Three different levels of investment are illustrated by the investment schedules, I_1, I_2 and I_3, these correspond to the levels associated with the three different values of the rate of interest in part (a). Along the horizontal axis in part (c) are shown the three equilibrium income levels, $(I = S)$, associated with the three different levels of the investment function. Part (b) of the diagram brings together the information contained in the other two parts to yield the *IS* curve, the locus of pairs of values of the rate of interest and real income which yield equilibrium in the goods market. Only three points have been drawn, but it is obvious that by considering other values of the rate of interest, and hence investment, that additional equilibrium combinations of the rate of interest and real income

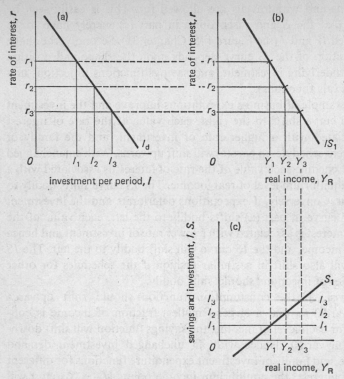

Figure 188 The derivation of the *IS* curve

could be established, and they would lie on the curve connecting the three points already drawn.

The resultant *IS* curve slopes down from left to right, indicating that, other things being equal, lower values of the rate of interest are associated with higher levels of real income. The intuitive explanation of the negative slope of the curve is that a fall in the rate of interest leads to a rise in the level of investment. An equilibrium level of real income requires that investment equals savings, so that as investment increases income must also increase, via the multiplier process, until the desired level of savings is increased to match the increase in investment.

Two things concerning the derivation of the *IS* curve should be apparent. Firstly, that the curve can also be derived for more general 'simple' models of income determination, in which other sources of injections and withdrawals are allowed for. This is easily seen by noting that the S and I schedules in part (c) merely have to be relabelled W and J (see Figure 145, Chapter 31). Secondly, the shape and position of the IS curve depends upon the shape and position of the underlying investment, and savings functions (injections and withdrawals functions).

For example, if business expectations improve and the investment demand curve shifts to the right, each value of the rate of interest is associated with a higher rate of investment, and the family of investment schedules in part (c) will shift upwards. With an unchanged savings schedule each value of the rate of interest is associated with a higher equilibrium level of real income. The IS curve shifts bodily to the right. Conversely, if expectations deteriorate and the investment demand curve in part (a) shifts bodily to the left, each value of the rate of interest is associated with a lower rate of investment and hence level of income, and the IS curve will shift bodily to the left. The IS curve will also shift in a similar fashion if the schedules for other categories of injections should shift bodily.

Likewise, if the consumption function should shift upwards (downwards) so that a larger (smaller) fraction of income is consumed for each level of income, the savings function will shift downwards (upwards). Hence with an unchanged investment demand schedule, and family of investment expenditure functions for different rates of interest, the equilibrium income points ($I_1 = S_1$, etc.) will alter and the IS curve move bodily to the right (left).

We can summarize these important results as follows:—

The IS *curve will shift to the right (left) if the investment demand curve shifts to the right (left), other things being unchanged.*
Likewise for similar changes in the functions for other categories of injections.

The IS *curve will shift to the right (left) if the savings function shifts downwards (upwards).*
Likewise for similar changes in the functions for other categories of withdrawals.

Turning to the slope, or elasticity, of the IS curve it should be noted, and self-evident, that its slope will depend upon the slopes of the investment demand curve and the savings function. The steeper the slope of the investment demand curve, i.e. the lower the interest elasticity of investment, and the steeper the slope of the savings function, i.e. the higher the marginal property to save, the steeper the slope of the IS curve. Conversely, the more interest elastic the investment demand curve, and the flatter the slope of the savings function, i.e. the lower the marginal property to save, the flatter will be the IS curve. As will become apparent later, these possibilities have important consequences for the relative efficiencies of monetary and fiscal policy changes.

The derivation of the LM curve is illustrated in Figure 189. The key to understanding the derivation of the LM curve is the distinction between the transactions demand for money, (M_{DT}) which relates the demand for money to the level of income, and the asset demand for money (M_{DA}) which relates the demand for money to the rate of interest.

In practice the demand for money functions is not separable, and for the economy as a whole we observe a total demand for money function, (M_D), which, at its most basic, is a function of the rate of interest and level of nominal income (or, if the demand for money is expressed in real terms, real income). For expositional purposes, it is convenient to treat the total demand as separable.

Given the institutional framework of the economy the transactions demand for money depends solely upon the level of income, and thus when plotted against the rate of interest is completely interest inelastic. This is illustrated in Figure 189, where three transactions demand for money functions are shown, corresponding to different levels of real income, $Y_1 < Y_2 < Y_3$. The asset demand for money, on the other hand, is an inverse function of the rate of interest, so that when the asset and transactions demands are combined to give the total demand for money function (M_D), this also slopes downwards from left to right against the rate of interest (see Chapter 28, Figure 138). The asset demand for money function may be constant, but the total demand for money curve will shift about as income changes, and with it the transactions demand for money. This is seen in part (a) where three separate total demand for money functions are shown, corresponding to the three transactions demand functions in part (c). If the supply of money is held constant, (M_S), as shown in part (a), the shift to the right of the total demand for money function, as income increases, will cause the rate of interest to

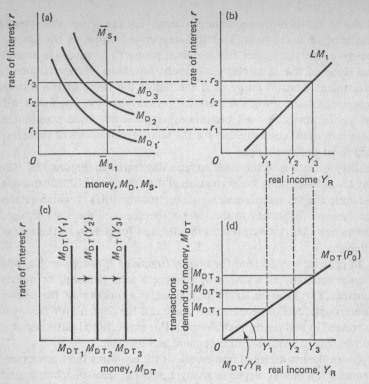

Figure 189 The derivation of the *LM* curve

increase to maintain equality between the supply and demand for
money. Thus in part (a) the maintenance of equilibrium between the
supply and demand for money causes the rate of interest to rise from
r_1 to r_3 as income increases. If the relationship between income and
the transactions demand for money is assumed to be proportional,
the information contained in part (c) can be expressed by a single
line as in part (d). Real income is plotted on the horizontal axis and
the transactions demand for money on the vertical axis, the curve
labelled M_{DT}, the slope of which measures the factor of proportionality between income and the transactions demand, then relates
changes in the transactions demand directly to changes in the level
of real income. Part (b) of the diagram brings together the information continued in parts (a) and (d) to yield the *LM* curve, the locus

of pairs of values of the rate of interest and real income which maintain equilibrium in the money market. As before, only three points have been drawn, but it is again obvious that other points could be added and that they would all lie along the curve labelled *LM*.

The resultant *LM* curve slopes upwards from left to right, indicating that, other things being equal, higher levels (of real income) are associated with higher values (of the rate of interest). The intuitive explanation of the slope of the *LM* curve is that, given a fixed supply of money, as income increases the growing transactions demand for money can only be satisfied by inducing people to hold less for asset purposes. People will only be prepared to reduce their asset demand for money as the rate of interest increases. Hence to maintain equilibrium between the supply of and total demand for money the rate of interest must increase as income increases. The derivation and general slope of the *LM* curve are the same for different theories of the demand for money, provided they include the rate of interest and real income as determinants of the total demand. More importantly, the slope and position of the *LM* curve depends upon the slope and position of the underlying transactions and asset demand curves, and the supply of money.

For example, taking the latter first, if the demand for money curve remains unchanged but the supply of money is increased (decreased) the whole *LM* curve will shift bodily to the right (left). Because the demand for money balances is a demand for real rather than nominal money balances the position of the *LM* curve is also dependent upon the general price level. That is, a decrease in the general price level, with an unchanged nominal money supply, will cause the *LM* curve to shift to the right, and an increase in the general price level will cause the LM curve to shift bodily to the left. The similarity of effects for changes in the nominal money stocks and the general price level arises because both result in a change in the *real value* of the money supply. In analytical terms an increase in the nominal money supply, with a constant general price level, is equivalent to a decrease in the general price level, with a constant nominal money stock. In both cases, the initial effect of the change is an increase in the real value of the money stock. Likewise, a decrease in the nominal money supply, with the general price level held constant, is equivalent to an increase in the general price level, with the nominal money supply held constant; both lead to a fall in the real value of the money stock.

If either the asset demand for money should increase, in the sense of a greater asset demand for money at an unchanged rate of interest, or the income demand for money increases, in the sense of a greater transaction demand for money at an unchanged level of real income, the total demand for money curve will shift to the right. If the supply of money is constant, a shift to the right of the total demand for money curve will cause the *LM* curve to shift to the left. Conversely, if either the asset or transactions demand for money should decrease, in the sense that the total demand for money curve shifts to the left, with a constant money supply, the *LM* curve will shift to the right. These movements of the *LM* curve should not be confused with movements along a given *LM* curve, which take place when the demand for money changes in response to a change in either income or the rate of interest.

We can summarize these important results as follows:—

The LM *curve will shift to the right (left), if the supply of money is increased (decreased), other things remaining unchanged.*

The LM *curve will shift to the right (left), if the general price level falls (rises), other things remaining unchanged.*

The LM *curve will shift to the left (right), if the total demand for money curve moves to the right (left), other things being equal.*

As in the case of the *IS* curve, the slope, or elasticity, of the *LM* curve depends upon the elasticities of the demand and supply of money curves. The more interest elastic the demand for money, the flatter the slope of the *LM* curve. At the limit of an infinitely interest elastic demand for money curve (the liquidity trap case), the *LM* curve will be horizontal. While at the other extreme, if the demand for money is completely interest inelastic the *LM* curve will be vertical. Although we have assumed the supply of money is given, there is reason to believe that it is interest elastic and slopes upwards to the right, in which case this will tend to make the *LM* curve less steep. All of these elasticity possibilities are of great significance in assessing the relative effectiveness of fiscal and monetary policy measures.

We can now bring the two curves together in one diagram and see how they jointly determine the general equilibrium values of the

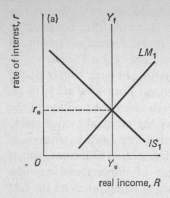 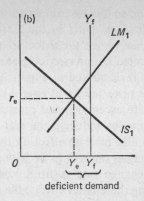

Figure 190 (a) The *IS* and *LM* curve intersection – the simultaneous determination of equilibrium in the money and goods markets.
(b) Macro equilibrium at less than full employment

rate of interest and the level of real income. This is done in part (a) of Figure 190, in which both curves are drawn with slopes which indicate that the underlying functions are interest elastic.

In deriving these curves, the general price level is held constant, so that any change in the value of nominal income is necessarily a change in the value of real income, and it is real income which is measured along the horizontal axis. This allows us to introduce a maximum real output curve into the diagram, corresponding to the level of real output which is possible when labour and capital are fully employed. This is represented in part (a) by the vertical line labelled Yf. The *IS* and *LM* curves have been drawn to intersect at a point on the Yf line, which means that the situation depicted in part (a) is one of full employment general equilibrium. This is only one of many possible equilibrium positions, since the economy can be in equilibrium at less than full employment. If unemployment exists in the economy, in the sense that the equilibrium level of real output is less than Yf, the *IS* and *LM* curves will intersect to the left of the Yf line, as illustrated in part (b) of Figure 190. An indication of the deficiency in the level of aggregate demand is provided by the shortfall in real output $Ye - Yf$, which can be translated into a measure of unemployment by use of the aggregate production function. When analysing situations involving deficient aggregate effecttive demand it is reasonable to assume that the general price level is constant, so that no complications are introduced into the analysis by price induced shifts in the *LM* curve. However, this ceases to be true when we use the model to analyse excess demand situations, as represented by intersection points to the right of the *Yf* line.

This is illustrated in Figure 191, part (a). In such situations the general price level will rise. As the general price level rises, in response to excess demand pressures, it will affect the position of the *LM* curve by reducing the real value of the nominal money stock. It may also have an effect on the *IS* curve through the influence of rising prices on savings decisions, the distribution of income, and, if the exchange rate is fixed, the volume of imports and exports. Ignoring these latter effects, the influence of rising prices on the *LM* curve is illustrated in Figure 191. Initially the general price level is P_0, and the *LM* curve is LM_1. This intersects the *IS* curve to the right of the *Yf* line which indicates that the economy is suffering from excess demand, as indicated by the horizontal distance, $Ye - Y^*$. As in all supply and demand analysis the existence of excess effective demand leads to a bidding up of prices and a rise in the general price level. If the nominal money supply is held constant, the rise in the general price level will cause the real value of the money stock to fall and this will lead to a shift to the left in the *LM* curve. When the general price level has risen to P_1 the fall in the real value of the

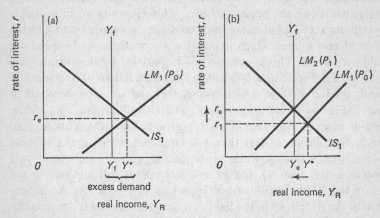

Figure 191 (a) The *IS* and *LM* curves — excess effective demand. (b) The *IS* and *LM* curves — elimination of excess demand. The general price level rises from P_0 to P_1 and the *LM* curve shifts leftward to LM_2

money stock, and the consequent rise in the rate of interest, will be such as to eliminate the excess demand and restore price stability. This is shown in the diagram by the second LM curve, LM_2, which intersects the IS curve at a point on the full employment line. The second LM curve is based on the same nominal money stock as the first, but embodies a higher general price level, i.e. $P_1 > P_0$. You should check your understanding of this sequence of events by constructing the LM curve, as shown in Figure 189, for two different price levels and hence two different transactions demand for money curves.

This particular example provides a formal analysis of one of the propositions discussed in Chapter 37. For inflation to continue, the nominal money supply must be continually expanded, otherwise as the general price level increases, it will eliminate the pressures which caused it to rise in the first place.

The model is useful for the light it throws on the operation and relative effectiveness of monetary and fiscal policy measures. Before using the model for this purpose we would like to stress that it only provides an approximate guide to the choice of alternative policy measures. There are two reasons for this note of caution. The first, which was mentioned earlier, is that the model can only be used to yield comparative static predictions about the effects of different policy measures. It yields no information on the dynamics of adjustment following a particular policy action, information which may be crucially important in choosing between policies. The second is less obvious, but no less important, and concerns the question of how fiscal policy measures are financed, and hence the extent to which monetary and fiscal policy actions are interdependent. This involves the broader question: how does money enter into the economy? This is one of the issues discussed in the appendix to this chapter. At this stage it is sufficient to note that it is not always meaningful to talk about monetary and fiscal policy measures as though they were independent alternatives. Depending upon how some fiscal policy measures are financed, they may also involve changes in the supply of money. Further, the effectiveness (multiplier value), of certain fiscal policy measures may vary depending upon the degree of monetary support given to the fiscal measure. For example, the effectiveness of an expansionary fiscal policy is more likely to be enhanced if it is accompanied by a policy of keeping interest rates

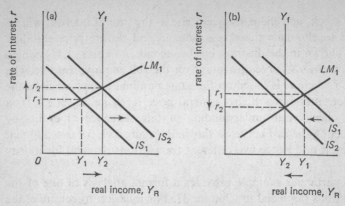

Figure 192 (a) An expansionary fiscal policy, represented by the shift to the right of the IS curve IS_2, causes the equilibrium level of real income to increase from Y_1 to Y_2. With this policy the rise in income is associated with a rise in the rate of interest. (b) A deflationary fiscal policy represented by the shift to the left of the IS curve to IS_2 eliminates excess demand and leads to an equilibrium level of income at the full employment level, Y_f. With this policy the elimination of excess demand is associated with a fall in the rate of interest

constant (which involves monetary expansion), than if it is associated with a rise in interest rates (a constant supply of money).

Figure 192 illustrates the operation of fiscal policy. In part (a) the economy is initially in equilibrium at less than full employment, Y_1, and the government introduces an expansionary fiscal policy, increase in government expenditure, which via the multiplier process causes real income to increase to Y_2, the full employment level. (In these examples the IS curve is constructed by adding a government expenditure function to the investment function.) The operation of the policy is represented by the shift to the right of the IS curve to IS_2, so that it intersects the LM curve at a higher output/employment level. Because the policy is 'pure' in that it involves no accompanying monetary expansion (the LM curve remains the same), the increase in real income, and hence in the transactions demand for money leads to a rise in the equilibrium value of the rate of interest to r_2.

Part (b) illustrates the operation of a deflationary fiscal policy. The initial position is one of excess effective demand, represented by the intersection of the IS and LM curves at Y_1, which is to the right of the full employment line. This position cannot be maintained since the desired level of output exceeds the economy's productive capacity. If we assume a closed economy, so that the excess demand cannot spill over into imports, the situation will lead to a rise in the general price level. A fiscal policy designed to eliminate the excess demand would serve to moderate or even forestall, the inflationary process. Such a policy would involve a cut in government expenditure and/or measures to restrain private expenditure. This is represented in the diagram by the shift to the left of the IS curve to IS_2. If the measures operate with precision (which is rare in practice), the IS curve would shift to the left and intersect the unchanged LM curve at Y_2, the full employment, zero excess demand, level of output. This policy action also leads to a fall in the demand for money and thus is associated with a decrease in the equilibrium value of the rate of interest to r_2.

Figure 193 illustrates how the same problems can be dealt with using monetary policy measures. In the unemployment case, part (a), an expansionary monetary policy shifts the LM curve to the right, to LM_2, and the stimulus to demand causes real income to

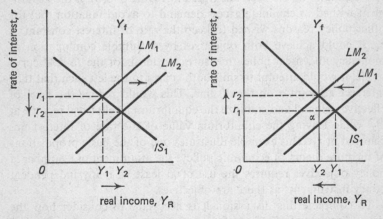

Figure 193 (a) An expansionary monetary policy, represented by a shift to the right of the LM curve to LM_2, causes the equilibrium level of income to increase from Y_1 to Y_2. With this policy the rate of interest falls. (b) A deflationary monetary policy, represented by a shift to the left of the LM curve to LM_2, eliminates excess demand and leads to an equilibrium level of income at the full employment level, Y_f. With this policy the rate of interest rises.

Fitting the Pieces Together 713

increase to Y_2, the full employment level. In contrast with the expansionary fiscal policy discussed above, this policy is accompanied by a fall in the equilibrium value of the rate of interest. More correctly, it is the policy induced decrease in the rate of interest which helps to stimulate demand.

In part (b) a deflationary monetary policy, represented by the shift to the left of the LM curve to LM_2, eliminates excess demand and prevents inflation. The economy returns to equilibrium at the full employment level of output, Y_2. In this case demand is checked by the rise in the rate of interest, which moves to a higher equilibrium level.

The difference in the behaviour of the rate of interest with respect to the operation of fiscal and monetary policy measures is due to the fact that in one case demand, and hence income, changes are associated with changes in the supply of money, while in the other they are not. This difference is of considerable importance. If the government has an interest rate policy objective as well as employment and price level objectives, it will often need to use a combination of fiscal and monetary measures to reach its policy objectives. For example, in the case illustrated in Figure 193(b), if the government wished to eliminate excess demand to avoid inflation, but for other policy reasons wished to keep the rate of interest constant at r_1, it could achieve both objectives by a suitable combination of monetary and fiscal policy measures. In terms of the IS-LM curve model it would attempt to shift both curves to the left such that they intersect at point α on the Y_f line. This would reduce the level of effective demand and stabilize the equilibrium level of real income at Y_2, while leaving the equilibrium value of the rate of interest unchanged at r_1. This example illustrates one of the basic propositions of the pure theory of economic policy: the attainment of a number of policy objectives requires the use of at least as many independent policy instruments as there are objectives.

To complete this discussion it is necessary to consider how the slopes (interest elasticities) of the two curves influence the effectiveness of different policy measures. As mentioned earlier, the slopes of the IS and LM curves depend upon the interest elasticities of the underlying functional relationships. The greater the responsiveness of investment (and consumption) expenditure to changes in the rate of interest, the more elastic the IS curve will be. With an exogenously determined supply of money, the more interest elastic the demand for money, the more interest elastic the *LM* curve will be. If the supply of money is assumed to be positively related to the rate of interest this elasticity would also affect the slope of the *LM* curve. However, since the interest elasticity of the supply of money is likely to be low, in the short run at least, we will continue to assume that it is zero, i.e. that the supply of money is exogenously determined. (This is another simplifying assumption which could prove to be misleading. When you have read this chapter it would be a useful exercise to see how relaxing this assumption modifies some of the results derived in this section.)

Figure 194 below illustrates how different values of the interest elasticities of investment and the demand for money determine the relative effectiveness of monetary and fiscal policy measures. The examples shown all illustrate expansionary policy measures, since the conclusions derived for expansionary policies apply equally to deflationary policies.

In part (a) the *IS* curve has a moderate slope, which indicates that the underlying investment demand curve is interest elastic. We will refer to this as the 'normal' case. The *LM* curve, on the other hand, is shown to be nearly horizontal, which, on our assumption about the supply of money, indicates that the demand for money is highly interest elastic. In this case it is apparent that fiscal policy is very effective. The shift to the right of the *IS* curve, caused by an expansionary fiscal policy, has a large impact on the level of real income and a small impact on the rate of interest. The fiscal policy multiplier is large in this case. The reason why fiscal policy works well in this case is because the demand for money is highly responsive to variations in the rate of interest. Thus, as income increases, and with it the demand for money, a small increase in the rate of interest is sufficient to induce people to make do with less money. Consequently the expansion of real income is not thwarted by monetary stringency.

Although the case is not illustrated separately, the same combination of elasticities reduces the effectiveness of monetary policy. That is, the effectiveness of fiscal policy in this case is at the expense of monetary policy. This is made plain by considering what happens when the demand for money is perfectly interest elastic (the liquidity trap case). When the demand for money is perfectly interest elastic, the *LM* curve becomes horizontal, and variations in the supply and

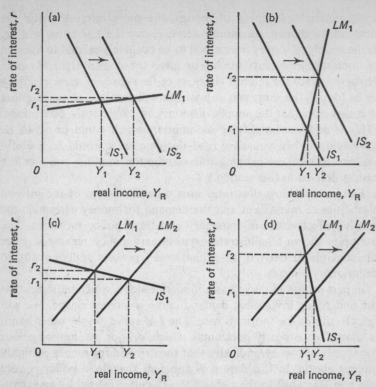

Figure 194 The influence of interest elasticities on the effectiveness of monetary and fiscal policy. (a) Demand for money highly interest elastic, monetary policy weak, fiscal policy strong. (b) Demand for money highly interest inelastic, monetary policy strong, fiscal policy weak. (c) Investment demand highly interest elastic, monetary policy strong, fiscal policy weak. (d) Investment demand highly interest inelastic, monetary policy weak, fiscal policy strong

demand for money have no effect on the rate of interest. Consequently fiscal policy measures have a significant impact on the level of real income. In direct contrast, monetary policy measures have no effect on either real income or the rate of interest (variations in the supply of money do not alter the position of the LM curve).

The situation depicted in part (b) involves a combination of elasticities which reverses the above conclusions. The IS curve has the same slope as before, but the LM curve is nearly vertical, indicating that the interest elasticity of the demand for money is very low.

In this case an expansionary fiscal policy has only a weak effect on the level of real income and a much more pronounced effect on the level of the rate of interest. The fiscal multiplier is weakened in this case because the demand for money is interest inelastic. The demand boosting effect of the fiscal expansion rapidly runs up against monetary stringency. A large rise in the rate of interest is required to induce people to hold less money for asset purposes and provide the extra money for transactions purposes. But as the rate of interest rises private investment (and consumption) expenditure is cut back and it is this reduction in private expenditure which causes the fiscal multiplier to be small. If the demand for money was totally interest inelastic the *LM* curve would be vertical, and the interest rate 'crowding out' effect would completely nullify any expansionary fiscal policy. That is, in this extreme case the fiscal multiplier would be zero, and changes in the level of government expenditure would merely serve to alter the equilibrium level of the rate of interest.

The same combination of elasticities as depicted in part (b) have the opposite effect on the efficiency of monetary policy, as fiscal policy becomes less effective monetary policy becomes more effective. Although the case is not illustrated separately, it can be readily deduced from the diagram, that the steeper the *LM* curve, the greater the impact of monetary policy (changes in the supply of money), on the equilibrium level of real income.

We can summarize these results as follows:—

Given a reasonably interest elastic IS curve, and other things being equal, the relative effectiveness of monetary and fiscal policy measures depend upon the interest elasticity of the demand for money.

The more interest elastic is the demand for money the stronger is fiscal policy and the weaker is monetary policy.

The less interest elastic is the demand for money the weaker is fiscal policy and the stronger is monetary policy.

Parts (c) and (d) of Figure 194 illustrate how the interest elasticity of investment expenditure (the slope of the *IS* curve), influences the relative effectiveness of monetary and fiscal policy. In both diagrams the *LM* curves are drawn so as to indicate that the demand for money is moderately interest elastic. We will refer to this as the 'normal' case for the *LM* curve. Taking both diagrams together, it is apparent that the effectiveness of monetary policy depends crucially upon the interest elasticity of the *IS* curve. In part (c) the *IS* curve is fairly interest elastic and an expansionary monetary policy, represented by the shift to the right of the *LM* curve, has a marked impact on the equilibrium level of real income, and a fairly moderate effect on the level of the rate of interest. In sharp contrast, part (d), when the *IS* curve is interest inelastic, monetary policy is largely ineffective in its influence on the equilibrium level of real income. At the limit of a completely interest inelastic *IS* curve monetary policy would have no effect on the level of real income and merely serve to determine the equilibrium level of the rate of interest.

As in the other two cases, an improvement in the effectiveness of one policy is at the expense of the other policy. Thus in part (c) as investment expenditure becomes more interest elastic (the *IS* curve becomes flatter), monetary policy becomes more effective and fiscal policy less effective. Conversely, in part (d), as investment expenditure becomes less interest elastic (the *IS* curve becomes steeper), monetary policy becomes less effective and fiscal policy becomes more effective, in terms of the impact of the policy measure on the level of real income.

We can summarize these results as follows:

Given a reasonably interest elastic LM *curve, and other things being equal, the relative effectiveness of monetary and fiscal policy measures depends upon the interest elasticity of investment expenditure.*

The more interest elastic is investment expenditure the stronger is monetary policy and the weaker is fiscal policy.

The less interest elastic is investment expenditure the weaker is monetary policy and the stronger is fiscal policy.

Hopefully by now you should have a firm understanding of this kind of reasoning so there is no further need to describe in detail how the relative effectiveness of monetary and fiscal policy measures varies as other elasticity possibilities are considered. We will confine our discussion to just one more example. If both curves are highly interest inelastic (a combination of the *LM* curve in (b) with the *IS* curve in (d)), monetary and fiscal policy measures will both be ineffective.

The question you should now be asking, with due regard to our earlier warnings about the limitations of the *IS–LM* curve model, is:

what do the curves look like in practice? The answer has already been given when we referred to a reasonably interest elastic *IS* curve and a moderately interest elastic *LM* curve as representing the 'normal' cases. That is, although the evidence relating to these questions is less than perfect, and circumstances can be envisaged in which one of the curves approximates fairly closely to one of the extreme elasticity possibilities, if only for a short period of time, the two curves normally exhibit sufficient interest elasticity, for both monetary and fiscal policy measures to be effective. If this is accepted, and it is not by all economists, the question of the choice of policy instruments is not an either/or one between monetary and fiscal policy measures, but rather that of the choice of the 'best' combination of the two to achieve the chosen objectives of macroeconomic policy.

Extension of the model to the open economy

The *IS–LM* model depicts the workings of a closed economy and to extend the analysis to the open economy it is necessary to use the *BB* (balance of payments) curve which we constructed in Chapter 36. Figure 195(a) reveals that the equilibrium of an open economy requires the intersection of the *IS*, *LM* and the *BB* curve at one point; that is, there must be simultaneous equilibrium of the domestic goods market, the money market and the foreign trade market. Several points from Chapter 36 now need to be observed. Firstly, the *BB* curve indicates balance of payments equilibria for given rates of interest, income levels and exchange rate, the trade account need not balance since any deficit could be offset by a surplus on the capital account. Secondly, all points above the curve denote a surplus and all points below the curve indicate a deficit. Thirdly, the curve slopes upward because at low income levels imports are low and the small amounts of short-term capital required for balance can be attracted at low interest rates whilst at high income levels net imports tend to be high and require high interest rates and capital inflows to maintain balance. Fourthly, an exchange rate appreciation shifts the curves upward and a depreciation shifts it downward.

Now let us suppose, as in Figure 195(b), the economy is in domestic and foreign equilibrium at point *A* but that this equilibrium is an underemployment equilibrium. The balance of payments is only kept in equilibrium by keeping incomes, output and employment low. If

Extension of the Model to the Open Economy 719

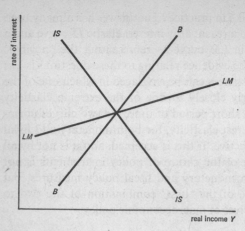

Figure 195 (a)

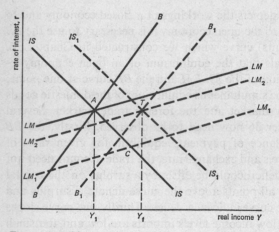

Figure 195 (b)

the government wished to attain full employment income Y_1 it could expand the money supply to LM_1. The domestic goods and money markets could then move into equilibrium at C. But if the expansion of the money supply lowered interest rates it would attract less capital from abroad and the balance of payments would become worse. The solution might, therefore, be to let the exchange rate fall and shift the BB curve to BB_1. Because devaluation has a switching effect it would shift the IS curve to IS_1 and because devaluation has a real balance or expenditure-reducing effect, the LM curve would shift from LM_1 to LM_2. Eventually, a full employment equilibrium could be attained at T.

In combining the foreign trade sector with the IS–LM diagram we omitted to mention why the BB curve was steeper than the LM curve. This was deliberate because the analysis of curves with different slopes becomes complicated. However, our analysis does provide a justification for drawing the BB curve steeper than the LM curve. Devaluation increases net injections and raises the level of income, and with a given money supply raises the interest rate. If the slopes were reversed monetary and fiscal policies would give different results under fixed and flexible exchange rate regimes.

Finally, we note that if a fixed exchange rate was in operation then the removal of unemployment in Figure 195(b) would involve expansionary fiscal policies to move the IS curve and restrictive monetary policies to shift the LM curve until the new IS and LM curves intersected on an unchanged BB curve at a point above T.

Appendix: The monetarist controversy

In recent years, few issues in economics have aroused as much interest as the 'Monetarist Controversy'. In this controversy, as in most others, much of the debate was engendered by confusion as to the real issues involved, and even over the meaning of some of the terms used. One aspect of this confusion concerns the name of the controversy, since it has been misleadingly referred to by some as the 'Monetary versus Fiscal Policy Controversy' and by others as the 'Keynesian versus Monetarist Debate'. We say these are misleading because while they do refer to aspects of the controversy they nevertheless distract attention from the fundamental issues involved in it, namely the importance of the supply of money and the role of monetary policy.

The controversy has its origins back in the 1950s with the pioneering work of Professor Milton Friedman of Chicago University, on the demand for money and the role of monetary policy. Friedman, and subsequently his followers, a term used to describe all those with similar views, stressed the importance of the supply of money in determining the behaviour of prices and the level of economic activity, and hence argued the case for the revival of monetary policy, which at the time had fallen into disrepute. Consequently, they became known as *monetarists*. The participants on the other side of the controversy formed two distinct, but not unrelated, groups. Those who challenged the theoretical, empirical and methodological basis of the monetarists' arguments, and those who set themselves up as the defenders of fiscal policy, which they thought was under attack by the monetarists. This latter group became known as the Keynesians.[1]

With hindsight it is clear that participants on both sides of the controversy were responsible for creating confusion. To avoid adding to this confusion we will describe the monetarist position, and the main issues involved in the controversy, by means of a set of straight-forward propositions.

1 The demand for money function is a stable function of a relatively small number of economic variables.

2 The relationship between the demand for real money balances and the nominal supply of money is one of the key macroeconomic relationships.

3 There is a predictable relationship between changes in the supply of money and the level of nominal income, the *money multiplier relationship*.

4 The money multiplier relationship is at least as good a predictor of the response of the level of economic activity to changes in the supply of money, as the *fiscal multiplier* is for changes in the level of autonomous expenditure.

5 Changes in the supply of money exert their influence on nominal income with a long, and sometimes variable, lag.

6 In the long run, the influence of changes in the supply of money is mainly on the price level and not real output. Money is neutral in the long run.

7 The interest rate relevant to economic decision making is the *real* and not the *money* rate of interest. Because the real rate of interest depends upon price expectations, it is unobservable. Consequently,

1. The development of the controversy is discussed by H. G. Johnson:
'The Keynesian Revolution and the Monetarist Counter Revolution',
American Economic Review, May 1971. The article is reprinted in Johnson:
Further Essays in Monetary Economics.

variations in the money rate of interest do not provide a good indication of variations in the real rate of interest, nor of the strength of monetary policy.

8 The target variable of monetary policy should be the supply of money (a monetary aggregate) and not the rate of interest (credit market conditions).

9 Because of lags in the transmission of monetary impulses, steady growth of the money supply is likely to be more stabilizing than discretionary variations.

10 Fiscal policy is important, but in using fiscal policy allowance must be made for the monetary consequences of different fiscal policy actions.

11 Monetary expansion is essential for the continuation of an inflationary process. Control of the money supply is an essential ingredient of any policy to stop inflation.

This rich menu of monetarist propositions clearly demonstrates why it is inappropriate to appraise the monetarist controversy solely in terms of monetary versus fiscal policy. It also dispels the myth that monetarism is synonymous with crude quantity theory predictions. Monetarism is concerned with the role of money in the economy, and the appropriate monetary policy for minimizing monetary and real disturbances in the economy. It does not imply that money alone is important, nor that monetary policy is more important than fiscal policy. It recognizes that both are important, but stresses that to use them effectively they must be used to attain the ends to which they are best suited. It further emphasizes that because changes in the supply of money, for whatever reason, exert specific and pronounced effects on the level of nominal income, the monetary consequences of fiscal policy actions must be allowed for. That is, monetarists recognize that in some cases the terms monetary and fiscal policy refer to the same policy actions, in that the policy actions involve changes in the supply of money.

The propositions also reveal that the influence of changes in the supply of money on the level of economic activity involves time lags and expectations effects. This means the *IS–LM* curve model is often unsuited for the purpose of analysing monetarist arguments, since the model assumes that the price level and expectations are given, and, because of its comparative static nature, ignores time. Not surprisingly then, attempts using the model to spell out the issues involved in the controversy have often served to confuse rather than enlighten. This said, when it is properly used, the model can throw some light on the issues in question.

In Figure 196 we draw on the analysis of the preceding chapter to illustrate the conditions under which the supply of money, and hence monetary policy, can have an influence on the level of economic activity. What the model cannot reveal is the full nature of this influence (the transmission mechanisms involved) and, more importantly, from the point of view of economic policy, the time scale over which the influence operates. To simplify our discussion Figure 196 contains three diagrams in one.

The two IS curves which intersect the horizontal section of the LM curve illustrate the case in which, because of an infinitely interest elastic demand for money, fiscal policy is effective. Changes in the level of government expenditure affect the equilibrium level of real income, without affecting the level of the rate of interest. Monetary policy, in contrast, has no effect on either the level of real income or the level of the rate of interest. Because of the association of Keynesian economics with fiscal policy, this situation is referred to as the extreme *Keynesian Case*.

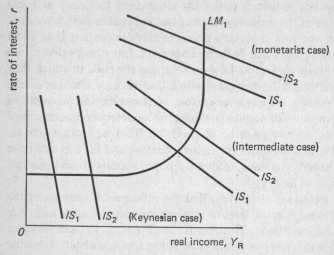

Figure 196 Fiscal versus monetary policy

724 Fitting the Pieces Together

The opposite situation is illustrated in the diagram by the intersection of the two *IS* curves with the vertical section of the *LM* curve. In this case, in which the demand for money is perfectly interest inelastic, fiscal policy has absolutely no effect on the level of real income and merely alters the equilibrium level of the rate of interest. Monetary policy, in marked contrast, affects both the level of real income and the level of the rate of interest. For these reasons this situation is referred to as the extreme *monetarist case*.

The third situation illustrated in the diagram, referred to as the *intermediate case*, is that in which both monetary and fiscal policy affect the level of real income and the level of the rate of interest. Obviously, if the real world approximated to either of the two extreme cases, the monetarist controversy would have been readily resolved since it reduces to an either/or issue between fiscal and monetary policy. Moreover, the issue in question is one which hinges solely upon the magnitude of the interest elasticity of the demand for money, and thus lends itself to empirical investigation. However, empirical studies clearly indicate that the relevant interest elasticities are such as to indicate that the intermediate case best describes the real world. This implies that both monetary and fiscal policy are potentially important. This in turn implies that the *IS–LM* curve model is severely limited in the additional light it can throw on the issues involved, for the reasons mentioned above.

It is necessary to use dynamic macroeconomic models to examine the validity of many monetarist propositions. Since some of these models incorporate relationships based on the interpretation of historical evidence, and hence involve judgements linking association with causation, they are subject to the problem of differing interpretations of the 'facts'. Despite this, progress has been made. On the basis of theoretical analysis, and the large body of empirical findings which have been accumulated in testing monetarist propositions, some of the issues have been resolved. It is now possible to conclude that the case for the importance of money, and the effectiveness of monetary policy, has been established beyond reasonable doubt. It is no longer possible to claim that 'money does not matter', or that 'money alone matters'. Indeed, it now seems surprising to think that either of these two views were ever seriously advocated, yet they did represent the polarization of views in the early stages of the controversy. Other aspects of the controversy are still being debated, just as differences remain as to the degree of importance to be attributed to monetary policy.

Questions

1 Outline some of the problems encountered in analysing the interdependence between macroeconomic variables.

2 Using one of the approaches described in this chapter, describe the channels of operation through which the devaluation of a country's currency will effect the main macroeconomic variables in the economy. (Hint: clearly specify the initial state of the economy and which magnitudes are being assumed constant.)

3 Describe the construction of the *IS–LM* curve model and use the model to analyse the consequences of:
(a) a change in the supply of money;
(b) a change in the price level;
(c) a change in the level of injections.

4 Is the rate of interest determined by monetary or real forces or jointly by the interaction of the two?

5 Use the *IS–LM* curve model to assess the usefulness of the 45° model of income determination.

6 'The *IS–LM* curve model conceals more than it reveals.' Is this a valid criticism of the model? If you answer in the affirmative, what approach would you recommend for analysing the problems the *IS–LM* curve model is meant to deal with?

7 'An increase in the level of money wages has the same macroeconomic consequences as a decrease in the supply of money.' Discuss.

8 Will an increase in government expenditure, paid for by an increase in the rate of income tax, have the same impact on the economy as an equivalent increase in government expenditure, paid for by printing money?

9 An economy is in equilibrium with everything unchanging from one period to the next. Now imagine that as a result of too much wine at lunch the chief of the central bank orders the money supply to be

increased. Trace out the impact on interest rates, the balance of payments, output, prices, income, government tax income etc. If it helps, try imagining that the economy is that of the UK.

10 'Monetarism is not synonymous with the Quantity Theory of Money, nor directly concerned with the issue of monetary versus fiscal policy.' Elucidate.

Part Nine
The State

That the state is a good and not a bad is something that the British school of economists, from Smith down to Keynes, has always accepted. True, they could warn of dangers, but there was never any doubt that they saw the state as something more than an appendix. This view of the British tradition has come to be rejected by one strand of contemporary British economists and an influential group of American economists whose philosophic outlook seems to have been influenced as much by continental thinkers as by aberrations of the British tradition. Briefly, in the opinion of these latter groups, it is so difficult to control the state that a strong preference is expressed for market production and distribution. So much so that every attempt is made to squeeze decision-making into the confines of the market.

Science, so the history books demonstrate, has advanced by solving the easy problems first. Physics appeared successful as compared with the other natural sciences, because it found a group of problems where classification and measurement made prediction and understanding possible. The contrast with biology, chemistry and metallurgy was striking. Likewise economics among the social sciences seemed successful because it appeared to indulge in measurement: psychology tended to follow the same path. Sociology and politics differ strikingly. Sociology appears to be the residual legatee of all that is non-quantifiable and politics appears to have languished since economics was severed from its Siamese twin, political economy. But these were early and cheap successes. The willingness of physicists to move into a strange and difficult terrain like thermodynamics is, however, in sharp contrast to those economists who seem reluctant to consider institutions other than the market. 'Truth', said William Blake, 'can never be told so as to be understood, and not be believed.' Perhaps we understand the market propagandists even if we do not always believe them.

Chapter 41
The Role of the State

In an earlier chapter (Chapter 38) we discussed the impact of the government's revenue/expenditure processes on the level of employment and the general level of prices. Now we turn to a discussion of the need for government action to ensure a particular pattern of resource allocation and distribution of incomes. In this chapter, therefore, we are concerned with one of the longest-standing debates in economics: what constitutes the right 'mix' of economic activities undertaken by the public and private sectors of the economy?

The analysis of government's role is based upon a value judgement, arrived at through consensus, that society should aim at making the best possible use of its scarce resources which have alternative uses. Thus the study of government's economic role applies certain conclusions derived from *positive economics*, concerning the relative efficiencies of various institutional arrangements for production and distribution, to the field of *normative economics* which is concerned with discovering the best set of these institutional arrangements. Now since the state, as we saw earlier, is no more than another institutional mechanism for the transformation of scarce resources into goods, to refer (as people often do) to government's role in terms of 'interference' with the economic system is to deny the state's identity with that system. A system may comprise a sharing of the transformation processes between private and collective production; or it may comprise only one institution, the state, in which case all production is collective. Which system a society adopts is largely determined by the social and political, as well as the economic, desires of that society. In other words, the politico-economic system itself becomes a good, satisfying the philosophic ideals (wants) of the community which adopts it. Such goals, alongside all other community desires, constitute what the economist terms a 'social welfare function'.

Objectives

Taking the role of the State to be the promotion of the best use of society's scarce resources, what constitutes the 'best'? Presumably the best use is that which maximizes community happiness or 'welfare'. But such a guideline is somewhat imperfect since the determinants of welfare constitute a multifarious array, creating severe measurement problems for the public decision-makers. The greatest problem facing the economist, as adviser to government, is that welfare is subjective. Now the economist usually makes objective calculations of things subjective via the use of the measuring rod of money; subjective motivations may promote activities which have a quantifiable impact on prices and incomes. In so far as welfare is determined by consumption of goods and services which carry market prices, then community welfare can also be measured in this way, i.e. in terms of national income. Indeed it is this measure of welfare which has traditionally been adopted by economists,[1] but total reliance upon it will always result in an inaccurate estimate of community welfare since the latter depends on many things which do not carry a market price. (We encountered some of these difficulties in the very first chapter of this book.)

The subjective nature of welfare also creates another serious problem – how to aggregate individual welfare levels. How can we measure the impact on community welfare of, say, an increase in the production of a particular good if some people benefit and others suffer as a result? Suppose the public decision-maker decides to promote an increase in the production of butter and a reduction in the production of ships. Suppose further that shipbuilders are totally unsuitable for employment in butter production without extensive re-training. Other things being equal, the income of factors involved in the production of butter will rise, while shipbuilders' short-run income will fall. On the narrow interpretation of welfare one group in society is made better off, another worse off; how then are we to measure the welfare effect of the policy change?

To avoid this problem of interpersonal welfare comparisons economists have adopted the somewhat negative *Pareto criterion*[2] which states that for a policy change to lead to an increase in

1. The term *economic welfare*, first coined by Pigou (1912), is usually employed.
2. After Vilfredo di Pareto (1848–1923).

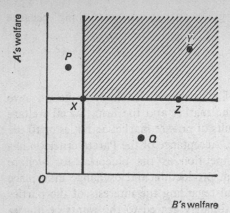

Figure 197

community welfare it must make *at least one* community member better off and *no* community members worse off. In terms of Figure 197, a policy change which moves the community (two individuals) from welfare level X to any level within the shaded area is acceptable, but not a change which results in a move from X to a point outside the shaded area, e.g. P or Q.

As a practical policy guide the Pareto criterion is of little use since real public decisions will nearly always result in one section of the community being made better off and another one worse off. Furthermore, a rigid adherence to the rule would always maintain the *status quo* and constitute a severe obstacle to changes in the law. A less conservative approach is to allow for compensation to take place, whereby potential gainers from a policy change can, if required, compensate potential losers. In this way, a policy change is acceptable even when one section of the community gains at the expense of another, so long as the former gains more than the latter loses. Although presenting problems, both theoretical and practical, this approach does give hope of a practical compromise.

We should note of course that concern for compensation is only characteristic of an economic system in which distribution of social justice is defined in terms of private exchange. A rigid central planner, on the other hand, may simply decree that the unequal bestowal of private benefits resulting from his decisions is a cost far outweighed by the social benefit thereby created. In this system the individual loses his autonomy and any policy change is a 'good thing' because the economic dictator says so.

Private or public markets?

Turning to the definition of government's economic role we have two models to guide us – the market and the firm. Social welfare can be largely left to the results of private market activities or to the planning powers of the state. Acceptance of the Pareto criterion has led many to postulate competition as the blueprint for welfare maximization. In this system production and exchange take place in markets which are neutral regarding the interests of the parties concerned. Production is ultimately geared to the wants of households, each of which faces the same price for any particular product and the same financial reward for the rendering of factor services owned by the household. All producers face a common set of relevant factor prices and they equate the marginal cost of production with the price of their product. In this way society maximizes output from its given supply of scarce resources and consumers pay for the last unit of a commodity produced an amount exactly equal to the cost to the producer of producing that unit, i.e. to the cost to the community in foregone alternatives.

This extreme form of the market system merely minimizes the role of government, it by no means renders such a role unnecessary. No economic system can operate without some production activities being undertaken by the state. Even the perfectly competitive economy requires some minimum provision of government services since markets can only function properly against a backcloth of state protection. Such protection must at least include laws to prevent contractual default and violation of the institution of private property. Also required is the physical manifestation of these laws, both domestically and internationally, via a police force and a national defence network. (Equally important in a monetary economy is the maintenance of a stable value of the medium of exchange.)

Such goods as a legal system and a national defence network are examples of what we have termed 'collective goods'. A unit of national defence is equally available to all consumers – individual A's consumption of that unit can in no way diminish the consumption by individual B of that same unit. The private sector cannot undertake production of such goods since the exclusion principle cannot operate – no one can be excluded from the benefits of collective goods once they are supplied. In the absence of exclusion the price mechanism cannot operate since, in a free market, potential consumers would not reveal their true preferences, knowing that as long as one unit of the good is purchased by someone the benefits of that unit may be enjoyed by everyone. This difficulty is often referred to as the 'free-rider' problem. But the state possesses coercive powers to extract payment for such goods and can determine supply, assuming a democratic political framework, via reference to information collected in the ballot-box. Thus it is possible for the voting mechanism to constitute a proxy market-place wherein consumer preferences for various quantities of collective goods are expressed not in terms of money bids but in terms of votes.

We should note at this stage that 'public provision' merely refers to the fact that total supply of certain collective goods is determined by a political, rather than a market mechanism. The actual physical manifestation of these goods, in the form of inputs into the collective goods production process, may quite easily be undertaken by private enterprise. To continue with the example of national defence, it is not military hardware that constitutes this particular collective good but defence policies, the amount and nature of defensive protection. Production of the intermediate goods – machine guns, tanks and aircraft carriers (even trained manpower) – may be undertaken by the private sector in response to the placing of government contracts.

The provision of the two collective goods mentioned so far, a legal system and a defence network, is the necessary condition for an economy to operate smoothly. But is it sufficient? If, as suggested earlier, the perfectly competitive market system has so many attractive features, what is the case for extending state activity beyond the provision of law and order, defence of the realm and the financing of these provisions? The answer is twofold:

1 Several of the conditions necessary to achieve a perfectly competitive equilibrium are not features of the free enterprise system of reality.

2 The perfectly competitive model may be a world of allocative efficiency but it contains no in-built guarantees about an equitable distribution of incomes.

The major problems facing the real world market system collapse into two groups: (a) problems of monopoly; and (b) spillover problems (or 'externalities').

Let us now consider these problems and their consequences in some detail.

Monopoly

A feature of the 'unregulated' market economy is that market-power may become concentrated in the hands of a few producers, or only one producer. As we saw in Chapter 18 this may result in a welfare loss for society. Because marginal cost is not equal to price under conditions of monopoly, consumer surplus is not being maximized. It is true, as we saw earlier, that output of a commodity may rise and its price be lowered when a perfectly competitive industry is 'monopolized'. This result obtains from the realization of economies of scale. But even if all monopolies were to be created via the reaping of scale economies a social optimum would still not be reached since marginal cost would still not equal price. As a result of increased output and a lower price consumer surplus from a particular commodity might be increased relative to the amount enjoyed under competition but unrealized consumer surplus would still exist. This is illustrated by Figure 198 which is a modified reproduction of Figure 110 (horizontal marginal cost curves have been chosen for simplicity).

Industry output under competitive conditions is OX_c and price per unit is OP_c (equals marginal cost, MC_1). Scale economies are realized; the industry merges into a production/sales unit and the marginal cost (equals average cost) curve shifts downwards. The monopoly output is OX_m. In the initial situation consumer surplus was equal to the area EP_cD but in the monopoly situation it has increased to EP_mC. However, despite the increase in consumer surplus (P_cDCP_m) the monopoly situation is not ideal as it stands since society is forgoing potential surplus P_mCBA. Of this potential, P_mCFA is in fact gained by the monopolist in revenue (constituting a problem of income distribution, a separate issue at this stage), but CFB is forgone. Only if marginal cost is equated with price, if output OX_s is produced, will the community gain the full benefit from this technical, or 'natural', monopoly.

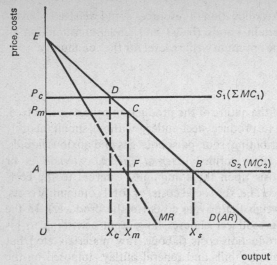

Figure 198

How might the State ensure maximum consumer surplus is enjoyed? One method would be for the community to subsidize the monopolist by an amount equal to $AFCP_m$ (the monopolist's surplus) to enable him to produce amount OX_s and be no worse off. Alternatively the State could 'nationalize' the monopoly and operate a marginal-cost pricing policy, thus producing OX_s. Which method is chosen will depend partly on a comparison of relative costs – the subsidization costs of the first method compared to the acquisition costs of the second, including the extent of X – inefficiency under public ownership. Choice will also depend upon prevailing views on income distribution since public ownership redistributes away from the monopolist to the community at large.

Spillovers

The collective goods referred to earlier cannot be traded in the market place. But many goods which *are* produced and traded under market conditions also exhibit degrees of collectiveness. The case for perfect competition rests on the assumption that all goods are purely private, i.e. privately produced and privately consumed. In the real world, however, many goods are privately produced but few are absolutely privately consumed. Now, if most goods are collectively consumed free market allocation of resources could well lead to over-consumption of certain goods (bads) and under-consumption of others in terms of the optimum welfare level for the community.

Over-consumption

Suppose, because of the nature of the production processes involved, it was not possible to produce steel cutlery without simultaneously producing (and distributing) soot, poisonous gas and noxious liquids. Such by-products, often termed *external effects*, *externalities* or *spillovers* impose costs upon the community external to the costs borne by the producer, i.e. the social costs, or total community costs, of production outweigh the private costs (to the producer). In the cutlery example the producer chooses his output according to his private marginal production costs (labour, raw materials etc.) but ignores the extra laundry bills and funeral outlays imposed on the community at large as a result of his activities. Free market allocation might ensure that the supply of knives and forks is optimal in terms of private costs and benefits, but in terms of *social* costs knives and forks are being over-produced.

Our analysis would seem to suggest that the rule to be followed to maximize community welfare is to produce units of a commodity until the marginal social costs of production are equal to the marginal social benefits from consumption. But choosing the most efficient mechanism for ensuring that this rule will be pursued is an exceedingly difficult task. Nor is it certain that an available mechanism will be adopted. The calculus of social costs and to a large extent the corrective mechanisms employed are largely determined by political and social considerations since the latter reflect the community's hierarchy of wants. The true (inter-generational) social costs of, say, despoliation of the countryside may be grossly underestimated or deliberately ignored by a community for which the major day-to-day concern is adequate food and shelter. We see evidence of this in Western Europe where current environmental problems are largely the inheritance of economic activities from an earlier period of relative under-development.

Measures taken to equate marginal social costs and benefits may operate through the market mechanism or they may take effect outside it. Where net social benefit from private production and/or distribution is likely to be negative for all ranges of output, then output may be controlled via an extension of that necessary collective good referred to earlier – the legal system. Hence in the UK we currently outlaw the private production (for purposes of market resale) of mustard gas and heroin. But where net social benefits from private production are likely to be positive for a considerable output range, products may be permitted to be bought and sold through the market mechanism subject to certain controls at the margin.

Controls on marginal outputs may again be physical although this can present problems. Referring again to noxious emissions, a method of control which has been tried in many western countries is the setting of legally permitted ceilings on the output of noxious materials. But this control mechanism presents serious scrutiny problems, e.g. how to discover which of a dozen firms established along the banks of a river exceeded the permitted noxious output limit and poisoned thousands of fish a hundred miles downstream. Obviously the larger the number of enterprises within an industry the greater the incentive for each one to ignore the law.

Alternatively the fitting of anti-pollution devices could be made compulsory on all outlets of noxious materials, both industrial (factory chimneys) and domestic (motor car exhaust systems). But if no such devices are available in the short term some alternative solution may initially be called for. Note·that both the mechanisms referred to so far require the use of further resources. The pollution problem is not simply that the environment is unpleasant but also that resources must be diverted from production of goods to the reduction of bads. If we wish to rely upon the market mechanism to solve its own problems, presumably an ideal way is to encourage research into pollution-minimizing production techniques. The market itself might provide such an incentive via increased waste-disposal costs as the sources of free goods – disposal space – are gradually exhausted; or via consumer dissatisfaction with commodities which pollute. However, the market may be very tardy in providing such response, perhaps due to the availability of seemingly unlimited disposal space in the early stages of economic development; or due to reasons suggested earlier in relation to the hierarchy of wants. Despite over two hundred years of industrialization several areas of the world are only now discovering a shortage of waste-disposal space; and Nader's 'Raiders' are a recent phenomenon.

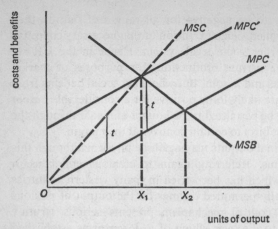

Figure 199

A possible means of speeding up market response is to raise the costs of existing production methods by forcing firms to incorporate *all* costs into their output calculations. The object of this would be to ensure that private costs, the costs actually borne by the polluter, are equal to the social costs. This could be achieved via the imposition of a tax on each unit of output, the tax so calculated as to equal the difference between private and social costs, as in Figure 199.

Figure 199 depicts a polluter. *MPC* is the curve of marginal private costs; *MSC* the curve of marginal social costs; and *MSB* the curve of marginal social benefits. There is no divergence between private and social benefits (the *MSB* curve stands for both) but social and private costs do diverge (*MSC* lies above *MPC*). Left to its own devices the firm will want to produce OX_2 units of output, equating *MPC* with *MSB*. Yet this level of output is not optimal for society since *MSC* is greater than *MSB*. Optimal output for society is OX_1 where *MSC* and *MSB* are equal. If a tax is imposed on each unit of output, equal to the difference between the private and social costs of each unit, then *MSC* becomes the firm's effective marginal cost curve and production is cut back to OX_1 which is also the optimum output level for society.[3]

Since it would be impossible to apply a different tax rate to every

3. This analysis and the illustrative diagram is applicable to all forms of congestion or pollution, e.g. road traffic, air traffic, effluent in rivers, overpopulation.

tax unit produced, a compromise must be adopted. This could be achieved by levying, on each unit produced, a tax equal to the difference between the producer's costs and the cost to society at output level OX_1. By a vertical shifting of the producer's cost curve to MPC' the optimum output level of OX_1 is produced. The gains in pollution reduction from moving to OX_1 outweigh the costs in terms of forgone output and the fact that the available output is offered at a higher price.

The above example does, of course, violate the rigorous version of the Pareto criterion since the producer is harmed in order to secure a net gain to society. Once again we see the criterion's limitation as a policy guide. Another important point to note is that even though pollution has been reduced in the example it has not been eradicated. Some individuals are still suffering external effects from output level OX_1. Should they, therefore, not receive some compensation for the loss of benefits incurred through activities beyond their control? There may still remain some ethical problems for society to resolve.

An interesting feature of the divergence between private and social costs is that the 'social optimum' output level is the same whether it is the producer who is forced to compensate the consumer or whether the consumer pays the producer to cut back production. Suppose an extra unit of firm's output would impose external costs of £50 upon local residents. The residents are, then, prepared to pay up to £50 to the firm as an inducement not to produce the marginal unit. Hence, to produce the extra unit would cost the firm (over its production costs) £50 in forgone income. If, instead, the firm is legally compelled to compensate those who suffer from the marginal output, it will again incur an extra cost of £50. The output effect, therefore, is the same regardless of which side pays for the marginal externality.

But again there is an ethical difference in the above example. Since it is the firm, rather than the consumer, which controls production, society may consider it more 'just' for the creator rather than the sufferer to pay. The state may, therefore, frame its laws as if the property rights reside with the sufferers.

The indivisibilities problem again

What if the benefits to the producer from the extra production outweigh the external costs? Then, neither a bribe nor compulsory compensation equal to the external cost will prevent the production increase. When this is the case it is even more 'just' that the producer pays, since the sufferer's bribe would be inadequate to prevent the increase in production. In the example represented by Figure 199 it was assumed that the externality problem could be dealt with by minute changes in output and in the money value of costs and benefits. But what if the nature of the good being produced is such that it cannot be produced and utilized in minute bits?

Let us consider a single example which, although an exaggeration, does demonstrate the crux of the difficulty. Suppose that a married couple, the Browns, who have one child, and who live in a block of flats, decide to produce a second child. Their neighbours, the Meanies, dislike the noise and general disturbance which children create and on hearing the news decide to spend more time away from home and to install sound-proof walls. These costs they evaluate at £150 in present value terms and they receive no benefits. The Browns estimate their costs at £400 and their benefits at £600 (both in present value terms), giving them a potential net benefit of £200.

Now, although the private cost to the Browns is £400, the true social cost of the extra child is £550, i.e. the £400 borne by the Browns *plus* the £150 borne by the Meanies. However, in this case a corrective marginal tax would not equate social costs and benefits. Since the choice involves a whole baby or no baby the Browns would still enjoy a net benefit even if the government taxed them the amount of the costs imposed on their neighbours. If the Browns were to be taxed £150 for having the extra child, their private costs would be £550; but since their private benefit from the child is worth £600 they would still pursue their intention. Furthermore, if the government were to impose the tax penalty such action would merely increase total (i.e. social) costs. The Browns would face costs of £550 and the Meanies would still bear costs of £150, a total of £700.[4] A bribe by the Meanies would be similarly ineffectual since they would only be prepared to offer £150. The only means by which all costs can be accounted for (so that $MPC = MSC$) is if the Meanies *actually receive the £150 as compensation*, i.e. if the government operates as a transfer agency. The example is summarized in Table 59

4. We are assuming that government's use of the tax proceeds does not benefit the Meanies.

Table 59

	Private costs (£)	Private benefits (£)	Uncompensated external costs (£)	Total costs (£)	Total benefits (£)
costs and benefits without corrective tax or compensation	400	600	150	550	600
costs and benefits with corrective tax	550	600	150	700	600
costs and benefits with direct compensation	550	600	nil	550	600

(the table does not include an external benefits column since the example assumes such benefits to be nil).

Let us finally remind ourselves that the problem in the example arose because the Browns were unable to produce their extra child in minute pieces. Both the benefits and costs of a minute bit of the extra child would be extremely small, so small as to be easily equated via some form of penalty imposed on the producers. But when production is all or nothing (i.e. a whole child or none) then benefits from the extra unit produced may so outweigh the costs that even if the producers are forced to incorporate all costs into their calculations they may still proceed with production. When this happens direct compensation must be effected. We need only substitute for the extra child an extra 'jumbo' jet or oil tanker to appreciate the significance of the problem in reality.

Under-consumption

Just as too much of certain goods may be consumed, according to the prevailing aims and values of society, so it is possible for *too little* of many other goods to be consumed, according to the set of values. Such under-consumption may be general or specific. A household under-consumes *generally* when its means are inadequate to finance the enjoyment of a standard of living considered to be adequate by the majority of the population. The unfortunate who are in this position are usually classified as living in *primary* poverty. *Specific* under-consumption results when households consume too little of those goods and services which benefit everyone; a range including toothbrushes, milk, good quality housing, medical services, education and any other good which yields spillover benefits.

Poverty and inequality. The definition of 'adequacy' will be based upon value judgements reflecting both the cultural and moral standards of the majority of the population as well as the economic strength of the community as a whole. Thus poverty comprises both an absolute and a relative component. Absolute poverty relates to some objectively defined standard of subsistence needs, basic physiological requirements which all individuals have regardless of their cultural environment.

Relative poverty, on the other hand, relates to culturally determined needs and its income threshold will vary from one society to another.

The causes. What causes poverty? Primary poverty is not synonymous with inequality but it often reflects how incomes are distributed in the market-oriented economy. In principle the market system provides the basis for the satisfaction of everyone's material needs in so far as specialization and the division of labour enable Man to produce as much as he can from his given supply of resources. The market system helps members of society to enjoy the fruits of this efficiency by the provision of opportunities to earn income. However, principles are notorious for breaking down in practice and the guarantee of market opportunities is not enough to ensure that everyone can enjoy the fruits of the market place since not everyone is capable of *pursuing* these opportunities.

In the market system the standard of living of each individual household is circumscribed by its ownership of something marketable, either property or labour services. In other words how much a household can buy is largely determined by how much it can sell. But as we saw in Part Eight the cyclical movements of aggregate demand in such a system prevent the guarantee that outlets for household services will always be plentiful. Furthermore, even if such a guarantee could be given, not all households possess something which markets desire – people are often limited in their capacity to learn; are subject to illness; and always grow old.

Not only does the market system provide opportunities to earn income but it also provides opportunities to accumulate wealth, i.e. a stock of net assets.[5] Such a stock provides a flow of benefits to its owner. The benefits thus derived are in excess of the regular flow of money income from the stock of assets since the ownership of wealth increases the household's range of expenditure opportunities – it provides protection against contingencies and enables periodic spending sprees; and magnifies the owner's total economic power giving access to privileges both economic, social and political.

But, as with earned income, there is no guarantee of equal access to wealth opportunities. Wealth derives initially from surplus income, that is, from income over and above consumption requirements. Thus, since opportunities for earning incomes are not equally distributed, neither are the opportunities for accumulating surplus income. Furthermore such inequality, left unchecked, is self-perpetuating. Once accumulated, a stock of wealth may be handed on from generation to generation. A household may thus enjoy a greater share of economic and political opportunities simply because it has inherited a stock of wealth.

It would seem, then, that to organize economic life in such a way as to permit purely market-determined results is to create two problems: a problem of inequality and a poverty problem. They are related but nevertheless distinct – it is possible (remember the example of Mauritius in Chapter 3) for the distribution of incomes to be perfectly equal within a community yet for everyone to be poor simply because community output is consistently very low. However, when poverty is the norm we no longer treat it as a spillover problem but as a problem of economic development. The role of the state in this respect has been discussed in earlier chapters.

Why should a community consider the distributional consequences of market activities to be problems? We can suggest two major reasons why there is concern:

1 Improvements in the distribution of incomes and wealth can lead to improvements in the allocation of resources since the latter is

5. 'Wealth' is synonymous with 'net worth', i.e. assets minus liabilities.

determined by effective demand, that is, demand backed by purchasing power, by income.

2 Utility functions are usually interdependent. Unless people wear blinkers they cannot exist in society without observing the plight of their fellows. Such awareness does not allow severe inequalities in income and wealth to persist indefinitely. The rich eventually desire to improve the welfare of the poor. Such concern may derive from an altruistic or from a selfish basis. The rich may have a genuine unselfish desire to improve the lot of the poor but the desire for improvement could equally stem from a fear of revolution or a fear of the spread of contagious diseases, poverty and disease being long-standing bedmates.

Market failure again. If the rich are concerned about the welfare of the poor and the market is an efficient signalling device, why is the poverty problem not attacked via the market mechanism itself? To some extent it is, via private charitable institutions which provide information on the location of poverty. In the small group case, like the Bushmen of the Kalahari, or the local neighbourhood in a city, the information problem may not be severe since most individuals in these cases are aware of the location of poverty and can act accordingly. But in the large group of the modern mass society individuals are aware that poverty exists but are unaware of its precise location. It is in this context, then, that the market plays its role and charitable organizations are established to channel income transfers from the 'haves' to the 'have-nots'.

The reason the market fails to solve the poverty problem is that filling the information gap by the establishment of private charities is not enough. If the problem is to be overcome the actual amount of income transferred must suffice and it is in this respect that the market is unreliable, for two reasons: the absence of efficiency checks and the existence of free riders. Charitable organizations may be inefficient because only minimal efficiency checks operate upon them. An altruistic donor loses interest once he has donated; he does not pursue, like a tenacious shareholder, the organization's use of his donation. But even if charitable organizations were efficient in terms of minimizing the costs of giving to the poor, the amount of transfers from the rich would be unlikely to suffice for solving the poverty problem. The reason for this is that not all who wish to see the position of the poor improved will themselves actually donate an income transfer. A transfer of £1 from rich to poor presents a £1 increase in the incomes of the poor regardless of who actually effects the transfer. In other words, a charitable donation is a collective good, it confers an equal benefit on all potential donors and the total supply of voluntary transfers is likely to be inadequate.

Some possible cures. Thus, in the absence of effective private arrangements, the state may take on the responsibility for income-redistribution and for solving the poverty problem by pursuing policies to minimize those market tendencies which promote inequalities and by adopting the role of a collective transfer agency to channel income transfers from rich to poor. The state can apply coercion to raise revenue, thus ensnaring the free riders, and it is conceivable that through economies of scale the state may be able to channel aid to the poor at a lower cost than when private agencies effect such transfers. Private charitable organizations do, however, continue to play an important role in pinpointing any holes in the State's programme and in discovering new areas of need, that is, they are important as *pioneers* (a role which was recognized by the Charities Act of 1960).

Furthermore, the state's role is not that of a Robin Hood. Indeed, this gentleman found so much to keep him busy simply because the state at that time was not fulfilling its role as protector of everyone, including the lower income groups. Rather, we are assuming that the whole community, including the rich, is in favour of transfers to the poor and the state is *chosen* as the most efficient means of effecting such a programme.

A necessary programme

In the context of market corrections there are certain minimum tasks which the state must perform if a positive attack is to be made upon the problems of poverty and inequality. First, any government must ensure that the level of aggregate demand is always sufficient to guarantee full employment (or else provide equivalent household means in the world of automation) and it must construct a programme whereby individuals can be helped to finance investment in new skills when their old ones become obsolete. The maintenance of stability in the value of money, the second task, is equally important since inflation breeds inequalities. It is also essential that the state destroy all unwarranted discriminatory practices which either prevent defined sections of the population from acquiring market skills, or prevent other sections from exercising skills which have already been acquired. Finally the state must do all it can to iron out any undesirable inequalities (although the consensus may deem some given amount of inequality as *desirable*) and this may involve using the tax mechanism to bring *disposable* incomes, both earned and inherited, in line with the desired distribution.

The above aims are no more than the necessary conditions for an effective programme against poverty and inequality; they are not sufficient. No matter how 'tight' the prevailing labour market nor how free from discrimination, there still remain the problems of the 'unemployables' (the chronic sick, the aged, the mentally subnormal); temporary loss of earning power; and excessive family size. These difficulties highlight how ineffective would be a redistributive programme which merely concentrated upon maximizing the number of market opportunities and upon reducing incomes from the top via the tax mechanism. If poverty is to be seriously tackled the amounts deducted from higher incomes must also be transferred to those on lower incomes. Not only is the tax *and* transfer method more effective for the recipients of the transfer – it is also cheaper for the donors, that section of society which is giving up some of its income. Consider a rich man with £10 and a poor man with £5. The rich man considers that an income gap of £5 is too great and the poor man requires at least £6 if he is to adequately feed, clothe and house his family. If the rich man lights his fire with one of his £1 notes then he immediately reduces the income gap to £4. But although the poor man may receive some slight psychological boost from the knowledge of this new state of affairs it is cold comfort to his hungry family. If, on the other hand, the rich man *gives* £1 to the poor man, not only is the poor man enabled to purchase extra household needs, but the rich man's desire for a more equitable income distribution is doubly satisfied since the income gap is closed to £3. Put another way – £1's worth of redistribution can be achieved for only 50p (assuming away administrative costs). In this way, then, society is able to pursue two objectives at the same time – to redistribute incomes and to relieve absolute poverty.

The mechanics

The above example is deliberately simple for illustrative purposes and, consequently, it disguises a very thorny problem: *how* are transfers to be effected? There can be, and is, much conflict over the choice of transfer methods. If one group in society is to self-impose coercive transfers of a part of its income and wealth to another group, it is going to want the main say in how the transfer should be achieved. Thus the nature of the transfer mechanism will depend upon two things:

1 The motives of those who make the transfers. Altruistic motivations are likely to yield different policies to those based upon a fear of revolution or a belief in the doctrine of self-help. One set of principles gave Britain the Poor Law Amendment Act of 1834 and the consequent reliance upon the workhouse 'solution'. A quite different philosophy led to the Beveridge Report of 1942,[6] which laid the foundations of the post-war social security system.

2 The relative effectiveness of different methods of transfer. The best method of transfer is presumably that which channels a given amount of aid to those who need it most. To many this suggests the use of some form of means test. But in a society where social status is largely determined by economic success, potential recipients of state aid may be reluctant to disclose eligibility if this is dependent upon demonstration of inadequate household means.

The question of means-tested transfers has dominated the thoughts of both economists and social administrators for most of the post-war period. Much research time has been spent looking for an 'acceptable' selective tax/transfer mechanism. Currently, much thought is being devoted to the concept of *negative taxation* as a solution to the problem. We shall consider this concept in Chapter 42. In the meantime we should note that society has another powerful mechanism at its disposal, the *social contract*. Under this alternative system eligibility for aid is determined not by lack of means but according to the categorization of the *causes* of poverty – old age, sickness, etc. Such is the essence of the 'pay-as-you-go' social insurance system which the United Kingdom has operated since the Second World War. In this system the currently healthy provide for

6. Social Insurance and Allied Services, HMSO Cmd. 6404, 1942.

the sick, the currently employed provide for the unemployed and the young provide for the old, all out of national insurance contributions and general taxation. The arrangement suits the donors on the understanding that the next generation will do the same for them, that is, in the belief that future governments will not renege on the contract. It is very tempting to pursue these arguments further at this point but in order that the basic principles may be digested and so that we may discuss all unsolved problems together, we shall leave further discussion on this topic also to Chapter 43.

Spillover benefits

Finally, let us take a brief look at the problem created when commodities yield, in consumption, benefits to society in addition to those enjoyed by the individual. What we see here is the complete opposite of the problem of social costs discussed earlier in this chapter – in the case of goods such as education and health services, social benefits (i.e. total benefits) are in excess of private benefits. It is possible, therefore, for individuals to consume too little of these beneficial goods relative to the optimum consumption level for society. This specific under-consumption may have a primary cause, household income may simply be inadequate to purchase the socially desirable amounts of goods like education and health services, or even milk. But the problem can still prevail even when household means *are* sufficient to permit consumption of the socially optimum level, as the result of ignorance, self-interest, apathy or myopia. (Remember that the individual may be maximizing his own, private benefit, not social benefit.)

When households do socially misspend for these reasons the problem is often labelled as one of 'secondary poverty', a curious phrase since the rich are well capable of misspending, indeed in an increasingly overpopulated environment they may well be the worst culprits. We can illustrate the problem of social under-consumption resulting from spillover benefits in a way analogous to the way we used to discuss the problem of over-production of spillover bads.

In Figure 200 marginal social benefit (MSB) exceeds marginal private benefit (MPB) at all levels of production and consumption. The social optimum is where MSB equals MSC (marginal social cost) at output OX_1. (We are assuming for convenience that $MSC = MPC$.)

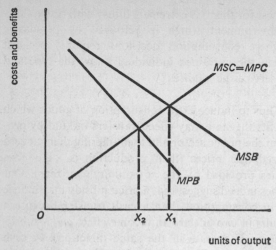

Figure 200

If we rely on private markets then consumption and output will be at OX_2, a lower total than the social optimum OX_1. Now we shall briefly discuss how we can move consumers from OX_2 to OX_1.

Income transfers. In so far as inadequate income is one root cause of under-consumption the answer may lie in an extension of the tax/transfer mechanism which aims at solving primary poverty. But if under-consumption results from ignorance, self-interest or apathy a cash transfer may be totally ineffectual in promoting a consumption rise. If Fred Smith receives cash but chooses to buy beer instead of extra education the social purpose of the transfer is defeated. To argue for cash transfers in the face of ignorance of spillover benefits, or decisions to ignore them because the individual is maximizing his private welfare is to expect people to spend in such a way as to (somehow) maximize social welfare. This expectation is based on two assumptions: that the individual knows what he wants and that allowing complete freedom of purchase (consumer sovereignty) will maximize community well-being. This latter argument is obviously ill-founded when we take the objectives of the donor into account – a cash transfer given in the hope that it will be spent on education can only reduce the welfare of the donor if it is spent on beer. Furthermore, the assumption that the consumers know what they want (and what is best for them) is extremely flimsy with respect to a highly technical environment which is befogged by persuasive advertising and where consumption decisions require specialist knowledge. How can the untrained individual know the type and quality of medical services he requires?

Transfers in kind. Thus to induce extra consumption of goods which yield spillover benefits the state may effect transfers in kind by producing such goods in the public sector and then offering them at zero or heavily subsidized user prices (their production is, of course, financed by revenues provided by the community's citizens). Our consumer theory does indeed suggest that a price subsidy may induce a greater increase in consumption than a cash transfer because a price reduction results in two effects: an income effect *and* a substitution effect (which may operate in the same direction). A cash transfer, on the other hand, relies on only one effect – the income effect. The actual magnitude of the required price reduction will depend upon the nature and strength of individual tastes. When the commodity is very low on the individual consumers' hierarchies of wants, as may be the case with medical services, a zero or even negative price may be required to promote the optimum level of consumption; but when the good is a little higher in their hierarchies, as is the case with housing, the required price reduction may not be so massive.

Other methods. But even an offer at zero price may not be taken up if the good is considered highly inferior by individual consumers. This would seem to suggest two possible avenues by which the socially optimal level of consumption may be achieved. First, so long as individuals would be prepared to buy at least some units (no matter how few) of the commodity at zero price, the state can offer a choice to the individual of either consuming all the units offered by public provision, or none at all. Since the individual is prepared to consume some units without this choice he may not wish to lose these benefits and may opt for a big increase in his consumption as a result of the 'all or nothing' scheme. The second avenue is in fact the last resort, that of coercion. When the commodity is very high on the community's hierarchy of wants but believed to be so low on individual hierarchies that even an all-or-nothing scheme would be unsuccessful, compulsory consumption will be the outcome. The United Kingdom has opted for this course of action with regard to education.

A final word on the all-or-nothing scheme. Many of the goods which rank high on the community's hierarchy of wants are subject to constraints on the supply side. A lengthy time period is involved in building schools and hospitals and it takes a long time to train teachers, nurses and doctors. Thus even if the ignorance or self-interest problems could be overcome (by, say, a non-transferable voucher scheme) supply of these commodities is likely to be highly inelastic in any short-run period. Thus, how can supply be rationed if the price mechanism is ruled out because of the massive spillover benefits involved and because access to supplies must be given to the poor as well as the rich? One method is to operate production in two sectors, a small private sector and a large public sector, giving the population equal access to each. Since supplies are relatively scarce and the price mechanism does not operate, a queue system serves to allocate resources in the public sector. Those who do not wish to queue and who have the means to pay for consumption can opt for the private sector where the price mechanism operates. In this way, access to essential services is guaranteed to all the population. The rich cannot gain a disproportionate share of scarce resources since the only queue-jumping permitted is that which involves a jump into a completely different sector. Britain's supply of medical services operates in this fashion with the National Health Service existing alongside private practice. The housing stock as we saw in Chapter 9 is also distributed along these lines in so far as two sectors operate side by side and the alternatives are to join a queue for public authority housing or pay a market price in the private sector. A cynical view might suggest that a qualitative all-or-nothing scheme operates with housing since the choice within the public sector is a characterless red-brick block or nothing, and the rich are not likely to starve the population of public housing resources, preferring to buy in the private market.

Summary

Reaching conclusions on the topics discussed in this chapter is difficult. To say what society's problems are is one thing, to state categorically how they should be dealt with is quite another. As we have tried to underline, the way in which society chooses to deal with its problems depends upon the value judgements which are operative within the community at large. If people like to live in an environment in which essential services are offered free of direct charge, then they will opt for this form of provision despite the queues which may go with it. If the consensus prefers alternative arrangements then these alternatives will be chosen. This chapter, then, has been very much a mixed bag; some positive economics has been used alongside a lot of analysis which is not quite so rigorous, but nonetheless very important. Some of the problems referred to have been, or soon will be, solved; others *must* be solved if the future is going to be a pleasant time in which to live.

Questions

1 What is the Pareto criterion? Do you think it is a universally acceptable criterion? Who decides whether someone might be made 'worse off' by a move from an optimum?

2 What criteria would you choose for deciding whether particular goods and services should be supplied free of charge by the government or provided through the market?

3 'The role of the state as defined in this chapter is so extensive that we may as well advocate complete central planning.' Discuss.

4 How could the model of perfect competition provide guide-lines for a 'liberal socialist' economy in which the state owns all the means of production except labour services, a central planning unit decides what prices are to be charged for goods and services, but consumer preferences still dictate the use of productive resources?

5 This chapter has not made specific reference to *local* government. Do you think this is because local government is unimportant?

6 'Unless resources allocated to the public sector of the health services are legally prevented from transferring to the private sector (full time or part time) the rich can always command the lion's share of health services.' Discuss.

Is complete public ownership of health resources a better system?

7 Why is it that country villagers were able to shunt around the proposed sites for London's third airport while in most large cities

hundreds of families live in close proximity to dirty, noisy factories and roadways?

8 Why is the 'free-rider' problem important?

9 Does the ethical behaviour of individuals depend upon the size of the group to which they belong?

10 What factors will determine the optimum mix of private and collective goods in an economy?

11 Is there any connection between indivisibilities in production processes, joint supply of goods, externalities, exclusion in consumption and market failure?

12 'Economics is the study of the whole system of exchange relationships. Politics is the study of the whole system of coercive or potentially coercive relationships' (J. M. Buchanan). Discuss.

Chapter 42
Financing the State

The previous chapter concentrated upon the production side of the state's activities on the implicit assumption that the necessary finance was always available. But this assumption avoids many interesting questions regarding the determinants of how much finance the state can raise; what methods of fund-raising the state can adopt; and what economic effects are likely to result from the various methods. Only a simple guide to the answers to some of these questions can be attempted at first-year level.

At several stages in this book the point has been underlined that what distinguishes households, private firms and government (the public firm) is not only the products of these institutions but also their relative access to sources of finance. Of these three institutions the activities of government are the least circumscribed by financial constraints. Households and private firms rely upon two methods of financing their activities – the net revenue they gain from selling their goods and services, and net borrowing. Government also uses these sources of finance but has access to an additional source: governments can print money. Furthermore, the determinants of how much revenue can be raised from the first two sources differ in the case of the state from those affecting a private institution: the state can effect a *compulsory* transfer of resources from the private to the public sector and a government has access to an international capital market unrivalled by that enjoyed by private institutions.

How the public sector gains resources

The government activities referred to in the previous chapter create a demand for productive resources and unless there are unemployed resources in the economy this demand must compete with the demands of the private sector. We can distinguish four methods by which the state may achieve a transfer of resources from the private to the public sector: taxation, borrowing, printing money and government directives (commandeering). What, then, determines which method the state will choose? For a given resource demand the method of finance should be chosen on a comparative costs basis, i.e. the least cost method should be chosen. The costs arise from any subsidiary reallocation of resources (which may include effects on inducements to work, save, take risks, etc.) plus any redistribution of incomes which accompanies the transfer of resources from private to public ownership. Thus the rule would seem to point to that method of finance which creates minimum disturbance of resource allocation (assuming this to be efficient) and has the most equitable impact on the distribution of incomes and wealth. Let us now take a closer look at the various methods of satisfying a government's demand for resources.

Strong-arm tactics

The state could achieve a coercive transfer of resources to the public sector at prices below those prevailing in the private sector. Conscription into the armed forces is the prime example of this method of transfer. The obvious inequities that this method creates require little elaboration except to remind ourselves that the ramifications of resource commandeering by the government may spread the burden of finance well beyond those immediately affected. Indeed, in a situation of full employment the burden may extend its inequitable tentacles very far afield as a result of price inflation. Because a coercive transfer of resources to the public sector does not involve an automatic compensatory reduction in private demand, the prices of resources to the private sector will rise as a result of the newly denuded supplies to that sector. Commandeering in, say, a national emergency such as wartime may not have the same inflationary impact since, in such times, the transfer to the public sector is usually accompanied by price controls and/or physical rationing. Nevertheless, while recognizing that in such emergencies state directives might be necessary to speed up market processes, this does not excuse the state paying its resources rewards below what they could obtain in the private sector.

The printing press

Since the central government controls the supply of money to the economy, including the issue of new notes and coins, why does it not always finance its activities with newly printed money? The reason is that unless there are unemployed resources in the economy the net impact of financing public expenditure by the printing of money is, like commandeering, inflationary and therefore constitutes no more than an inefficient and inequitable form of taxation.

When resources are idle, printing money may be the most efficient means of financing state activities since it is entirely neutral with regard to the allocation of resources and the distribution of incomes.[1] But when resources are already being fully utilized within the private sector the effect of increased resource demand from the public sector is to drive up resource prices unless a parallel contraction in private demand takes place. No such parallel adjustment takes place as a result of the government printing money. Resource prices rise in both sectors and a proportion of this increase in income is spent on goods and services produced in the private sector, thus causing a further rise in private-sector resource prices and, hence, in the prices of those goods produced by these resources.

Thus the financing of public expenditures with newly printed money is neither neutral nor equitable when resources are already fully employed. Indeed, inflationary finance, as we saw in Chapter 37, creates a three-fold burden. Production planning becomes extremely hazardous in the face of unpredictable price movements. Some sections of the community, those consuming out of relatively fixed incomes, face a bigger consumption cut-back than other sections. Finally, as an unchecked inflation gathers so much momentum that the rate of price increases outstrips the rate of growth of the money supply, the community experiences ever-increasing transactions costs. This latter part of the burden might be viewed as a tax on cash balances.

It would appear that any government which chooses to compete with the private sector by bidding up resource prices, financing the

1. Assuming, of course, that the existing states of allocation and distribution are ideal, given the community's desires. Where this is not the case the community may deliberately choose a method of finance which interferes with the prevailing economic order.

bidding with newly printed money, is choosing an inefficient and inequitable means of competition although, if subtly handled, it is potentially a method which minimizes the likelihood of public accountability.

Loan finance

Another way the public sector can gain productive resources is for the government to finance its expenditure through borrowing and, given certain circumstances, this method may not bid up resource prices. The state can borrow from its citizens on the strength of a promised fixed rate of interest, using the funds so raised to purchase resources. If the community's supply of investment funds is financed (eventually) out of saving and the latter is a residual income remaining after consumption, the new issue of government bonds must compete alongside existing (low-yield) paper assets for the available supply of investment funds. In this way the government's demand for resources does not constitute a net increase in aggregate demand since resources are released to the public sector via a compensatory reduction in private capital expenditure following the community's switching from private to public bonds. Furthermore, neither does this method of raising finance create any of the inequities associated with inflationary finance. On the contrary, since those individuals who purchase the government bonds do so voluntarily the expected benefits from lending to the government must outweigh the costs (the forgone use of the funds).

Yet the national debt is often referred to as a burden in some sense. Why is this? Two reasons have been put forward as explanations of why loan finance imposes a burden on the community and in both cases the problem is considered to be an inter-generational one. The first reason refers to extra tax payments which a future generation may have to face in order to service the debt. This is not a very convincing argument for the existence of a burden of debt. 'Burden' must refer to the incidence (who actually bears the burden) of the taxes required to finance the interest payments on the original loan. As such the debt does not add to the general problem of tax incidence unless the state's use of the loan funds does not generate sufficient extra community income with which to finance the debt servicing. If the state's use of the original funds is sufficiently productive the debt can be serviced from existing taxes. (It should be noted also that raising taxes to service debt involves income redistribution.)

The second reason advanced for considering that public debt imposes a burden on a future generation presents a more complex argument. The analysis hinges on how the purchase of government bonds is financed, as the results of financing a loan by forgoing consumption will be different from those which will follow financing it out of savings. Since savings are a residual we can postulate that at any point in time the community's supply of investable funds (savings) is given. Now, as mentioned earlier, with a given supply of loanable funds a public loan will be largely financed out of a reduction in private capital formation, i.e. the community switches from one type of asset to another. This in itself cannot impose any burden on a future generation since the reduction in private capital is compensated for by the addition of publicly provided capital goods and the future generation merely inherits a different private/public capital mix. However, the total amount of capital goods inherited by the next generation is less than it would have been if the original expenditure had been financed by taxes. It is in this sense that loan financing might be considered to impose a burden. An increase in taxation reduces disposable incomes and assuming that households consume out of current disposable income (see Chapter 33), private consumption is likely to decrease. The new public expenditure is thus financed mainly out of a reduction in private consumption and hence the next generation inherits a larger capital stock than it would do following loan financing.

Perhaps we can summarize the above arguments by a simple example. Imagine a community which currently possesses capital worth £100 million. The community's government has decided to add to this stock by a new capital investment programme of £1 million. Let us assume that the community consumes, on average, 80 per cent of its disposable income and saves the remaining 20 per cent. If the government decides to finance the new programme via a voluntary loan it presents the community with a simple choice, either to ignore the new bonds or to buy them. The community's consumption of goods and services is unchanged since nothing has happened to disposable income (consumption remains at a proportional rate of 80 per cent). Thus, if the community decides to make the loan, it must do so out of existing loanable funds (20 per cent of disposable income). The government's capital expenditure is financed ultimately by a reduction in private capital expenditure. However, if the government chooses to increase taxes to finance the new project then the immediate impact will be a reduction of disposable income and therefore of private consumption. Tax financing thus enables a larger capital stock to be handed by one generation to another than is possible under loan financing.

It would seem from the above analysis that it can only be with reference to the *relative* effects of loan and tax finance that the former might constitute a burden. What the above analysis also highlights is the potential confusion surrounding the use of the term 'burden'. The use of this term conjures up a picture of future generations staggering, like Pilgrim, beneath a great weight, the Public Debt. Yet we have seen many times in this book that economic decisions involve *choice*, they require a sacrifice or cost to be realized. But this cost, gladly borne in expectation of an even greater benefit, cannot constitute a burden in the uncompensated sense. However, when the costs of obtaining given benefits are *greater than they might be*, then a true burden (previously referred to as an 'excess burden') does exist. It is in this context that the term 'burden' must be employed in relation to the relative results of loan and taxes, for if the term is meant to be merely synonymous with sacrifice then why should the reduced inheritance of a future generation, resulting from loan finance, be more of a burden than the reduced private consumption of the *present* generation as a result of tax financing?

Note that to consider the relative burden of debt in the manner of the above paragraph is to assume that the present generation is willing to make sacrifices for future generations. But why should one generation be prepared to do this for another? Why, for example, should people forfeit the use of resources which could provide them with consumption goods in order to provide young people with universities? When one generation expects to benefit, before it dies, from the education of another generation then part of the answer to this question is to be found in the collective-goods discussion of earlier chapters. But how can we explain such behaviour when practised by a generation which will not live to reap the spillover benefits of a well-educated society? The answer must have something to do with charity, albeit in an inter-generational sense. One generation derives psychic benefit from passing on goods and services to the next generation and just as parents provide for their children's future consumption of private goods so they may seek to provide for their children's future consumption of collective goods.

A final point that should be made in our discussion of government domestic borrowing concerns the possible impact of borrowing on interest rates. If the government intends to change its borrowing it will affect the total demand for funds, the demand for money, and this will affect the level of interest rates. Other things being equal an increase (decrease) in the level of government borrowing will raise (lower) interest rates. A change in the level of interest rates will affect consumption/saving decisions (Chapter 33), investment decisions (Chapter 34), and the balance of payments (Chapter 36), and thus governments must take these ramifications into account.

Foreign loans

Foreign borrowing may be preferred to domestic borrowing. At the time the loan is granted additional resources are made available from abroad without a consequent reduction in domestic resource use (normally such imports would need to be financed by exports). Thus in a time of full employment of domestic resources a foreign loan may be of immense benefit. When the debt has to be repaid, however, resources are drained from domestic use. If the original loan has been productively employed, repayments may not present too great a problem unless the balance of payments is in difficulties for other reasons.[2] Furthermore foreign loans may often be raised on very favourable repayment terms as countries play the inter-national-relations game. Access to this sort of capital market *may* greatly benefit emerging countries.

Tax finance

Finally, let us turn to a discussion of taxation. Owing to the myriad complex issues raised in a study of taxation our analysis will be kept brief and somewhat restricted.

2. It will be appreciated that foreign loans, like foreign investment and foreign indebtedness through trade, will involve monetary adjustments (under regimes of either fixed or flexible exchange rates) as analysed in Chapter 35.

Currently the UK employs a whole range of different taxes but each one is an example of a particular form of taxation and the interesting question is: which form is best, given the state's concern for an efficient allocation of resources and an equitable income distribution? We broadly classify the two forms as taxes on income and taxes on outlay. In each case taxes are defined according to the tax *base*, i.e. the source at which the tax is aimed. Thus an income tax is aimed at releasing resources through a fall in private expenditure induced by a reduction in disposable income. An outlay tax, on the other hand, reduces private real expenditure by raising the prices of items of expenditure resulting in smaller quantities being purchased.

The tax base

Why do we not term outlay taxes 'expenditure taxes'? The reason is historical rather than academic. Outlay taxes, as employed by the UK and by most of the other countries of the world, have always been levied on *specific* items of consumption rather than on *total* household expenditure for a given time period. At the present time the UK fiscal system exhibits both *ad valorem* outlay taxes (levied as a proportion of the sales value) such as value added tax; and unit taxes (levied per unit of measure) such as the tobacco tax. An *expenditure* tax, however, means precisely that to the economist. It is a tax levied on households' total expenditure for a specific time period. Now, if by 'total expenditure' we mean to include not only consumption expenditure but also savings (investment expenditure); and if we also adopt a comprehensive definition of income (see below) then income and expenditure become the same tax base since an expenditure flow during a given time period cannot exceed the income flow of the same period.

What do we mean by a 'comprehensive' definition of income? In a nutshell, we mean a true measure of *economic power*, the command over productive resources. Thus, income for a specified time period relates to all net additions to economic power between the beginning and end of that period. The major problem in defining income so comprehensively is one of computation: not all forms of income carry a monetary tag. Income which derives from the sale of market goods and services is readily calculable if in a monetary form, but if services are paid for in kind then the income of a particular resource owner may be exceedingly difficult to measure. Even more complicating is the case of 'imputed income'. which is income derived from non-market resources. As such, imputed income includes any income in kind which does not constitute the result of a market transaction – receipt of a durable good as payment for work done does not constitute imputed income since it is a non-monetary reward for market services but the value of the flow of services from the good to its owner does constitute imputed income. A prime example of the concept is the flow of non-monetary returns from a dwelling to its owner-occupier.

It is apparent then that a truly comprehensive tax base would create such administrative complexities that the costs of collection would outweigh the benefits to society from the use of the proceeds. If the reader is not convinced, ponder on how leisure, an important source of imputed income, might be incorporated into the tax base. Thus a practical compromise must be adopted whereby a feasibly comprehensive definition of income is adopted. Such a definition would at least include those forms of income which are fairly readily translated into money form. Many payments in kind, plus gifts and bequests, could be so translated, as well as capital gains and all forms of wealth, including property and other material possessions (painting, antiques etc.). The inclusion of sources of wealth is important since, as we saw in the previous chapter, wealth produces a flow of services to its owner and if this flow cannot be taxed comprehensively a tax on its source, the wealth stock, is an alternative means of transferring economic power to the public sector.

We should note finally that if a sufficiently comprehensive definition of income is not adopted then the aims of the state cannot be adequately pursued. The narrower the definition of income, the greater the scope for tax avoidance. For example, if a taxpayer faces the choice of receiving income in the form of £100 cash, or groceries valued at £100, and only money income is subject to tax, a strong incentive exists to choose the groceries. When the tax system contains many such loopholes, three results emerge. First, as tax units juggle their sources of income to avoid tax, the actual incidence of taxation may differ greatly from the intended incidence. Secondly, the certainty that a given amount of revenue can be raised is much reduced. Finally, as the actual tax base is steadily eroded, ever higher tax rates are required to raise a given level of revenue. The problems created by these results are discussed in the course of our analysis.

The benefit principle

Why should taxation be such an apparently complex issue? Why can't the state simply charge a price for its services in the same way that other institutions do?

Such a system of taxation according to benefit has been advocated many times and there is a wealth of literature on the subject going back to the popular prevalence of the idea among seventeenth-century political and economic philosophers. The essence of the approach is that beneficiaries pay in direct proportion to the benefits they enjoy from publicly provided goods and services. It is claimed that this method of taxation is both fair and efficient since no one enjoys benefits without paying for them, and therefore, no one pays for benefits not received. Thus, no governmental expenditure is undertaken which is 'wasteful' since community demand and state supply meet, as in the market place, to determine the optimal size of the public sector.

Figure 201 depicts a community of two taxpayers, a simple model of a much larger society. The curve SS represents the supply curve of a state-provided good. As such it reflects marginal costs in terms of forgone private goods. Curves $D_A D_A$ and $D_B D_B$ represent the demand curves for the state-provided good by the taxpayers. These curves are assumed to reflect the marginal benefits to each consumer from consuming varying amounts of the services provided by the state good. Thus $D_A D_A$ shows the benefit which A enjoys from successive amounts of the service and $D_B D_B$ shows the same for B. The combined benefits of the varying amounts are shown by the curve $D_{A+B} D_{A+B}$ which is constructed by the vertical summation of D_A and D_B and, as such, it shows the 'collective demand' for this particular state service. Demand and supply meet at output OQ. For this output taxpayer A pays a unit price (tax) of Oa, i.e. he makes a contribution of forgone consumption of private goods to the value of area $OQda$. B pays a unit price of Ob, making his contribution $OQeb$. The total contribution is thus $OQfc$.

In this way an 'optimum' output level is determined which is analogous to the market solution. But how true is it that the two

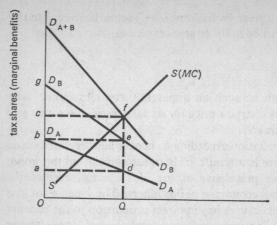

Figure 201

individuals pay according to the benefits they receive? Since the state services are a collective good they are provided in a lump sum and individuals cannot consume more or less by offering different prices. In our example both A and B consume OQ units once this amount is provided. Thus the total benefits enjoyed by A equal the area $ObdQ$ and B's benefits equal $OgeQ$. Yet A pays only $OadQ$ and B pays only $ObeQ$; apparently neither is paying according to the true magnitude of the benefits he receives and total benefits do not equal total costs.

The above problem is not the only drawback to the 'benefit principle' as a blueprint for taxation policy. Further difficulties surround whether or not consumers will reveal their true preferences for state-provided goods and services. (We assumed away this problem in order to construct ·Figure 201.) First, given the collective nature of state-provided services, preferences have to be somehow revealed via a political process (or else services are provided according to the dictates of a political authority, regardless of private preferences). But political processes are notoriously inefficient at determining true preferences, as discussed later in Chapter 43. Finally, even if all other problems surrounding the benefit approach could be solved, society might still want to reject it on the grounds that it does not fit in with the aims of a programme against inequality. A rich man may be able to afford to pay for his benefits, a poor man may not. Whereas society may find this acceptable in the case of toffee consumption it is unlikely to find it so regarding national defence. Thus, benefit taxation permits maintenance of the *status quo* and unless society considers this to be ideal, some alternative guide to taxation policy will be adopted.

Although payment according to benefit is not an acceptable principle on which to base a taxation system, certain taxes do approximate to this principle. The criterion is most likely to be adhered to when public services are considered to confer identifiable private benefits. In the UK for example, the television licence and the 'road tax' follow the benefit principle, representing payments for specific publicly provided services. Such payments are outlay taxes levied on items of expenditure. Despite the fact that revenues so raised disappear into the government's general pool, this does not prevent taxpayers from regarding such taxes as *earmarked* for a specific purpose. Earmarked taxes may of course be aimed not at specific benefits (goods) but at specific disbenefits (bads). Thus the gin tax of the eighteenth century was imposed to reduce consumption of cheap gin.

But to decide properly upon the relative merits of income and outlay taxes we must scrutinize more carefully the way in which taxation policy must be geared to fit the general aims of the state. Our discussion of the state's activities has always revolved around the basic aims of efficiency and equity – society's concern for the best allocation of resources and an equitable distribution of incomes. In terms of these basic objectives a tax on income wins hands down.

The goal of efficiency

At the beginning of this chapter we suggested that the best method of raising revenue would be that which interfered the least with the existing states of distribution and allocation, assuming these states to be the ones desired by society. Given this assumption we can employ Figure 202 to demonstrate the case for an income tax *vis-à-vis* a tax on a specific commodity. The diagram makes further use of the consumer-surplus concept employed in earlier chapters and in this case, perhaps more than in any of the others, we must beware of what the analysis presumes – that the specific circumstances have no ramifications beyond those reflected in the diagram.

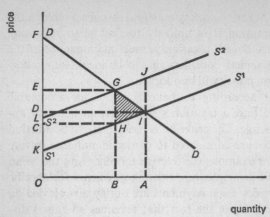

Figure 202

The initial situation depicted in Figure 202 is one of market equilibrium, where the demand for a specific good equals supply of that good, at price OD. At this price consumer surplus is equal to area FDI and producer surplus to area KDI. A unit tax equal to $IJ(=HG)$ is levied on the output of the commodity and the supply curve shifts vertically upwards by this amount. As a result, a new (post-tax) equilibrium is established at price OE and quantity OB. At this new equilibrium consumer surplus has been reduced to FEG and producer surplus to KCH, a total reduction equal to area $EGIHC$. But this loss of surplus is greater than the amount of revenue taken by the government. Tax revenue raised on output OB is equal to area $EGHC$, the number of units sold, $OB(=EG)$, multiplied by the tax rate per unit, $GH(=IJ)$. Thus the true burden of the tax is in excess of the resource transfer ($EGHC$) from private to public sector by an amount equal to GHI.

The existence of the excess burden is due to the distortion of relative prices which follows the imposition of the specific tax. In a perfectly competitive environment, market equilibria occur where marginal costs equal prices and marginal utilities. When a unit tax is imposed on one particular commodity, X, it drives a wedge between marginal cost and price – the post-tax price of the commodity is higher than the pre-tax price (i.e. the tax has been partially passed on) but marginal costs are unchanged. It would now benefit society if more were produced of X since its (post-tax) price has risen while other prices have remained the same. But since nothing has simultaneously happened to resource prices, that is, marginal costs are unchanged, resources will not move out of the production of other goods into production of X. A comprehensive tax on incomes, on the other hand, has no such distorting effect on the prices of commodities.

The goal of equity

In our analysis of public policies we have observed how society gives much weight to considerations of equity and our brief discussion of taxation gives similar attention to equity considerations. Equity, we have seen, is a two-dimensional concept. Horizontal equity, which has been implicit throughout our analysis of state activities, relates to that concept of justice which most societies have readily accepted – *equal treatment of equals*. Vertical equity, to which we have already devoted considerable space, relates to society's ethical views on the distribution of economic power. As a guideline for taxation the concept of vertical equity roughly translates into *unequal treatment of unequals*.

Horizontal equity

To aim at achieving horizontal equity is to accept a value judgement, but one unlikely to cause conflict. In the context of taxation, fairness demands that tax units possessing identical economic power face identical tax demands. Thus, if two tax units are in receipt of the same income (taken to be a measure of true economic power) then, under an income tax, they should each face the same tax demand from the state to ensure that post-tax incomes are also equalized. As in the case of the efficiency objective, it is essential that the tax base be comprehensively defined if horizontal equity is to be achieved. Therefore, if an outlay tax is not levied on all items of expenditure but only on some commodities, or groups of commodities, it will offend this criterion. For example, suppose the community comprises two sets of taxpayers, each possessing the same spending power but different tastes: one set prefers boiled sweets. Suppose, now, that the government decides to finance a particular level of expenditure by levying a tax on each ounce of boiled sweets supplied to retailers, who raise the price of boiled sweets accordingly. Consequently, the state extracts relatively more revenue from one section of the population simply because that section enjoys eating boiled sweets; and regardless of the fact that the economic power of this section is identical to that of those who abstain from consuming boiled sweets.

The need for a comprehensive base is equally important in the case of an income tax. If some forms of income are omitted from the income-tax base then taxpayers will not pay according to the magnitude of their income but according to its nature. Thus suppose two individuals receive income of £1000 p.a. but while all of the income of one is in monetary form, the income of the other is partly in kind – he works for a market gardener who pays him £750 p.a. plus fruit and vegetables which the recipient values at £250. If the revenue authorities, for administrative convenience, define 'income' to include only monetary returns, then the tax bill which each of our taxpayers must face will differ. If the tax rate applied is 25 per cent of income, as defined by the authorities, then the individual whose income is wholly in money form pays £250, while the other faces a demand for only £187.50, despite enjoying the same total amount of economic power.

Vertical equity

It is in the context of vertical equity that the inferiority of specific-outlay taxes *vis-à-vis* a tax on incomes is really highlighted. If we are to continue with our assumption of a society committed, for whatever reason, to a more equitable distribution of incomes than that which results from market transactions, taxation policy must be brought into line with the general programme of redistribution. As we shall see, to tax items of expenditure is to pursue a policy which does not further such an aim.

If taxation policy is to reflect the community's desire for vertical equity then taxes must be levied according to the principle of *ability-to-pay*. Whereas the benefit principle seeks to link taxes paid with benefits received, ability-to-pay relates tax bills to true capacity to pay, thus, for a given level of state-provided services, yielding equal benefits to two individuals possessing different degrees of economic power, a relatively higher tax demand is made of the individual

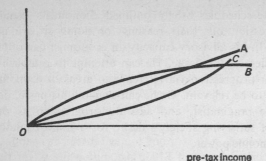

Figure 203

possessing the most economic power.[3] Under a comprehensive income-tax system a rich man pays more in tax than a poor man. But how much more? The ability-to-pay doctrine merely sets the tenor of an equitable taxation policy, it does not provide formal rules for the execution of such a policy. The obvious guide to formulating such rules is the range of tax *rates* which can be applied. Now, the range of rates at which resources are released to the public sector can be *regressive*, *proportional*, or *progressive*. The proportion of income (economic power) transferred to the public sector from any individual diminishes as his income rises, when tax rates are regressive. Under a proportional tax rate the proportion of income transferred remains constant as income rises. Finally, when tax rates are progressive an increasing proportion of any individual's income is transferred to public use as his income rises. These various rates are illustrated in Figure 203.

OA represents a proportional rate: the slope of the schedule remains constant. A regressive-rates schedule is depicted by *OB* – the slope of this line flattens as income rises. *OC* represents a progressive-rates schedule – the slope of *OC* increases as income rises. (Progressive tax rates, then, do not simply require the rich to pay more than the poor. Indeed a rich man with income of £10 000 pays more than a poor man with income of £1000 under a regressive-rates schedule of 5 per cent and 10 per cent respectively.)

3. It is an interesting observation that when the rich want to live in a healthy environment, amidst a well-educated population, the distinction between the benefit and ability approaches tends to become blurred. The beneficiaries are also those with the ability-to-pay, i.e. the rich.

Of the three rate schedules briefly outlined economists usually recommend progression but their reasons for doing so are not always legitimate. In his advisory capacity an economist can adopt one of two attitudes on this issue. He can attempt to establish a 'scientific' case for progression via reference to areas of economic theory he believes to be relevant. Or he can swallow his pride, don the mantle of the pragmatist, and advance progression as one potential means of satisfying society's desire for a more equitable distribution of economic power.

The sacrifice doctrine

Given our existing knowledge of the world, a truly scientific case for progressive taxation is impossible. The hypotheses upon which an analysis must be attempted are those which have never progressed beyond the armchair in which they were conceived: they are untestable. Such is the criticism aimed at the *sacrifice* doctrine. This doctrine was given a precise formulation in the heyday of marginal analysis after its fairly innocent beginnings as a seed sown in the writings of John Stuart Mill. As a general proposition the sacrifice principle is quite acceptable, suggesting no more than the idea that surrendering resources to the state involves a sacrifice for the taxpayers. Neither is its preliminary extension particularly objectionable: that, generally speaking, the greater a taxpayer's ability to pay, the less the sacrifice he suffers from paying a given amount of tax. But to refine the analysis beyond this, in the hope of ultimately making a case for progressive taxation, is fruitless.

We cannot at this level delve too deeply into the intricate formulation of the sacrifice concept, but we can consider its essence. The sacrifice assumed to be suffered in paying taxes relates to the forgone utility which could have been derived from the income surrendered to the state. A guideline for an equitable tax system would seem to be: equate the sacrifices made by all tax units.

In fact the guideline might be refined even further to the equating of *marginal* sacrifices,[4] that is, transferring resources from the com-

4. Students who eventually tackle more advanced literature will discover two other sacrifice measures: equal *absolute* sacrifice, and equal *proportional* sacrifice. For ease of exposition we have omitted consideration of these

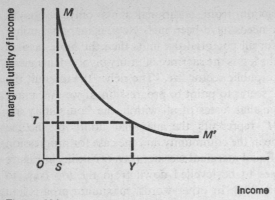

Figure 204

munity until the last unit of income taken from each represents the same sacrifice to each. In this fashion the total sacrifice of the community is minimized or, put another way, the total (after-tax) utility of the community is maximized. Suppose, for example, that the utility from the additional £1 of income differs for two tax units A and B: A's £1 represents 10 utils to A, whereas B's has a subjective value of only 7 utils. Now, if £1 less were transferred from A to the public sector and £1 more were transferred from B, then total money transfers to the public sector would be unchanged but total utility of the community would rise by 3 utils (B loses 7 but A gains 10).

At first sight, the analysis above seems quite harmless. Indeed it seems no more than a further application of the marginal rule that we have met several times in this book. Could it not be used to substantiate a case for progressive taxation? Some economists in the past have believed that it could be so used. Such an extension of our analysis requires one basic assumption – that the utility derived from additional units of income diminishes as total income rises. A curve of diminishing marginal utility of income is illustrated by MM' in Figure 204.

Along the income axis of the above diagram OS represents a subsistence level of income. Additional units of income prior to this subsistence level being reached are assumed to have an infinite utility

concepts from our analysis. The criticisms we shall aim at the equal marginal rule, which sets the limit to egalitarianism, also apply to those alternative concepts which are somewhat removed from the marginal limit.

value, hence satisfaction from additional units only begins to diminish when basic needs have been met. Now, if marginal utility of income declines for all potential tax units then the more income each one possesses, the less is the sacrifice of utility involved in a given transfer of income to public sector use. 'The richer the tax unit the smaller the sacrifice' seems to point to progression. If we now make a second assumption, that tastes of all within the community are identical, then MM' represents the marginal utility of income schedule for everyone in the community and the case for progression seems indisputable. Equal marginal sacrifice (say, OT utility in Figure 204) requires incomes to be levelled down from the top (say, to OY income in Figure 204). In other words, maximum progression should be used to completely equalize post-tax incomes.

Some problems

However, despite the apparent rigour of this case for progression its core is somewhat hollow. In the first place there exists no mechanism by which to cardinally measure the amount of utility a tax unit derives from a given amount of income. Therefore, we cannot establish, *a priori*, that an extra bit of income means less to a rich tax unit than to a poor one; and we cannot make interpersonal comparisons of the amounts of utility sacrificed by different tax units. (We met this problem of interpersonal comparisons of utility early in the previous chapter.)

Even if we could obtain cardinal measures of the amount of utility derived from different levels of income we could not guarantee that the schedule of marginal income utility for everyone in the community would look the same as that in Figure 204. Indeed, it is extremely unlikely that tastes would be so uniform. When tastes do differ then the amount of utility derived from an extra amount of income will differ among tax units – sober Mr Brown does not receive the same enjoyment from an extra £1 of income as the riotous Mr Spender.

Finally, the basic assumption that marginal utility of income schedules slope continually downwards is very open to challenge. While such a curve is conceivable in relation to a given *level* of wants, in terms of a *hierarchy* of wants its shape is likely to be very different. Although tax units may experience diminishing marginal

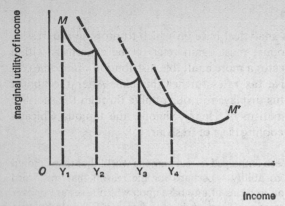

Figure 205

utility from income within any particular income bracket, it is quite probable that marginal utility rises in the region of the threshold to each bracket. Figure 205 depicts a marginal utility of income schedule which exhibits such characteristics.

MM' is the marginal utility of income curve for a particular tax unit. OY_1 is the subsistence level of income. Within each income bracket ($Y_1 - Y_2$; $Y_2 - Y_3$; etc.) the utility curve slopes downwards until the tax unit is within sight of the following bracket, at which point the curve slopes upwards until this bracket is actually reached. (Effectively, the curve is shifting as income rises, as shown by the dotted continuations in the diagram.) The major consumption item within the first bracket may be a family car; within the second it may be foreign travel; the third brings hope of a weekend cottage; and the fourth may mean a yacht. Now, very often in economics (as we have seen many times by now) we can legitimately iron out any minute indivisibilities when the general relationship between two variables does at least approximate a smooth curve. But we cannot do so in the present example. Although we may postulate many steps in the hierarchy of wants the number of upturns in the marginal utility of income curve will always be discrete since each tax unit must spend considerable time within each income bracket. Thus, given such a schedule, a tax structure based on the utility sacrifice approach would require tax rates levied on certain levels of income (when the utility schedule slopes upwards) to be regressive.

Some Problems 775

Some common sense

Lacking a rigorous analytical base on which to propose progressive tax rates the economist must again refer to the consensus within society which advocates a more equitable distribution of incomes. In principle, progressive tax rates further this end. After the almost pretentious apparatus displayed in our ramble through the sacrifice doctrine, the pragmatism of Henry Simons, the famous Chicago economist, is like a cooling blast of fresh air.

Tons of paper have been employed in teaching the world that taxes should be levied according to ability – perhaps for the reason that this word utterly defies definition in terms of any base upon which taxes are or ever might be levied. Whereas the question is as to how taxes should be allocated with respect to income, consumption, or net worth, the answer is that they should be proportional to ability or faculty, which cannot be conceived quantitatively or defined in terms of any procedure of measurement. . . . The case for drastic progression in taxation must be rested on the case against inequality – on the ethical or aesthetic judgement that the prevailing distribution of wealth and income reveals a degree (and/or kind) of inequality which is distinctly evil or unlovely.

Written over thirty years ago by Simons (1938).

If we accept the ability-to-pay doctrine as part of a programme against inequality then outlay taxes are again shown in an adverse light. An outlay tax, whether *ad valorem* or levied per unit of output, does not discriminate among taxpayers according to their ability-to-pay – the rich face the same tax rates as the poor. An attempt to reduce the regression may be made by exempting from tax those consumption items considered to be basic wants, e.g. food. But, given the interrelationships among markets, unless *all* the inputs which help produce basic goods are also exempt, then tax effects may filter through to the final price of these items of consumption. For example, if food were exempt but not petrol, if the tax on petrol were to be shifted forward (wholly or partly) food prices would still rise. Yet to exempt many goods greatly reduces the tax base, necessitating ever-increasing rates of tax to raise the same amount of revenue, thus creating further inequities. Furthermore, the very aim of protecting basic wants, like food, conflicts with the aim of raising a given amount of revenue. When outlay taxes are designed to raise revenue they will have to be placed upon goods which are price-inelastic in demand. The goods satisfying this criterion will be satisfying basic wants.

Efficiency again

Before leaving the subject of progressive taxation we must give some consideration to the spectre of disincentives. In a market-oriented economy the actions of economic agents are motivated by the rewards from the sale of assets, both human and non-human. If the supply of a particular asset is price-elastic then if its price should fall its supply will contract. Such contraction may result from taxation since this reduces real disposable incomes. The disincentives we are mainly concerned with in this context relate to the supply of work effort, savings, and the taking of risks. Progressive taxation in particular may have disincentive effects since it lowers the return from the extra hour of effort, the extra £1 saved and so on. Thus, the redistributive aims of a progressive tax system could be thwarted by a consequent reduction in the total product to be shared out.

Our knowledge of the incentive effects of taxation is very limited. What empirical information is available suggests that in reality reactions to price changes, including changes in factor prices, are difficult to predict. But is this not what our theory warns? In so far as a tax changes relative prices, reactions to it will depend upon the relative strengths of taxpayers' income and substitution effects. The best and most often quoted example of this relates to the effect of progressive income tax rates upon the supply of work effort. Since a progressive rate reduces the remuneration from an extra hour's work it changes the relative prices of work and leisure. The price of leisure in terms of forgone income from work is reduced. But whether or not a taxpayer reacts by consuming more leisure depends upon his relative preferences for income and leisure. He may in fact work more hours in order to maintain some desired income level. Similar analysis can be applied to other sources of income and to other types of incentive. But it is important to remember that although we have no cast-iron basis for predicting that progressive taxation creates disincentives, the danger does exist. Society should not become hysterical either way but should devise a system of taxation which, given administrative constraint, satisfies the state's objectives with minimum disincentive effects. Needless to say this requires that a comprehensive definition be applied to the tax base.

Summary

We have succeeded in no more than briefly contemplating the tips of many icebergs. What should emerge from our discussion is that the state possesses several methods of raising finance each of which will have different consequences for the economy and society generally. Which method will be adopted depends upon the prevailing circumstances. Several observations have been made. We have seen that printing money is not necessarily the monster of popular thought. If there are unemployed resources in the economy this may be the best method of raising finance. Borrowing, as opposed to taxing, is a mechanism which could be used more often, particularly where inter-generational considerations are paramount. To rely on taxation as a major source of finance requires the adoption of a fully comprehensive tax base; taxing according to ability is not a sufficient principle to ensure satisfaction of general rules of fairness and efficiency unless such a base is adopted.

Finally, since different methods of transferring resources from private to public use can affect the prevailing states of allocation and distribution, they place at the disposal of governments various mechanisms for enabling society to reach desired ends. Thus, the raising of revenue may often be a secondary issue in the adoption of a particular method of reducing private consumption. This is very true, as we have previously implied, in the case of taxation where a tax may be imposed purely as a corrective mechanism. When discussing the relative merits of income and outlay taxes we have assumed most of the time that prevailing resource allocation is efficient, but when this condition is not met these taxes may appear in a different light in relation to their ability to change the course of economic events.

Questions

1 Compare the relative merits of (a) confiscation, (b) printing money, (c) borrowing and (d) taxation as means of financing the goods and services provided by the state.

2 Can efficiency and equity be reconciled in a tax system?

3 What changes in the current UK tax system would seem to be required by the introduction of a comprehensive income-tax base?

4 What tax principles can be derived from (a) the benefit principle, and (b) the least-sacrifice principle?

5 What do you understand by the concepts of (a) horizontal, and (b) vertical equity? How are these concepts implemented in the UK tax system?

6 Newtown is a commuter town near London. Its population consists of large numbers of 'business reps' who stay on average about three years. The council proposes to build a municipal golf course and swimming pool. A referendum is conducted to decide on the method of financing the projects. Which method of financing do you think will be chosen?

7 Given the existence of a hierarchy of wants certain interpersonal comparisons of income utility are possible. For example we may advocate income redistribution from those who own luxury yachts to those who are struggling to feed themselves but not to pony-trekkers. Discuss.

8 Since Hitler was defeated, in what sense can the government debt incurred as a result of the Second World War be considered a burden?

9 What effect do you think that government borrowing would have on the level of interest rates? Assuming that interest rates rose what effect would this have upon the balance of payments? (In attempting this question you may wish to refer to the analysis in Chapters 29, 33, 34, 35 and 36.)

10 During and after the Second World War the UK borrowed from the US. Both countries were on a fixed exchange rate. How did the US manage to transfer resources to the UK? Were the Americans who lent made worse off? Were the Americans who did not lend made worse off? Did the UK citizens during the war feel better off? How was repayment effected?

Chapter 43
Poverty and Inequality

One of the incongruous facts of life is that poverty is not confined to poor countries but is a problem which even the affluent nations of the western world are continually fighting. The United Kingdom is no exception and this chapter contains a brief summary of the post-war efforts to overcome the poverty problems of this country. As we saw in Chapter 41, although poverty and inequality are two distinct problems their solutions are necessarily linked. Poverty is unlikely to be overcome until market opportunities are more equal; until discrimination is completely eliminated and access to skills (including re-training) becomes a possibility for all; and until massive concentrations of wealth are eliminated. The reason that these are such immediate problems for the UK is that despite being a 'public' problem since 1611 poverty still persists, all the more disappointing since over the short run, since 1944, we have had a supposedly firm commitment to the eradication of this particular evil. But our refusal to accept that the poor are not 'always with us' has still to reap its aims despite the intensive programme since 1944.

Inequality in the UK

We shall concentrate, then, on the years since 1944 to try to judge the effects of the UK's most comprehensive programme to date. Our conclusions will be disappointing. Despite the social and economic progress of the post-war years, including full employment for a quarter of a century, the distribution of incomes remains stubbornly fixed and wealth is still heavily concentrated. Tables 60 and 61 present the distribution trends.

As Table 60 demonstrates, a policy of full employment is not sufficient to guarantee a continual closing of the distribution gap. The existence of rigidities in the economic system, for example fixed-

Table 60 Percentage distribution of incomes before tax, UK, selected years

Group of income recipients (%)	Percentage of total income received			
	1949	1957	1963	1967
top 1%	11·2	8·2	7·9	7·4
5%	23·8	19·1	19·1	18·4
10%	33·2	28·1	28·7	28·0
40%	68·1	65·7	67·7	66·9
70%	87·3	88·8	90·3	89·7
bottom 30%	12·7	11·3	9·7	10·3

Sources: Lydall (1959), Nicholson (1967); Walsh (1972)

Table 61 Percentage distribution (concentration) of private wealth, UK, selected years

Percentage of population (over twenty-five years of age)	Percentage of total wealth owned				
	1911–13	1936–8	1960	1963–7	
				(a)	(b)
1	69	56	42	29	22
5	87	79	75	54	41
10	92	88	83	67	52

Sources: Revell (1967); Atkinson (1972)
Note: the figures in column (a) do not take account of state annuities whereas those in column (b) do.

dividend policies and scarce supplies of land, impose a limit to the degree of equality automatically created by a growing economy. Coupled with changes in the occupational structure, such as an increase in the numbers of salaried workers relative to the numbers of wage-earners, these rigidities can have a very significant impact on the pre-tax distribution of incomes. The movement towards greater equality in the distribution of incomes in the UK was negligible after 1957. For the period 1949 to 1957 both wages and salaries, the dual components of employment income, were growing at a faster annual rate than either self-employment income or rents, interest and dividends. But the rate of growth of wages slowed alarmingly in the years from 1957 to 1963 and for the next four years grew more slowly than all other forms of personal income (with the exception of farmers' incomes – a problem we considered in Chapter 10).

Inequalities in the distribution of wealth are even more startling than inequalities in income distribution. Over the course of this century there have been improvements, but wealth remains heavily concentrated, as shown by Table 61.[1] Although the share of the top 1 per cent of wealth owners has fallen considerably over a period of fifty years the share of the top 10 per cent (or even the top 5 per cent) has not fallen very markedly. In other words what redistribution has taken place has done so among the extremely rich and the rich. By 1960 there was still over 80 per cent of wealth in the hands of the top 10 per cent and current estimates put the figure above 50 per cent. The major reason for the persistence of wealth concentration is that the UK lacks an effective mechanism for tackling the problem – we do not have a comprehensive wealth tax.

Personal taxation and distribution

Income

Since the UK income-tax system is based upon the principle of progression we should expect distributional changes to be achieved with the tax mechanism. But, as we can see from Table 62, this has not been the case and the post-tax distribution picture is disappointingly similar to the pre-tax pattern.

Table 62 Percentage distribution of incomes, UK after tax

Group of income recipients		1949	1957	1963	1967
		Percentage of total incomes received			
top	1%	6·4	5·0	5·2	4·9
	5%	17·7	14·9	15·7	15·0
	10%	27·1	24·0	25·2	24·4
	40%	64·1	62·5	64·7	64·0
	70%	85·4	86·5	88·2	88·3
bottom	30%	14·6	13·4	11·8	11·7

Sources: Lydall (1959); Nicholson (1967); Walsh (1972)

1. Because of data deficiencies the situation may be even worse than our table suggests. Concentration figures are based on Estate Duty returns which omit many forms of wealth and constitute only a small sample of the wealth-owning population at any time.

Why has the personal income-tax system failed to achieve more post-tax equality? There are certain specific reasons regarding technicalities of the personal allowances and reliefs within the personal income-tax structure, but these are beyond the scope of our discussion of general problems. The overriding reason why the tax system fails to achieve more equity, either vertically or horizontally, is the narrowness of the tax base. As we have suggested many times by now, only under a fully comprehensive income tax can post-tax equity objectives be satisfied. A less than comprehensive definition of income provides an incentive (to those who possess the means) to choose tax-avoiding forms of income. To establish that certain forms of income are non-taxable very often requires a legal battle with the consequent result that the definition of taxable capacity becomes established through case law. As more tax units opt for tax-avoiding forms of income and as others establish further case-law precedents, the gradual erosion of the tax base is inevitable. As a consequence ever higher tax rates are imposed, fostering further iniquities and promoting new legal wrangles.

Wealth

As mentioned earlier, the major reasons why wealth is still heavily concentrated in the UK is that wealth has been taxed even less comprehensively than income. Estate Duty, the tax adopted by the UK, is not a tax on wealth but a tax on estates passed on at death or within some prescribed period prior to death (currently, seven years). As such it is a notoriously easy tax to avoid, but the main criticism which can be aimed at such a tax is that it does not promote a breakdown of wealth concentration in the way that a tax on *inheritance* does. We mentioned in Chapter 41 that wealth may be self-perpetuating over time and thus remain concentrated. However, if a tax is levied on amounts of wealth inherited rather than on amounts passed on, wealth donors face an incentive to break up the fortunes they intend handing to the next generation. If inheritances are taxed then small amounts of wealth donated to many different recipients means a smaller tax liability, under a progressive rates system, than if the same total amount is handed on to just one recipient. But under an estates system, tax liability is the same. For example, compare the differing effects on estates and inheritances for a wealth transfer of £60 000 when tax rates for both are 5 per cent on the first £20 000; 10 per cent on the second £20 000; and 20 per cent on the third £20 000.

Estate	Tax	Inheritance (three recipients)			Tax	Inheritance (one recipient)	Tax
		A	B	C		A	
£60 000	£7000	£20 000	£20 000	£20 000	£3000	£60 000	£7000

Under the estates-tax system the tax bill is £7000 regardless of how many receive inheritance from it – the actual size of the estate cannot be reduced by increasing the number of inheritors. Under the inheritance-tax system, however, the liability can be altered. If three recipients A, B and C each receive an equal share, £20 000, the total tax bill is only £3000 but if only one recipient inherits the full £60 000, the tax bill increases to £7000. The donor faces an incentive to spread his inter-generational gifts as widely as possible.

Thus a short-term improvement might involve a switch of emphasis away from estates towards inheritances. Over the longer run, however, the real solution to the problem of wealth concentration lies (again!) in the adoption of a fully comprehensive tax base to include *all* additions to net worth (i.e. not just inheritances) as well as other forms of command over society's scarce resources. A step towards this goal could be the introduction of an *annual* net worth (wealth) tax.

Poverty in the UK

Freedom from want cannot be forced on a democracy or given to a democracy. It must be won by them. Winning it needs courage and faith and a sense of national unity: courage to face facts and difficulties and overcome them; faith in our future and in the ideals of fair play and freedom for which century after century our forefathers were prepared to die; a sense of national unity overriding the interests of any class or section. The Plan for Social Security in this Report is submitted by one who believes that in this supreme crisis the British people will not be found wanting for courage and faith and national unity, of material and spiritual power to play their part in achieving both social security and the victory of justice among nations upon which security depends.

It was with these words that Sir William Beveridge (1942) concluded his famous report. The unashamed optimism which emanates from this final paragraph reflects the mood of a nation wearied from a decade of economic depression and still in the throes of a near-global war. Whether this hope for the future was well founded is something of a moot point since, while poverty has not been seen again on the pre-war scale, the nation as a whole has not achieved 'freedom from want'.

The fact that poverty still existed on a large scale in the United Kingdom came as a rude shock to the nation in the early 1960s. The heady atmosphere of the preceding fifteen years with full employment backed by a comprehensive social-security system à la Beveridge had lulled the community into the belief that poverty was just a bad memory. But illusions were shattered by the publication in 1965 of the findings of two sociologists (Abel-Smith and Townsend), showing that 3·8 per cent of the population in 1960 were living in poverty. Further reports, authorized by government[2] in the following years substantiated these earlier findings. Yet, despite this evidence and some piecemeal alterations in the state programme, those in poverty still constituted 3·4 per cent of the population in 1969.

Why did the scheme envisaged by Beveridge not prevent this situation from arising? After all, the plan formulated in the Report, the principles of which were implemented in subsequent legislation, seemed all-embracing: a comprehensive social-insurance scheme; a national-assistance 'safety net' to catch those not covered by the insurance provisions; and family allowances to take care of the financial problems created by excessive family size. The major reason for the relative failure of the plan lies in the neglect of successive governments to maintain the aims of the Beveridge proposals. A scheme so comprehensive and discretionary requires constant revision and overhaul if it is to adapt to structural changes in the economy and in society at large. Such checks have not been exercised on the social-security system, despite many structural changes in the United Kingdom in the last twenty-five years. Demographic changes have resulted in proportional increases in the dependent sectors of population – the pre-school sector; those in full-time education; and the retired sector. Changes have occurred in the occupational

2. Ministry of Pensions and National Insurance (1966); Ministry of Social Security (1967); Department of Health and Social Security (1971).

structure and hence in the incidence of unemployment. Even the concept of poverty itself has undergone change as general living standards have risen.

Given these changes and the lack of government monitoring of the poverty situation, the post-war system has failed the Beveridge principles in one very important respect. The Report proposed that both retirement pensions and family allowances should be adequate to provide at least a subsistence level of income. Neither of these conditions has been satisfied, a major contributory factor in the concentration of poverty among the aged and among families with small children. In the latter case, small children, failing to satisfy one of the Beveridge principles has been compounded by the fact that one of the Report's important assumptions has not been borne out by reality. This was the assumption that, given full employment, work income would be adequate in all cases to provide for the needs of a one-child family. However, in 1966 25 per cent of families with incomes below the national assistance scale (the 'official' poverty line) had a father in full-time employment.[3] It would seem that a full-employment policy is not enough to protect the lowly skilled from inadequate remuneration.

What is to be done?

The growing concern about the existence of poverty in a so-called advanced economy and the apparent failure of the post-war programme to solve the problem, has led many academics and policy-makers to call for a radical departure from the existing social-security arrangements. Very often this call has been for the implementation of some sort of negative income-taxation plan whereby individuals are not only compelled to transfer resources to the state when income rises above some defined level, but also they receive *automatic subsidies* from the state when incomes fall below some defined level.

The term *negative taxation* is an umbrella which covers many types of anti-poverty plan. Indeed the term can be applied to any earnings-related transfer scheme. But generally we may distinguish between two types of plan which are referred to under this heading:

Negative-rates taxation;
Social-dividend taxation.

3. Ministry of Social Security (1967).

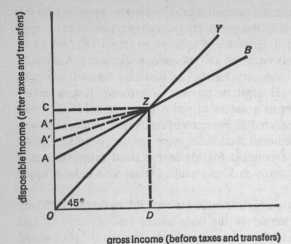

Figure 206

Negative rates

Negative-rates taxation represents a simple extension of the existing income-tax structure – above the level of minimum taxable income a tax unit pays positive taxes; below this level it receives transfers ('pays' negative taxes).

The relationships in Figure 206 relate to a tax unit of given size and structure. OY represents a guideline – along OY gross income and disposable income are identical (OY has a slope of 45°). AB represents the actual relationship between gross income and disposable income for the prevailing tax régime: thus the vertical distance between OY and AB at any point indicates the amount of tax, positive or negative, associated with that particular level of gross income. As can be seen, this distance diminishes as gross income approaches D, that is, as gross income approaches the level of minimum taxable (positive) income C. Hence the actual rate of negative tax is given by the ratio A/C; for example, if $A/C = \frac{1}{2}$, the negative tax rate is 50 per cent.[4] To summarize, D is the 'break-even' level of gross income – when gross income is less than D the tax unit is a net beneficiary from the scheme (AB lies above OY); above this level the tax is a net contributor to the scheme (AB lies below Y).

4. Note that our simple example assumes positive and negative rates to be identical. This may not be the case in a real world negative-rates plan.

Negative-rates taxation epitomizes the 'selective' approach to the poverty problem – only the genuinely poor derive benefit from state transfers. As such, it faces the disclosure problem referred to in Chapter 41. A drawback of the Beveridge National Assistance programme ('supplementary benefit' as it is now termed) has been that eligibility for aid must be proven by a means test, a device notoriously deficient as a means of estimating true needs. In 1966, for example, an estimated 39 per cent of retirement pensioners who were eligible for National Assistance were not receiving it. Dislike of the means test accounted for at least a third (approximately) and possibly for as many as 50 per cent of those who did not apply for benefit.[5]

It is claimed that a negative-rates plan would avoid this difficulty since a tax return would be the only means test required. If this argument is assuming that a tax return under this sort of plan would not be viewed with hostility by potential transfer recipients, it is not very strong. Why should an individual with, say, zero income be more prepared to disclose this fact under this system than any other? However, if the argument is based on the fact that tax returns would be compulsory then it may carry some weight.

But whatever the basis to the argument it ignores an important point – how regular would negative-tax returns need to be? If such returns were made annually then alternative arrangements would be required for those suffering *unforeseen* hardship during the following tax year. Yet if some secondary mechanism were established to assess temporary needs of this kind the problem of eligibility disclosure reappears in full force. The alternative – to file tax returns regularly, say monthly or, better still, weekly – renders a compulsory scheme administratively impossible and the alternative of a voluntary system would be no improvement upon the current arrangements.

Neither is eligibility disclosure the sole problem under negative-rates taxation. Even more difficult to resolve are the problems surrounding the fixing of the break-even-level of income, i.e. the income level at which negative-tax payments cease and positive payments commence. If this level is established as the poverty line then negative-tax rates of less than 100 per cent would not place tax units beyond poverty. Thus, in the example of Figure 206, if *OC* represents the official poverty line then the negative tax rate depicted

5. Ministry of Pensions and National Insurance (1966).

by *AB* fills only a portion of the poverty gap. *A'Z* and *A"Z* represent rate improvements but only when the negative rate is depicted by *CZ* (when all the poverty gap is filled in) could the plan hope for a comprehensive attack on poverty. However, the price of filling the poverty gap this way is the disincentives likely to result since, under this alternative, marginal increments to income below *OD* would not improve disposable income beyond *OC*, so why work when *OC* disposable income is guaranteed for zero effort? While recognizing that we cannot predict on such matters in the absence of empirical information about income and substitution effects, the sheer size of the potential disincentive seems very likely to make it effective.

Social dividend

The aim of social-dividend taxation is to provide a guaranteed minimum income (at least subsistence) for all – the social dividend – and to classify all income, including the social-dividend transfer,[6] as taxable. Such a scheme is illustrated in Figure 207 where a proportional tax rate is applied to all forms of income.

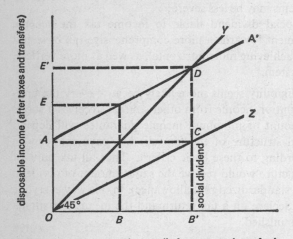

gross income (before taxes and transfers)

Figure 207

6. Some types of social-dividend scheme have been advanced in which the social dividend is excluded from the tax base, but such schemes do not satisfy the generally acceptable tax criteria.

In the above diagram OY again represents a guideline. A guaranteed minimum income is fixed at A for the given tax unit. As the unit's gross income (income from other sources) rises above zero, positive tax payments are made. The rate at which these taxes are extracted (50 per cent for simplicity) is indicated by OZ – points on this line show income net of tax but not of transfer. To show income net of both taxes and transfer OZ is shifted vertically by the amount of guaranteed minimum income, A. Thus points along AA' show total disposable income, after allowing for both taxes and transfer. We can see, then, that the tax unit's break even level of income is OB' gross $(= OE'$ net). At this point tax payments equal the minimum income guarantee $(AA'$ crosses $OY)$; for gross income levels below OB' the tax unit is a net beneficiary of the scheme but when gross income rises above OB' the unit is a net contributor $(OY$ lies above $AA')$.

The concept of social dividend is more attractive than that of negative-rates taxation for three important reasons:

Disclosure of eligibility is more likely;
Despite *everyone* being guaranteed a minimum level of income, disincentive problems may be less severe;
By making the social dividend liable to income tax the scheme facilitates a movement towards a more comprehensive tax base and therefore towards achieving more horizontal, as well as more vertical, equity in the tax system.

1 Disclosure of eligibility seems more likely because every tax unit, regardless of amount of income from other sources, receives a social dividend. The amount of minimum income guarantee will depend upon the size and structure of the tax unit but payments can be standardized according to these basic criteria. Thus all tax units of equal size and structure would receive the same amount of dividend (inclusive of some standardized rent allowance). In this way everyone has something to declare on a tax return and the means-test stigma is consequently diminished.

2 As always, we can only make tentative suggestions regarding potential disincentive effects. It does seem that there could be dangers in this respect regarding a social dividend scheme since the *positive* rate of tax may have to be high, say 30 to 40 per cent, to help finance the scheme. But potential disincentives exist under any income-

tax scheme, particularly, as we have seen, negative-rates taxation and it can be argued that such effects may be less severe at lower income levels under a social-dividend scheme. One reason for this cautious optimism is that since some minimum income level is guaranteed additions to the *gross* income above zero level also represent net additions to disposable incomes (assuming the *positive* tax rate to be less than 100 per cent); whereas under negative-rates taxation this was not the case when the break-even level equalled the poverty threshold since the negative-tax rate would then be 100 per cent.

A second possible argument is that providing a secure income floor may induce households to offer more labour hours than in the absence of such a guarantee. Consider Figure 207 again: in the absence of a minimum guarantee of *OA* a household would need to earn *OB* gross income to achieve this same amount. But under the social-dividend scheme a gross income level of *OB* translates into disposable income of *OE* – it may now appear worthwhile to offer the number of work hours necessary to yield *OB* gross income whereas previously it did not. In other words the social dividend provides a foundation upon which it is worthwhile to build – in the absence of the foundation this incentive does not exist.[7]

3 Finally, a social dividend scheme may facilitate all-round improvements in the tax structure. A guaranteed minimum for all could replace all existing social-security benefits, some of which may not have been included in the definition of taxable income. Since the social dividend would be taxable this may be a means of achieving a more comprehensive tax base. In so far as any scheme did achieve this end it would immediately help create more horizontal equity in the tax structure and over the longer run more vertical equity as tax avoidance is reduced. This latter possibility would also alleviate the financing of the scheme – the broader the tax base the lower the tax rate for a given level of redistribution.

Despite its relative attractiveness a social-dividend scheme suffers from a basic drawback – what to do about those individuals whose needs are not catered for by the transfer mechanism. The benefits from a social dividend derive from the *automatic* establishment of an income floor beneath every tax unit but to achieve this type of

7. There is some empirical evidence to suggest that savings are increased in similar fashion as a result of providing some secure floor such as a state pension. See, for example, Cagan (1965).

mechanism requires social-dividend payments to be standardized according to general circumstances, mainly the size and structure of the tax unit. However, many needs will be *specific* to the tax unit and will not be easily catered for by a tax return, very often because they cannot be foreseen. This problem would seem to return us full circle to some separate arrangement, some form of safety net, and the problems of means testing. Yet, as previously hinted at, this is not a problem peculiar to social-dividend taxation. Indeed, it must be faced by all types of tax/transfer mechanism since no system can cater for every individual need and circumstance by standardized transfers. The best that can be aimed for is a plan which gives as comprehensive a standardized coverage as possible, so minimizing the areas and occasions of specific needs.

True to Beveridge

This question of stand-by arrangements must be faced, then, by the third alternative to existing arrangements which is to establish firmly for the first time a social-security system which is true to Beveridge principles. Such a plan would require all benefits, including retirement pensions and family allowances, to satisfy subsistence requirements. In this way families in and out of work could be given an income floor, thus lessening the need to rely on such schemes as minimum-wage legislation which has not been very successful in the UK, for reasons suggested by our theory in Chapter 10. The great drawback to such a scheme is that it is administratively unwieldy whereas a social-dividend plan can provide an income floor and create economies of scale in administration. These potential economies plus the other benefits from a social dividend which we discussed earlier are in large part dependent upon a general overhaul of the system of personal-income taxation. The social dividend seems the necessary longer-run objective, in the meantime the adoption of truly Beveridge principles may bring immediate gains.

Questions

1 'Poverty is unacceptable whereas inequality is acceptable.' Discuss.

2 How can we say that one distribution of income (or wealth) is more unequal than another? Does our answer depend upon value

judgements? Do the same arguments apply to the monopoly concentration ratios of Chapter 20?

3 'The case for a social dividend or negative income tax founders upon the problem of incentives.' Discuss.

4 'The distribution of personal income depends upon genes and nothing can be done about them.'
'The distribution of personal income depends upon chance.'
'The distribution of personal income depends upon the "taste" for making money.'
'The distribution of ability is normally distributed whereas the distribution of incomes is skewed so making money has nothing to do with brains.'

Comment on these statements.

Chapter 44
Political Processes

The state and the market

So we come to the issue we have been avoiding: the efficiency of the state. Whenever we encountered a problem – monopoly, unemployment, collective goods and so on – we referred the problem to the state for a solution. But we always avoided explaining what this thing called the state was and how it worked. The state was something, a divine intervention, that wrought the necessary miracles. But even a casual glance at history suggests that the state, the political process, is not above reproach. And in this chapter we shall, in fact, stress the point that both our instruments – market and state – are imperfect instruments whose use needs care and whose improvement must always be sought. So if the impression is one of despair tinged with cynicism then the reader should realize that the world is not perfect but needs perfecting.

The state may be defined as a geographical segment of society which is united by a common obedience to a sovereign. Of especial importance to economists are the phrases 'common obedience' and 'sovereign will'. Politics is concerned with problems of power, authority and legitimacy and these issues follow from our earlier analysis of collective goods which demonstrated that some goods cannot be provided by the market because of the free rider problem. Some means must therefore be found whereby people can be coerced into accepting collective financing of those goods. And this is in line with beliefs of the early political theorists, Hobbes, Locke and Rousseau. For Rousseau, people had to force themselves to be free – in order, as economic jargon puts it, to get on to higher indifference curves. This viewpoint stands in contrast to much economics which is concerned with constructing theories of exchange from which power and coercion are absent. Indeed, economics may be regarded as an attempt to overcome or reduce the magnitude of the political problem by indicating areas where exchange might take the place of coercion or by suggesting rules which might most efficiently reduce the costs of coercion.

Rules for decision making

The problems of political decision making are, of course, simplified if it is known in advance what should be done. Then there can be a simple rule: 'Implement decision X' and the people could elect or nominate someone to do X. Some economists do believe that such rules can be formulated and we have encountered such rules in Chapter 38 in connection with discretionary monetary and fiscal policies. But, more commonly, there is a feeling that rules, at best, can only be guidelines and that what is required is a search process to find the most efficient methods of catering for wants. It is this search process that we call political processes and like the market solution, the political solution is a product of trial and error.

The constitution

The set of rules governing the methods by which searches should be carried out is known as the *constitution* and may be written or un-written. At the elementary level the UK constitution may be said to comprise the electorate and a group of institutions which includes parliament and the judiciary. The people, in effect, delegate the task of searching for optimum solutions to some of their number and exercise control over them through periodic elections.

Problems of political processes

Majority voting and the problem of group choice

The essence of the political process is the acceptance of the will of the majority with due consideration of the wishes of the minority. What is, however, interesting is the manner in which opinions are obtained for there is an apparent lack of any attempt to measure the relative intensities of preferences. The insistence on equality in democracies leads to the principle of one man–one vote. Unfortunately this insistence on equality can lead to the absence of clear-cut majorities. Consider, for example, the following problem. A report of a Monopolies Commission concludes that the lollipop industry is monopolistic and the government is therefore faced with the following courses of action:

Policy A – regulate prices;
Policy B – nationalize the lollipop industry;
Policy C – reduce tariffs in order to allow foreign competition to break up the domestic monopoly.

These three policies, we may suppose, are placed before the heads of the government departments most likely to be involved and we may imagine that they rank their preferences as follows:

Table 63 Group choice

Minister for	Regulate	Nationalize	Import
private industries	1	2	3
public sector	2	3	1
foreign trade	3	1	2

What is apparent from Table 63 is that no basis exists for a group decision: each alternative receives as much support (i.e. votes) as every other one. Before examining how this apparent paradox arises and how it may be resolved, it is worth noting that the same problem can occur within the individual. In the individual the id and the ego may pull in different directions and somehow the individual has to produce a unified approach to problems lest his personality disintegrates and he becomes a schizophrenic.

Now coherence can be produced by either a dictatorship (note how this harks back to centralization discussed in Part Two) or some way of trading preferences as in the market. This last solution points to the essential difference between political trading and private market trading. In the example given above each Minister behaves rationally in the sense that he ranks the alternatives and does not then behave inconsistently with respect to his preferences. Now this is what happens in the markets for private goods. A housewife may prefer meat to eggs or cheese and we would normally expect her to always purchase meat unless her tastes changed. Another housewife might prefer eggs to meat or cheese and we should always expect to observe her buying eggs. We could introduce further housewives but the general point is that what appears to be an identical situation does not produce stalemate. Why should this be so?

The answer to our question seems to lie in the lack of a means for expressing the relative strength of political preferences whereas in private markets money measures the intensity of preferences. As a result compromises are much more easily achieved in the markets for private goods.

The efficiency of corruption

Of course money has been, and is, sometimes used in the political decision-making process. Stalemates and disequilibria are undesirable and methods must be found to obtain solutions. But the use of money for vote-buying is frowned upon on the grounds that the distribution of income and wealth should not be allowed to dictate the workings of a democracy. Paradoxically, it may be the 'back-door' use of money which yields political stability. Bribery and corruption can be efficient means of achieving ends – even if the ends and the means are not always respectable to some.

Small and large groups

Within a small group the problems posed by the paradox of voting can be overcome. Face-to-face contact allows group members the opportunity to gauge each other's intensity of preferences. But the state is a large group and that causes a difficult problem, and the problem is compounded by further issues that the individual does not encounter in private markets:

1 The buyer of a private good is likely to be more knowledgeable about what he is being offered since he is continually shopping in the market. Moreover the goods are easier to judge in terms of the relationship between physical characteristics and presumed utilities. In contrast the political buyer may only shop once every four or five years.

2 In buying private goods the buyer is buying only for himself whereas in buying political possibilities he may be buying for others. What this means is that market man and political man may have different frames of reference. Sometimes the political man may

behave like the market man as, for example, when he buys defence or law and order, but sometimes he may have in his mind the image of the good society.

3 In buying private goods the buyer is usually confronted by many sellers whereas in the political market there are usually a few sellers, and this difference in market situations can considerably affect the possibilities of many electors obtaining satisfaction at the polling booths.

The similarity of political parties

An important feature of party politics is the tendency of their programmes to be similar. Although British political parties were founded on class differences these differences have seemingly become irrelevant. Labour Party candidates tend to be drawn from the middle class and many working-class voters are Conservative. There is a great deal of homogeneity in the electorate which has tended to make the parties appeal to the middle of political spectrum. Like Woolworths, Marks and Spencer and British Home Stores, they have concentrated where the mass of votes are. This similarity in manifestos makes it difficult for the electorate to decide who to vote for and bewilderment is confirmed by the tendency of parties to renounce their programmes as a result of external factors such as the balance of payments, inflation and unemployment. The similarities of the parties and their inability to solve major problems accounts for the volatility of voting behaviour, the inability of pollsters to predict election results, the low majorities of successful parties and the tendencies of governments to lose by-elections.

Why vote?

When we consider the obstacles in the way of political man obtaining what he wants the surprising thing is that he bothers to vote. During the post-war period there have been ten general (national) elections and the percentage of the electorate voting has never been less than 72·0 per cent and has in fact been as high as 82·5 per cent (Table 64). In addition there is the interesting feature that the difference in votes cast for the leading contenders has usually been slight, which suggests that a large number of voters have been doomed to disappoint-

Table 64 Voting behaviour at general elections, 1945–74

	1945[1]	1950	1951	1955	1959	1964	1966	1970	1974 (a)	1974 (b)
Conservatives										
percentage votes cast	39·8	43·5	48·0	49·7	49·4	43·4	41·9	46·4	37·8	35·8
number of seats	213	298	321	345	366	304	253	330	297	277
Labour										
percentage votes cast	48·3	46·1	48·8	46·4	43·8	44·1	47·9	43·0	37·1	39·2
number of seats	393	315	295	277	258	317	363	287	301	319
Liberal										
percentage votes cast	9·1	9·1	2·5	2·7	5·9	11·2	8·5	7·5	19·3	18·3
number of seats	12	9	6	6	6	9	12	6	14	13
Other										
percentage votes cast	2·8	1·3	0·7	1·2	0·9	1·3	1·7	3·2	5·8	6·6
number of seats	19	4	3	2	—		2	7	23	26
total electorate (millions)	32·8	34·3	34·7	34·9	35·4	35·9	36·0	39·3	39·8	40·0
percentage voting	73·3	84·0	82·5	76·8	78·7	77·1	75·8	72·0	78·1	72·8

Source: Butler and Pinto-Duschinsky (1971)

1. University seats excluded: other 1945 figures adjusted to eliminate the distortions introduced by double voting in the fifteen two-member seats then existing

ment. This problem of wasted votes is also the phenomenon of key constituencies and wasted majorities.

It has been frequently suggested that general elections are determined by the results of certain key (marginal) constituencies. These constituencies are ones in which the margin by which the victor won at the previous election falls short of the expected swing to his opponent in the forthcoming election. Thus if a Conservative won a seat in 1970 with a 4 per cent majority and it is expected that the swing to Labour will be 10 per cent then the seat would be deemed marginal. Now the number of marginal seats is usually small which means that the electorate may be governed by the votes of a few whom they can little influence.

The problem of wasted votes also occurs when some candidates win by massive majorities only to discover that they are not members of the ruling party. Thus in the general election of 1951 the Labour candidates obtained 48·8 per cent of the votes but only 295 seats whereas the Conservatives got less votes and more seats. Since it is seats and not votes which count many Labour votes were apparently wasted (see Table 64).

We have therefore the problem of why people vote, and as yet we have only a few guesses.

1 Since the right to vote is exercised so infrequently national elections are a novelty or carnival. If they happened more often, as with local elections, people might see the folly of voting and become disinterested.

2 Universal adult suffrage is so recent an innovation that people still regard it as a novelty, privilege or duty to vote.

3 People recognize that it is as important to vote for an opposition, an alternative government, as it is for a victorious party.

The irrelevance of elections

In theory, elections are supposed to give the electorate a chance to participate in decision making, to choose a government which will be strong enough to carry through its programme, a chance to participate in a quasi-referendum on issues of the day and a means of legitimizing change in the state. All these reasons have, however, become undermined. A major reason for thinking that elections are irrelevant is that they are so infrequent. Unlike voters in other countries, the British electorate has no opportunity to vote for members of the Second Chamber, there are no primaries in which candidates can be tested and there are no referendums on specific issues (save the Common Market). Furthermore, when elections do take place, and parties swap roles, nothing else seems to change. The civil service does not change nor do the trade unions.

Of course, we should not expect political man to be content with so few opportunities of shopping. Man operates in a variety of political environments; he is a member of many clubs – a trade union, a church and so on. He can be a member of a pressure group which petitions, bullies or cajoles politicians. But more than that he can belong to an organization which, by its rejection of an incomes policy, destroys a government. He may operate a multinational corporation which dictates to or flaunts governments. Wasted majorities can sometimes exert their influence. Moreover, new political parties can emerge and a striking feature of recent UK elections is the rise in the vote for newer parties. This does carry dangers. It may lead to a substitution of party bargaining for bargaining between a party and the electorate. And, since many of the newer parties are regional parties, it could lead to the abandonment of universal standards for such things as poverty.

The irrelevance of politics

The problems surrounding political processes raise the question: is politics important? Most of the major problems in society seem to be incapable of being solved by politicians, such as the balance of payments, the rate of growth and inflation and so on. So why not abandon politics for the market? The answer probably lies in the fact that we expect too much of politicians and we encourage them to believe that they can solve difficult problems. But some of the difficult problems are problems for the market. A clearer distinction between market and political might therefore help to resolve the relative efficiencies of the two systems.

Summary

The problems of ensuring efficiency in political processes are two-fold. First, there is the simple point that voting processes can fail to reflect the intensity of voters' preferences. Secondly, the market so infiltrates the political that appeals to the state to correct the imbalances of the market may be otiose.

Questions

1 In countries where there is only one political party what purpose do you think is served by elections?

2 According to Marx the state would wither away with the emergence of Socialism. Does your reading of Chapters 41 and 42 lead you to the

same conclusion? Do you think that Marx employed a different definition of the state to that employed in those chapters?

3 The internal operations of a university are conducted without money. There is one fairly well-defined task of teaching and another objective, research, which is ill-defined. Consider how a university's constitution is framed so as to reconcile and permit the efficient pursuit of both objectives.

4 'Politics are, as it were, the market-place and the price mechanism of all social demands – though there is no guarantee that a just price will be struck; and there is nothing spontaneous about politics – it depends on deliberate and continuous individual activity' (Crick, 1962). Comment on this statement.

5 In his book, Crick (1962) sets out certain conditions for a stable political system. Examine these stability conditions in the light of your understanding of the workings of markets.

6 It has been suggested that (a) the political system produces too much of some goods, such as defence, because of outmoded attitudes, and (b) too little of other goods, such as health, because of the attempts of people to avoid paying taxes (i.e. because of the existence of free riders). What do you think?

7 Can voting behaviour be analysed along the same lines as standard consumer behaviour (recall Chapter 11)?

8 What objections would you raise against the vote-maximizing theory of political party behaviour?

9 'It is impossible to construct a political constitution which is capable of resolving any interpersonal differences brought to it while at the same time satisfying certain reasonable and desirable assumptions.' Discuss and indicate whether the statement suggests that the lot of man is either civil discord or life under Big Brother.

10 In the political system the distribution of political money (votes) is equal yet the distribution of political power is unequal. Why should this be?

References

Abel-Smith, B., and Townsend, P. (1965), *The Poor and the Poorest*, Bell.
Aspinall, A. (1949), *The Early Trade Unions*, Betchworth Press.
Atkinson, A. B. (1972), *Unequal Shares*, Allen Lane The Penguin Press.

Ball, R. J., Eaton, J. R. and Steuer, M. D. (1966), 'The relationship between United Kingdom export performance in manufactures and the internal pressures of demand', *Economic Journal*, September.
Baumol, W. J. (1959), *Business Behavior, Value and Growth*, Harcourt Brace Joranovich.
Beckerman, W. (1968), *An Introduction to National Income*, Weidenfeld & Nicolson.
Butler, D. E., and Pinto-Duschinsky, M. (1971), *The British General Election of 1970*, Macmillan.

Cagan, P. (1965), *Effect of Pension Plans on Aggregate Saving: Evidence from a Sample Survey*, National Bureau of Economic Research.
Crick, B. R. (1962), *In Defence of Politics*, Weidenfeld & Nicolson; Penguin, 1969.

Deane, P., and Cole, W. A. (1960), *British Economic Growth 1685–1959*, Cambridge University Press.
Department of Health and Social Security (1971), Statistical Report Series No. 14, *Two-Parent Families*, HMSO.

Friedman, M. (1957), *A Theory of the Consumption Function*, Princeton University Press.
Friedman, M. (1962), *Capitalism and Freedom*, University of Chicago Press.

Graaf, J. de V. (1967), *Theoretical Welfare Economics*, Cambridge University Press.

Haberler, G. (1969), Reading 5 in R. N. Cooper (ed.), *International Finance*, Penguin.
Harcourt, G. C., and Laing, N. F. (eds), *Capital and Growth*, Penguin.
Harrod, R. F. (1951), *The Life of John Maynard Keynes*, Macmillan.

Hicks, J. R. (1937), 'Mr Keynes and the "Classics": a suggested interpretation', *Econometrica*.

International Monetary Fund (1971), *Direction of Trade Annual, 1966–70*.

Keynes, J. M. (1971a), *The Economic Consequences of the Peace*, Macmillan. (First published in 1919.)
Keynes, J. M. (1971b), *Treatise on Money*, vol. 1, Macmillan. (First published in 1930.)
Keynes, J. M. (1931a), 'Economic possibilities for our grandchildren', in *Essays in Persuasion*, Macmillan, 1931.
Keynes, J. M. (1931b), 'The economic consequences of Mr Churchill', in *Essays in Persuasion*, Macmillan, 1931.
Keynes, J. M. (1936), *The General Theory of Employment, Interest and Money*, Macmillan.
Knight, F. H. (1971), *Risk, Uncertainty and Profit*, University of Chicago Press.

Lydall, H. F. (1959), 'The long-term trend in the size distribution of income', *Journal of the Royal Statistical Society*.

Maddison, A. (1964), *Economic Growth in the West*, Allen & Unwin.
Malthus, T. R. (1970), *An Essay on the Principle of Population*, Penguin. (First published in 1798.)
Marris, R. (1964), *Economic Theory of Managerial Capitalism*, Macmillan.
Marx, K. (1970), *Capital, Volume 1*, Lawrence and Wishart. (First published in 1867.)
Matthews, R. C. O. (1959), *The Trade Cycle*, Cambridge University Press.
Meade, J. E. (1961), 'Mauritius: a case study in Malthusian economics', *Economic Journal*.
Merton, R. C. (1972), *The Collected Scientific Papers of Paul A. Samuelson*, vol. 3, MIT Press.
Ministry of Pensions and National Insurance (1966), *Financial and Other Circumstances of Retirement Pensioners*, HMSO.
Ministry of Social Security (1967), *Circumstances of Families*, HMSO.
Morris, V., and Ziderman, A. (1971), 'The economic return on investment in higher education in England and Wales', *Economic Trends*.

Nicholson, R. J. (1967), 'The distribution of personal income', *Lloyds Bank Review*.

Phillips, A. W. (1958), 'Unemployment and wage rates', in R. J. Ball and P. Doyle (eds.), *Inflation*, Penguin, 1969.
Pigou, A. C. (1912), *Wealth and Welfare*, Macmillan.
Pratten, C. F. (1971), *Economies of Scale in Manufacturing Industry*, Cambridge University Press.

Radford, R. A. (1945), 'The economic organisation of a POW camp',
Economica.
Revell, J. (1967), *Wealth of the Nation*, Cambridge University Press.
Robertson, D. H. (1952), *Utility and All That*, Allen & Unwin.

Saunders, P. G. (1973), 'The current inflation – an academic view',
The Bankers' Magazine, May.
Sawyer, M. C. (1971), *Concentrations in British Manufacturing Industry*,
Oxford University Press.
Sen, A. K. (1970), *Growth Economics*, Penguin.
Servan-Schreiber, J.-J. (1969), *American Challenge*, Penguin.
Sheppard, D. K. (1971), *The Growth and Role of UK Financial Institutions
1880–1962*, Methuen.
Simons, H. C. (1938), *Personal Income Taxation*, University of Chicago Press.
Stolper, G. (1967), *The German Economy 1870 to the present*,
Weidenfeld & Nicolson.
Sumner, M. T. (1973), 'The current inflation – a programme for control',
The Bankers' Magazine, May.

Times Newspapers (1971), *British Economy: Key Statistics 1900–1970*.
Turner, H. A. (1969), *Is Britain Really Strike-Prone?*,
Cambridge University Press.

Utton, M. A. (1971), 'The effects of mergers on concentration in UK
manufacturing industry, 1954–1965', *Journal of Industrial Economics*.

Walsh, A. J. (1972), 'Tax allowances and fiscal policy' in P. Townsend and
N. Bosanquet (eds.), *Labour and Inequality*, Fabian Society.
Williamson, O. E. (1964), *The Economics of Discretionary Behaviour*,
Prentice-Hall.

Further Reading

American Economic Association/Allen and Unwin, London 1948–1972.
 Readings in Business Cycles.
 Readings in Business Cycle Theory.
 Readings in Fiscal Policy.
 Readings in the Theory of Income Distribution.
 Readings in International Economics.
 Readings in the Theory of International Trade.
 Readings in Monetary Theory.
 Readings in Price Theory.
 Readings in the Economics of Taxation.
 Readings in Welfare Economics.
E. H. Chamberlin, *The Theory of Monopolistic Competition*,
Harvard University Press, 1933.
I. Fisher, *The Theory of Interest*, Macmillan, 1930.
N. Georgescu-Roegen, *Analytical Economics*, Harvard University Press, 1966.
N. Georgescu-Roegen, *The Entropy Law and the Economic Process*,
Harvard University Press, 1970.
J. R. Hicks, *Value and Capital*, 2nd ed., Oxford University Press, 1946.
C. Hill, *Reformation to Industrial Revolution*, Penguin, 1970.
E. J. Hobsbawm, *Industry and Empire*, Penguin, 1970.
S. Jevons, *The Theory of Political Economy*, 1870; Penguin edition, 1971.
M. Kalecki, *Selected Essays on the Dynamics of the Capitalist Economy*,
Cambridge University Press, 1971.
J. M. Keynes, *The Collected Writings of John Maynard Keynes*, Macmillan, 1971.
 vol II, *The Economic Consequences of the Peace.*
 vol IV, *A Tract on Monetary Reform.*
 vols V and VI, *A Treatise on Money.*
 vol VII, *The General Theory of Employment, Interest and Money.*
A. Marshall, *Principles of Economics*, 8th ed., Macmillan, 1920.
K. Marx, *Collected Works*, Penguin edition, 1973–5.
 Grundrisse, 1973.
 The Revolution of 1848, 1973.
 Surveys from Exile, 1973.
 Early Writings, 1975.
 The First International and After, 1974.
 Capital vol. 1, 1976.

Capital vol. 2, forthcoming.
Capital vol. 3, forthcoming.
J. E. Meade, *Efficiency, Equality and Ownership of Property*, Allen & Unwin, 1964.
R. A. Musgrave, *The Theory of Public Finance*, McGraw-Hill, 1959.
A. Nove, *An Economic History of the USSR*, Penguin, 1972.
A. C. Pigou, *The Economics of Welfare*, Macmillan, 1924.
M. M. Postan, *Medieval Economy and Society*, Penguin, 1975.
D. Ricardo, *The Works and Correspondence of David Ricardo*, Sraffa edition, Cambridge University Press, 1951–71.
J. Robinson, *The Economics of Imperfect Competition*, Macmillan, 1930.
P. A. Samuelson, *The Collected Scientific Papers of Paul A. Samuelson*, edited by J. Stiglitz and R. Merton, MIT Press, 1967–72.
J. Schumpeter, *History of Economic Analysis*, Allen & Unwin, 1954.
C. Shoup, *Public Finance*, Weidenfeld & Nicolson, 1970.
A. Smith, *An Inquiry into the Causes of the Wealth of Nations*, Cannan edition, Methuen, 1961.

Penguin Modern Economics Readings

G. C. Archibald, *The Theory of the Firm*.
A. B. Atkinson, *Wealth, Income and Inequality*.
R. J. Ball and P. Doyle, *Inflation*.
H. Bernstein, *Underdevelopment and Development*.
J. Bhagwati, *International Trade*.
J. Bhagwati, and R. S. Eckaus, *Foreign Aid*.
M. Blaug, *Economics of Education*, vols. 1 and 2.
G. P. Clarkson, *Managerial Economics*.
R. W. Clo·· r, *Monetary Theory*.
M. H. Cooper and A. J. Culyer, *Health Economics*.
R. N. Cooper, *International Finance*.
J. H. Dunning, *International Investment*.
M. Gilbert, *Modern Business Enterprise*.
G. C. Harcourt and N. F. Laing, *Capital and Growth*.
J. F. Helliwell, *Aggregate Investment*.
M. Hodges, *European Integration*.
R. W. Houghton, *Public Finance*.
M. C. Howard and J. E. King, *Economics of Marx*.
J. Hughes and R. Moore, *A Special Case?*
E. K. Hunt and J. G. Schwartz, *A Critique of Economic Theory*.
A. Hunter, *Monopoly and Competition*.
R. Jolly, E. de Kadt, H. Singer, F. Wilson, *Third World Employment*.
D. M. Lamberton, *Economics of Information and Knowledge*.
R. Layard, *Cost-Benefit Analysis*.
I. Livingstone, *Economic Policy for Development*.
B. J. McCormick and E. O. Smith, *The Labour Market*.
D. Munby, *Transport*.
L. Needleman, *Regional Analysis*.

A. Nove and D. M. Nuti, *Socialist Economics.*
E. S. Phelps, *Economic Justice.*
H. Radice, *International Firms and Modern Imperialism.*
P. Robson, *International Economic Integration.*
N. Rosenberg, *Economics of Technological Change.*
K. W. Rothschild, *Power in Economics.*
A. K. Sen, *Growth Economics.*
P. Temin, *New Economic History.*
H. Townsend, *Price Theory.*
K. A. Tucker and B. S. Yamey, *The Economics of Retailing.*
R. Turvey, *Public Enterprise.*
J. Vanek, *Self Management.*
A. A. Walters, *Money and Banking.*
B. S. Yamey, *Economics of Industrial Structure.*

Penguin Modern Economics Texts

C. M. Allan, *The Theory of Taxation.*
A. D. Bain, *The Control of the Money Supply.*
M. Barratt-Brown, *The Economics of Imperialism.*
M. Blaug, *Introduction to the Economics of Education.*
A. Bose, *Marxian and Post Marxian Political Economy.*
M. Bromwich, *Economics of Capital Budgeting.*
B. Carsberg, *Economics and Business Decisions.*
B. J. Cohen, *Balance-of-Payments Policy.*
G. Dalton, *Economic Systems and Society.*
P. Dorner. *Land Reform and Economic Development.*
W. Elkan, *Introduction to Development Economics.*
R. Findlay, *Trade and Specialization.*
C. Freeman, *The Economics of Industrial Innovation.*
H. J. Green, *Consumer Theory.*
H. G. Grubel, *The International Monetary System.*
E. K. Hawkins, *The Principles of Development Aid.*
G. K. Helleiner, *International Trade and Economic Development.*
M. B. Johnson, *Household Behaviour.*
B. J. McCormick, *Wages.*
D. Metcalf, *The Economics of Agriculture.*
H. Myint, *Southeast Asia's Economy.*
G. L. Reid and K. Allen, *Nationalized Industries.*
H. W. Richardson, *Elements of Regional Economics.*
H. W. Richardson, *Urban Economics.*
D. Swann, *The Economics of the Common Market.*
J. M. Thomson, *Modern Transport Economics.*
M. A. Utton, *Industrial Concentration.*
D. M. Winch, *Analytical Welfare Economics.*

Index

Abel-Smith, B., and Townshend, P. 785
Absolute advantage 66
Accelerators
  inventory 586
  revenue changes 574–6
Accountants, supply and demand
  160–61
Accounting 284–302, 359–62
  information 291
Accounts 284–7
  national 291–302
  private firm's 284–5
  profit-and-loss 286–7
  unit of 77–8, 479
Adjustment costs 571–2
Advantage
  absolute 66
  comparative 66. 73, 593
Advertising 362, 368, 434
Affluence, routes to 34
Aggregate behaviour 518–19
Aggregate consumption 545
  production function 700
Aggregate demand 457, 518–19,
  529–31, 532–3
  exports and imports 602–3
  householders' contribution to 545–62
  investment by firms 566–91
Aggregate supply 518, 525–8, 530
  inflation and 634–59
Agricultural policy 157–60
Agriculture 32, 34
  developing economies 679
  diminishing returns in 55, 332–3
  industrialization and 72
  problems 155–6

stabilization 156
surplus 157
Aid, foreign 680
Algebra 138–40, 149–50, 490, 522–4,
  537–9
  see also Simultaneous equations;
    Functions; matrix algebra
Allocation 96, 134–5
  overheads 215–16
Anti-monopoly legislation 373–5
Assets 285–7, 492
Automatic stabilizers 671–2
Automation 60–62, 400
Average propensity to consume 548

Balanced budget 663–4
Balance effect, real 478
Balance of payments 604–33
  accounts 629–31
  deficit 663–5
  devaluation and 459, 595, 720–21
  IS–LM curve model 719–21
  policy and control 618–23
Balance sheets 285–91
Banks
  central 496, 501–2
    control of money supply 493
  commercial 483–8
  creators of money substitutes 493
  credit 483–92
  secondary 497–8
Bank of England 496, 501, 503–4
Banking
  cloakroom theory of 483
  fractional reserve 483–91, 493
Barter economy 74–5, 454

Behavioural theory of the firm 279–80
Behaviour, consumers' 179–81, 407
Beveridge Report 784–6, 792
Black market 133–4
Blood transfusion 133–4
Bonds 473, 499, 504, 699, 700, 759, 760
Books 377–8
Booms 516–17
  contra-cyclical spending 461
  money supply 458
Borrowings 546, 655
  foreign currency 621
Break-even chart 360
Bretton Woods Agreement 627
Budget
  balanced 663–4
  constraint, consumers' 194–9
Buffer stocks 679

Calculus 220, 229–59
  golden rule 316–18
Cambridge K 467–8
Capital
  account, eqilibrium 617
  accumulation 400
  demand for 574–5
  flows 629
  goods 72, 82, 203–5, 295–6, 430, 693
  goods, industries 575n
  human 436–7
  increase in 27–8
  investment, state 760
  market 276–7, 303, 422, 578
  neoclassical theory 429, 433
  theory 570
  units of measurement 568n
Capitalism, nineteenth-century 397–401
Capital-output ratio 575, 576
Cartels, international 679
Cash balance 489
Cash–deposit ratio 487–90, 491
Cash-reserve ratios 491, 493
Central banks see Banks: central
Centralization 97, 454

Change, technical see Technical change
Charity 44, 746–7
  market 134
Choice 185
  collective 795–8
  group 795–8
  scarcity and 36–7
  theory of 179
  unemployment 508
Churches 800
Circular flow of income 511–14
  equilibrium 514–17
  instantaneous 512–13
Civil Service 800
Class, social 798
Closed community 293–7
Closed monopoly 341–5
Closing down, time for 313–14
Coal output and wages 168
Cobweb cycle 162, 165
Coercion 794–5
Collective
  bargaining 445–7
  choice 795–8
  goods 41–3, 177, 216, 266, 401, 461, 735
Collectivization 44–5
Commonwealth Immigration Act 59
Community, closed 293–7
Companies' Acts 287
Company
  firm and 583n
  joint stock 276, 401
  profits 583–4
  see also Firm
Comparative advantage 66, 73, 593
Comparative statics 354, 456
Compensation
  pollution 741–3
  principle 733
Competition 304
  labour 446
  monopoly versus 366–73
  perfect see Perfect competition
Competition and Credit Control 501–2
Concentration ratios 369–70

Confederation of British Industry
    574
Confiscation 655
Constant returns to scale 50
Constitution 795
Consumer
  behaviour 185, 411
  demand 546, 584
  durables 557–9
  protection 374
  spending 579–81
  surplus 127, 189–90
  theory 179–81, 549–55,
    557–9
Consumption
  age structure and 687, 689
  aggregate 545
  demand for sterling 604–5
  excess 738–41
  function 547–9
    long- and short-run 554–6
  lag 524–5
  propensity
    average 548
    marginal 549, 552, 558
  saving and 560
  social optimum 752
  statistics 564–5
Consumption goods trades,
    fluctuations 575n
Contra-cyclical spending 461
Contraception 680
Contracts 264
Control
  economic 303
  industry 34
  monetary 478, 693ff
  monopolies 372–81, 384–94, 736–7
  ownership and 401
  prices 130, 371
  rents 130–32
Corporate
  economy 280–81
  world 281–2
Corporations 274–82
Corruption 797
Cost–benefit analysis 176, 202

Cost curve
  monopoly 343
  production functions and 212–14,
    218
Costing 203
'Cost plus' pricing 279–80
Cost–price ratio 357, 365, 368
Cost pricing, marginal 386–8
Cost-push inflation 637
Costs
  acquisition 204–5
  average 214, 279–80
  avoidable 205–6
  benefit 201
  constant 48, 265, 330–31, 361
  decreasing 208–9, 332–3
  empirical aspects of 217
  escapable 205
  factors 298
  fixed 205, 300
  increasing 48, 68–9, 207, 331–2
  investment 573
  marginal 206, 310–11, 386–8
  obsolescence 204
  operating 204–5
  opportunity 48
    investment and 88–90
  prices and 203–5
  private 216–17
  production and 208–14
  social 216–17
    and benefits 738–9, 750–51
  subjective 203
    and objective 389
  supply and 208–18
  transaction 74
  uncertainty 362
  utility and 175–7
  variable 205, 214, 265
Credit
  bank 483–91
  ceilings 500
  control, competition and 501–2
  money, creation of 481–91
  multiplier 491–2
Crowding out 666
  interest rates 717

Cultural heritage squandered 41
Currency system, unified 481
Current
  account, equilibrium 618
  balance 629
Cycle
  cobweb 162, 165
  damped 165
  explosive 165
  trade 165

Damped cycle 165
Death rates 33
Debt
  acknowledgements 480
    see also Government debt; Loan
    finance; National Debt
Defence
  industries 280–81
Deficits
  government spending 664–5
  spending 663
Deflation 459, 620, 712, 714
Demand 99–120
  aggregate see Aggregate demand
  consumer 546
  cross elasticity 113–15, 368–9
  curve 99, 179
    derived 187
    elasticity 108–13
    monopoly 341–3, 356–7
    movements along 105, 151, 154
    perfect competition 323–4
    shifts 104, 144–6, 151, 154, 181
    substitution 102
  definition 99
  derived 403–7, 413–14
    price elasticity of 411–12
    shifts in 413–14
  determinants 100
  effective 99
  ex ante 99, 413
  ex post 99, 413
  excess, 131–2, 142, 455, 710, 712–13
  income and 99–102
  income elasticity of 115, 118
  laws of, and supply 304

management 671
market 104–6
money 463–70, 472–5, 487
price elasticity 106–13, 115, 118,
  153–6, 411–12, 608
prices and 102–4, 179–82
production factor 403
resources 403–14
revenue elasticity 114–17
sterling 604–13
stocks and 607
supply and, involuntary
  unemployment 511
theory 96, 152–3
total 456
variations 456
Demand-pull inflation 634
Democracy, economic 401
Deposits
  creation by banks 503
  special 500
Depreciation 291, 361
Derivative 234, 238
  higher order 244–5, 259
  partial 257, 259
  second 246–9
Devaluation 459, 595, 720–21
Development economics 678–81
  strategies 680–81
Differentiation 235–43, 249, 257
Disaggregation 558
Discount houses 497
Discounting 80–84
  approach to education 84–8
Discretionary policy 630–63
  monetary 502–3
Discrimination
  labour 747–8
  price 347–51
Disequilibrium see Equilibrium
Disincentives 777–8
Disinvestment, demand changes 455
Distribution
  central planning approach 395
  global problem 397–402
  income 72, 97, 745–7, 780–83
    see also Wages, distribution of

market procedure 395
theory 395–6
  lack of 434
wealth 781–3
Disturbances 456
Dividends 583
Dollar 282
  standard 627–8
Durable goods 203–5, 557–9
  consumer 557–9

Econometric models 692
Economic
  forecasts 668
  growth see Growth
  instability 684
Economics
  art 678
  development 678–81
  measurement 176
  non-market 11
  normative 38, 678
  positive 38, 678
Economies
  centrally planned 510
  of scale 208–9, 339–40
    monopolies 736–7
    organizational behaviour and 345–7
    public ownership and 384–5
Economists' tasks 19–20
Economy
  control 492–6
  corporate 280–81
  macroeconomic behaviour
    relationships 702
  money 74–8, 474–5
  one-commodity 58
  open 297, 671, 719–21
  stabilization 663–5
Education
  compulsory 752–3
  discounting approach to 84–8
  subsidized 132
Efficiency
  marginal see Marginal efficiency
  nationalized industries 392
  tax 767, 777

Elasticities
  arc 110, 112
  cross 113–15, 118–19, 368–9
  demand 106–19, 153–6, 180–81,
    368–9, 708
  derived 116
  empirical measures of 117–19
  income 115, 117, 118
  interest 714–18
  investment 704
  marginal revenue 116
  negative 119
  point 110–11
  price 106–13, 115, 117, 118–19, 153–6
  supply curve 123
  supply of factors 411–12
  revenue 114–17
  taste 114
Elections, irrelevance 800–801
Employment
  full 661
  level 531
  total demand 456
Energy, crisis 686 see also Oil, prices
Entropy 513
Equal pay 272
Equilibrium 311
  balance of payments 719–21
  circular flow of incomes 514–17
  exchange rate 611
  firms 570
  foreign exchange market 615–18
  general 98, 454, 456–8
  income level 521, 524, 529, 536, 698
  interdependence of real and monetary
    variables 699–720
  investment and 696, 698
  long-run 326
  market 98, 139–40
  monetary 516
  money market and 697
  monopoly 345, 736
  partial 98, 455–6, 561
  perfect competition 326
  short-run 326, 681
Equity 286, 783
  horizontal 769–70

Equity – *continued*
  taxation 769–72, 783
  vertical 770–72
Estate duty 783–4
Eurodollar market 498
European Economic Community,
  Common Agricultural Policy
  159–60
Ex ante 327, 328, 332, 579, 668
Exchange
  consumption possibilities and 67
  costs 462
  medium of 77–8, 480, 482
  trade and 65–73
Exchange rate 458
  equilibrium 611
  expectations 612
  fixed 515, 681–5
  flexible 146, 515, 681–5
  floating *v.* fixed 621–3
  foreign investment in U.K. 606
  freely floating 618
  stability 661
  sterling supply and 611
Expansion, fiscal policy 712
Expectations 704
  exchange rates 612
  general 464
  investment decisions 573–4
  of life 29, 32
  Phillips curve 'breakdown' 647–9
  profits 566
  total demand 456
Expenditure 519
  autonomous 513–14
  definition 511
  household 101
  inducement 510
  investment 573–4
  national 292, 294, 297, 300
    see also Government expenditure
  taxation 763
Explosive cycles 165
Exports 458, 595–8
  circular flow of income 512
  equilibrium analysis 617
  price elasticity 613

  prices 458
  subsidies 621
    see also Foreign trade
Ex-post 328–9, 332, 579
Externalities 63, 388, 738
  see also Spillovers

Factor-payments lags 514
Factors of production, demand
  403
Fairs 76
Fair Trading Act 375–6
Farmers' incomes 155–60
Federal Reserve Banks 460
Feudalism 30
Finance 756–78
Financial
  assets 491
  evolution 491
Firms
  accounts 284–5
  aims 277–9, 305
  behaviour of 303, 566
  capital formation by 570
  company and 583n
  decisions of 308–9, 323–6
  equilibrium 570
  investment 566–91
  market and 270–71
  monopoly 290, 337, 341, 356
  net worth of 306–8
  ownership and control 401
  perfect competition 321–8
  short-run supply curve 327
  size of 267–71, 275
  theory of 263, 279–80
  time to close down 313–14
  see also Company
Fiscal
  drag 656
  policy 668–71, 723
  deflation 712
  discretionary, destabilizing effects
    668–71
  expansionary 712
  financing 711
  inflexibility 665–6

interdependence of monetary policy 711
long run 673–5
monetary policy 666
short run 662–3
Fisher, Irving 465, 466
Fix-price 515, 681–5
Flex-price 146, 515, 685
Flows
capital 629–31
demand for sterling 607
distinguished from stocks 567
Football 79, 84, 134
League 379–81
Foreign aid 680
Foreign exchange
market 604–33
rate see Exchange rate
reserves 620–21, 623
speculation 606, 609
Foreign trade 65–73, 592–600
aggregate demand and 592ff, 602–3
changing pattern of 25–6
obstacles to 600–601
prices see Exports; Imports;
International trade
Fractional reserve banking 483, 485–91, 493
Free reserves 491
Freedom 319
economic 319
from want 784–5
Free trade 34, 600
Frictional unemployment 508–9
Friedman, Milton 319n, 458, 553, 649–50
Functions 135, 137, 220–28
cubic 225–8
inflectional points 251–3
linear 223
maxima and minima 245–9, 251
power 235
quadratic 224–5
several variables 255–7
Funds-flow statement 288, 290

Galbraith, J. K. 280

General disequilibrium 454–8
General equilibrium 98
Geographical mobility 440, see also
Labour: mobility
Germany, inflation 459
Giffen goods 181, 187
Giffen, Sir Robert 119
Gladstone, W. E. 662
Golden rule 309–13
calculus of 316–18
Gold exchange system 625
Gold standard 459, 625–7
Goods
collective 41–3, 216, 266, 401, 461, 734–5, 786
durable 203–5, 557–9
free 386
Giffen 181, 187
inferior 183
market 699–701
private 40–41, 461, 546
see also Capital goods; Product
public 546
total demand 456
Government
aims 732–5
borrowing 546, 621, 655, 759–62, 778
closed economy 296–7
decision-making 732, 795, 797
economic role of 731–2, 734–5, 747
expenditure
balance of payments 620
circular flow of income 512
crowding-out effect 666
deficits, with and without 664–5
financing 661
long run fiscal policy 673–5
prestigious 689
statistics 190
intervention 127–34, 372–5
money supply 492–503
investment 677, 760
incentives 584–5
opportunism 669
revenue 655–9
see also Taxation

Great slump 460
Gross domestic fixed capital
  formation (GDFCF) 578, 579–80
Gross investment 566
Gross National Product (GNP)
  295–301
Growth
  economic 661, 681–7
  export-led 654
  fix-price model 681–5
  flex-price model 685
  rates 462

Health 132
Hicks, J. R. 699
Hicks-Hansen model 699
Hire purchase, control 502
Historical approach 9–11
History, monetary theory of 458–61
Hobbes, T. 794
Hours of work, decline in 29
Households 63, 271–3
  aggregate demand 545–65
  expenditure 101, 118–19
Housing
  new 559–60
  rent control 130–32
Human capital 436–7
Hume, David 453–4
Hyper-inflation 463, 637, 658

IS–LM curve model 699–721
Identification problem 155
Ignorance, accounting for 354–62
Illiteracy 33
Immigration 58–60
  see also Migration
Imperialism 70–71, 680
Imports 597–601
  circular flow of income 512
  demand for sterling 607–9
  elasticity of demand 609
  equilibrium analysis 617
  substitution 680–81
  supply of sterling 612

Income
  definition 511, 764
  demand and 99–102, 115 118
  determination of 518–33
  distribution 661, 685
  effects 186–7, 439
  elasticities 115–18
  disposable 546–51, 561
  distribution 72, 97–8, 745–6, 780–83
    see also Wages, distribution of
  equilibrium level of 521, 524, 529,
    536, 696–8
  farmers', 155–60
  marginal utility 773–5
  measurement of 287
  models for determination 703–4
  minimum 157
    see also Minimum wages
  multiplier effect 618–19
  national see National income
  permanent 541
  personal 781
  tax 672, 783
  transfers 750–52
  utility 192, 196, 773–5
    see also Circular flow of income
Income-consumption lags 514
Income–expenditure approach 508–17
Income-leisure choice 546
Incomes policy 621, 653
Independent variable 222, 256, 656
Indifference curve 188, 198, 794
Indivisibilities 334, 339–40, 741–3
  public ownership 386–8
Industrialization
  agriculture and 72
  imperialism and 70–71
  misery due to 30
Industrial Revolution 24–5, 30
Industry supply curve 328–33
Inequality 780–84
  poverty and 744–50, 780–92
Inferior good 183
Inflation 460
  aggregate supply and 634–54
  causes 635–41
  cost-push 637

credit control 502
definition 634
demand for sterling 613
demand-pull 634
devaluation 721
exchange rates 621, 622
gold standard 627
hyper- 463, 637, 658
inside and outside money 503
money supply and 470–71, 637–41, 711, 758
Phillips curve 647
problem 635
source of government revenue 655–9
suppressed 634
trade unions and 637–9
unemployment and 531–3, 641–9, 654
wages and 642
Inflectional points 251–3
Injections 512, 520, 536, 538–9, 542
Injections–withdrawals diagram, 521–2
Inside money 503–5
Instability 693–5
Institutional change 28
Institutions, non-profit 134–5
Interactions, simultaneous 691
Interdependence 691–2
real and monetary variables 699–720
Interest rates
balance of payments 619, 620
booms and slumps 516
Competition and Credit Control 502
demand for sterling 614–15
elasticities 705, 714–18
equilibrium 698
fiscal policy 714
foreign investment in UK 606
investment and 81, 84, 494, 568–71, 705, 718
machine lives 574
money and 457, 468–71, 472–3, 499–500, 516, 714
planning and 421
post-Second World War 460
real 582n, 722–3
and monetary 421–2

relative to profits 609
Interest theory 421–2
International Bank for Reconstruction and Development (World Bank) 627
International Monetary Fund 627
International trade 65–73
consumption possibilities and 65–8
pattern of 69–73
services 593, 596
specialization and 68–9, 71
see also Foreign trade
Introspection 192
Inventions 60–62, 577
Inventory accelerator 586
Inventory investment 586–7
Investment
actual compared with planned 578
age structure and 687
aggregate demand and 566–91
consumer demand 583
consumer spending 579–81
costs 573
decision 457
demand 455, 702, 704–5, 715
equilibrium and 696, 698
ex ante 579
expectations 573–4
ex post 579
flows 629, 631
future revenue 572
foreign, in U.K. 605–7, 617
goods
flow demand 572
gross 566
government 677, 760
incentives 584–5
gross and net 566
interest 81, 84, 494, 568–71, 582–3, 705, 718
inventory 586–7
marginal efficiency 572, 577, 579
nationalized industries 389–91
net 566
opportunity cost and 88–90
overseas 609–11, 617, 680
private 559–60

Investment – *continued*
  reasons for 567–8
  replacement 566
  revenue 574–6
  and savings functions (*IS* curve) 699ff
  technology and 573, 576–7
  theory of 570, 577–8
  U.K., 1952–72 579
  U.K. unwillingness 688
Involuntary unemployment 509–11
Ireland, potato consumption 119

Job information 644
Johnson, H. G. 722n
Joint stock company 276, 401

Kahn, Lord 535
Keynes, J. M. 19, 20, 397–9, 400,
    456–8, 471–4, 459, 461, 509, 528–9,
    536, 579, 655, 663, 693, 722

Labour
  competition 446
  demand, wages and 445
  discrimination 748
  division of 56
  human resource 436–7
  marginal product of 437–8
  market 127–30, 160–65, 436–7, 445,
    449, 643, 699, 700
  mobility 440–42, 644
  monopoly and 446
  non-agricultural 33
  rent 417–19
  supply 437n
  theory of value 188–9, 427–9, 679
  unions *see* Trade unions
  working hours 29
  see also Wages
Labour-saving inventions 60–62
Labour Standard 459
Lags 456, 585, 668
  autonomous expenditure 513–14
  factor-payment 514
  monetary equilibrium 516
  money supply 722, 723

Laissez-faire 28
Land tenure, reform 679
Law, John 275
Law of diminishing returns 49, 51–5,
    59–60, 526
Leisure 438, 546, 689
Lending 546
Lenin, V.I. 274, 656
Liabilities 285, 290–91, 306
Liberalism 42
Licensing 338–9, 767
Life expectancy 29, 32
Limit, concept of 231
Limited liability 275–6
Liquidity trap 471–4, 715
Literacy, poverty and 32
Living standard 22–3, 302, 551, 678
Loan finance 759–62
Loans, foreign 762
Locke, J. 794

Machines 568
  lives 574
  price determinants 568
Macroeconomics 545–8
Malthus, T. R. 20, 58, 687
Management 264, 268–9
Manifestos 798
Manpower
  policies 654
  supply 437
  see also Labour market
Margin, concept of 229
Marginal cost
  curve 310–11
  pricing 386–8
Marginal efficiency 573
  investments 572, 577
Marginal product 51–2, 53, 55
  curve 61, 404–6
  doctrine 58–9, 432
  labour 437
Marginal propensity
  to consume 549, 552, 558
  to stock build 587
  to withdraw 538–9, 541

Marginal revenue 324, 341
  curve 310–13, 324
  derivation of 116
  elasticities 116
  monopoly 341, 343
  product 407–11, 413
Marginal sacrifice 761–2, 772–4
Marginal utility
  income 773–5
  money 472
  theory 184–91
Market 95–7, 125–70
  analysis 10–11, 98, 135–40
  behaviour 182
  blood 133–4
  book 377–8
  capital 276–7, 422
  charity 134
  colour-film 378
  coordination 454
  demand 104–6
  disadvantages 97–8
  distinction needed 801
  disturbances 455
  distribution procedure 395
  equilibrium 98, 139–40
  failure 457, 746–7
  firm and 270–71
  interactions 454, 462
  intervention in 127–34
  labour see Labour market
  money 697
  monopoly power and 367
  power 314
    equal distribution of 320–21
  price 354–5, 362
  private or public 734–6
  stability 126
  state and 794–5, 798n
  stock 276–7, 494–5, 583
  surpluses 126–7
  system, poverty and 744–6
  tax effect on 147–50
Marriage allowances 272–3
Marshall, Alfred 20, 137, 268,
  455–7
Marx, Karl 20, 270, 399–400, 427–9

Mathematics 135–40, 216–59
  see also Algebra
Matrix algebra 455
Maxima 245–7, 249, 251
Measurement, in economics 176
Merchants 76
Mergers 375
Microeconomics 545–8
Migration 58–60, 442–4, 687, 688
Mill, John Stuart 679
Minima 245–9, 251
Minimum income, farmers' 157
Minimum wages 128–9, 792
Middlemen 76
Models, econometric 692
Monetarism 721–6
  judgements in 725
Monetary
  control 478, 693ff
  equilibrium 516
  policy 500, 666, 721, 723
  theory of history 458ff
  variables 699–720
Money
  balances, relationships with supply
    722
  Cambridge approach 467–8
  capital good 693
  cheap 460
  circulation, transactions velocity of
    565, 466–7, 695
  commodity 77–8, 480–81
  compatibility with knowledge 464
  control of production 478
  credit and 482, 483–91
  definition 464, 479–80
  demand for 463–70, 472–5, 487, 695,
    705, 707, 708, 711, 716–17, 722
  economy 74–8, 475, 695
  elasticities 708
  high-powered 492
  illusion 647–8
  inside and outside 503–5
  interest rates and 457, 468–70, 472–3,
    498–500
  managed 482
  market 496–8, 699, 701

Money – *continued*
  marginal utility 470, 472
  measuring rod 454
  medium of exchange 303, 492
  and net wealth 504
  neutrality 453
  opportunity cost 657
  output effect 503
  prices and 469–70, 693n
  printing 461, 655–6, 758
  quantity theory of 453–4, 459, 464–8,
    470–71, 636
  as a set of values 693
  store of value 693
  supply 470, 473, 478
    balance of payments 620
    contraction 721
    control of 492–6, 696, 723
    demand curves (*LM* curve) 699ff
    destabilizing effects 478
    importance 721
    inflation and 471, 637–41, 758
    interest elasticity 715
    involuntary unemployment 510
    open market operations 498–500,
      653, 711
    real value 707, 710
    rules versus discretion 502–3
    slumps and booms 457–8
    relationship with balances 722
  token 481
  uncertainty and 464
  value of a quantity 177
  wage rate 457, 526, 528–9, 643
Monopolies Commission 373, 375
Monopoly 303, 332, 341, 351
  bilateral 304
  case for and against 364–7
  causes of, 338–40
  closed 341–5
  cost curve 343
  demand curve 341–3, 356
  economies of scale 736
  equilibrium 345, 736
  firm 290, 337, 341, 356
  legislation against 373–5
  marginal revenue 341, 343

  policy 370–71
  power
    market structures and 367
    measurement of 344–5, 367–8
  price 356–7, 365
    discrimination 347–51
  profits 357–9
  public control of 372–81, 384–92,
    737
  pure 304
  regulation of 364–81
  strategies for 356–9
  subsidization of 737
  supply curve 343–4
Monopsony 447
Morals, income distribution and 97–8
Multinational corporations 281–2
Multipliers 535–43, 561, 662, 668
  effects, income 618–19
  fiscal policy 711, 715, 717, 722
  instantaneous versus period 541–3
  money 722
  process 703
  real versus money 542
  theorem of balanced budget 663–4

National Debt 493, 499, 759
National expenditure 292, 294, 297,
  300
National income 292–302
  behaviour of 21–5
  demand for sterling 613–14
  determination of 518–33
  real 22–3
  statistics, measuring 190
  welfare measure 732
National product
  calculating 292–302
  composition of 24
Nationalized industries 384–92
Negative inventory investment 586
Net Book Agreement 377–8
Net investment 566
Net present value 572, 573, 580–81,
  585
Non-profit institutions 134–5

Obsolescence cost 204
Occupational mobility *see* Labour:
    mobility
Oil prices 623, 628, 671
Oligopoly 304, 349–50, 368
Open economy 297, 671
Open market operations 493,
    498–500
Opportunity cost 48, 88–90
Optimal factor combination 406–7
Optimism
    investment decisions 585
    volatility 573–4
Organizational behaviour 305–18
    economies of scale versus 345–7
Organizational slack 278
Output
    definition 511–12
    effect 410–11
    investment and 575
    lags 514
    total demand 456
Outside money 503–5
Over-consumption 738–41
Over-production 660
Overheads 359, 387
    allocation of 215–16
Overpopulation 58
Ownership and control 401

Pakistan, Green Revolution 679
Paradox of value 187–8
Parallel money market 498
Pareto criterion 732–3, 741
Partial equilibrium 455–6
    demand for sterling 613–15
Parties, political 798–801
Perfect competition 319–34
    assumptions of 320–22
    buyers 323
    demand curve 323–4
    equilibrium 326
    firm in 321–8
    producers 322
    supply curves 327–33
Period analysis 456, 462
Period multiplier 541–2

Permanent income hypothesis 553,
    554
Pessimism
    investment demand 585
    volatility 573–4
Phelps, E. S. 650
Phillips, A. W. 643
Phillips curve 643–51
Piece rates 265
Pigou, A. C. 20
Planning 96–7, 140, 263, 280
    approach to distribution 395
    compensation and 733
    interest rate and 421
Political
    parties, similarities 798
    processes 794–802
Politics
    definition 794
    distinction needed 801
    irrelevance 801
Pollution 30, 41, 60–61, 739–40
    compensation for 739–43
    taxation and 740–42
Population
    development economics 680
    diminishing returns and size of 56–60,
        462, 686–8
    optimum 56–60
    over- 58
Poverty 784–6
    causes of 744
    cure of 746–8, 751–3, 786–92
    inequality and 744–50, 780–92
    literacy and 32
    primary 744
    relief of 130, 132
    secondary 750
    universal standards 801
Power
    functions 235
    in firms 270–71
    market 314, 320–21
    monopoly 367
Present values 82, 308
Pressure groups 800
Price–cost ratio 357, 365, 368

Price elasticities 106–13, 115, 117, 118, 153–6, 608, 613
Price leadership 350
Prices
  constant 298–9
  control of 130, 371, 460
  costs and 203–5
  demand and 102–4, 179–82, 187, 456
  determinants 455
  discrimination in 347–51
  export 458
  fluctuation of 22–3
  foreign trade and 58, 609, 613
  incomes policies 653
  inflation, demand for sterling 613
  international relationships 623
  international stabilization agreements 679
  market 354–5, 362
  models, fix- and flex- 681–5
  money and 469–70, 478, 691–4
  monopoly 356–7, 365
  production factor 122
  public and private 757–8
  resources 406, 686
  sluggish movements 681
  stable 661
  subsidization 752
  supply curve and 123
  taxation and 768–9
  uncertainty 362
Price system 96–7
Pricing
  cost 386–8
  cost-plus 279–80
  nationalized industries' policy 385–9
  two-part 388
Producer
  rent 127
  surplus 126–7
Product
  average 51–3
  cycle theory 282
  marginal see Marginal product
  total 52–4

Production 46–63
  costs and 208–14
  doubling 50, 56
  factors
    demand 403
    demand and supply 416–20
    price 122
  function 46–8, 55, 63, 361, 525–6
    aggregates 700
    cost curves and 212–14, 218
  gross and net 299
  laws 49–51
  measures of 299, 302
  national calculating 292–302
  open system 62–3
  perfect competition 322
  public and private 753
  roundabout techniques 88–9
  social institutions of 263–73
Production-possibility curve 46–8
Productivity, Phillips curve 645–6
Products, good and bad 62–3, 98, 266
Profits 307, 424–35
  company 583–4
  expectations 566
  foreign investment in U.K. 606
  interest/profit rates 609
  Marxist theory 427–9
  maximization 278–9, 303–5, 308–13, 315–18, 341, 350, 357–8, 404
  monopoly 357–9
  neoclassical theory 429–33
  Ricardian theory 425–7
  uncertainty 425
  undistributed 566
Profit-sharing 266
Property laws, revision of 273
Protectionism 341, 600–601
Public ownership 384–92
  economies of scale and 384
  externalities 388
  indivisibilities 386–7
Public sector
  diversion of resources to 674
  growth 461, 651
  optimum size 462
  see also Government

Quantity theory of money 453–4, 459, 464–8, 470–71, 636
Quasi-rent 419, 530
Quotas, import 600–601
Quotient, differentiating 242–3

Rates, local 200
Rationalization 372
Rationing 132–3, 460
Raw materials crisis 686
Recessions 503, 642
Referenda 800
Regression analysis 585
Rent
  control 130–32
  economic 417–19
  labour 417–19
  producer 127
Replacement investment 566
Resale price maintenance 374–5
Reservation wage 644
Reserves 620–21, 623
Residuals 685
Resources
  allocation of 454, 515
    price mechanisms 686
  demand 403–14
  diversion to public sector 674
  efficient use of 661
  owners 265–6
  prices 406
Restrictive Trade Practices Act 373
Retail price fluctuations 22–3
Retirement, postponement 688
Returns
  diminishing 49, 51–5, 59–60, 526
  increasing 55–6, 333, 339
  rate of 82–3, 612
  to scale, constant 50
Revealed preference 198–9
Revenue
  average 343
  changes, accelerator principles 574–6
  elasticities 114–17
  future 572
  marginal see Marginal revenue
  total 324

Ricardian theory of profit 425–7
Ricardo, D. 20, 65, 73, 417, 419
Risk 431
Road tax 767
Rousseau, J-J. 794

Sacrifice
  doctrine 761–2
  marginal 772–3
Sales, inventory investment
    relationships 587
Satisficing behaviour 279–80
Savings
  1974–5 560–61
  circular flow of income 512
  collective bargaining 685
  consumption and 559–60
  level of 702
  marginal propensity 705
Scarcity, choice and 36–7
Schumpeter, J. 576
Search
  strategy, jobs 644
  unemployment 644
Secular stagnation 457
Securities
  market 699
  money supply aspects 493
  see also Stock Exchange
Self-sufficiency 44, 90
Services
  international trade in 593, 596
  total demand 456
Share, uncertainty 457
Shareholders 275, 277, 303
Simons, Henry 776
Simultaneous equations 135–40, 149–50, 220, 454–5, 692
Slumps 455, 457–8, 460, 516–17
  balanced budgets 662
  contra-cyclical spending 461
Smith, Adam 20, 56, 275, 440, 679
Social
  class 798
  costs 216–17
    and benefits 738–9, 750
  dividend, taxation and 786, 789–92

Social – *continued*
  institutions of production 259–73
  mobility 440
  security 785–6
  welfare 732–3, 738
Spatial distribution, mobility of labour
    440
Special deposits 500
Specialization 68–9, 71, 268
Speculation, foreign exchange 606, 609
Speculators 455
Spending lags 514
Spillovers 42–3, 270, 322, 392, 737–50
  benefits of 750–53
  excess demand 713
Stability, market 126
Stabilization
  agricultural 156
  automatic 671–2
  policies 677
Stagflation 502, 647
Stagnation, secular 457
Standard of living 22–3, 302, 551
State 731–55
  control of industry 34
  definition 794
  finance 756–78
  market and 794–5, 797–8
  see also Government; National
Statics, comparative, 456
Statistics 21
  errors in 119
Sterling
  demand for 604–15
    consumption 604–5
    equilibrium rate of exchange 611
    flow *v.* stock 607
    foreign investment in U.K. 605–7
    imports 607–9
    investment overseas 609–11, 612
    price inflation 613
    supply of 610, 612
Stock Exchange 276–7, 494–5, 583
Stockpiling 165
Stocks
  buffer 679
  changes in 296

demand and 607
demand for sterling 607
demand curve 568
flows and 567, 693
uncertainty 457
  see also Inventory
Strikes 372, 448
Structural unemployment 509
Subsidies
  agricultural 157–8
  control of money supply 493
  educational 132
  health 132
  market effect of 147
  monopolies 737
  nationalized industries 388
  price 752
  training 160–62
Substitution 186–7, 189, 190, 196, 199,
    410, 439, 573, 594, 613
Supervisors 264–5
Supply
  aggregate *see* Aggregate supply
  costs and 201–18
  curve
    elasticity 123
    firm's short-run 327
    industry 328–33
    monopoly 343–4
    movements along 131, 145–7, 151
    perfect competition 327–33
    price and 123
    shifts 123–4, 147, 151
    short-run 327
  determinants of 121–4
  laws of demand and 304
  manpower 160–65, 654
    see also Labour market
  money *see* Money supply
  production factor 416–20
  sterling 610, 612
  technology and 123
  theory 153
Surplus
  agricultural 157
  consumer 127, 189–90
  market 126–7

producer 126–7
value 399, 427–9

Tariffs 600–601, 621, 628, 680–81
Tastes 114
Taxation 546, 576–7, 637, 655
  ability to pay 771, 776, 778
  avoidance of 783
  balance of payments 620
  base 657, 763–9
  benefit principle 765–7
  circular flow of incomes 512
  control of money supply 493
  conundrum 151–2
  depressing effects 651
  earmarked 767
  efficiency 767–9, 777–8
  equity 769–72, 783
  exemption 776
  expenditure 762
  finance 761, 762–3
  income 672, 783
  inflation 655–8
  investment incentives 585
  laws, revision of 273
  lump sum 371
  market effect of 147–50
  nationalized industries and 387–8, 391
  negative rates 786–7
  outlay 762–3
  personal 763, 782–3
  progressive 771–2, 776, 777
  proportional 771
  reduction 664
  reliefs 272–3
  sacrifice doctrine 761–2
  social dividend 786, 789–92
  unit 147, 740–41, 763–4, 768
Tax-transfer mechanism 751
Technical change 566, 573, 576–7, 585, 685
Technology
  investment and 673, 576–7
  supply and 123
Theft 44

Thrift 539–40
Time
  preference 81
Trade 44
  account, equilibrium 618
  cycle 509
  domestic 65, 69
  foreign see Foreign trade
  over time 79–84, 90–92
  unions 400, 469, 443–8, 480
    collective bargaining 445–7
    inflation and 637–9
    strength 689
    wage negotiations 647
    wage reductions 457
Trades Union Congress 128
Transaction costs 462
Transactions velocity of money
  circulation 445, 466–7
Transfer earnings 417–19, 424
Transfers
  income 751–2
  in kind 752
Treasury Bills 497–8

Uncertainty 177
  management and 269
  money and 464
  prices and costs 362
  profits and 425
  risk and 431
Under-consumption 743–6
Under-production 660–61
Underdeveloped countries 34–5, 58
  industrialization and 70–71
Unemployment 30–31, 97, 427, 454–6, 677
  balance of payments 620
  benefits, automatic stabilizers 672
  cyclical 509
  devaluation 720–21
  inflation and 531–4, 641–9, 654
  involuntary 509–11
  migration and 642–4
  natural rate 644–5
  persistence 457
  Phillips curve 643–51

Unemployment – *continued*
relief 535
search 644
types 508–11
U.K. economy 1945–77 689
voluntary 509
United Kingdom
economy 1945–77 688–9
monetary theory of history 458ff
United States of America
as a cause of world inflation 651
monetary theory of history 458ff
Utilities, negative 202
Utility
analysis 184
cardinal 175, 192
cost and 175–7
curve 184
income 192, 196, 773–5
marginal *see* Marginal utility
maximized 202, 303
measurement 200, 304
money's worth 184
ordinal 175
substitution effect 196, 199
theory 200
total 184, 187, 189
units of 176
Utton, M. A. 370

Value
judgement 11
labour theory of 188–9, 427–9, 679
paradox 187–8
surplus 399, 427–9
theory 177, 457
Values, changing 28
Variable costs 205, 214, 265
Variables 222–3
independent 222, 256, 656
real and monetary 699–720
several 255–7
Velocity of circulation of money 465,
466–7, 695
Vietnam war, as a cause of world
inflation 623, 651
Voting 401, 731, 795, 798–800

Wage–price spiral 639–40, 647
Wages 59
change, substitution effect 439
distribution of 128, 442
see also Income distribution
inflation and 642ff.
labour demand and 445
labour supply and 437–9
leisure and 438, 546, 689
minimum 128–9, 643–51, 792
money rate 526, 528–9
piece rates 265
raising 445–8
real 457, 643
reductions in 510, 641
reservation 644
theory 434
value 427–9
Walras, Leon 20, 454–5, 457, 691
Walras's Law 700, 701
Want, freedom from 784–5
Wants
cultural determinants 38
goods and 36–45
hierarchy of 38–40, 187, 188, 738
mechanism for satisfaction of 43,
188
Waste 513
disposal costs 739
Wealth
distribution of 781–2
inside and outside money 504
tax 783–4
Welfare 732–3, 738
gains, currency unification 481
Williamson, O. E. 278
Withdrawals 512, 536, 538–41
Workers' control 266
World, corporate 281–2
World Bank 627

X-inefficiency 347

Yarn Spinners' Agreement 376–7
Yields, liquid assets 492

More about Penguins and Pelicans

Penguinews, which appears every month, contains details of
all the new books issued by Penguins as they are published.
From time to time it is supplemented by *Penguins in Print*,
which is our complete list of almost 5,000 titles.

A specimen copy of *Penguinews* will be sent to you free on
request. Please write to Dept EP, Penguin Books Ltd,
Harmondsworth, Middlesex, for your copy.

In the U.S.A.: For a complete list of books available from
Penguins in the United States write to Dept CS, Penguin
Books, 625 Madison Avenue, New York, New York 10022.

In Canada: For a complete list of books available from
Penguins in Canada write to Penguin Books Canada Ltd,
2801 John Street, Markham, Ontario L3R 1B4.

Industrial Concentration
M. A. Utton

This book neatly considers the whole range of arguments for and
against high levels of industrial concentration. Early chapters
explain the factors governing levels of and changes in concentration,
and review the strengths and weaknesses of the measures that
empirical studies have used. Three central chapters then follow:
they form a survey of the available evidence on concentration levels
and trends both in Britain and the United States, and are the core
of the book. Included are such questions as whether concentration
levels in the two countries have shown a persistent tendency to
increase throughout the twentieth century.

In chapter 7 the author, emphasizing that his subject is useful only to
the extent that it can indicate market performance, considers in
particular whether profit levels in concentrated industries are
significantly higher than in more competitive industries.

The final chapter considers the whole range of attitudes to
concentration that governments may adopt in the search for better
industrial performance.

Nationalized Industries
Graham L. Reid and Kevin Allen

The authors examine the economics of the nationalized industries in
six areas: electricity, gas, coal, the railways, road haulage and
airlines.

Each industry is dealt with in separate chapters which together
offer a spectrum of the many interesting special problems of
nationalized enterprises. Thus *electricity* supply is a case-study in
continuous growth, technological change and economies of scale –
the basic unit of plant has multiplied seven-fold in twenty years.
Within one decade *gas* supply has changed from coal to naphtha and
from naphtha to natural gas. With the long-term contraction and
redeployment of *coal* runs the complementary contraction of *rail
transport*; while *air transport* offers insights into the working of an
international industry.

Economics of Retailing

Edited by K. A. Tucker and B. S. Yamey

Everyone knows about retailing but, in much economic theory and analysis, the treatment of it is as if producers sold directly to consumers – retailers are scarcely present. This volume of Readings presents the major aspects of the economics of these missing intermediaries.

In Part One are short extracts from J. S. Mill, A. Marshall and others on pricing policies and the behaviour of retail prices. Competition and concentration in retailing are the central topics of Part Two, while Part Three considers cost functions in retailing as well as cost structures and differences among different sizes of firms. The articles in Part Four examine competition, factor prices, technology and consumer preferences as constraints on the individual retailer. The last part investigates various pricing arrangements such as resale price maintenance and includes a well-known piece on retail trading in Nigeria.

The Economics of the Common Market

Dennis Swann

This clearly written book describes the social and political origins of the Common Market, traces its evolution through the practical decisions that have been taken since 1958, and indicates the possibilities of future development.

The attitudes of the member states towards central issues such as the Common Agricultural Policy, movements of labour and capital, and the coordination of social security are clearly brought out. The reader is given real insights into the decision-making functions of the Council of Ministers on such matters as the attainment of economic and monetary union, the methods of achieving the objectives of the Rome Treaty in the face of tremendous difficulties, and the spur to integration that the American challenge affords.

This thoroughly revised edition is written in the context of Britain's membership of the EEC and has a postscript on the changed situation since the return of a Labour Government committed to important renegotiations.

'This is an excellent text to put in the hands of university students of economics and should satisfy also the wider public' – *Economic Journal*

Economic Justice
Edited by Edmund S. Phelps

This volume of readings presents classic and recent contributions to the theory of economic justice, and explores the implications for social policy – especially taxation in public expenditure programmes – of some of the principal conceptions of distributive justice that so far have emerged.

Part One contains an introductory essay on the choice of public policies towards income distribution. Parts Two and Three review the Pareto-type modern welfare economics and analyse the inability of 'democratic' decision-making systems unaided by a consensual ethic to escape certain voting paradoxes. Kant's notion of natural rights and the succeeding ideas of the classical utilitarians are surveyed in Part Four as well as modern development in neo-utilitarianism, culminating in the fundamental reformulation of the social contract doctrine by John Rawls. The last part analyses the nature of taxation and public expenditure policy in economies conforming to utilitarian and Rawlsian principles.

The Economics of Industrial Innovation
Christopher Freeman

In the world of computers, space travel and energy crises we may curse or bless technical innovation, but we cannot escape its impact on our daily lives, nor the moral, social and economic dilemmas with which it confronts us. Least of all can economists afford to ignore innovation – an essential condition of economic progress and adaptation and a critical element in the competitive struggle of enterprises and nation states.

In Part One of this book, Professor Freeman illustrates historically three basic aspects of the rise of the professionalized Research and Development system – the growing complexity of technology, the increased scale of process, and the specialization of scientific work. The whole of Part Two is devoted to an examination of empirical evidence which might support or refute various contemporary theories of innovation, particularly in relation to the behaviour of firms. Part Three deals with some national-policy implications for technical innovation, and especially with the problem of 'consumer sovereignty'.

Economic Systems and Society

George Dalton

It is less useful today to group economic systems under the traditional headings of capitalist or communist, because both kinds continue to change structurally and ideologically in unforeseen ways.

In this historica l account of changing systems, George Dalton has traced the development of these economies, from the Industrial Revolution to the present. He deals first with nineteenth-century capitalism, the contrasting responses of utopian, Marxian and democratic socialism, the welfare-state capitalism of the 1930s and 1940s, and the policies and practices of Stalin's Russia. Later chapters explore recent change in both developed and developing economies: the author shows in particular how the Industrial Revolution is being relived today in Africa and Asia.

This book very clearly shows how the policy goals, policy instruments and economic institutions of each country are shaped by its historical and political tradition. It is intended for students just starting an economics course as well as others involved with political science or social history.